BENJAMIN DISRAELI LETTERS: 1860–1864

BENJAMIN DISRAELI LETTERS

The Disraeli Project, Queen's University at Kingston

VOLUME EIGHT 1860–1864

Edited by

M.G. WIEBE
General Editor

MARY S. MILLAR
Co-editor

ANN P. ROBSON
Co-editor

ELLEN L. HAWMAN
Research Associate

University of Toronto Press   Toronto, Buffalo, London

Toronto Buffalo London
www.utppublishing.com
Printed in Canada

ISBN 978-0-8020-9949-5

Printed on acid-free paper

Library and Archives Canada Cataloguing in Publication

Disraeli, Benjamin, 1804–1881
[Correspondence]
Benjamin Disraeli letters / edited by J.A.W. Gunn ... [et al.].

Vol. 3–8 edited by M.G. Wiebe ... [et al.]
Includes bibliographical references and index.
Contents: [v. 1] 1815–1834 – [v. 2] 1835–1837 – [v. 3] 1838–1841 – v. 4. 1842–1847 – v. 5. 1848–1851 – v. 6. 1852–1856 – v. 7. 1857–1859 – v. 8. 1860–1864.
ISBN-10: 0-8020-5523-0 (v. 1). – ISBN-10: 0-8020-5587-7 (v. 2). – ISBN-10: 0-8020-5736-5 (v. 3). – ISBN-10: 0-8020-5810-8 (v. 4). – ISBN-10: 0-8020-2927-2 (v. 5). – ISBN-10: 0-8020-4137-x (v. 6). – ISBN-10: 0-8020-8728-0 (v. 7). – ISBN-13: 978-0-8020-9949-5 (v. 8)

1. Disraeli, Benjamin, 1804–1881 – Correspondence. 2. Prime ministers – Great Britain – Correspondence. 3. Great Britain – Politics and government – 1837–1901. I. Gunn, J.A.W. (John Alexander Wilson), 1937– II. Wiebe, M.G. (Melvin George), 1939– III. Title. IV. Title: Correspondence.

DA564.B3A4 1982 941.081092 C820-941697- rev

The Disraeli Project has received generous funding from the Social Sciences and Humanities Research Council of Canada. Publication of this volume is made possible by a grant from the Canadian Federation for the Humanities, using funds provided by the Social Sciences and Humanities Research Council of Canada.

CONTENTS

ILLUSTRATIONS

ACKNOWLEDGEMENTS

We again acknowledge with gratitude our deep indebtedness to the sources of our financial support, both public and private, as listed in previous volumes, especially the continuing support of the Social Sciences and Humanities Research Council of Canada and of Queen's University.

We remain indebted to the individuals and institutions named in the earlier volumes to which lists we add:

Douglas C. Anderson, Montserrat; Colin Barr, Ave Maria University, Florida; Belinda Beaton, St Peter's College, Oxford; David Bebbington; Erika Behrisch, Royal Military College, Kingston; Jessie Binns, Community Learning Officer, Hughenden Manor; Eileen Curran, Colby College, Waterville, Maine; Timothy Duke, Chester Herald, College of Arms, London; David Elverson, Norfolk County Council; Major Charles R.C. Elverson; Zachary W. Elder, Duke University Libraries, RBMSCL Research Services; Judith Flanders; Linda Freeman; Chris Fanning, Queen's University; Mr Gordon; Linda Henderson, Northwood University; Geoffrey Hicks, Norfolk Record Office; Miloš Kovič, Department of History, University of Belgrade; Geoffrey Leboldus, Queen's University; David McLees, Cadw, Cardiff, Wales; Philip Montgomery, Fondren Library, Rice University; Robert Morton, Chuo University, Tokyo; Esther Ormerod, Somerset Archive and Record Service; Elaine Penn, Rothschild Archive; Ginger Pharand, Disraeli Project; Michel Pharand, Disraeli Project; Andrew Prescott, University of Sheffield; Nigel Roche, St Bride Foundation Library; Mrs M.A.L. Saunders, Diocesan Church House, Oxford; Helen Tiffen, University of Tasmania; the anonymous assessors of the typescript of this volume and the editors at University of Toronto Press.

Special Acknowledgements

As this will be the last volume of this edition before it is continued with a revitalized Disraeli Project at Queen's University, the General Editor, Dr Mel Wiebe, with deep gratitude acknowledges the Project's great indebtedness to Dr Mary S. Millar, Dr Ann P. Robson and Ms Ellen L. Hawman.

INTRODUCTION

Volume VIII of Disraeli's correspondence contains 916 letters. The main body, covering 1860-4, addresses 176 recipients and is made up of 556 letters, of which 409 have never before been published, in part or in whole. These include, for example, all 10 to Samuel Wilberforce, 25 of the 40 to Lord Derby and nearly half of the 123 to Sarah Brydges Willyams. In addition, 323 for which there is evidence are described at the end of the Chronological List. Appendix I contains 37 letters to 26 correspondents from the years before this volume. Other Appendixes provide the guest lists for the political dinners in 1863 at which Disraeli tried to bring together MPs from both Houses of Parliament (Appendix II), and reproduce his evocative descriptions of the wedding of the Prince of Wales and his own later interview with Queen Victoria after his eulogy of Prince Albert (Appendix III). Appendix VII is the journalist Thomas Kebbel's somewhat bemused account of a visit to Disraeli's country house, Hughenden, while Appendix VIII lists the entries from Mary Anne Disraeli's account books that document her extensive renovation and refurnishing of Hughenden.

Appendix VI contains perhaps the most exciting discovery in this volume, the complete text of an anonymously published sixteen-page pamphlet arguing for Jewish political rights, which four Appendix I letters show resulted from a hitherto unknown collaboration between Disraeli and Lionel de Rothschild, with research from Lord George Bentinck (**1617**X, **1619**X **1619**XA, **1619**XB). The pamphlet, *Progress of Jewish Emancipation since 1829* (published by Effingham Wilson in January 1848 and discovered in the Rothschild Archive), was put together in the context of events in 1847 – Rothschild's election for London and his subsequent refusal to take the parliamentary oath 'on the true faith of a Christian,' Disraeli's and Bentinck's vocal support of Lord John Russell's bill to remove Jewish disabilities in parliament, and Bentinck's resignation as Protectionist leader at the end of the year because of his own party's hostility to his action (IV **1607**&nn3&5). The proofs of the pamphlet, corrected, revised and heavily supplemented by Disraeli, show how actively he was preparing for the bill's second reading in the next session as well as managing Rothschild's strategy to help pass the bill (**1617**xnn1-5). On 3 January 1848, for example, he sent Rothschild two packets of papers with his interpretation of their argument, judiciously arranged for maximum effect on those MPs as yet undecided, and warned Rothschild: 'There is not a name introduced without a special reason' (**1619x**). When the draft came back from Rothschild on the 7th, Disraeli again extensively revised, amplified and corrected it: 'You sent me the "General abolition of oaths Bill," by mistake, instead of the "Sheriffs De[c]lar[ati]on Bill," & therefore you must take care that I have properly described its object' (**1619xA**&nn2-3). On the 9th, less than a week before publication, he again inserted material that he thought essential for their success (**1619xB**&n1). The extent of his contribution to the pamphlet is yet further evidence (if more were needed now) of how deeply committed he was to the Jewish cause in parliament, even at this relatively insecure point in his political career.

In February 1863 Disraeli summed up the theme of the letters in this volume: 'The external public world is more interesting & active than the internal political life' (**3783**). These were years of international upheaval: Garibaldi and the Italian revolution, constant nervousness about Napoleon III's intentions in Europe, the American Civil War and its effects on the British cotton industry, the Polish revolt against Russia and the continuing Schleswig-Holstein conflicts involving Austria, Prussia and Denmark – to the despair of Queen Victoria, who had family in both the latter nations. Visiting the Duke of Wellington at Apsley House, Disraeli viewed the portraits there of the envoys to the Congress of Vienna and recognized the contrast with current European affairs, 'most interesting ... when the past has really become history, & the famous settlement of 1815 is disturbed, & perhaps about to be superseded' (**3486**). The balance of power that the great Metternich had stressed to him was disappearing (**3896**), and, with the arrival of Bismarck, he wondered: 'What is preparing? A greater revolution, perhaps, in Austria, than ever occurred in France. Then it was "the rights of *man*" – now, it is, "the rights of *nations*"' (**3531**).

Disraeli made speeches on each revolt, war and annexation, sometimes forcefully, as in his censure of the Liberal government's policy (or lack of it) on Schleswig-Holstein (**3680-1**, **3791**, **3818**, **3895**, **3927**, **3929**, **3933**; and *see* Chronology). Although he down-played the significance of French threats and opposed what he called 'bloated armaments' expenditure on national defence, he thought Garibaldi's rebellion would lead to a 'general conflagration' in Europe (**3471**). Unlike Gladstone and many Conservatives, he refused to meet the Italian leader in London and criticized Prince Albert for doing so: 'For a quasi-crowned head to call on a subject is strange – & that subject a rebel!' (**3919**). Despite occasional descents into gloom (**3694**) on foreign affairs – 'I only anticipate a new chapter of political conundrums' (**3455**) – the sense of being involved in international history exhilarated him: 'It is a privilege to live in this age of rapid & brilliant events. What an error to consider it an Utilitarian age! It is one of infinite Romance. Thrones tumble down, & crowns are offered, like a fairy tale, & the most powerful people in the world, male & female, a few years back, were adventurers, exiles, & demireps. Vive la bagatelle!' (**3750**). When it seemed that his friend Lord Stanley would be offered the Greek throne but would refuse it, his comment had a touch of envy: 'Had I his youth, I would not hesitate, even with the Earldom of Derby in the distance' (**3783**).

His enchantment with foreign affairs stemmed from the stark contrast with domestic politics, which were at a standstill. 'Everything,' he lamented to Bulwer Lytton, 'is dead in the House; dangerously dead – one cannot conceive, how a popular assembly can exist for six months in such inertness & apathy' (**3784**). These were five years of a quiet agreement between Conservative and Liberal leaders *not* to bring about a government defeat, in order, Derby stated, to spare the country the constant changes of weak governments that had characterized earlier years (**3574**n2). Disraeli's own comment, to the Saxon ambassador, Count Vitzthum, had a slightly different slant: 'We shall not form a weak Ministry a third time' (**3774**n1). Parliamentary life thus became a waiting game that Disraeli, as leader of the opposition, did not enjoy; after all, as he put it to Derby, 'the Opposition is a body prepared to take office' (**3975**). Contemporaries observed that there was little to distinguish the parties. When in 1860 Gladstone had to revise a proposed increase in income tax, Disraeli told Mary Anne, 'I cd. not, myself, have brought forward a more Conservative Budget,' although he added, 'I would sooner have cut off my right hand, than have done so under the same circumstances. Gladstone looked like a beaten hound, & ate no ordinary quantity of dirt' (**3485**). Nevertheless, he followed his leader's policy: 'our tactics are to watch circumstances, & not to attempt to create them. The cards will fall into our hands if we are quiet' (**3475**).

Even when, in May 1860, Gladstone's bill to repeal the paper duty was defeated in the Lords, Disraeli maintained the necessity of the truce: 'The Government has not recovered, & is still reeling, but, it is to be hoped, we shall keep them on their legs a little longer' (**3473**). In part, his expressions of content with the situation were based on his own expectations. The old-guard Tories, he reckoned, were disappearing. 'Fate seems to pursue the Peelites like the House of Atreus. A series of tragedies. One cannot believe, that Peel, Goulburn, Dalhousie, Herbert, Graham, should all have departed, & that their senior, Palmerston, should remain, playing his tricks with the volatility of inexperience!' (**3627**). Although his old friend Lord Lyndhurst died in 1863 at 91 (**3861**), he expected that Palmerston, a mere 80, would retire or die soon, leaving the Liberals in a disarray on which the Conservatives could capitalize (**3543**n3). The difficulty meantime was to keep the Liberals in; when the 1861 session opened, he could have argued for a reform bill, but instead focused on a Liberal strength, its foreign policy: 'tho' I could ... have destroyed the government, I was wise enough to refrain' (**3555**).

The result for Disraeli was often complete boredom, which historians have sometimes construed as apathy, loss of purpose or just plain aging – he was now approaching 60, a statistic he habitually reduced to correspondents (**3460**&n2). The party policy explains such apparent anomalies as (after his own reform bill in 1859) his refusal to support Russell's in 1860. His unusual lack of aggression, however, exacerbated party discontent with his leadership in the Commons. In January 1860, Derby warned him of a Conservative cabal (led by George Bentinck and Henry Baillie) that accused Disraeli of an 'understanding' with Radical members and readiness to abandon his party over reform (**3441**n4). Although Mary Anne Disraeli told Mrs Brydges Willyams he was 'never on better terms with his party' (**3466**n2), the dissatisfaction with Disraeli was reflected in party members' refusal to support him against Gladstone's 1860 budget, and in a viciously critical attack in the April *Quarterly Review* by Lord Robert Cecil, alleging that Disraeli had betrayed his party by colluding with non-Conservatives over the 1859 reform bill: 'To crush the Whigs by combining with the Radicals was the first and last maxim of Mr. Disraeli's tactics.'

Disraeli was clearly hurt by the article, by the son of his friend Lord Salisbury; there was bitterness in his Biblical description of Conservative hostility: 'they chalk the walls in the market place with my opprobrium' (**3478**&n9). A few weeks later, after Russell had used the article in questioning Disraeli's leadership, Disraeli wrote to Sir William Miles that he wanted to resign the post, 'to which it is my opinion, that fourteen years of unqualified devotion have not reconciled the party.' Even if there was an element of testing the party waters, his frustration was real. 'I read with pain, but I felt the truth of the statement in [the *Quarterly Review*] ... that my leadership of the party was one of "chronic revolt, & unceasing conspiracy"' (*ibid*). In some alarm, Miles consulted with prominent party members with 'gratifying' results and was able to assure Disraeli that moderation and promotion of the established Church would solve the problem (*ibid* n9).

Perhaps he took Miles's advice to heart. After this low point, he undertook one of his most energetic, and perhaps surprising, roles as champion of the established Church, in alliance with the Bishop of Oxford, Samuel Wilberforce. Apart from regular attendance at St George's, Hanover Square (**3452**n3), Disraeli had not elsewhere shown himself very religious, but his support of the Church as an institution central to national stability was perfectly consistent; as long ago as *Tancred*, he had declared it 'the main remedial agency in our present state' (*Tancred* II ch 1). The letters in this volume, however, show his concept seriously challenged by political issues such as church rates and a dissidents' burial act, by theological criticism such as *Essays and Reviews*, and by new science, specifically Darwinism. Like Carlyle, Disraeli saw man as a creature to whom belief was essential; without it mankind would turn to false gods such as materialism or nationalism, or would acquire the darker view of human existence that a later age would call modernism. Unlike Matthew Arnold a few years later, he did not think that an established Church reflecting a common faith could be supplanted by a national culture as the antithesis of anarchy, or that a greater emphasis on 'Hellenism' ('spontaneity of consciousness') was needed to offset the dominance in their time of 'Hebraism' ('strictness of conscience') (*Culture and Anarchy* ch 4 and *passim*).

The force with which Disraeli argued the dangers to the established Church, both from within and without, can be seen in the considered speeches he brought to its defence. Perhaps the most serious threat from without during this period was the Bill to abolish church rates, *ie* the state Church's power to levy rates on non-members of the Church. Both in and out of Parliament Disraeli took a no-compromise position. In December 1860 at Prestwood, Bucks, he declared church rates vital to the survival of the established Church, and hence of the parochial system of local government on which the constitution was based (**3523**&n2). Conservative colleagues such as Lord Derby acknowledged the issue's importance but doubted the political wisdom of such an extreme position (**3534**&n3); Lord Stanley thought Disraeli's ideas 'very wild' (**3556**n1). Disraeli, however, as a lay trustee of the Church (defence) Institution, justified his position on political grounds: 'I took the step after great enquiry & reflection; & I think if I had not taken it, our counties would have slipped away' (**3551**). Two months later, awaiting debate on the Church Rates Bill, he told Malmesbury: 'in internal politics there is only one question now, the maintenance of the Church. There can be no refraining or false Liberalism on such a subject' (**3556**&n1). He saw the bill as 'only part of a concerted movement, comprising other measures against the union between Church and State' (**3567**). Disraeli's confidence that the measure would be defeated (**3557**&n2, **3563**&n8, **3594**) was vindicated on 19 June 1861 when, after Disraeli rallied his troops (**3587**&n1), the Speaker cast his tie-breaking vote against it (**3596**&n1). It would again be defeated in 1862 and 1863.

Nevertheless, in Disraeli's view the Church remained vulnerable, largely because of internal division. As he put it to Mrs Brydges Willyams in November 1861: 'The state of the Church is critical – from dissensions & heresy – among its own children. If it were to fall, philosophy would not profit: we should only be handed over to a narrow-minded & ignorant fanaticism' (**3628**). At a diocesan meeting at Aylesbury next day, he presented an orthodox defence of the Church against the essayists and higher critics and called for a united front in support of pro-Church legislation (**3626**&n1, **3628**n1). When the Bishop of Natal, John Colenso, challenged the literal truth of the Pentateuch, Disraeli echoed the storm of Church protest in calling Colenso's book 'a great scandal' (**3741**&n4). He saw Palmerston's policy of appointing only Evangelical or Low Church clergy to bishoprics as another divisive factor; his attempt to get Wilberforce appointed Archbishop of York in 1862 was an effort to counter it (**3742**&n4). He bemoaned the 'systematic hostility always shown by the Catholic members of the House of Commons to the Church of England', which he thought 'most unwise. We live in times when Churches should act together' (**3803**). He opposed relaxing the requirement that clergy subscribe to all of the Church's Thirty-Nine Articles of faith (**3821**&n2). He opposed the Burials Bill (which would have allowed Dissenters access to Church of England cemeteries), and hailed its defeat as a 'great triumph', although he supported the Prison Ministers Bill (allowing prisoners to choose the religion of the chaplains visiting them and therefore a predominantly pro-Catholic measure) even though it was seen by some as a threat to the established Church (**3803**&nn1-4, **3805**). Addressing the National Conservative Registration Association in June 1863, he identified maintaining the union of church and state as a major issue distinguishing Conservatives from Liberals, who, he said, wished to abolish the union (**3824**&n6).

It was in this embattled context that, at Wilberforce's request on 25 November 1864, he delivered to an audience of clergymen at Oxford his well-known 'apes and angels' speech (**3970**&n1). In this he reproached clergy who 'embraced the perspective of the new criticism and philosophical scepticism yet remained within the church,' behaviour which Disraeli saw as a major threat to the Church from within. Discounting much new criticism as 'second-hand,' he challenged his audience with his own version of 'spontaneity of consciousness': 'there is something in original research so invigorating to the intellect, which so braces and disciplines the human mind that those who have undergone that process arrive at their conclusions with great caution and with great circumspection'. It was from this perspective that he approached the conflict between science and religion. Here he made a distinction, between 'the most advanced, the most fashionable, and modest school of modern science' – evidently the social sciences in the development of which Disraeli had strongly supported Stanley (VII **2980**&n1) – and the 'later teaching' (*ie*, Darwinism), which he was not prepared to admit was 'more scientific' in relation to 'the highest nature ... Man'. The current glib question the distinction produced, he said, was whether man was 'an ape or an angel? (A laugh.) Now,' he famously pronounced, 'I am on the side of the angels. (Cheers.)'.

In this context, his declaration is no simplistic creationist position. It actually resembles that of some modern humanist intellectuals who, while fully aligned with evolutionary science, also insist against reductionist interpretations of human nature and culture, and who argue for approaching all aspects of the human phenomenon with appreciation of Man's potential higher nature. For Disraeli, the anchor of this perspective was the Church, teaching that 'man is made in the image of his Creator (cheers) – a source of inspiration – a source from which alone can flow not only every right principle of morals, but every Divine truth' (**3970**n1). Infamous as this speech has in some contexts become, in it Disraeli was defending the Church as 'the main remedial agency in our present state,' that is, as one of the key institutions, along with the Monarchy and the Constitution, that uphold the Conservative view of civil society. He was obviously wrong about the scientific validity of Darwinism, but that need not detract from his emphasis on the human need for spirituality in a materialistic world.

As well as his alliance with the Church, these letters indicate his increasing acceptance into the social establishment. He was appointed a trustee to the British Museum (**3801**) and to the National Portrait Gallery (**3917**); he dined often at Buckingham Palace (**3455-6**, **3480**), and in 1861 Mary Anne received her first invitation to Windsor (**3547**); he was invited to converse with King Leopold (**3480**, **3537**, **3594**), and he hobnobbed with French princes (**3555**, **3578**, **3594**), the Egyptian Pasha (**3697**) and the Speaker of the House (**3598**, **3610**, **3920**). He and Mary Anne mingled with Wellingtons (**3486**, **3962**), Salisburys, Northumberlands (**3628**, **3625**), Derbys (**3815**), Jerseys (**3849**) and a Grand Duke (**3698**, **3702**). His relationship with the Jerseys remained close, as he continued to grapple (as he had since 1855) with the murky finances of their son Francis Villiers. An unknown amount of Disraeli's energies went into correspondence with London agents and distant would-be profiteers. 'I have no confidence,' he wrote, 'in any of the parties with whom we have to deal in this matter' (**3714**). The comparative paucity of surviving Disraeli letters on the subject belies (judging from the voluminous correspondence from the Jersey family) the extent of his work in unravelling the mess, which culminated in Villiers's early death abroad (**3714**).

These years also mark the growing rapport with Queen Victoria in the aftermath of Prince Albert's death in 1861. Disraeli was genuinely shocked at the Prince's death. Privately, he told Vitzthum: 'With Prince Albert we have buried our Sovereign. This German Prince has governed England for twenty-one years with a wisdom and energy such as none of our kings have ever shown' (**3654**n6). Publicly, he delivered an eloquent parliamentary eulogy, which perhaps over-stated the Prince's virtues but which drew the Queen's deep gratitude and a gift of portraits of herself and Albert (**3662**&n1, **3666**, **3667**&n2, see illustration p lvi). Later, his fulsome speech in support of funds for Albert's memorial (**3809**&nn1&3) again brought thanks, a personal interview at Windsor and an inscribed copy of the Prince's collected speeches (**3813-14**). The groundwork was being laid for the important future bond between politician and monarch.

In this period Disraeli at last found his way cleared through his labyrinthine finances, some of whose persistent debts charged a ruinous 10% in interest. Many details are lacking (perhaps destroyed by Philip Rose) for the steps that accomplished his liberation, and it is still hard to follow the threads that were left available, or to determine which of his many advisors and/or creditors were involved at each stage. Henry Padwick, for example, somehow a participant with Disraeli in dealing with Villiers's affairs, may also have helped in managing Disraeli's own (**3766**). The principal agent, however, was undoubtedly the enterprising Philip Rose, by now an international financier but still faithfully giving Disraeli advice on investments, and in some cases loans (**3906**). The 'great affair' (**3748**) in 1862-4 was the consolidation of Disraeli's debts into a manageable whole, engineered by Rose through the benevolence of the wealthy Conservative landowner Andrew Montagu. As early as January 1862, Disraeli and Rose were discussing consolidation, 'the basis of everything, &, if effected quickly, may have the happiest results' (**3649**). Although Montagu is not mentioned by name in the letters until May, Disraeli evidently met with him on 4 March; documents in the Bucks Record Office show that many of the deeds involved were transferred to Montagu on 14 March (**3683**&nn1&2). In return, Montagu took a mortgage on Hughenden at only 3% instead of 10%, meaning that Disraeli, who had been paying out £6,000 a year, now paid only £1,800, which could be covered by his party pension of £2,000. His congratulations to Rose were fervent: 'This is a great year, commencing, as it did, with yr. masterly consolidation' (**3737**). In addition, a large loan was negotiated, initially for £35,000 but finally for £60,000, partly secured by a second mortgage (**3740**, **3748**). When Lionel de Rothschild, who had made previous gifts to Disraeli but disliked loans, was suggested as co-lender, Disraeli was not optimistic about the chances. By a stroke of luck – 'it must be Fate,' he exulted – he and Mary Anne found themselves in the same Torquay hotel over Christmas 1862 and he was able to get Rothschild's agreement. 'I shd., indeed, have been a blunderer, to have lost the marvellous opportunity of the last fortnight!' (**3767**)

Now he had solid financial ground beneath his feet, perhaps the best indication of which was the full-scale renovation of Hughenden house and gardens and the replacement or refurbishment of its contents in order to hold suitably illustrious house parties like those to which they were regularly invited. The lists of guests in the letters read like a mid-century *Who's Who* of politicians, aristocrats, writers and handsome young men (**3944**, **3950**, **3962**). Mary Anne, whose health had not been good at the start of 1860 (VII **3430**, **3432**), now exhibited in her seventies the vigour and spirits of a woman half her age. Sir Stafford Northcote thought her 'great fun,' with a warmth of personality that compensated for some of her less inhibited remarks to Disraeli's aristocratic friends (**3445**n3). As a surprise for her husband, she commissioned an obelisk at Hughenden as a monument to Isaac D'Israeli (**3707-8**; and *see* illustration p lviii) before tackling the progressive Gothicization of the house itself. For details of the renovations see Appendix VIII. Even before renovation began, the house parties, Disraeli complained, were 'as hard work as having a playhouse – or keeping an Inn' (**3715**); once work did start, in November 1862, Hughenden became 'a chaos'. Outdoors, Mary Anne superintended more than twenty navvies who levelled the ground for broad grassy terraces, and there were as many workmen inside the house, 'for altho' I always thought, that, both from form, & situation, I was safe from architects, it turns out that I was wrong, & Hughenden House will soon assume a new form & character' (**3747**). By January 1863, he was welcoming the prospect of a week with the Salisburys at Hatfield, where he could work in peace (**3777**). By August, however, although they were confined to two rooms in the house, he boasted to Mrs Brydges Willyams (with some poetic licence): 'We have realised a romance we had been many years meditating: we have restored the House to what it was before the civil wars' (**3853**). Workmen were still there in November, but, as he totted up builders' accounts, he comforted himself: 'She has been very much amused, wh: is something for your money' (**3875**). The cost was over £3,000 (**3876**), probably not including the new furnishings, linens, carpets and curtains Mary Anne ordered from London, or the statues and shrubbery she bought to place around the estate (**3876**&n1).

With the timely good fortune that so often marked Disraeli's career, the renovations were barely over when another source of great expectations became a reality. Between 1860 and 1863, the Disraelis travelled dutifully to Torquay to spend Christmas and New Year with the aging Mrs Brydges Willyams. Over this time Disraeli also devoted considerable time and research, amid his political concerns, to establishing what exactly should be included in her personal coat of arms, only to find at the end that all she wanted was forty engraved bookplates (**3600**, **3650-51**, **3669**, **3673**). Both he and Mary Anne, however, were always solicitous for her comfort, and it is thanks to his letters to her that we have the full and entertaining descriptions of his life at this period. During their 1862 visit, he realized that she was failing, and in early November 1863 received the news that she had died at Torquay, refusing to have him summoned because he was 'a Statesman & must not be disturbed' (**3877**n1). As she had promised him, Disraeli inherited from her £40,000 (**3887**), a substantial legacy to go with the debt consolidation. As he had promised her, she was buried at Hughenden, though, by a quirk of recent law, it could not be in the church itself (**3884**&n1).

She appreciated the frequency with which he wrote to her: 'Your incomparable letters,' she told him shortly before her death, 'are my admiration and my comfort' (**3842**n1). Though she probably did not fully understand much of what he wrote to her – international diplomacy, by-election results and parliamentary debates as well as social doings – her death, following that of his sister, Sarah, in 1859, left him without a sympathetic female correspondent; his letters to Lady Londonderry drop off sharply in these years. As a result, the letters in 1864 show some diminution in epistolary brilliance and much less of his social life. Disraeli absolutely required at least one intelligent correspondent. It is likely that his secretary, Ralph Earle, helped to fill this role, although the mere nine surviving letters here do not reflect the volume of correspondence between them at this period, and only partly the extent to which Disraeli relied on his advice, sometimes quoting his words verbatim to other correspondents or in his speeches (**3584**n5, **3789**n1). The same may be true of Lord Henry Lennox, whose long letter about the impact of Albert's death on the court (**3637**) Disraeli reproduced the same day, without attribution, in a letter to Lady Londonderry (**3638**). He cultivated other correspondents, notably the Lygon brothers, Henry (by now Lord Beauchamp) and Frederick, putting Beauchamp in a personal pantheon with Count D'Orsay and George Smythe (**3854**) and addressing Lygon as 'my most brilliant aide-de-camp' and 'Mon cher' (**3910**, **3912-13**). In late 1863, he even tried to regale a gouty Derby with London gossip about Palmerston's rumoured sexual escapades (**3866**). Perhaps foreseeing Mrs Brydges Willyams's demise, he shows signs in 1863 of wanting to inaugurate a correspondence with Lionel de Rothschild's wife, Charlotte, 'of bright mind & glowing pen' (**3843**); in this volume it resulted in only seven letters, although an appreciative Charlotte used his example to scold her son Leopold: 'remember that a great man, while lavishing the pearls of thought and the gems of style, does not disregard the graces of penmanship' (**3861**n1).

Despite his age, his health was generally good, and he bore the long hours of tedious Commons debate well, managing eight hours sleep between 4 *am* and noon (**3486**). In 1863 he suffered an unspecified leg injury, which led to gratifying concern among the Conservatives (**3851**n4, **3858**&n1). Like Derby, he began to suffer from gout, which, Northcote mischievously commented, was 'a good omen for a future premier' (**3894**n1). Although in the midst of the 1864 session he wrote to Lady Dorothy Nevill, 'I envy you in your exotic groves' (**3919**), politics were his driving force and his tonic their 'fascinating velocity' (**3702**). When there was a chance of action, optimism replaced boredom and he grew full of energy; about one imminent debate, Northcote recorded that he was 'in the highest spirits because the battle is to be fought by tactics and not by brute force' (**3586**n1). Similar vigour went into rallying his troops for debate on military expenditure in Gladstone's 1862 budget (**3682**, **3684-7**); he reminded Derby, who was nervous of confrontation: 'We drifted once into war. To drift into chronic deficits is not less dangerous,' words that Derby meekly adopted for his own speech in the Lords (**3688**n4). In fact, albeit cautiously, they were beginning to look forward again. They made lists of new and able MPs and potential cabinet appointees as though anticipating power (**3653**, **3837**) – although Derby pointed out that 'one of our great difficulties will be, not the selection of new [men], but the discarding of the old' (**3837**&n14). In late 1863, Disraeli was gleefully counting up by-elections won by Conservatives (**3859**, **3862**, **3866**), and by the end of 1864 both he and Derby were hearing rumours of dissolution (**3959**&nn1&4). 'Everyone says, the pear is ripe,' he wrote, but 'I wish, that it should deserve a stronger, scarcely a more refined, epithet, before it is introduced to the political dessert' (**3859**).

Perhaps the most significant aspect of the letters in this volume is Disraeli's ability to play a waiting game and to adapt at the same time. He was no longer an outsider; his leadership had been threatened but re-confirmed. He had presented himself as capable of moderation as well as vehemence; his finances had achieved stability, and he had championed the established Church as a cornerstone of order. He had reached a new level of security, and, though his time was not yet, it was not far off.

EDITORIAL PRINCIPLES

For the complete description of the editorial principles and conventions used in this edition see VOL I xxvii, reprinted in VOL II vii. The following is an abbreviated list summarizing the main points.

Headnote ADDRESSEE: the name is given in the shortest form consistent with clear identification.

DATE: square brackets indicate the parts of the date not actually in the text or on the cover. A question mark is placed after any parts of the date about which doubt remains (see dating note in EDITORIAL COMMENT).

LOCATION OF ORIGINAL: given in short form: see Abbreviations. A PS indicates a printed source, the MS not having been found (see PUBLICATION HISTORY).

REFERENCE NUMBER: the archival number used by the holder of the original MS, numbers in square brackets added by us if necessary. In the case of a PS, the number refers to the Project's system of reference.

COVER: vertical solidi indicate line divisions in the address. Integral covers and separate envelopes are not distinguished.

POSTMARKS: see VOL I xxxiii for illustrations of the most common ones.

PUBLICATION HISTORY: not exhaustive; first and perhaps subsequent important publication, especially in M&B and Blake, are cited.

EDITORIAL COMMENT: *Sic*: list of words and phrases from the text that are incorrect (according to SOED), unusual or otherwise puzzling; includes incorrect, but not omitted, accents and punctuation. *Dating*: cites the logic by which a date has been attributed.

Text No silent corrections have been made. D's erasures have been noted whenever possible. Square brackets have been used to add material to facilitate easy reading. When abbreviations ending in periods are thus expanded, the periods have been dropped unless otherwise needed for punctuation. Editorial comments in square brackets are italicized. Catchwords are not repeated or noted, and are given before the page break sign (/). **NEW IN THIS VOLUME**: D's insertions have been indicated by up and down arrows (↑ ↓) at the beginning and end respectively of each insertion. VERTICAL SOLIDI (|) are used to indicate line divisions in the date, address, addressee and signature sections to allow us to render them in continuous form.

DIAGONAL SOLIDI (/ with space both before and after) indicate page breaks. This is a change from the usage in VOL I and VOL II.
DATE, ADDRESS AND ADDRESSEE, if present in the text, are always given at the beginning of the letter (unless it is a fragment), regardless of where D put them in the MS.
[?] follows any reading on which some doubt remains.
Italics indicate single underlining.
Small capitals indicate multiple underlining.
D's abbreviation of 'the' as 'ye', *ie* using the thorn to represent 'th', has been rendered as 'the'.

Annotations

Sources cited are given a short form (see List of Abbreviations and Short Titles) if used more than a few times. Standard reference works (*eg* DNB, *EB* XI, *OED*) are cited only if directly quoted. Each name is normally identified by a main note (in bold type in the index) the first time it occurs in the text of a letter, and thereafter only as required for clarification of a letter. Of the material in the appendices, only the pre-1860 letters in Appendix I have been annotated. In transcriptions of MA's writing, we have eschewed the use of '*sic*', despite her unconventional grammar and spelling. We also do not comment on eccentric punctuation (*eg* Lennox's).

Index

All names in the text and annotation of the letters have been indexed, main notes being indicated by bold type. The subject matter of the letters and notes has also been indexed. All references are to letter numbers, not pages. Except for the pre-1860 letters in Appendix I, the appendices and introductory materials have not been indexed.

DISRAELI CHRONOLOGY 1860–1864

1860

1 Jan	at Grosvenor Gate (since 2 December 1859)
24 Jan	opening of Parliament; Address replying to Speech
26 Jan	comment on Friday adjournments
30 Jan	question on annexation of Savoy to France
2 Feb	question on annexation of Savoy to France
6 Feb	comment on postponing budget
8 Feb	speech on Church Rates Bill
9 Feb	comment on Friday adjournments
10 Feb	comment on postponing budget
15 Feb	at Queen's levee
17 Feb	question on exchequer bonds; speech on commercial treaty with France
20 Feb	speech on Customs Acts
24 Feb	question on House business; speech on budget
28 Feb	comment on annexation of Savoy and Nice to France; comment on Customs Acts
29 Feb	dines at Buckingham Palace
1 Mar	comment on Reform Bill
2 Mar	comment on Franklin expedition
5 Mar	comment on commercial treaty (Savoy and Nice)
6 Mar	comment on France's annexation of Savoy and Nice
8 Mar	comment on East Indian labourers; comment on commercial treaty with France
9 Mar	speech on commercial treaty with France
12 Mar	comment on annexation of Savoy and Nice to France
13 Mar	speech on Italian affairs
16 Mar	comment on supply (China)
19 Mar	speech on Reform Bill
22 Mar	comment on Reform Bill
23 Mar	speech on annexation of Savoy and Nice to France
26 Mar	comment on army establishments; speech on income tax; comment on Licences Bill

1860 *continued*

29 Mar	comment on order of business
30 Mar	comment on Easter recess; speech on income tax
31 Mar	comment on Stamp Duties Bill
2 Apr	comment on public business
4 Apr	at Hughenden
17 Apr	at Grosvenor Gate; comment on parliamentary proceedings
20 Apr	comment on church rates; comment on Duchy of Cornwall
23 Apr	comment on Reform Bill
26 Apr	comment on Reform Bill; comment on Paper Duty Bill
27 Apr	speech on Church Rates Bill
30 Apr	comment on House business
7 May	questions on House business; speech on Walter and Horsman
8 May	speech on Paper Duty Bill
11 May	question on public business; speech on House practice
14 May	questions on order of business
15 May	question on order of business
17 May	comment on civil service estimates
24 May	speech on civil service estimates
25 May	on taxes committee; to Hughenden
30 May	at Grosvenor Gate
31 May	comment on General Grey
2 Jun	at Commons meeting at Derby's
4 Jun	speech on Reform Bill
6 Jun	Lord Henry Bentinck breaks with D
7 Jun	speech on Reform Bill
11 Jun	proposes to resign House leadership; speech on Reform Bill
12 Jun	comment on supply (China)
18 Jun	meets King Leopold at Buckingham Palace
21 Jun	dines with Queen Victoria; comment on petitions
22 Jun	chairs Society of Arts dinner; at Queen's state ball
3 Jul	question re tax bills
5 Jul	speech on tax bills
16 Jul	comment on House late sittings
17 Jul	speech on paper duties
19 Jul	questions and speech on public business
23 Jul	comment on fortifications; questions re paper duty
26 Jul	speech on public business
27 Jul	speech on public business
6 Aug	speech on paper duty
9 Aug	speech on Galway mails
16 Aug	at Hughenden
28 Aug	Parliament prorogued
12 Sep	Hughenden fête to 100 children and others
26 Sep	speech at Royal Bucks Agricultural Association
2 Oct	at Cumberland Lodge, Windsor (Col Wood)

1860 *continued*

3 Oct	speech at South Bucks Agricultural Association
4 Oct	at Hughenden
15 Oct	at Quarter Sessions, Aylesbury
3 Nov	at Grosvenor Gate
6 Nov	at Berwick election inquiry
7 Nov	at Hughenden
14-15 Nov	entertains Bishop Wilberforce at Hughenden
19 Nov	at Mentmore
21 Nov	at Hughenden
4 Dec	speech on church rates at Prestwood, Bucks
19 Dec	at Grosvenor Gate
23 Dec	letter to King Leopold
27 Dec	at Haldon House, Exeter (Palks)
31 Dec	at Torquay

1861

12 Jan	at Grosvenor Gate
14 Jan	at Hatfield
18 Jan	at Grosvenor Gate
23 Jan	at Windsor Castle
25 Jan	at Grosvenor Gate
30 Jan	at Mentmore
1 Feb	at Grosvenor Gate
4 Feb	Grosvenor Gate parliamentary dinner
5 Feb	Parliament opens; speech on foreign policy
7 Feb	speech on House business; on House business committee
8 Feb	comment on Red Sea Telegraph Company
14 Feb	comment on Charity Trustees Bill; comment on excusing MPs from committees; vote of thanks to army in China; comment on Red Sea Telegraph Company
18 Feb	speech on Highways Bill
19 Feb	speech on County Franchise Bill
27 Feb	speech on Church Rates Bill
1 Mar	question on inquiry into Chancery Funds; comment on Admiralty committee
2 Mar	Scottish MPs at Grosvenor Gate
4 Mar	at Hughenden; Bucks Lent Assizes; dines at Carrington's
5 Mar	at Grosvenor Gate; speech on hop duties
7 Mar	at Aston Clinton, for Rothschild's dinner to judges
8 Mar	at Grosvenor Gate
12 Mar	speech on Admiralty committee
13 Mar	speech on County Franchise Bill
14 Mar	comment on China war
15 Mar	responds to Peel's personal remarks
16 Mar	death of Duchess of Kent

1861 *continued*

18 Mar	seconds Address of condolence on Duchess of Kent; comment on Bankruptcy Bill
19 Mar	comment on East India income tax; speech on Afghan war
26 Mar	at Cardiff
28 Mar	visits Pantgwynlais
30 Mar	at Tredegar (Lord Tredegar)
3 Apr	at Grosvenor Gate
4 Apr	at Wimpole (Lord Hardwicke)
6 Apr	at Grosvenor Gate
10 Apr	American Civil War begins
22 Apr	comment on Ways and Means Committee
24 Apr	comment on Nonconformist Burial Bill
29 Apr	comment on bribery at Berwick; speech on ways and means; comment on income tax
2 May	comment on income tax; comment and speech on tea and sugar
3 May	comment on Princess Alice's marriage
6 May	comments on paper duty
7 May	speech on Ireland Tramways Bill; comment and speech on Ways and Means report
9 May	speech on Army estimates; comments on Ways and Means report, duties and revenue
13 May	speech on Inland Revenue Bill
15 May	speech at Royal Literary Fund dinner
16 May	question on public business; speech on Inland Revenue
18 May	at Hughenden
22 May	at Grosvenor Gate
27 May	comment on Inland Revenue Bill
28 May	comment on Derby Day adjournment
30 May	speech on Inland Revenue Bill
3 Jun	rumours of his resignation
5 Jun	at opening of Horticultural Gardens, Kensington
10 Jun	comment on Appropriation of Seats Bill
12 Jun	speech at Agricultural Benevolent Institution
14 Jun	speech on Galway Postal Contract
17 Jun	speech on Appropriation of Seats Bill
18 Jun	audience with King Leopold
19 Jun	defeat of Church Rates Bill
24 Jun	speech on reinforcements for Canada; speech on civil service estimates
27 Jun	comment on East India Council
28 Jun	at Buckingham Palace concert
1 Jul	comment on civil service estimates
4 Jul	comments on House business, civil service estimates
5 Jul	speech on Wakefield new writ

1861 *continued*

8 Jul	comment on civil service estimates
10 Jul	at Apsley House
11 Jul	at Lord Montrose's
16 Jul	comment on Bankruptcy Bill; speech on Galway Postal Contract
18 Jul	comment on Duke of Modena
25 Jul	comments on Ecclesiastical Registry, civil service estimates
26 Jul	speech on Navy estimates
30 Jul	Russell elevated to peerage
31 Jul	at Hatfield
2 Aug	at Knebworth; death of Lord Herbert
5 Aug	at Grosvenor Gate
6 Aug	Parliament prorogued
8 Aug	at Hughenden
15 Aug	Ralph Disraeli marries Katherine Trevor
4 Oct	death of Eglinton
16 Oct	at Grosvenor Gate
18 Oct	at Hughenden
25 Oct	death of Graham
8 Nov	*Trent* incident
14 Nov	speech at Diocesan meeting, Aylesbury
19 Nov	at Grosvenor Gate
22 Nov	at Alnwick Castle (Northumberland)
29 Nov	at Seaham Hall (Londonderry)
2 Dec	speech inaugurating Londonderry monument at Durham
10 Dec	at Grosvenor Gate
14 Dec	at Gunnersbury; death of Prince Albert
16 Dec	at Grosvenor Gate
17 Dec	at Torquay

1862

1 Jan	at Grosvenor Gate
22 Jan	at Hatfield
25 Jan	at Grosvenor Gate
5 Feb	Grosvenor Gate parliamentary dinner
6 Feb	Parliament opens; eulogy of Prince Albert
11 Feb	speech on House estimates
13 Feb	speech on education regulations
17 Feb	comment on estimates for Canada
20 Feb	speech on Gloucester City writ
21 Feb	comment on education regulations
25 Feb	Queen sends portraits of herself and Prince Albert
27 Feb	comment on education regulations
28 Feb	question and comment on education regulations
6 Mar	at Bucks Lent assizes

1862 *continued*	
7 Mar	at Grosvenor Gate
10 Mar	question on Italian proclamations
14 Mar	Hughenden mortgage transferred to Andrew Montagu
16 Mar	influenza
17 Mar	question on income tax; speech on maritime law
18 Mar	speech on education, science and art
28 Mar	comments on education regulations
1 Apr	question on Easter recess
5 Apr	Grosvenor Gate parliamentary dinner
7 Apr	speech on budget taxes
24 Apr	at Mentmore
26 Apr	at Grosvenor Gate
28 Apr	speech at Lord Mayor's banquet
29 Apr	comment on prisons
1 May	at opening of International Exhibition, Kensington
8 May	death of Francis Villiers; comment and speech on budget and foreign policy
14 May	speech on Church Rates Bill
19 May	speech on budget and national security
24 May	party meeting on budget at Derby's
1 Jun	party meeting at Derby's
3 Jun	comments and speech on national expenditure
5 Jun	comment on civil service estimates
7 Jun	at Mentmore
10 Jun	at Grosvenor Gate
13 Jun	speech on Italian outrage on Mr Taylor
20 Jun	comment on suppression of *British Star*
23 Jun	at Royal Agricultural show; speech on fortifications
24 Jun	comment on Church Rates Bill
Jun	monument to Isaac D'Israeli at Hughenden
5 Jul	interview with Prince Napoleon; speech at banquet to Viceroy of Egypt
10 Jul	comments on fortifications
20 Jul	Grosvenor Gate dinner to Grand Duke of Weimar
25 Jul	speech on defence of Canada
30 Jul	comments on Union Relief Bill
31 Jul	comment on Union Relief Bill
1 Aug	speech on Palmerston administration
7 Aug	Parliament prorogued
9 Aug	at Hughenden
28 Aug	Hughenden luncheon
16 Sep	at Addington Manor, Bucks (Hubbard)
17 Sep	speech at North Bucks Agricultural meeting
18 Sep	at Hughenden
22-9 Sep	Hughenden house party

1862 *continued*	
30 Sep	at Aston Clinton
1 Oct	speech at Central Bucks Agricultural meeting
3 Oct	at Hughenden
13 Oct	at Quarter Sessions, Aylesbury
16 Oct	Hughenden school opening; Hughenden house party
29-31 Oct	Hughenden house party for Bishop Wilberforce
30 Oct	speech to Diocese Benefices Society, High Wycombe
6 Nov	at Grosvenor Gate
13 Nov	sale of Taynton property
17 Nov	at Hughenden
18 Nov	Hughenden renovations begin
2 Dec	starts fund for Bucks families in Lancs
13 Dec	at Grosvenor Gate
20 Dec	at Torquay

1863	
5 Jan	at Plymouth (Normanby)
8 Jan	at Grosvenor Gate
9 Jan	meets Rose re agreement with Rothschild and Montagu
21 Jan	at Hatfield
24 Jan	James Disraeli's paralysis; at Grosvenor Gate
4 Feb	Grosvenor Gate political dinner
5 Feb	Parliament opens; speech responding to Queen's Speech
11 Feb	Grosvenor Gate political dinner
14 Feb	Grosvenor Gate political dinner
17 Feb	comment re Prince of Wales's marriage; speech on commercial treaty with Italy
18 Feb	Grosvenor Gate political dinner
19 Feb	comment re Prince of Wales's marriage
25 Feb	at Prince of Wales's levee
27 Feb	speech on Poland
28 Feb	Grosvenor Gate political dinner
4 Mar	Grosvenor Gate political dinner
7 Mar	Grosvenor Gate party to watch pre-wedding procession
10 Mar	at wedding of Prince of Wales to Princess Alexandra
13 Mar	at Duchess of Cambridge's
20 Mar	at Waleses' party at St James's Palace
25 Mar	elected British Museum trustee
27 Mar	parliamentary Easter recess
30 Mar	at Hughenden
6 Apr	at Aylesbury meeting; at Wotton (Duke of Buckingham)
8 Apr	at Hughenden
11 Apr	at Grosvenor Gate
13 Apr	Parliament resumes
14 Apr	comment on death of Sir George Cornewall Lewis
15 Apr	speech on Burials Bill

1863 *continued*

18 Apr	Grosvenor Gate political dinner
20 Apr	speech on Prison Ministers Bill
22-3 Apr	at Windsor Castle
23 Apr	audience with Queen; speech on Prince Albert's memorial
24 Apr	Queen sends copy of Prince Albert's speeches
28 Apr	speech on Army
4 May	comment on public business; speech on Inland Revenue Bill
7 May	comment on Brazil; speech on Prison Ministers Bill
8 May	speech on commerce with Naples
9 May	Grosvenor Gate political dinner
13 May	at Derbys' dinner
16 May	at Princess of Wales's drawing room; at Stanhopes' dinner
18 May	comments on civil service estimates
20 May	at Northumberlands' dinner
21 May	at Hughenden
28 May	at Grosvenor Gate
4 Jun	comment on Holyhead Harbour
8 Jun	at Guildhall banquet
9 Jun	speech on Uniformity Act
10 Jun	at unveiling of Prince Albert statue
11 Jun	speech at Merchant Taylors banquet to Prince of Wales
12 Jun	at Northumberlands' dinner to Waleses
15-18 Jun	at Oxford Commemoration festivities
18 Jun	at Grosvenor Gate
22 Jun	speech on Poland
25 Jun	at Miss Copley's wedding; comment on Mhow court martial; speech on army expenses
26 Jun	speech at Conservative Association dinner; at Guards' ball for Waleses
29 Jun	comment on diplomatic service
30 Jun	at Miss Lowther's wedding
2 Jul	comments on Exhibition buildings purchase
9 Jul	comment on British subjects in Japan
27 Jul	at Hatfield
28 Jul	death of Normanby; Parliament prorogued
29 Jul	at Grosvenor Gate
3 Aug	at Hughenden
16? Aug	at Carringtons' dinner, Wycombe Abbey
1 Sep	at Cliveden (Duchess of Sutherland)
4 Sep	at Osterley (Jerseys)
16 Sep	speech at Rayners Harvest Home, Bucks
post-18 Sep	injures leg
23 Sep	unable to attend Central Bucks Agricultural Association
24 Sep	unable to attend Hughenden Harvest Home
12 Oct	death of Lyndhurst
13 Oct	*Times*'s eulogy of Lyndhurst (by D?)

1863 *continued*

11 Nov	death of SBW; at Torquay
18 Nov	at Grosvenor Gate
19 Nov	at Hughenden; SBW's funeral
20? Nov	at Torquay
28 Nov	at Grosvenor Gate
9 Dec	at Stowe (Duke of Buckingham)
12 Dec	at Grosvenor Gate
23 Dec	at Hatfield
28 Dec	at Grosvenor Gate

1864

1 Jan	to Hughenden and back
4 Jan	at Quarter Sessions, Aylesbury; at Mentmore (Mayer de Rothschild)
6 Jan	at Grosvenor Gate
13 Jan	at Burghley (Lord Exeter)
16 Jan	at Grosvenor Gate
20 Jan	at Tedworth (Lord Broughton)
22 Jan	at Grosvenor Gate
27 Jan	at Aston Clinton (Anthony de Rothschild)
29 Jan	at Grosvenor Gate
3 Feb	Grosvenor Gate political dinner
4 Feb	Parliament opens; speech replying to Queen's Speech
9 Feb	questions on war between Prussia and Denmark
13 Feb	Grosvenor Gate political dinner
15 Feb	question re armistice rumours
22 Feb	speech and comments on Schleswig-Holstein
27 Feb	Grosvenor Gate political dinner
29 Feb	speech on policy re Schleswig-Holstein
7 Mar	question on Jutland; comment on Annuities
8 Mar	question on Schleswig-Holstein
12 Mar	Grosvenor Gate political dinner
14 Mar	speech on Stansfeld and Mazzini
17 Mar	questions and speech on Stansfeld; comment on Denmark
18 Mar	MA has haemorrhage; D at Lionel de Rothschilds'
31 Mar	at Hughenden
4 Apr	at Quarter Sessions, Aylesbury
7 Apr	at Grosvenor Gate
14 Apr	speech on sugar duties
15 Apr	questions on under-secretaries
18 Apr	comment on Merthyr Tydvil writ; comment on Lowe; speech on privilege
19 Apr	speech, comment and question on Treaty of London
21 Apr	comment on ways and means
29 Apr	question on Germany and Denmark; comment on Mr Bewicke

1864 *continued*

5 May	question on London conference
9 May	question on Danish-German war
10 May	at Apponyi's
11 May	at Buckingham Palace
17? May	new edition of *Revolutionary Epic*
28 May	'At Home' for 300 at Grosvenor Gate
2 Jun	speech on education reports
6 Jun	speech on London conference
10 Jun	question on armistice
17 Jun	speech on Ashantee war
20 Jun	questions on London conference
23 Jun	question on 'Gladiator' troopship; questions on London conference
25 Jun	London conference ends in failure
27 Jun	speech on foreign policy
4 Jul	speech of censure on government
7 Jul	at Miss Carrington's wedding, Whitehall; comments on censure of government
8 Jul	speech on censure of government
19 Jul	At Strawberry Hill (Waldegrave)
21 Jul	at Hatfield
23 Jul	at Grosvenor Gate
29 Jul	Parliament prorogued
8 Aug	at Hughenden
28 Aug	25th wedding anniversary
6 Sep	to and from London
21 Sep	speech at Central Bucks Agricultural meeting, Aylesbury
26-30 Sep	Hughenden house parties
5 Oct	speech at South Bucks Agricultural meeting, Salt Hill
6-11 Oct	Hughenden house parties
17 Oct	at Quarter Sessions, Aylesbury
24 Oct	in London
2-5 Nov	Hughenden house parties
10 Nov	at Grosvenor Gate
21 Nov	at Hughenden
24 Nov	at Cuddesdon Palace (Bishop of Oxford)
25 Nov	'apes and angels' speech at Oxford
26 Nov	at Hughenden
29 Nov	at Strathfieldsaye (Wellington)
2 Dec	at Beckett (Barrington)
5 Dec	at Hughenden
20 Dec	at Grosvenor Gate
22 Dec	at Hatfield
27 Dec	at Grosvenor Gate
30 Dec	at Hughenden

ABBREVIATIONS IN VOLUME EIGHT

A	denotes an additional letter to be inserted into the sequence
ABPC	*American Book Prices Current*
ADM	Gordon Adamson, collection of
AES	A.E. Scanes
app	Appendix
AR	*Annual Register* (followed by year)
ATM	*Autographic Mirror*
BA	British Almanac (followed by year)
BAR	Baring Brothers, collection of
BCP	Lady Beauchamp, collection of (now deposited at BL)
BEA	Belvoir Castle, Lincolnshire
Bell *Palmerston*	Herbert Bell *Lord Palmerston* (1936 repr 1966)
BH	*The Bucks Herald*
BHF	Chris Cook and Brendan Keith *British Historical Facts* (1975)
BL	The British Library, London
Blake	Robert Blake *Disraeli* (1966)
Boase	Frederick Boase *Modern English Biography* (1892 repr 1965)
BODL	Bodleian Library, Oxford
Bourne	H.R. Fox Bourne *English Newspapers* 2 vols (1887)
Bradford	Sarah Bradford *Disraeli* (1982)
BRI	Christopher Briggs, collection of
Bright	John Bright *The Diaries of John Bright* (1930)
BRN	Brandeis University, Waltham, MA
BSP:HC	*British Sessional Papers: House of Commons* (followed by year)
BUC	Buckinghamshire Record Office, Aylesbury
BUL	Birmingham University Library
C	Conservative
CARR	Carrington Collection, Bodleian Library, Oxford
Chadwick	Owen Chadwick *The Victorian Church* 2 vols (New York 1966)
Clapham	J.H. Clapham *An Economic History of Modern Britain* 3 vols (Cambridge 1932; repr 1967)
Clergy List	*The Clerical Guide and Ecclesiastical Directory* publ by Rivington, later *The Clerical Directory* publ by Crockford (followed by year of edition)

CUL	Columbia University Library, New York
Cunningham	Peter Cunningham *Hand-Book of London Past and Present* (1850)
D	Benjamin Disraeli (and thus also 'the DS' = D and MA)
DA	Douglas C. Anderson, collection of
DBP	Derby Papers, 14th & 15th Earls, Liverpool City Libraries
Dickens Letters	Graham Storey ed *The Letters of Charles Dickens* 12 vols (Oxford 1974-2002)
Dino	Duchesse de Dino *Chronique de 1831 à 1862* (Paris 1909), followed by volume number
Disraeli, Derby	John Vincent ed *Disraeli, Derby and the Conservative Party: Journals and Memoirs of Edward Henry, Lord Stanley 1849-1869* (Hassocks, Sussex 1978)
Disraeli Newsletter	The Disraeli Project *Newsletter* (1976-81)
DNB	Sir Leslie Stephen and Sir Sidney Lee eds *The Dictionary of National Biography* (1917 repr 1973)
DR	Helen M. Swartz and Martin Swartz eds *Disraeli's Reminiscences* (1975)
DUR	Durham County Record Office
DURG	Durham University Library (Grey Papers)
EB XI	*Encyclopædia Britannica* Eleventh Edition (1910-11)
ec	Editorial comment section of the headnote
EH	*The Evening Herald*
EIC	East India Company
EJM	ex-Jewish Museum (see abbreviations in Volume II)
Ellens	J.P. Ellens *Religious Routes to Gladstonian Liberalism: The Church Rate Conflict in England and Wales* (University Park, PA, 1994)
FIT	Fitzwilliam Museum, Cambridge
Foster	J. Foster *Alumni Oxonienses* (1887, 1888)
Frances Anne	Edith, Marchioness of Londonderry *Frances Anne: The Life and Times of Frances Anne Marchioness of Londonderry ...* (1958)
Furtado	Peter Furtado *et al* eds *The Ordnance Survey Guide to Historic Houses in Britain* (New York 1987)
GLA	John F. Glaser, collection of
Gladstone Diaries	M.R.D. Foot and H.C.G. Matthew eds *The Gladstone Diaries* (1968-94)
GM	*The Gentleman's Magazine*
GMF	John Simon Guggenheim Memorial Foundation
Greville	Lytton Strachey and Roger Fulford eds *The Greville Memoirs, 1814-60* 7 vols (1938)
GRI	Grinnell College Archives, Iowa
H	The Hughenden papers, Bodleian Library, Oxford
H acc	H WMA 4498 – MA's account book
HAL	Halifax Central Library, Calderdale, Halifax, UK
Hansard	*Hansard's Parliamentary Debates*
HARV	Harvard University, Baker Library, Cambridge, MA

HAS	Hon Mrs Hastings, collection of
HAV	Haverford College, Quaker Collection, Haverford, PA
Haydn	Joseph Haydn *The Book of Dignities* 3rd ed (1894 repr Baltimore 1970)
HCC	Hampshire County Council
HCR	Hertford County Record Office
HEY	Robert Heyneman, Chapel Hill, NC
H/LIFE	Monypenny papers in H for his *Life of Disraeli*
Holt *Risorgimento*	Edgar Holt *Risorgimento: The Making of Italy, 1815-1870* (1970)
HUL	University of Hull
HUNT	Huntington Library, San Marino, California
HWD	Denis Hill-Wood, collection of
ILLU	University of Illinois, Urbana-Champaigne, Illinois
INL	National Library of Ireland, Dublin
INU	Indiana University, Bloomington
Isaac	Isaac Disraeli
JAH	Jacobs & Hunt Fine Art Auctioneers, Petersfield, Hampshire
James or Jem	James Disraeli
Jenkins *Gladstone*	Roy Jenkins *Gladstone* (1995)
JHC	*Journal of the House of Commons*
JWA	John Wilson Autographs, London
KCR	Kent County Record Office, Maidstone
Kenealy	Arabella Kenealy *Memoirs of Edward Vaughan Kenealy, LL.D, by his daughter Arabella Kenealy* (1908)
Koss *Political Press*	Stephen Koss *The Rise and Fall of the Political Press in Britain* (Chapel Hill, NC 1981)
L	Liberal
Lady Londonderry	The Marchioness of Londonderry ed *Letters from Benjamin Disraeli to Frances Anne Marchioness of Londonderry 1837-1861* (1938)
Law List	*Clarke's New Law List* compiled by S. Hill and later by T. Cockell (followed by year of edition)
LCC	Lowry-Corry Collection
LGB	Benjamin Disraeli *Lord George Bentinck: A Political Biography* (1st ed 1852)
LIS	Raymond Lister, collection of
LIV	Liverpool City Libraries and Record Office
Londonderrys	H. Montgomery Hyde *The Londonderrys: A Family Portrait* (1979)
Longford *Victoria R.I.*	Elizabeth Longford *Victoria R.I.* (1964)
Lowell	A. Lawrence Lowell *The Government of England* (1921) 2 vols
LPOD	*London Post Office Directory* (followed by year of edition)
LQV	Arthur C. Benson and Viscount Esher eds *The Letters of Queen Victoria: A Selection from Her Majesty's Correspondence between the Years 1837 and 1861* (1908)

*LQV*B	George Earle Buckle ed *The Letters of Queen Victoria: A Selection from Her Majesty's Correspondence and Journal between the Years 1862 and 1878* (1926)
LUC	Loyola University Chicago, E.M. Cudway Memorial Library
MA	Mary Anne Disraeli
Malmesbury	3rd Earl of Malmesbury *Memoirs of an Ex-minister* (1884) 2 vols
M&B	William Flavelle Monypenny and George Earle Buckle *The Life of Benjamin Disraeli, Earl of Beaconsfield* (1910-20) 6 vols
MC	*The Morning Chronicle*
McCalmont	*McCalmont's Parliamentary Poll Book: British Election Results 1832-1918* (1971)
Meacham *Lord Bishop*	Standish Meacham *Lord Bishop: The Life of Samuel Wilberforce, 1805-1873* (Cambridge, MA 1970)
Meynell	Wilfred Meynell *Benjamin Disraeli: An Unconventional Biography* (1903)
MH	*The Morning Herald*
MHS	Massachusetts Historical Society, Boston
MOPSIK	The Donald and Delores Mopsik Collection
Morley *Cobden*	John Morley *The Life of Richard Cobden* (14th ed, 1910)
Morley *Gladstone*	John Morley *The Life of William Ewart Gladstone* (1903) 3 vols
MP	*The Morning Post*
NCMH	J.P.T. Bury ed *The New Cambridge Modern History X 1830-70* (Cambridge 1971)
NOR	Duke of Northumberland, Alnwick Castle, collection of
Northcote	Andrew Lang ed *The Life, Letters, and Diaries of Sir Stafford Northcote* 2 vols (1890)
Norton Rose	Andrew St George *A History of Norton Rose* (1995)
NOT	University of Nottingham
NRO	Norfolk Record Office, Norwich
NYM	New York Public Library (Montague Collection)
Ogden	James Ogden *Isaac D'Israeli* (Oxford 1969)
ODNB	Colin Matthew and Brian Harrison eds *Oxford Dictionary of National Biography* (Oxford 2004)
OED	*Oxford English Dictionary*
Parker *Graham*	Charles Stuart Parker *Life and Letters of Sir James Graham* 2 vols (1907)
Pevsner	Nikolaus Pevsner *The Buildings of England: Buckinghamshire* (Harmondsworth 1960)
ph	Publication history section of the headnote
PML	Pierpont Morgan Library
PP	Palmerston Papers, Southampton University Library
Prest *Russell*	John Prest *Lord John Russell* (1972)
PRIN	Princeton University Library
PRO	Public Record Office, London
PS	Printed Source, identified in ph, used when the original MS has not been located

QUA	Disraeli Papers, formerly in the Queen's University Archives, Kingston, Ontario
R	denotes a letter now available from a manuscript or a more complete or reliable printed source replacing a fragmentary letter published in a previous volume (*eg* '**123R**' replaces '**123**')
RAC	Royal Archives
RD or Ralph	Ralph Disraeli
RIC	Rice University, Fondren Library
Ridley *Palmerston*	Jasper Ridley *Lord Palmerston* (1970)
RLF	Royal Literary Fund
RN	Royal Navy
ROSE	Lady Rosebery, collection of
ROTH	The Rothschild Archive, London
RTC	Lord Rothschild, collection of
RUL	University of Rochester Library, Rochester, NY
Sa or Sarah	Sarah Disraeli
SBW	Sarah Brydges Willyams
SCR	Somerset County Record Office
Sheahan	James Joseph Sheahan *History and Topography of Buckinghamshire* (1862 repr 1971)
SIL	Juliet Silcock, collection of
SPI	Harry and Brigitte Spiro, collection of
STCL	Strathclyde Regional Archive, Glasgow
Stenton	Michael Stenton *Who's Who of British Members of Parliament: Volume I, 1832-1885*; *Volume II, 1886-1918* (Hassocks, Sussex 1976, 1978)
Stewart *Conservative Party*	Robert Stewart *The Foundation of the Conservative Party 1830-1867* (1978)
Stewart *Writings*	R.W. Stewart *Benjamin Disraeli: A list of writings by him, and writings about him, with notes* (Metuchen, NJ 1972). Citations are of item numbers.
TCC	Trinity College, Cambridge
TEXU	University of Texas, Austin
TIA	Archives of *The Times*
UCLA	University of California, Los Angeles
ULR	John Ulrich, collection of
UO	A source that cannot be divulged for reasons such as requested confidentiality (rarely used)
URI	University of Rhode Island, Kingston, RI
Venn	John Venn and John Archibald Venn eds *Alumni Cantabrigienses* (1922-54)
VH-B	*The Victoria History of the Counties of England: A History of Buckinghamshire* (1969)
Victorian Travellers	*The Victorian Travellers Guide to 19th Century England and Wales* (1864 repr 1965)

Vitzthum	Count Charles Vitzthum von Eckstaedt *St. Petersburg and London in the Years 1852-1864: Reminiscences* 2 vols (1887)
Weintraub *Charlotte and Lionel*	Stanley Weintraub *Charlotte and Lionel: A Rothschild Love Story* (2003)
Weintraub *Disraeli*	Stanley Weintraub *Disraeli: A Biography* (New York 1993)
Weintraub *Edward*	Stanley Weintraub *Edward the Caresser* (New York 2001)
Weintraub *Victoria*	Stanley Weintraub *Victoria: An Intimate Biography* (New York 1987)
Wellesley Index	Walter E. Houghton ed *Wellesley Index to Victorian Periodicals* 5 vols (1966-89)
Whibley	Charles Whibley *Lord John Manners and His Friends* 2 vols (1925)
Woodham-Smith *QV*	Cecil Woodham-Smith *Queen Victoria: Her Life and Times Vol I 1819-1861* (1972)
WRC	Worcestershire Record Office, Shirehall
WSRO	West Sussex Record Office, Chichester
X	denotes an entirely new letter or fragment to be placed in chronological sequence after the corresponding letter number in a previous volume (*eg* '**123x**' follows '**123**')
YAU	Yale University, New Haven, CT

CHRONOLOGICAL LIST OF LETTERS 1860–1864

NO	DATE	TO	PLACE OF ORIGIN	LOCATION OF ORIGINAL
3438	1 JAN '60	SARAH BRYDGES WILLYAMS	[LONDON]	RTC
3439	[JAN '60]	LADY FRANKLIN	[LONDON]	PS
3440	4 JAN '60	LORD DERBY	GROSVENOR GATE	DBP
3441	8 JAN '60	LORD DERBY	GROSVENOR GATE	DBP
3442	[12 JAN '60]	BARON L. DE ROTHSCHILD	GROSVENOR GATE	ROTH
3443	14 JAN '60	LORD DERBY	GROSVENOR GATE	DBP
3444	16 JAN '60	SARAH BRYDGES WILLYAMS	GROSVENOR GATE	RTC
3445	16 JAN '60	SIR STAFFORD NORTHCOTE	GROSVENOR GATE	BL
3446	18 JAN '60	LORD DERBY	GROSVENOR GATE	DBP
3447	[19 JAN '60]	LORD DERBY	[LONDON]	DBP
3448	25 JAN '60	LORD DERBY	GROSVENOR GATE	DBP
3449	28 JAN '60	SARAH BRYDGES WILLYAMS	GROSVENOR GATE	RTC
3450	3 FEB ['60]	[JOHN DELANE?]	[LONDON]	MOPSIK
3451	4 FEB '60	LORD GREY	GROSVENOR GATE	DURG
3452	7 FEB '60	EDITOR OF MORNING STAR	GROSVENOR GATE	PS
3453	[15] FEB '60	SIR JOHN PAKINGTON	GROSVENOR GATE	WRC
3454	18 FEB '60	SIR JOHN PAKINGTON	GROSVENOR GATE	WRC
3455	29 FEB '60	SARAH BRYDGES WILLYAMS	[LONDON]	RTC
3456	2 MAR '60	SARAH BRYDGES WILLYAMS	GROSVENOR GATE	RTC
3457	4 MAR '60	SIR WILLIAM JOLLIFFE	GROSVENOR GATE	SCR
3458	6 MAR '60	FRANCIS ESPINASSE	GROSVENOR GATE	MHS
3459	24 MAR '60	SARAH BRYDGES WILLYAMS	GROSVENOR GATE	RTC
3460	27 MAR '60	FRANCIS ESPINASSE	GROSVENOR GATE	H
3461	30 MAR '60	WILLIAM CARLISLE	CARLTON CLUB	TCC
3462	4 APR '60	SARAH BRYDGES WILLYAMS	GROSVENOR GATE	RTC
3463	13 APR '60	SARAH BRYDGES WILLYAMS	HUGHENDEN	RTC
3464	21 APR '60	SAMUEL WILBERFORCE	GROSVENOR GATE	BODL
3465	21 APR '60	SARAH BRYDGES WILLYAMS	GROSVENOR GATE	RTC
3466	1 MAY '60	SARAH BRYDGES WILLYAMS	H OF COMMONS	H
3467	2 MAY '60	THOMAS KEBBEL	GROSVENOR GATE	H H/LIFE
3468	[2] MAY '60	LADY DOROTHY NEVILL	GROSVENOR GATE	PS
3469	10 MAY '60	WILLIAM CARLISLE	GROSVENOR GATE	MOPSIK
3470	12 MAY '60	LORD DERBY	CARLTON CLUB	DBP
3471	14 MAY '60	SARAH BRYDGES WILLYAMS	GROSVENOR GATE	RTC
3472	15 MAY '60	HENRY PADDON	GROSVENOR GATE	H H/LIFE
3473	24 MAY '60	SARAH BRYDGES WILLYAMS	GROSVENOR GATE	RTC

NO	DATE	TO	PLACE OF ORIGIN	LOCATION OF ORIGINAL
3474	27 MAY '60	SIR WILLIAM JOLLIFFE	HUGHENDEN	SCR
3475	27 MAY '60	LORD DERBY	HUGHENDEN	DBP
3476	[6? JUN '60]	[LORD HENRY BENTINCK]	[LONDON]	H
3477	[10 JUN '60]	LORD DERBY	[LONDON]	DBP
3478	11 JUN '60	SIR WILLIAM MILES	[LONDON]	H
3479	20 JUN '60	HENRY EDWARDS	GROSVENOR GATE	HAL
3480	20 JUN '60	SARAH BRYDGES WILLYAMS	CARLTON CLUB	RTC
3481	29 JUN '60	LORD DERBY	H OF COMMONS	DBP
3481A	[30 JUN? '60]	LORD DERBY	CARLTON CLUB	DBP
3482	[JUN '60?]	[MARY ANNE DISRAELI]	[LONDON]	QUA
3483	3 JUL '60	MARY ANNE DISRAELI	[LONDON]	H
3484	12 JUL '60	[N.M.ROTHSCHILD & SONS]	GROSVENOR GATE	ROTH
3485	[16 JUL '60]	MARY ANNE DISRAELI	[H OF COMMONS]	H
3486	23 JUL '60	SARAH BRYDGES WILLYAMS	GROSVENOR GATE	RTC
3487	29 JUL '60	THOMSON HANKEY	GROSVENOR GATE	H
3488	29 JUL '60	WILLIAM TRUSS	GROSVENOR GATE	MOPSIK
3489	[29 JUL '60?]	SIR HENRY STRACEY	[LONDON]	PS
3490	7 AUG '60	HENRY PADWICK	GROSVENOR GATE	LCC
3491	11 AUG '60	SARAH BRYDGES WILLYAMS	GROSVENOR GATE	RTC
3492	15 AUG '60	SARAH BRYDGES WILLYAMS	GROSVENOR GATE	RTC
3493	15 AUG '60	JOHN WALCOT	GROSVENOR GATE	MOPSIK
3494	16 AUG '60	WILLIAM FERRAND	GROSVENOR GATE	PS
3495	20 AUG '60	SARAH BRYDGES WILLYAMS	HUGHENDEN	RTC
3496	[23 AUG '60]	[KING LEOPOLD]	[HUGHENDEN]	H
3497	25 AUG '60	RALPH DISRAELI	HUGHENDEN	BL
3498	7 SEP '60	SARAH BRYDGES WILLYAMS	HUGHENDEN	RTC
3499	16 SEP '60	SARAH BRYDGES WILLYAMS	HUGHENDEN	RTC
3500	19 SEP '60	SARAH BRYDGES WILLYAMS	HUGHENDEN	RTC
3501	28 SEP '60	WILLIAM W.F. HUME	HUGHENDEN	BRN
3502	1 OCT '60	SARAH BRYDGES WILLYAMS	HUGHENDEN	RTC
3503	8 OCT '60	JOHN KNOTT	HUGHENDEN	YAU
3504	16 OCT '60	LORD STANLEY	HUGHENDEN	DBP
3505	18 OCT '60	SARAH BRYDGES WILLYAMS	HUGHENDEN	RTC
3506	21 OCT '60	PHILIP ROSE	HUGHENDEN	H
3507	26 OCT '60	LORD STANLEY	HUGHENDEN	DBP
3508	[27? OCT '60]	[JOSEPH LOVEGROVE]	[HUGHENDEN]	H
3509	2 NOV '60	SIR WILLIAM JOLLIFFE	[HUGHENDEN]	SCR
3509A	7 NOV '60	CHARLES CLUBBE	[HUGHENDEN]	RIC
3510	8 NOV '60	LORD STANLEY	HUGHENDEN	DBP
3511	9 NOV '60	SAMUEL WILBERFORCE	HUGHENDEN	BODL
3512	9 NOV '60	W.H. BAKER	[HUGHENDEN]	NYM
3513	11 NOV '60	SARAH BRYDGES WILLYAMS	HUGHENDEN	RTC
3514	12 NOV ['60]	J. CHAPMAN	CARLTON CLUB	PS
3515	18 NOV '60	SARAH BRYDGES WILLYAMS	HUGHENDEN	RTC
3516	25 NOV '60	THOMAS KEBBEL	HUGHENDEN	PS
3517	27 NOV '60	CHARLES COLERIDGE	HUGHENDEN	H
3518	1 DEC ['60?]	[THOMAS MILNER GIBSON?]	CARLTON CLUB	MOPSIK
3519	2 DEC '60	SARAH BRYDGES WILLYAMS	HUGHENDEN	RTC
3520	3 DEC '60	WILLIAM CARLISLE	[HUGHENDEN]	MOPSIK
3521	5 DEC '60	RALPH DISRAELI	[HUGHENDEN]	BL
3522	5 DEC '60	EDITOR OF *MORNING STAR*	HUGHENDEN	HUL

NO	DATE	TO	PLACE OF ORIGIN	LOCATION OF ORIGINAL
3523	6 DEC '60	JOHN DELANE	[HUGHENDEN]	TIA
3524	7 DEC '60	THOMAS EVETTS	HUGHENDEN	GLA
3525	7 DEC '60	RALPH DISRAELI	HUGHENDEN	BL
3526	8 DEC '60	LORD DERBY	HUGHENDEN	DBP
3527	8 DEC '60	LORD JOHN MANNERS	HUGHENDEN	BEA
3528	11 DEC '60	ERASTUS HOLBROOK	[HUGHENDEN]	H
3529	12 DEC '60	RALPH DISRAELI	[HUGHENDEN]	BL
3530	12 DEC '60	PHILIP ROSE	HUGHENDEN	H
3531	13 DEC '60	SARAH BRYDGES WILLYAMS	HUGHENDEN	RTC
3532	18 DEC '60	SARAH BRYDGES WILLYAMS	HUGHENDEN	RTC
3533	18 DEC '60	JOHN MACMAHON	HUGHENDEN	MOPSIK
3534	21 DEC '60	LORD MALMESBURY	GROSVENOR GATE	HCC
3535	21 DEC '60	RALPH DISRAELI	GROSVENOR GATE	BL
3536	[21 DEC '60]	RALPH DISRAELI	[CARLTON CLUB]	BL
3537	23 DEC '60	KING LEOPOLD	[LONDON]	H
3538	24 DEC '60	SARAH BRYDGES WILLYAMS	CARLTON CLUB	RTC
3539	29 DEC '60	SARAH BRYDGES WILLYAMS	[HALDON HOUSE]	RTC
3540	31 DEC ['60]	SARAH BRYDGES WILLYAMS	[TORQUAY]	RTC
3541	[7 JAN '61?]	SARAH BRYDGES WILLYAMS	[TORQUAY]	RTC
3542	16 JAN '61	N.M. ROTHSCHILD & SONS	HATFIELD	ROTH
3543	18 JAN '61	LORD STANLEY	GROSVENOR GATE	DBP
3544	18 JAN '61	SIR WILLIAM JOLLIFFE	GROSVENOR GATE	SCR
3545	18 JAN '61	SIR JOHN PAKINGTON	GROSVENOR GATE	WRC
3546	19 JAN '61	[CONSERVATIVE MPS]	HUGHENDEN	INL
3547	19 JAN '61	SARAH BRYDGES WILLYAMS	CARLTON CLUB	RTC
3548	19 JAN '61	EDWARD KENEALY	GROSVENOR GATE	BRN
3549	22 JAN '61	SIR WILLIAM JOLLIFFE	GROSVENOR GATE	SCR
3550	23 JAN '61	G. CHAMBERS	GROSVENOR GATE	H H/LIFE
3551	28 JAN '61	LORD DERBY	GROSVENOR GATE	DBP
3552	28 JAN '61	PHILIP ROSE	CARLTON CLUB	H
3553	30 JAN '61	EDWARD SELBY LOWNDES	[LONDON]	H
3554	30 JAN '61	[JOSEPH WOLFF]	GROSVENOR GATE	H
3555	9 FEB '61	SARAH BRYDGES WILLYAMS	GROSVENOR GATE	RTC
3556	22 FEB '61	LORD MALMESBURY	H OF LORDS	PS
3557	[28] FEB '61	SARAH BRYDGES WILLYAMS	GROSVENOR GATE	RTC
3558	[1 MAR '61]	MARY ANNE DISRAELI	[LONDON]	H
3559	2 MAR ['61]	EDITOR OF *THE TIMES*	GROSVENOR GATE	PS
3560	[6 MAR '61]	MARY ANNE DISRAELI	[LONDON]	H
3561	11 MAR '61	LORD DERBY	GROSVENOR GATE	DBP
3562	[11 MAR '61]	MARY ANNE DISRAELI	H OF COMMONS	H
3563	16 MAR '61	SARAH BRYDGES WILLYAMS	GROSVENOR GATE	RTC
3564	20 MAR '61	N.M. ROTHSCHILD & SONS	H OF COMMONS	ROTH
3565	20 MAR '61	SARAH BRYDGES WILLYAMS	H OF COMMONS	RTC
3566	24 MAR '61	WILLIAM GLADSTONE	GROSVENOR GATE	BL
3567	24 MAR '61	HENRY ALMACK	GROSVENOR GATE	PS
3568	[30 MAR '61]	SARAH BRYDGES WILLYAMS	CARDIFF	RTC
3569	11 APR '61	SARAH BRYDGES WILLYAMS	H OF COMMONS	RTC
3570	[16 APR '61]	[UNKNOWN]	[LONDON]	QUA
3571	16 APR '61	[OCTAVIAN BLEWITT]	H OF COMMONS	RLF
3572	16 APR '61	N.M. ROTHSCHILD & SONS	H OF COMMONS	ROTH
3573	24 APR '61	LADY DOROTHY NEVILL	CARLTON CLUB	PS

NO	DATE	TO	PLACE OF ORIGIN	LOCATION OF ORIGINAL
3574	24 APR '61	SARAH BRYDGES WILLYAMS	CARLTON CLUB	RTC; H
3575	25 APR '61	SARAH BRYDGES WILLYAMS	CARLTON CLUB	RTC
3576	10 MAY '61	SARAH BRYDGES WILLYAMS	H OF COMMONS	H
3577	13 MAY '61	OCTAVIAN BLEWITT	GROSVENOR GATE	RLF
3578	17 MAY '61	SARAH BRYDGES WILLYAMS	H OF COMMONS	RTC
3579	23 MAY '61	WILLIAM STIRLING	H OF COMMONS	STCL
3580	24 MAY '61	MONTAGU PEACOCK	GROSVENOR GATE	SPI
3581	24 MAY '61	THOMAS BARING	[LONDON]	BAR
3582	25 MAY '61	SARAH BRYDGES WILLYAMS	GROSVENOR GATE	RTC
3583	26 MAY '61	MONTAGU PEACOCK	GROSVENOR GATE	SPI
3584	[28 MAY '61]	[SIR WILLIAM HEATHCOTE]	[LONDON]	H
3585	29 MAY '61	[CONSERVATIVE MPS]	GROSVENOR GATE	H
3586	30 MAY '61	SIR STAFFORD NORTHCOTE	[LONDON]	BL
3587	2 JUN '61	EDGAR BOWRING	GROSVENOR GATE	PS
3588	3 JUN '61	SARAH BRYDGES WILLYAMS	H OF COMMONS	RTC
3589	5 JUN '61	[FRANCIS VILLIERS?]	[LONDON]	H
3590	7 JUN '61	SIR MATTHEW WHITE RIDLEY	GROSVENOR GATE	H
3591	9 JUN '61	SIR JOHN PAKINGTON	GROSVENOR GATE	H
3592	11 JUN '61	SARAH BRYDGES WILLYAMS	CARLTON CLUB	RTC
3593	19 JUN '61	LADY OLLIFFE	GROSVENOR GATE	PS
3594	19 JUN ['61]	SARAH BRYDGES WILLYAMS	H OF COMMONS	RTC
3595	[22 JUN '61]	WILLIAM W.F. HUME	CARLTON CLUB	BRN
3596	27 JUN '61	SARAH BRYDGES WILLYAMS	CARLTON CLUB	H
3597	28 JUN '61	[FRANCIS VILLIERS]	[LONDON]	H
3598	3 JUL '61	JOHN EVELYN DENISON	GROSVENOR GATE	NOT
3599	8 JUL '61	SARAH BRYDGES WILLYAMS	H OF COMMONS	RTC
3600	12 JUL '61	SARAH BRYDGES WILLYAMS	CARLTON CLUB	RTC
3601	15 JUL '61	LORD JOHN MANNERS	GROSVENOR GATE	BEA
3602	[MID-JUL '61]	LADY STRANGFORD	[LONDON]	H
3603	17 JUL '61	SARAH BRYDGES WILLYAMS	[LONDON]	RTC
3604	[18?]JUL '61	[GEORGE SCHARF]	GROSVENOR GATE	PS
3605	21 JUL '61	ALFRED AUSTIN	GROSVENOR GATE	BRN
3606	[25 JUL '61]	MARY ANNE DISRAELI	[H OF COMMONS]	H
3607	26 JUL '61	WILLIAM FOLLETT SYNGE	[LONDON]	PS
3608	28 JUL '61	RICHARD CHENEVIX TRENCH	GROSVENOR GATE	H
3609	30 JUL ['61]	SARAH BRYDGES WILLYAMS	CARLTON CLUB	RTC
3610	6 AUG '61	JOHN EVELYN DENISON	GROSVENOR GATE	NOT
3611	16 AUG '61	SARAH BRYDGES WILLYAMS	HUGHENDEN	RTC
3612	22 AUG '61	SARAH BRYDGES WILLYAMS	HUGHENDEN	RTC
3613	4 SEP '61	SARAH BRYDGES WILLYAMS	HUGHENDEN	RTC
3614	12 SEP '61	[SIR STAFFORD NORTHCOTE]	[HUGHENDEN]	H H/LIFE
3615	12 SEP '61	CHARLES ADDERLEY	HUGHENDEN	H H/LIFE
3616	16 SEP '61	WILLIAM CARLISLE	HUGHENDEN	MOPSIK
3617	20 SEP '61	SARAH BRYDGES WILLYAMS	[HUGHENDEN]	RTC; H
3618	22 SEP '61	WILLIAM FERRAND	HUGHENDEN	PS
3619	23 SEP '61	JAMES SHEAHAN	[HUGHENDEN]	H
3620	1 OCT '61	WILLIAM PARTRIDGE	HUGHENDEN	GMF
3621	2 OCT '61	[FRANCIS VILLIERS]	[HUGHENDEN]	H
3622	3 OCT '61	SARAH BRYDGES WILLYAMS	HUGHENDEN	RTC
3623	6 OCT '61	THOMAS TAYLOR	[HUGHENDEN]	H H/LIFE
3624	[MID-OCT '61]	SIR STAFFORD NORTHCOTE	[HUGHENDEN]	H

NO	DATE	TO	PLACE OF ORIGIN	LOCATION OF ORIGINAL
3625	4 NOV '61	SIR WILLIAM JOLLIFFE	HUGHENDEN	SCR
3626	7 NOV '61	JOHN DELANE	HUGHENDEN	H H/LIFE; M&B
3627	9 NOV '61	LADY LONDONDERRY	HUGHENDEN	DUR
3628	13 NOV '61	SARAH BRYDGES WILLYAMS	HUGHENDEN	RTC
3629	15 NOV '61	LORD DERBY	HUGHENDEN	DBP
3630	18 NOV '61	LORD ADOLPHUS VANE	HUGHENDEN	DUR
3631	24 NOV '61	SARAH BRYDGES WILLYAMS	ALNWICK CASTLE	RTC
3632	27 NOV '61	JAMES VINCENT	ALNWICK CASTLE	QUA
3633	8 DEC '61	SARAH BRYDGES WILLYAMS	SEAHAM HALL	RTC
3634	11 DEC '61	LADY LONDONDERRY	GROSVENOR GATE	DUR
3635	14 DEC '61	LADY LONDONDERRY	GROSVENOR GATE	DUR
3636	14 DEC '61	ACHILLE FOULD	GROSVENOR GATE	PS
3637	19 DEC '61	LORD HENRY LENNOX	TORQUAY	NYM
3638	19 DEC '61	LADY LONDONDERRY	TORQUAY	DUR
3639	20 DEC ['61]	HENRY PHILPOTTS	TORQUAY	BODL
3640	25 DEC '61	SARAH BRYDGES WILLYAMS	[TORQUAY]	RTC
3641	[28 DEC '61]	SARAH BRYDGES WILLYAMS	[TORQUAY]	RTC
3642	31 DEC '61	SARAH BRYDGES WILLYAMS	TORQUAY	RTC
3643	31 DEC '61	EDWARD KENEALY	TORQUAY	UO
3644	1 JAN '62	SARAH BRYDGES WILLYAMS	TORQUAY	RTC
3645	1 JAN '62	HENRY PHILPOTTS	TORQUAY	BODL
3646	7 JAN '62	[CONSERVATIVE MPS]	HUGHENDEN	WSRO
3647	9 JAN '62	SARAH BRYDGES WILLYAMS	GROSVENOR GATE	RTC
3648	11 JAN '62	N.M. ROTHSCHILD & SONS	GROSVENOR GATE	ROTH
3649	12 JAN '62	PHILIP ROSE	[LONDON]	H
3650	14 JAN ['62]	SARAH BRYDGES WILLYAMS	[LONDON]	RTC
3651	18 JAN '62	SARAH BRYDGES WILLYAMS	GROSVENOR GATE	RTC
3652	20 JAN '62	WILLIAM CARLISLE	GROSVENOR GATE	MOPSIK
3653	22 JAN '62	LORD DERBY	GROSVENOR GATE	DBP
3654	22 JAN '62	SARAH BRYDGES WILLYAMS	GROSVENOR GATE	RTC
3655	26 JAN '62	CHARLES ADDERLEY	GROSVENOR GATE	PS
3656	27 JAN '62	SAMUEL WILBERFORCE	GROSVENOR GATE	BODL
3656A	28 JAN '62	EMILY CLUBBE	GROSVENOR GATE	RIC
3657	29 JAN '62	GEORGE POTTS	GROSVENOR GATE	QUA
3658	29 JAN '62	SARAH BRYDGES WILLYAMS	GROSVENOR GATE	RTC
3659	31 JAN '62	SIR HENRY STRACEY	GROSVENOR GATE	BUL
3660	1 FEB '62	JOHN FANE	GROSVENOR GATE	BODL
3661	4 FEB '62	SARAH BRYDGES WILLYAMS	[LONDON]	RTC
3662	9 FEB '62	SIR CHARLES PHIPPS	GROSVENOR GATE	RAC
3663	12 FEB '62	SIR WILLIAM JOLLIFFE	[LONDON]	ATM
3664	12 FEB '62	SIR E. BULWER LYTTON	GROSVENOR GATE	HCR
3665	17 FEB '62	SIR WILLIAM JOLLIFFE	[LONDON]	SCR
3666	24 FEB '62	SARAH BRYDGES WILLYAMS	H OF COMMONS	RTC
3667	25 FEB '62	[SIR CHARLES PHIPPS]	[GROSVENOR GATE]	H
3668	5 MAR '62	LORD JOHN MANNERS	GROSVENOR GATE	BEA
3669	6 MAR '62	SARAH BRYDGES WILLYAMS	GROSVENOR GATE	RTC
3670	[13 MAR '62]	LORD DERBY	H OF COMMONS	DBP
3671	16 MAR '62	LORD DERBY	GROSVENOR GATE	DBP
3672	17 MAR '62	LORD DERBY	GROSVENOR GATE	DBP
3673	20 MAR '62	SARAH BRYDGES WILLYAMS	GROSVENOR GATE	RTC
3674	6 APR '62	SIR JOHN PAKINGTON	GROSVENOR GATE	WRC

NO	DATE	TO	PLACE OF ORIGIN	LOCATION OF ORIGINAL
3675	14 APR '62	SARAH BRYDGES WILLYAMS	GROSVENOR GATE	RTC
3676	19 APR '62	THOMAS HANSARD	GROSVENOR GATE	ILLU
3677	29 APR '62	SARAH BRYDGES WILLYAMS	H OF COMMONS	RTC
3678	2 MAY '62	LORD DERBY	H OF COMMONS	DBP
3679	9 MAY '62	LORD ELMLEY	[LONDON]	BCP
3680	9 MAY '62	SARAH BRYDGES WILLYAMS	H OF COMMONS	RTC
3681	13 MAY ['62]	THOMAS HAMBER	GROSVENOR GATE	BRN
3682	21 MAY '62	LORD DERBY	GROSVENOR GATE	DBP
3683	21 MAY '62	PHILIP ROSE	GROSVENOR GATE	H
3684	22 MAY '62	LORD DERBY	H OF COMMONS	DBP
3685	22 MAY '62	SIR WILLIAM JOLLIFFE	H OF COMMONS	SCR
3686	22 MAY '62	WILLIAM STIRLING	H OF COMMONS	STCL
3687	23 MAY '62	SIR E. BULWER LYTTON	[LONDON]	HCR
3688	25 MAY '62	LORD DERBY	GROSVENOR GATE	DBP
3689	27 MAY '62	SARAH BRYDGES WILLYAMS	H OF COMMONS	RTC
3690	31 MAY '62	LORD DERBY	GROSVENOR GATE	DBP
3691	1 JUN '62	SIR STAFFORD NORTHCOTE	GROSVENOR GATE	BL
3692	6 JUN '62	PHILIP ROSE	GROSVENOR GATE	H
3693	7 JUN '62	LORD DERBY	GROSVENOR GATE	DBP
3694	13 JUN '62	SARAH BRYDGES WILLYAMS	GROSVENOR GATE	RTC
3695	23 JUN '62	SIR GEORGE BOWYER	H OF COMMONS	PS
3696	26 JUN '62	SIR STAFFORD NORTHCOTE	GROSVENOR GATE	MOPSIK
3697	8 JUL '62	SARAH BRYDGES WILLYAMS	GROSVENOR GATE	RTC
3698	15 JUL '62	LADY HARRY VANE	GROSVENOR GATE	KCR
3699	16 JUL '62	LADY HOLLAND	GROSVENOR GATE	BL
3700	22 JUL '62	CHARLES ADDERLEY	GROSVENOR GATE	HARV
3701	23 JUL '62	SIR WILLIAM JOLLIFFE	GROSVENOR GATE	SCR
3702	26 JUL '62	SARAH BRYDGES WILLYAMS	GROSVENOR GATE	H
3703	8 AUG '62	SIR WILLIAM JOLLIFFE	GROSVENOR GATE	SCR
3704	8 AUG '62	RALPH DISRAELI	GROSVENOR GATE	BL
3705	19 AUG '62	WILLIAM FERRAND	HUGHENDEN	PS
3706	21 AUG '62	DUKE OF BUCKINGHAM	HUGHENDEN	BUC
3707	21 AUG '62	SARAH BRYDGES WILLYAMS	HUGHENDEN	RTC
3708	LATE AUG '62	BARONESS L. DE ROTHSCHILD	[HUGHENDEN]	PS
3709	1 SEP '62	SARAH BRYDGES WILLYAMS	HUGHENDEN	RTC
3710	3 SEP '62	JOHN HUBBARD	HUGHENDEN	QUA
3711	4 SEP '62	FREDERICK LYGON	HUGHENDEN	BCP
3712	8 SEP '62	RALPH EARLE	HUGHENDEN	H H/LIFE
3713	10 SEP '62	LORD ST ASAPH	HUGHENDEN	PS
3714	12 SEP '62	BURLEY & CARLISLE	HUGHENDEN	MOPSIK
3715	15 SEP ['62]	SARAH BRYDGES WILLYAMS	HUGHENDEN	RTC
3716	18 SEP '62	ROBERT HARVEY	[HUGHENDEN]	PS
3717	20 SEP '62	PHILIP ROSE	HUGHENDEN	H
3718	26 SEP '62	SARAH BRYDGES WILLYAMS	HUGHENDEN	RTC
3719	30 SEP '62	BARONESS L. DE ROTHSCHILD	HUGHENDEN	ROTH
3719A	30 SEP '62	CHARLES CLUBBE	HUGHENDEN	RIC
3720	3 OCT '62	SAMUEL WILBERFORCE	HUGHENDEN	BODL
3721	[4?] OCT '62	GEORGE FELL	[HUGHENDEN]	H
3722	6 OCT '62	LORD JOHN MANNERS	HUGHENDEN	NOT
3723	11 OCT '62	JOHN GRAVES	HUGHENDEN	CUL
3724	11 OCT '62	CALEDON DU PRE	HUGHENDEN	PML

NO	DATE	TO	PLACE OF ORIGIN	LOCATION OF ORIGINAL
3725	14 OCT '62	SARAH BRYDGES WILLYAMS	HUGHENDEN	RTC
3726	14 OCT '62	MARY ANNE DYCE SOMBRE	HUGHENDEN	QUA
3727	14 OCT '62	CECIL FORESTER	HUGHENDEN	QUA
3728	20 OCT '62	THOMAS TAYLOR	HUGHENDEN	H H/LIFE
3729	21 OCT '62	SIR WILLIAM JOLLIFFE	HUGHENDEN	SCR
3730	22 OCT '62	LADY VERE CAMERON	HUGHENDEN	TEXU
3731	24 OCT '62	SPENCER WALPOLE	HUGHENDEN	QUA
3732	28 OCT '62	SAMUEL WILBERFORCE	HUGHENDEN	BODL
3733	[LATE OCT?' 62]	JAMES FARRER	[HUGHENDEN]	H
3734	2 NOV '62	SARAH BRYDGES WILLYAMS	HUGHENDEN	RTC
3735	4 NOV '62	SIR WILLIAM JOLLIFFE	HUGHENDEN	SCR
3736	5 NOV '62	ANNE GILCHRIST	HUGHENDEN	LIS
3737	14 NOV '62	PHILIP ROSE	[LONDON]	H
3738	16 NOV ['62]	LORD DERBY	CARLTON CLUB	DBP
3739	21 NOV '62	CHARLES PYNE	HUGHENDEN	PS
3740	23 NOV '62	PHILIP ROSE	HUGHENDEN	H
3741	23 NOV '62	SARAH BRYDGES WILLYAMS	HUGHENDEN	RTC
3742	30 NOV '62	SAMUEL WILBERFORCE	HUGHENDEN	BODL
3743	30 NOV '62	LORD CARRINGTON	HUGHENDEN	CARR
3744	2 DEC '62	EDITOR OF *BUCKS HERALD*	HUGHENDEN	PS
3745	2 DEC '62	EDWARD KENEALY	HUGHENDEN	MOPSIK
3746	2 DEC '62	LADY G. CODRINGTON	HUGHENDEN	QUA
3747	5 DEC '62	LADY DOROTHY NEVILL	HUGHENDEN	EJM
3748	6 DEC '62	PHILIP ROSE	HUGHENDEN	H
3749	7 DEC '62	PHILIP ROSE	HUGHENDEN	H
3750	9 DEC '62	SARAH BRYDGES WILLYAMS	HUGHENDEN	RTC
3751	11 DEC '62	LORD CARRINGTON	HUGHENDEN	CARR
3752	15 DEC '62	JAMES HANNAY	[LONDON]	PRIN
3752A	15 DEC '62	CHARLES CLUBBE	LONDON	RIC
3753	16 DEC '62	SAMUEL WILBERFORCE	GROSVENOR GATE	BODL
3754	17 DEC '62	SARAH BRYDGES WILLYAMS	GROSVENOR GATE	RTC
3755	17 DEC '62	JAMES HANNAY	GROSVENOR GATE	PS
3756	19 DEC '62	[MILFORD] REED	GROSVENOR GATE	PS
3757	19 DEC '62	PHILIP ROSE	GROSVENOR GATE	H
3758	19 DEC '62	HENRY PADWICK	GROSVENOR GATE	LCC
3759	20 DEC '62	SARAH BRYDGES WILLYAMS	[TORQUAY]	RTC
3760	20 DEC '62	SARAH BRYDGES WILLYAMS	TORQUAY	RTC
3761	25 DEC '62	HENRY PADWICK	TORQUAY	LCC
3762	31 DEC '62	CONTRIBUTORS TO FUND	[TORQUAY]	H
3763	[LATE DEC '62?]	CHARLES CLUBBE	[TORQUAY]	QUA
3764	[JAN '63?]	JOHN SKELTON	[LONDON]	H
3765	1 JAN '63	PHILIP ROSE	TORQUAY	H
3765A	1 JAN '63	CHARLES CLUBBE	TORQUAY	RIC
3766	3 JAN '63	HENRY PADWICK	TORQUAY	LCC
3767	4 JAN '63	PHILIP ROSE	TORQUAY	H
3768	4 JAN '63	RALPH EARLE	TORQUAY	H H/LIFE
3769	[5 JAN '63?]	SIR JOHN NEELD	[TORQUAY]	PS
3770	5 JAN '63	PHILIP ROSE	PLYMOUTH	H
3771	8 [JAN '63]	SARAH BRYDGES WILLYAMS	[LONDON]	RTC
3772	10 JAN '63	SARAH BRYDGES WILLYAMS	GROSVENOR GATE	RTC
3773	14 JAN '63	[PHILIP ROSE]	CARLTON CLUB	H

NO	DATE	TO	PLACE OF ORIGIN	LOCATION OF ORIGINAL
3774	14 JAN '63	SARAH BRYDGES WILLYAMS	GROSVENOR GATE	RTC
3775	15 JAN '63	SIR WILLIAM JOLLIFFE	GROSVENOR GATE	SCR
3776	15 JAN '63	[CONSERVATIVE MPS]	HUGHENDEN	WSRO
3777	21 JAN [63]	SARAH BRYDGES WILLYAMS	GROSVENOR GATE	RTC
3778	23 JAN '63	PHILIP ROSE	HATFIELD	H
3779	26 JAN '63	MARY ANNE DISRAELI	[EATON TERRACE]	H
3780	26 JAN '63	SARAH BRYDGES WILLYAMS	GROSVENOR GATE	RTC
3780A	27 JAN '63	CHARLES CLUBBE	GROSVENOR GATE	RIC
3781	3 FEB '63	HENRY BRAND	[LONDON]	UO
3781A	4 FEB ['63]	PHILIP ROSE	6 VICTORIA ST	H
3782	6 FEB '63	PHILIP ROSE	H OF COMMONS	H
3783	7 FEB '63	SARAH BRYDGES WILLYAMS	[LONDON]	RTC
3784	8 FEB '63	SIR E. BULWER LYTTON	GROSVENOR GATE	HCR
3785	[10 FEB '63]	SARAH BRYDGES WILLYAMS	H OF COMMONS	RTC
3786	11 FEB '63	PHILIP ROSE	6 VICTORIA ST	H
3787	[12] FEB '63	MARY ANNE DISRAELI	EATON TERRACE	H
3788	[13 FEB '63]	SARAH BRYDGES WILLYAMS	H OF COMMONS	RTC
3789	20 FEB '63	LORD SYDNEY	[LONDON]	FIT
3790	20 FEB '63	LORD JOHN MANNERS	H OF COMMONS	BEA
3791	[23 FEB '63]	SARAH BRYDGES WILLYAMS	H OF COMMONS	RTC
3792	25 FEB '63	SARAH BRYDGES WILLYAMS	[CARLTON CLUB]	RTC
3793	25 FEB '63	MARY ANNE DISRAELI	[CARLTON CLUB]	H
3794	28 FEB '63	QUEEN VICTORIA	GROSVENOR GATE	QUA
3795	4 MAR '63	SARAH BRYDGES WILLYAMS	GROSVENOR GATE	RTC
3796	13 MAR '63	ROBERT NEWMAN	GROSVENOR GATE	BRN
3797	21 MAR '63	SARAH BRYDGES WILLYAMS	GROSVENOR GATE	RTC
3798	23 MAR '63	LORD CARRINGTON	GROSVENOR GATE	CARR
3799	25 MAR '63	SARAH BRYDGES WILLYAMS	[H OF COMMONS?]	RTC
3800	25 MAR '63	BURLEY & CARLISLE	[LONDON]	MOPSIK
3801	26 MAR '63	LORD PALMERSTON	GROSVENOR GATE	PP
3802	4 APR '63	LORD STANHOPE	HUGHENDEN	KCR
3803	10 APR '63	LORD CAMPDEN	HUGHENDEN	PS
3804	10 APR '63	SARAH BRYDGES WILLYAMS	HUGHENDEN	RTC
3805	15 APR '63	SARAH BRYDGES WILLYAMS	H OF COMMONS	RTC
3806	17 APR '63	SIR HENRY STRACEY	[LONDON]	PS
3807	[20 APR '63]	HENRY WHITMORE	[LONDON]	PS
3808	[24 APR '63]	QUEEN VICTORIA	[LONDON]	H
3809	26 APR '63	QUEEN VICTORIA	GROSVENOR GATE	RAC
3810	27 APR '63	SARAH BRYDGES WILLYAMS	GROSVENOR GATE	RTC
3811	27 APR '63	BENJAMIN LUMLEY	GROSVENOR GATE	MOPSIK
3812	[APR '63]	JOHN GRAVES	[LONDON]	PS
3813	[5 MAY '63]	ARTHUR HELPS	[LONDON]	H
3814	5 MAY '63	SARAH BRYDGES WILLYAMS	GROSVENOR GATE	RTC
3815	14 MAY '63	SARAH BRYDGES WILLYAMS	GROSVENOR GATE	RTC
3816	15 MAY '63	CHARLES GREY	GROSVENOR GATE	RAC
3817	21 MAY '63	SARAH BRYDGES WILLYAMS	H OF COMMONS	RTC
3818	27 MAY '63	SARAH BRYDGES WILLYAMS	HUGHENDEN	RTC
3819	30 MAY '63	SIR THOMAS [UNKNOWN]	CARLTON CLUB	UO
3820	13 JUN '63	[ANTHONY PANIZZI]	[LONDON]	MOPSIK
3821	14 JUN '63	SARAH BRYDGES WILLYAMS	GROSVENOR GATE	RTC
3822	14 JUN '63	DUKE OF NORTHUMBERLAND	GROSVENOR GATE	CUL

NO	DATE	TO	PLACE OF ORIGIN	LOCATION OF ORIGINAL
3823	22 JUN '63	LORD CAMPDEN	GROSVENOR GATE	BL
3824	25 JUN '63	SARAH BRYDGES WILLYAMS	[LONDON]	RTC
3825	30 JUN ['63]	CHARLES GREY	GROSVENOR GATE	RAC
3826	[3 JUL '63]	CHARLES GREY	[GROSVENOR GATE]	RAC
3827	3 JUL '63	FREDERICK LYGON	GROSVENOR GATE	BCP
3828	6 JUL '63	SARAH BRYDGES WILLYAMS	GROSVENOR GATE	RTC
3829	9 JUL '63	PHILIP ROSE	H OF COMMONS	H
3830	20 JUL '63	LORD DERBY	GROSVENOR GATE	DBP
3831	20 JUL '63	FREDERICK FURNIVALL	GROSVENOR GATE	HUNT
3832	21 JUL '63	SARAH BRYDGES WILLYAMS	GROSVENOR GATE	RTC
3833	29 JUL '63	SARAH BRYDGES WILLYAMS	HATFIELD	RTC
3834	31 JUL '63	REES HOWELL GRONOW	GROSVENOR GATE	GLA
3835	[AUG '63?]	[LADY NORMANBY?]	[HUGHENDEN?]	H
3836	2 AUG '63	BARON L. DE ROTHSCHILD	GROSVENOR GATE	ROTH
3837	[5?] AUG '63	LORD DERBY	GROSVENOR GATE	DBP
3838	7 AUG '63	SARAH BRYDGES WILLYAMS	HUGHENDEN	RTC
3839	7 AUG '63	RALPH EARLE	[HUGHENDEN]	H H/LIFE
3840	7 AUG '63	LORD DERBY	HUGHENDEN	DBP
3841	14 AUG '63	LORD DERBY	HUGHENDEN	DBP
3842	15 AUG '63	SARAH BRYDGES WILLYAMS	HUGHENDEN	RTC
3843	21 AUG '63	BARONESS L. DE ROTHSCHILD	HUGHENDEN	ROTH
3844	22 AUG '63	LORD MALMESBURY	HUGHENDEN	HCC
3845	22 AUG '63	SARAH BRYDGES WILLYAMS	HUGHENDEN	RTC
3846	29 AUG '63	BARON L. DE ROTHSCHILD	HUGHENDEN	ROTH
3847	2 SEP '63	LORD DERBY	HUGHENDEN	DBP
3848	3 SEP '63	SIR ANDREW BUCHANAN	HUGHENDEN	NOT
3849	12 SEP '63	SARAH BRYDGES WILLYAMS	HUGHENDEN	RTC
3849A	17 SEP '63	CHARLES CLUBBE	HUGHENDEN	RIC
3850	18 SEP '63	WILLIAM ROSE	HUGHENDEN	DA
3851	20 SEP '63	SARAH BRYDGES WILLYAMS	HUGHENDEN	RTC
3852	[25? SEP' 63]	CHARLES CLUBBE	[HUGHENDEN]	PS
3853	28 SEP '63	SARAH BRYDGES WILLYAMS	HUGHENDEN	RTC
3854	28 SEP '63	LORD BEAUCHAMP	HUGHENDEN	BCP
3855	7 OCT '63	PHILIP ROSE	HUGHENDEN	H
3856	8 OCT '63	PHILIP ROSE	[HUGHENDEN]	H
3857	8 OCT '63	PHILIP ROSE	HUGHENDEN	BODL
3858	10 OCT '63	LORD CAMPDEN	HUGHENDEN	PS
3859	17 OCT '63	SARAH BRYDGES WILLYAMS	HUGHENDEN	RTC
3860	19 OCT '63	EDWARD KENEALY	HUGHENDEN	H H/LIFE
3861	21 OCT '63	BARONESS L. DE ROTHSCHILD	HUGHENDEN	ROTH
3862	21 OCT '63	RALPH EARLE	HUGHENDEN	H H/LIFE
3863	21 OCT '63	W.W. FITZWILLIAM HUME	HUGHENDEN	BRN
3864	29 OCT '63	FREDERICK LYGON	HUGHENDEN	BCP
3865	29 OCT '63	LADY LONDONDERRY	HUGHENDEN	DUR
3866	30 OCT '63	LORD DERBY	HUGHENDEN	DBP
3867	1 NOV '63	RALPH EARLE	HUGHENDEN	H H/LIFE
3868	1 NOV '63	BARON L. DE ROTHSCHILD	HUGHENDEN	ROTH
3869	4 NOV '63	LORD STANLEY	HUGHENDEN	DBP
3870	5 NOV '63	RALPH EARLE	HUGHENDEN	H H/LIFE
3871	5 NOV '63	PHILIP ROSE	[HUGHENDEN]	H
3872	5 NOV '63	SARAH BRYDGES WILLYAMS	HUGHENDEN	RTC

NO	DATE	TO	PLACE OF ORIGIN	LOCATION OF ORIGINAL
3873	7 NOV '63	LORD CARRINGTON	HUGHENDEN	CARR
3874	8 NOV '63	RALPH EARLE	HUGHENDEN	H H/LIFE
3875	8 NOV '63	SIR JOHN PAKINGTON	HUGHENDEN	WRC
3876	9 NOV '63	R.E. ROBERTS	HUGHENDEN	MOPSIK
3876A	12 NOV '63	CHARLES CLUBBE	TORQUAY	RIC
3877	13 NOV '63	JAMES BUTLER	TORQUAY	PRIN
3878	13 NOV '63	LORD CARRINGTON	TORQUAY	CARR
3878A	14 NOV '63	CHARLES CLUBBE	TORQUAY	RIC
3879	15 NOV '63	RALPH EARLE	TORQUAY	H H/LIFE
3880	17 NOV '63	PHILIP ROSE	TORQUAY	H
3881	17 NOV '63	LORD DERBY	TORQUAY	DBP
3882	21 NOV '63	MARKHAM SPOFFORTH	TORQUAY	ILLU
3883	21 NOV '63	LORD DERBY	TORQUAY	DBP
3883A	21 NOV '63	CHARLES CLUBBE	TORQUAY	RIC
3884	1 DEC '63	PHILIP ROSE	6 VICTORIA ST	H
3885	[2? DEC '63]	LORD STANLEY	CARLTON CLUB	DBP
3886	13 DEC '63	LORD JOHN MANNERS	GROSVENOR GATE	NOT
3887	13 DEC '63	JOHN DELANE	GROSVENOR GATE	TIA
3887A	14 DEC ['63]	JOHN MAGUIRE	GROSVENOR GATE	PS
3888	3 JAN '64	CATHERINE OSBORNE	HUGHENDEN	SIL
3889	12 JAN '64	[CONSERVATIVE MPS]	HUGHENDEN	WSRO, BCP
3890	18 JAN '64	LORD JOHN MANNERS	GROSVENOR GATE	BEA
3891	18 JAN '64	SIR JOHN PAKINGTON	GROSVENOR GATE	WRC
3892	20 JAN '64	SIR GEORGE SINCLAIR	[LONDON]	H
3893	26 JAN '64	G.[F.]SMITH	GROSVENOR GATE	H
3894	29 JAN '64	DUKE OF WELLINGTON	GROSVENOR GATE	ADM
3895	2 FEB '64	LADY ELY	[LONDON]	RAC
3896	12 FEB '64	LORD STANHOPE	GROSVENOR GATE	KCR
3896A	15 FEB '64	CHARLES CLUBBE	LONDON	RIC
3897	17 FEB '64	MONTAGU SCOTT	GROSVENOR GATE	ILLU
3898	24 FEB '64	LORD STANLEY	GROSVENOR GATE	DBP
3899	18 MAR '64	BARONESS L. DE ROTHSCHILD	GROSVENOR GATE	ROTH
3900	20 MAR '64	BARONESS L. DE ROTHSCHILD	GROSVENOR GATE	ROTH
3901	[20 MAR '64]	BARONESS L. DE ROTHSCHILD	[LONDON]	ROTH
3902	22 MAR '64	WILLIAM CARLISLE	GROSVENOR GATE	MOPSIK
3903	23 MAR '64	PHILIP ROSE	GROSVENOR GATE	INU
3904	24 MAR '64	A. BAILLIE-COCHRANE	GROSVENOR GATE	HAS
3905	3 APR '64	PHILIP ROSE	HUGHENDEN	INU
3906	6 APR '64	PHILIP ROSE	HUGHENDEN	H
3907	[8 APR '64]	PHILIP ROSE	GROSVENOR GATE	H
3908	10 APR '64	PHILIP ROSE	GROSVENOR GATE	H
3909	11 APR '64	SAMUEL WILBERFORCE	GROSVENOR GATE	BODL
3910	[16 APR '64]	[FREDERICK LYGON]	GROSVENOR GATE	BCP
3911	[17 APR '64]	FREDERICK LYGON	GROSVENOR GATE	BCP
3912	17 APR '64	FREDERICK LYGON	GROSVENOR GATE	BCP
3913	[17 APR '64]	FREDERICK LYGON	[LONDON]	BCP
3914	[18 APR '64]	PHILIP ROSE	H OF COMMONS	H
3915	[18]APR '64	MARY ANNE DISRAELI	[H OF COMMONS]	H
3916	19 APR '64	JOHN E. DENISON	GROSVENOR GATE	NOT
3917	19 APR '64	LORD STANHOPE	GROSVENOR GATE	LIV
3918	19 APR '64	PHILIP ROSE	6 VICTORIA ST	H

NO	DATE	TO	PLACE OF ORIGIN	LOCATION OF ORIGINAL
3919	[27?]APR '64	LADY DOROTHY NEVILL	GROSVENOR GATE	EJM
3920	29 APR '64	JOHN EVELYN DENISON	GROSVENOR GATE	NOT
3921	9 MAY '64	LORD AUGUSTUS LOFTUS	GROSVENOR GATE	LUC
3922	11 MAY '64	DUKE OF WELLINGTON	GROSVENOR GATE	HUNT
3923	13 MAY '64	LORD DERBY	GROSVENOR GATE	DBP
3924	14 MAY '64	PHILIP ROSE	GROSVENOR GATE	H
3925	20 MAY '64	LORD SHREWSBURY	CARLTON CLUB	H H/LIFE
3926	[PRE21MAY'64]	HENRY GEORGE WARREN	[LONDON]	PS
3927	27 MAY '64	PHILIP ROSE	6 VICTORIA ST	H
3928	[27?]MAY '64	MARY ANNE DISRAELI	[H OF COMMONS?]	H
3929	29 MAY '64	LORD DERBY	GROSVENOR GATE	DBP
3930	5 JUNE '64	FREDERICK LYGON	GROSVENOR GATE	BCP
3931	9 JUNE '64	LORD BEAUCHAMP	GROSVENOR GATE	BCP
3932	18 JUNE '64	LORD DERBY	GROSVENOR GATE	DBP
3933	[3 JUL '64]	[LORD MALMESBURY]	GROSVENOR GATE	HCC
3934	5 JUL '64	[CHARLES ROSS]	CARLTON CLUB	HUNT
3935	11 JUL '64	THOMAS KEBBEL	GROSVENOR GATE	H H/LIFE
3936	[LATE JUL'64]	ELIZA FOX BRIDELL	[LONDON]	H
3937	27 JUL '64	MR HARVEY	GROSVENOR GATE	MOPSIK
3938	30 JUL '64	GEORGE B. MATHEW	GROSVENOR GATE	PS
3939	[2 AUG '64?]	PHILIP ROSE	CARLTON CLUB	H
3939A	3 AUG '64	EMILY CLUBBE	GROSVENOR GATE	RIC
3940	4 AUG '64	SIR E.BULWER LYTTON	GROSVENOR GATE	HCR
3941	[15?]AUG '64	SIR HENRY JAMES	HUGHENDEN	PS
3942	24 AUG '64	LADY DE ROTHSCHILD	HUGHENDEN	QUA
3943	31 AUG '64	LORD CLANWILLIAM	HUGHENDEN	PS
3944	31 AUG '64	LORD JOHN MANNERS	HUGHENDEN	BEA
3945	4 SEPT '64	LADY EMILY PEEL	HUGHENDEN	NYM
3946	4 SEPT '64	LORD STANLEY	HUGHENDEN	DBP
3947	9 SEPT '64	OCTAVIAN BLEWITT	HUGHENDEN	RLF
3948	12 SEPT '64	LADY LOVAINE	HUGHENDEN	NOR
3949	13 SEPT '64	CHARLES ADDERLEY	HUGHENDEN	H H/LIFE
3950	15 SEPT '64	SIR WILLIAM JOLLIFFE	HUGHENDEN	SCR
3951	16 SEPT '64	[LORD HENRY LENNOX]	HUGHENDEN	PS
3952	19 SEPT '64	SIR E.BULWER LYTTON	HUGHENDEN	HCR
3953	24 SEPT '64	[EDWARD] GRIFFIN	HUGHENDEN	PS
3954	26 SEPT '64	PHILIP ROSE	HUGHENDEN	H
3955	1 OCT '64	SIR WILLIAM JOLLIFFE	HUGHENDEN	SCR
3956	3 OCT '64	SAMUEL WILBERFORCE	HUGHENDEN	BRN
3957	[5 OCT '64]	PHILIP ROSE	[HUGHENDEN]	H
3958	14 OCT '64	PHILIP ROSE	HUGHENDEN	H
3959	18 OCT '64	LORD DERBY	HUGHENDEN	DBP
3960	18 OCT '64	PHILIP ROSE	HUGHENDEN	H
3961	22 OCT '64	C.H. HAWKINS	HUGHENDEN	RUL
3962	24 OCT '64	LADY LOVAINE	HUGHENDEN	NOR
3963	24 OCT '64	MARY ANNE DISRAELI	[LONDON]	H
3964	26 OCT '64	FREDERICK LYGON	HUGHENDEN	BCP
3965	30 OCT '64	JAMES SHEAHAN	HUGHENDEN	UCLA
3966	2 NOV '64	RALPH EARLE	HUGHENDEN	H H/LIFE
3967	15 NOV '64	LORD STANLEY	GROSVENOR GATE	DBP
3968	19 NOV '64	OCTAVIAN BLEWITT	GROSVENOR GATE	RLF

NO	DATE	TO	PLACE OF ORIGIN	LOCATION OF ORIGINAL
3969	20 NOV '64	LORD NEVILL	GROSVENOR GATE	H H/LIFE
3970	29 NOV '64	SAMUEL WILBERFORCE	HUGHENDEN	BRN
3971	1 DEC '64	SIR JOHN PAKINGTON	STRATHFIELDSAYE	WRC
3972	1 DEC '64	EDWARD KENEALY	STRATHFIELDSAYE	QUA
3973	9 DEC '64	FREDERICK LYGON	HUGHENDEN	BCP
3974	11 DEC '64	LORD DERBY	HUGHENDEN	DBP
3975	12 DEC '64	LORD DERBY	HUGHENDEN	DBP
3976	14 DEC '64	LORD HENRY LENNOX	HUGHENDEN	QUA
3977	18 DEC['64]	WILLIAM LOVELL	HUGHENDEN	BL
3978	26 DEC '64	JOHN MOWBRAY	HATFIELD	PS

The following is the available information (source indicated) about Disraeli letters that have not been located, for which no significant portion of the text is available, but which seem to belong to the 1860-64 period, or earlier. Some of them have been used in the notes of this volume, as indicated. The references to items in H *are to items from which a specific* D *letter can be inferred. For pre-1860 letters newly found see Appendix* I.

26 Jun '58	To Robert Hume. **App I 3111x**n1 (cover).
['60?]	To Lady Drogheda, invitation. H B/XXI/D/368.
['60?]	To Lady Jersey, several letters. H A/IV/J/139.
before 6 Feb '60	To J.R. McCulloch. H B/XXI/M/30.
before 15 Mar '60	To Joseph de Schler. H B/XXI/S/58.
before 10 Apr '60	To E. Bickersteth, church rates. H B/XXI/B/484.
before 14 Apr '60	To W.S. Lindsay, re calling. H B/XXI/L/209.
before 24 Apr '60	To W.H. Hale, re church rates. H B/XXI/H/9.
before 22 Apr ['60?]	To James Disraeli. H A/I/D/18.
before 9 May '60	To Sir George Sinclair, political. H B/XXI/S/250.
before 30 May '60	To T.S. Estcourt, to meet. H B/XXI/E/258.
Jun '60	To W.S. Lindsay, re Reform. H B/XXI/L/207.
10 Jun '60	To R.B. Harvey. Pearson catalogue II: 6, 121.
before 11 Jun '60	To F. Villebois. H B/XXI/V/69.
before 12 Jun '60	To Joseph de Schler. H B/XXI/S/65.
before 17 Jun '60	To duc d'Orleans, invitation. H B/XXI/O/46.
before 23 Jun '60	To Emily Hardinge, *ditto.* H D/III/D/282.
29 Aug '60	To Ralph Disraeli. **3497** (cover).
before 2 Sep '60	To Lord Henry Lennox. H B/XX/LX/138.
before 12 Sep '60	To Thomas Loftus, re Williams. H D/II/B/147.
before 20 Sep '60	To Lord Henry Lennox. H B/XX/LX/139.
8 Oct '60	To Samuel Wilberforce, invitation. **3505**&n6.
before 9 Oct '60	To Philip Rose, re Berwick election. H R/I/B/67.
before 12 Oct '60	To Sir John Neeld, to cancel visit. **3505**.
before 18 Oct '60	To Poulett Scropes, *ditto.* **3505**.
before 18 Oct '60	To Lord Bath, *ditto.*
before 18 Oct '60	To T.S. Estcourt, *ditto.*
before 18 Oct '60	To Walter Long, *ditto.*
before 18 Oct '60	To FitzWilliam Hume, *ditto.*
before 25 Oct '60	To Colonel Taylor. H B/XX/T/6.
before 28 Oct '60	To Lord Henry Lennox. H B/XX/LX/140.
before 1 Nov '60	To Charles Lennox. H B/XX/LE/5.
before 6 Nov '60	To Charles Coleridge, re Berwick. **3506**n1.

before 7 Nov '60	To Samuel Wilberforce, invitation. H B/XXI/W/354.
before 10 Nov '60	To Philip Rose, invitation. H R/I/B/71.
before 15 Nov '60	To Thomas Baring. H B/XXI/B/59.
22 Nov '60	To Charles Coleridge, re Berwick. **3517**n3.
before 27 Nov '60	To George Denison, church rates. H B/XXI/D/110.
[Dec '60?]	To C.P. Villiers. H B/XXI/V/76.
before 12 Dec '60	To Salisbury, re Trelawny. **3531**n4.
before 14 Dec '60	To Maria Palk, re invitation. H B/XXI/P/69.
before 17 Dec '60	To Gerard Noel, re duties. H B/XXI/N/98.
before 26 Dec '60	To Lord Malmesbury, re church rates. **3551**n1.
before 27 Dec '60	To Colonel Taylor. H B/XX/T/11.
['61?]	To Lord Salisbury, invitation. H B/XXI/C/145.
[18 Jan '61]	To Lord J. Manners, Queen's speech. H B/XX/M/118.
23 Jan '61	To [M. Margoliouth?]. *Wilson Autographs* (Mar 1994) 3626.
before 30 Jan '61	To Richard Long, re Parliament. H B/XXI/L/247.
before 4 Feb '61	To W.H. Hale. H B/XXI/H/17.
26 Feb '61	To Lord Cardigan, church rates. H B/XXI/C/46.
before 5 Mar ['61?]	To Lord Holmesdale. H B/XXI/H/604.
before 12 Apr '61	To Thomas Loftus, re finance. H D/II/B/150.
before 17 May '61	To Lord Pevensey. H B/XXI/P/221.
before 21 Jun '61	To Rev T. Evetts, re church rates. H B/XXI/E/286.
26 Jun '61	To Francis Villiers. H A/IV/J/148.
before 30 Jun '61	To Countess Persigny, invitation. H B/XXI/P/219.
before 14 Jul '61	To Lord Bath, invitation. H B/XXI/B/168.
before 31 Jul '61	To William Cubitt. H B/XXI/C/610.
Aug '61	To Lady Jersey, re F. Villiers. H A/IV/J/157.
before 28 Aug '61	To Laurence Peel, *ditto.* H A/IV/J/155.
before 28 Aug '61	To Lady Jersey, *ditto.* H A/IV/J/154.
before 15 Sep '61	To Henry Padwick, *ditto.* H A/IV/J/160.
20? Sep '61	To J. Sheahan, *History of Bucks.* H B/XXI/S/159.
before 24 Sep '61	To Francis Villiers. H A/IV/J/163.
before 27 Sep '61	To Charles Greville, invitation. H A/IV/J/165.
[before 15 Oct '61]	To Lady Glengall, *ditto.* H B/XXI/G/183.
before 23 Oct '61	To E. Bickersteth, re meeting. H B/XXI/B/487.
before 10 Nov '61	To SBW. RTC [436Q].
before 27 Nov '61	To Lady Londonderry, re visit. H B/XX/V/225.
before 30 Nov '61	To Lady Jersey. H A/IV/J/170.
[Dec '61?]	To Lady Jersey. H A/IV/J/173.
before 4 Dec '61	To Sir George Sinclair. H B/XXI/S/257.
11 Dec '61	To Sir Archibald Alison. **3634**&n2.
14 Dec '61	To Thomas Taylor, re Durham. **3635**&n2.
before 18 Dec '61	To Charles Adderley, re pamphlet. H B/XXI/A/77.
'62	To Lord Norton, re Canada. H H/Life.
before 1 Jan '62	To Duke of Northumberland, visit. H B/XXI/N/189.
before 4 Jan '62	To Lady Londonderry. H B/XX/V/229.
before 12 Jan '62	To Col E.W. Fane, re Oxford election. **3649**n2.
before [23?] Jan '62	To James Whiteside. H B/XXI/W/303.
before 30 Jan '62	To E. Kenealy, re judgeship. **3643**n1.
before 8 Feb '62	To E. Kenealy, *ditto.* H B/XXI/K/93.
before 9 Feb '62	To Lord Coventry, invitation. H B/XXI/C/544.
before 12 Feb '62	To Lord Henry Lennox, *ditto.* H B/XX/LX/151.
before 16 Feb '62	To Lord Lonsdale, invitation. H B/XXI/L/278.
before 17 Feb '62	To Lady Jersey. H A/IV/J/187.
24 Feb '62	To Sir R. Mayne, re police watch. **3485**n4.

before 8 Mar '62	To Frank Fowler, re 'ruin'. H B/XIX/ADD.
before [22 Mar '62]	To Andrew Montagu, invitation. **3683**&n2.
before 24 Mar '62	To Lord Exeter, invitation. H B/XXI/E/304.
before [24?] Mar '62	To Lord Lonsdale, *ditto.* H B/XXI/L/277.
before 6 Apr '62	To Francis Villiers. H A/IV/J/188.
14 Apr '62	To J. Lovegrove, re Taynton sale. **3737**&n1.
before 23 Apr '62	To J. Lovegrove, re insurance. H D/II/B/302.
[May?] '62	To Georgiana Bentinck. H B/XXI/B/321.
before 15 May '62	To Count Reventlow, invitation. H B/XXI/C/373.
22 May '62	To Lord Lovaine, to meet. **3684**&n1.
before 23 May '62	To Sir William Heathcote, *ditto.* H B/XXI/H/433.
[Jun?] '62	To Lady Jersey, re F. Villiers. H A/IV/J/208.
about 6 Jun '62	To T.S. Estcourt, re speech. **3693**&n2.
before 10 Jun '62	To Thomas Baring, invitation. H B/XXI/B/64.
about 19 Jun '62	To Charles Adderley, re Canada. **3700**n2.
before 23 Jun '62	To William Powell, re registration. **3706**n2.
28 Jun '62	To unknown. F. Edwards catalogue 406: 124.
[Jul '62?]	To Baron Brunnow, invitation. **3698**.
[Jul '62?]	To Lady Hardwicke, *ditto.* H B/XXI/H/190.
Jul '62	To Lord Forester, *ditto.* H B/XXI/F/202.
Jul '62	To Lady Glengall, *ditto.* H B/XXI/G/184.
before 7 Jul '62	To Mortimer Collins, re book. H B/XXI/C/324.
before 9 Jul '62	To Sir George Sinclair, to meet. H B/XXI/S/258.
before 9 Jul '62	To Charles Adderley, re Canada. **3700**n2.
before 15 Jul '62	To Lady Malmesbury, invitation. **3698**n1.
before 15 Jul '62	To Lord Granby, *ditto.* H B/XXI/R/340.
before 15 Jul '62	To Lord Bath, *ditto.* H B/XXI/B/170.
15 Jul ['62]	To Lady Cowley, *ditto.* *ABPC* (1974) 1013.
15 Jul '62	To George Carrington, Jr, *ditto.* H B/XXI/C/84.
before 16 Jul ['62?]	To Lord Forester, *ditto.* H B/XXI/F/203.
before 16 Jul '62	To Charles Lennox, *ditto.* H B/XX/LE/6.
before 8 Aug '62	To SBW. RTC [465Q], **3702**n7.
before 22 Jul '62	To T.S. Estcourt. H B/XXI/E/272.
before 20 Aug '62	To Philip Rose. H R/I/B/86A.
before 21 Aug '62	To Henry Edwards. H B/XXI/E/50.
before 26 Aug '62	To Count L. Corti, invitation. H B/XXI/C/463.
before 1 Sep '62	To William Lowndes. H B/XXI/L/361.
3 Sep '62	To William Powell, re registration. **3706**n2.
before 4 Sep '62	To Lord Stanley. H B/XX/S/709.
before 5 Sep '62	To Lord Elmley, invitation. H B/XXI/L/426.
before 8 Sep '62	To Lady Hardwicke, *ditto.* H B/XXI/H/191.
before 9 Sep '62	To Lady G. Codrington, *ditto.* H B/XXI/C/299-300.
14 Sep '62	To Elliott Bros, re telegraph. H A/V/G/233.
before 11 Sep '62	To Lady Mary Hood, invitation. H B/XXI/B/933.
before 13 Sep '62	To Ralph Earle. H B/XX/E/257.
before 13 Sep '62	To William Peel, invitation. H B/XXI/P/189.
before 13 Sep '62	To Henry Drummond Wolff, *ditto.* H B/XXI/W/477.
before 16 Sep '62	To Lord G. Gordon-Lennox, *ditto.* H B/XXI/L/126.
before 22 Sep '62	To W. Lovell, with enclosure. H A/V/G/196.
22 Sep '62	To S. Triscott, re charges. **3718**n1.
before 23 Sep '62	To Ralph Earle. H B/XX/E/259.
before 25 Sep '62	To Lady G. Codrington. H B/XXI/C/302.
before 26 [Sep '62?]	To Philip Dauncey, re Aylesbury. H B/XXI/D/40.
before 26 Sep '62	To J. MacDonald, invitation. H B/XXI/M/32.

before 29 Sep '62	To John Delane, *ditto.* H B/XXI/D/76.
before 4 Oct '62	To E. Bickersteth, re Hughenden. **3723**&n1.
before 9 Oct '62	To William Powell, re registration. H B/I/D/41.
before 13 [Oct?] '62	To Mrs E.W. Fane, invitation. H B/XXI/F/49.
14 Oct '62	To Lady Vere Cameron, invitation. **3730**&n1.
14 Oct '62	To J. Lovegrove, re Taynton sale. **3737**n1.
before 16 Oct '62	To Lady Jersey, re F. Villiers. H A/IV/J/255.
before 17 Oct '62	To Robert Bourke, invitation. H B/XXI/B/666.
before 17 Oct '62	To J.G. Hubbard, invitation. **3732**&n6.
before 18 Oct '62	To Duke of Northumberland. H B/XXI/N/189.
before 20 Oct '62	To Lord Stanley, invitation. H B/XX/S/710.
20 Oct '62	To J. Lovegrove, re Taynton sale. **3737**n1.
before 21 Oct '62	To Lord Lyndhurst. H B/XXI/L/481.
before 22 Oct '62	To Lady Londonderry, re marriages. H B/XX/V/233.
22 Oct '62	To J. Lovegrove, re Taynton sale. **3737**n1.
before 23 Oct '62	To Rev T. Evetts, invitation. **3732**&n6.
before 23 Oct '62	To Lady Jersey, re F. Villiers. H A/IV/J/227.
before 24 Oct '62	To Ralph Earle. H B/XX/E/263.
before 27 Oct '62	To E. Bickersteth, invitation. H B/XXI/B/492.
before 26 Oct '62	To Lord Malmesbury, *ditto.* H B/XX/HS/110.
before 27 Oct '62	To Rev W.E. Partridge, invitation. H B/XXI/P/130.
before 28 Oct '62	To E. Kenealy, re book. **3745**n1.
before 31 Oct '62	To J. Lovegrove, re Williams. H D/II/B/312.
before 2 Nov '62	To Philip Rose, re meeting. H R/I/B/87.
before 3 Nov '62	To J. Lovegrove, re Taynton sale. **3737**n1.
before 5 Nov '62	To Lady Campden, re France. H B/XXI/G/29.
5 Nov '62	To William Powell, re registration. **3706**.
before 6 Nov '62	To E. Bickersteth, re D speech. **3734**n1.
9 Nov '62	To J. Lovegrove, re Taynton sale. **3737**n1.
before [11?] Nov '62	To W.H. Hale. H B/XXI/H/20.
18 Nov '62	To Fred. Villiers, re F. Villiers. H A/IV/J/229.
before 20 Nov '62	To M. Spofforth, re newspaper notice. H B/XXI/S/393.
before 25 Nov '62	To R.W. Miles, re investments. H D/II/B/226A.
before 27 Nov '62	To T. Hamber, *Morning Herald.* H B/XX/A/116.
before 27 Nov '62	To E. Kenealy, re book. **3745**n1.
before 27 Nov '62	To E.B. Lamb, re Hughenden gardens. H A/V/G/234.
before 27 Nov '62	To Sir R. Mayne, Jobson threats. H B/XXI/M/316.
8 Dec '62	To W.M. Rossetti, re Blake etchings. **3736**n1.
before 9 Dec '62	To Philip Dauncey, re relief fund. H B/XXI/D/33.
about 15 Dec '62	To unknown recipient, re relief fund. **3752A**n2.
about 19-20 Dec '62	To Philip Dauncey, *ditto.* **3744**n2.
31 Dec '62	To Miss Warrington, autograph. Sotheby's (Oct 1977): 208.
['63?]	To Ralph Earle. H B/XX/E/311.
['63?]	To Ralph Earle. H B/XX/E/313.
12 Jan '63	To J. Sheahan, on D letter. **3619**n1.
16 Jan '63	To J. Sheahan, to buy his book. H B/XXI/S/164.
before 22 Jan '63	To Lord Normanby, invitation. H B/XXI/P/287.
before 22 Jan '63	To Sir E.B. Lytton, re House. H B/XX/LY/137.
before 22 Jan '63	To Lord Henry Lennox, *ditto.* H B/XX/LX/169.
before 30 Jan '63	To Henry Lowry-Corry, on Italy. H B/XXI/C/437.
before 31 Jan '63	To Duke of Buckingham, invitation. H B/XXI/B/1215.
before 4 Feb '63	To Percy Wyndham, invitation. H A/IV/L/66.
before 12 Feb '63	To Lady Londonderry. H B/XX/V/235.
before 14 Feb '63	To Sir R. Mayne, re police watch on Jobson. H B/XXI/M/317.

before 17 Feb '63	To Charles Trefusis, invitation. H B/XXI/C/273.
before 18 Feb '63	To Sir P.P. Duncombe, invitation. H B/XXI/D/419.
before 27 Feb '63	To Duke of Northumberland. H B/XXI/N/190.
before 3 Mar '63	To J. Parrott, re London meeting. H B/XXI/P/115.
before 6 Apr '63	To Lord Lyndhurst. H B/XXI/L/483.
before 20 Apr '63	To Thomas Collins, re a Whip. H B/XXI/C/322.
before 20 Apr '63	To W. Pennington, re Slough committee. H C/XI/29.
before 1 May '63	To C.H. Stewart, re Ceylon laws. H A/IV/J/239AA.
before 8 May '63	To Lady Derby, re Knatchbulls. H B/XX/S/520.
15 May '63	To W. Pennington, re Slough donation. H C/XI/30.
before 18 May '63	To C.H. Stewart, on Ceylon laws. H A/IV/J/239BB.
before 30 May '63	To Lord Arundel, invitation. H B/XXI/A/214.
before 9 Jun '63	To George Vernon, re Hughenden work. H A/V/G/17.
before 13 Jun '63	To Lord Palmerston, re House votes. H B/XXI/P/93.
before 18 Jul '63	To William Powell, re registration. H B/I/D/45.
before 27 Jul '63	To Duchess of Westminster, books. H B/XXI/W/240.
14 Aug '63	To SBW. **3842**&n1.
before 16 Aug '63	To Lady Londonderry, on Durham. H B/XX/V/237.
before 20 Aug '63	To James Disraeli, re visit. H A/I/D/21.
before 21 Aug '63	To Col Edwards, on his regiment. **3843**n1.
before 21 Aug '63	To Lady Exeter, on harvest. H B/XXI/E/307.
1 Sep '63	To Cavendish, salutation only. H B/II/87.
before 5 Sep '63	To C.P. Barrett, re meeting. H A/V/G/[unnumbered].
before 5 Sep '63	To T.S. Estcourt. H B/XXI/E/274.
before 6 Sep '63	To R. Michell, re pruning machine. H B/XXI/M/362.
before 8 Sep '63	To H. Wellington, re investments. H D/II/B/230.
before 13 Sep '63	To Duke of Wellington, on Sevigné. H B/XXI/W/158.
before 9 Oct '63	To J. Lovegrove, on Taynton sale. H D/II/B/317.
before 12 Oct '63	To Ralph Earle, re Lord Campden. **3858**n3.
before 14 Oct '63	To Philip Rose, on finance. **3858**n1.
before 24 Oct '63	To Sir H. Stracey, re speech. H B/XXI/S/601.
before 24 Oct '63	To H. Wellington, re Glyn & Co. H D/II/B/231.
before 30 Oct '63	To Lady Jersey. H A/IV/J/244.
before 31 Oct '63	To Lord H. Lennox, on Palmerston. H B/XX/LX/179.
before 16 Nov '63	To Rev. C. Clubbe, on SBW's funeral. **3884**n1.
before 16 Nov '63	To Margaretta Rose, re Bishop. **3880**&n1.
before 17 Nov '63	To Lord Vane, on Lady Londonderry. H B/XX/V/239.
before 8 Dec '63	To J.W. Chetwode, on SBW's death. H A/V/G/150.
before 9 Dec '63	To J. Lovegrove, on Loftus. H D/II/B/318.
before 11 Dec '63	To Sir E.B. Lytton. H B/XX/LY/142.
before 14 Dec '63	To Elizabeth Russell. H B/XXI/R/317.
before 14 Dec '63	To Lord Henry Lennox, invitation. H B/XX/LX/181.
before 25 Dec '63	To Ralph Earle. H B/XX/E/305.
['64?]	To H.A.B. Johnstone, his motion. H B/XXI/J/116.
about Jan '64	To S. Laing, re Land Mortgage Bank. H A/V/G/235.
before 5 Jan '64	To Lord Malmesbury, re new club. H B/XX/HS/113.
before 11 Jan '64	To Thomas Hamber, re meeting. H B/XX/A/120.
before 14 Jan '64	To T.S. Estcourt, re dinner. H B/XXI/E/275.
before 20 Jan '64	To Sir E.B. Lytton, re his wife. H B/XX/LY/143.
before 25 Jan '64	To A. Austin, several letters. H B/XXI/A/241.
before 26 Jan '64	To J. Lovegrove, on finance. H B/D/III/B/324–5A.
before 28 Jan '64	To Lady Jersey. H A/IV/J/251.
before 28 Jan '64	To Sir J.C.D. Hay, re assize. H B/XXI/H/294.
before 28 Jan '64	To R.W. Williams, on finance. H D/III/B/235.

before 30 Jan '64	To Stark & Co, re Mt Braddon sale. H A/V/G/173.
before 31 Jan '64	To Lord Buchan. H B/XXI/B/1106.
about Feb '64	To H.A.B. Johnstone. H B/XXI/J/114.
12 Feb '64	To W. Jenkins, re Dowlais. H A/V/G/74.
before 19 Feb '64	To Duke of Wellington, on reading. H B/XXI/W/160.
before 30 Mar '64	To J. Hannay, re Ellice. H B/XXI/H/145.
before 1 Apr '64	To W. Lovell, re SBW legacies. H A/V/G/158.
before 13 Apr '64	To Stark & Co, re books. H A/V/G/161.
before 25 Apr '64	To Stark & Co, re SBW's funeral. H A/V/G/163.
before 12 May '64	To E. Edwards, invitation. H B/XXI/E/57.
before 13 May '64	To R.B. Harvey, re battalion. H B/XXI/H/278.
before 18 May '64	To J. Skelton, compliments. H B/XXI/S/277.
before 25 May '64	To A. Montagu, with 'Revolutionary Epick'. H B/XXI/M/408.
before 5 Jun '64	To G.A. Denison, re denomination. H B/XXI/D/130.
before 10 Jun '64	To Lord Cranstown, re meeting. H B/XXI/C/589.
before 13 Jul '64	To J.W.P. Watlington. H B/XXI/W/142.
before 16 Jul '64	To M. Collins. H B/XXI/C/325.
before 17 Jul '64	To G.E. de Michele, invitation. H B/XXI/M/358.
before 29 Jul '64	To W. Powell, re Bucks registration. H B/I/D/49.
before 21 Aug '64	To Lady Jersey. H A/IV/J/226.
before 22 Aug '64	To Lord Napier. H R/I/B/98.
27 Aug '64	To Mr Simpson, Additional Curates Society. Paul Richards Autographs 106 (1979): 118.
before 29 Aug '64	To Stark & Co, re a clock. H A/V/G/169.
before 31 Aug '64	To Mrs Loraine, Royal Literary Fund. H A/IV/M/84.
before 31 Aug '64	To J. Lovegrove, re rents. H D/II/B/333.
before 1 Sep '64	To Lord Beauchamp, invitation. H B/XXI/L/429.
before 2 Sep '64	To Lord St Germans, *ditto*. H B/XXI/S/6.
before 5 Sep '64	To J. Sheahan, re his book. H B/XXI/S/166.
before 7 Sep '64	To Count Apponyi, invitation. H B/XXI/A/182.
before 8 Sep '64	To Arthur Russell, *ditto*. H A/IV/L/109.
before 8 Sep '64	To Lord Wilton, *ditto*. H B/XXI/W/419.
before 8 Sep '64	To Lady Ely. H B/XIX/D/149.
before 10 Sep '64	To Lady Brownlow, invitation. H B/XXI/B/1045.
before 11 Sep '64	To Lord Loughborough, *ditto*. H B/XXI/R/165.
before 12 Sep '64	To Lady G. Codrington, *ditto*. H B/XXI/C/304.
before 12 Sep '64	To A. Montagu, *ditto*. H B/XXI/M/409.
before 12 Sep '64	To J. Sheahan, re his book. H B/XXI/S/167.
12 Sep '64	To R.H. Barrett, re meeting. H A/V/G/[unnumbered].
before 13 Sep '64	To Thomas Baring, invitation. H B/XXI/B/66.
before 17 Sep '64	To Lady Mary Hood, *ditto*. H B/XXI/B/930.
before 17 Sep '64	To Lord Henry Lennox, *ditto*. H B/XX/LX/201.
before 20 Sep '64	To Lady Chesham, *ditto*. H B/XXI/C/186.
before 22 Sep '64	To Lord Napier, letter for Rose. H R/I/B/98.
22 Sep '64	To Ralph Earle. H B/XX/E/340.
before 23 Sep '64	To Lord Carrington, invitation. H B/XXI/C/79.
before 27 Sept '64	To Lord Courtenay, *ditto*. H B/XXI/C/474.
before 30 Sep '64	To Philip Dauncey, *ditto*. H B/XXI/D/38.
before 6 Oct '64	To T.E. Kebbel, *ditto*. H B/XXI/K/23.
before 8 Oct '64	To Lady Normanby, a kind letter. H B/XXI/P/293.
before 13 Oct '64	To C. Carlton, invitation. H B/XXI/C/49.
before 15 Oct '64	To Lord Loughborough, *ditto*. H B/XXI/R/167.
before 18 Oct '64	To Lord Loughborough, *ditto*. H B/XXI/R/167.
before 19 Oct '64	To Charles Carrington, *ditto*. H B/XXI/C/86.

before 19 Oct '64	To J. Du Pre, on dissolution. H B/XXI/D/447.
before 20 Oct '64	To Sir G. Jenkinson, re Bristol. H B/XXI/J/28.
before 20 Oct '64	To Lady Willoughby. H B/XXI/W/382.
before 22 Oct '64	To W. Powell, re registration. H B/I/D/52a.
before 23 Oct '64	To Lord Stanley, re meeting. H B/XX/S/719.
before 24 Oct '64	To Samuel Wilberforce, invitation. H B/XXI/W/368.
24 Oct '64	To Julian Fane, re return. **3963**&n2.
before 25 Oct '64	To Sir G. Jenkinson. H B/XXI/J/30.
before 25 Oct '64	To Count Vitzthum, invitation. H B/XXI/V/84.
before 27 Oct '64	To Lord Coventry, *ditto.* H B/XXI/C/545.
before 28 Oct '64	To Henry Wyndham, *ditto.* H A/IV/L/87.
before 1 Nov '64	To J. Du Pre, re election. H B/XXI/D/446.
before 3 Nov '64	To G.C. Du Pre, on dissolution. H B/XXI/D/439.
before 23 Nov '64	To Lord Loughborough, invitation. H B/XXI/R/168.
before 23 Nov '64	To Mrs E. Poulett Scrope. H B/XXI/S/90.
before 24 Nov '64	To J. Sheahan, re Literary Fund. H B/XXI/S/170.
1 Dec '64	To J.A. Roebuck, on railways. **3971**&n2.
before 14 Dec '64	To W. Lovell, on picture sale. H A/V/G/202.
before 22 Dec '64	To Lady Ehrenfield, re portrait. H B/XXI/E/113.
before 26 Dec '64	To Lady Brownlow. H B/XXI/B/1049.

'Princess Beatrice of Battenberg' by John Jabez Edwin Mayall. Hand coloured albumen carte-de-visite. February 1861. National Portrait Gallery NPG Ax46715. See **3557**&n1.

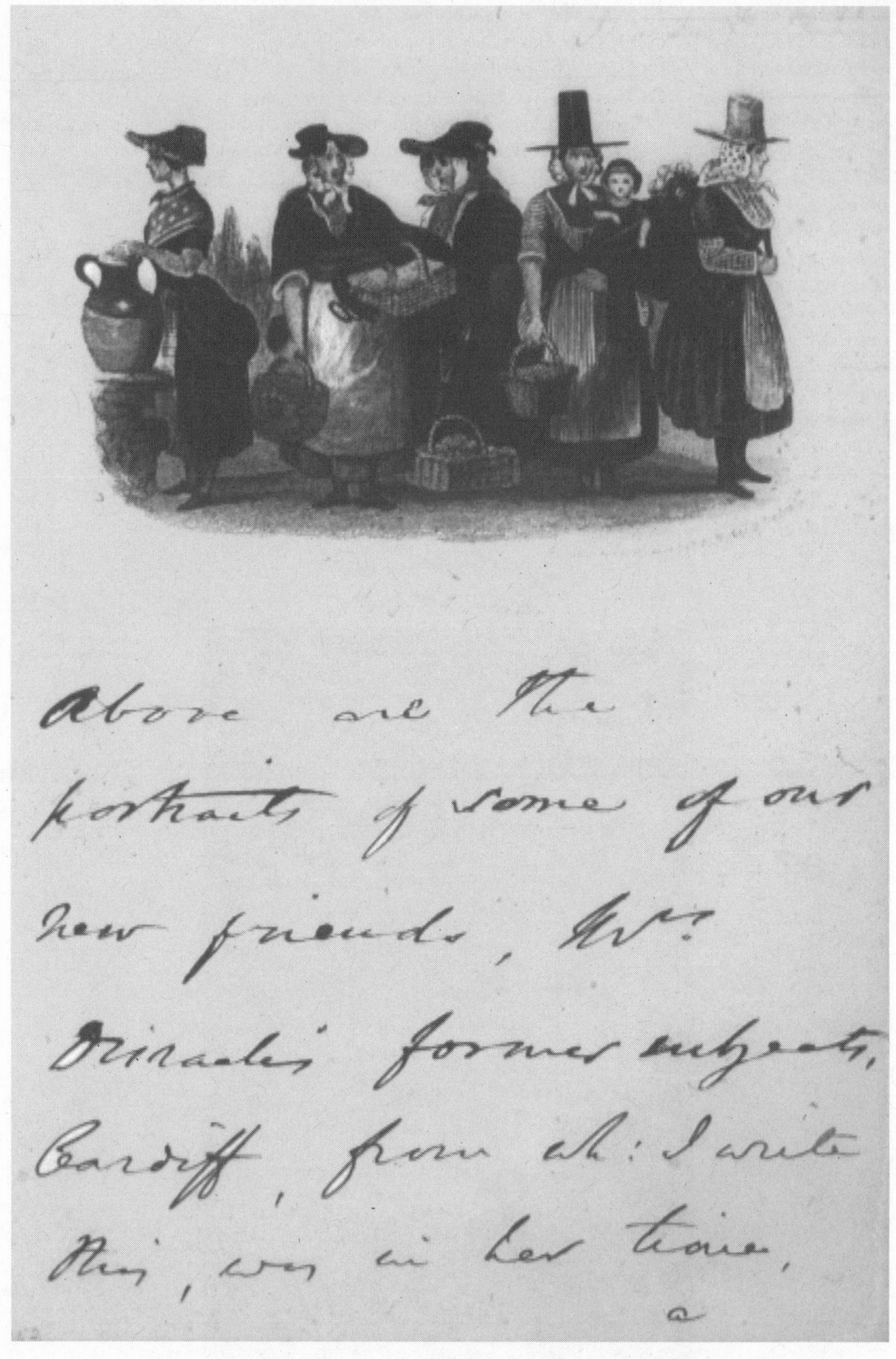

Above are the portraits of some of our new friends, Mr. Disraeli's former subjects, Cardiff, from wh: I write this, was in her time, a

'Welsh costumes. Engraved by Newman & Co 48 Watling St London.' See **3568**.

'Lord Palmerston Addressing the House of Commons During the Debates on the Treaty of France in February 1860.' Engraved by T.O. Barlow after a picture by John Phillip. See **3610**&nn1&2&4.

'Queen Victoria' (1843) and 'Prince Albert' (1859) by Francis Xavier Winterhalter. Hung in the South Bedroom at Hughenden Manor. NT/HVG/C/110. See **3667**&n2.

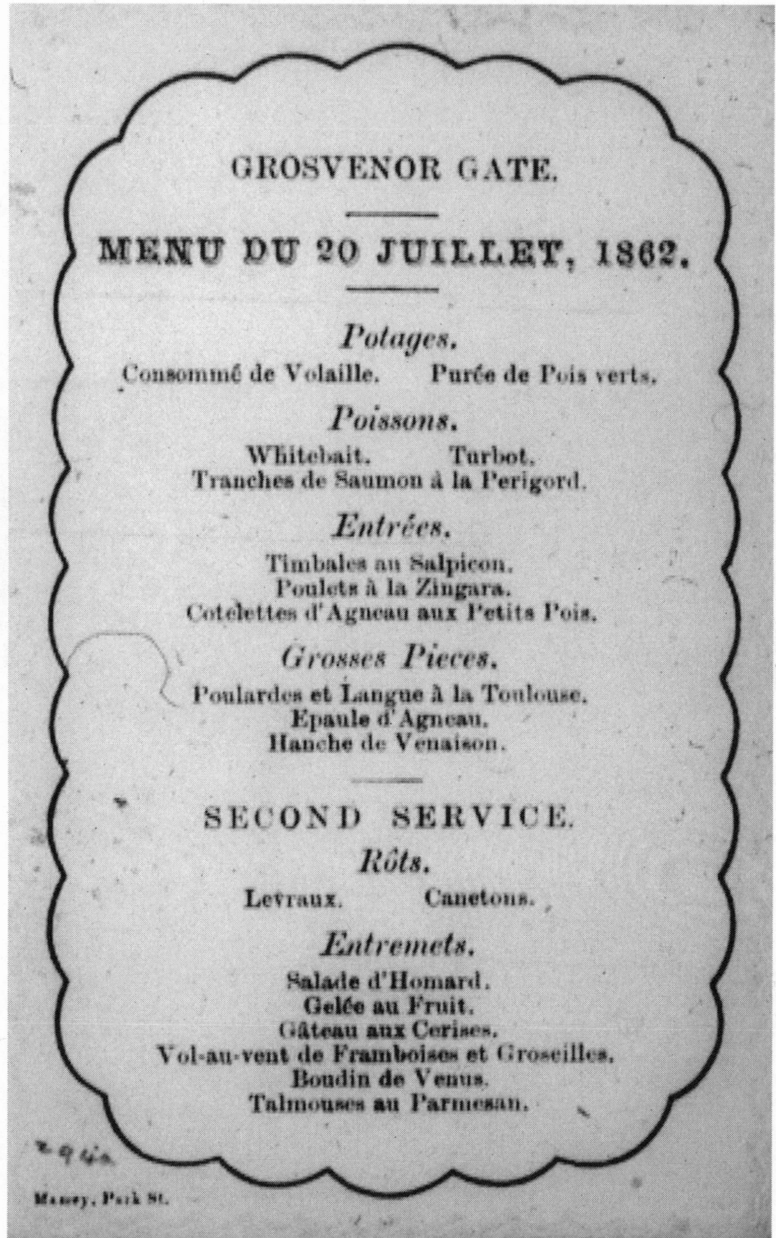

GROSVENOR GATE.

MENU DU 20 JUILLET, 1862.

Potages.

Consommé de Volaille. Purée de Pois verts.

Poissons.

Whitebait. Turbot.
Tranches de Saumon à la Perigord.

Entrées.

Timbales au Salpicon.
Poulets à la Zingara.
Cotelettes d'Agneau aux Petits Pois.

Grosses Pieces.

Poulardes et Langue à la Toulouse.
Epaule d'Agneau.
Hanche de Venaison.

SECOND SERVICE.

Rôts.

Levraux. Canetons.

Entremets.

Salade d'Homard.
Gelée au Fruit.
Gâteau aux Cerises.
Vol-au-vent de Framboises et Groseilles.
Boudin de Venus.
Talmouses au Parmesan.

Massey, Park St.

Menu for a Grosvenor Gate Dinner, 20 July 1862. See **3702**&n6.

The monument to Isaac D'Israeli, erected by Mary Anne Disraeli at Hughenden in June 1862. See **3707**&n3, **3708**&ec, **3725**&n2, **3818**&n2.

E.B. Lamb's proposed elevation for the north front of Hughenden, 1862. Now in the Bartolozzi Room at Hughenden Manor. See **3747**&n2.

'The Marriage of the Prince of Wales, 10 March 1863' by William Powell Frith, 1865. Queen Victoria watching at upper right. See **3797**&n2.

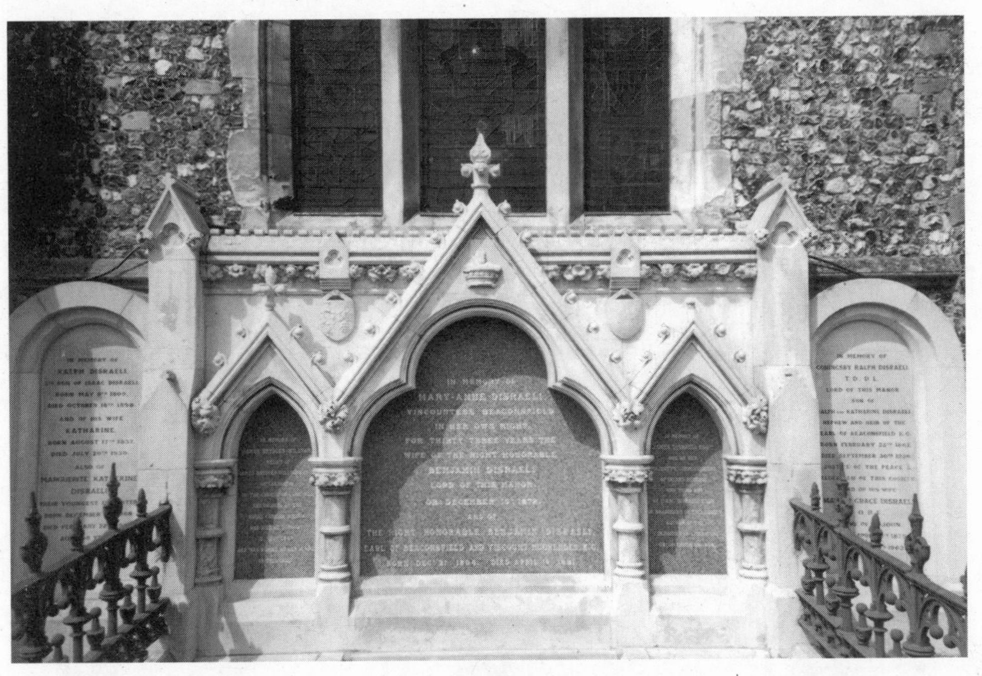

IN MEMORY OF
SARAH BRYDGES-WILLYAMS
RELICT OF
JAMES BRYDGES-WILLYAMS ESQ^{RE}
OF CARNANTON
IN THE COUNTY OF CORNWALL
AND COLONEL OF THE
ROYAL CORNISH MILITIA
SHE DIED AT TORQUAY
11 : NOV. 1863
AND WAS BURIED AT HER DESIRE
IN THIS VAULT

The grave (second from left) of Sarah Brydges Willyams at the Church of St Michael and All Angels, Hughenden. See **3884**&nn1&2.

'Dressing for an Oxford Bal Masqué' from *Punch* (10 December 1864). Disraeli as not ape but angel. See **3969**&n2.

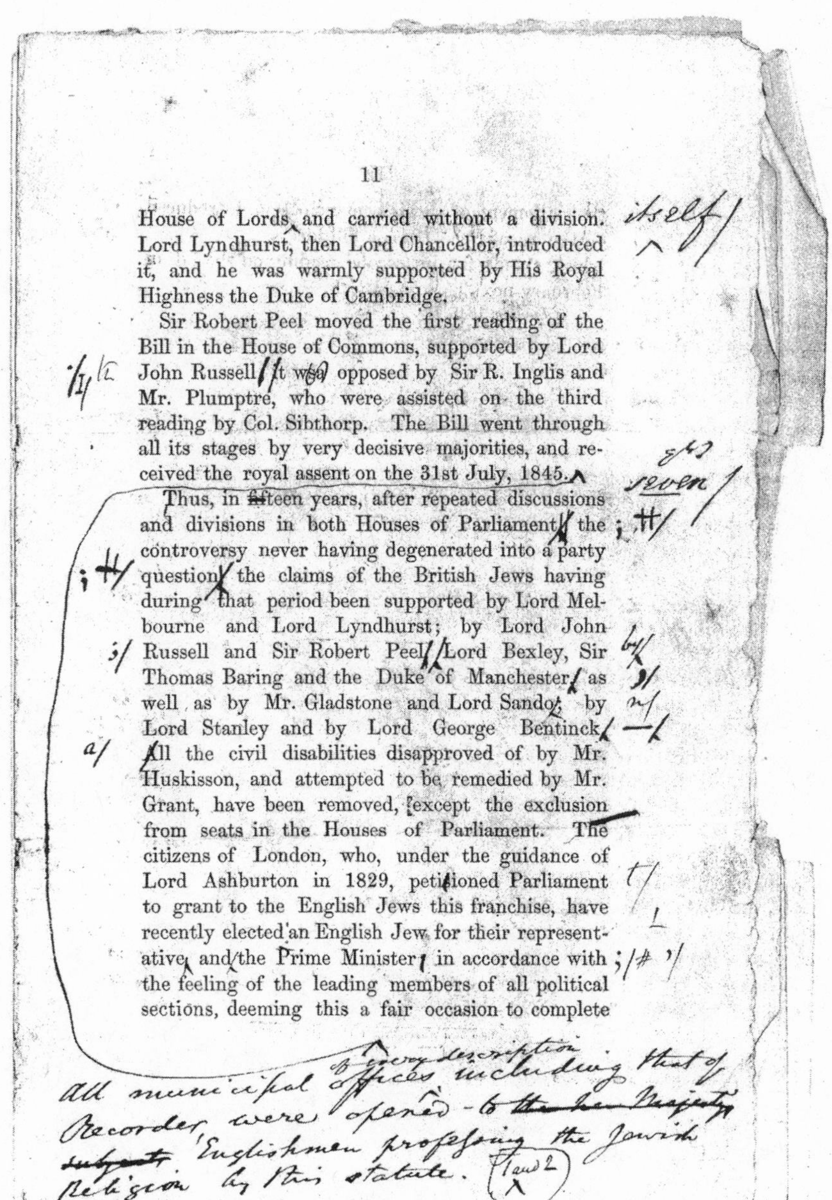
11

House of Lords and carried without a division. Lord Lyndhurst, then Lord Chancellor, introduced it, and he was warmly supported by His Royal Highness the Duke of Cambridge.

Sir Robert Peel moved the first reading of the Bill in the House of Commons, supported by Lord John Russell. It was opposed by Sir R. Inglis and Mr. Plumptre, who were assisted on the third reading by Col. Sibthorp. The Bill went through all its stages by very decisive majorities, and received the royal assent on the 31st July, 1845.

Thus, in fifteen years, after repeated discussions and divisions in both Houses of Parliament, the controversy never having degenerated into a party question, the claims of the British Jews having during that period been supported by Lord Melbourne and Lord Lyndhurst; by Lord John Russell and Sir Robert Peel, Lord Bexley, Sir Thomas Baring and the Duke of Manchester, as well as by Mr. Gladstone and Lord Sandon, by Lord Stanley and by Lord George Bentinck. All the civil disabilities disapproved of by Mr. Huskisson, and attempted to be remedied by Mr. Grant, have been removed, except the exclusion from seats in the Houses of Parliament. The citizens of London, who, under the guidance of Lord Ashburton in 1829, petitioned Parliament to grant to the English Jews this franchise, have recently elected an English Jew for their representative, and the Prime Minister, in accordance with the feeling of the leading members of all political sections, deeming this a fair occasion to complete

All municipal offices of every description including that of Recorder, were opened to Englishmen professing the Jewish Religion by this statute.

Proof page from ‘Progress of Jewish Emancipation Since 1829.’ See App I **1619XA**&n2.

BENJAMIN DISRAELI LETTERS: 1860–1864

TO: SARAH BRYDGES WILLYAMS [London, Sunday] 1 January 1860 **3438**

ORIGINAL: RTC [131]

PUBLICATION HISTORY: M&B IV 355, dated New Year's Day, 1860, the third (first sentence omitted), fourth and fifth paragraphs

EDITORIAL COMMENT: Black-edged paper. SBW has written 'mankind' over D's 'mankind' in the third paragraph and 'Church' over D's 'Church' in the fourth paragraph as though she had to have help reading these words. *Sic:* Thuilleries.

My dearest friend, New Years Day 1860.

Altho' there is no post today, I wish, that my first letter in this year should be addressed to you. It will bear you my ardent wishes for your prosperity, & for the continuance of that / matchless health, which is an honor to Nature, & which alike shames & baffles physicians.

The year ends gloomily to me,[1] but I will not trouble you with such thoughts, but will rather indulge in a sanguine future.

What an imbroglio! is politics. Only think of our living / to see the Pope on his last legs – & to be betrayed, too, by "the eldest son of the Church."[2] A great Roman Catholic Lady told me yesterday, that the truth was too obvious – mankind wd. no longer endure Clerical authority. She pitied them, but was consoled by the conviction of their eventual / misery, & that no other authority could long endure.

"As for your Church of England" she added "– what are we to think of that? Four theatres hired, [*illegible deletion*] ↑every↓ evening, for "divine" service! A Bishop preaching at Sadlers Wells, I believe![3] If Theatres will do, what is the use of Churches? And why not one of the usual performers / to preach, instead of an ordained Priest?"

Do you know, I thought her remarks unanswerable – & did not much care to prove she was wrong, altho' she thought she was confounding me.

To day, the Emperor of the French is to say something at the Thuilleries, wh: may reassure the faithful.[4] Everybody is / agog, & being Sunday, there is no foreign news stirring. I have no doubt, that our Ministers will have a telegram before sunset – & very little doubt, that the sayings will be as ~~Spinxl~~ Sphinxlike as usual.

Mr. Wilson called on me a day or two ago! I like him very much – & when I am Chancellor of the Exchequer again, which, according to all appearances, / may be sooner than I care for, he is to give me a secret plan of his own to pay off the na-

1 Sarah Disraeli had died on 19 December 1859, and MA was in poor health; see VII **3431**n1 and **3436**&n2.

2 Napoleon in an anonymous pamphlet, 'Le Pape et Le Congrès', had called on the Pope to give up control of the papal states to enable the success of the proposed congress on Italian affairs (see VII **3421**n2); a translation had been published in *The Times* on 22 December 1859. On 31 December Napoleon had written directly to the Pope to repeat the request as the only means of securing peace in Italy. *AR* (1859 History) 260-1.

3 Archibald Campbell Tait (1811-1882), since becoming Bishop of London in 1856, had encouraged the building of churches, the opening of Westminster Abbey and St Paul's for special evening services (both resuming series on 1 January, with the Bishop preaching at the latter), and the use of theatres and public halls (Exeter Hall, St James's Hall, Sadler's-Wells Theatre, the Garrick Theatre at Whitechapel, the Britannia Theatre at Hoxton) for evangelistic services at which he himself occasionally preached. *The Times* (2 Jan 1860). He would become Archbishop of Canterbury in 1869, on D's nomination.

4 Napoleon on this day, 1 January, would assure the diplomatic corps assembled in the throne room at the Tuileries that all his efforts were aimed at maintaining peace. *The Times* (2 Jan 1860).

tional debt, or do without taxes, or something of the kind. He has a hearty disposition & a lively mind. His daughter accompanied him, & must be invaluable to him.[5]

Your Xmas basket came rather apropos to us poor Cockneys – passing, I believe, our first Xmas in London & / away from all our halls & bowers. It was a capital cargo – & seemed to smell of the sweet freshness of your Devonian farm – with its casket of cream, its rich brown fruit, & its white tender poultry.[6]

Adieu! with 1000 good wishes.

Yrs e[ve]r, | D.

3439 TO: LADY FRANKLIN [London, early January 1860]

ORIGINAL: PS 679

PUBLICATION HISTORY: Francis J. Woodward *Portrait of Jane: A Life of Lady Franklin* (1951) 303

EDITORIAL COMMENT: *Dating:* by context; see n1.

These are deeds which will claim the page of history and the name of the true heroine of the tale will never be forgotten.[1]

3440 TO: LORD DERBY Grosvenor Gate [Wednesday] 4 January 1860

ORIGINAL: DBP Box 146/1

PUBLICATION HISTORY: M&B IV 269, dated 4 January 1860, part of the third paragraph

EDITORIAL COMMENT: Black-edged paper. Endorsed by Derby on the last page: 'Disraeli B. *Ansd*'.

Secret Grosvenor Gate | Jan 4. 1860

Rt Honble | The Earl of Derby | K.G.

My dear Lord,

I hope it is true, that you will be in town on the 20th:, & I trust you may find it convenient to see me on the same day.[1] Indeed, / I ought to see you now, but I have neither the energy to run down to Knowsley, nor the spirit to write at the necessary length.

As to F. Affairs: the whole of the Cabinet wish to get rid of the Congress,[2] except

5 Stephen Wilson was a trustee of one of SBW's legacies; see VII **3426**&n1. He would die a few weeks after meeting D at Grosvenor Gate; see **3463**&n2 and **3487**&nn1&2.

6 See VII **3435**n2. The DS had spent Christmas 1857 at Twickenham; see **3007**n4.

---

1 Lady Franklin had written to D on 31 December 1859 from 13 Park Place, St James's Square, enclosing Captain F.L. McClintock's *In the Arctic Seas. A Narrative of the Discovery of the Fate of Sir John Franklin and his Companions* (1859), which McClintock had dedicated to her (dated 24 November 1859): 'The accompanying volume was intended for your dear sister as an affectionate & grateful acknowledgment on my part of her kind feelings in seeking to renew our ancient friendship. On this ground alone you would perhaps allow me to transmit it to yourself, but I am glad also of an opportunity of making it testify to my grateful remembrance of the kind advocacy which in past times you have never refused me when my efforts for Arctic search needed support in Parliament.' H A/IV/N/10. See VII **3424**n3 for Sarah Disraeli's dinner invitation to Lady Franklin that had to be cancelled because of the illness of which she died on 19 December 1859; see **3431**n1 and **3432**n1, to which should be added that she was buried in Paddington Cemetery, London. John McLeod 'Genealogy of the Disraeli Family' *Genealogists' Magazine* Vol 24 No 8 (December 1993) 344. For D's involvement in the Franklin affair, see V **2122**n11 and VI **2649**nn1&3.

---

1 Derby at Knowsley on the 5th would reply: 'The newspapers announce my return to London for one day earlier than I propose, as I cannot be there before the 21st. but I shall be up in ample time to see you, if you think it necessary, the same afternoon.' H B/XX/S/259.

2 See VII **3421**n2 for the proposed congress on Italian affairs.

Ld. P[almerston] & Ld. J.R[ussell] but as the first has entirely / revived his ancient, & uncompromising, alliance with the Emperor Napoleon, who is using all his energies for the Congress, there is no doubt the majority of the Cabinet will suffer the fate usually allotted to minorities.

But what is most pressing, is the Reform Question. / It is quite on the cards, that an offer will be made to settle the affair out of the House. A Cabinet Minister has sounded me, & said communications would be confined, & ~~solely~~ strictly confined, to P. & J.R. I replied I was ready to listen, of course telling you everything, / tho' engaging, that, at present, it shd. not go further.[3] I think I ~~find~~ found out, pretty well, all that has taken place in the Committee of the Cabinet.

It is necessary, therefore, to bring your mind to this subject, as you may be called upon for a decision.

For / my own part, I should like to see a Conservative Reform Bill carried, & the Congress meet, as I know no combination of circumstances more calculated, at the ensuing general Election, to bring about, what has not been seen since 1841, an absolute Conservative / majority.

I apprehend the wish to settle the Reform Question out of Parliament is strong with the Court: but, probably, all this time, I am writing to you about matters of wh: you know much more than I do.[4]

Yours sincerely, | D.

3 The cabinet minister was D's friend C.P. Villiers, at this time president of the poor law board; see **3446**n3. There are three notes from him of this period; the first is dated 7 December 1859: 'I saw our friend *Lionel* the other night, & in consequence of a communication that he made to me, I am very desirous of seeing you for a few minutes.' Another is dated only 'Sunday': 'I have called on you, really to explain to you, *why*, after the note I troubled you with before, I had not communicated with you since. I have trusted, however, to our friend Lionel telling you how the matter stood, & I have called again today rather to feel sure that he gave you my message, than from our proceedings being in that state as should make it important that I should allude again to the subject of our former interview.' In the third, evidently written after Sarah Disraeli's death, he wrote that he did not expect to have anything further to report until after Christmas: 'If any other course is adopted, I will, if you will allow me, address a letter to you in the country ... P.S. My communication of what passed the other day has been *exclusively* to the 2 Members of the Cabinet that I named to you, & I shall not extend it. They are disposed I am sure to give a calm & respectful consideration to the views of all parties upon the question.' H B/XXI/V/72, 74, 76.

4 Derby (n1) would reply: 'As to Foreign Affairs, they appear to me every day to be farther from a solution, and you rather puzzle me by the expression of your opinion that the meeting of a Congress would tend in any way towards the strengthening of the Conservative party. I presume however that it will meet, as the Emperor seems determined that it shall; and that we shall take a part in it, since Palmerston, following in his wake, and supported by John Russell, will force his Colleagues into it. But it certainly cannot now meet till after the meeting of Parliament; and if we are to take any part in it, we must have from the Government a clear explanation of the basis on which it is proposed to treat. So far as I can make out, there is, up to this moment, no agreement whatever among the Powers on this head; and I think we ought to protest against entering upon a general and undefined discussion of all subjects of European interest, and to insist upon the questions to be treated of in conference being strictly and clearly limited. I entirely agree with you as to the desirableness, if possible, of passing a Conservative Reform Bill, and I should be very glad if it could be accomplished by previous concert; but I own I doubt the possibility. That the Court anxiously desire it I have no doubt; and I cannot but think that a trifling circumstance in itself was intended the other day to mark the Conservative disposition in those regions. This was the appointment by the Queen, on the recommendation of the Prince, of Lord Colville, our Whipper-in, to the Honorary Office of Colonel of the London Artillery Company, in the room of H. Fitzroy. To return however to Reform – the D. of Newcastle assured me not long ago that the measure would be a very mild one, and that we should have no difficulty in supporting it – and the old Bear has been holding similar

3441 TO: LORD DERBY Grosvenor Gate [Sunday] 8 January 1860

ORIGINAL: DBP Box 146/1

PUBLICATION HISTORY: M&B IV 270-1, dated at Grosvenor Gate, 8 January 1860, omitting part of the first and the last five paragraphs

EDITORIAL COMMENT: Black-edged paper. Two of the sheets are numbered: '2.', '3.' Endorsed by Derby on the first page: 'Disraeli B. *Ansd*'. *Sic*: burthern.

Secret Grosvenor Gate | Jan. 8 1860

Rt Honble | The Earl of Derby | K.G.

My dear Lord,

The Cabinet will meet on Tuesday, with a strong intention to come to some decision on the Reform Bill. As at present advised, it is on the / cards – nay, probable – that the following proposition will be submitted to you:[1]

1. 10£ County franchise – if the Lords carry £20; to be accepted:
2. 7£ value – Boroughs.
3 Disfranchisement in a separate Bill, & to take its chance.

I shd / like to have had your view of this proposition without troubling you with my own, but as we are separated, & time is hurrying on, I will venture to observe, tho' with great diffidence, that these seem terms, wh: we may substantially obtain without entering into any engagement, & that / they are prompted as much by the feelings of their own party, as by a desire to conciliate ours.

I doubt, whether the difference between a £6, & a £7, value, is one of conservative importance: while, at the same time, it keeps up the mischievous imposture that there is a conservative, party in the Cabinet, on wh: the Peelites intrigue, / as they are doing already, & trying to break up our ranks.[2]

A majority of the Committee was in favor of an £8 value; but ultimately yielded to the sense of the ridiculous in turning us out for identity,[3] & then proposing £10 & 8£. An £8 would have estranged the Radicals: they will grumble about the £7 – but take it, I think.

I was / asked, what we considered a "temperate measure", assuming, that after what had occurred in Parlt, identity was out of the question. I declined to give an opinion on the subject, but said I thought, that public opinion would recognise, as a temperate measure, equal to the occasion, £20 for county; 8£ for Boros; & the scale of disfranchisement in Ld. Derby's bill.

It / was said, if that course were taken, the Radicals would take the first opportu-

language to Rosslyn. On the other hand Malmesbury's information is that after a hard struggle Palmerston has knocked under to Johnny, and accepted the £6 franchise, though Cornewall Lewis & Elgin still hold out. The latter is unimportant: but they would not like to quarrel with the former. The language of yesterday's Times however seems to intimate, with an air of authority, that there is, as yet, no agreement as to the details of the Bill. I own that I should myself look with great apprehension at the result of a £6 franchise in the Towns. It would however be accepted by the Radicals, but only as an Instalment. I doubt exceedingly its being popular with the Ten pounders, though they probably would not venture to offer any opposition to it.'

1 See **3440** for the prospect of an offer to settle the reform question out of the House.

2 Derby would address this point in his 15 January letter; see **3443**&n1.

3 See VII **3323**&n1; the Conservative bill provided for identity of qualifications for boroughs and counties.

nity of turning them out. I replied, we were *sincerely* desirous of not disturbing the Govt. at present, & that if we agreed on a Reform Bill, we shd., as a matter of course, wish to give them a general support till it had passed, wh: alone would carry them – thro' the Session.[4]

I was pressed as to our conduct in case of a motion on For: Politics.

I / declined to hold out any expectation of our binding ourselves on that subject. We must always be free to assert our own principles & policy on such a subject, but I did not hesitate to say, that we certainly shd. not encourage any motions on F. Pol: brought forward by the Radicals to disturb them; that we should deplore returning to power by their aid. /

I have made memoranda of what occurred: but these are the chief features, & will do for / the present.

If a conservative Bill could have been carried, & if, by the Congress, the Roman Catholic interest had become permanently detached from the Liberal party, I think the general Election of 1861, if one take place, would ~~have~~ giv~~en~~ you, at last, a working majority.

I hear from Paris, that the Emperor has proposed to our Government to enter into a / *treaty*, for the settlement of Italian affairs, & that Palmn. is highly favorable to the proposition, wh: was, no doubt, concocted between them witht the knowledge of Ld P's colleagues. Such a treaty will, I think, be looked ~~uep~~ upon by the country with very great suspicion, to use the mildest term; & I should think the Cabinet will hesitate before they enter into it. But the Emperor is positive & peremptory. / It is the only way ↑by wh:↓ he can extricate himself, with dash & lustre, from his difficulties, & he offers everything – Suez canal to be opposed;[5] Peace between Spain & Morocco[6] &c &c.; & government by us to be always impossible. It will be rather ludicrous, after the volunteers & the 10 million loan, ~~that~~ ↑shd↓ the new Session ~~is~~ be inaugurated with not only une entente cordiale, but an absolute alliance.[7]

4 In his brief reply from Bulby of 11 January Derby would promise to write at length when he got back to Knowsley, but warned: 'I think I ought to tell you that I hear of a cabal getting up among our people, some of whom will have it that you have come to an understanding with the Radicals, and mean to throw them over on Reform. I only name this, that you may be very guarded in your communications on the subject. I hear that Big Ben [*George Bentinck*] (of course) is among the Leaders of this fronde, and I was not surprised to hear H. Baillie mentioned as another.' H B/XX/S/260.

5 Palmerston's policy of opposition to the Suez canal, which he regarded as a French threat to British naval superiority, had succeeded, via the Sultan of Constantinople, Abd-ul-Mezid, in stopping the scheme. In 1859, however, Napoleon had got work on the canal started by direct intervention with the Khedive of Egypt and without the Sultan's approval. Palmerston's further opposition would amount to little more than attempts to give the enterprise bad publicity. Ridley *Palmerston* 536-7.

6 Because of ongoing territorial disputes, war between Morocco and Spain had broken out in October 1859, and was currently at a decisive stage. Britain, perceiving a threat to Gibraltar, had obtained from Spain a promise (which it kept) not to keep any relevant African territory after the war. Peace was restored in 1860 on the terms of the victorious Spanish, Morocco ceding to Spain the contested territories plus compensation.

7 To offset the reduction in the standing army, a volunteer force had been authorized by the secretary at war (Jonathan Peel) in a 12 May 1858 circular to the lord-lieutenants of counties; the policy, which actually increased the nominal size of the army and therefore was seen as threatening by elements in France, was continued by the current government until 1863. *EB* XI XXVIII 208; *The Times* (2 Dec 1859). Derby on 5 January had written (see **3440**&nn1&4): 'There will be four main subjects for consideration and

I have / written at greater length than I contemplated, & have touched upon two of your four points – Reform & Congress: as for China,[8] I shall be anxious to have your views when we meet as something must be said upon it, I apprehend, the first night. On that occasion, finance need not be noticed, but nothing will persuade me, until I hear the official declaration, that Gladstone will propose a loan in time of peace; nor do / I believe, that Rothschild & Baring, united, could float 10 millions of terminable annuities. They are the most impracticable, the most unpopular, & the most expensive, of public securities. The public will not touch them, as was seen in the last moderate experiment of Sir George Lewis,[9] & if the contractors then had not, by / giving a good bonus ↑(for wh:, in the price, they must be themselves re-couped)↓, induced the public companies to absorb them, they would themselves have been saddled with the burthern. My opinion is, that if the New Alliance does not terminate the project altogr, that Gladstone will bring in some bill empowering the Treasury to / raise money, when they require it, to a certain amount, for the avowed object – & spread over some years – three at least, & that he will get his cash as he can – probably by a large recurrence, at protracted dates, of Exchequer Bonds.

I ought to have reminded you of the position we took in / the Ho: of Comm:, at the end of the Sess:, respecting Congress, & the inexpediency of entering one. I commenced the question, & the effect it produced induced Ld. Elcho & Co. to give notice of a motion in the same vein.[10] I apprehend the Ho: is still in the same humor. This is an important consideration.

Yours sincerely, | D.

3442 TO: BARON LIONEL DE ROTHSCHILD

Grosvenor Gate
Thursday [12 January 1860]

ORIGINAL: ROTH RAL 000/848
EDITORIAL COMMENT: Black-edged paper. *Dating:* see n1. *Sic:* Government.

Private — Grosvenor Gate | Thursday morning

Baron Rothschild | M.P.

discussion in and out of Parliament, Foreign Affairs, China, Reform, and Finance. On the latter all that I know is, that the Estimates are likely to be very large; and the decision certainly had been taken some time ago to provide for the Military expenditure on Fortifications &c by a loan, I presume by way of terminable annuities. This, as you know, is a course which I should have considered advisable when we were in Office, but was deterred from taking by your strong objections, and your estimate of the opposition it would encounter in the House of Commons.' For the course actually taken (an increase in the income tax to offset an estimated deficit of £9.4 million), see **3448**n2. In his reply (n4) Derby would write: 'The Flahaults are here. I sat by Madame at dinner yesterday, and extracted from her, what I think is very likely, that there is an understanding between the two Governments for considerable reductions of duty in the manufactures of the respective Countries, including wine on ours. This will give them some popularity, and will strengthen the impression of the entente cordiale – but it will add to their financial difficulty.'

8 War with China had broken out again when a naval force sent in 1859 to ratify the treaty of 1858, settling the conflict arising from the late-1856 *Arrow* incident, was attacked and repulsed. The war would end with the treaty of Peking, signed in October 1860 after a British and French expedition captured the Taku forts and occupied Peking; see VII **2916**n1 and **2947**&n2.

9 Lewis's budget of 1855 proposed to raise £16 million by perpetual annuities at 3%. *Hansard* CXXXVII cols 1897ff.

10 See VII **3397**&n2.

My dear Lionel,

I hear, from a high quarter, that there is "an understanding between the *two* Government (France & England) for considerable / reductions of duty on the manufactures of the respective countries, including Wine in ours."

Is this so? It would strengthen the impression of the entente cordiale, & have, I shd think, in that sense, a very good effect, / tho' I don't yet see, how it would relieve the financial difficulties, but, I suppose, you cd manage that.[1]

Yours ever, | D.

TO: LORD DERBY Grosvenor Gate [Saturday] 14 January 1860 **3443**

ORIGINAL: DBP Box 146/1

EDITORIAL COMMENT: Black-edged paper. Endorsed by Derby on the last page: 'Disraeli B *Ansd*'.

Secret Grosvenor Gate | Jan 14. 1860

Rt Honble | Earl of Derby | K.G

My dear Lord.

Up to Thursday morning last, the Reform Bill had not been mentioned *in the Cabinet, or out of the Cabinet.* All the rumors, therefore, rife, founded on the assumption, that the meeting of Ministers, on Tuesday / last, was to settle the question, are canards – the Cabinet being occupied, that day, with a very different matter.

Lord Cowley came over from the Emperor with a distinct proposal for an alliance "*offensive & defensive*". And, strange to say, enforced it, as his own opinion, in the strongest manner. The Emperor had completely got over him. The Court, finding this out, was much / disgusted – & countermined. Ld. Palmn. & Ld. John had held out to the Emperor every hope of success. Gladstone, furiously Italian, was gained to absolute interference, by the mirage of a Commercial Treaty – but when the Cabinet met, the business being opened by Ld. John, the strong opinion of Ld. Cowley duly dwelt on, & Ld. Palmerston very decisive, they / were thoroughly beaten by the Court party!

This is the real state of affairs. You may depend upon its accuracy; & form your own conclusions as to the probable result.[1]

Yours ever sincerely, | D.

1 D is conveying an extract from Derby's letter of 11 January; see **3441**n7.

---

1 Derby at Knowsley the next day (15th) would respond to D's last two letters: 'The contents of this latter, if their accuracy can be depended upon, are of the highest importance, and may, I fear, be productive of no little embarrassment.' All his other information tended to confirm D's 'report of the offer of an Alliance Offensive and Defensive having been made, and accompanied by a proposal for a Commercial Treaty. I certainly was not prepared to learn that the Cabinet had been too much for Palmerston, Johnny, the Emperor and Cowley combined. One hardly sees how after such a defeat on a vital question of Foreign Policy, the two former can meet Parliament in their present posts.' He thought this development left the Emperor with no alternative but a congress; 'I have not forgotten the language which we held last year as to the inexpediency of our being made parties to such a measure: and I still retain my opinion on that subject: but I think while we intimate the objections to it under any circumstances, we should limit our active opposition to entering into it without the previous establishment of clearly defined bases. I believe it to be impossible for France, Austria, Russia & Prussia, to agree upon any such bases. If they could, and those bases involved, as they must, material alterations in the Treaties of Vienna, it would not be possible for us, as one of the Great Powers, to stand wholly aloof, and see the work in which we

3444 TO: SARAH BRYDGES WILLYAMS

Grosvenor Gate
[Monday] 16 January 1860

ORIGINAL: RTC [132]

PUBLICATION HISTORY: M&B IV 318, dated at Grosvenor Gate, 16 January 1860, the second paragraph

EDITORIAL COMMENT: Black-edged paper. There is no salutation.

Grosvenor Gate | Jan 16 1860

I merely write you this, to show you, that I am alive. We have remained in this foggy land, tho' my agent, who came up yesterday, tells me, that Hughenden is golden in the Sun!

The Emperor of the French has introduced a / new system of governing mankind – by anonymous pamphlets,[1] & by letters from himself addressed to Mr. Reuter of the Electro-Telegraph![2] Wonderful man! He delights England with his Protestantism & Free Trade – & when public opinion is conciliated & regained, he intends to propose, / that Savoy shall be surrendered to France, in order to ~~ga~~ guard her fertile plains from Sardinia, who will then be too powerful for him.[3] And the people of England, who, last month, believed he was going to conquer them, will also believe that. The fact / is, the Emperor is in a scrape, but he is so clever, ~~that his scrapes are so clever,~~ that his scrapes are preferable to other persons' success.

Yrs e[ve]r, | D.

Pray give my kind Complts. to the Butlers.[4]

had taken part, set aside without giving, or being asked for an opinion.' He did not see 'that we are in the least degree called on to relieve L.N. from his difficulties, which, great as they are, have been chiefly of his own making'. D's letters seemed contradictory as to the state of cabinet discussion on reform: 'I presume you mean that no later discussion had taken place. Of that plan, I will only say that I think it will greatly dissatisfy the Radicals, while of course it will not please our people. They will however attach more importance than you seem to do (and I agree with them) to the difference between a £7 and a £6 qualification; and I think that the returns which they will produce will show that between those figures there would be a very great increase of the lowest class of Voters.' He thought they could discuss China when they met, in the meantime suggesting that a formal declaration of war was necessary to avoid difficulties, in the event of a blockade, with neutral powers such as the U.S. and Russia. H B/XX/S/261.

1 See **3438**&n2.

2 Paul Julius Reuter (1816?-1899), born Israel Beer Josaphat in Cassel, Germany, a baron of Saxe-Coburg and Gotha (1871, with privileges recognized in England), had moved his fledgling news agency to London from Paris in 1851 and in 1858 had persuaded *The Times* to use material from his Paris agent; the agency rapidly expanded into a world-wide service. On 14 January 1860 *The Times* had published an unsigned '"extract of a letter received at Mr. Reuter's office"', dated 12 January at Paris; it described Cowley's London mission (see **3443**&n1) as failing to renew Anglo-French negotiations for an agreement to regard any European power's intervention in Central Italy's affairs as a *casus belli*: '"The British Cabinet having thus declined the propositions to enter into engagements having such an important bearing, the question of an early meeting of the Congress is again revived."' On this day (16 January) it published Napoleon's letter (not identified as a Reuter's item) to his minister of state (Fould), proposing free-trade policies to stimulate agriculture, industry and commerce. A *Times* leader applauded Napoleon's courage in confronting both clergy (in suppressing the St Vincent de Paul Society) and commerce at once, and declared his free-trade initiative the best prospect of lasting peace.

3 See **3449**&n4.

4 James Butler in 1836 had married Emily Mary Fitzgerald (d 1897), only daughter of Sir William Fitzgerald, 2nd Bt, of Carrygoran, co Clare. In her 2 January letter SBW had mentioned that they were with her. RTC [395Q].

3445

TO: SIR STAFFORD NORTHCOTE — Grosvenor Gate [Monday] 16 January 1860

ORIGINAL: BL ADD MS 50015 f513
EDITORIAL COMMENT: Black-edged British Museum paper. *Sic*: cause.

Private — Grosvenor Gate | Jany. 16 1860

Sir Stafford Northcote | Bart: M.P.

My dear Northcote,

Since we left you,[1] we have experienced a great sorrow – as sudden as it was sad – wh. has shaken me to the centre, & / quite incapacitated me for business.

However, I can delay the exertion no longer, &, indeed, affairs are very critical – both foreign & domestic. Every hour something happens, & adds to the complications, & difficulties, of / the situation. But I have neither time, nor energy, to write a despatch. When shall you be up? Lord Derby will be here mid-day on Saturday, & I shall have to see him directly.[2] Shall you be in town before that, / or when? – as I sho[ul]d like to have a long, & confidential, *cause* with you on all heads – &, if it might be, before I saw him.

Mrs Di unites with me in the kindest remembrances to your charming wife, & we embrace the children[.][3]

Yours sincerely, | D.

3446

TO: LORD DERBY — Grosvenor Gate [Wednesday] 18 January 1860

ORIGINAL: DBP Box 146/1
PUBLICATION HISTORY: M&B IV 271, dated at Grosvenor Gate, 18 January 1860, part of the first and all of the third and seventh paragraphs
EDITORIAL COMMENT: Black-edged paper. Endorsed by Derby on the last page: 'Disraeli B. *Ansd Encl retd*'.

Confidential — Grosvenor Gate. Jany. 18 1860

Rt Honble | The Earl of Derby K.G.

My dear Lord,

There was a Cabinet on Monday (See No *1* enclosed) but it was suppressed ↑in the journals↓. My friend came yesterday according to No 2 (also enclosed), but he came so late, & stayed so late, that it was impossible to write to you.[1]

As it is, I have not sufficient energy for the affair, & it is, at all times, difficult, in writing, to deal with such immense detail. Here is the result.

1 See VII **3421**&n1 for the 23-25 November 1859 visit.

2 Derby had written on 15 January (see **3443**n1) that he would leave Liverpool on a 9:00 *am* train, to be in his house by 3.

3 Northcote in 1843 had married Cecilia Frances Farrer (1823-1910), eldest daughter of Thomas Farrer and sister of the future 1st Baron Farrer; they had six sons and two daughters living. Shortly before the DS' visit Northcote had written to his wife: 'Mrs Disraeli is great fun ... though I could not help occasionally pitying her husband for the startling effect her natural speeches must have upon the ears of his great friends. Still there is something very warm and good in her manner, which makes one forgive a few oddities.' Northcote I 161.

---

1 Charles Villiers, D's informant (see **3440**&n3), had written on the 17th that he would be with D between 4 and 5, or later if D preferred. The letter is marked 'No 2' on the last page. H B/XXI/V/73. The other enclosure ('No 1') has not been found.

Nothing settled. The Committee of the Cabinet, being quite unable to come to any agreement, & it being impossible any longer to delay some general discussion, the question, quite crude, was thrown, like a piece of raw meat, into the / assemblage of sixteen last Monday. My correspondent told Palmn & Lord John, that having commenced the negotiation with me, & after ~~having~~ what had passed, it was impossible, he felt, to continue silent, & they agreed, that, whatever might occur, they were bound to deal frankly with us. /

All agreed that the Lords, as a house of proprietors, should deal, as they thought fit, with the County Franchise, & their amendment, if any, on the Ministerial proposition of £10 occupation shd be accepted.

All agreed, that the Lords ought not to be permitted to deal with the decision of the H of Commons with respect to the Boro' franchise, but that the Govt. would accept any amendment made by the Commons.

It was, therefore, still more important, that the / ministerial proposition shd. not be a mistake. But what shall it be?

I gathered, that the moderate party is much stronger in tone at this moment, & that Lord John is checked. I suspect he has enough on his hands of another character.

My friend said he had ~~it~~ little doubt that 6£ *rating* would have been adopted, had it not been shown conclusively to the Cabinet, that, witht. a public valuation as in Ireland,[2] it was quite impracticable. He said they were ashamed of taking an 8£ value – after having turned us out. I endeavoured to encourage him. He said that the Borough qualification was more a Whig, than a Tory, question. The great towns now were theirs, & £6 ↑value↓ would very little affect the moderate & small towns. I told him, that if they proposed 6£ value it would be carried, & they would be in a scrape – that if they / feared the taunts of Bright, they would as surely be subjected to them by proposing £7 as 8£ – and after all, the thing was to carry a bill – & that £8 would really conciliate the conservative feeling of our benches. He said £8 had a greater chance than before, that he could not clearly see his way, but had a strong conviction, that a temperate bill would be introduced, wh: would please nobody.

Ld. J. very strong about disfranchising the small Boros. I have said little on this head; as the Whigs ~~will~~ ↑wo[ul]d↓ be the principal victims, & I know the invincible difficulties wh: await them when they come to practice. But what I suspect, & fear, is that they meditate giving largely a third member to Counties. This would furnish a number of safe Whig seats, & must be opposed. ↑I told him that the Country gentlemen of all shades on our side were against this.↓[3]

2 Qualifications in Ireland were currently based on a uniform system (called Griffith's Valuation, after Sir Richard Griffith, commissioner of valuation) of annual valuations of all rateable properties; a bill dealing with the cost of the valuation process was currently before the House. *Hansard* CLVI cols 1541-3, 2054.

3 Derby would reply from Knowsley on the 19th: 'I must confess that the signature of your Correspondent rather startled me, for a correspondence with a Member of the Cabinet on such a subject has rather a *suspicious* appearance; but if the correspondence be sanctioned by the Head of the Government and his chief supporter (and rival) I do not see that it is our duty to remonstrate on the part of the rest of the Cabinet; and we are certainly under no obligation to abstain from such communications. The secrets of the Cabinet indeed do not appear to be very strictly guarded, since you are apprized, and kept au courant, of what passes, through "Lionel." I do not at all concur in the view which the Cabinet seem to take as to what amendments the Lords can, and cannot, be allowed to make. On the our [*sic*] hand it must

This is a wretched letter, but I write it with difficulty; living in perpetual fogs, to say nothing of moral vapors.

Sincerely yrs, | D.

TO: LORD DERBY Grosvenor Gate, Thursday [19 January 1860] **3447**

ORIGINAL: DBP Box 146/1

PUBLICATION HISTORY: Blake 429, undated extract

EDITORIAL COMMENT: Black-edged paper. Endorsed by Derby on the last page: 'Disraeli B'. *Dating*: by context; see nn1&2.

G. Gate | Thursday.

The division in the Cabinet, on Tuesday week, on the French Alliance, was 12 to 4.

Ayes

Ld. Palm: Ld. John: Gladstone & M. Gibson.[1]

D. T.O. /

I wrote to you yesterday, with Enclosures, on the other matter.[2]

be recollected that we ourselves having proposed a £10 franchise for the Counties, should have great difficulty in opposing it when proposed by our Successors, and sent up by the Commons; added to which you are aware that many of our best friends are of opinion that a £10 franchise in the Counties would be anything but disadvantageous to the Conservative interest. The offer therefore to accept an Amendment on this point seems to me illusory. On the other hand there will be very great and general objection, not on our side of the House alone, to a very low Borough franchise; and a very great probability that if such be proposed, it will be rejected. I hardly know whether its rejecton by the Lords after its adoption by the Commons, or its final adoption by the Legislature, is most to be deprecated. It is therefore, as I think, of the first importance that the proposal of the Government should be such as we can conscientiously and cordially support; and should they make up their mind to offer £8 value, they shall hear no taunt from me, and I will do my best to carry their proposal for them through both Houses. I wish that our Cabinet had adopted my suggestion, when we were discussing this subject before the introduction of the Bill, of £12 & £8 as in Ireland; but the present Government could not now make such an offer, and it is useless to regret. Rating seems now discarded as a basis by all parties; and the question is narrowed to the amount of value. I should think £6 *very dangerous,* £7 less so, and considerably; but still likely to give an undue preponderance to the lowest class of voters in Towns. Although therefore, if £7 were carried in the Commons, I should probably advise the Lords to acquiesce rather than run the risk of a collision on such a question, we should be very cautious not to hold out the slightest hope of our supporting, or concurring in, such a proposal; whereas I think £8 would be a fair basis on which to close. As the Radicals would probably oppose filling up the blank with the word 7 as well as ourselves, though on different grounds, the Government might very likely be placed in a minority. They would then have to choose between £8, with a certainty of carrying it, and £6, with all the consequences of such a proposition, and under the disadvantage of a previous defeat. You do not say whether they propose to adopt our "Lodger," on any of the "Fancy" franchises – probably the question has never yet been discussed among them. I should look with as much jealousy as yourself at the proposition of giving third members to many of the Counties. It was a mistake in the first Reform Bill; and the motive for its adoption now would be so palpable, as to taint their whole measure in public opinion. As to disfranchisement of small Boroughs, they cannot carry a very large measure; and as far as party interests are concerned, there is no principle which they can lay down, by which, if fairly worked out, they can obtain any undue advantage on the balance. I conclude that J. Russell will not be allowed to indulge any of his crotchets about giving votes to the minority – though the "Unicorn" Counties would indirectly have that effect. I need hardly caution you to be extremely guarded in your communications with C.V. on this delicate question; and the more so, in consequence of what I named to you in a former letter. If there exist in any quarters, such suspicions and jealousies as I told you of, they would be greatly strengthened by the knowledge of such pour parlers as are going on at present.' H B/XX/S/262.

1 See **3443**&n1.

2 See **3446**.

3448 TO: LORD DERBY Grosvenor Gate [Wednesday] 25 January 1860

ORIGINAL: DBP Box 146/1

PUBLICATION HISTORY: M&B IV 271, dated [25 January 1860], the second paragraph

EDITORIAL COMMENT: Black-edged paper. Endorsed by Derby on the first page: 'Disraeli B *Ansd*'. The numerals of the date are oddly (over?)written, but the date is confirmed by context.

Private Grosvenor Gate | Jan 25. 1860

Rt Honble | The Earl of Derby | K.G.

My dear Lord,

I hear but one opinion, of approval & admiration, of your speech of last night, at wh: I am not surprised, having just risen from its attentive perusal.[1]

I have frequently observed, that, until the Houses / meet, it is impossible to hit upon what will be the question of the Session, often very different from that anticipated. From all I hear, & observe, it will be the Commercial Treaty.

It touches a greater amount of ~~taxation~~ revenue, than generally supposed, if, as I apprehend, brandy & / silk are included, as well as wine – not less, than three millions.

It will, if adopted, involve the continuance of the war duties on tea & sugar; probably an increase of the Income Tax; & certainly the permanence of the paper / Duty. There is a very active party wh: counted on its repeal.

I think, under these circumstances, we ought to insist upon the Financial Statement being made before we consider the Treaty.[2]

Yours sincerely, | D.

1 Parliament had opened on 24 January, when Derby had spoken in the Lords on the Address in response to the Queen's speech. Of its many topics, he confined his comments to the recent commercial treaty with France, the war with China, and the proposed congress on Italy. He thought the commercial treaty was of immediate benefit to France but of only prospective benefit to Britain, and questioned several of its provisions; on China, they must clarify whether they were at war or not; Britain should not join in any congress but, if it did, it should be very clear about its objects in doing so. He would reply from St James's Square on the 26th: 'I am glad to hear that you, and our friends generally, are satisfied with my Speech on Tuesday. We seem to have followed very much the same line, and to have taken up all the topics which we had talked over in the morning.' *Hansard* CLVI cols 44-62 (D 88-107); H B/XX/S/263.

2 Derby (n1) agreed 'that the Commercial Treaty is likely to be the most prominent subject of discussion. The reception of its announcement must, I think, have disappointed the Government ... I think that after Palmerston's declaration that it was entered into subject to the approval of Parliament, you are quite entitled to require that it shall not be ratified until after we have had the financial statement.' He would write again on the 29th: 'After I saw you on Thursday, I looked again at Gladstone's Speech; and I see he says that the Treaty contains an express provision that its provisions are subject to the approval of Parliament, that it was to be ratified within ten days, and that he should therefore be able to lay it on the Table towards the end of the present week, and would make his Financial Statement tomorrow week. I do not think, under these circumstances, that we could ask for a delay of the ratification'; he would check whether he was right about the parliamentary procedure in the matter. He wrote again on 2 February, having just seen Gladstone: 'It is, I think very doubtful whether the Treaty will be ratified (though he did not say so) before Tuesday ... I told him that considering the great extent of the measure believed to be included in his Budget ... I thought it was impossible to ask the House of Commons to express an opinion on propositions which must be considered as parts of a whole ... He at once admitted that it was a case in which, if time were asked for, it could not be refused ... I can see that he is disposed to make the adoption of the treaty a question of confidence'. H B/XX/S/263-5. The treaty, signed at Paris on 23 January with ratifications exchanged on 4 February, abolished duties on brandy and silk and reduced those on wine, with further provisions to be recommended to parliament. It would be put on the table on 10 February, just before Gladstone presented his budget (postponed because of illness from the 6th, when Palmerston

TO: SARAH BRYDGES WILLYAMS — Grosvenor Gate [Saturday] 28 January 1860 — 3449

ORIGINAL: RTC [133]
PUBLICATION HISTORY: M&B IV 318, dated at Grosvenor Gate, 28 January 1860, the second paragraph
EDITORIAL COMMENT: Black-edged paper. There is no salutation.

Grosvenor Gate | Jan: 28. 60

I have sent you some pheasants, half of those which arrived, from Lord Salisbury's, last night[1] and I have sent you some "forbidden fruit,"[2] / believing that you sufficiently share the weakness of your sex as to taste it. If you sin, I am confident, that your sin will be original, & not commonplace, or you must have changed / much, since our last visit to Torquay.[3]

Politics most absorbing, &, more mysterious than ever. The Imperial Free Trader is now going to seize Savoy & Nice. / The "natural boundaries" of the Empire are fast developing, & in 1861, he will be on the Rhin[e]. It is said, that all nations, that speak French, belong to France![4] Our uncle at Belgium does not like affairs.[5]

Yrs ever, | D.

TO: [JOHN DELANE?] — [London] Friday 3 February [1860] — 3450

ORIGINAL: MOPSIK [83]
EDITORIAL COMMENT: Black-edged paper. For Delane as recipient cf VI 2756; Henry Padwick is also a possibility. *Dating*: the year is evident from context; see n1. *Sic*: Th [*started to write 'Thursday'?*]; Clarke.

PRIVATE — Th[?] Friday Feby. 3

Clarke *v.* Ld Clifden

This is a case of iniquity. Four years ago, Clarke produced a list of bills of Mr Villiers & Ld Clifden, & on his personal and solemn declaration to Mr. Chas Greville, that this list contained all with wh: he was connected, he was settled with. Now he

told D the doctor's advice) while the House was in committee on the customs acts. H B/XXI/P/87. In his budget, Gladstone would renew the taxes on tea and sugar, impose a new duty on chicory, abolish the excise duty on paper, reduce the duty on hops and malt, and continue the income tax at an increased rate. *Hansard* CLVI cols 812-72.

1 MA on 30 January would write to Lady Salisbury: 'We are very much obliged to Lord Salisbury, for his kind present of game which arrived on Saturday.' H D/III/C/270.

2 MA recorded buying on this day (28th) some 'forbiden fruite' along with chestnuts and 'Tops & Bottoms' (rusks). H acc. The epithet has been attached to a number of fruits (see *OED*).

3 The DS had last been at Torquay 9-23 November 1859.

4 When Napoleon's congress failed to materialize, it was proposed to cede Savoy and Nice to France in return for his consent to the unification of the central Italian provinces with the Italian kingdom. The French press took up the idea enthusiastically, but a question in the Lords on 27 January brought the government's assurance that it knew of no treaty between France and Sardinia annexing Savoy and Nice to France, and that France knew Britain's opposition to any such arrangement. *Hansard* CLVI cols 214-19. A *Times* leader on the 28th facetiously accepted this assurance, and then reviewed the French press's claims much as D does here.

5 Queen Victoria on 31 January would try to reassure her uncle Leopold, King of the Belgians, on this point: 'There has been a strong despatch written relative to Savoy – and altogether I think matters are taking a better turn.' He however replied on 3 February: 'Things look in most directions very gloomy; my neighbour is creating dangers for himself by the constitutional Government he gives to Italy.' *LQV* III 386.

produces another for £2000: & if this were discharged, there is no security, the manufacture wd. not proceed.[1]

It is a case of pure extortion, in wh: Clarke uses the Press as his instrument to terrify a woman, already overwhelmed with unusual sorrows.[2]

D.

3451 TO: LORD GREY Grosvenor Gate [Saturday] 4 February 1860

ORIGINAL: DURG [1]

EDITORIAL COMMENT: Black-edged paper. Endorsed in another hand on the last page: 'Mr Disraeli Feb 4/60'. *Sic*: de Republicâ.

Confidential Grosvenor Gate | Feby. 4. 1860

Rt Honble | The Earl Grey

Dear Lord Grey,

I wish you would permit me to come & talk with you, de Republicâ.[1]

1 See VI **2756**&n1. The *Times*'s law notices for this day (3 February 1860) scheduled 'Clark v. Clifden' for the court of Queen's Bench. Next day, it would report Edward Rawson Clark's testimony that in 1855 he had paid Francis Villiers £1,850 for the £2,000 bill due three months later on 19 May, and that Villiers had endorsed it before witnesses. Clark's barrister did not challenge Clifden's statement that the bill was not in his handwriting, and the jury found for the defendant.

2 Lady Jersey's husband, the 5th Earl of Jersey, had died on 3 October 1859, followed on 24 October by her eldest son, the 6th Earl (brother of Francis); her second youngest daughter, Lady Clementina, had died on 5 December 1858.

---

1 Cicero's *De Re Publica* takes the form of a dialogue based on Plato's *Republic*. The topic to be discussed with Grey (an independent since 1852) was presumably the controversial way in which parliament was considering the commercial treaty with France (see **3448**&n2); on 24 January Grey had objected that the treaty entrenched actual rates rather than general principles, and he would subsequently help D and Derby in their strategy on the matter. *Hansard* CLVI cols 13-27. In the Commons on Friday 17 February, D would ask how the government proposed to proceed with the treaty, citing Pitt's 1787 treaty and protesting that proceeding in committee on the customs duties would leave many provisions unconsidered. Palmerston's reply that every article would be considered in due course did not satisfy D: 'When [Pitt] moved that the Treaty should be taken into consideration he first of all gave a full exposition of the financial policy of the Government. The next step taken was to call upon the House to take the Treaty into consideration, thus giving the House an opportunity of expressing its opinion upon every Article of the Treaty. That, in my mind, was the proper and constitutional course.' *Ibid* cols 1244-58 (D 1248-9, 1257-8). Derby in a letter dated 'St. James's Sqr. Sunday Night [*19 February*] 10 P.M' would write: 'I send you, as *most important*, a note which I have just received from Lord Grey. I had thought it right, as I had told him of my intention of only asking a question tomorrow, to let him know that after what passed in the H. of Commons on Friday, I should alter my course, and say what I had to say on the Constitutional question tomorrow. I think him *entirely* right, as to the Amendment which he proposes that you should move – and his argument seems to me conclusive. Whether you can do it, according to the forms of the House, I can hardly say, but if you can, it is *on every account* most desirable that his advice should be followed. The Amendment will be entirely, and almost singularly, in accordance with the line of argument which I mean to take tomorrow. I shall be able to explain to Lord Grey the difficulty to which he admits in the end of his note.' H B/XX/S/278. On Monday 20 February, Derby turned his previously announced question about the 20th article of the treaty (that the treaty was not valid until authorized by parliament) into a speech on the way the treaty was being handled in parliament. He also contrasted this with Pitt's handling of his 1787 treaty with France, and cited 2nd Earl Grey (father of the colleague who supported him later in the debate) as having taken part in the debate on that occasion. Also on the 20th, in the Commons, D would address the constitutional implications of parliament considering the terms of a ratified treaty, and move, as an amendment, that the treaty be considered by the House before going into committee on the customs acts affected by it. *Hansard* CLVI cols 1320-50 (D 1355-75). After debate, the amendment was defeated 293-230. *Ibid* 1375-1448.

This request, I feel, would / be a great liberty, had not some confidential passages taken place between us, some years ago, thro' the medium of one, whose memory, I presume to say, I scarcely less cherish, than / yourself.[2]

I could call upon you tomorrow, after Church, ½ pt 2 o'ck, or to day even at 5 o'ck.[3] I have the honor to remain,

Yours faithfully, | *B. Disraeli*

TO: EDITOR OF *THE MORNING STAR* Grosvenor Gate 3452

[Tuesday] 7 February 1860

ORIGINAL: PS 756 (see EC)

PUBLICATION HISTORY: *Morning Star* (8 Feb 1860) under the heading 'MR. DISRAELI AND COLONEL RATHBORNE.'

EDITORIAL COMMENT: The text is that of a clipping in H E/III/16/11.

TO THE EDITOR OF THE "STAR."[1] Grosvenor Gate, Feb. 7, 1860.

Sir, –

Although opposed to my political views, your paper is so honourably and ably conducted, that I do not for a moment hesitate to respond to your appeal respecting Colonel Rathborne.[2]

Colonel Rathborne was introduced to me, at his own request, in the year 1857, previously to my bringing before the House of Commons the subject of the Indian Revolt. I was then in the daily habit of conferring with gentlemen connected with India. I never heard, until that time, that Colonel Rathborne was a writer in the *Press* newspaper. His entire statement, therefore, as to his solicited labours in that journal from 1853, so far as I am concerned, and, I have little doubt, the whole of the Conservative party, is a mere romance. The "chief editor"[3] of the *Press* was the late Mr. Coulton, a distinguished man of letters, and a gentleman, and one who was never in the habit of mentioning the names of the contributors to his journal.

2 The editors presume that D is presuming to cherish the memory of Grey's father, the 2nd Earl.

3 Grey responded: 'I shall be happy to see you this afternoon at five o'clock. This would suit me better than tomorrow after church.' H B/XXI/G/360. The DS were parishioners of the church in which they had been married, St George's, Hanover Square, where, according to Cecil Roth's undocumented statement, D attended 'regularly ... every Sunday'. H acc (12 May 1863); Cecil Roth *Benjamin Disraeli* (New York 1952) 77.

---

1 The *Morning Star*, a Cobdenite London daily founded in 1856, was currently edited by Bright's brother-in-law Samuel Lucas (1811-1865), not to be confused with the quondam editor of the *Press*); see further Koss *Political Press* 123-30.

2 For Rathborne's grievance against D and his party, which the *Morning Star* had now taken up, see VII **2960**&ph&n1 and the references cited there and in the index. In 1858 Rathborne had published D's correspondence with him (*Mr. Disraeli to Colonel Rathborne*) and now (1860) he had published an 88-page pamphlet, *Mr. Disraeli, Colonel Rathborne, and The Council of India. A Letter Addressed to ... Palmerston ... and the other ... Members of the House of Commons, in Explanation of a Petition for Enquiry, presented from Colonel Rathborne, on the 9th August, 1859*. Rathborne's letter to Palmerston is dated 1 January 1860. Stanley on 14 June 1859 had warned D, after a letter from Rathborne, that there would be an appeal to Stanley's successor to reopen Rathborne's case: 'His style is very offensive, so much so that if he publishes he can do us no harm.' H B/XX/S/688.

3 Rathborne in his publication had referred to D throughout as chief editor of the *Press*.

I endeavoured to serve Colonel Rathborne in 1858, because I thought him a man of abilities, knowledge, and honesty, who had been hardly treated in life, and who, from his peculiar temper and isolated habits, had little chance of the advancement which he merited. I regretted much at the time that I failed in my cordial endeavours to aid him.

The statement that the omission of Colonel Rathborne's name in the Indian Council was made in deference to Lord Derby, in opposition to the rest of the Cabinet, and even at the instigation of H.R.H. the Prince Consort,[4] is one of those extraordinary narratives which can only be accounted for by a degree of diseased vanity bordering on aberration of intellect; and is as groundless as it is absurd.

No person has ever been authorised by me, either directly or indirectly, to hold the slightest communication with Colonel Rathborne, in order to obtain the return of any letters which I have written to him.[5] There is no letter I have ever written in the course of my life the return of which I would condescend to solicit. The publication of private letters may hurt my feelings, but can never impugn my honour.

Colonel Rathborne has, however, himself refuted this wild declaration. For he confesses that, somewhat incredulous of the authority of the unknown envoy, he deemed it discreet to address me himself on the matter, and he received from my secretary, at my dictation, an answer of defiance and contempt.

Colonel Rathborne has, I am informed, published this reply of mine in his pamphlet,[6] though it completes the refutation of his incoherent case. But Colonel Rathborne is no rogue. He is only a wrongheaded man: of ungovernable temper; and vexed by nature with an infirmity of suspicion touching on insanity: one of those men who are always playing into the hands of their enemies, by quarrelling with their friends. – I have the honour to remain, sir, your faithful servant,

B. DISRAELI.[7]

4 *Mr. Disraeli* ... 45-6.

5 Rathborne identified the person who had decreed that nothing could be done for him until he returned all of D's letters only as 'a literary gentleman of the party, a friend of Mr. Disraeli's and my own, who had received a public appointment through his influence'. He was careful to distinguish this friend from Rose and Earle; earlier he had not hesitated to name Lord Henry Lennox as the one who had approached him in 1857. *Mr. Disraeli* ... 27, 45-6, 62-6. In an undated note Earle wrote: 'I was right in my anticipation, as to Rathborne's pamphlet. The anonymous writer spoken of must be our friend.' H B/XX/E/116. Rathborne would respond to D's letter with another publication, *Mr. Disraeli and the Unknown Envoy: A Letter to Lord Palmerston.* Haydon on 28 May 1860 would write: 'There is nothing in Col. Rathborne's new letter but a statement that Lord Stanley carried away the Rathborne correspondence entirely, when he left office. The rest is a fierce denunciation of the unknown Envoy.' H B/XXI/H/364.

6 Rathborne stated that he had sent the letter to D on 10 January 1858 and received a reply from 'the gentleman, who had taken so active a part in the negociations', renewing the letter-return offer. When Rathborne rejected it, he received a note from Earle acknowledging receipt of the 10 January letter: Earle told him that D as a minister of state was dissociating himself entirely from Rathborne's private affairs, and terminating further correspondence. The letter is given in paraphrase. *Mr. Disraeli* ... 65.

7 The *Saturday Review* on 18 February 1860 (198-9) thought that D, in his attempt 'to snuff the Colonel ingeniously out ... has rather burnt his own ingenious fingers.'

TO: SIR JOHN PAKINGTON Grosvenor Gate 3453

Wednesday [15] February 1860

ORIGINAL: WRC 705:349 BA 3835/7(ii)14

EDITORIAL COMMENT: Black-edged paper. *Dating*: the Wednesday date is confirmed by context; see n4. *Sic*: Feb 18.

Wednesday Feb 18. 60 | Grovr Gate

Rt Honble | Sir John Pakington | G C B

My dear Pakington,

The enclosed[1] I drew up last night, & showed it to Baring, Hubbard,[2] Jolliffe & Cairns, whom I had occasion to see. I missed you, or should have asked you to consider / it. I send it by this messenger to Lord Derby, who has also this morning, sent me a sketch of his own[3] – but I don't like it, because it talks of "direct" & "indirect" taxation, wh: I think unwise. I will consider yours, & I hope we may meet at the Levée.[4]

Yrs ever | D.

TO: SIR JOHN PAKINGTON Grosvenor Gate 3454

[Saturday] 18 February 1860

ORIGINAL: WRC 705:349 BA 3835/7(ii)12

EDITORIAL COMMENT: Black-edged paper. Endorsed in another hand on the fourth page: '*1860 Disraeli* Politics, & Bp of Rochester's death'.

Grosvenor Gate | Feb. 18 1860

Rt Honble | Sir J. Pakington | G.C.B.

1 The enclosed draft amendment to Gladstone's budget reads: 'That, while this House, recognises the importance of developing the resources of the Country by extending our commercial intercourse with other nations, & by removing such burdens upon trade or manufactures, as can be dispensed with consistently with a due regard to the exigencies of the / public service, it is not prepared to adopt measures, wh:, by adding to our existing deficiency, would render necessary a large increase of the Income Tax, & thus disappoint the just expectations of the Country.' Gladstone had submitted his budget, including a proposed increase in income tax, on 10 February, when D had asked him to postpone debate for two weeks to allow for due consideration; after discussion it was set for Monday 20 February. On the 17th, Du Cane would give notice of an amendment essentially identical to D's draft, but on the 20th defer to D's amendment on procedure. *Hansard* CLVI cols 812-89 (D 872-4), 1226-7, 1354-5. See further **3454**&n2. For D's 20 February amendment on the motion to go into committee on the customs acts see **3451**n1.

2 John Gellibrand Hubbard (1805-1889), merchant, director since 1838 of the Bank of England, was MP (C) for Buckingham 1859-68, for London 1874-87, chairman of the public works loan board 1853-75, PC 1874, created Baron Addington 1887. He was a recognized authority on (among other topics) the income tax, on which he published several pamphlets, and in 1861 would carry a motion against the government for a select committee on the tax; see **3581**&n2.

3 Derby had written on 'Tuesday Night ... I send you the result of my cogitations as to the form of our Amendment for Monday next. I have put one or two alternatives which I hope you will comprehend: but the substance of the whole must be the question whether the proposed financial sacrifices, and attendant advantages, are to be set in the scale against the necessity for the increased and permanent Income Tax. I shall see you at the Levée tomorrow, if you are there *before* we go in'. H B/XX/S/279. His enclosure has not been found.

4 The Queen held her first levee of the season on 15 February, at St James's Palace; Pakington, Derby and D are listed as having attended. *MP* (16 Feb 1860). Pakington replied the same day (15th) with two suggestions: 'It may be worth consideration whether our amendment should not express our views rather more fully, and if so, whether they should not be embodied in a series of about three resolutions.' H B/XX/P/55.

My dear Pakington,

Affairs have been so anxious, & fitful, that it has been impossible for me to write to you; changing, as they have done, every moment, / in a capricious & uncertain house. The papers, & the votes, will show you what took place last night.[1] It is supposed, that, if our men are well up on Monday, the Government will be beaten on the / motion of wh: I have given notice[2] – many Whigs, Harry Vane among others, supporting it.[3] If the Govt. adopt the suggestion, it will cause at least four days delay, in order, that they may prepare, & we peruse, their / resolutions. This delay is of the last importance – the prospects for Du Cane's motion not being favorable, tho' time may mend them.[4]

I sincerely condole with you. I greatly respected & regarded him; having known him from my youth, at Stowe.[5]

Yours sincerely, | D.

3455 TO: SARAH BRYDGES WILLYAMS [London, Wednesday] 29 February 1860

ORIGINAL: RTC [134]

PUBLICATION HISTORY: M&B IV 278, extract dated February [1860]

EDITORIAL COMMENT: Black-edged paper. There is no salutation. *Sic*: March 1. 1860.

March 1. 1860

The World is getting sick of a provisional existence. Tomorrow, the Emperor of the French is to enlighten mankind, wh: is exhausted with perplexity.[1] I only anticipate a new chapter of political conundrums. It is the Gordian Knot. /

1 See **3451**&n1 for the Commons events of 17 February. Pakington had written on the 16th: 'I hope ... that you will make an arrangement tomorrow in what shape the opinion of Parliament as to the Treaty is to be expressed, in the event of our amendment being rejected. If our amendment is carried, I suppose that will be considered as a rejection of the Treaty.' H B/XX/P/56.

2 D had given notice of the procedural amendment that he would move on 20 February, while the amendment he had previously drafted (see **3453**&n1), currently in the form of a motion of which Du Cane had given notice, would be deferred. Pakington replied that he had read the proceedings with 'great interest & entire concurrence', and was glad to see D's notice 'which of course will supersede Du Cane's.' H B/XX/P/57.

3 Vane during the debate on the 17th had argued for 'such a course as would enable the whole subject of the Treaty, to be submitted to the deliberation of the House'. *Hansard* CLVI cols 1253-4. D on the 20th would insist that his was not a party motion, and that he would have preferred it to have been made by an independent member. *Ibid* cols 1355-75.

4 Du Cane's deferred motion (n2) would not appear again.

5 Pakington's father-in-law, the Right Rev George Murray (1784-1860) DD, Bishop of Rochester 1827-54 and Dean of Worcester 1828-54, grandson of 3rd Duke of Atholl, had died on 16 February after a long illness; Pakington on the 15th (**3453**n4) had thought the Bishop had rallied a little, but on the 16th (n1) had written that 'the poor Bishop is dying'. The Bishop in 1843 had mildly attacked *Tracts for the Times*. D recorded seeing his sister at Stowe in 1840 (see III **1085**&n11 – *contra* that note, Lady Frankland Russell was born in 1790 and was the bishop's sister).

---

1 The current focus of the post-Villafranca anxieties about Italy's future was whether France would risk renewal of war by annexing Savoy and Nice; because of distressing rumours the Commons on the 28th had extensively discussed a motion for the foreign office's relevant correspondence with France and Sardinia to be laid before the House. At the opening of the French Legislative Chamber on 1 March, the Emperor would be vague about his plans except for his intention to claim part of Savoy; see **3456**&n7. *Hansard* CLVI cols 1933-70; *The Times* (1 Mar 1860).

I have misdated my letter – forgetting it was a Leap-Year. I must say with the Emperor Titus – *Perdidi diem.* I have lost a day – tho' in a different manner – from the Roman.[2]

I went to see your book plate just now, wh: you will receive, with other / things, very shortly.[3]

We have had some noisy parliamentary fights, but they have been sham battles.

We dine at the Palace to day, &, if not very late, shall go afterwards to the Prussian Ministers, who calls his house in Carlton / Terrace, *Prussia House.*[4]

I hope you are quite well. To day, here, is a burst of spring; but you always have spring in your land of violets & myrtles.

Yours ever, | D.

TO: SARAH BRYDGES WILLYAMS — Grosvenor Gate — 3456
[Friday] 2 March 1860

ORIGINAL: RTC [135]
EDITORIAL COMMENT: Black-edged paper. There is no salutation. *Sic:* ArchBishop.

Private — Grosvenor Gate | March 2. 1860

The dinner at the Palace was amusing, given in honor of the return of Prince Alfred, who sate at table on the Queens right hand. He is sixteen, but only looks ten, in face, & stature; a pretty, & very little, Midshipman. He has / not grown an inch during his eighteen months of absence.[1] This is very unfortunate. His father is a handsome man, & above the middle height, & tho' the Queen herself is very short, she comes from a tall family, & it ought to have come out in her offspring. I attribute it all to the inter-marriage / of first cousins. The breed always degenerates.[2] The Princess Alice, who is very lively & agreeable, told me with an air of triumph, one day last year at Windsor,[3] when I sate next to her at dinner, that the Prince of Wales, had written home from Italy, that he had grown an inch. But he too is very short. We / had the Marquis & Marchioness of Normanby there on Wednesday, the ArchBishop of Canterbury who had christened Prince Alfred, Sir George Lewis, the Secretary of State,

2 The Emperor Titus (39-81 CE) considered a day lost on which he had not bestowed a benefit on anyone. In an undated letter, SBW thanked D: 'Your little calendar is the *best* and most comprehensive I ever saw.' RTC [502Q].

3 See **3459**&n1. An invoice (marked as paid on 15 April 1861) from John & Richard Longman, Waterloo Place, engravers to Her Majesty, has entries for 5 December 1859 and 1 March 1860; the former is for 'Engraving Arms Quarterly & Coronet Bloodstone & fine Gold Seal 7.3.6'; the latter is for three items: 'Engraving Paper Dio Arms & Coronet 2.12.6', '1 quire Notepaper & Envelopes stampd plain & colord 0.1.6' and 'Engraving Bookplate Arms Quarterly Coronet & Initials 3.3.0'. H A/V/G/[unnumbered, following 240].

4 The Queen's dinner party at Buckingham Palace on 29 February included the Ds; see further **3456**. The Count and Countess de Bernstorff after their dinner party had a small musical party. *MP* (1 Mar 1860).

---

1 Prince Alfred (1844-1900), the Queen's fourth child, had been away on naval training; he had entered the RN in 1858. He would live to become, as Duke of Saxony, Prince of Saxe-Coburg-Gotha and Duke of Edinburgh, admiral in 1887 and commander-in-chief of the Mediterranean Fleet 1886-9.

2 *Cf* VII **2980**&n1 for D's approval in 1857 of Stanley's views on racial degeneration.

3 See VII **3283-4**.

& Lady Theresa,[4] & many other very agreeable people. The Queen in high spirits, but complaining of the storms,[5] wh: had uprooted some fine elms in her gardens round the Palace.

Yesterday Lord John Russell brought forward a new Reform Bill,[6] & the Emperor of the French announced the annexation of Savoy.[7] Two tolerable events.

Yrs ever, | D.

3457 TO: SIR WILLIAM JOLLIFFE Grosvenor Gate, Sunday 4 March 1860

ORIGINAL: SCR DD/HY C/2165 [57]

EDITORIAL COMMENT: Black-edged paper. *Sic:* St. James'.

Grosvenor Gate | Sunday night | Mar: 4. 60

Rt Honble | Sir W.H. Jolliffe

My dear Jolliffe,

Affairs are critical. I shall be with Lord Derby early tomorrow morning, & it would be well for me to see / you afterwards. I should think I could be at the Carlton about noon – but, perhaps, the best wd. be for you to meet me in St. James' Sqr. I count on being there a little / after eleven o'ck[.]

In the meantime, you must move heaven & earth to have a good muster in the evening.[1]

Yours ever, | D.

4 Lady Theresa, born Lady Maria Theresa Villiers (1803-1865), sister of 4th Earl of Clarendon, in 1830 had married Thomas Henry Lister (d 1842) and secondly, in 1844, Sir George Cornewall Lewis, Bt, currently home secretary. In 1852 she had published her major work, *The Lives of the Friends and Contemporaries of Lord Chancellor Clarendon* (3 vols).

5 The storm of 27-28 February had caused much damage and even loss of life throughout much of England and the continent. *MP* (29 Feb 1860).

6 The main features of Russell's bill were a £10 county franchise, a £6 borough franchise, twenty-five two-seat boroughs reduced to one seat each, nine of these going to other boroughs, fifteen to counties and one to London University. *Hansard* cols 2050-73.

7 See **3455**n1. Manners on 3 March would write to suggest D 'move an Amendment on the Treaty Address against the annexation of Savoy'. H B/XX/M/144. Sardinia would cede Savoy and Nice to France, after almost unanimous votes to that effect in both places, in a treaty of 24 March ratified on 12 April. *AR* (1860, History) 218-20.

---

1 Palmerston had given notice of the motion he would make on Monday 5 March, to give immediate priority to the motion for an address on the commercial treaty with France. Derby at St James's Square wrote to D this day (4 March): 'I should like much to know what course you intend to take when the Address, approving of the Treaty, is moved, rather suddenly, tomorrow. Even the words have not been given to Parliament; but if those quoted in the Observer are correct, they only furnish an additional proof of the extreme carelessness with which this whole business has been conducted. The Commons are made to state that having considered the Treaty &c "they shall proceed to take such steps as may be necessary for giving effect to a system which" &c &c. Now these words are nearly copied from Pitt's Address, to which they were as appropriate, as they are here the reverse. For Pitt's Address was moved when Resolutions had been carried only in a Committee on the Treaty, and not in a Committee of Customs; and when consequently all which was necessary to give effect to the Treaty remained to be done; whereas in the present case full effect has been given by reporting the Resolutions, to the financial part of the Treaty, and I do not understand that with regard to the remainder, they contemplate anything more than the Address. If so, the terms as given in the Observer, are unmitigated nonsense ... I should be inclined to doubt the policy, after all that has occurred, of your taking a substantive division against the Treaty. You would probably have a bad division, you would take a step very offensive to France, and that to no

TO: FRANCIS ESPINASSE Grosvenor Gate [Tuesday] 6 March 1860 **3458**

ORIGINAL: MHS Guild Library [2]

PUBLICATION HISTORY: Francis Espinasse *Literary Recollections and Sketches* (1893) 411, undated extract

EDITORIAL COMMENT: Black-edged paper. Endorsed in another hand on the fourth page: 'Later, Lord Beaconsfield'.

Private Grosvenor Gate | March 6 1860

Francis Espinasse | Esqr[1]

Dear Sir,

Let me thank you for your kind & gentlemanlike letter. My life, since I emerged from the crowd, has been / passed in a glass-house – tho' its windows have often been broken – & I don't think there is much of its career, that can be unknown to you – but, with regard to what you properly describe as its mythic period, I will / endeavour to send you some memoranda of *facts,* wh: may be useful to you, tho' I think you will find it no easy labor to penetrate more than thirty years of studied misrepresentation, with wh:, as it never involved my honor, I / have never contended.[2]

Believe me, dear Sir, | Very faithfully yrs | *B. Disraeli*

I will try to send you the notes in a few days.

purpose even if you carried your point; for the reductions of duty on our side being now a fait accompli, you would only, if you rejected the Treaty, sacrifice whatever advantage it holds out to our Commerce, without escaping the grave financial difficulties which it involves. Jolliffe tells me he has a whip out, which is all right – but I should be glad to see you sometime before you go down to the House.' H B/XX/S/266. On Monday, after discussion, the motion would be withdrawn. *Hansard* CLVI cols 2228-64. The treaty in June (ratified on 1 July) would be divided into three categories of goods each to be negotiated separately before 1 November. *AR* (1860) 210-31.

1 Francis Espinasse (1823?-1912), currently writing for the *Imperial Dictionary of Universal Biography* (undated, but catalogued as published 1857-63, again in 1863 only, then a 'New Edition' in 1877-84, and finally in 1890), and other periodicals, later (1864-7) editor of the *Edinburgh Courant,* in 1893 would publish his *Literary Recollections and Sketches* (see n2). No letters of his to D have been found.

2 In his *Recollections* 407-26 Espinasse gives an account of his dealings with D that does not exactly fit all the details that can be confirmed: 'I cannot now recollect whether ... I neglected to send the usual proof to Mr. Disraeli ... However this may have been, it was from headquarters that I first received the intimation that Mr. Disraeli had notified [*letter not found*] his discovery of mis-statements in my sketch of him. On learning this, I wrote to him to say ... that I should be happy to correct any errors ... In reply to what he styled my "gentlemanlike letter," he asked me to call on him, naming a day and hour for my visit. Very soon afterwards he wrote [*letter not found*] to me naming another day ... [because] he had received a summons to attend the King of the Belgians [*on 19 June; see* **3480**&n2] ... On the new-appointed day ... Mr. Disraeli conducted me to what he called his "den," at the top of the house, a very plainly furnished room. The immediate subject of my visit having been briefly discussed, he promised me some autobiographical notes, and then the dialogue, if dialogue it can be called, became general. He talked to me on men and things political with great frankness ... I remarked particularly that when he spoke of his Conservative colleagues and followers he always said "they," not "we," as if he regarded himself as with them, not of them. "They," he said, were urging him to make an effort for restoration to office, but he had had enough of office with a majority against him ... Soon after this first interview, I duly received Disraeli's autobiographical and autograph notes [*see* **3460**]. I found that they corrected only two errors of fact ... One of these errors regarded the name of the firm of solicitors to whom he had been articled. The other was my statement that he had "aided" not only "in founding" but in "conducting" the once much-talked-of *Representative,* but this was an error universally prevalent at the time, and not extinguished until years after Disraeli's death ... Most of Disraeli's notes related to his earlier years. Among the exceptions were two ... The first was one unknown to any of his former biographers, namely, that in his second candidature for High Wycombe in 1835, he was supported by Sir Robert Peel ... The other was that his becoming both

3459 TO: SARAH BRYDGES WILLYAMS

Grosvenor Gate
[Saturday] 24 March 1860

ORIGINAL: RTC [136]
PUBLICATION HISTORY: M&B IV 273, dated 24 March [1860], extract from the last paragraph
EDITORIAL COMMENT: Black-edged paper. There is no salutation. *Sic:* forsee.

Grosvenor Gate | March 24 1860

I enclose a proof of the plate: I think the initials are not happily executed. They are too common. The letters, I think, should be more fanciful – but I will not give the final directions, / till I hear from you.

I do not understand what is your objection against the arms & coronet on the note paper. They are quite correct. I send you three specimens. The only *alteration,* that I would / suggest, is an *addition* "Mount Braddon" underneath the shield. Would you like this?[1]

Public business has been so active & engrossing since Parliament met, that I have scarcely had time to attend to any private affairs. Every day brings a great event – & greater ones are preparing. I / forsee immense changes in Europe – England, I hope, may escape. The new Reform Bill[2] is like the "Great Eastern" & sticks on its stays.[3] It will not be launched, & if ever it do float, I think it will founder.[4] Then, all will be right.

Yours ever, | D.

Chancellor of the Exchequer and leader of the House of Commons without having held office previously was a twofold event which had never happened before, except in the case of Mr. Pitt'. In the next chapter, Espinasse compares J.A. Froude's 1890 biography of D with his own on the reason for D's placement in a solicitor's office: 'Very soon after receiving [*D's version*] I incorporated it with other of his statements in a second edition, so to speak, of my memoir ... A proof of this second edition was sent immediately to Mr. Disraeli, who by returning it unaltered "with thanks," [*letter not found*] indorsed its accuracy. I used, as far as possible, Disraeli's own words'. Espinasse subsequently describes his role in an 1881 controversy involving conflicting accounts of D's role on the *Representative,* resulting in two letters from D (9 and 14 February 1881) and an interview in February 1881 during which Espinasse returned D's notes to him.

---

1 See **3455**&n3. SBW, whose letter evidently in response to **3455** is missing its opening page(s) and to which D is here responding in turn, on 26 March would reply: 'According to my english ideas my coat of arms with that of my Husband shd be in a lozenge shield but whether it be Spanish fashion I do not know. As an Heiress I fancy I am entitled to the crest of my ancestors which I have hitherto used and I have no hesitation in using the seal for which I am so much indebted to you as I consider them my antient right Family distinctions but a Coat of Arms only on recent note paper I fancy might be questionable this is the reason I prefer a Crest on note paper. The arms for the Book plate is beautifully defined I admire it very much and I am quite of your opinion, so I return the book plate with fancy letters pined to it for you to do as you please.' On the paper with the ornate intertwined letters 'SMDC' (for Sarah Mendes da Costa), SBW has written: 'If you approve, the initials may be something in this way with *da* instead of the capital letter D'. RTC [397Q].

2 See **3456**&n6.

3 See VII **2997**&n4 for the troubled launch of the *Great Eastern.* On 16 September, 1859, on its first voyage, there had been a dreadful explosion, causing five deaths and several injuries. It however would not founder, on 17 July 1860 sailing successfully to New York in unfavourable conditions in ten and a half days. *AR* (1859 Chronicle) 136-41; (1860 Chronicle) 84-7.

4 It did; see **3477**&n1.

TO: FRANCIS ESPINASSE Grosvenor Gate [Tuesday] 27 March 1860 3460

ORIGINAL: H A/X/B/1

PUBLICATION HISTORY: Bradford 244, dated 27 March 1860, one sentence plus description

EDITORIAL COMMENT: Black-edged paper. A.E. Scanes (the first organizer of H), whose signature is attached to the correction of D's birth year, '1804 AES', may have made all the corrections in another hand. 'Confidential' is repeated at the top of the first page of each sheet (pages 5, 9, 13). *Sic:* mistatement; 1805; Ecologue; 18312; 29; Wycomb [*three times*]; Marybone; 1848; Viney Evans; son of; sister of.

Confidential Grosvenor Gate. Mar. 27. | 60

Francis Espinasse Esqr

Dear Sir,

As I understand, that the Memoir of my father, in the "Univ: Bioghy", is to precede mine, it will be unnecessary for me to touch upon some points I must otherwise have noticed. Nor, indeed, in this confidential memorandum is there, probably, anything, that will be of absolute use to you as regards myself, but it may prevent the repetition of mistatements, wh: have, perhaps, been too long permitted to pass unnoticed.[1]

I was born Dec: 21. 1805[2] [*written above in another hand:* 1804 AES] & my education / was strictly private, wh: is perhaps all that need be said. I was at school for two or three years under the Revd. Dr Cogan, a Greek scholar of eminence, who had contributed notes to the Æschylus of Bishop Blomfield, & was himself the Editor of the Greek Gnomic Poets.[3] After this, I was with a private tutor for two years in my own County, & my education was severely classical. Too much so: in the pride of boyish erudition, I edited the Adonisian Ecologue of Theocritus wh: was privately printed.[4] This was my first production: puerile pedantry.

My father, who always lived in seclusion, / & during the last thirty years of his life almost uninterruptedly in Bucks, had one powerful friend, who offered to provide for me in one of the offices of the Court of Chancery.[5] It was a post, wh:, in routine, would have given me, in due course, a better income than any other public office, &, if pursued with diligence & ability, led to some of the highest prizes in the profession. To be admitted as a Solicitor was a necessary qualification, & an intimate friend of my father assisted me in this respect – but altho' my life was, & wd. have been, little more than a form, I ↑soon↓ relinquished it, from a restlessness wh: /

1 See **3458**&n2. The entry for his father would immediately follow the one for D in the *Imperial Dictionary of Universal Biography* of which D had been sent the proof.

2 See V app VI, the corrected 1851 draft of the entry on D in *Men of the Time* in which D allows the erroneous birth year of 1805 to stand; 1805 would still appear in the *Dictionary* entry for D in the 'New Edition' in which the latest date mentioned is 1876.

3 Eliezer Cogan (1762-1855), a Presbyterian, some say Unitarian minister and Greek scholar, taught D at his famous school at Higham Hill, Walthamstow, and is recorded as having said '"I don't like Disraeli; I never could get him to understand the subjunctive".' *DNB* IV 675. Bishop Blomfield's earliest edition of Æschylus was his *Prometheus Vinctus* in 1810, with notes and glossary; in the 1833 edition available to the editors, Cogan is not mentioned. Cogan's edition, *Moschi Idyllia tria, Graece* was published in 1795.

4 Espinasse claimed this as 'unknown to any of his biographers' except himself: 'If there survives a copy of the young Disraeli's edition of the fifteenth idyl of Theocritus, its possessor ... should make haste to inform the world of his possession of it.' Evidently to date nobody has done so.

5 The powerful friend was T.F. Maples; see I **4**&n3, **5**&n1, **6**, M&B I 32-3, 56 and James Ogden *Isaac D'Israeli* (Oxford 1969) 139-40. According to *Espinasse* 419, D's name was on the books of Lincoln's Inn from 11 November 1824 to 25 November 1831.

then influenced ↑me↓, & rendered travel absolutely necessary. In due course, my brother was offered the same opportunity, & the pursuit being one adapted to his character, he has, at a comparatively early period of life, risen to the post of Registrar of the Court of Chancery – one of dignity & great emolument.[6]

Both my brothers were at Winchester, for wh: I was intended. This is the reason of my being often described as an alumnus of that public school.

When I was quite a youth, I made the acquaintance of the late Mr. Lockhart, & hung about him, as boys do about the / first distinguished man with whom they become acquainted. In the year 1825, Mr Lockhart, who then lived in Scotland, undertook, with the countenance of Mr Canning, to edit the Representative newspaper. In making his preliminary arrangements, he often made use of me, & I was delighted with his confidence.[7] Sometime after, when in Italy, I took up an English magazine, & found "a son of Mr Disraeli" described as the Editor of that paper, wh: had been a failure. I never was Editor of the paper; I never wrote a line in the paper; I was never asked to write a line in the paper. At the time of its appearance, I did not know I cd. write. But the mythus was established, & effected its object, it shielded Mr Lockhart, who was an expert in / all the nebulous [*illegible deletion*] ↑chicanery↓ of these literary intrigues. Unfortunately, in this case, the man of straw he had fixed on, became eminent, & a newspaper failure, of nearly forty years ago, is remembered from its being the subject of a literary forgery.

Being upon this subject, I may venture to observe, that I do not suppose that any man of literary habits, who has so long been connected with public life, ever wrote less in the newspapers than myself. But I have never contradicted any assertion to the contrary; & for an obvious reason. I shd. have hurt the feelings of every Journalist in the country.

With respect to the statement in the "Gentleman's / Mag[azin]e" respecting my father & Mr. Murray, & of wh: I was unaware, it is hardly necessary to enter into the reasons why, nearly forty years ago, my father withdrew his confidence from Mr Murray. The ~~af~~ incident could have had no reference to any relations between myself & Mr Murray, for that gentleman subsequently published several works for me, & among them "Contarini Fleming" (18312). [*Here D has drawn a short line.*]

Vivian Grey was published 26-7. anonymously

Young Duke – 29.

In that year, I left England, for the second [*1 word written above in another hand:*] third time, in order to travel more extensively than hitherto. I was absent until the end of 1831, & shd. not have returned but as a Candidate for the Boro' of High Wycomb, in / the immediate neighbourhood of my father's residence, against the Hon: Chas Grey, the son of the Prime Minister.

I was brought forward by the old Corporation, & proposed by the Tory Mayor, John Carter Esqr. The Tories were influential men, but a very small minority. I made a coalition betn them & the Radicals, whose leader obtained the famous letters of Hume & O'Connell, neither of whom I had ever seen; & wh: led to the other mythus of my being sent down to Wycomb by those gentlemen.[8]

6 See VI **2826**&n2.

7 See I **23** to **48** *passim*.

8 See I **198** to **203**.

I never stood for Marybone, tho' I was asked immediately after the loss of the Wycomb Election, & issued an address.[9]

I may mention, that the contest betn. myself & Colonel Grey was a neck & neck race; & it was repeated in 1835 when I stood for the Boro' at / the request of Sir Robert Peel, & was supported by precisely the same combination.[10]

I ought to have mentioned, that I published in 1831-2 [*written above in another hand:* 1832-3] "C. Fleming" & "Alroy" – both written while I was abroad – & the latter planned & partly composed at Jerusalem, wh: I believe I have mentioned in the preface of the later popular editions. ↑In these days of rapid locomotion, my travels go for nothing - but I was in Syria, Asia Minor, & ascended the Nile to Nubia.↓

1836-7 "Henrietta Temple" & "Venetia."

Returned to Parliament for Maidstone *1837* ↑The Queen's↓ first Parliament, & I have never been out of Parliament since.

Returned for Shrewsbury 1841 & sate for it six years.

1844-5. 6 "Coningsby", "Sybil", & "Tancred" tho' the latter was not published until the / spring of 1848 – having been too much engaged in Parliament to finish it.

After the death of Ld. George Bentinck, was chosen leader of the Tory party in the House of Commons ~~184~~; – at the commencement of the Sess: 1849. Sir John Buller & Mr. Miles were deputed formally to announce to me the choice – & I had the satisfaction in due season, of recognizing their undeviating fidelity to myself, by making one a Baronet, & elevating the other to the Peerage.[11]

I found the Tory party ↑in the Ho: of Commons↓, when I acceded to its chief management, in a state of great depression & disorganisation: Lord George Bentinck had only numbered 120 in his motion on the Irish Railways,[12] wh: was to / try our strength in the new Parliament. By a series of motions to relieve the agricultural Interest by revising & ↑partially↓ removing the local taxation of the country, I withdrew the Tory party gradually from the hopeless question of Protection, rallied all those members who were connected either personally, or by their constituencies, with the land, & finally brought the state of parties in the House of Commons to nearly a tie.

This led, in 1851, to the offer of the Government of the Country to Ld. Derby, wh: he declined, but wh: he accepted in 1852.

I was then called to the Privy Council, appointed Chanr of the Exchequer, / & ~~was~~ became Leader of the House of Commons without ever having been in office, wh: I believe never happened before, except in the case of Mr Pitt, when he was ↑made↓ Chanr. of the Exchequer in Ld Shelburne's Government; & for as short a period.[13]

9 See I **248**.

10 See II **362** to **365**. Espinasse (413-14) notes that it was 'unknown to any of his former biographers ... that in his second candidature for High Wycombe in 1835, he was supported by Sir Robert Peel, a disclosure which one would have hardly expected from him who made it.'

11 Miles was made a baronet on 19 April 1859, and Buller was created Baron Churston on 2 August 1858. For an account of D's rise to the leadership, see V Introduction pp xi-xv.

12 See IV **1533**n1.

13 Pitt was chancellor of the exchequer 6 July 1782 to 31 March 1783.

In 1853 The University of Oxford conferred on me the degree of D.C.L. with a demonstration of feeling, on the part of the University, wh: has never been equalled, & is still remembered.[14]

I ought to have observed, that, ~~in~~ at the general election of 1847, I was ~~returned~~ chosen Member for the County of Buckingham witht. a contest, & I have ↑been↓ returned five times for that County. This is the event in my public life wh: has given me the greatest satisfaction. /

Lord George Bentinck was very firm to me, & in 1850 or 51, I took the opportunity of recording his career in a work in ↑which I↓ have attempted to treat cotemporary politics with truth.

In ↑Feby↓ 1858, I was again appointed C of Excr, ↑& leader of the Ho: of Comm:↓ & resigned June 1859.

I have answered your appeal witht. reserve. Perhaps, probably, there is nothing in all this of wh: you can avail yourself. It is rather to tune your mind, than to guide your pen. Details in cotemporary biography can hardly be touched witht. great delicacy & reserve. One shd. only record events, but it is desirable that they shd. be true. I have written this with haste, for your / letter has reached me at a moment of great pressure. I hope it is rather egotistical, than vain; but at all events excuse it.

I shd. have said that in *1839* I married, & it is the complete domestic happiness wh: I then achieved, wh: has mainly sustained me in a career of considerable trial.

My wife, ↑with↓ whom I had been long acquainted, was the widow of my colleague at Maidstone Mr. Wyndham Lewis, & was herself the daughter of Captain Viney Evans R.N son of ~~Sir~~ General Sir James Viney by a sister / of the late William Scrope Esqr., ↑of Castle Combe, Wilts↓ with whose distinguished works you are well acquainted, & who represented in his person the most ancient family of noble blood in England.[15]

Have the kindness to acknowledge the receipt of this packet & believe me, | faithfully yours | D.

T.O. /

The late Ld. Strangford, unknown to me, drew a sketch of my character & career, especially with reference to my political position, wh: is written with great power – & worth looking at. It appeared, I believe, in some periodical – & anonymously. My attention has been recently drawn to it by a work called "Leaders of Parties", or some title of that kind, by the late Mr. O. Maddyn. I found the article, devoted to myself, a reprint of Ld. Strangford's (Hon: G.S. Smythe) production. Coming from one, who tho' a personal friend, was a follower of Sir Robert Peel, & who had a very fine taste & quick perception, & was behind the scenes of political life, it is very interesting.[16]

14 See VI **2533**n2.

15 William Scrope was a descendant of 1st Baron Scrope, whose barony was created in 1371. He in turn was a descendant of Robert de Scrupe, a feudal baron in the time of Henry II.

16 For the background to this article, and D's participation in it, see VI **2613**&n1.

TO: WILLIAM CARLISLE Carlton Club [Friday] 30 March 1860 **3461**

ORIGINAL: TCC [84]

EDITORIAL COMMENT: Black-edged Carlton Club paper.

– Carlisle Esqr March 30 1860

Dear Sir,

I have been wishing for some weeks to see you, but I have been so much engaged, / that I have been unable to take my chance of seeing you at Lin: Inn, & could not make an appointment to receive you at Grosvenor Gate.

Could / you do me the favor of calling there on Monday morning next? Anytime will suit me from 11 o'ck to 3.[1]

Yours faithfully | *B. Disraeli*

TO: SARAH BRYDGES WILLYAMS Grosvenor Gate [Wednesday] 4 April 1860 **3462**

ORIGINAL: RTC [137]

EDITORIAL COMMENT: Black-edged paper. There is no salutation.

Grosvenor Gate | April 4. 1860

We depart this morning for Hughenden, where we have not been for six months![1] A long while to be away from home, when home is only thirty miles from town.

The parliamentary campaign has been very satisfactory. The Ministers went off like a rocket; & / will come down like a stick. The Reform Bill is like the Great Eastern;[2] it won't move; & all their other affairs, worse. They were brought in to carry a Reform Bill, & because they were the only men, who could manage France! Their Reform Bill is dead, &, if they continue in office, we shall have war with our / great ally![3] I should not be surprised, if they went out.

I shall send you your book plate when I return. It will then be finished. I am glad you like the seal so much. I think the note paper had better wait till we meet, & can hold a council on the matter[.] I took / down your instructions in writing, & fulfilled them literally – but the affair will keep.[4]

1 For the on-going process of dealing with Francis Villiers's debts by negotiating through Carlisle the sale of Villiers's Ceylon estates, see VI **2817**&n1, **2840**&n1, VII **2942**&n1, **2986**&nn1&2, **2988**&n1, **3012**&n1 and **3380**&n1. See also **3450**&n1. No correspondence related specifically to this letter has been found.

---

1 Since 19 October 1859; see VII **3411**&n2. MA also recorded the departure for Hughenden on Wednesday 4 April. H acc.

2 *Cf* **3459**&n3.

3 For the reform bill see **3456**&n6. Debate on second reading had begun on 19 March (when D opened the strong Conservative opposition to the bill) and would be prolonged until 3 May, when second reading was finally passed without a division. See further **3475**&n1 for the troubled committee stage that would begin on 4 June; the bill would be abandoned on 11 June. With respect to France, Lord John Russell on 26 March had called her proposed annexation of Savoy an act of aggression that threatened England's friendship with her. *Hansard* CLVII cols 839-915 (D 839-58, 866, 915) 1252-60, CLVIII cols 564-652, CLIX cols 225-70 (D 231-6).

4 See **3455**n3 and **3459**&n1. SBW on 5 April would reply: 'Having looked into Elements of Heraldry I have gained an idea that it is best not to procede farther with the book plate and note paper till we have held the Council you propose'. RTC [398Q].

The glass is high & the sun is bright; & I shall be delighted to see once more my woods, wh: must be about to burst forth.

I hope you are quite well.

Ever yours, | D.

3463 TO: SARAH BRYDGES WILLYAMS Hughenden [Friday] 13 April 1860

ORIGINAL: RTC [138]

EDITORIAL COMMENT: Black-edged paper. There is no salutation. *Sic:* embarassment.

Hughenden Manor | April 13 1860

It was the first moss Rose of the season for me! which added to its sweets – moreover, I fancied it bore also the perfume of friendship.[1]

I return you the letter. I regret his loss, for I was pleased with him, when I made his acquaintance – but the event shows how provident & wise we were, so that an event, which under / ordinary circumstances, might have occasioned you much embarassment, & some anxiety, is now only accompanied with that serene sorrow, wh: attends the loss of one, to whom we have been long ~~accompani~~ accustomed, & for whom we entertain a quiet regard.[2]

The Engraver would finish his corrected proof, but I have told him to adjourn his further labors *sine die* – & I only enclose it, that you may observe, that your wishes are always attended to.[3]

Here there is no spring: no bud or blossom, but our trout stream, which, for three years, has been as dry as a Spanish torrent in summer, rolls now a brawling volume! When I say there is no spring, I was in error, for the whole of Hughenden, park, woods, & fields, is covered with violets – & the air is literally perfumed / in our walks, tho' the primroses scarcely peep forth. I introduced their Devonshire relations to our Buckinghamshire violets, & they were very much pleased with their new friends. Some of them return the visit.

Yours ever, | D.

3464 TO: SAMUEL WILBERFORCE Grosvenor Gate [Saturday] 21 April 1860

ORIGINAL: BODL MS Wilberforce c12 ff196-7

EDITORIAL COMMENT: Black-edged paper.

The | Lord Bisp of Oxford Grosvenor Gate | April 21. 1860

My dear Lord,

Your letter, of the 18th., Inst., directed to Hughenden, reached me here, for, alas! our / holidays are over.[1] Ive no prospect of quitting town, even for an hour, for

1 SBW on 17 April would tell MA: 'This is the first and only Moss Rose which has opened this season'. RTC [399Q].

2 Presumably this refers to the death of Stephen Wilson, a trustee of one of SBW's legacies, and the wisdom of having appointed a number of trustees; see **3438**&n5 and **3487**&n1. The 'letter' would then probably have been the official notification SBW had received from his firm.

3 See **3462**&n4.

---

1 Bishop Wilberforce had written on 18 April 1860: 'We are about to make a great effort in favour of the three Diocesan Societies, which are the right areas for doing the Church's work amongst our people. We

many weeks, &, therefore, it will be quite out of my power to assist you at Oxford on the / 24th., wh: wd:, otherwise, have been to me a gratification, & an honor.

Yours sincerely, | D.

TO: SARAH BRYDGES WILLYAMS Grosvenor Gate [Saturday] 21 April 1860 **3465**

ORIGINAL: RTC [139]
EDITORIAL COMMENT: Black-edged paper. There is no salutation.

Grosvenor Gate | Apl. 21. 1860

The roses open more every day, & some of them are now full blown, tho' still perfect. Their place is on my table, & they are my companions during my / morning labors.

We returned to Grosvenor Gate on Tuesday last,[1] & the pressure of business is very great. These are stormy times, & will be wilder.[2] The age / of nationalities will not be of short duration, or of a very tranquil character.[3]

Yours ever, | D.

TO: SARAH BRYDGES WILLYAMS House of Commons [Tuesday] 1 May 1860 **3466**

ORIGINAL: H R/II/E/384
EDITORIAL COMMENT: The text is from a fair copy in another hand in the Rose papers.

House of Commons | Library | May Day 1860

Has brought me roses worthy of such an anniversary![1] Never were they equalled for form, color, and fragrance. Some of their brethren were still alive upon my table to welcome them; but it was evident they were born in April.[2]

My table has never been so adorned with my favorite flowers, as this year – and it was a great pleasure to me, that they came not from Cashmere, but Devonia!

Yours ever, | D.

greatly want by calling attention to the needs of our Parishes & to these instruments for supplying that need to obtain for them a largely increased support. For this purpose We propose to hold a public meeting at Oxford on Tuesday April 24th: at 2 p.m. in the Town Hall, at which meeting I venture earnestly to ask you to attend, and by your presence & voice to support this good work.' H B/XXI/W/352. Parliament had resumed sitting, after the Easter recess, on 17 April.

---

1 MA recorded the return to Grosvenor Gate on Tuesday 17 April. H acc.

2 D may have had in mind Earle's report of his recent interview with Napoleon: 'The Emperor then entered into some general considerations about the English alliance. He said he considered the present state of things most critical. Interested politicians who were exciting exaggerated alarms, would learn, when it was too late, that they had been playing a dangerous game.' H B/XX/E/187. See **3462**&n3.

3 See Introduction p x.

---

1 Among the festivities associated with May Day was Wellington's birthday, still widely celebrated at this time.

2 MA on 4 May would write to SBW: 'D was never on better terms with his party – he is quite well and glories in your lovely roses. I have found out a way to keep them fresh a long time.' RTC [400Q]. See further **3471**&n4.

3467 TO: THOMAS KEBBEL — Grosvenor Gate [Wednesday] 2 May 1860

ORIGINAL: H H/LIFE

PUBLICATION HISTORY: *Standard* (14 August 1906) 'Some Beaconsfield Recollections (no 7): Personal Traits'; T.E. Kebbel *Lord Beaconsfield and other Tory Memories* (1907) 61

EDITORIAL COMMENT: The text is taken from the *Standard* clipping in H H/LIFE.

Grosvenor-gate, May 2, 1860.

My dear sir, –

I have read your article with much satisfaction. Generally speaking it shows a knowledge of politics which is not usual, and is, therefore, calculated to influence opinion.

Personally speaking, I feel indebted to you for a generous and, I trust, not altogether unjust survey of a difficult career, and I shall not easily forget your effort.[1]

Believe me, | Yours sincerely, | B. DISRAELI

3468 TO: LADY DOROTHY NEVILL — Grosvenor Gate [Wednesday 2] May 1860

ORIGINAL: PS 738

PUBLICATION HISTORY: James Drake catalogue 205 (1929) item 56: '4 pp ALS Grosvenor Gate 3 May 1860 to Lady Dorothy Nevill'

EDITORIAL COMMENT: *Dating:* D's reference to 4 May as 'Friday' instead of 'tomorrow' suggests that '3 May' (ph) is a mistranscription.

Dearest Dorothy,

May Day brought me from you an offering as bright as the season & as sweet as yourself![1] ... All the world is full of a wonder picture by Landseer, which is to be revealed at the Exhibition on Friday – a farm on fire! The most marvellous representation of every species of escaping life, from mankind to rats & mice.[2]

Ever, dearest Dorothy, | Your affectionate, | D.

1 Thomas Edward Kebbel (1827-1917), BA (Oxford 1849), later briefly a barrister (Inner Temple 1862), was primarily a journalist and political biographer; as a *Press* writer from 1855, he had got to know D, and in 1888 would publish his *Life of Lord Beaconsfield.* In 1907 he would reprint one of his journalistic pieces on D (see ph) in his *Lord Beaconsfield And Other Tory Memories.* He there explains (60-1) that in 1860 he wrote 'an article on him and his career down to that date, of which he corrected the proofs, enriching it at the same time with marginal notes of the greatest interest in his own handwriting'. For D's 1859 correspondence with Kebbel, see App I **3331X**&n1. On 7 February 1860 Kebbel had written to arrange an interview with D for the *Universal Review,* and on 11 (14?) April that the *Review* editor had requested an article on D for the next number; he asked if there was anything D would like him to include. H B/XXI/K/18, 44. The essay as reprinted in Kebbel's 1864 *Essays upon History and Politics* 326-62, dated 'May, 1860' (the date of Volume 3 of the *Universal Review*), is a highly laudatory analysis of D's career since 1848 contending that D was 'one of the greatest leaders of a party that England has ever seen' (328). MA on 4 May would send SBW, 'by this post, 2 notices of Dear Dizzy, one from an enemy quarter, the Saturday Review, the other the Universal Review. I like both for who would not be delighted to be thought like so great a man, as the Emperor.' SBW would reply on the 13th: 'The Emp. of the French may well be pleased with comparison to dear Dizzi'. RTC [400-1Q].

---

1 Lady Dorothy had evidently sent the strawberries she had promised when she had written to MA on 15 April: 'It would have done your heart good to have seen the magnificent strawberries I had destined for Mr D. but I hope there will be some equally fine when he returns to L[ondon].' H D/III/C/1514.

2 Landseer's *Flood in the Highlands* (now in the Aberdeen Art Gallery) had the place of honour when the Royal Academy Exhibition opened to private view on Friday 4 May; it depicts 'every species' escaping a raging torrent. *The Times* (5 May 1860). Earlier accounts had predicted that Landseer would show it at the Exhibition. *MP* (10 Apr 1860).

TO: WILLIAM CARLISLE Grosvenor Gate [Thursday] 10 May 1860 3469

ORIGINAL: MOPSIK [36]

EDITORIAL COMMENT: Paper imprinted 'Grosvenor Gate'. Endorsed in another hand on the first page: '*10 May/60 Honble B Disraeli*'.

W.T. Carlisle Esqr Grosvenor Gate | May 10. 1860

Dear Sir –

The difficulties of effecting a sale of the estates in question, are, at this moment, so great, that I must request / you to decline the offer of Messrs Dunbar.

With regard to your client, the system, heretofore pursued, can continue, wh:, as respects his interests, I doubt not you will consider satisfactory, tho' I cd. have wished for the / final settlement of Mr Villiers' affairs, & as facilitating the eventual sale of the estates, that Mr Magenis would have been satisfied with receiving his interest only at present, and wd. have permitted the balance of the rents to be / applied to the general liquidation referred to. Is this impossible?

I am highly dissatisfied with Messrs Dicksons' conduct as to the arrears, & I certainly understood, that, in terminating the stewardship of Captn Fisher, we were not to be subject to commission.[1]

Yrs faithfully | *B. Disraeli*

TO: LORD DERBY Carlton Club [Saturday] 12 May 1860 3470

ORIGINAL: DBP Box 146/1

EDITORIAL COMMENT: Carlton Club paper. Endorsed by Derby on the last page: 'Disraeli B.'

Rt Honble | The Earl of Derby K.G. May 12. 1860

My dear Lord,

Sir Stafford has got the Report of the Contracts Committee on *Tuesday* – & it will, probably, be a long business – & also a very / important one. He has two heavy committees on Thursday, & a Board to attend on Saturday – wh: wd. also be rather late for Monday's debate.[1]

He proposes to come to you on Tuesday, tho' it / may be as late as four o'ck. His presence wd. not be necessary in the House of Commons that day, & he cd. remain with you as long as might be agreeable, tho' I fear yr presence in / the House of Lords may curtail your interview.[2]

He will bring all his papers – & have everything in a condensed form.

Yours sincerely, | D.

1 See **3461**&n1. See further **3520**&n2. Lady Jersey on this day (10th) wrote to D: 'I only write this line to tell you Frederick will be in Town from abt. one to 4, tomorrow, if you wish to see him.' H D/III/C/2746.

---

1 In the Lords on Monday 21 May, Derby would continue Conservative opposition to the Paper Duty Repeal Bill (see **3471**&n1), citing extensive figures to show that the loss of revenue could not be afforded at present. Sir Stafford Northcote had opened the opposition on 8 May in the Commons, moving an amendment to the same effect; the bill would be passed in the Commons but defeated in the Lords. *Hansard* CLVIII cols 920-70, 1525-48. On 7 February (as also on 12 July 1859) Northcote had been appointed one of 19 MPs to the select committee on packet and telegraph contracts (for mail transport), which had held its hearings in March. *Hansard* CLIV col 1082, CLVI col 633. Northcote was also on the miscellaneous expenses and civil service appointments committees. *MP* (7, 16, 19, 21, 26, 28 Mar, 11 May 1860).

2 On Tuesday 15 May, the Lords met only briefly, and adjourned until Monday the 21st; Derby is not recorded as having spoken. *Hansard* CLVIII cols 1263-83.

3471 TO: SARAH BRYDGES WILLYAMS Grosvenor Gate [Monday] 14 May 1860

ORIGINAL: RTC [140]

PUBLICATION HISTORY: M&B IV 321, dated 14 May 1860, the third paragraph

EDITORIAL COMMENT: Black-edged paper imprinted 'Grosvenor Gate'. There is no salutation. *Sic:* recal.

Private May 14. 1860

We are in the midst of a most brisk campaign; indeed, I never remember a session where the interest was so unflagging. On Tuesday last, I drove the enemy into their trenches, & nearly annihilated them. / The struggle is to be renewed in the House of Lords on this day week.[1]

Gladstone's reputation has collapsed, more suddenly, & completely, than anything since Jonah's gourd.[2]

Affairs abroad very critical, & great events may / be expected every day. Garibaldi's pirate expedition is a spark, that will lead to a general conflagration. Who was its promoter?[3]

In the meantime, there is no house in London, wh: can vie with Grosvenor Gate for roses! In splendor, fragrance, & profusion, we / beat the noblest mansions in the town. The succession has been so rapid, & Mrs. D. is so clever in a discovery, wh: she has made, of retaining their life, that my table is always crowned with them, & not only mine.[4]

You recal yourself to us, hourly, with sweet thoughts.

Ever yrs | D.

3472 TO: HENRY PADDON Grosvenor Gate [Tuesday] 15 May 1860

ORIGINAL: H H/LIFE

EDITORIAL COMMENT: Taken from a manuscript copy.

Copy Grosvenor | Gate | May 15. 1860

The Revd | H. Paddon[1]

Dear Sir

Your letter being directed to the House of Commons only reached me last night.

The only petition from Your town respecting Church Rates that has arrived at this

1 See **3470**&n1. On Tuesday 8 May in the debate on Northcote's hostile amendment on third reading of the Paper Duty Repeal Bill, D had stated that he now opposed a measure he had supported two years earlier because of the reduced state of the revenue, which he put down to the failure of all of Gladstone's tyrannically imposed financial projects. The ensuing division defeated the amendment by only 9 votes, 219-210, causing much cheering on both sides of the House. *Hansard* CLVIII cols 920-70 (D 957-66); *The Times* (9 May 1860).

2 See Jonah 4:6-10. Greville (VII 475-6) confirms D's assessment of the sudden collapse of Gladstone's reputation, his treaty with France and now his budget being seen as dangerous blunders by both sides of the House. See further Jenkins *Gladstone* 226-27.

3 The press of this day published the first reports of the landing in Sicily of Giuseppe Garibaldi (1807-1882), the Italian patriot. It would transpire that he had been assured of England's support by Sir James Hudson, the envoy at Turin, and had landed under the protection of two British vessels.

4 See **3466**n2. SBW on 13 May had promised the next day to forward 'the remainder' of her 'happy roses'. RTC [401Q].

1 The Reverend Thomas Henry Paddon (1807-1887), BA (Oxon) 1830, was vicar of High Wycombe 1844-69.

house is one addressed to the House of Lords, & I have forwarded it to a Peer, in order that it may be presented.

I conclude the petition to the House of Commons has been by an analogous mistake forwarded to some noble Lord.[2]

I have the honor to remain

Yours faithfully | (sd) *B. Disraeli*

TO: SARAH BRYDGES WILLYAMS — Grosvenor Gate [Thursday] 24 May 1860 — **3473**

ORIGINAL: RTC [141]

EDITORIAL COMMENT: Paper imprinted 'Grosvenor Gate'. There is no salutation. *Sic:* Tuesday night.

May 24 1860

There was quite a coup d'etat in the House of Lords on Tuesday night.[1] The Government has not recovered, & is still reeling, but, it is to be hoped, we shall keep them on their legs a little longer.

The Duke of Marlboro', who / dined here a few days ago,[2] has the finest gardens in the world, at Blenheim, & the greatest number of gardeners. He was much struck by your roses, which, at dinner, reposed, before him, in an Italian basket of alabaster. / He said, he thought he could equal the flowers, but "the leaves" he added "beat me".

I have before noticed to you the singular beauty of your rose leaves. They are quite immaculate, & / their form complete.

We go to Hughenden tomorrow, for the burst of spring, & have a Whitsun-holiday of five days[3] – very grateful in the midst of this sharp campaign.

I hope you are as flourishing as your flowers!

Ever, | D.

2 The government early in the session had addressed the perennial church-rate issue with an abolition bill that met with much opposition, especially from established-Church clergy. See VII **3296**n1 for the Conservatives' unsuccessful compromise attempt to resolve the problem in 1859; see also **3503** for D's position (that the bill threatened the survival of the critically important established Church), which he had argued at length on 8 February (second reading) and on 27 April (third reading). On the latter occasion the bill had been approved 235-226, but it would be defeated in the Lords 128-31 on 19 June; as had happened in the Commons, petitions (mostly opposing the bill) were presented in the Lords at almost every sitting, often in batches too large for reporters to list individually. *Hansard* CLVI cols 634-86 (D 672-6), CLVIII cols 259-301 (D 291-9), CLIX cols 618-65.

---

1 The Lords' sitting on Tuesday 22 May was relatively uneventful, and adjourned early. *Hansard* CLVIII cols 1587-1608. For the defeat of the government's Paper Duty Repeal Bill in the Lords on Monday night (the House adjourned right after the division at 1:45 *am* on Tuesday morning) see **3470**&nn1&2 and **3471**&n1.

2 The DS on Saturday 19 May had entertained at dinner sixteen noble guests including the Duke of Marlborough, the Duke of Rutland and the Bishop of Oxford. H acc; *MP* (21 May 1860).

3 MA recorded that the DS left for Hughenden on Friday 25 May and returned to Grosvenor Gate on Wednesday the 30th. H acc.

3474 TO: SIR WILLIAM JOLLIFFE Hughenden [Sunday] 27 May 1860

ORIGINAL: SCR DD/HY C/2165 [58]

EDITORIAL COMMENT: Paper imprinted 'Hughenden Manor'.

Rt Honble | Sir W.H. Jolliffe Bart MP May 27 1860

My dear Jolliffe,

Ld. Derby will have returned to town by Friday, & wishes you to summon a meeting of the Commoners (who previously consulted on the Reform Bill) at his house on Saturday ↑next↓ for *one* o'ck[.][1] And pray remember to add Northcote.

I think also you had / better whip strongly for a full attendance on Monday 4th. June.[2]

Yours ever, | D.

3475 TO: LORD DERBY Hughenden [Sunday] 27 May 1860

ORIGINAL: DBP Box 146/1

PUBLICATION HISTORY: M&B IV 273, dated at Hughenden, 27 May 1860, omitting the first and last sentences

EDITORIAL COMMENT: Paper imprinted 'Hughenden Manor'. Endorsed by Derby on the last page: 'Disraeli B *Ansd*'.

Rt Honble | The Earl of Derby | K.G. May 27 1860

My dear Lord,

I have written, by this post, to Jolliffe, as you desired.[1]

The front bench has long been restless – desiring many things, either dangerous, or impracticable. Pakington wants a Royal Commission to enquire into the whole subject of Reform, wh: is / madness: John Manners wants to meet the motion by "previous question", wh: can't be moved on going into Committee: Estcourt wants "something to be done", but has no conception of what it shd. be.[2] The fact is, our tactics are to watch circumstances, & not to attempt to create them. The cards will play into our hands if / we are quiet. I fully expect, however, that the Bill will come

1 Derby had written to D on the 25th and 26th outlining his movements and asking D, if he agreed, to get Jolliffe to call 'another small meeting of the H. of C. as we had before'. H B/XX/S/271-2. See also **3475**&n1.

2 The Commons on 4 June would go into committee on the government's reform bill. Jolliffe would write on 28 May that, before the current holiday, Derby had thought a meeting prior to the committee not desirable, but Jolliffe had discounted it as an after-dinner opinion. On the 29th he would send D a copy of the circular he was sending to the enclosed list of MPs (seventeen, including D and Northcote, all recent office holders) summoning them to the 2 June meeting on the reform bill. H B/XX/J/84-5. For the committee see VII **3227**&n1 and **3228**.

---

1 See **3474**&nn1&2. Derby had written on 26 May: 'the language of the Times intimates pretty plainly that it is intended to give up the Reform Bill, though it is not yet quite clear how the operation is to be performed. I presume that supply will prevent its coming on on the 4th. for which it stands at present; but we ought to be agreed as to the mode in which we should deal with it, if it is brought forward, and our "front bench" are, I hear, getting restless on the subject'.

2 These men were holding meetings during the break, with Pakington and Estcourt writing reports to D, frustrated that he was not attending. H B/XXI/E/256-7, XX/P/59.

on 4th. June – our movement on Thursday, tho' advantageous, was not sufficiently decided to prevent that.[3]

Yours sincerely, | D.

TO: [LORD HENRY BENTINCK] [London, Wednesday 6? June 1860] 3476

ORIGINAL: H B/XXI/B/376a

PUBLICATION HISTORY: Blake 423, undated extract

EDITORIAL COMMENT: *Dating:* see n1.

My astonishment exceeds my sorrow, if that be possible! I solemnly declare, that I have never had even a thought respecting yourself, except that of absolute / devotion. That ~~sentiment~~ feeling has never swerved for an instant. ~~in the course of all the various years.~~ You have too high a spirit thus to treat / a man on whom you have conferred ~~immeasurable kindnesses~~ ↑such oblig[at]ions↓ without ↑supposing you have↓ a cause.

Let me at least know on what ground I am deprived / of the friendship wh: was the pride & consol[ati]on of my life![1]

TO: LORD DERBY [London] Sunday [10 June 1860] 3477

ORIGINAL: DBP Box 146/1

PUBLICATION HISTORY: M&B IV 273-4, dated Sunday [10 June 1860], 7 o'clock, the first two paragraphs, omitting the second sentence

EDITORIAL COMMENT: Endorsed by Derby on the 4th page: 'Disraeli B.' There is no salutation. *Sic:* Macinnon.

Private Sunday | 7 *o'ck*

I have seen the Bear [Ellice]. He says, he thinks the Govt. will give up the Bill tomorrow: he hopes so. They can do it with some dignity after the late division; if / they persist, they will, probably, be put in a minority, when the withdrawal will be humiliating. The division was exactly the right thing; the Govt expected betn. 40 / & 50 majority, wh: wd. have encouraged the violent party – but a small majority indicates the only honorable course – withdrawal.

He has seen Johnny, who, he says, is low, but / he thinks, resigned. By his own account, he appears to have said to him everything most disagreeable – having ex-

3 Horsman had given notice on Thursday 24 May that, on the motion for the House to go into committee on the Reform Bill, he would move an amendment to proceed by resolution to determine the provisions of an acceptable reform bill. In the event, he did not make the motion. *The Times* (25 May 1860). See further **3477**&n1.

1 This is a draft of D's reply to a letter dated 6 June 1860 at 45 Lower Brook Street (Claridge's Hotel): 'Lord Henry Bentinck hopes that Mr Disraeli will not give himself the needless trouble of calling at Claridge's Hotel tomorrow. Ld H. will not be at home and there is no subject whatever that he has the slightest inclination to discuss with Mr Disraeli.' H B/XXI/B/376. For some background see VII **2945**&n1. Next to D's draft an almost illegible letter (H B/XXI/B/377) possibly indicates earlier correspondence between D and Lord Henry: 'Lincoln Tuesday My Dear D This Evenings Post has brought me No 3 & really Horrified me. I wd not have been so indolent in answering No 2 had I been quite sure that you were in earnest. In Truth I almost fancied you were "poking fun" at me. I do hope that you will not suffer the Maggot to bother your Brain again – & that you cant believe me to be quite so childish. Yours very Truly HB.'

plained to him, that he does not understand the question, & that if Reform is ever treated again, / it must be treated on quite different principles.

The Bear added, that we must be cautious about supporting Macinnon – because he thinks the majority against M. will be / very considerable, & that in the face of a large majority on any point, it will be difficult for the government to withdraw.

But he hopes, that Palmerston will prevent / the Debate going on by making a statement at ½ past four o'ck.[1]

Yrs sincerely, | D.

3478 TO: SIR WILLIAM MILES [London, Monday] 11 June 1860

ORIGINAL: H B/XXI/M/387b

PUBLICATION HISTORY: M&B IV 289-92, dated at House of Commons, 11 June 1860, omitting part of the last two paragraphs, but including the postscript; Blake 427, extract; Bradford 252, dated 11 June 1860, extract.

Sir William Miles Bart: | M.P. 11 June 1860

My dear Sir William,

You were speaking to me, the other night, of the state of the party, your regret at its discontented condition, & your hope, that, before you left us,[1] those, sitting behind me, might yet become my supporters. I could not, / at the moment, pursue the conversation, because our position was then so critical, that it required unceasing vigilance & I cd. not venture to be frank.

Out of those dangerous waters, we have now steered, & the course, wh: I pursued some months ago in great difficulties, has succeeded, &, I hope, saved us. I may now, therefore, / communicate to you, without reserve.

I think it is fourteen years ago, since yourself, then the Leader of the Country gentlemen, & another County member – alas! no more![2] called upon me at my private residence, & appealed to me to assist you at a moment of apparently overwhelming disaster. I, ultimately, agreed to do so, but with / great unwillingness, & only because, ultimately, I found Lord George Bentinck, with whom I had no acquaintance, had undertaken to fulfil the duties of leadership, if I, with others, wd. support

1 During the debate in committee on the reform bill on 4 June, W.A. Mackinnon on the government side had moved that reform deliberations be postponed until the results of the 1861 census were known, an idea strongly rejected by Russell. Derby on 26 May (see **3474**&n1) had told D that the motion, when it came on, would be left an open question for government supporters. Debate on the motion had opened on 7 June, when a motion to adjourn the debate was defeated 269-248, D accepting Palmerston's challenge to a division. Earle on 9 June had told D that the government expected a very large majority against Mackinnon's motion, and that the Conservatives risked losing supporters if they supported it. H B/XX/E/103. As D here predicts, on 11 June Russell would withdraw the bill and Mackinnon his motion. *Hansard* CLVIII cols 1951-2038, CLIX cols 26-144 (D 130-7), cols 225-70. R.P. Dawson would write to MA on the 11th: 'Your Husband has just told me that Lord John will withdraw the Bill in 5 minutes time, & we are to receive the announcement in solemn silence.' H D/III/C/540. William Alexander Mackinnon (1813-1903), of Acryse Park, Kent, and Belvedere, Broadstairs, after 1870 34th chief of Clan Fingon (Mackinnon), JP and DL for Kent, high sheriff 1885, JP for Middlesex and Hants, was MP (L) for Rye 1852-3, for Lymington 1857-68.

---

1 Miles, created a baronet by the Conservatives in 1859, would retire in 1865.

2 Probably George Bankes (d 1856); see IV xxxii and **1482**n2.

him; & because, from my earliest years, my sympathies had been with the landed interest of England.

I need say nothing of the years 1846 – 7 – 8. They were not inglorious / to the country party.

When the catastrophe occurred at the end of 1848, & we lost Lord George, Lord Derby, with whom I had very slight relations, wrote to me, & asked me to undertake, under certain conditions, the management of our party.[3] I declined to do so, tho' honoring duly the offer. I saw personal difficulties ahead, & the engagement on my part would / have involved the sacrifice of several thousands a year, wh: I wd. willingly, having no children, have relinquished, if I possessed the confidence of the gentlemen of England, but wh: witht. that great reward, I was not willing to give up.

After long & earnest representations, principally urged by Ld. Derby, the present Duke of Rutland, yourself & Lord Henry Bentinck, I undertook the / office of leading the somewhat ↑shattered↓ remnants of the Country party. They had divided on Ld. G. Bentincks great party motion on Irish Railways *120*.[4] This was the condition in wh: affairs were put in my hands. Before three years had passed, by a series of motions on Agricultural Burdens made by myself, they had become a / moiety of the House of Commons, while I left no stone unturned to reconstruct the Tory party by bringing back the Peelite section to our colors.

This was my unvarying effort, &, for this, I have always been prepared to make the greatest personal sacrifices. The Leadership was offered twice to Ld. Palmerston[5] & once, even so late as 1858, after the Ellenboro' disaster, to Sir James / Graham:[6] frequent offers, if not of a precise, of a flattering, nature have been made to Mr Gladstone[7] – & all ~~by~~ ↑at↓ my instance, &, generally, personally.

Nevertheless, they failed, & altho' Ld. Derby & myself were unwilling to accept office ever without this reconstruction, we were obliged, in order to save the party from political annihilation, on two occasions to accept this responsibility.

Always / in a great minority, on the last occasion, the minority was *120*.[8] It was clear that such a state of affairs must always conclude in a dissolution; it was as clear, that a dissolution could only restore Tory strength, not establish Tory power.

Of course our measures cd. not be carried, after such dissolutions, great as might be our gain. But the strength of the / party was restored. I have, however, to bear the brunt of disaster, & the measures of the Cabinet, are called my measures, & I am held as alone to blame for their production.

This from my opponents, I cd. bear, as I have had to bear much – but it is unreasonable that ~~it~~ I shd. endure it from those who ought to be my friends.

3 At the end of 1848 Derby (then Lord Stanley) had asked D to support Herries as leader; see V **1755**&n1.

4 See IV **1533**n1 for the 118 (plus two tellers) who supported Bentinck's railway motion.

5 See VI **2232**n1 and **2448**&n2.

6 See VII **3118**&n1 and **3128**&n1.

7 See VII **3128**&nn3&7 for the most recent of these offers.

8 Kebbel's May 1860 article (see **3467**n1) 345 gives the 1858 Conservative government's minority as 120; see also VII **2918**&n4 and **2928**&n5 for the 1857 election results and the difficulty in determining party strengths. Stewart *Conservative Party* 319 puts the Conservative strength after the 1857 election at 260, while F.W.S. Craig *British Parliamentary Results 1832–1885* (1977) 622 tallies the 1857 results as 264 Conservatives (including Peelites) to 390 Liberals, for a Liberal majority of 126.

The / Tory party, as an Opposition, has never stood in a more solid – I wd. say prouder & more powerful – position, than at this moment[.]

The finance of Mr Gladstone has blown up:

The House of Lords exercises a real authority in the State:

For the first time, since 1841 ↑(say 1839)↓, there has been a real Church Party in the House of Commons: /

The question of Parliamentary Reform has ceased to be a party question, & the Tories are cleared of the taint of opposition to popular franchise.

They command half the House – & stand high in the country.

So long as they were in distress, I have borne without a murmur, the neglect, the desertion, the personal insults that I have experienced: / so long ~~as~~, even, as these were confined to our own ranks, & not the scandal of the world, I would, for party sake, have been silent. But the Tories are no longer in distress – they have abundance of friends; & with respect to the privacy of their feelings towards me – they chalk the walls in the market place / with my opprobrium.

I must, therefore, now take a step, wh: I wished to have done at the meeting of Parliament, & wh: nothing but the extreme difficulties & dangers of the Party prevented my fulfilling. I must resign a Leadership, ~~to~~ which I unwillingly accepted, & to which it / is my opinion, that fourteen years of unqualified devotion have not reconciled the party.

I will not communicate this resolve in the first instance to my Colleagues, because I do not think that is a fair course to them, or to the party generally.

Your position is independent: you were originally deputed to solicit my undertaking the office: & you are / in every respect best qualified to take the steps necessary in the present conjuncture.

They shd. be taken with tact, & witht. unnecessarily exciting attention until all arrangements are completed. What I wd. suggest is, that: you shd. call together some of the principal members of the party, & arrive at yr. general result: & that when you have, pretty generally, made / your new arrangements, you shd. communicate your conclusion ↑to Lord Derby↓. I shd. wish to say nothing to him, until you have agreed upon my successor, as, otherwise, I might be involved in distressing appeals & explanations.

I will not conclude this hastily written, but well considered, communication / witht. expressing to you my sense of the undeviating kindness & unbroken support, wh: I have always had the satisfaction of experiencing from your hands, thru' long, difficu[l]t, & trying years.

Yours sincerely, | My dear Sir William, | *B. Disraeli* T.O /

I read ~~the~~ with pain, but I felt the truth of the statement, in a Liberal Journal, a day or two ago, that my leadership of the party was one of "chronic revolt, & unceasing conspiracy"[.][9]

9 An article, 'The Budget and the Reform Bill', in the April 1860 issue of the *Quarterly Review* (Vol 107, 267-87), widely known to have been written by D's colleague Lord Robert Cecil (confirmed in *Wellesley Index* I 743, item 1322), had viciously criticized D's leadership of the party. For a full discussion of the article, Russell's citing of it in his speech of 4 June to question D's leadership, the attempt by *The Times* on 6 June somewhat to offset its attack, and the degree of disaffection with D's leadership in the party indicated by it, see M&B IV 284-93 and Blake 426-7. Miles would return D's letter with his lengthy response on 16 June;

TO: HENRY EDWARDS Grosvenor Gate [Wednesday] 20 June 1860 3479

ORIGINAL: HAL [1]

EDITORIAL COMMENT: Paper imprinted 'Grosvenor Gate'.

Major Edwards | M.P. June 20 1860

My dear Major,

I shd. have liked, above all things, to have met our friends under your roof, but I am sorry to say I am engaged every Wednesday, & Saturday until / we leave town, wh:, I hope, may be towards the end of next month.[1]

I hope Mrs Edwards[2] received Mrs Disraeli's card for the 23rd – & that we may have a sunny / day.[3]

Yours sincerely, | D.

TO: SARAH BRYDGES WILLYAMS Carlton Club [Wednesday] 20 June 1860 3480

ORIGINAL: RTC [142]

PUBLICATION HISTORY: M&B IV 280-1, dated at the Carlton Club, 20 June [1860], omitting the last paragraph

EDITORIAL COMMENT: Carlton Club paper. There is no salutation. *Sic:* manouvres; Yesterday; St James'.

confidential June 20. 1860

It is a long time since I wrote, but the course of affairs has been very critical, & indeed is so intense at the present moment, that I have not been able to free myself from the absorption of public duties sufficiently to realize / private correspondence.

The withdrawal of the Reform Bill[1] was the culminating point of three months of masterly manouvres on the part of the Opposition, & has shaken the Government to the centre. They are dispirited & discredited: & have to cope with numerous difficulties to meet & / manage which requires both reputation & courage. I myself wish to maintain them for a season, but I begin to doubt the possibility of doing so.

he had discreetly consulted Walpole, Henley, Baring, Trollope, Hotham and Seymer (only the last two being told of D's letter) with 'gratifying' results. He gave examples of how the cavillers in a pinch had come to the support of the party 'like men'; nevertheless, there had been talk of D playing too much into the Radicals' hands, thereby endangering the prospect of fusion with the moderate Whigs. Miles concluded: 'I do not think you are sensitive to attacks from our Enemies: do not be too susceptible of the follies of our friends, & all will go well ... depend upon it, that by advocating well considered & moderate progress, & the necessity for the cause of religion *of an Established Church* your luke warm friends may be converted into ardent Supporters: and so through a bond of union may be established between yourself & party as may render you irresistible.' H B/XXI/M/387. MA in sending to SBW the 6 June *Times* leader on D would identify the *Quarterly Review* author as Cecil, 'angry because Dizzy did not give him office'. RTC [402Q].

1 On this day (20th) Edwards, though aware that D would probably not be disengaged, had invited him to 'a dinner party of twenty *old fashioned* TORY *MP's* on the 27th Inst. all (with perhaps one exception) political WORSHIPPERS of your own.' H B/XXI/E/41.

2 Edwards in 1838 had married Maria Churchill Coster (d 1906), eldest daughter of Thomas Coster, of Regent's Park, London.

3 On Saturday 23 June MA would give a *déjeuner* to a throng of distinguished guests; see further **3480**&n6. The half-column list of guests (including, *eg,* Landseer) in the press does not mention the Edwardses. *MP* (25 Jun 1860).

1 See **3477**n1.

Yesterday the King of the Belgians sent for me at Buckingham Palace[2] & I had a most interesting conference with him on foreign affairs. He / is the wisest Prince in Europe: natural abilities & great experience; his judgment of men & things very mature[.] He proposed, that we should in future maintain together a confidential correspondence. Tomorrow, we ~~wi~~ dine with the Queen. It is unusual to ask the Leader of Opposition to dine more than once during the season at the Palace, & I suspect this second / invitation will excite comments.[3] There was a leading article in some of the Radical Journals, a few weeks ago, on the enormity of Lord Derby having dined three times at Court since December.

Friday will be a very hard day ↑for me↓: for at twelve o'ck, the Committee of the House of Commons meets, which is to draw up / the report on the famous question of the right of the Lords to throw out the Bill for the Repeal of the Paper duty[4] – at 6 o'ck precisely, I am to take the chair for the Prince Consort, at the anniversary dinner of the "Society of Arts, Manufactures & Commerce"; & as soon as I can get away from St James' Hall, where the / dinner of four hundred of the ablest men in London takes place, I am going with Mrs. Disraeli, to a ball at the Palace.[5]

I would, for her sake, gladly escape the latter, as on the following day, Saturday, she gives a great morning fête, in honor of the Queen's review of the Volunteers in Hyde Park, & has / invited upwards of seven hundred members of the beau monde. I fear the terrible weather will foil the fête, & that we shall all be drowned[.][6]

The town abounds with royal Princes, many of whom will be her guests, but I would rather see you there.

I trust you are quite well & am

Ever yours, | D.

2 On 17 June Van de Weyer, Belgian minister in London, had sent in French the King's desire to meet D for an hour at Buckingham Palace on Monday (18th); he asked D to reply to 50 Portland Place. Later the same day, he responded to D's reply (not found): 'The King will be happy to see you tomorrow at *twelve*.' H B/XXI/V/7-8. See further **3496**.

3 The only other active politician among the distinguished guests at the Queen's dinner party on 21 June was Russell. *MP* (22 Jun 1860). For the previous dinner with the Queen this season, see **3455**&n4 and **3456**.

4 The Lords' rejection of the Paper Duty Repeal Bill (see **3473**&n1) had raised the constitutionality of their apparent encroachment on the Commons' exclusive privilege on revenue. On 25 May D had been one of twenty-one MPs appointed to a committee to ascertain each House's previous practice on bills imposing or repealing taxes. The report would be presented on 29 June, when it was tabled and ordered to be printed. *JHC* CXV (1860-1) 272, 341. See further **3481**&n2.

5 On Friday 22 June, at the 106th anniversary dinner at St James's Hall, Piccadilly, of the Society for the Encouragement of Arts, Manufactures, and Commerce, D in the chair would propose the toast to the Prince Consort, the Society's president, and to the success of the proposed 1862 international exhibition; he would focus on the important role of such societies to the education of the English artisan. D would be listed among those who that evening attended the Queen's state ball, to which 1,921 were invited. *MP* (23, 25 Jun 1860).

6 There would be a review of over 20,000 of the Queen's volunteers in Hyde Park on Saturday 23 June; reportedly it was a huge success, with 'cool-and-cloudy' weather after the feared rain showers blew over. *The Times* (25 Jun 1860). For MA's fête see **3479**n3. On 27 June MA would send SBW the *MP* report: 'We receiv'd about 350. Most of our visitors on the top of the House, which was boarded & carpeted for the occasion. The Duke of Cambridge & some of the foreign Princes were to have been here, but they had orders to be near her Majesty. I receiv'd a kind little note from H R H. [*see* **3491**&n4] after the Review...' RTC [403Q].

TO: LORD DERBY House of Commons [Friday] 29 June 1860 **3481**

ORIGINAL: DBP Box 146/1

EDITORIAL COMMENT: House of Commons paper. Endorsed by Derby upside down on the last page: 'Disraeli B. *Ansd*'.

confidential June 29 1860

R. Hble. | Earl of Derby K G.

My dear Lord,

Collier[1] has given a hostile notice on Privilege for Tuesday next.[2] I don't think in ~~with~~ any concert with / the government.

Walpole, who has had a confidential conversation with Graham, thinks we ought ↑*immediately*↓ to have a conference with you, Cairns alone included. / Walpole will come up tomorrow from Ealing, & will be at Grosvenor Gate, ¼ to one. Could you receive us at ½ past one or two? Or when, or / at all? – as in that case, I will write to Cairns, & try to get him.[3]

Yrs ever | D.

TO: LORD DERBY Carlton Club, Saturday [30 June? 1860] **3481A**

ORIGINAL: DBP Box 146/1

EDITORIAL COMMENT: Carlton Club paper. Endorsed by Derby on the last page: 'Disraeli B.' *Dating*: Although the letter has in another hand been dated 'May 12', a not impossible date (see **3470**&n1), the more likely date is 30 June 1860 (see n1).

Saturday 6 o'ck

I have just seen Cairns, who seemed a little perplexed last night, but who came up

1 Robert Porrett Collier (1817-1886), a barrister (Inner Temple) 1843, QC 1854, was MP (L) for Plymouth 1852-71, judge advocate of the fleet and counsel to the admiralty 1859-63, knighted 1863, solicitor-general 1863-6, attorney-general 1868, PC 1871, created Baron Monkswell 1885.

2 In the Commons on the afternoon of 29 June the select committee on the two Houses' handling of tax bills (see **3480**&n4) had presented its report; reviewing practice since 1628, it found a few rather inconclusive precedents for the Lords' rejection of the Paper Duty Repeal Bill. In the evening, Collier had given notice that on the following Tuesday he would move a resolution that the Lords' rejection of a Commons bill repealing a tax was a breach of constitutional usage. *The Times* (30 Jun 1860).

3 Derby had written on 27 June: 'Lord Stanhope told me last night, with much annoyance, that he had just heard from Walpole [*deputed by the select committee to make its report to the House*] himself, that he had inserted in his report three propositions for modes of preventing the Lords from again adopting their late course with respect to the Paper Duties .... [A]ll these proposals assume that the House of Lords has been guilty of an usurpation upon the privileges of the Commons, which may be technically within their powers, but against which it is the duty of the Commons to protect themselves for the future by such expedients as they can devise. This is a low, and, I think a false, view of the Constitutional question – it concedes much more than I should be inclined to do; and I am not surprised to hear that Lord John is not indisposed to acquiesce in it, and assume it to be the legitimate exposition of his principles. We all know Walpole's tendency to endeavour to smooth down difficulties by making concessions; but I am very anxious that our friends in the Committee should not carry this disposition so far as to lead them to sacrifice true Constitutional principles to a desire to produce, for the moment, apparent harmony.' H B/XX/S/274. On Monday 2 July, Palmerston would give notice of his own resolutions (tabled on 3 July) derived from the report and postpone debate to Thursday 5 July, when Derby would urge D to show strong support for Palmerston. H B/XX/S/275. In the 5 July debate, Collier would reply to Palmerston's mild resolutions by dissecting the report to argue that the Lords had assumed a new precedent-setting power over the Commons; D would speak heartily in support of Palmerston, whose resolutions would be agreed to. *Hansard* CLIX cols 1383-1507 (D 1484-99). M&B IV 279 summarizes the constitutional dispute: 'Gladstone and the Radicals advocated violent measures against the Lords; the Conservatives rallied to the Prime Minister.'

to me today, to say, that he had, since fully considered / the objections of the enemy, as to privilege &c, in all their hearings, & was convinced they were "a complete mare's nest".

The fallacy was ~~to~~ confusing annual taxation with / permanent ~~ways & mea~~ revenue.[1] I urged him to call on you, wh: he did – in vain – but will see you on Monday at your Comm[itt]ee, being himself / engaged in the Ho: of Lords.

D.

3482 TO: [MARY ANNE DISRAELI] [London, late June 1860?]

ORIGINAL: QUA 422

EDITORIAL COMMENT: Written on an envelope. *Recipient*: conjectural; see n2. *Dating*: by Bruce-Pryce's letter (see n2). There is no salutation.

Private

Our neighbours have a habit of rather too indiscriminately distributing 'fivers'. It seems charitable; & saves trouble. If they subscribed to the Mendicity Socy.,[1] they wd. know more of their correspondents. This is a practised mumper: return him his enclosure.[2]

D.

3483 TO: MARY ANNE DISRAELI [London, Tuesday] 3 July 1860

ORIGINAL: H A/I/A/306

EDITORIAL COMMENT: Endorsed by MA: '1860 July 3d – Dizzy'.

½ past five

Dear Darling

I am now going to walk down slowly to the House, where I shall expect you.[1]

Your own, | D.

1 See **3481**&n3. In his 5 July speech, D would use this distinction in his argument.

---

1 The Society for Repression of Mendicity, founded in 1818, was an association for relief of the poor. Its London office was at 13 Red Lion Square, High Holborn. *LPOD* (1856, 1865). Subscribers received tickets to give to beggars for presentation at the Society's office, where their needs were assessed. They might be given paid work or provided with meals and money for lodging. James Greenwood, 'The Seven Curses of London' (1869), Victorianlondon.org/publications.

2 On 26 June 1860, John Bruce-Pryce (1784-1872) of Duffryn, Cardiff, had written to MA asking for a donation to a clergy widows and orphans fund and enclosing the fund's last statement. He cited a list of donors, such as Lady Bute and Lady Jersey, whose gifts ranged from 1 to 5 guineas. MA docketed his letter: 'Mr Bruce Price not answered.' H D/III/D/482. Bruce-Pryce was in fact a JP and DL and father of the future Baron Aberdare.

---

1 The House would begin its 3 July evening sitting at 6 o'clock, during which Russell, in Palmerston's absence, would respond to D's query that the resolutions promised the previous evening would be tabled later that evening for discussion on Thursday. The House would be counted out at 8:10 *pm. The Times* (4 July 1860).

TO: [N.M. ROTHSCHILD & SONS] Grosvenor Gate [Thursday] 12 July 1860 3484

ORIGINAL: ROTH RAL 000/848
EDITORIAL COMMENT: Calculations (in another hand?) on the verso:

'7.6
3.9
11.3'

Grosvenor Gate | London 12 July 60
£75

Will you have the kindness to credit Mr Vance of Bilbao?[1]
D.

TO: MARY ANNE DISRAELI [House of Commons, Monday 16 July 1860] 3485

ORIGINAL: H A/I/A/307
PUBLICATION HISTORY: M&B IV 281, dated 16 July 1860
EDITORIAL COMMENT: Endorsed by MA: '1860 July 16th 16th [*sic*] Dizzy from the House of Commons'.

8 o'ck

My dearest

No Income Tax.[1] I cd. not, myself, have brought forward a more Conservative Budget; tho' I would / sooner have cut off my right hand, than have done so under the same circumstances.

Gladstone looked like a beaten hound, & ate no ordinary quantity / of dirt.[2]

Bright has not only to pay ~~an income~~ a paper Tax, but it is to be applied to a China War![3] What a combination of injuries / & insults.

Yours | D.[4]

1 *Ie,* Francis Villiers.

1 Gladstone on 16 July presented his plan to raise £3.8 million more than the £2.5 million already voted for the China war (see **3441**&n8); there would be no increase in income tax, but continued paper duties, an increased tax on spirits, and spending of the surplus in the exchequer. *Hansard* CLIX cols 1963-90.

2 Gladstone received severe criticism, first from Roebuck for supporting an immoral war in China, and, after his financial statement, by Lord Fermoy for using the paper duties, which, Fermoy contended, acquiesced in the Lords' usurpation of Commons' privileges. *Hansard* CLIX cols 1948-51, 1982-3.

3 Bright, who had supported Gladstone's February budget and the commercial treaty with France, was one of the more vociferous critics of the paper duties and of the China war.

4 On this day (16 July) D appeared as a prosecution witness in a charge of libel brought by Sir James Fergusson, 6th Bart, against David Wemyss Jobson, who had accused Fergusson's family of murder and stealing his inheritance. When D testified that Jobson had sent him verses accusing Sir James of cowardice in the Crimea, Jobson challenged his testimony as that of a Jew whose oath was invalid. He would do so again on trial on 14 August, when D further testified that he had asked for a police watch on Jobson because he constantly haunted the House of Commons. On 14 September 1862 Jobson would write to the *Daily Telegraph* accusing D of perjury, and on 3 November would try to have him arrested for it. On 24 November D would ask (letter not found) Sir Richard Mayne, first police commissioner, to have Jobson watched, to which Mayne would agree on the 27th, and send a report of the surveillance on 14 February 1863. H B/XXI/M/315-17a; *The Times* (29 Mar, 10, 17, 18, 24, 28 Jul, 15, 17 Aug 1860, 4 Nov 1862).

3486 TO: SARAH BRYDGES WILLYAMS

Grosvenor Gate
[Monday] 23 July 1860

ORIGINAL: RTC [143]

PUBLICATION HISTORY: M&B IV 281-2, dated at Grosvenor Gate, 23 July [1860], omitting the second and part of the last paragraph

EDITORIAL COMMENT: Paper imprinted 'Grosvenor Gate'. There is no salutation. *Sic:* last night.

July 23 1860

An interesting, & exhausting, Session is drawing to a close. Until the last ten days, the existence of the Government, in its integrity, has been in daily danger – so it beat fox-hunting. The hours very late, sometimes four o'ck: in the morning. I have borne it well, as I have contrived to sleep my hours all the same, & with a due quantum / of sleep, health & vigor seem to me a matter of course. But rising thus at noon, & being obliged to be in your place in the House at four o'ck, your day is necessarily very brief, & all correspondence, & general business, fall into terrible arrear.

With endless rain, Hyde Park a swamp, & the Serpentine more boisterous than Torbay, one can scarcely sigh for the bowers of Hughenden, & yet I am getting weary, / & should like to see my home in summer – but alas! a summer without a sun. This year, London was visited by a *Parsee* millionaire from Calcutta, whom the Queen has made an English Baronet – Sir Cursetjee Jejeebhoy![1] He wears the native dress, tho' he speaks our language with fluency. Descended from the ancient Persians, he is a disciple of Zoroaster & worships the Sun! I envied him his religion.

It has been a very gay & / brilliant social season; at least Mrs. Disraeli tells me so, for I never go anywhere except Wednesdays & Saturdays; with rare exceptions. I went, however, to two fêtes on Thursday & Friday last, which amused me. The first was at the Russian ambassadors,[2] at Chesham House, & was really like a festival in a play, or a masquerade. There were a dozen servants in scarlet liveries, who never left the Entrance Hall, only bowing to those who arrived, & ushering you to one of the finest & most fantastical staircases / in London, reaching to the roof of the house, & full of painted & gilded galleries. All the other attendants, who swarmed, were in court dresses & wore swords.

The other entertainment, which amused me, was ~~given~~ a ball, given by the Duchess of Wellington, at Apsley House. I had never been there since the death of the famous old Duke. This magnificent mansion has been entirely re-decorated, & with / consummate taste & splendor. The gallery, where he used to give his Waterloo banquets, now hung with ruby silk & covered with rare pictures the spoils of Spain & Portugal, is one of the most effective rooms in this city. The banquetting room, hung with the full-length portraits of the sovereigns & notabilities at the Congress of Vienna, most interesting at this moment, when the past has really become history, / & the famous settlement of 1815 is disturbed, & perhaps about to be superseded.

1 D has conflated father and son; Sir Jamsetjee Jejeebhoy (1783-1859), a wealthy Parsee Bombay merchant and philanthropist, had been created a knight bachelor in 1842 and a U.K. baronet in 1857. On 14 April 1859 he had been succeeded by his eldest son, Sir Jamsetjee Jejeebhoy (1811-1877), 2nd Bt, who changed his name from Cursetjee Jejeebhoy; on 1 May 1860 an act of legislative council of India had ordained that future holders of the baronetcy would also perpetuate the first holder's name. The 2nd Bt, JP for Bombay, FRS, fellow of Bombay University 1862, continued his father's charity.

2 The ambassador was Baron von Brunnow.

I closed my season last night by making my bow to the wife of my rival, Lady Palmerston, whose crowded saloons at Cambridge House were fuller even than usual, for she had invited all the Deputies of the Statistical Congress,[3] a body of men, who, for their hideousness, the ladies declare were never equalled: I confess myself / to a strange gathering of men with bald heads, & all wearing spectacles. ~~Your~~ You associate these traits often with learning & profundity, but when one sees 100 bald heads & 100 pairs of spectacles, the illusion, or the effect, is impaired.

I hope you are quite well. Summer has set in, as Horace Walpole says, with its usual severity.[4] Lady Ebury said to me the other night, that she lived only for climate & ~~her~~ ↑the↓ affections. (Her children happen to be scamps, & I sho[ul]d think the skies hardly made up for them.)[5]

Adieu! Adieu! | D.

TO: THOMSON HANKEY Grosvenor Gate [Sunday] 29 July 1860 3487

ORIGINAL: H A/V/G/138

EDITORIAL COMMENT: Paper imprinted 'Grosvenor Gate'.

Private & C July 29 1860

Thomson Hankey Esq | M.P.

My dear Hankey,

I consented, at the beginning of this year, to become a trustee for *two* sums in the funds, held in trust for Sarah Brydges Willyams.

It was an old trust, & my colleagues were Stephen Wilson, Edward Wilson, &, I think, a gentleman named Oldham.[1] I only knew Mr. S. Wilson, & entirely trusted to him to fulfil the duties of our office, / wh: he had discharged for many years. Unfortunately, a very few weeks after he had called at Grosvenor Gate to see me on the matter, he died;[2] &, tho' I have signed a paper since, accepting the trust, I am really without any information of the matter, & I do not wish to make any enquiry of those interested. I wish to ascertain, whether my name has been introduced into the trust according to my acceptance of it; who are my fellow trustees; & what are the precise sums confided / to us.

I should like to know also, what sums are in the name of Sarah Brydges Willyams alone, which are not in trust, as I was informed there were several such.[3]

3 The International Statistical Congress had concluded on Saturday 21 July; many of the delegates had attended Lady Palmerston's assembly that evening at Cambridge House. *MP* (23 Jul 1860). On 24 July, Prince Albert's secretary, Charles Grey, would send D a copy of the Prince's opening address to the congress. H A/IV/N/45.

4 In a 9 May 1826 letter to Vincent Novello, Lamb attributes this observation to Coleridge. Alfred Ainger ed *Letters of Charles Lamb* (1888) II.

5 Lady Ebury had seven children, at this time aged 12 to 28.

---

1 An undated list apparently of SBW's intended bequests designates £300 for both 'Ed. Wilson' and 'Jos: Oldham' and £500 for 'Step: Wilson'. The first was probably Edward Wilson, a director of the General Life and Fire Assurance Co whose bankers were Messrs Hankey. RTC [489Q]; *LPOD* (1856). See also n3. For D's expectations from SBW, see VI **2493**&n1 and, in this volume, **3887**&n1.

2 See VII **3426**&n1 and, in this volume, **3438**&n5.

3 Hankey on 31 July would reply: 'No account in any of the Funds in the joint names of Stephen Wilson, Edward Wilson, – Oldham & Benjn Disraeli[.] In the name of Sarah Bridges [*sic*] Willyams ... £4406.1.9

Your invariable kindness to me must be my excuse, emboldened by your previous permission, for thus troubling you.

Yours very sincerely, | D.

3488 TO: WILLIAM TRUSS Grosvenor Gate [Sunday] 29 July 1860

ORIGINAL: MOPSIK [189]

EDITORIAL COMMENT: Paper imprinted 'Grosvenor Gate'.

The | Rev. W.N. Truss | M.A.[1] July 29 1860

Dear Sir,

I thank you, very much, for your great consideration & courtesy in forwarding me a copy of the old pamphlet – "The history of the Minority".[2] / The instance, to wh: you call my attention, is appropriate to these times, & I read the book, after an interval of many years, with renewed interest.

Believe / me, | dear Sir, | Your obliged & faithful | Servant, | *B. Disraeli*

3489 TO: SIR HENRY STRACEY [London, Sunday 29 July 1860?]

ORIGINAL: PS 741

PUBLICATION HISTORY: Christie's catalogue (4 Nov 1981) item 44, one of 'a series of twenty-six A.LS.S. (*some initialled*), to Sir Henry Stracey'

EDITORIAL COMMENT: *Dating:* conjectural; see n1.

[trading political gossip with a Conservative Party stalwart ... with whom Disraeli communes on opposition legislation such as the introduction of paper duty in 1860] that parliamentary supporter, whose friendship & fidelity never failed[1]

Consols[;] £500 - Bank Stock[;] £1000 - New 3PCts – ... in this acct Power for Divds to Edward Wilson'. H A/V/G/138a. On 9 November Lovell would write to D: 'I am progressing satisfactorily in the matter of the Trusteeship. The Sums of £5500 New £3 pr Cts & £3500 reduced are quite correct & are held under the will of Mr Ford. The £10,500, or £10000 (I rather think the latter sum is the right one) is held under the Settlement made in *1794* on Mrs Brydges Willyams's marriage. I have copies of the appointments of Mr Stephen Wilson & Mr Edward Wilson as Trustees in 1849, of Mr Oldham Junr also in 1849, and of yourself. In reply to a Letter received this morning from Messrs Fox & Co I have requested them to prepare an appointment under the *Settlement* immediately.' H A/V/G/139.

1 William Nicholas Truss (1834-1921) MA (Cambridge 1856), ordained deacon 1857, priest 1858; curate of Paulton, Somerset, 1857-8, of Holy Trinity, Forest of Dean, Gloucs, 1858-9, of Guilsborough, Northants, 1859-64, of Donington, Salop, 1864-9; chaplain of H.M. Prison, Knutsford, 1869-1907. No letter from him to D has been found.

2 John Almon *The History of the late Minority, exhibiting the conduct, principles, and views of that party during the years 1762, 1763, 1764, and 1765* (1765, pp x, 9-332 [*sic*]).

1 This catalogue extract warrants inclusion here as a means of noting the substantial correspondence D exchanged with Sir Henry Stracey; see ph. There are in H two dozen letters from Stracey to D 1860-74 (including a request for a barony), to any of which this snippet may be part of D's response. The first, dated 28 July 1860 at the Carlton Club, explains that Taylor (the whip) has asked Major Edwards to organize some of their friends to write to 90 'absentees' to urge their attendance on 6 August (when the paper-duties issue would come to a division); on behalf of the group he asks D to approve this plan and 'to condense [the accompanying description of the intention of Govermt] so that it may be clearly understood by all ... to whom we write so that they may know the object for which we invite their presence'. He says D's name will not be used, and what they write will be confirmed by Jolliffe's circulars. H B/XXI/S/597. Sir Henry Stracey (1802-1885), 5th Bt, JP and DL for Norfolk, was Conservative MP for Norfolk East 1855-7, for Great Yarmouth (Norfolk) 1859-65, for Norwich 1868-70.

TO: HENRY PADWICK Grosvenor Gate [Tuesday] 7 August 1860 3490

ORIGINAL: LCC LC.1 Item 5

EDITORIAL COMMENT: Paper imprinted 'Grosvenor Gate'.

Private Augt 7 1860

H. Padwick Esqr

My dear Sir,

Read the enclosed. I must give a definitive reply. Was I right in understanding from you, that I have no power of sale?[1]

I am preparing to leave town.[2] / Is the other business advancing?[3] Perhaps, I may see you on Thursday? as, I hear, you will be absent tomorrow.

Yrs very flly | D.

TO: SARAH BRYDGES WILLYAMS Grosvenor Gate [Saturday] 11 August 1860 3491

ORIGINAL: RTC [144]

EDITORIAL COMMENT: Paper imprinted 'Grosvenor Gate'. There is no salutation.

Augt 11 1860

When I wrote to you last, I thought the Session was on the point of expiring, & that, by this time, we should have been at Hughenden.

But the campaign broke out again in increased force, / & we have even had a great party struggle. I am not at all sorry, myself, that it ended by Ld Palmerston remaining in, for I have no wish, at this moment, to see a change of government – but it was a very close fight, & had not some of the Tories / voted for him, he would have been beaten.[1]

I am very tired, but very well – tho' I feel, rather in mind than body, this sunless year!

You I hope are as well as ever: we must soon be thinking of again meeting!

1 The 'enclosed' has not been found, but was presumably an offer on Francis Villiers's Ceylon estates; see **3469** and **3520**&n2.

2 The DS would not leave for Hughenden until 16 August (see **3491** for the cause of the delay). H acc.

3 Possibly D's own financial matters; see VII **2895**&n1.

1 The latest test of strength for which there had been much preparation (see **3489**n1) had occurred on 6 August, when Gladstone introduced two resolutions (one for France and one for other countries) to reduce the duties on foreign paper to the level on domestic, arguing that the first at least was required by the commercial treaty with France. Christopher Puller then moved an amendment to postpone consideration of the first resolution. D supported Puller's amendment, citing the precedent of France's delays in implementing the treaty with respect to other commodities. At 1:30 *am*, Puller's resolution had been defeated 266-233, and both resolutions agreed to. *Hansard* CLX cols 698-814 (D 795-804, 813). *MP* on 8 August had suggested that the Conservatives were blaming the failure of their concerted attempt to regain office on D's 'indifferent generalship'. Derby, writing to D on the 13th, would blame not the Tory but the Liberal defectors: 'I hear you have left Town, not a little disgusted at the result of last Monday's Division ... It is however satisfactory that if we were defeated on Monday, it was from no defection of our own people, nor even any miscalculation on the part of our Whips – but a gross violation of pledges on the part of the so-called Liberals. I send you a ... list, from which you will see the numbers of broken promises. Had only a fair proportion of them been kept, the Government must have been in a minority.' H B/XX/S/276. See further **3496**&n3.

Lady Brownlow has been very ill this season in London.[2]

I / often ~~seer~~ ↑see↓ your new Devonshire Baronet, *Sir* Lawrence Palk, who wants us to pay him a visit this year at Haldon, but all the time we can spare to Devon, must be given to you.[3]

As you like an interesting autograph now & then, I send you a letter of H.R. Highness the Duke of Cambridge[4] – for yr collection.

Yrs ever, | D.

3492 TO: SARAH BRYDGES WILLYAMS Grosvenor Gate [Wednesday] 15 August 1860

ORIGINAL: RTC [145]

EDITORIAL COMMENT: Paper imprinted 'Grosvenor Gate'. There is no salutation.

Augt 15 1860

I sent you three brace of grouse yesterday – the first of the season, killed by one of my warm supporters, Major Edwards, M.P. for Beverley.[1] / They were in fine condition, & I hope ~~yo~~ found you in the same.

Tomorrow, after seven months of great labor & excitement, we shall reach the / tranquil towers of Hughenden.

Foreign affairs look most serious, & if Garibaldi attack ↑Venetia↓, I don't see how a general war can be long avoided.[2] We / shall, however, find peace in Bucks, & I hope, in the course of the autumn, by the blue waters of Torbay.

Ever yours, | D.

3493 TO: JOHN WALCOT Grosvenor Gate [Wednesday] 15 August 1860

ORIGINAL: MOPSIK [68]

EDITORIAL COMMENT: Paper imprinted 'Grosvenor Gate'. *Sic:* today; beleive.

V. Adml Walcot | M.P. Aug 15 1860

My dear Admiral,

I must have the pleasure of thanking you for your magnificent haunch before I leave town, wh: I do today. It / was very kind, indeed, of you to remember us.

Affairs on the Continent seem very serious, & if Garibaldi attack Venetia, it will be difficult to prevent a general war.

2 Lady Brownlow would write to MA on 29 August, just before leaving London although still very weak, 'to thank you both for all your amiable enquiries after me during my tedious illness. For five weeks I never left my room'. H D/III/C/163.

3 Sir Lawrence Palk, MP (C) for S Devonshire, had succeeded as 4th baronet on 15 May; on 14 September he would again invite the DS to visit at Haldon, in mid-October. H B/XXI/P/43. The DS would not get to Haldon until 27 December and to Torquay until 31 December. H acc.

4 See **3480**n6. SBW on 15 August would thank D for the 'valuable autograph'. RTC [405Q].

---

1 For the warmth of his support see, for example, **3489**&n1.

2 Garibaldi at this point was in Sicily marshalling his forces. D is echoing a report from Paris published in *The Times* on this day (15th) about the probable Austrian response should Garibaldi move against Austrian possessions, *ie* Venetia.

Pray, / make my compliments acceptable [to] Mrs. Walcot & your daughter,[1] & beleive me, always,

My dear Admiral, | Very sincerely yours | *B. Disraeli*

TO: WILLIAM FERRAND Grosvenor Gate [Thursday] 16 August 1860 **3494**

ORIGINAL: PS 424

PUBLICATION HISTORY: J.T. Ward 'Correspondence between Disraeli and W.B. Ferrand' in *Disraeli Newsletter* 2,1 (Spring 1977) 11-21

Grosvenor Gate | Augt. 16. 1860.

My dear Ferrand,

A hasty line to thank you for your kind remembrance of us – your birds will be our companions, today, to Hughenden, where we get at last.

I trust your sport, this year, may turn out much better than was anticipated.[1]

What of the Harvest? Foreign affairs very critical. I hope you have good news from Paris.[2]

Yours sincerely, | D.

TO: SARAH BRYDGES WILLYAMS Hughenden [Monday] 20 August 1860 **3495**

ORIGINAL: RTC [146]

EDITORIAL COMMENT: Paper imprinted 'Hughenden Manor'. There is no salutation.

Augt 20 1860

I have sent you five birds to day, being half a basket received from Lord Powis, & which I think you will find young, fresh, & tender – worthy of your own eating. My friends are very kind, & / almost every day has brought some spoil, but, I fear, from all I hear, that it is only a transient burst, & that the wind & rain, this year, have played havoc with the grouse. We can hardly expect the continued / arrivals of the last golden autumn.

Here, everything is damp & dripping, notwithstanding our high situation & dry soil. My tenants have not, unlike their neighbours, suffered from / the wind & water-spouts. Their crops are magnificent, but, alas! quite green.

Yours ever, | D.

1 Walcot (for whom see VII **3214**&n1), of Winkton, Hants, in 1819 had married Charlotte Anne Nelley (1796-1863), daughter of Col John Nelley; the Walcots had two surviving daughters, Agatha and Constance. No correspondence relevant to this letter has been found.

---

1 The exceptionally cold and wet summer of 1860 (there was snow in Yorkshire on 28 July) caused continuing concern. As late as 24 August letters to *The Times* suggested postponing the opening of the partridge shooting season from 1 September to 22 September because no crops were ready for harvest and the game birds were very small. *The Times* (6, 24 Aug 1860).

2 On 5 April, Ferrand had mentioned that he and Mrs Ferrand were going to Paris so that she could consult French doctors; possibly this consultation was continuing. H B/XXI/F/134.

3496 TO: [KING LEOPOLD] [Hughenden, Thursday] 23 August 1860

ORIGINAL: H B/II/54

PUBLICATION HISTORY: M&B IV 282-3, dated 23 August 1860, to the King of the Belgians

EDITORIAL COMMENT: A draft in D's hand; deletions have been indicated as much as possible, but insertions in this instance have not been identified. For a clear version, see PH. *Dating:* by the archivist's docket on the first page: '23 Augt. 1860'.

1. Sir, as the Session

As the Sess: of Parlt. is about to close[1] it may be convenient to place before Yr Majesty its results so far as ~~the~~ it has influenced the pos[iti]on of the two great parties.

In the audience wh: yr Majesty was graciously pleased to grant to me ~~in during yr visit to our Court will not render it necessary for me to weary Yr Majesty's att[enti]on to~~ in the month of June,[2] I ~~provided called yr Majestys~~ indicated to yr Majesty ~~how the consolid[ati]on of the Conservative party during this year had been mainly accomplished~~ the three causes wh: had mainly contributed to the consolid[ati]on of the Cons. party [*illegible insertion deleted*] during this year:

1st. ~~By~~ The withdrawal of ~~the~~ by the Govt of their Reform Bill

2ndly. ~~By~~ the successful assertion of the authority of the H of Lords ~~in the question of the Paper duty~~

3rdly. [*start of block deletion:*] ~~By~~ the first time, since 1840, of an organised Church party in the H of C, & the clergy [*sign marking the following deleted passage:*] throughout the country again generally acting with the Conservatives ~~Party~~ [*end of block deletion*]. The appearance of a Ch: party in the House of C for the first time since 1840, & the fact of the Clergy throughout &c. vide [*sign as above indicating where the above passage is to be inserted.*] /

~~Later in the Sess:~~ Later in the Session [*original start of the page:*] The discontent with the French Treaty, & probably a jealousy of Mr Glad[ston]e wh: a section of the Whig Party wished publickly to express rendered it expedient that a decided opposition shd be given to the repeal of the Duty on For: paper. This struggle elicited another important ~~result~~ feature in the relative state of parties: vizt. the ~~en entire~~ complete alienation of the Roman Catholic party ~~in England~~ from the present Government ~~occasioned~~ avowedly caused by their Italian policy. On that occasion, while ~~all the~~ many Independent Roman Cath: Irish members voted with the Conservatives as has been ~~for some time their wont~~ their custom of late: the Whig R.C. members for the first time evinced their disappro. of the Ministry, rose & in a body left the House, including among many others, the leading names of Lord Ed. Howard, Mr More O'Ferrall, Mr Monsell & Sir Jno. Acton.[3]

1 Parliament would be prorogued on 28 August; D had left London on 16 August.

2 See **3480**&n2.

3 See **3489**n1 and **3491**&n1. None of these names appears in the 6 August division list. Lord Edward Howard (1818-1883), younger brother of 17th Duke of Norfolk, vice-chamberlain to the Queen 1846-52, PC 1846, deputy earl marshal of England 1861, was MP (L) for Horsham 1848-52, for Arundel 1852-68, created Baron Howard of Glossop 1869. Richard More O'Ferrall (1797-1880), of Ballyna, co Kildare, son-in-law of 3rd Viscount Southwell, JP and DL, a lord of the treasury 1835-9, secretary to the admiralty 1839-40, secretary to the treasury 1841, governor of Malta 1847-51, PC 1847, was MP (L) for Kildare 1830-47, 1859-65, for Longford 1851-2. William Monsell (1812-1894), of Tervoe, co Limerick, brother-in-law of 3rd Earl of Dunraven, JP and DL (later LL), high sheriff 1835, clerk of the ordnance 1853-7, PC 1855, president of the

Had not the very Whig Section wh: had originated the ~~motion agst the Governmt~~ resistance agst. the repeal of the For: duty on paper wheeled round ~~during the last~~ in this emergency & supported ~~them~~ the Govt, ~~the Govt they~~ Ld P wd have been in a minority, wh:, ~~had it led to an~~ [*illegible deleted word*] I was far from desiring [*phrase changed from* was not to be desired] & had never contemplated. /

Yr. Majesty will, therefore, perceive, that the course of Italian politics may have a most important influence upon ~~affairs~~ [*marked* stet] ~~the dispos[iti]on of power~~ in this country.

What that course may be, I will not ~~proceed to spe~~ presume to speculate on ~~while,~~ when addressing so wise & well informed a Prince as yr Majesty. I shd. rather be grateful were I to receive on this head an intimation [*word order originally* an intimation on this head] of Yr Majestys views. But assuming I was right in my ~~views~~ observ[ati]ons expressed more than two years ago in Parlt ~~in answer to Ld J. Russell~~ that Ld. J.R. was counting witht. his host in supposing that ~~the Liberal psrty party in Italy wd. be~~ Italian Lib: wd be content merely to take the mild form of Eng: Whiggery, & that *he* must be prepared to encounter the long matured machinations of the secret societies in whose existence Ld John then wd never believe,[4] events may / occur wh: may render war & even a general war a necessity for L.N. ~~In that case, if there is to~~ The English will enter into a war with France with reluctance, but once embarked in it they will never cease ~~when they have begun~~, until their entire object is attained. *If there is to be that war, it is of importance that Ld P. shd. begin it.*

I have the honor &c.[5]

TO: RALPH DISRAELI Hughenden [Saturday] 25 August 1860 **3497**

ORIGINAL: BL ADD MS 59887 ff 78-9

COVER: R. Disraeli Esqr | 73 Gloucester Place | Hyde Park | London [*imprinted on verso:*] Hughenden Manor

POSTMARK: [*recto:*] penny postage stamp postmarked (in double circle): 3 [*illegible*]; [*verso:*] in circular form: London | 8C | AU29 | 60 | W.

EDITORIAL COMMENT: Although the cover is with this letter in BL, it would seem from its postmarks to be the cover for D's (unfound) letter in response to RD's of the 27th (n1).

R. Disraeli Esqr Hughenden | Augt 25. 1860

My dear Ralph,

I want you to execute a little piece of business for me, but I won't bore you about

board of health 1857, vice-president of the board of trade and paymaster-general 1866, under-secretary for the colonies 1868-70, postmaster-general 1871-3, was MP (L) for co Limerick 1847-74, created Baron Emly 1874. The historian Sir John Emerich Edward Dalberg-Acton (1834-1902), 8th Bt, of Aldenham, Salop, stepson of 2nd Earl Granville, JP and DL, FSA (1876), DCL (Oxford 1887), LLD (Cambridge 1888), regius professor of modern history at Cambridge 1895, KCVO (1897), was MP (L) for Carlow 1859-65, for Bridgnorth 1865, created Baron Acton 1869. Greville (VII 481) writes of the 6 August debate: 'As late as eleven that evening ... the division seemed very doubtful. The Irishmen held off, indignant at Palmerston's having mentioned with approval the landing of Garibaldi on the mainland. This was held to be an insult to the Pope, so More O'Farrell [*sic*], Monsell, Sir J. Acton, and eight or ten more would not vote at all.'

4 See VI **2857**&n2 for D's 14 July 1856 speech on Italy. See further **3501**&n3.

5 For the King's response, see **3537**n1.

it, until I / am sure you have not left town. Let me have a line, by return if you can, saying whether you are still in London[.][1]

Ever yrs, | D.

3498 TO: SARAH BRYDGES WILLYAMS Hughenden [Friday] 7 September 1860

ORIGINAL: RTC [147]

EDITORIAL COMMENT: There is no salutation.

Hughenden Septr 7. 60

Here we live in profound solitude – not even seeing a parson, except on Sundays. In this district, & especially on this estate, the harvest will be magnificent, & the fields are full of life. Being a light dry soil, it can stand any quantity of rain, provided it has some sun at the right time; for / the in gathering.

On Wednesday ↑next↓, Mrs. Disraeli gives a rural fête to her school children, eighty in number, & invites all her neighbouring friends to dance, with them, on the turf, & feast in the park ↑under the trees↓.[1] I wish you were here.

The political world is very interesting. The Italian Revolution is only commencing, & / the future is most obscure. It is such an imbroglio, not the least confusing element the presence of the French garrison at Rome, wh: will have to act, probably, against the Regenerators.[2] ~~WH~~ Whether the French succeed or fail, the position of the French Emperor will be equally perilous.

1 RD would reply on Monday the 27th from London, to which he had just returned and had hoped to leave immediately: 'Your mysterious note has a little bothered me as I am quite unprepared to stay in London & I want to get to the Hombourg waters as soon as possible. I shall stay to see the post on Wednesday but the Ides of Sepr. are close at hand.' RD's next letter is dated 18 October 1860 at Gloucester Place: 'My dear Brother[,] It was always my wish to come to Hughenden before the end of the vacation, but a sad & terrible shock greeted my arrival in London. I tell it to you for I am sure my dear Mary Anne & yourself will sympathise with me in my great & sudden affliction. On my arrival in London I hastened to where I ever met, & now for many years, a fond & cheering welcome. The first thing I saw was that all the blinds were down. I rushed by the scared & astonished servant who could not answer me. All things so familiar to me remained in her room as I had left them six weeks ago. I went on & a funeral pall seemed to wave a lasting farewell to all our happiness. Oh it was terrible. I had only heard from her scarcely a week before apparently well & happy. I came to settle when we were to spend a week at the seaside. On Tuesday in the pouring rain I followed her to her last home. This sad story will now explain my apparent carelessness in other things. She was so genuine, so thorough, whatever annoyances I might have were always forgotten or softened when with her. Sometimes I may have felt in a worldly view that there was something wrong; but never when with her. Altho no explanation took place with our darling Sa, I am sure she was well aware of it. I felt there could be no jealousy, & now all are gone. I never felt so sad so utterly alone. I am obliged to write this, it is so cruel to suffer so & suffer in silence and secrecy. I cannot help telling you & Mary Anne my great grief, I could not come to you without. I understand James arrived in London yesterday. I am now going to enquire after him & will not close this till I hear of him. If he is tolerable I will try to come to you on Saturday for tho' incog in London I have several things I must attend to. ... P.S. James is better. He seems to have had the gout in the stomach & had to send off to Worcester in the middle of the night for an additional Doctor. To day is more rainy than ever. He was in his bedroom for more than a week.' H A/I/E/72-3. For a possible clue to the 'business' mentioned, see **3506**&n1 and **3513**&n1. For RD's marriage in 1861, see **3609**n7.

---

1 See **3499**.

2 The French garrison in Rome, according to press reports, was being increased by 3,500 men the better to protect the city and the person of the Pope against the nationalists whom Napoleon otherwise supported and did not want to fight. The term 'regeneration of Italy' occurs in some reports, from which

Not a grouse has reached / us – & I learn, with sincere regret, that my old & faithful friend & supporter, the Duke of Richmond is dying![3]

This is a very dull note, but it comes from a hermit, &, I thought, you would not dislike me saying "How d'ye do?"[4]

Yours ever, | D.

TO: SARAH BRYDGES WILLYAMS Hughenden [Sunday] 16 September 1860 3499

ORIGINAL: RTC [148]

PUBLICATION HISTORY: M&B IV 321, dated 16 September 1860, the last paragraph; Blake 416, extract dated 16 September 1860

EDITORIAL COMMENT: There is no salutation.

Hughenden – Septr 16 1860

Our rural fête↑, on Wednesday,↓ was very successful – the weather was divine; balmy & golden; the first summer day, & the last!

There were 100 school children, as many farmers & peasants with their wives; & all the county families for ten miles round[1] – Sir George & Lady Dashwood;[2] Lady Frankland Russell; Colonel & Mrs. Fane;[3] Sir Anthony & Lady Rothschild & a great assemblage of squires & / clergymen. Lord Tredegar, who never forgets, that I made him a peer,[4] sent me a buck. They feasted in the open air, & danced until sunset, amid trees that were planted in the reign of Queen Anne, & when Lord Bolingbroke was Secretary of State.[5]

This is the only adventure of our lives of entire solitude. As I see no one, I will give you an account of some old acquaintances of yours, who though not human, are beings, perhaps, more charming. And first of all, do you remember the Microfolia Rose which you sent / to Hughenden?[6] That has become a bush five foot high, & is, at this moment, covered with thirty or forty beautiful flowers – but it has sent out

D may have coined the term 'Regenerators'. *The Times* (1, 3, 5 Sept 1860). It was Mazzini's concept that nationalism in Italy and Europe would be awakened by a religious regeneration in Italy. Frank J. Coppa *The Origins of the Italian Wars of Independence* (1992) 174. The troops would remain in Rome until a treaty of 1864 stipulated the terms for their withdrawal within two years.

3 The Duke of Richmond would live only until 21 October; Lord Henry Lennox on 2 and 20 September sent D reports of his father's illness, and on 28 October would thank D for his 'most kind letter [*not found*] ... [and] the assurance of your friendship'. H B/XX/LX/138-40.

4 See VII **3143**&n1 for D's previous use of Mr Weston's greeting with SBW, who on 9 September would write of her delight in anticipating the DS' visit. RTC [406Q].

---

1 MA recorded the county families attending as totalling '38 with ourselves & 9 children'. H acc.

2 Lady Dashwood, née Elizabeth Broadhead (1801-1889), and her cousin Sir George Henry Dashwood, Bt, of West Wycombe, MP, had married in 1823.

3 John William Fane (1804-1875), of Wormsley, Oxon, JP and DL, Lieut-Col Oxfordshire Militia, high sheriff 1854, in 1856 had married fourthly Victoria Temple (d 1912), daughter of Sir William Temple KCB; Col Fane, whose late third wife was Lady Dashwood's sister Charlotte, would be MP (C) for Oxfordshire 1862-8. Mrs Fane in 1880 would marry secondly Lieut-Col Sir John Terence O'Brien, KCMG.

4 See VII **3268**n7; Lady Tredegar had written to D on 14 April 1859: 'As *you* have, I feel sure been the chief means of our being raised to the Peerage, by kindly interesting yourself in our cause, I *must* write you one line to thank you myself for so doing'. H C/I/A/29b.

5 The dates are 1702-14 and 1710-14 respectively.

6 *Cf* VI **2780**.

colonies, this parent stem, in the shape of cuttings, & I think we must have raised some dozens in pots, so that the microfolia, generally so scarce, is now almost the predominant rose at Hughenden.

Do you remember, the little Spanish Pinsapo, that you were also so kind as to send us?[7] That has immensely grown during this humid season, as almost all evergreens have. To / complete yr triumph, you must know, that we, the "aristocracy," at our fête, lunched at a series of round tables, & in the centre of the one over wh: my wife presided, in a silver vase, was your orange tree,[8] ~~under~~ ↑in↓ the shade of whose branches birds of paradise might have reposed.

What an immense event is the Italian revolution! Since 1792 we have not had such affairs! This is real history. And what an imbroglio! A race between the red flag of Mazzini wafted on by the passions of centuries & the cold diplomatic standard of mere Sardinian ambition.[9] The sovereigns & statesmen of Europe have raised a spirit they will find it difficult to quell. Look out for great events.

Yrs ever, | D.

3500 TO: SARAH BRYDGES WILLYAMS

Hughenden [Wednesday] 19 September 1860

ORIGINAL: RTC [149]

EDITORIAL COMMENT: Paper imprinted 'Hughenden Manor'. There is no salutation.

September 19 1860.

A basket of grouse – three brace – 6 birds – arrived here this morning from a Yorkshire moor.[1] I sent them on to you at once by the train; so / they are perfectly fresh, & I expect also, from the quarter from which they arrive – quite young & tender.[2]

Yrs e[ve]r | D.

3501 TO: WILLIAM W.F. HUME

Hughenden [Friday] 28 September 1860

ORIGINAL: BRN [26]

EDITORIAL COMMENT: Endorsed in another hand on the first page: 'B.D. '60'; on the fourth page in a second hand: '*Disraeli*'; and in a third hand: 'Right Hon. B Disraeli'. *Sic:* a-head.

W.W.F. Hume Esq | M.P. Hughenden Manor | Septr 28, 1860

7 For the cuttings, see VII **3397**. Possibly the plant with the mysterious name mentioned there is 'the little Spanish Pinsapo', a pyramidal fir tree with an annual growth rate of less than 12 inches but which can reach 60 feet with a spread of 30 feet. SBW in her 17 September grateful acknowledgement of D's letter would remark the 'flourishing state of everything under yr controul'. RTC [407Q].

8 See VI **2780**n1.

9 Sardinia at this time, in response to the beginning of outright war by the incursion into the papal states of the Mazzini-inspired forces led by Garibaldi, had also entered the papal states in an attempt to contain the revolutionaries' advance before it drew all of Italy into war with Austria.

---

1 Frederic Haydon had sent them on the 18th, hoping they would be tender: 'I can hardly promise any more this year, there is so little prospect of any shooting'. H B/XXI/H/367.

2 SBW on 21 September would report with gratitude having received the grouse the previous afternoon. RTC [408Q].

My dear Hume,

I fear from a letter, wh: Mrs Disraeli received from Lady Bisshopp[1] this morning, that we may, very unintentionally, be occasioning you some inconvenience.

You were so kind as to express a wish, that if we were wandering in the West this year, we should pay you a little / visit at your new residence, & I said, that if we could have that pleasure, I would give you timely notice of our intention to avail ourselves of yr obliging invitation. But we have no intention of leaving Hughenden this autumn, where the claims upon our continued presence are irresistible – & if we manage to get to Torquay at the beginning of the winter, our visit must be brief & direct.[2]

He / is a bold man, who can see so far a-head, as the beginning of the winter, in these days of revolution. I hope Lord John Russell has now had enough of attempting to govern Italy on Whig principles. I told him, four years ago, & have repeated it since, that he would find the secret societies too strong for him; & if he does not take care, he will have both Hungary & Poland in insurrection.[3]

I / am amused by the attempts – alternate – to coax & scold Garibaldi into good behaviour. Garibaldi is only doing that, wh: everyone, who knew Italy, was convinced he would do, & what he has in fact been attempting to do all his life. I think the Whig Ladies ought to have their subscriptions returned.[4]

Yours very sincerely, | D.

TO: SARAH BRYDGES WILLYAMS Hughenden [Monday] 1 October 1860 **3502**

ORIGINAL: RTC [150]

EDITORIAL COMMENT: Paper imprinted 'Hughenden Manor'. A fragmentary draft version of paragraph 3 is in H B/II/132. There is no salutation.

Octr. 1. 1860

I have sent you today a couple of brace of grouse, wh:, I trust, have reached you.

1 Lady Bisshopp in 1849 as Mary Taylor (*c*1830-after 1899), daughter of Rear-Adm Taylor of the Brazilian Navy, had married Sir Edward Cecil Bisshopp, 11th (and last) Bt, of Parham Park, Sussex; in 1880 she would marry secondly Count Quarto, of Italy. Her letter to MA has not been found.

2 Hume at Monkton Farleigh, Bradford-on-Avon, Wilts (presumably the 'new residence') would reply on 2 October: 'I don't know how Lady Bishop [*sic*] came to name me to Mrs Disraeli in reference to any visit you might have contemplated here – for certainly I had no conversation with her on the subject nor indeed any other, for I am not one of her admirers.' He had expected the DS only enroute to Torquay in winter, as it would be directly on their way. H B/XXI/H/753. There is no evidence the DS visited them this year.

3 See **3496**&n4 and, further, **3527**&n2. Earle in a note dated only 'Saturday' wrote: 'The Italian movement has evidently passed into [the] hands of the Secret Societies according to your anticipation.' H B/XX/E/112.

4 Russell had extended moral support to Garibaldi for his conquest of Sicily and Naples; see also **3471**n3. For the efforts now to contain and direct him see **3499**&n9 and (also for a fuller version of the remark about subscriptions) **3502**&n2. Hume (n2) would agree that the future was difficult to foretell, and continue: 'To me however & the conservative party in Ireland there is one satisfaction in all that has occurred – namely the "fix" the Irish Papal Priests find themselves in – for the last 20 years they have been preaching Liberal principles – simply because they imagined they were destroying the Protestant Constitution and weakening British power in Ireland – they in fact by their aiding to sustain in office such men as Palmerston & Lord John Russell – sowed broadcast the seeds of Revolution over Europe'. He concluded by asking what had been done about replacing Jolliffe as whip.

I hear from Paris, that the Emperor & Cte. Cavour are resolved to annihilate Garibaldi, & that, probably, in a fortnight, the Dictatorship will be a dream / of the past![1]

In this case, Lady Palmerston & her friends who subscribed for Garibaldi, will probably discover, that it ~~way~~ was by mistake, & that they intended to take boxes for the opera of Masaniello.[2]

On Wednesday, I take the chair for the South Bucks Agricultural Association; a society / under the immediate patronage, & active management of the Court,[3] & as it is rather far to return to Hughenden after the dinner, we go tomorrow to stay a couple of days with Colonel & Lady Mary Hood, who live at Cumberland Lodge in Windsor Park. Colonel Hood is one of the equerries, & the eldest son / of Lord Bridport.[4] They are very agreeable people. It is, however, a great effort to leave the complete seclusion of this place, where, however, there is always a great deal to do. At present we are clearing the stream, wh: runs thro' our park, & wh:, having been dry for three years, is now a Nile![5]

Yrs e[ve]r, | D.

1 D's source has not been identified. Garibaldi had declared himself dictator of Sicily on 13 May 1860, and was also briefly dictator of Naples. On this day (1 October), *The Times* published comments from the Paris papers about the despatch of another division to Rome (presumably the act to which D is referring) and quoted the *Constitutionnel:* '"This measure is taken in consequence of the late events accomplished in Italy, and the revolutionary character of Garibaldi's last acts. In 1860, as in 1849, France will protect Rome and the Papacy against the attacks of demagogues."' Holt *Risorgimento* 238, 245.

2 The Ladies Garibaldi Fund was one of a number of committees raising subscriptions for Garibaldi. Holt *Risorgimento* 243; *MP* and *The Times* (19, 20 Sep 1860). Several operas had been composed by this time based on the story of Tommaso Aniello Masaniello (1622-1647), who led a revolt against Spanish rule in Naples in 1647. One example is Auber's *La Muette de Portici* (1828), also referred to as *Masaniello.*

3 D had already spoken at the meeting of the Royal Bucks Agricultural Association (the second since its amalgamation with the Central Bucks association) at Aylesbury on Wednesday 26 September. *The Times* on the 28th had taken exception to D's approval of the society's recognition of meritorious service by labourers, seeing this to be the responsibility of masters. On Wednesday 3 October, D would take the chair in place of Prince Albert (see **3505**) at the Royal South Bucks Agricultural meeting at Salt Hill, near Slough. He would urge the society to show leadership by including all classes involved in agriculture and moving to a federation of agricultural societies which would focus on the advancement of agriculture and the improvement of the condition of the agricultural labourer. *BH* (29 Sep, 6 Oct 1860). The Queen and Prince Albert from 22 September to 17 October were on the continent; see Stanley Weintraub *Uncrowned King* (1997) 391-4.

4 One of D's supporters at Salt Hill (n3) would be Col Hood, elder son of Samuel Hood (1788-1868), 2nd Baron Bridport, and his wife, Duchess of Bronté (Sicily). Alexander Nelson Hood (1814-1904), 3rd Baron Bridport 1868 (January), 1st Viscount Bridport 1868 (July), also Duke of Bronté (Sicily) 1873, lieut-col Scots Fusilier Guards, major-general 1862, general 1877, equerry to the Queen 1858-84, extra equerry and lord-in-waiting 1884-91, hon equerry to the King 1901-4, clerk marshal to Prince Albert 1853-61, KCB 1885, in 1838 had married Lady Mary Penelope Hill (1817-1884), second daughter of 3rd Marquess of Downshire. Lady Mary on 10 September had written to MA to invite the Ds to stay with them; they stayed at Windsor Forest 2-4 October. H D/III/C/2879; acc.

5 See VII **3399**&n6, in which D in August 1859 thinks the stream will never reappear.

TO: JOHN KNOTT Hughenden [Monday] 8 October 1860 3503

ORIGINAL: YAU [4]

EDITORIAL COMMENT: Paper imprinted 'Hughenden Manor'. There is in H B/II/55, also on Hughenden Manor paper, a version of this letter evidently originally intended to be sent (*eg*, 'C & S' is there written out in full); in it the second 'abolition' herein changed to 'termination' is not altered, and after 'all parties' it reads: '& sections in the Church, & if this condition be wanting, it would be unwise, & might be disastrous, to make the effort. [*New paragraph:*] I refrain / from suggestions, wh: however important, would be premature at this moment. [*Signature block:*] Believe me, dear Sir, | Yours very faithfully | *B Disraeli*'.

Private Oct 8. 1860

J.M. Knott Esq

My dear Sir,

I duly received yr letter of the 29th. Ulto:[1]

Fully impressed with the responsibility of offering counsel ~~of~~ ↑on↓ such a subject, but speaking on one wh: constantly occupies my thought, my opinion is that the period has arrived, / when the Church should take the initiative, & that Parliament shd be prayed to maintain the constitutional connection between C & S; & to resist the abolition of Ch. Rates, as a measure tending to the ~~abolition~~ ↑termination↓ of that Alliance.

If the / action, on the part of the Church, be conducted with the requisite vigor & perseverance, the beneficial effects will be incalculable; but the condition of success is cordial & co-operative energy by all parties in the Church, & without that, the effort would be unwise, / perhaps disastrous.

Yours very faithfully, | *B. Disraeli*

3504

TO: LORD STANLEY Hughenden [Tuesday] 16 October 1860

ORIGINAL: DBP Box 47/2

EDITORIAL COMMENT: Endorsed by Stanley on the last page: 'Disraeli. Oct. 60 x'. *Sic:* Neopolitan.

The | Lord Stanley. M.P Hughenden | Octr. 16 – 60

Dear Stanley

I am much obliged to you by yr report of Ld. Derby's condition.[1] I have been dis-

1 John M. Knott (for whose earlier correspondence with D see V **2031**&n1), Baptist pamphleteer and honorary secretary of the Committee of Laymen, on 12 June had sent D a pamphlet by the 'Church Defence Association' arguing that the 1851 census carefully analysed was not as disadvantageous to the established Church in church-rate debates as was generally assumed, and urging churchmen to be more careful in submitting their returns for the 1861 census. On 29 September 1860 he had written again, from Kenilworth, enclosing a circular (not found) 'which has just been issued to the Archdeacons of England & Wales in preparation for Church defences in the next Session of parliament. The question is, whether petitions should be presented immediately on the opening of parliament or whether they should focus in on some aggressive movement ... I have a strong opinion that the preservation of our parochial system and the identity of Church rates with it, will form an important rallying point of real conservatism ... Any remarks from you, at your convenience, will be highly esteemed.' On 8 December he would congratulate D on his church-rate speech (see **3523**&n2) and enclose a copy of the circular (dated November 1860) he was sending to all rural deaneries urging everyone to petition parliament against any bill abolishing church rates; it included a model petition representing agitation against the church rates as an attack on the union of church and state. H B/XXI/K/166-8b. See also **3472**&n2. Knott would later publish pamphlets such as *The Established Church and the Political Non-Conformists of 1866* (1866).

1 Stanley had written from Knowsley on 13 October: 'As there have been so many conflicting reports about my Father's health, you may like to know the facts. He has suffered from a long and very sharp attack of gout, not such as at any time to alarm us, but which has greatly weakened him'. H B/XX/S/702.

tressed for his sufferings, but not alarmed. The newspapers always exaggerate the illness of great men. I assumed, that he had one of his severe attacks – similar to that of 1858[2] – but, provided he does not avail himself of Colchicum for his / cure, I believe the visitation, tho' at first exhausting, has ultimately a clearing & renovating influence. Yesterday at Q Sess:, I sate at dinner, next to a retired Indian Judge, one Sir Yardley,[3] who told me a new specific had been discovered for gout, wh:, with all the remedial effects of Colchicum, was inspiriting, instead of depressing. Its name, I collected, was Lithia; but / tho' my neighbour was rather intelligent, & apparently Scientific, I was not successful in eliciting from him a more definite account; tho' I tried. Do you know anything about it?

We have been here more than two months, & except an occasional agricl dinner, I have, literally, never been off my own manor; nor have we had a single guest; but the time has flown like water amid changes in our microcosm more considerable, / than those projected in the map of Europe. I have arrived at that stage of life & feeling, that I like a Westminster campaign, & the perfect solitude of this place – but nothing intermediate.

I look upon the presence of a congenial companion as a heightener, not a disturber, of the charms of solitude – & if, therefore, you have had enough of the north for the present, & will come to us before the leaf quite falls, you will have / a cordial reception. Will you come at once?[4]

I hear that all the streets & Boulevards, of Paris are crowded with Neopolitan Dukes & Princes, who have arrived, in order to supplicate the Emperor to save Southern Italy, & give them a redeemer in the shape of a Murat![5]

My last words to yr father, when I quitted him, was that we shd. have immense events this autumn. In short after five & twenty years of statistical imposture, / real politics have commenced. But nobody's house is in order, except Englands – but that will not prevent the war, tho' it may postpone it. It will be a very long war, for all the great questions will tumble into it, & when it closes, the face of Europe will be more changed, than 1815 compared with 1780.[6]

I am sorry about the Westminster but believe some martyr will yet advance, / & prevent the catastrophe.[7] There are no fanatics like the initiated.

2 See VII **3143**.

3 Sir William Yardley (1811-1878), a barrister (Middle Temple) 1837, knighted 1847, had been puisne judge at Bombay 1847, chief justice 1852-8. For D's encounter with him in 1841, see III **1168**&n2. He had been one of the magistrates in attendance with D at the Bucks Michaelmas Session at Aylesbury on 15 October. *BH* (20 Oct 1860).

4 Stanley would reply on 24 October that, because his father was still ill, he could not come immediately, and suggested 10 November, as he had a London engagement on the 9th. H B/XX/S/703.

5 Joachim Murat (1767-1815), who served under Napoleon in Italy and was made King of Naples in 1808, had augmented the trappings of royalty and created a new nobility.

6 Stanley (n1) had asked if D had any information 'as to the solution of the Italian trouble. Every thing I hear, see, or read, makes me believe more & more in the probability of a European war. Surely the Emperor will never allow a single Italian State to be formed – nor give up Rome? It is a state of affairs such as the world has not seen since 1815.'

7 Stanley (n1) had written: 'Philosophy is at a discount. Our friend Chapman, whom you so nearly forced on the orthodox Walpole, writes to me that the West. Rev. will not pay its way, and must stop unless subsidised ... I advised him to try and reunite with the "National" which seceded some years ago, being one degree less heretical.' John Chapman, who had bought the *Westminster Review* in 1852, survived its 1860

Ld Hastings, that little wretched Jacob Astley – who really has fifty thousand a year – has gone & married a member of the demi-monde, with whom he was already on intimate terms. This Stamford system, wh: is spreading, will, I fear, be a hedge for the "conservative re-action."[8] It is very vexatious, & so idiotic!

Edward Thynne has written to me, tho' that hussy, his wife, dared not.[9] The appointment would be scandalous.

Yours ever, | D.

TO: SARAH BRYDGES WILLYAMS Hughenden [Thursday] 18 October 1860 3505

ORIGINAL: RTC [151]

PUBLICATION HISTORY: M&B IV 321, dated 18 October 1860, the last paragraph; M&B IV 355, dated 18 October 1860, extract from the seventh paragraph

EDITORIAL COMMENT: There is no salutation. *Sic:* Virgimia; flaggon; Moncton.

Hughenden | Octr. 18. 1860

When I wrote to you last, I think I was going to take the chair in South Bucks. We went on a visit for two days to Colonel & Lady Mary Hood at Cumberland Lodge, in Windsor Park – a large uncouth red-brick pile in the worst style of the Georgian age, situate in the most exquisite sylvan scenery / in the world. Have you ever been at Virginia water? An artificial lake – one hundred & fifty acres in extent, winding amid wooded banks like the forests of Spenser, or "As you like it."

Colonel Hood told me, what I did not know before, that Virgimia Water was made by the Duke of Cumberland's army after / the battle of Culloden. On their return from Scotland, 10,000 strong, they were quartered at Windsor, & this was their employment.[1]

My host, an agreeable man, is Equerry to the Prince, & has the management of the Royal farms, 4000 ↑acres↓ in extent, in wh: every invention of modern science, as / applied to agriculture, is introduced – & wh: may serve as a normal school to

financial crisis with contributions of money and unpaid articles, and by selling his publishing business. *Wellesley Index* III 550. In the spring (6 April 1860) Stanley had written: 'Have you seen either the last Westminster or the last National Review? They are both, as you know, organs of what are called advanced Liberal opinions in a philosophical sense: and both are strong against the Govt: scheme of Reform, as giving too much power to the working class. You ought to read the articles – when philosophers grow Conservative, there is real reaction.' H B/XX/S/701.

8 Jacob Henry Delaval Astley (1822-1871), since 27 December 1859 17th Baron Hastings, on 19 May 1860 had married Frances Cosham (d 1884); she in 1873 would marry secondly Robert Heane, of Barnwood, Gloucs. 'This Stamford system' is a reference to George Harry Grey (1827-1883), 7th Earl of Stamford and Warrington, who in 1855 had married his second wife, Catherine Cocks (d 1905), an Astley's (no relation) Royal Circus equestrienne and a former mistress of (presumably among others) the late Lord Strangford (D's friend George Smythe); see VII **2982**n6.

9 Stanley (n1) had written: 'I have a letter from Ly E. Thynne, who professes to write without her husband's knowledge, asking for him the office which Jolliffe has vacated, & hinting that [4th Marquess of] Bath supports his claim. You are a better judge than I as to his probable efficiency in that line – between ourselves, I should doubt it'. Lord Edward Thynne (1807-1884), younger brother of 3rd Marquess of Bath, MP (L-C) for Frome 1859-65, in 1853 had married secondly Cecilia Anne Mary Gore (d 1879).

---

1 William Augustus (1721-1765), Duke of Cumberland, third son of George II, defeated Prince Charles Edward Stuart at the Battle of Culloden in 1746. According to Thomas Eustace Harwood *Windsor Old and New* (1929) 179-80, the work on the lake was begun after the Duke's return from Holland in 1748.

the cultivators of the soil, & breeders of cattle & stock, throughout the United Kingdom.[2]

The Colonel is the eldest son of Lord Bridport, the head of the Hoods, a famous house of naval conquerors. Lord Bridport married the Duchess of Bronte, the / daughter & heiress of Earl Nelson, the brother of the hero. Their son, Colonel Hood, married Lady Mary Hill, who was a Wellesley by her mother's side; so that in his numerous offspring, & in them alone, the blood of Nelson & Wellington is blended![3]

At this dinner at Salt-hill, wh: was held the day after our arrival at Cumberland Lodge, I gave the Prince Consorts / prize for the best crop of roots. It was a splendid silver flaggon. It was at the especial desire of the Prince, that I took the chair.

We have a very busy rural season here, tho' we live in profound solitude. The volunteer movement[4] greatly increases our duties. Today, there is much silver-bugling, & a firing for prizes in my neighbour's park, the Lord / Lieutenants,[5] wh: is to last, I believe, three days. I have got to dine with him & meet what they call "the County." I have just come from Quarter Sessions; which is our Provincial Parliament.

In addition to all this, I have another claim upon my time & exertions this season. This year is the triennial visitation of our Diocesan, & I / have to receive the Bishop at this place. This is no slight affair, for, on these occasions, a Bishop is like a Highland chief, & moves with a tail. Besides the descendant of the Apostles, I have to extend hospitality to

His Chancellor
His Chaplain
His Secretary
&
The Archdeacon of Bucks

& all their servants. / This great ecclesiastical visitation comes off on the 14th. of next month,[6] & as soon after as possible, we shall commence bending our steps

2 The Windsor Home Farm had been made profitable by Albert. Robert Rhodes James *Albert, Prince Consort* (1983) 114.

3 See **3502**n4. The naval hero Horatio Nelson (1758-1805), 1st Viscount Nelson, had been given the title Duke of Bronté by Ferdinand IV, King of Naples and Sicily, in 1801; it had then passed to his brother, the Rev William Nelson (1757-1835), 1st Earl Nelson. In 1786 the latter had married Sarah Yonge (d 1828), daughter of the Rev Henry Yonge and, on the Earl's death, the title had passed to their only surviving child, Lady Bridport (1787-1874), who as Lady Charlotte Mary Nelson in 1810 had married Samuel Hood, 2nd Baron Bridport 1814. Their eldest son, as already noted, had married Lady Mary Penelope Hill. Her mother, the Marchioness of Downshire, as Lady Maria Windsor (1790-1855), eldest daughter of 5th Earl of Plymouth, in 1811 had married 3rd Marquess of Downshire. Lady Mary's perceived link to the Wellesley line evidently was Wellington's mother, born Lady Anne Hill, eldest daughter of 1st Viscount Dungannon.

4 See **3441**&n7.

5 Lord Carrington, Wycombe Abbey, Bucks.

6 Bishop Wilberforce on 15 October had responded to D's 8 October invitation (not found) by proposing he stay with the DS on 14 November until after breakfast on the 15th. D is anticipating his further request, on 7 November, that D extend his invitation to include those accompanying him. H B/XXI/W/353-4. The learned jurist Robert Joseph Phillimore (1810-1885), a barrister (Middle Temple) 1841, MP (L-C) for Tavistock 1852-7, QC 1858, knighted 1862 and created a baronet 1881, was chancellor of the dioceses of Oxford, Salisbury and Chichester. The Venerable James Randall (1790-1882), Archdeacon of Berks since 1855, had been chaplain to the Bishop since 1846. John Marriott Davenport (1809-1882), an Oxford so-

towards the West. What with agricultural societies, volunteer reviews, & episcopal visitations, I think I have done my duty to Church & State. All this, however, will not materially affect our meeting, as we have written / to give up all our intended visits, on the way, in Wiltshire especially, & shall at once proceed from this place to Torquay[.] We had promised, after many solicitations, to have made a sort of Wiltshire progress this autumn. My wife's relations, the Poulett Scropes reside in that county, at Castle Combe;[7] & we were to have visited, at the same time, several of my supporters & colleagues; the Marquis of Bath at Longleat; Mr Estcourt, who was Secretary of State, at Estcourt; Sir John Neeld at Grittleton; Mr. Long at Rood Ashton. He is the M.P. for the County & an expectant peer[8] – & Mr. FitzWilliam Hume at Moncton Farleigh. I assure you to have to write to all these persons, & throw them over, as the phrase is – has not been a very easy business – especially as I could not / say I was not going into the West – & my annual visit to Torquay is now a national event. However it is done.

Strange news came from Naples last night[9] – more confounding than anything that has happened. Garibaldi is like an eel. Is he playing a cross with Cavour? Is he a Masaniello? Is he a Washington? A great many other questions will be asked before it is all finished.

Ever yours, | D.

TO: PHILIP ROSE Hughenden [Sunday] 21 October 1860 **3506**

ORIGINAL: H R/I/A/143

EDITORIAL COMMENT: *Sic:* embarasses.

Private

P. Rose Esqr Hughenden. Octr 21: 60

My dr Rose,

I have written to the Secretary proposing the 5th. Novr.[1]

licitor, had been legal secretary to the diocese since 1854. The Venerable Edward Bickersteth (1814-1892) was Archdeacon of Bucks 1853-75, Dean of Lichfield 1875-92. See further **3515**.

7 See VII (app I) **919**xn1. Emma Phipps Scrope (d 1866), daughter and heir of the late William Scrope, of Castle Combe, Wilts (see III **801**n6), in 1821 had married George Poulett Thomson (1797-1876), who assumed the name of Scrope; he was JP and DL for Wilts, FRS, FGS, Liberal MP for Stroud 1833-67.

8 Long (for whom see III **922**n2) would die in 1867 without having the expectation fulfilled.

9 *The Times* on 17 October 1860 had published a report from Naples of 13 October that Garibaldi had ordered his troops to fire on anyone shouting republican slogans and had issued a proclamation announcing and welcoming Victor Emmanuel's imminent arrival (the latter had just published a proclamation accepting the proffered fealty of Southern Italy). On the 18th *The Times* published a report received from Paris the previous evening: '"As soon as the annexation of Naples and Sicily to Sardinia shall have been proclaimed Garibaldi will resign his [dictatorship], and will assume the title and functions of Commander-in-Chief of the Land and Sea Forces of Southern Italy. He will exclusively occupy himself in preparing for war next spring, and will make an appeal for volunteers from all Europe."'

---

1 Attempts to keep D and Rose from being called before the Berwick election commission (see VII **3309**&n1) had failed, and efforts were now focused on preparing for the hearing. The commission had concluded its hearings at Berwick-on-Tweed on 1 September, and had adjourned the further inquiry (to examine D and Rose) until 30 October, in London. *The Times* (4 Sep, 7 Nov, 1860). On 19 October Rose had written: 'I wrote to [commission secretary C.E.] Coleridge asking as a personal favor that he would not call me in the week commencing on the 28th. inst: ... I enclose his reply. Would it not be well to write

Will you have the kindness to bring the Enclosure Award to conclusion? Its delay stops, & embarasses, us.[2]

Yrs ever scly | D.

3507 TO: LORD STANLEY Hughenden [Friday] 26 October 1860

ORIGINAL: DBP Box 47/2

EDITORIAL COMMENT: Paper imprinted 'Hughenden Manor'. Endorsed by Stanley on the last page: 'Disraeli. Oct. 60. Accepted for 13th'.

Dear Stanley, October 26 1860

I forwarded yr letter to Mr P., of wh:, I entirely approved.[1] This Prowett has, for many years, pestered me with letters asking for interviews, wh: I never granted, in order to render his "organ" more efficient, &c &c. I never saw him, or wrote to him, until the day before yesterday, when having received a letter from the "Carlton", suggesting that the "party" shd take a share in the "John Bull" & furnish it with information & advice, in order to render the Conservative Press more "efficient",[2] / I sent him a reply, of wh: I enclose copy, that you may exactly know how I stand with all these gentry.

As I don't see many papers here, I don't exactly apprehend the circumstances to wh: his letter to you refers. I conceive 'tis some freak of Ingestre. His surplus energy is not content with saving the Constitution, but must, also, reform the press.[3]

and fix a day for your own examination and I would venture to suggest as early a day in the following week commencing the 5th. as you can as I think your evidence will throw such ridicule on the Brodie case that the Commissioners will be disposed to shut up as soon as they can ... Will you let me know the day you name to the Commrs.' The enclosed letter from Coleridge, dated 18 October, acceded to Rose's request without specifying a date, and continued: 'I wrote to Mr. DIsraeli some time since asking him to fix his own day but have had no answer. If you see him will you please mention it to him.' D's letter proposing the 5th has not been found. H R/I/B/70a,b. See further **3513**&n1 and **3517**&nn1-3.

2 For the ongoing enclosure process affecting Hughenden, see V **1749**&n4, **1872**, and VI **2224**n2. In 1857, George H. Hussey (see VII **2884**n2) had disputed the 'Enclosure Award', the portion awarded to Hughenden; Rose on 16 January 1858 had reported that D's claim had been allowed except for the woodland, which remained procedurally entangled. Rose on 17 October had suggested another aspect of the matter: 'I am in communication with the Commissioners & the Valuers and hope to bring about an immediate settlemt of the enclosure. I have given a distinct refusal on your part to any setting out of the road, or any appropriation beyond the existing width or any interference with the Gates or any requirement as to fencing, and as this difficulty [*sic*] there is nothing for it but for the Commissioners to accept what I previously offered.' H R/I/B/36, 69a. There would be a meeting of the enclosure commissioners on 26 November in Wycombe to deal with the 'Inclosure and particularly with ... the School Allotment.' *BH* (21 Nov 1857, 10 Nov, 8 Dec 1860).

---

1 Stanley had written on 24 October 1860 enclosing 'an enquiry which as it is addressed to others besides myself, I should like you to see, with my reply, before it is disposed of. I suppose we have no official relations with the Press now? If you think a different answer ought to be given, send the papers back to me at Knowsley, where I go this afternoon, and tell me what to say.' H B/XX/S/703.

2 C.G. Prowett had written from the Carlton Club on 'Wednesday' (docketed 17 October 1860 by an archivist) to draw D's attention to his article 'Conservative Journalism' in *John Bull;* identifying himself as its editor and proprietor, he asked D to support a scheme whereby shares in it would be taken up 'by active members of the party who would further promote the success of the paper by information and contributions.' H B/XX/A/70. Charles Gipps Prowett (1818-1874), born Topcroft, a barrister (Inner Temple) 1848, and contributor to several periodicals, would be editor of *John Bull* until 1865. No prior letters from him have been found.

3 More than a year earlier, on 20 September 1859, Earle had suggested that Ingestre be considered to replace Lucas at the *Press.* H B/XX/E/175. See VII **3422**n1 for Ingestre's 'energy' and Rose's description of it.

Will you come to us on the 13th. November?

I heartily hope, that you have found yr father improving.[4]

Ever yrs | D. /

(Copy)[5]

Sir, H. Oct: 24. 1860

In reply to yr letter without date, I beg leave to say, that in my opinion the sole cause of the inefficiency of the Conservative Press is its want of ability. No party sympathy, or connection, can compensate for this deficiency. They rather render it more glaring, & tend to reciprocal injury.

I have no doubt, that able writers on the Tory side would command public attention; as they have often done before, & in worse times; but until men of sufficient capital / will embark their property, as a matter of trade, in such enterprises, & adequately remunerate competent writers, the present contemptible state of the Conservative Press will remain unchanged.

I have the honor &c | [*a squiggle*]

To | C.G. Prowett Esqr

TO: [JOSEPH LOVEGROVE] [Hughenden, Saturday 27? October 1860] 3508

ORIGINAL: H D/II/B/300a

EDITORIAL COMMENT: *Recipient and dating*: written to Lovegrove on the back of an appeal to D dated 25 October 1860; see n1. H D/II/B/300a.

Return me this [*illegible deletion*] letter, & tell me, what is the size of the Parish of Taynton.[1]

Yrs | D.

TO: SIR WILLIAM JOLLIFFE Hughenden [Friday] 2 November 1860 3509

ORIGINAL: SCR DD/HY C/2165 [59]

Rt Honble | Sir Willm. Jolliffe Nov. 2. 1860

My dear Jolliffe,

If it happen to blend with yr engagements, we shd. be delighted to see you here on the 15th. Inst: – to stay as long as you like.[1]

Yrs ever, | D.

4 Stanley on the 28th would reply that the 13th suited him 'perfectly well'; his father was 'mending slowly'. He thought Prowett would 'not ask for a second.' H B/XX/S/704. Stanley and Manners would be at Hughenden 13-18 November; see **3513**. H acc.

5 There is an extensively revised draft of this letter (but dated 25 October) in H B/II/57.

1 The curate (William Hughes) and churchwardens (Samuel Cadle and Thomas Wintle) of Taynton parish church had written to D on 25 October asking him, as one of 'the principal Land Proprietors of the parish', for a donation toward church repairs; they hoped to raise £100. Lovegrove at Gloucester would return the letter on 1 November and report: 'the parish contains about 1800 acres with a population of about 500.' He named some of the other land owners and concluded: 'I know the Parish Church and can say that it is in a most delapidated [*sic*], if not disgraceful, condition.' H D/II/B/300-300a.

1 Jolliffe on 5 November would accept, for the 16th; he would be at Hughenden 16-18 November. H B/XX/J/86, acc.

3509A TO: CHARLES CLUBBE [Hughenden, Wednesday] 7 November 1860

ORIGINAL: RIC [013]

COVER: The | Revd. C.C. Clubbe, A.M. | The Vicarage. | *B. Disraeli*

EDITORIAL COMMENT: *Sic:* C.C.

The | Rev. C.C. Clubbe | A.M. Nov. 7. 1860

Dear Mr Clubbe,

I hope you will give me the pleasure of yr company at dinner, on Wednesday the 14th. Inst:, at ¼ to 8 o'ck, to meet the Bishop.[1]

Yours very faithfully | *B. Disraeli*

3510 TO: LORD STANLEY Hughenden [Thursday] 8 November 1860

ORIGINAL: DBP Box 47/2

EDITORIAL COMMENT: Paper imprinted 'Hughenden Manor'. Endorsed by Stanley on the first page: 'Disraeli Nov. 60.'

The | Lord Stanley Nov. 8. 1860

Dear Stanley,

The Rothschilds, understanding you were coming here, have asked you to Mentmore. We could not go there before Monday 19th Inst., / as we have guests here for the previous week. I hope, however, you may be able to go, as the visit has been so long promised & so long planned – & the / Queen of the Vale ought not to be visited except descending the Chilterns, wh: is really rather fine.[1]

I send this, therefore, that you may not unnecessarily hamper yourself / with engagements.

We expect you here on the 13th.

You can get to town, f or to anywhere else, from Mentmore with great ease.[2]

I hope Ld. Derby continues mending.

Ever yours, | D.

3511 TO: SAMUEL WILBERFORCE Hughenden [Friday] 9 November 1860

ORIGINAL: BODL MS Wilberforce c12 ff236-7

EDITORIAL COMMENT: Paper imprinted 'Hughenden Manor'.

The | Lord Bp of Oxford Nov 9 1860

My dear Lord,

I quite count on the pleasure of receiving yr Chancellor; an old acquaintance of mine – & shall trust to you to express, to him, this / hope on my part.[1]

1 At the dinner, both the 'Revd C & Mrs Clubbe' would be among the guests. H acc.

1 Baron Meyer Amschel de Rothschild had married in 1850 Juliana Cohen (1831-1877), eldest daughter of Isaac Cohen. For D's earlier rapturous description of Mentmore Towers, see VII **2936**&n4. For a fuller account of the visitors to Hughenden at this time, see **3513**.

2 Stanley would reply from Knowsley on the 11th: 'I shall be with you on Tuesday – leaving London by the 5 P.M. train, so as to arrive in time for dinner. I wish I had known a little earlier about Mentmore: I *have* hampered myself with engagements, but will try and get free, for it is, as you say, a long promised visit, and one I should regret to miss.' ROSE [29]. Evidently he did not make the visit; the Ds would be at Mentmore 19-21 November. H acc.

1 See **3505**&n6; Wilberforce had reminded D that he might remember Phillimore from the Commons.

John Manners will be with us, &, therefore, we may settle our next Church campaign with that chief of "ecclesiastical laymen" – perhaps, we may convert Stanley, who / is also here.[2]

Yrs sincerely, | D.

Pray give my kind remembrances to yr host![3]

TO: W.H. BAKER [Hughenden, Friday] 9 November 1860 3512

ORIGINAL: NYM [10]

EDITORIAL COMMENT: Endorsed in several hands on the first page: (at the top) 'From *Benjamin Disraeli,* Esq. M.P.'; (at the bottom) 'Disraeli'; 'with portrait'; '30/'; '334'.

Mr. W.H. Baker Novr 9 1860

Sir,

I have the honor to acknowledge your letter of the 24th. Ulto:

I have no copy of my works in my own library, nor do I know where one could be obtained; other, / than the railway editions, over wh: I have no control.

Some years ago, I presented, if I remember right, your Institution with a copy of the Library Edition of my fathers "Curiosities of Literature", a beautiful & costly work,[1] & now not / to be obtained – but I observe, in the printed Report of yr affairs, that you have been recently purchasing a copy of the same work, tho' a much less valuable edition.

The books were sent by Mr. Moxon to the accredited officer of your Society, / & to an individual in that capacity alone. If he have misappropriated the volumes, ↑as you intimate,↓ I should have him up before the Magistrates. At all events, the result is not stimulating to donors, & to those, who wish to assist you.[2]

I have the honor to be, Sir, | yr obedt servt, | *B. Disraeli.*

TO: SARAH BRYDGES WILLYAMS Hughenden [Sunday] 11 November 1860 3513

ORIGINAL: RTC [152]

PUBLICATION HISTORY: M&B IV 355, dated 11 November 1860, the second paragraph

EDITORIAL COMMENT: Paper imprinted 'Hughenden Manor'. There is no salutation.

Private Nov. 11 1860

I have been obliged to go up to town to answer the charge of a maniac. It might have been very troublesome, as he was egged on by cunning men, but the force of truth,

2 Manners had accepted the DS' invitation on 30 October, proposing to arrive on 12 November; he and Stanley would be at Hughenden 13-18 November. H B/XXI/M/115; acc. Stanley would be the only one there with broad church leanings; he would later record finding some of D's ideas on church rates, currently the major church issue, 'very wild'. *Disraeli, Derby* 166 (4 February 1861).

3 Richard Benyon (1811-1897), born Fellowes, changed to Benyon (1854), of Englefield House, Berks, a barrister (Lincoln's Inn) 1837, JP, DL, high sheriff 1857, chairman of Quarter Sessions, was MP (C) for Berks April 1860 to 1876. Wilberforce (n1) had written that he would be staying with Benyon for 'the next few days'. *Law List* (1845).

1 For the edition see V **1644**&n1.

2 Baker's letter has not been found, nor his 'Institution' identified. For D's role in the public-library movement that emerged in the 1830s and 1840s, see Sally Mitchell ed *Victorian Britain* (1988)450-2.

&, I hope, the influence of character, entirely frustrated the plot; the article in the "Times" is / an impartial & vigorous summary of the whole case, & coming from a leading Journal, favorable to the existing government, its effect is doubled.[1]

On Tuesday, Lord John Manners & Lord Stanley come down here, to assist me in my great episcopal reception, wh: commences on Wednesday. On Thursday, Lord Malmesbury & Lord & Lady Salisbury. I hope to clear my house by the / end of the week, but I rather doubt it. Sir William Jolliffe & Colonel Taylor, the chief of my staff, arrive on Friday.[2]

When all this hubbub is over, we shall begin to wind up our affairs of the Province, & our thoughts will turn westward. So many of our friends are going, or are gone, to Torquay, that I must take care to give Mr. Webb ample / notice.[3] I suppose the disturbed state of the Continent favorably affects the English Baden-Haus. Ld. & Lady Willy. have just joined you:[4] Lady Glengall writes to my wife, that she & her daughter, Lady Matilda,[5] are ordered to Torquay immediately; my colleague William Cavendish, Lord Chesham's eldest son, is there, with his family.

Sir Lawrence Palk writes me, that all the Russians have paid him a visit to Haldon.[6]

Adieu! dear friend, | D.

3514 TO: J. CHAPMAN — Carlton Club [Monday] 12 November [1860]

ORIGINAL: PS 740

PUBLICATION HISTORY: Carnegie Bookstore catalogue 307 (20 May 1969) item 111: 'A.L.s., "B. Disraeli." 4 full p., 8vo. "Carlton Club, Nov. 12," (1860). To J. Chapman'

EDITORIAL COMMENT: *Sic:* had occasion.

[... pertaining to some matter concerning] the settlement of my affairs ... I have no wish to enter into any details of business, & I regret that the conduct of any person had occasion this trouble – but I write these few lines, which I do in the midst of

1 See VII **3309**n1 and, in this volume, **3506**&n1. According to D's testimony at the Berwick enquiry, the 'maniac' was a Sgt Alexander Brodie whom D had tried to help get a position (sergeant-saddler – Brodie had lost a similar post at Weedon for whistle-blowing) until learning that he had a 'predisposition to insanity.' D had however earlier (on 14 April 1859) given him a note: '"The bearer of this, by name Brodie, wants very much to see Mr. Rose. I know nothing about his business, but have promised to try and get him a hearing."' Brodie had immediately shown the note to a Liberal as evidence that he was D's personal agent to bribe voters on Earle's behalf in the Berwick election; the story before it reached the Berwick commission had evidently blossomed into a major scandal. *The Times* on 8 November was relieved to have learned the truth about 'the famous story of Mr. Disraeli and Sergeant Brodie ... for Mr. Disraeli himself has been called upon to relate it; and he has done so with the circumstantiality and point of an Eastern storyteller.' It then gave a detailed account of the affair and spoke approvingly of D, especially for having refused to allow the police to arrest Brodie despite being constantly harassed by him on the street. *The Times* (7, 8 Nov 1860).

2 All these arrangements correspond with MA's accounts, except for Lady Salisbury, who begged off because of a sick child; she would arrive at Hughenden on the 17th, the day after her husband left. H acc; D/III/C/273; *MP* (20 Nov 1860).

3 Webb was the proprietor of the Royal Hotel, where the Ds always stayed when in Torquay; see VI **2763**n1.

4 *MP* on 13 November would announce the departure of Lord and Lady Willoughby de Eresby for Torquay.

5 Lady Matilda Butler (1836-1861) was the second (eldest unmarried) daughter of Lady Glengall and the late 2nd Earl of Glengall.

6 Palk had written on 23 September and again on 29 October about the continental royalty and aristocracy appearing at Torquay since Nice was annexed, in the latter mentioning that he had been 'receiving a quantity of Russian friends'. H B/XXI/P/44-5.

great noise, merely that you shd not misapprehend ... that there was any change in the friendly feelings which I trust will always exist betn your house & mine.[1]

TO: SARAH BRYDGES WILLYAMS Hughenden [Sunday] 18 November 1860 3515

ORIGINAL: RTC [153]

PUBLICATION HISTORY: M&B IV 355-6, dated 18 November 1860, omitting the last sentence; Blake 417, undated extract

EDITORIAL COMMENT: Paper imprinted 'Hughenden Manor'. There is no salutation. *Sic:* not the greatest effort; Wycomb.

Private Nov. 18. 1860

You could not have sent us a more acceptable offering to our banquets, & one, I assure you, more appreciated, than the rosy-colored tribute of Torbay, wh: quite delighted us for their own merits, & their evidence of the kind / thoughts of their donor. The Bishop was quite delighted. Prelates love delicacies, & as he is a wit as well as a priest, he was very playful about Devonian fairies & magic gifts. It certainly arrived most opportune, & was precious from its history / – because no one in Bucks would have tasted a prawn from London, whereas, direct from the balmy waters of the West, they were a delight.[1]

Our house has been brimful, & is not yet quite emptied. Sir William Jolliffe & Col. Taylor still linger & leave us tomorrow – all the rest have / departed. It has been a week of great & unceasing bustle – not the greatest effort, the Bishop's charge at Wycomb, wh: I, & Ld. John Manners, thought it but right to attend, & wh:, irrespective of divine service, was three hours long![2] Its rightly called a *Visitation*. I have sent you some papers, wh: will amuse you.

Yours ever, | D.

TO: THOMAS KEBBEL Hughenden [Sunday] 25 November 1860 3516

ORIGINAL: PS 1433

PUBLICATION HISTORY: T.E. Kebbel *Lord Beaconsfield and Other Tory Memories* (1907) 27.

HUGHENDEN, | *Nov.* 25, 1860.

MY DEAR SIR, – I am not an admirer of contemporary biography, and I dislike to be the subject of it. When I pass through town, which will be in the course of next month, I will, however, see you if you wish it.[1]

1 Possibly the 'J. Chapman' (see ph) was John Chapman (1822-1894), author, book-seller, publisher, physician and editor and proprietor since 1851 of the *Westminster Review;* see **3504**&n7.

---

1 MA would record receiving a 'box of prawns from Mrs B Willyams, from Wyc[omb]e 6d'. H acc.

2 *BH* on 17 November would notice the DS' hosting of the Bishop during his triennial visitation of South Bucks, and that D and Manners on Thursday had accompanied him to Wycombe to deliver his charge (for which see further **3551**&n3).

---

1 T.E. Kebbel (see **3467**) had written from 6 South Square, Gray's Inn, on 13 November. The letter, marked 'Answd.', docketed '? 1868' by an archivist and with the postmark on the envelope (addressed to D at Grosvenor Gate) smudged, is clearly the one to which D is here responding; it reads: 'Mr Kebbel has long been anxious to have the honour of writing Mr Disraeli's Life ... [and having now] a period of leisure ... writes to ask Mr Disraeli whether he could make it convenient ... to give him any assistance in the matter.' He then outlined his plan for a 3-volume work, 'aware that there are likely to be many persons and events about which it may not be desirable to tell the whole truth immediately'. H B/XXI/K/28.

I have always been desirous that a gentleman of your talents, acquirements, and character should have the opportunity of bringing them to bear on public opinion in a manner advantageous to the country and beneficial to himself. But no occasion has yet offered itself to me by which I could satisfactorily accomplish this end. You are, however, fortunately yet young, and I hope to see you succeed in life.[2]

Believe me, | Very truly yours, | DISRAELI.

3517 TO: CHARLES COLERIDGE Hughenden [Tuesday] 27 November 1860
ORIGINAL: H B/XIII/235b

(Copy)

C.E. Coleridge Esq[1] Hughenden Manor | Nov 27. 1860

Sir,

Yr letter of the 19th Inst: wh: I recently received on my return home from Mentmore, expresses the wish of the Sen: Commissr., that I shd. "*forward the name of the Lord of the Treasury whom I employed to speak in Mr. Earle's interest.*"[2]

As I never "employed any Lord of the T. to speak in Mr. Earle's interest," it was not in my power to reply to what was seemingly a hasty enquiry, wh: subsequent reflection had probably shown to the enquirer to be / inaccurate.

Your letter of today informs me, that it is "*The unanimous, determination of the Commissrs. that it is necessary that they shd. be put in possession of the name of the Lord of the T., to whom I referred in my last communication to yourself.*"

In that communication, there is no mention of my "employing a Lord of the Treasury to speak in Mr E's interest"; but merely, so far as an imperfect recollection of what then seemed an insignificant circumstance could guide me, my ~~belief~~ impression that a member of Parlt, then a Lord of the T.; writing from the Ho: of Commons, was / the medium of communicating, from myself to Mr. Earle, ~~of~~ a piece of public information: vizt, that the Govt. were about to send down a person to inspect the Ber[wic]k barracks.

I can have no difficulty in giving the Comm[issi]oners the inform[ati]on wh: they now require. ~~I believe~~ My impression is that Mr Whitmore, M.P. for Bridgnorth, who was in the habit of assisting me in my correspondence from the Ho: of Comm:,

2 Although Kebbel's *Life of Lord Beaconsfield* would not be realized until 1888, well after D's death, judging from Kebbel's letters (see also his section on D in his 1907 *Lord Beaconsfield and Other Tory Memories* 1-70), D at this time helped him with advice and information for his *Universal Review*, even in 1864 inviting him to Hughenden and eventually establishing a cordial relationship with him. H B/XXI/K/17ff.

---

1 Charles Edward Coleridge (1827-1875), a barrister (Middle Temple) 1853, of 1 Paper Buildings EC, on the South Wales and Chester circuit, Glamorganshire session, was secretary of the Berwick election commission.

2 After D's appearance before the Berwick commission on 6 November (see **3513**&n1), Coleridge had written on 9 November with a question the commission had omitted asking: '"What is the name of the person by whom the information obtained from the War office was communicated to Mr Earle?"' (It had been alleged that Earle had used information about work on the Berwick barracks the war office was planning as an election promise.) Coleridge, on instructions from 'Mr Vaughan, senior Commissioner', had written again, on 19 (14?) November, as D describes. H B/XIII/232-3. James Vaughan, a barrister (Middle Temple) 1839, was parliamentary counsel. *Law List* (1860).

was the gentleman, who forwarded the infor[m]a[t]ion ↑in question↓ to Berwick.[3]

I have &c

TO: [THOMAS MILNER GIBSON?] Carlton Club [Saturday?] 1 December [1860?] 3518

ORIGINAL: MOPSIK [192]
EDITORIAL COMMENT: For recipient and dating see n1.

Carlton Club | Dec 1

Dear Sir,

The bearer of this, Henry Kitchen, has applied to me for a recommendation to your office, where he is extremely anxious to / obtain employment. I have explained to him, that I have no claim upon your attention, but as he is one of my constituents, & you / were my schoolfellow, I wo[ul]d not refuse him this note; which I trust you will pardon.[1]

Believe me, dear Sir, | with great respect | your *faithl Sert* | *B. Disraeli*

TO: SARAH BRYDGES WILLYAMS Hughenden [Sunday] 2 December 1860 3519

ORIGINAL: RTC [154]
EDITORIAL COMMENT: Paper imprinted 'Hughenden Manor'. There is no salutation.

Private Dec 2 1860

The letter, wh: I return with thanks, is interesting from the trail of Garibaldi's war.[1] With respect to what it says of myself, the future is in the womb of time,[2] & I keep myself, as much as I can, in retirement, / wh: has many advantages, when everybody wants to see you, or hear what you have to say. Speech is silver – but silence, sometimes, Gold.

The state of Italian affairs is most interesting & critical. Everyone is trying / to gain time – but I don't think six months will pass without greater events occurring there, & in other places, than even we have yet witnessed.

3 Coleridge had written yet again, as D describes, on 26 November, the same day that Henry Whitmore had also written: 'Your letter of the 22nd [*not found*] has only just reached me ... You were quite correct in the statement you made and I should have no hesitation in saying, if necessary, that I was frequently your medium of communication in matters of business but that I have not the slightest recollection of the affair to which you allude or of the nature of the communication which I probably *may* have made to Mr. E. on your behalf.' On 2 December he would write that the commission had asked again if he had any recollection of writing a letter for D to Earle about the Berwick barracks; he had answered that he had no recollection of writing any such letter. H B/XIII/234, 236. Henry Whitmore (1813-1876), of Apley Park, Bridgnorth, Shropshire, a lord of the treasury and keeper of the privy seal to the Prince of Wales 1858-9, 1866-8, was MP (C) for Bridgnorth 1852-65, 1866-70.

---

1 The only person known to have been D's schoolfellow and to have held public office is Thomas Milner Gibson, president of the board of trade 1859-60. No information on Henry Kitchen has been found.

---

1 In her 16 December letter SBW would enclose a letter from one of the Butlers at Nice (see **3532**&n1); possibly this was an earlier one from the same source. Nice, where Garibaldi had landed in 1848 in a previous endeavour, had now been ceded to France (12 April 1860; see **3449**&n4), indignation at which fact would bring Garibaldi out of retirement in 1861.

2 *Othello* I iii 377: 'Many events in the womb of time will be delivered.'

Our thoughts are now turning very *westward,* & we are making all preparations / to strike our flag here. It seems, that all the world is at Torquay; at least I hear of nothing, but our acquaintances being there. It is often a consolation to me to remember, that it is a place, wh: contains, for me, at least *one devoted friend.*

Hers ever, | D.

3520 TO: WILLIAM CARLISLE [Hughenden, Monday] 3 December 1860

ORIGINAL: MOPSIK [37]

EDITORIAL COMMENT: Endorsed on the last page: '3 Decr. 1860'.

Private Dec 3 1860

W.T. Carlisle Esq

Dear Sir –

As from your letter of 27th. Augt. last,[1] it is quite clear, that I can't act under the deed, & as Captn. Fisher has no power of att[orn]ey to aid us, & the difficulties, in general, are insuperable – I think I might really withdraw from / this business – but I yield to the entreaties of all to make one more effort.

Will Mr Magenis be satisfied, for a time, with receiving his interest merely, but, of course, regularly thro' yr hands? If so, & he will repay us the monies, wh: he may have received beyond the arrears that were due, I think it probable, that we may be able to obtain a / sum, wh: would settle the very few controverted claims on Mr. Villiers, &, when that is arranged, there wd be no difficulty, I think, in obtaining a direct sale of the estate from Mr Villiers himself.

He is strongly of opinion, that Mr. Magenis, on whose kind disposition he seems to ~~acc~~ count, wd. agree to this suggestion. I will not / presume to offer any opinion on that head, but having tried to help this unfortunate business, thro' innumerable difficulties from the first, I cannot refuse him, in sorrow & in trouble, making this last effort.[2]

Yours very faithfully, | D.

1 This letter has not been found, but see n2; see also **3469**&n1.

2 Carlisle would respond to D's letter on 26 December, after seeing Magenis: 'he is willing to accept payment of the principal and interest due to him out of the remittances and not to press a Sale without your full consent, but he cannot consent to give up any part of the remittances so long as his debt remains. It therefore only remains for your decision whether the Estates are to be kept or sold. During the last 18 months there has been considerable negociation as to the Sale for you thought it better to sell the Plantations if a proper price could be had. Mr. Thomas Dickson Mr. Magenis' Attorney in the Island and also one of the Lessees of the Middleton Plantation wished to buy his holding and required terms. It was arranged not to sell the Plantations separately, and ultimately Mr. Thomas Dickson and his agents Messrs. Duncan Dunbar & Co. agreed to our terms and consented to give £6000 for the property as from the 4th. Jany. 1860. These circumstances were communicated to you and the only question was how the sale could be made and after some interval you informed me that Mr Villiers' concurrence could not be obtained and that the Sale must be made if possible without. I enquired into the matter and inspected the Deed Mr. Villiers signed, a copy of which Mr. Padwick sent me and I wrote to you in August last that a Sale must be made by the Court in the Island unless Captn. Fisher had a power of Sale. Matters have proceeded so far in regard to the Sale to Mr. Dickson that I feel some doubt of the propriety of not carrying it out even by asking for a Judicial Sale in his favor at the sum agreed upon, but this Mr. Magenis does not wish done in opposition to you. Mr. Magenis has had all his interest to the 1 March 1860 and on striking the amount to that day it appeared that there was a sum of £156.4.5 to go in reduction of the principal of his debt which thus was reduced to £2977.17.1. On the 8th. May 1860 Mr. Magenis received

TO: RALPH DISRAELI [Hughenden, Wednesday] 5 December 1860 3521

ORIGINAL: BL ADD MS 59887 ff80-1

R. Disraeli Esq Dec 5. 1860

My dear Ralph,

The Bucks Shrines may be got at Hall Virtue & Co.[1] I wd. have sent you a copy pr post, but the / cost wd. be more than the price.

We have never had a line from you since yr visit here – &, of course, we never hear from James.[2] This is not the / way to keep the family together – poor darling Sa's last hope & prayer.

Yrs ever, | D.

TO: EDITOR OF *THE MORNING STAR* Hughenden [Wednesday] 5 December 1860 3522

ORIGINAL: HUL [1]

EDITORIAL COMMENT: Paper imprinted 'Hughenden Manor'.

Private December 5 1860

from Mr. Thomas Dickson an account shewing the receipts and payments he had made up to the 4th. Jany. 1860 from which time he proposed to become the Purchaser at £6000 with interest at £5 per Cent until payment. There was a sum of £303.5.9 appearing due from Mr. Thomas Dickson to the 4th. Jany 1860 and which sum he wished to retain if he became the purchaser at £6000. I refused to allow this and Messrs. Duncan Dunbar & Co. say it will be paid when the treaty is settled. It now only remains for you to decide whether to urge Mr. Villiers to concur in the Sale, or to abandon the Contract with Mr. Thomas Dickson and leave the Rents of the Plantations to be remitted to Mr. Magenis until his debt is satisfied. I beg to enclose a copy of the last letter from Mr. Thomas Dickson.' Dickson's letter is dated 15 November 1860 in Colombo: 'Mr. D. Dunbar has forwarded me a copy of your letter settling the terms of Sale of the Gallegedere and Middleton Estates and the only question is now how a legal Title is to be obtained. Mr Villiers' Attorney here has not the power to convey and some means must be obtained by which the Estates can be put up to Auction and bought in from the Fiscal for £6000.' He was fearful that any of Villiers's creditors could force a sale of the estates before their titles were transferred to him, and required protection for his previous offer to stand. He also reported that the lessees were applying for a reduction in the terms of their leases. See further **3616**. D evidently sent this correspondence to Lady Jersey, who in an illegible letter dated only 'Friday' wrote 'I return your letters' and asked to see D briefly at the House of Commons. H A/IV/J/139-40.

1 *A Pilgrimage to the Shrines of Buckinghamshire,* by John Leadbetter, of High Wycombe, bears the publication date 1861. Bradenham House is one of the 'shrines' included, as the residence of Isaac D'Israeli. The booklet was advertised as available at eighteenpence from establishments in Aylesbury, Wycombe and London; the one for London was Hall, Virtue and Co, booksellers and publishers at 25 Paternoster Row. *BH* (8 Dec 1860).

2 See **3497**&n1 for the correspondence leading up to RD's visit to Hughenden 20-29 October. H acc. James Disraeli's most recent letters to MA and D respectively are of 30 July and 22 April 1860. H D/III/B/57, A/I/D/18. RD would reply on 7 December: 'I should have written to Hughenden long ere this had I anything amusing or agreable to talk of. There is a dull monotony in my existence that I cannot break thro', & do not seem much to care to do so. Even my House that I want to get quit of is a source of annoyance, for I cannot conceive when I am to get another'. He commented on a number of topics, for example (in light of the Rothschilds' announcement on 6 December that they would pay the coupons of the Roman loan due on 1 December, reversing an announcement of 2 December, these published in the London press on 3 and 7 December respectively) remarking: 'I see that your friends the Jews are at last shelling out Peters pence.' H A/I/E/74.

Mr Disraeli presents his Compliments to the Editor of the "Star",[1] & wd. feel obliged, if he would state, that there is no sort of foundation for the announcement, / contained in the "Star" of Monday 3rd. Decr., that Mr Disraeli is about to visit Leeds, & take the chair at some public meeting.[2]

Mr Disraeli / is sorry to trouble the Editor on such a matter, but this mornings post has brought him a cloud of correspondence on the subject,[3] & he wishes / to prevent its continuance.

P.S. Mr. Disraeli never heard of the Society in question.

3523 TO: JOHN DELANE — [Hughenden, Thursday] 6 December 1860

ORIGINAL: TIA Vol 10/60

Private Dec 6. 1860

J. Delane Esqr

Dear Delane,

I attended a meeting on Ch: Rates on Tuesday, with the intention of making a public declaration on that subject & other matters connected with / the Ch:, but there were no reporters there except clerical Reporters for the "Guardian".[1] They sent me a summary of my observations, in wh: they confess they had broken down, to revise & fill up this morning, wh: / I have done – but as I have had the complete trouble of making the report, & as I am very anxious, that my views shd. be known at this moment, I have sent the MS. up to you. I am desirous that / it shd appear in the "Times", & at this season of the year, you may not find its insertion very inconvenient.[2]

Yours sincerely, | D.

1 The editor was Samuel Lucas, not to be confused with the quondam editor of the *Press; cf* **3452**&n1.

2 George Beecroft, MP (C) for Leeds since 1857, had written to D on this day (5 December) enclosing two clippings from the *Leeds Mercury,* of 1 and 4 December respectively. The first reported that D, through Beecroft's intercession, would preside at the annual soirée of the Bank Temperance Society, corrected in the second to the East Ward Mechanics' Institution. The prior notice had been premature, as Beecroft had only been asked to invite D. Beecroft wrote: 'I replied, that I did not think there was any probability of your accepting such an invitation, because, last year you had declined to preside at the Soirée of the Leeds Mechanics' & Literary Society, & I stated the reasons you gave me for declining.' He also enclosed a letter from the Leeds Astronomical Society asking to be included in D's visit. H B/XXI/B/296,a,b,c. Presumably the *Star*'s item was based on the erroneous report.

3 The only relevant letter is Lady Londonderry's of 4 December asking the DS to come to her from Leeds. H B/XX/V/222.

---

1 The *Guardian* (not to be confused with the *Manchester Guardian*) was a high-church weekly founded in 1846 by, among others, Gladstone. Bourne II 131.

2 See **3524** for D's response to the 'summary'. Delane the next day (7th) would write: 'Of course, I will publish your speech but another time I hope you will not forget that it takes more time & trouble to report your own speech than to send a note beforehand'. H B/XXI/D/74. *The Times* on 8 December would publish the speech D had made on Tuesday 4 December at a meeting of the rural deanery of Amersham at Prestwood, Bucks, on the church-rate question. D argued that the church rates were vital to the survival of the established Church and to the parochial system of local government on which the constitution was based, and attributed the weak defence of them to the current divisions in the church over ritualism. He urged that petitions in their favour be sent from every parish, that church unions be established in every part of England to foster joint action by clergy and laity, and that there be more political involvement by the clergy such as lobbying of MPS. The meeting adopted all three suggestions. In a leader on

TO: THOMAS EVETTS Hughenden [Friday] 7 December 1860 3524

ORIGINAL: GLA [1]

EDITORIAL COMMENT: Paper imprinted 'Hughenden Manor'. Endorsed in another hand on the first page: 'Lord Beaconsfield (Benjamin Disraeli) 1804-1881.'

Private Dec 7. 1860

The | Rev T. Evetts[1]

My dear Sir –

I tried to condense a summary of the views, wh: I wish, at this moment, to place before the Church, but, with all my effort, / they appear to me much too long for the medium you mean to avail yourself of. I think I shall send the memorandum up to town, to take its chance.[2] I enclose yr / report.

Yours faithfully, | D.

TO: RALPH DISRAELI Hughenden [Friday] 7 December 1860 3525

ORIGINAL: BL ADD MS 59887 ff82-3

EDITORIAL COMMENT: Paper imprinted: 'Hughenden Manor'.

R. Disraeli Esqr Decr. 7 1860

My dear Ralph

Ld Malmesbury writes to me, that at Solomons, Duke St Manchester Sqre,[1] there is D'Orsays original statuette of Louis Napoleon, / done in 1840 – price £1.

Pray call *directly* & buy it for me. If I write, Solomons will ask some monstrous sum. Malmy. found the original / of D'Orsay himself, & others, wh: he bought.[2]

Yrs ever | D.

10 December, *The Times* would dispute D's contention that the church-rates question involved that of the national church, and ridicule his idea that church rates should be incorporated into the general rates. Derby on 12 December would question D's wisdom at having made such a strong speech, in which he thought he detected the effect of Stanley's recent visit to Hughenden: 'You were quite right however in your recommendation to the Clergy to make this a prominent question in the exercise of their influence at Elections'. H B/XX/S/277. See further **3530**&n2.

1 The Reverend Thomas Evetts (1821-1898), BA (Oxford) 1842, perpetual curate of Holy Trinity Church, Prestwood, Bucks, 1849-63, rector of Monks Risborough, Bucks, 1863-98, was the rural dean of Bucks who had chaired the meeting at which D had made his speech on church rates; see **3523**&n2.

2 See further **3530**&nn2&3.

1 Zimlor Solomon is listed as 'picture dealer' at 15 Duke Street, Manchester Square, in *LPOD* (1856), and as 'dealer in ant. china' at the same address in *LPOD* (1860).

2 Malmesbury had written on 6 December: 'It is curious that 3 days after our conversation about Dorsey's [*sic*] statuette (done by himself) I found the *original* in *terra cotta* at a Jew's, as well as his original equestrian statuette of Napoleon I – both beautiful. There remains as a curiosity his original one of Nap III done in 1840 ... If you want it you will find it at Solomons Duke St Manchester Sqre for £1'. H B/XX/HS/104. RD would reply on 10 December: 'I have obtained the Napoleon for £1. I was just hastening off to court in the pouring rain when your letter marked "immediate" was put into my hand. You do not seem to have the least idea of my obligations or you would not be sending to me to do affairs at a moments notice. Old Solomon will not open his shop on the Sabbath but that did not prevent him immediately asking me £2. He says it is Terra Cotta. It looks to me like a cast.' H A/I/E/75. See further **3529**.

3526 TO: LORD DERBY Hughenden [Saturday] 8 December 1860

ORIGINAL: DBP Box 146/1

EDITORIAL COMMENT: Paper imprinted 'Hughenden Manor'. Endorsed by Derby on the first page: 'Disraeli B. *Ansd* '.

Rt Honble | The Earl of Derby, K.G. Dec 8. 1860

My dear Lord,

I would not add to yr sufferings by correspondence, but as I learn, indirectly, that you are yourself again, & even writing, I will not deny myself the gratification of congratulating you on yr recovery, wh: I should hope a little time would now / ratify.[1]

I doubt not you know more, than I do, of public affairs. From all I can learn there are so many plans on the tapis, equally impracticable, that I should judge they were chiefly taken up to gain time: by some, from exhaustion, by others, from perplexity; & that the 5th. Feby[2] will find the world as distant from solution as / now.

Notwithstanding the flagrant inconsistencies of the two despatches,[3] I suspect public opinion is strongly in favor of the government foreign policy. The public only judge of ~~forei~~ external affairs by the immediate results. They think, that an English interest has been established, & that France has been baffled. And this is enough for them. It / is probable, that there will be a pause in great events until the Spring.

I should fancy, from what reaches me, that the Ministry have no longer a majority; certainly not, if we show indifference. But, however this may be, it is expedient that they should be kept in.[4]

Believe me, | my dear Lord, | Yours sincerely, | D.

1 Malmesbury had written to D on 6 December (see **3525**&n2): 'You may be glad to hear that the Captain writes to me in his usual dapper hand "I eat well sleep well & am well in myself but have not recovered the use of my feet & ancles as yet" ... [he] has asked people to shoot after Xmas.' Derby on the 12th (see **3523**n2) would respond from Knowsley: 'I am still a prisoner (though slowly improving) chiefly from weakness in my feet and ancles; but fortunately for my writing, my right wrist is, of all my joints, the strongest ... My holidays have been rather spoilt, but by the time we are wanted for work again, I may hope to be quite myself again.'

2 The scheduled date for the opening of parliament; see **3543**n1.

3 Lord John Russell had issued despatches on Italy on 31 August and 27 October 1860 that seemed, not only not in accord with England's official position of non-intervention, but contradictory, as the second espoused the right of a people to call on aid from foreign powers against a government they perceived to be bad, the principle the first despatch had denounced. The later despatch was joyously received by Italian patriots, and succeeded in identifying England with the unification of Italy. Prest *Russell* 391-3.

4 Derby (n1) would reply: 'From [Malmesbury] I learn, what indeed is sufficiently obvious, that nothing can be, or have been, on worse terms than the English & French Governments. Persigny has had a violent quarrel with Palmerston, and according to his custom, has not kept it to himself. I agree with you that all Europe is at sea with regard to the future. Now, if ever, would have been the time, when, if France & England had been cordially united in their Policy, they might have dictated terms to Europe, and preserved the peace of the world – instead of which, as far as we can judge of a policy which is so much the creature of circumstance as the Emperor's appears to be, it is not possible for two countries to be wider asunder. That J. Russell's Italian policy, favouring the independence of Italy, meets with the general concurrence of public opinion, I do not dispute. At the same time it will be impossible, when Parliament meets, to avoid noticing with censure (I do not mean by a *vote*) both the argument of his second Despatch, and the utter recklessness and disregard of consequences with which, quite gratuitously, he dogmatizes upon some of the most doubtful and delicate questions of International Law. The arguments which he uses alike justify the Sardinian invasion of Venetia, and any Austrian intervention on the other side in favour of any of the deposed Princes. Meantime the question of Italian unity is only now beginning to meet its

TO: LORD JOHN MANNERS   Hughenden [Saturday] 8 December 1860   **3527**

ORIGINAL: BEA [O83]

PUBLICATION HISTORY: Whibley II 134-5, the first paragraph, undated

EDITORIAL COMMENT: Paper imprinted 'Hughenden Manor'.

Rt Honble | The Lord John Manners   Dec 8. 1860

My dear JM.

I shd. strongly recommend you to decline the proposition. Such a task could not be undertaken by a person, in yr position, except for the sake of enduring reputation. That is not to be obtained with the reserve & restrictions, wh: the recentness of the topic / would entail on the writer, especially when he had himself been a principal actor in the scene. The subject itself is good, but, if treated, must be kept in MS. for the next twenty years, when, probably, you yourself may be Prime Minister, wh: will add to the piquancy of the publication.[1] /

There are many other reasons against the course.

The flagrant inconsistencies of the two despatches must not be lost sight of – but, I suspect, public opinion is, at this moment, strongly in favor of the Govt. foreign policy. The public, in external affairs / judge only by immediate results. They fancy, that an English interest has been established, & that France has been baffled. And that's enough for them.[2] There are many plans on the tapis – all I think impracticable – &, therefore, I conclude, taken up to gain time: by some, from exhaustion, by others, from perplexity.

Good accounts from Knowsley: eats, sleeps, & *writes* well – & is well / [*written at right angles at the top of the first page:*] in himself: but feet and ancles still wrong. However, there is to be a shooting party after Xmas.[3]

My kindest remembrances to the Duke[.]

Yrs ever, | D.

first real practical difficulties ... I do not see a hope of escaping a general war in the Spring. As to Home affairs I look to a quiet Session – Law Reform, and questions of that kind will be put forward, and Political Reform bushed by very general assent. This will make matters go very easy, especially if we can hold our people to that which I agree with you is the true policy, keeping the present men in, and resisting all temptations to avail ourselves of a *casual* majority.'

1 Manners had written on 5 December: 'Saunders and Otley have asked me to write the History of the Country Party from its formation in 1845: before answering them I should like to have your opinion. First – is it expedient that such a work should be concocted at all? Secondly – if so, ought it to be written by one who has been as much engaged in the affairs of the Party as I have been? My own judgment would lead me to answer both questions in the negative'. Manners on 13 December would thank D for his opinion: 'I lost no time in acting upon it, coinciding, as it did, completely with my own.' H B/XX/M/116-17.

2 See **3526**&n3. Manners on 5 December (n1) had suggested: 'When the time approaches I think you should seriously consider whether Lord John's Despatch ought not to be attacked as soon as Parliament meets, and in a formal manner.' Manners on 13 December (n1) would respond: 'I own I should like to see a formal censure of the second Despatch proposed in both Houses simultaneously perhaps as an amendment to the Address if, as I presume, there is an Italian paragraph in it. Popular as the Italian cause is, I doubt whether much defence in argument could be found for that despatch, which would be attacked not on Italian, but on Belgian, Swiss, German or Ionian grounds.' The government's Italian policy would be a main focus of the debate on the address when parliament reconvened; see **3555**&n1.

3 Manners on 5 December (n1) had asked: 'What news have you from Knowsley of the Captain's health? All sorts of absurd stories connected with our pleasant party at Hughenden were hatched in London, as you no doubt heard.' See **3526**&n1.

3528 TO: ERASTUS HOLBROOK [Hughenden, Tuesday] 11 December 1860

ORIGINAL: H A/VIII/E/20

COVER: Erastus Holbrook Esq. | Yale University | New Haven | Connecticut | U.S. | *B. Disraeli*

POSTMARKS: *recto:* (1) a cancelled one-penny stamp; (2) in large circle: [*illegible*] | A. PKT. | DEC | 26 | [*superimposed stamps:*] 3 | 2 | 4; (3) stamped: JAN | 15; (4) stamped: SENT BACK TO ENGLAND | WITHOUT A REASON | FOR NON-DELIVERY; [*verso:*] (1) [*twice:*] in circle: HIGH WYCOMBE | C | DE 12 '60; (2) in larger circle: NEW HAVEN [*illegible*]; (3) stamped: SENT BACK TO ENGLAND | WITHOUT A REASON | FOR NON-DELIVERY

EDITORIAL COMMENT: A hoax? See n1.

Erastus Holbrook | Esqr Dec. 11 1860

Sir,

I accept, with a due sense of the distinction, the honor, which your University has conferred on me, in my unanimous election to a senior Fellowship / of the "Irving Historical Institute."[1]

I beg, that you will express, to the Rector & Fellows, my sentiments of profound respect, & that you will believe me,

with great consideration, | Sir, | Your faithful Servant, *B. Disraeli*

3529 TO: RALPH DISRAELI [Hughenden, Wednesday] 12 December 1860

ORIGINAL: BL ADD MS 59887 ff84-6

COVER: Ralph Disraeli Esqr | 73 Gloucester Place | Hyde Park | London | D. [*verso, in another hand (RD's?), a calculation:* 235 *minus* 155 *yielding* 80]

POSTMARK: [*recto:*] (1) a cancelled one-penny stamp; [*verso:*] (2) in circle: HIGH WYCOMBE | [*illegible*] | DE12 | 60; (3) in circular form: LONDON | W [*enclosing*] 8E | DE13 | 60

R. Disraeli Esq Dec 12 1860

My dear Ralph,

I am very much obliged to you, & very sorry, that I gave you so much trouble.[1] It was thoughtless on my part, but I wrote in a great hurry, / & only meant by "immediate", that you shd. take yr chance on yr return from yr official duties, & not delay the visit.

Malmesbury wrote to me it was a terra cotta. He bought D'Orsays original of / himself in terra cotta & D'Orsay's equestrian Nap: 1. "both beautiful" he says. I shd. like to have got poor dear D'Orsay, but I hope Malmesbury will continue to let me have a copy. I wonder he did not appropriate his old acquaintance / Nap. 3 – & ↑for↓ only £1!

It is, he says, as the Emperor used to appear at Lady Blessington's in 1840.

So, Layard is in! to the great disgust, I hear, of H.M's government.[2]

1 'Erastus Holbrook' on 31 October 1860 had written from Yale University to 'B. D'Israeli Esquire': 'I am directed to inform you that the Rector & Fellows of the Irving Historical Institute of Yale University have unanimously chosen you as an Honorary Senior Fellow of the First Rank. They request that you may communicate your acceptance of the same, so that your name and dignities may be appropriately recorded.' H A/VIII/E/19. D's acceptance was returned undelivered; see headnote (POSTMARKS). A person named Erastus Holbrook has been found in the Civil War Soldiers Database of the Rutherford B. Hayes Presidential Center (website): enlisted at age 39 on 2 May 1864 at Fremont, Ohio, in Regiment 169 of the Ohio National Guard for a four-month term as a private, discharged on 4 September 1864. There are no records at Yale of either the man or the institute.

1 See **3525**&nn1&2.

2 Austen Henry Layard, Radical, in an 11 December by-election at Southwark had defeated George Scovell, a former Conservative turned Liberal, by a substantial margin. *The Times* (12 Dec 1860). RD in his

I never hear of Jem. How is he? Letters in the country, from either of you, are very acceptable[.]

Yrs ever, | D.

TO: PHILIP ROSE Hughenden [Wednesday] 12 December 1860 3530

ORIGINAL: H R/I/A/144

EDITORIAL COMMENT: Paper imprinted 'Hughenden Manor'.

Private Dec 12 1860

P. Rose Esq

My dear Rose,

The Bishop of Chichester[1] has written to Lowndes for the three resolutions, wh: were passed at the Prestwood meeting.[2] He says, that he has ordered 1000 copies of / Mr. Disraeli's speech to be printed & circulated in his diocese, & has summoned a meeting of all his rural deans.

I think it would be expedient, that the resolutions shd. be published. In what paper? I don't see the "Herald," & therefore know / not, whether it has inserted the speech, or noticed it. The "Standard" I see. It curtailed the speech, wh: was not long, but well considered in every part, for I intended it as a manifesto – & then the "Standard" writes an article, calling the / attention of its readers to passages of the speech, wh: are the omitted portions of its report. Rather vexatious, as the portions omitted referred to the state of parties in Ch: & State both, & were highly important.[3]

7 December letter (see **3521**n2) had wondered whether Layard would win, and referred to a bragging speech Layard had made. In that speech, on 4 December, Layard had identified the *Standard,* 'the lowest of the Tory organs,' as the source of Scovell's abusive attacks on him; meanwhile, he had withdrawn a circular abusive of Scovell. *The Times* (5 Dec 1860). In June 1861, to keep the support of the Radicals and despite the Queen's objections because of Layard's attacks on the aristocracy, Palmerston would appoint him under-secretary of foreign affairs, a post he had briefly held in the 1852 Derby government; see VI **2291**n3. Ridley *Palmerston* 515.

---

1 Ashurst Turner Gilbert (1786-1870), DD 1822, fellow of Brasenose College, Oxford, 1822-42, vice-chancellor 1836-40, was bishop of Chichester 1842-70.

2 See **3523**n2. There is a two-page document in D's hand of the resolutions (the heading, 'PRESTWOOD RESOLUTIONS; moved after the speech of Mr. Disraeli on Church Rates', has been struck out): '1. That Petitions shd. at once be presented to Parliament generally praying for the maintenance of the Union between Church & State, & incidentally against the abolition of Church Rates. 2. That Associations of the Clergy & Laity ~~sh~~ for mutual counsel & co-operation in all matters affecting the interests of the Church, should be established, & encouraged, in every part of the Country. 3. That the Clergy of all political opinions, following the example of the Committee of Laymen, should bring their influence to bear on members of the House of Commons against the abolition of Ch: Rates, as a question affecting the constitution of the Country.' 'G.P. Newspapers' is written upside down in another hand at the bottom of the first page. H R/I/B/77.

3 Rose would reply the next day (13 December) that he had seen to it that the resolutions would be published in both the *Herald* and the *Standard,* with attention drawn to them: 'It was most annoying that the Speech should have been curtailed. Everybody thinks you have inaugurated a very important movement and one which will add strength to your own position. The worst of it is that many of our party are really the greatest radicals in their hearts, but the views you have enunciated are very popular with all the upper section of the Conservative party. What changes there are in this world, Gladstone going to Bradford with Bright & Cobden & Milner Gibson & you leading the Church party throughout the Kingdom.' H R/I/B/72a,b. The resolutions had been published in the *Sun* on 8 December and would also be published in *BH* on 15 December.

I shall be here for another week, & then pass thro' town to Torquay.[4]

Yrs ever, | D.

3531 TO: SARAH BRYDGES WILLYAMS Hughenden [Thursday] 13 December 1860

ORIGINAL: RTC [155]

PUBLICATION HISTORY: M&B IV 321, dated 13 December 1860, part of the second and the third paragaphs

EDITORIAL COMMENT: Paper imprinted 'Hughenden Manor'. There is no salutation. The postscript is written at the top of the first page.

Decr. 13. 1860

I shall be able to strike my flag next week; I think the earlier part. I shall be detained in London a few days, & must make one visit en route,[1] a short one, otherwise my visit / to Torquay will be curtailed, & I wish, on the contrary, to prolong it. But, under any circumstances, I count on having the pleasure, the very cordial gratification, of wishing you many, many, happy new years on / the 1st. Jany.[2]

I trust, & believe, they will be happy to both of us – but what will they be to the World? And what is preparing? A greater revolution, perhaps, in Austria, than ever occurred in France. / Then it was "the rights of *man*" – now, it is, "the rights of *nations*"[.]

Once, I said in "Coningsby", there is nothing like Race – it comprises all truths. The World will now comprehend that awful truth.[3]

Yrs ever, | D. /

My friend, Lord Salisbury has been shot at a battue. I enclose his letter to amuse – written by the hand of Lady Salisbury.[4]

4 The DS would be at Grosvenor Gate 19-27 December. H acc. Rose (n3) would ask that he be allotted a day with D in London.

---

1 To the Palks; see **3538**.

2 The DS would arrive in Torquay on New Year's Eve; see **3540**.

3 It was in *Tancred* (bk II ch 14) that D wrote 'All is race; there is no other truth', repeated in *LGB* ch 18, 'All is race'. The Italian war had revealed the Austrian empire's basic instability, with internal agitation against matters such as excessive taxation, and externally, especially for Hungarian independence; *The Times* on 12 December had published a report from Vienna of the crisis arising from the recent promise of a constitution granting Hungary a measure of autonomy.

4 *The Times* (8 Dec 1860) had reported the 'Accident to Lord Salisbury. – While out rabbit shooting in Hatfield-park the noble Marquis was unfortunately struck in the leg by several shots. We are happy to add that no further result is apprehended than a confinement to the house for a few days.' On 12 December Salisbury in a letter written by Lady Salisbury had thanked D for his letter (not found): 'I am as well as can be expected, but ordered to lie upon my back. I hope it will not be for long & that I shall be ready to witness the shots you purpose firing against Sir John Trelawny.' RTC [413Q]. For the debate on Trelawny's Church Rates Abolition Bill, see **3556**n1.

TO: SARAH BRYDGES WILLYAMS Hughenden [Tuesday] 18 December 1860 3532

ORIGINAL: RTC [156]
PUBLICATION HISTORY: M&B IV 321-2, dated 18 December 1860, the second and third paragraphs
COVER: Mrs. Brydges Willyams | Mount Braddon | Torquay | D.
POSTMARK: [*recto:*] a cancelled one-penny stamp [*verso not photographed*]
EDITORIAL COMMENT: Paper imprinted 'Hughenden Manor'.

Mrs: Brydges Willyams Dec 18. 1860

I return you yr pleasant letter from Nice.[1]

The Chinese news will greatly interest ↑you↓, & give you some capital reading in the "Times".[2]

It / is our privilege to live in a wonderful age of rapid & stirring events – & if time, as the poets say, is not to be counted by calendars, but by incidents & sensation, all our existences will be patriarchal.[3] Lord Mendip, / a friend of my fathers, used to say, that by the parish Register, & the Peerage, he was only 60 – but, having lived through the French Revolution, he ~~was~~ considered he was a 100, at least![4]

We have got Italian & Austrian Revolutions, & a / great many ~~more~~ others coming – & eastern wars, whether in India, China, or Japan, wh: beat all the marvels of the Arabian nights.

I strike my flag at Hughenden tomorrow.

I heard from the lawyers, that there was something to be done which was omitted, & was only too happy to be of use to you.[5]

Adieu! | D.

TO: JOHN MACMAHON Hughenden [Tuesday] 18 December 1860 3533

ORIGINAL: MOPSIK [202]
EDITORIAL COMMENT: Paper imprinted 'Hughenden Manor'. *Sic:* Macmahon.

Dec 18. 1860

Mr. Disraeli presents his Compliments to Mr. Macmahon, & begs leave to thank him

1 SBW in her 16 December letter had added a postscript: '(I enclose E.S.F.G. Butler's letter as it comes from Nice)'. RTC [414Q]. Emily Sarah Fitz-Gerald Butler was the James Butlers' 22-year-old eldest daughter.

2 The war in China (see **3441**&n8) had ended. The latest news was of the exchange of ratifications of the 1858 Treaty of Tientsin according to the convention signed in late October 1860, and of the 5 November allied withdrawal from Pekin. *The Times* of 17 December 1860 had published the texts of the ratifications along with the accompanying despatches to the foreign office, and a long report, dated 9 October at a camp before Pekin. SBW (n1) had written: 'Pray give my love and thanks to dear Mrs Disraeli for the regular visits of the Times at Breakfast after being in yr hand!'

3 D is perhaps referring to Byron's lines in *Manfred* (Act II, sc i): 'Think'st thou existence doth depend on time? / It doth; but actions are our epochs.' Philip James Bailey's *Festus* has the following lines (sc v *A Country Town*): 'We live in deeds, not years; in thoughts, not breaths; / In feelings, not in figures on a dial.'

4 Henry Welbore Agar Ellis (1761-1836), 2nd Viscount Clifden since 1789 in the Irish peerage, had inherited the English Barony of Mendip in 1802 and evidently was known by it.

5 See **3487**&n3. SBW (n1) had expressed 'many more grateful thanks for consenting to be one of my Trustees.'

for his volume on Metaphysics, wh: Mr Disraeli has recently had occasion to refer to with / much satisfaction.

It is a work of great interest, & real learning.[1]

3534 TO: LORD MALMESBURY Grosvenor Gate [Friday] 21 December 1860

ORIGINAL: HCC 9M73/459/11

EDITORIAL COMMENT: A copy, not in D's hand. *Sic:* (?); go bang [*for* 'go along'?].

Grosvenor Gate | Decr: 21st: 1860

My dear Malmesbury,

I am here – passing through to Devon.

I have obtained the following from a high source.[1]

There is a disturbance in the Cabinet, but about / finance. Gladstone wishes to pursue his democratic system, and begin at once with repeal of paper duties,[2] Lewis, Wood, G. Grey (the three baronets) moving heaven and earth against him.

[*illegible deletion*], ~~who told my~~ informant, in the country, and in confidence, said that / his relations with John Russell were as finished (?) as with Palmerston; that he and his friends only cared for Gladstone, to whom they were devoted; and that if he turned out, they would throw the Government into a minority when we like; / that we might have another innings ("two years") and that then the country would be really ripe for reform, which it is not now.

Under these circumstances it seems to me of the utmost importance that you should re-open your communications with the medium of last year, and let it be understood, / that if Palmerston goes straight on Reform and Finance, and holds by the aristocratic interests, we will keep him in, at all events, (not making even foreign policy an exception) just as Peel and his followers kept in J. Russell after '46. If any conditions or exceptions are made, Palmerston will / suspect a dodge. Let our support then be absolute, and let him keep the Government as long as he can.

Bright said that the Radicals would waive any pressure ~~about~~ of Reform, if Palmerston would go bang about the Paper. He feared he would not – "~~that~~ as the Whigs were / more against Gladstone's finance, even than the Tories". But I am not so sure of this. Palmerston might be glad to get rid of Reform with the tacit connivance of the Radicals, even at so bitter a cost as democratic finance which is worse than Reform in my mind. But, if / assured, as I intimate, the country might be saved, and the revolutionary party finally checked.

1 The Reverend John Henry MacMahon (1829-1900), classical scholar, BA 1852 (Trinity College, Dublin), ordained 1853, in 1860 published *A Treatise on Metaphysics, chiefly in reference to Revealed Religion.* He would retire from parochial work in 1869, after the disestablishment of the Irish church, to become chaplain to the lord lieutenant, and then, in 1890, to the Mountjoy prison. No letters from MacMahon to D have been found.

---

1 Probably C.P. Villiers; see **3440**&n3 and **3446**&n1.

2 For the recent history of the paper duty controversy, see **3470**&n1, **3471**&n1, **3480**&n4, **3481**&nn2&3, **3485**nn1-3 and **3491**&n1. See further **3578**&nn1&2, **3585** and **3586**&nn1&2.

Can you make all this out? My hand is frozen.

Yours Ever | D.

I shall be here three or four days: but always direct here.[3]

TO: RALPH DISRAELI Grosvenor Gate [Friday] 21 December 1860 3535

ORIGINAL: BL ADD MS 59887 ff87-8

COVER: R. Disraeli Esqr | 73 Gloucester Place | *Hyde Park* | D.

POSTMARK: (1) a cancelled one-penny stamp; (2) in circular form: LONDON [*enclosing*] 4 | DE21 | 60

EDITORIAL COMMENT: Paper imprinted 'Grosvenor Gate'.

Private My birth day 1860[1]

R. Disraeli | Esqr

My dear R,

I rather wanted three, to make a payment witht drawing on my bankers till the turn of the year – but if you can't do it, I entreat you, *sans ceremonie,* to put the smaller one in the / fire. Let me have the result, whatr. it is, tomorrow at the Carlton.[2]

Yrs ever, | D.

TO: RALPH DISRAELI [Carlton Club, Friday 21 December 1860] 3536

ORIGINAL: BL ADD MS 59887 ff 89-90

EDITORIAL COMMENT: *Dating and location: cf* **3535**. *Sic:* checque [*twice*].

R. Disraeli | Esqr 2 o'ck

My dear Ralph,

Many thanks – but, alas! I, of course, counted on finding yr checque *here.*

I am now obliged to draw / on Drummonds. All I must try to do now, is to restore the situation as soon as possible – &, therefore, I shall be glad to have yr checque / tomorrow at G.G. or here on Monday morning.

Yrs ever, | D.

3 Malmesbury would reply on 23 December: 'I perfectly understand yr views & entirely agree with them both as to national & party policy. I write to Derby in this sense & ask him *when* I ought to communicate with the medium.' H B/XX/HS/105. Derby on 26 December would reply to Malmesbury: 'I am obliged to you for a sight of Disraeli's letter, which I return. He had not written to me on the subject; and I hope has not taken offence at my telling him in my last letter that I thought he had gone rather too far in his declaration of "no compromise" on the subject of the Church-rates. In principle he is right; but it was our moderation and the refusal of the other side to listen to any terms which mainly caused the dwindling of the House of Commons majority and thus made *our* work the easier. I am afraid that Disraeli's outspoken declaration will lose us this advantage, which will not be counterbalanced by the increased support of the thoroughgoing Churchmen ... As to the main question of Disraeli's letter to you, I am very glad to find that he takes the view he does of our policy; and I shall be pleased to hear of the renewal of your confidential communications with *the Palmerstons,* for I suppose my Lady counts – *pour quelque chose.* I should not be afraid of entering on these *quasi* negotiations too soon. I believe Disraeli is quite accurate in his estimate of the relations between Government and the Bright and Cobden party.' He then made suggestions how Malmesbury might approach Palmerston. Malmesbury II 243-4. Malmesbury would write to D again on 2 January 1861: 'Palmerston being at Broadlands I wrote to him to say that as we believed him to be in a position analogous to that in wh he stood when I had my last interview I was deputed by Ld Derby & you to bold language also analogous to my former assurances – & I asked when he would be in London ... Enough has been said to shew him what we mean & keep up his pluck till I do [see him].' H B/XX/HS/106.

---

1 D turned 56 on this day.

2 See further **3536**.

3537 TO: KING LEOPOLD [London, Sunday] 23 December 1860

ORIGINAL: H B/II/56

PUBLICATION HISTORY: M&B IV 323-4, dated 23 December 1860

EDITORIAL COMMENT: A draft in D's hand, docketed by him on the *verso* of the last page: 'Decr. 23. 1860 | To the King of the Belgians'. *Sic:* condescention.

23. Dec 1860

Sir,

Yr Majesty's letter reached me only ~~last night~~↑~~this morning~~↓ today, but as I am informed that a courier leaves this for Bruss: tomorrow,[1] I will not hesitate to have the honor of addressing ↑to↓ you Sir, a few lines, feeling ~~persuaded~~ Yr M. will pardon them for being written currente calamo.

The leger de main wh: now distinguishes public affairs ↑& ↑to↓ wh: Yr Maj[es]ty so graphically refers↓ appears to me attributable to this circumstance wh: the Eng: Govt. ~~never~~ either does not recognise, or never suff[icient]ly appreciates. The French Emperor, to use a ~~colloquial metaphor~~ homely image, always runs two hares. His first hare was the old traditionary ~~Italian~~ policy of ~~France~~ the French cabt.: a divided Italy & French supremacy. Ld. John thought that in ~~esta~~ bringing about Italian Unity, he [*1 word added at bottom of page:*] ~~Your~~ / had checkmated Buonaparte – but he only threw the Emperor on his second hare, ↑a much more dangerous animal↓ in a ↑natural↓ head of the Latin race; – Venetia secured by France to Sardinia, & a ↑offensive &↓ defensive all: betn. France & Italy, in order, that France ~~in return~~ ↑in poss: of their united resources↓ may obtain some great object.

Had the treaty of Vill. F.[2] been sedulously supported, instead of ~~counteracted~~ ↑~~& is~~ system[aticall]y decried↓, by the Eng. Govt., there might have been a resting point, ~~at least~~ ↑perhaps↓ for some years, & during the interval, all our energies might have been applied to what shd. be the great object of ~~an~~ English Statesmen vizt. to terminate, ~~& if not~~ ↑or at least↓ to counteract the undersg. betn. F[rance] & Russia. /

At present, if all is dark & perplexing to Yr Majy. what must it be to me! There are

1 Sylvain Van de Weyer on 20 December had forwarded a letter to D from the King of the Belgians, and the messenger's return schedule should D wish to reply. H B/XXI/V/1. The King had written from Laeken on 19 December: 'You will think me very ungrateful not to have acknowledged sooner your kind communication [*see* **3496**], but I can plead not guilty to that. The state of Europe is very strange. There is after all a certain sameness in human affairs, but the present time is distinguished by a sort of *leger-de-main,* which is unlike to what history generally shows, and one is constantly tempted to ask: *qui trompe-t-on-ici?* Much is owing to the Oriental war; it has brought about, what at all times was justly feared, an understanding between France and Russia, and has given to France a complete supremacy on the Continent. Happily England has felt the necessity, for its own independence, of being well armed. If that had been neglected, England would have had a sort of existence on sufferance, and would have been exposed to great danger. I trust that the Conservative party will remain faithful to its policy, as it was the first that awakened to the danger. But it is not only in this case that the Conservative party is of the most vital importance; no constitutional Government can be carried on without it, and it is a great misfortune that in the present Parliament there is such a tendency to split into fragments instead of uniting for the public good. The affairs of Italy are very strangely appreciated in England. Whatever may be the future consequences, the immediate practical result is to give to France allies against Germany, and I don't think that by so doing the real interests of England are wisely consulted. Whatever weakens still more the power of Germany exposes us also here to new dangers, and we can only see this with just apprehension.' M&B IV 322.

2 For the Treaty of Villafranca, see VII **3388**&nn1&2.

no doubt ample materials in Italy, if France ~~ultimately~~ chooses to revert to her first policy, to disturb, perhaps destroy, Italian Unity ↑in the Spring↓. The coast (Liguria,), is republican; the country reactionary; & ~~ea~~ as for the great towns each of them ↑not only↓ desires, ~~&~~ ↑but↓ *expects,* to be the Capital. But these elements to be effective require French manipul[ati]on; & it is to be feared that the blind exertions of England will force France to the larger & more ~~dange~~ dangerous scheme – Scheme (Insert Mundy &c) (*Vid ~~OO~~ on other sheet*) / [*in another hand on a separate sheet:*]

Mundy O.O. Insertion before

Mundy, ~~the~~ ↑our↓ Adml.,[3] says the King spoke much agst the French, praised the English (tho' complaining of the Brigade)[4] & sd., that Ld. J's despatch[5] was "plus q'amical, c'était magnifique". When Mundy left the presence, the King shook his hand so violently, that he broke his nail. He does not think favorably of the King's prospects: he says he never witnessed so frigid a reception as that of V[ictor] E[mmanuel] at the Opera. [*End of passage to be inserted.*] /

One thing is quite clear – ~~that~~ Napoleon meditates next year, some accession of territory. Otherwise, he wd. not court the English people. One of his principles is always to distinguish betn. them & their government, in the hope, that when he makes the great coup, public opinion in England may restrain the Eng: Govt. from resisting him.

↑Mr. Cobden enforces these views very much on the Emperor, & we must remember that to the Emperor Mr Cn. is the minister x↓ [*on another sheet:*] x of the Queen of Gt Britain! This is another of the injurious consequences of that "untoward affair".[6] [*End of passage to be inserted.*]

With respect to the state of the Cons: party in the H of C. I can report very favorably of it. It has become very consolidated during the recess, & even increased its numbers by some elections.[7] ~~The~~ ↑Our charact[eristic]↓ ignorance respecting for[eign] pol[itic]s ~~wh: always prevails in Engl is a charact. of Engld~~ renders it ↑however↓ extremely difficult to direct this immense power to an effective / & beneficial end – but the difficulty is only one of time, & opportunities must be taken gradually & skilfully to ~~form~~ guide their sentiments. On the 5th. Feb on the address such an occasion wd. naturally offer – ~~In guiding~~ when ~~one is~~ I am expected to speak generally on affairs, ~~yet no division is under~~ witht. contemplating any ~~division~~ trial of strength. I trust I ~~don't~~ do not count entirely witht. reason on the condescension of Yr Majesty ↑in assisting me↓ in the interval by Yr. ↑~~gracious~~↓ counsel.

The Rom. Cath. party, as I anticipated in my last, has made an overture to me ↑for the overthrow of the Govt↓. ~~But~~ I discouraged the ~~pro~~ propos[iti]on tho' with courtesy.

3 George Rodney Mundy (1805-1884), KCB 1862, GCB 1877, rear-admiral 1857, was protecting British interests at Palermo and Naples 1859-60; he would be made vice-admiral 1863, admiral 1869.

4 About 1,400 young Irishmen, the Irish Papal Brigade (the Battalion of St Patrick), had responded to the Pope's call earlier this year to all European Catholics to help defend the papal states. See C.T. McIntire *England against the papacy 1858-1861* (1983) 200-4.

5 See **3526**n3.

6 Cobden had been in France from April to November negotiating the terms of the commercial treaty. He and Bright had had an audience with the Emperor on 27 November. Morley *Cobden* 756-7, 789-90.

7 In the ten by-elections during the recess held by this time, the Conservatives had won four.

3538 TO: SARAH BRYDGES WILLYAMS Carlton Club [Monday] 24 December 1860

ORIGINAL: RTC [157]
EDITORIAL COMMENT: Paper imprinted with the crest of the Carlton Club. There is no salutation.

Private Decr 24. 1860

I manage to wish you a happy Xmas, in the spirit, if not in the person.

We leave town on Thursday; stay two days at Sir Lawrence Palk's at Haldon, a long / -promised visit on his accession,[1] & which, if not accomplished now, would have broken up, & curtailed, our visit to Torquay – where I have directed our rooms to be prepared for us on the 30th: /

I never knew public affairs so involved, & involved on so great a scale. There has been nothing like it, since the great French Revolution. Apparently 1861 will witness the breaking up of the great Austrian Empire; the greatest political / dissolution since that of Rome.

I received, the day before yesterday, a letter from the King of the Belgians;[2] of extreme interest. I shall put it into my despatch box to show you.

Yours ever, | D.

3539 TO: SARAH BRYDGES WILLYAMS [Haldon House, Exeter] Saturday 29 December 1860

ORIGINAL: RTC [158]
EDITORIAL COMMENT: There is no salutation.

Saturday. Dec 29/60.

We have been ↑here↓ two days, blocked up by the snow – but count on being at Torquay on Monday, by an early train. Country / life, entirely within doors, & without, a Siberian waste – is not fascinating.

Eating without exercise, & dressing without guests (for the weather has prevented anyone / arriving) is what is called a merrie Xmas![1] Torquay will be as refreshing to us, as Grand Cairo to the pilgrims after the desert! /

We count on the great pleasure of seeing you, & seeing you quite well.

Ever | D.

3540 TO: SARAH BRYDGES WILLYAMS [Torquay, Monday] 31 December [1860]

ORIGINAL: RTC [159]
EDITORIAL COMMENT: Endorsed (by SBW?): '1860'. There is no salutation.

Decr 31 –

We have just arrived; it would be delightful to pay you a little visit now, if you are disengaged.

Ever yrs | D.

A *verbal* answer.

1 See **3491**&n3.
2 See **3537**n1.

1 Palk in his 9 December letter from Haldon House, after bemoaning the 'disgraceful' weather, had promised D that 'you shall dress as you please & your feeding shall be as seldom as circumstances will permit, I will keep all bores at a distance & you shall enjoy the Luxury of repose'. H B/XXI/T/46.

TO: SARAH BRYDGES WILLYAMS [Torquay] Monday [7 January 1861?] 3541

ORIGINAL: RTC [74]

EDITORIAL COMMENT: Endorsed in another hand: '1857'. *Dating*: by the weather; see n1.

Monday

It is freezing so hard, & the snow is so deep,[1] that Mrs. Dis thinks driving is hardly practicable – but proposes, that we shall / call on you at ¼ past three o'ck.

We send two papers.

Yrs ever, | D.

TO: N.M. ROTHSCHILD & SONS Hatfield [Wednesday] 16 January 1861 3542

ORIGINAL: ROTH RAL RFAM C/2/47

EDITORIAL COMMENT: Endorsed in another hand: 'B Disraeli 16 Jany 1861'.

Messrs Rothschild & Sons Hatfield[1] | Jan. 16 1861

Gentlemen,

Will you have the kindness to place £80, enclosed, to the acct. of Mr. F. Vance of Bilbao.[2]

Yrs truly | *B. Disraeli*

TO: LORD STANLEY Grosvenor Gate [Friday] 18 January 1861 3543

ORIGINAL: DBP Box 47/2

EDITORIAL COMMENT: Paper imprinted 'Grosvenor Gate'. Endorsed by Stanley on the fourth page: 'Disraeli. Jan. 61 Accepted.'

Rt Honble | The Lord Stanley, | MP. Jan. 18. 1861

Dear Stanley,

I hope you will give me the pleasure of yr company at dinner on the 4th. Feby. – to talk over the Queen's / speech – a very small party – only our late colleagues & one or two more – therefore business, & you will be much wanted.[1]

I am told the present / deficiency, on Gladstone's spirit estimate, is three mill &

1 The weather described best fits the conditions general in England on the second Monday of the DS' 1860-61 stay at Torquay; however, *cf* **3547** and **3555**.

1 Lady Salisbury had written to MA on 3 January 1861 to invite the DS to Hatfield 14-17 January; they had returned from Torquay on 12 January and left Grosvenor Gate for Hatfield on 14 January. H D/III/C/275, acc. See further **3547**&n1.

2 To Francis Villiers, that is; *cf* **3484**&n1. See further **3564**.

1 Parliament would open on 5 February. Of the political dinners given the previous evening to discuss the Queen's speech, D's at Grosvenor Gate would entertain 'a select party of members of the House of Commons, including the members of the late Cabinet.' *MP* (5 Feb 1861). MA recorded: '4th Monday dined here ↑Rt Honbl↓ Lord John Manners Rt Honl Lord Stanley Rt H. General Peel Rt Hon Sir John Pakington Rt Honl Sir William Jolliffe Rt Honbl T.S. Estcourt & Sir Stafford Northcote Total with Dizzy 8'. She also recorded that nine bottles of various wines were consumed. H acc.

½![2] A wonderful financier! There are only two things, wh: he does not understand: income / & expenditure!

I hope our chief continues mending.[3]

Yrs ever, | D.

3544 TO: SIR WILLIAM JOLLIFFE Grosvenor Gate [Friday] 18 January 1861

ORIGINAL: SCR DD/HY C/2165 [60]

EDITORIAL COMMENT: Paper imprinted 'Grosvenor Gate'.

Rt Honble | Sir W.H. Jolliffe | Bart: M.P. Jany. 18 1861

My dear Jolliffe –

I count on the pleasure of yr company at dinner on the 4th. Feby., to talk over the Queen's speech – a very / small party; only my late colleagues in the Cabinet[.]

Yrs ever, | D.

R.S.V.P. / dinner ½ pt. 7 precisely

3545 TO: SIR JOHN PAKINGTON Grosvenor Gate [Friday] 18 January 1861

ORIGINAL: WRC 705:349 BA 3835/7(ii)15

EDITORIAL COMMENT: Paper imprinted 'Grosvenor Gate'.

Rt Honble | Sir Jno. Pakington | G.C.B. Jany. 18. 1861

My dear Pakington,

I hope you will give me the pleasure of yr company at dinner on the 4th. Feby.; to talk over the Queen's speech – a very small party / – only our late colleagues, & one, or two, more.

We dine at ½ pt 7 precisely.

My compliments to Lady Pakington.

Yrs sincerely, | D. /

R.S.V.P.[1]

2 James Haig had written to D from Lincoln's Inn on 12 January that the latest excise revenue returns showed a decrease in spirits revenue of £1½ million instead of the expected increase of £2 million; he enclosed an article on the subject in that day's *John Bull*. H B/XIX/ADDS.

3 Stanley would accept the invitation next day 'with much pleasure. If Gladstone's estimates turn out as you expect, there is an end of him as a financier –, and what is more important, there is an end of the paper duty v. income-tax controversy, for the present.' He thought the elections showed 'a conservative leaning in the country, but if we have a majority can we use it? My father goes on as well as possible.' H B/XX/S/705. In his diary, he would also record a meeting with D on 29 January: 'D. repeated to me what he had said before in letters: that it was the business of Conservatives to support the ministry: he evidently looks to the death or retirement of Lord P. as an event not likely to be long delayed, and expects a general disruption of his followers to succeed. He said that it was certain there could be no reform bill: and probably the immense deficit now existing would check Gladstone in any attempt at financial change. As to Italian, and foreign affairs generally, he did not see his way: thought the Emperor himself undecided, thought there were no present designs on the Rhine: did not see what would come out of the Italian complication, and knew no one who could give any information. He appeared to expect a quiet session, so far as in the uncertainty of politics anything can be foreseen.' *Disraeli, Derby* 165.

---

1 Pakington is listed among those who attended. H acc.

TO: [CONSERVATIVE MPS] Hughenden [Saturday] 19 January 1861 3546

ORIGINALS: INL O'Hara Papers MS 20,346 (8)

EDITORIAL COMMENT: Several identical copies of the following text in D's hand have been found: H B/II/76a; PRIN C0077, Straus Autograph Collection, Box 1, Folder 63; WSRO Mitford Archives MS 55 f61a f25. See n1. Other examples are **3646**ec, **3776**ec and **3889**ec.

Sir, Hughenden Manor | Jany. 19. 1861

The meeting of Parliament being fixed for the fifth of February, I beg the favor of your attendance in the / House of Commons on the first day of the Session.

I have the honor to be, | Sir, | Your faithful Servt. | *B. Disraeli*[1]

TO: SARAH BRYDGES WILLYAMS Carlton Club [Saturday] 19 January 1861 3547

ORIGINAL: RTC [160]

PUBLICATION HISTORY: M&B IV 294, dated 19 January [1861], extract from the third paragraph, and 382, dated January 1861, the last sentence; Blake 430, extract dated 19 January 1861

EDITORIAL COMMENT: Carlton Club paper. There is no salutation.

Private Jany. 19. 1861.

We found a very large party at Hatfield – the Duc d'Aumale, the Duke of Wellington, the Austrian Ambassador & the Countess Apponyi, the Countess Cowley, our / Ambassadress at Paris, & two beautiful Ladies Wellesley, just launched into the ocean of life & fashion – but, alas! our own Ambassador at Paris, Earl Cowley, was prevented leaving that capital at / the last moment.[1] [*sentence added:*] There was a crowd of others.

Affairs are most critical!

The Conservative party is gaining every day. The Whig candidate won't ~~fing~~ fight in Aberdeenshire: the Whig Candidate is beaten / in Pembrokeshire: the Whig Candidates will be beaten in Wiltshire & Leicester![2] Pretty well!

1 Several visually identical copies of this circular written in D's most careful hand have been found; see ORIGINALS. Three are to unknown recipients, WSRO Mitford Archives is presumably to W.T Mitford, and INL O'Hara Papers to C.W. O'Hara, in a file marked '14 letters to C.W. O'Hara Jan 1861' and endorsed in another hand on the fourth page of the copy: '*1861* Right Hon *B Disraeli* Jany. 28th Meeting of Parliament'. Evidently a copying process (probably lithography) was used, as with previous circulars (*eg* VII **3042**&ec and **3280**&n1); see VII **3349**ec. Charles William O'Hara (1817-1898), of Annaghmore and Cooper's Hill, co Sligo, JP, DL for Sligo, high sheriff 1849, was MP (C) for Sligo 1859-65; in 1860 he had assumed the surname O'Hara instead of his patronymic Cooper, but seems to have continued to be known as Cooper.

---

1 Count Rudolph Apponyi in 1840 had married a daughter of Count Alexander Benkendorff and niece of Princess Lieven. Dino III. Lord Cowley, British ambassador at Paris, in 1833 as Henry R.C. Wellesley had married Olivia Cecilia Fitz-Gerald de Ros (1807-1885), 2nd surviving daughter of Lord Henry Fitz-Gerald and his wife, Charlotte, Baroness de Ros. The Cowleys' two daughters (who had come out in 1858 and 1859 respectively) were: Lady Feodorowna Cecilia Wellesley (1840-1920), who in 1874 would marry Sir Francis Leveson Bertie (cr Baron Bertie 1915, Viscount Bertie 1918); and Lady Sophia Georgiana Robertina Wellesley (1841-1923), who in 1863 would marry Viscount Royston (5th Earl of Hardwicke 1873); see **3790**&n5. *MP* (23 Apr 1858, 9 May 1859). Lady Salisbury's invitation (**3542**n1) had specifically asked the DS for 14-17 January 'to meet Lord & Lady Cowley whom we expect then from Paris'.

2 Aberdeenshire had been left vacant by the succession to the Lords of Lord Haddo (L). Sir Alexander Bannerman (L) had withdrawn, since he had only recently returned from the continent. On 13 February

Until ~~tod~~ to day, the weather has been most severe, & the sufferings of the people intense. We could not believe what we have seen & / felt, since we have left your soft shores, where we breakfasted with our window open![3]

It is impossible to give you any notion of the number of persons I have to see, / & the number of letters I have to write.

On Wednesday, the 23rd, we go to Windsor Castle, on a visit to the Queen, until the 25th. It is Mrs. Disraeli's first visit to Windsor, & / is considered very marked on the part of Her Majesty to the wife of the leader of the Opposition, when many Cabinet Ministers have been asked there *witht.* their wives.[4]

Yrs ever | D.

3548 TO: EDWARD KENEALY Grosvenor Gate [Saturday] 19 January 1861

ORIGINAL: BRN [27]
EDITORIAL COMMENT: Paper imprinted: 'Grosvenor Gate'.

E. Kenealy Esqr Jany. 19 1861

Dear Sir,

I shall be very glad to read yr pamphlet, as I always am anything written by you.

I am only passing thro' / town, but anything, sent here, will always reach me.[1]

Yours very faithfully, | *B. Disraeli*

William Leslie (C) would defeat Bannerman's substitute, Arthur Gordon. The seat for Pembrokeshire left vacant by the succession to the Lords of Viscount Emlyn (L) had been unexpectedly won on 17 January by G.L. Philipps (C) over Col Hugh Owens (L). In S Wilts, Capt (later Col) F.H. Bathurst (C) on 14 February would be returned unopposed for the seat left vacant by Sidney Herbert's elevation to the Lords; a requisition to him had been 'numerously signed in several parts of the division' on 17 January, and a 'severe contest' was expected with T.F. Grove (L), before Grove withdrew on 12 February (Grove would take the seat in 1865). *MP* (13, 18, 19 Jan 1861). The vacancy at Leicester caused by the sudden death of Dr J.W. Noble (L) had revealed a split in the local party that would allow W.U. Heygate (C, unsuccessful in 1859) to win on 7 February over two Liberals, J.D. Harris and P.A. Taylor; *The Times* on 21 January would report a clear Liberal majority of several hundreds by the current registration, though Harris was said to have been forced on the Liberals by a party minority and to be unpopular because of an alleged coalition with the Tories at the last election. Manners on this day (19th) wrote to accept D's invitation for 4 February, hoping, 'from what we hear, that before then Leicester will have sent us up a recruit.' H B/XX/M/118.

3 SBW had written to MA on 11 January, the Ds' last day in Torquay: 'I shall be happy to be with you and dear Dizzi as soon after your Dinner as you will admit me.' RTC [415Q].

4 The two other wives at the dinners on 23 and 24 January were the Marchioness of Westminster and the Countess of Tankerville, neither married to cabinet ministers. Palmerston on this day (19th) was staying without his wife. *MP* (21, 25-6 Jan 1861). The Ds were entertained at dinner by military bands and on the 24th by a performance of Lytton's play *Richelieu*. See also Introduction p xiv.

---

1 Kenealy had written on 16 January from 10 Gray's Inn Square asking where to send early copies of his anonymous pamphlet, due out on 'Monday next', which he thought would amuse D. '[It] is ... in the form of a letter to Lord Palmerston from a Major of the Volunteers: and if it should be successful I mean to follow it with another at the close of the Session of Parliament. I have not mentioned the authorship in the matter to any person except yourself.' H B/XXI/K/85. For D's previous contacts with Kenealy see IV **1496**&n3 and V **2004**&n1.

TO: SIR WILLIAM JOLLIFFE Grosvenor Gate [Tuesday] 22 January 1861 3549

ORIGINAL: SCR DD/HY C/2165 [61]

Grosvenor Gate | Jany. 22. 1861

Rt Honble | Sir W.H. Jolliffe | Bart: M.P.

My dear Jolliffe,

I must deprive Mrs. Disraeli, who much regrets it, & myself, of the pleasure of paying Lady Jolliffe a / visit. We are commanded to Windsor Castle tomorrow till Friday,[1] &, at the end of the week, we were engaged to go to Blenheim.[2] I have been obliged, howr, to ask the Duchess to receive / us on some other occasion, as I find the pressure of affairs now getting very great,[3] &, unfortunately, on the 30th., I have a Bucks Ball, where Royalty is to be present & from wh: we cannot / extricate ourselves.[4]

With our kindest remembrances to Lady Jolliffe & all at Merstham,

Ever yrs | D.

TO: G. CHAMBERS Grosvenor Gate [Wednesday] 23 January 1861 3550

ORIGINAL: H H/LIFE

EDITORIAL COMMENT: The following is from a copy in the Monypenny papers.

G. Chambers Esq Grosvenor Gate | Jan 23. 1861.

Sir

I thank you for your letter. It is a great crisis in Church affairs, but, with skill & courage, I trust we shall win.[1]

Yours faithfully | B. Disraeli

TO: LORD DERBY Grosvenor Gate [Monday] 28 January 1861 3551

ORIGINAL: DBP Box 46/1

PUBLICATION HISTORY: M&B IV 295, dated at Grosvenor Gate, 28 January 1861, the sixth and seventh paragraphs; M&B IV 358, dated at Grosvenor Gate 28 January 1861, the first three paragraphs; M&B IV 382, undated, the first sentence of the sixth paragraph; Blake 430-1, extract from M&B dated 28 January 1861; Ellens 181, dated 28 January 1861, extract from the third paragraph

EDITORIAL COMMENT: Paper imprinted 'Grosvenor Gate'. Endorsed by Derby on the last page: 'Disraeli B.'

Private Jany 28 1861

Rt Honble | The Earl of Derby | K.G.

My dear Lord,

I was in hopes, that twelve years of trying companionship might have assured you,

1 See **3547**&n4 and **3555**&n2.

2 The Duchess of Marlborough had written to MA from Blenheim on 19 January inviting the DS to visit for a few days from the 28th. H D/III/C/349.

3 See **3551**&nn2-6.

4 See **3555**.

---

1 The letter to which D is responding has not been found; possibly it was from the George Frederick Chambers who compiled *The Church-and-State Handy-Book of Arguments, Facts, and Statistics suited to the times* published in 1866. Another possibility is the Rev George Chambers currently chaplain to the Medway Union (1855). For the crisis, see **3551**&nn2-6.

that I was ever grateful for criticism, even from my adversaries – & that it was impossible I cd. resent the gentle comments of one, who, tho' I have committed / so many errors, has never reproached me.

The only reason of my silence was, that I had nothing to write about. The situation, wh: I intimated in my last letter, never altered.[1]

As for Ch. Rates, I took the step after great enquiry & reflection; & I think if I had not taken it, our counties would have slipped away. The moment was more than ripe. The enclosed will give you some idea how it / worked in Wales, where the clergy, & the Ch: generally, are weakest. It will work more powerfully in Wiltshire, – & from the numerous communications wh: reach me, I think I shall have effected my purpose.[2] All, that I am afraid of, are the Bishops, acted on by a coterie, who hate us, & have flattered themselves they had a monopoly of Church championship. Most of these people are now out of Parliamt: Roundell Palmer, B. Hope & Co: but they are unceasingly at work. / They can do the Ch: no good, for they are utterly incapable of managing England; being a finical & fastidious crew, who are more anxious about what they call the Church, than the Church of England. My own Diòcesan has left them, & in his triennial-charge, this autumn, declared against their projects: the Bp of Exeter, whom I saw at Torquay, is all right, & will be up for the meeting of Parliament.[3] I have unceasingly worked, since you wrote to me, to counteract any

1 Derby had written from Knowsley on 27 January 1861: 'I hope you were not displeased at the frankness with which I expressed my fears as to the effect of your Speech on the Church Rate question. I have not heard from you since.' H B/XX/S/280. See **3523**&n2 for D's 4 December 1860 church-rates speech and Derby's comments of 12 December. Derby on 26 December had written to Malmesbury: 'I am obliged to you for a sight of Disraeli's letter [*not found*], which I return. He had not written to me on the subject; and I hope has not taken offence at my telling him in my last letter that I thought he had gone rather too far in his declaration of "no compromise" on the subject of Church-rates. In principle he is right; but it was our moderation and the refusal of the other side to listen to any terms which mainly ... made *our* work the easier. I am afraid that Disraeli's outspoken declaration will lose us this advantage ...' Malmesbury II 243.

2 The 'enclosed' has not been found. Lord Robert Montagu on 2 January had written to D as '"Lay consultee" for the Rural Deanery of Amersham' that 202 rural deaneries had by that date joined 'us' (*ie* the Church Institution; see n3) and he had got D's form of words carried: 'I think it will be all right. Viz: that as the National Church is for the good of the poor &c of all the country, & as the Church is not fighting for any selfish rights of her own, but for ability to do her appointed duty by the nation, it is more a question for the Laity than the clergy &c &c. Did you write to the Archbishop?' H B/XXI/M/432. Sotheron-Estcourt had written on 8 January that, having seen a draft of the bill to abolish church rates, he was concerned that it would expose the party disagreement suppressed in the previous session by getting the bill withdrawn. H B/XXI/E/259. Archdeacon W.H. Hale had written on 2, 21 and 26 January, on the 21st that he had told Mr Selwyn (see n4) on 'Saturday' what occurred in 'our' meeting on Friday (18 January). He was anxious to hear from D about settling church rates. So many had pledged votes and attempted conciliation only because they considered it a hopeless cause, that when they suddenly saw fundamental principles recognized, they would see that their promises to vote against church rates were made under a false premise. On the 26th he had written: 'I have read with most painful interest the papers issued by the Liberation society and which I have forwarded to Mr Selwyn. They seem to me to confirm the ideas which I have entertained of the necessity under which we are placed, of recalling to the minds of Members of Parliament, Constitutional principles.' H B/XXI/H/13-15. Meanwhile, at S Wilts (see **3547**&n2), Capt F.H. Bathurst in accepting the requisition had declared himself opposed to abolishing the church rates while still open to moderate alternatives. *The Times* (23 Jan 1861).

3 When the Liberation (of religion from the state) Society in 1859 had reluctantly revealed that their motive in opposing the church rates was disestablishment, a split had developed in the Church (defence) Institution (of which D was evidently a member and indeed a lay consultee; see n2 and Ellens 173); the

mischief from my movement, & to secure all the good, wh: might accrue from / it, & if the Bishops will only be quick & not commit themselves any further on the subject, leaving the question to the Country & the Ho: of Commons, I have no fear whatever of ultimate success.

I think it would be worth while considering, whether, on the presentation of the Archdeacon's petition, notice shd. not be given of moving [a] resolution on it. It is / a great constitutional question, wh: might justify such a course. A man like Selwyn could do such a thing.[4] But of this, & all other matters, anon.

I only saw Malmesbury yesterday, when I heard the result of his conference.[5] I

dominant side (with which D had conspicuously aligned himself in his 4 December speech) now abandoned its inclination to compromise and adopted a 'no surrender' stance, while a number of (mostly anglo-catholic) members, who feared that identification of the church with the Conservative party would ultimately militate against church establishment and/or the potential unity of the universal Catholic body, resisted this change. The acrimonious division had surfaced conspicuously at a meeting of the Church Institution on 21 January 1861 when the clause in J.G. Hubbard's proposed bill exempting Dissenters was staunchly defended by Roundell Palmer and Beresford-Hope and attacked by Lord Robert Montagu. Also, two articles in the *Saturday Review* (of which Beresford-Hope was a founder and owner), 'Mr. Disraeli on Church Rates' (15 Dec 1860, 760) and 'Church-Rates' (26 Jan 1861, 92-3), had mocked D's '"No Surrender"' position as a cynical attempt to make the church beholden to the Conservatives. D may also have been aware of some of the other activities of the 'crew'; a number of high-church and anglo-catholic groups had been formed in the 1850s, such as the Association for the Promotion of the Unity of Christendom, that also involved Roman Catholic and Greek Orthodox members and initially had the blessing of the Pope. Another (the same?) group (nicknamed the Anglo-Continental Association) since about 1855 had been promoting the unity of the Christian Church by publishing books to explain the catholicity of the Church of England on the continent. Its membership included four English bishops, among them Wilberforce (Oxford) and Phillpotts (Exeter), with Roundell Palmer (L-C, out of parliament from March 1857 to July 1861) and Alexander Beresford-Hope (L-C, out of parliament from April 1859 to July 1865) – and others such as Lord Robert Cecil and Gladstone – among the lay members. Ellens Chap IV ('Church Defense: Opportunities Missed, 1859-1865'); Walter Walsh *The Secret History of the Oxford Movement* (3rd ed, 1898) 307ff; James Embry *The Catholic Movement and the Society of the Holy Cross* (The Faith Press 1931) introduction ('The Catholic Movement in the Early Fifties'). For Wilberforce's triennial visitation of Bucks, see **3515**&n2. The projects which in his charge he specifically opposed because he now knew they were used to promote disestablishment were abolition of church rates for the sake of fairness, the Deceased Wife's Sisters Bill because it would create a division between the law of the state and the law of the church, and revision of the prayer book. *BH* (10 Nov 1860). On 28 December 1860 Earle had sent from Florence insider diplomatic gossip and praise for D's church-rates speech: 'The high church people are great fools, if they do not close with the offer. That Beresford Hope, who wrote the article in his own paper, (very weak du reste) will do us all the mischief in his power, but I dont think we need fear him.' H B/XX/E/191.

4 Charles Jasper Selwyn (1813-1869), a bencher (Lincoln's Inn) 1856, QC 1856, was MP (C) for Cambridge University 1859-68, solicitor-general (and knighted) 1867, lord-justice of appeal (and PC) 1868. Selwyn, who on the 22nd had arranged to call on D on Sunday the 27th, wrote to D on this day, the 28th, from Lincoln's Inn: 'I have had a satisfactory interview with Mr. H. Davies the Secretary of the Church Institution. The proposed public meeting at Willis Rooms will probably be abandoned. He says that Mr Hubbard has only one supporter in the Committee of the Institution: and that there is no chance of any proposal coming from that body in favour of his Bill. I have suggested, (but without much hope of success) that Mr. Hubbard and Mr. Howes shall withdraw their Bills for the present for the sake of unity. I have also seen Archdeacon Hale, who is to call upon the Archbishop tomorrow and hopes that the Archbishops and Bishops will concur with the Archdeacons.' H B/XXI/S/100-1. See further **3556**&n1.

5 Derby had written (n1): 'I suppose you have heard from Malmesbury (as I know you were an assenting party to his interview with Palmerston) the result of his Conversation, which leads me to hope that the Radical party, in and out of the Cabinet, will find themselves checkmated in the approaching Session.' In his 26 December letter to Malmesbury (also n1) Derby had written: 'As to the main question of Disraeli's letter to you, I am very glad to find that he takes the view he does of our policy [of supporting the

had met Shaftesbury at Torquay, who talked to me very freely on public matters & private considerations, &, without interfering with Malmesburys more formal & authoritative mission, I assisted the result.[6] /

They were very gracious, & very communicative.[7] They appeared to me greatly distressed & disgusted with public affairs. I had occasion to mention the state of our party; its numbers, compactness, general good understanding; its increase of strength; & I ventured to say, that we should probably win every impending election.

"But you have no newspapers," he exclaimed pettishly "the Country is governed by newspapers! And all / the Liberal Journals are in the pay of Foreign powers.[8] So much for the Liberty of the Press. Howr, when Parliament is sitting, their influence is less."

I must reserve all details till Saturday at three o'ck.[9] I leave town on Wednesday, but shall return on Friday night.[10]

Yours sincerely, | D.

3552 TO: PHILIP ROSE — Carlton Club [Monday] 28 January 1861

ORIGINAL: H R/I/A/145

EDITORIAL COMMENT: Carlton Club paper. An 'Extract' from this letter is in H R/III/B/34. *Sic:* tolerably.

P. Rose Esqr — Jany. 28. 1861

My dear Rose,

There *is*↑, or perhaps *was*,↓ an insurance in the Westminster for £*2,500* – annual premium

£10..1.

It is of the time of Bryce, / but in my name. The policy was given to Routledge.[1]

government]'. On 2 January Malmesbury had written to D: 'Palmerston being at Broadlands I wrote to him to say that as we believed him to be in a position analagous to that in wh he stood when I had my last interview I was deputed by Ld. Derby & you to hold language also analogous to my former assurances.' H B/XX/HS/106. See also M&B IV 293-4 and LQV III 429-30.

6 Shaftesbury had written to D on 17 January: 'Lord Palmerston was much gratified by the communication which you impressed me to make to him. On the three points specified there will arise but little, or indeed, no difference. Reserving, of course, his own opinion, & freedom of action, in respect of Church rates, he distinctly said that there was no intention of making it a "Government question".' H B/XXI/S/116. See M&B IV 295.

7 Derby had written (n1): 'I see you and Mrs. Disraeli were at Windsor last week. I hope H.M. was gracious and communicative.' See M&B IV 295 and *Disraeli, Derby* 165. See also **3895**&n2.

8 Cobden recorded an interview he and Bright had with Napoleon in late November 1860 in which the Emperor told them as a secret that he had bought the *Chronicle* and offered to put it under their control. Cobden had surprised him by saying that such an arrangement could not be kept secret, as he had known of the purchase for some months. Morley *Cobden* 790.

9 Derby had written (n1): 'I shall be in Town on Friday night, but not till late; and if you can call on me at 3 o'Clock either on Saturday or Sunday, I shall be glad to have an opportunity of discussing with you our programme.'

10 The DS would be at Mentmore from Wednesday to Friday. H D/III/C/1906; acc. Stanley would visit them on the 29th. *Disraeli, Derby* 165.

---

1 Rose had written on 26 January: 'Routledge asserts that he received strict orders from *Mr Lovell* to *assure* the Books at your special request. This appears to me very unlikely but I shall feel obliged by your ascertaining whether there is any foundation whatever to the statement. It will make a considerable difference in settling the account as Routledge has charged nearly £20 per ann: for insurance only and I am satisfied

I shall send you immediately a good remittance. I have been only waiting for / the payment into Drummond of my foreign divds. now due a week ↑& more↓. I shall, probably, find the announcement on my return home.

Ever yrs | D. T.O. /

Routledge ought to engage to give me the right of correcting the press of new editions ↑or impressions.↓ Hitherto the state of affairs has been unsatisfactory. There is no tolerably library Edit: of my own works, & he has sold the partial Edit: of Bryce, wh: was miserable.

R. has in fact suppressed the works, as much as possible, of late.

TO: EDWARD SELBY LOWNDES [London, Wednesday] 30 January 1861 **3553**

ORIGINAL: H PH/WM/A/4498 Item 318

EDITORIAL COMMENT: The imprint on the first page, presumably 'Grosvenor Gate', has been cut out.

E. Selby Lowndes Esqr Jany 30 1861

My dear Selby Lowndes,

You are the most munificent of Chasseurs, & the kindest of friends: you are a manor in yourself; an estuary; a real River God, ordering clouds of yr subjects, in the shape of wild fowl; ducks, / teal, & snipes, to pay homage & tribute to yr friends. I cannot express to you, how kind I think yr constant, & too splendid, recollections of us! My wife requests me particularly to recall her to yr recollection.

We left the county early in ~~this~~ ↑last↓ month, after four months / delightful residence at Hughenden, mainly passed in planting – that seductive pursuit. I dread to hear the fortune of our evergreens in this winter! We have been since at Torquay, where we cheated the season – & then to Hatfield, where we found a very large & agreeable party – & thence to Windsor / castle – Now we are on the wing, for two days to Mentmore – & then return – to business.

The world seems quite topsy-turvy – but I hope the good County of Buckingham will experience no revolutions. At any rate, there can be none in the feelings, with wh: I subscribe myself, with Complimts. to Mrs. Selby Lowndes.[1]

Sincerely yrs | D.

TO: [JOSEPH WOLFF] Grosvenor Gate [Wednesday] 30 January 1861 **3554**

ORIGINAL: H B/II/58

EDITORIAL COMMENT: A draft in D's hand. Endorsed in another hand on the first page: 'To Dr Wolff'.

Grosvenor Gate | Jan. 30. 1861

that the claim is unjust. I doubt if he even had any authority from anyone & if he had I dont believe he ever acted on it. I will communicate with Mr Lovell if you prefer it. Apart from the settlement of the past accounts which is still pending Routledge offers to give £500 for the use of the Copyright for *three* years.' H R/I/B/80. See also V **1836**n1, VI **2571**n1, **2671**&n1, VII **3063**&n1 and **3066**n2.

1 Edward William Selby Lowndes (1813-1885), of Winslow House, Bucks, JP and DL of Bucks, in 1834 had married Mary Elizabeth Hartman (d 1877), daughter of Isaac R. Hartman.

Revd & Dear Sir,

I shall feel honored by the dedication to me of any of yr works.[1]

I know yr son, who is clever, & who will, I think, succeed in the world, but I am sorry to hear, that he is so weakminded as to be ashamed of his race. This is feebleness under any circumstances, but sheer folly in a man, who is sprung from / the great Semitic family, the organisation of wh: ranks among the highest. Everybody knows, that Mr. Drummond Wolff is yr son, & the only consequence of his not being mentioned in yr memoirs, is, that the world will scandalously imagine, that the parental tie may be of an ultra-morganatic character, & that / he may be the offspring of some of those dangerous dancing girls from whom you so properly fled, or, perhaps, with more appearance of probability of those forlorn damsels of Cashmeer, whom you met running away clothed in shawls & diamonds, & from whom yr ultimate separation is not so clearly indicated / in yr memoirs, as the religious public might desire.

I congratulate you on your approaching marriage. A happy marr[iag]e is the most fortunate lot of man, & I feel sure you will find one in entering the honorable family of my good friend & supporter the member for Herefordshire.[2]

Believe me | Revd & dr Sir | Yrs truly | D.

1 The Rev Dr Joseph Wolff (1795-1862), born in Germany the son of a rabbi, baptised 1812, with degrees from Vienna, Tübingen, Rome, the U.S., St Andrews and Trinity College Dublin (LLD), ordained in the U.S. 1837, currently vicar at Isle Brewers in Somersetshire, had several publications based on his missionary work in the middle east, such as *Sketch of the Life and Journal of Joseph Wolff* (1827), *Researches and missionary labours among the Jews, Mohammedans and other sects ...* (1835) and *Travels and adventures of the Rev. Joseph Wolff... late missionary to the Jews and Muhammadans in Persia, Bokhara, Cashmeer ...* (2 vols, 1860). In 1848 he had written to D at length to thank him 'for the kind support you give to the question of the Emancipation of the Jews from Gentile *Intolerance* and hatred'; in 1852 D had declined his request for a colonial bishopric. On 26 December 1860 he had written that he had asked his publisher to send D 'the 1st & 2d Vol. of my *Autobiography* as a token of my admiration of your great merits for Lit. and the State'. On 26 January 1861 he had advised D that Vol. 1 (earlier omitted) would be sent. He added that his son's name was missing from the book because 'my Son wishes that the Public should forget altogether that he was of Jewish descent'. The son, Henry Drummond Wolff (for whom see VII **3179**n2), most recently had been Malmesbury's assistant private secretary (1858) and had been 'opposed to the Publication of my Autobiography altogether ... for my part I always boasted having been a Jew – and I never found any inconvenience by openly declaring myself of being of Jewish Descent – neither among Roman Catholics nor Muhamedans nor Protestants'. Vol. 1 was dedicated to Gladstone, Vol. 2 to his first wife's nephew and niece, Hon. Henry and Mrs Walpole, and he now wished to dedicate a new edition to D. In signing the letters he addressed D as 'Right Honourable & Dear Sir'. H B/XXI/W/497-9, 502.

2 Wolff had written (n1, 26 Jan) that he was to remarry, to Louisa Decima King, sister of James King King (1806-1881), of Staunton Park, Herefordshire, JP, DL, high sheriff 1845, Conservative MP for Herefordshire 1852-68. The marriage on 14 May 1861 would be performed by Miss King's brother-in-law, James Garbett, Venerable Archdeacon of Chichester. Wolff would reply from 1 Portugal Street on 6 February: 'Right Honourable & dear Sir, Thousand thanks for your kind permission of dedicating my Works to you! I shall try to vindicate myself better against the accusations of *Cashmeer beauties!*' He was going to Yorkshire to finish a shorter edition; but in case he died, he asked D and King to be executors so that his son could not stop publication, 'for I perceive that the more my Life becomes popular the more he tries to suppress the Publication'. On 13 February 1861 he would ask D 'to write a Review of my Life lately published'. H B/XXI/W/500-1. The publication was the second edition of *Travels ...* (1861). It is dedicated to D, and contains descriptions of several of Wolff's encounters with dancing girls, on one occasion causing him to flee, but on others evoking brief tolerance. The encounter with the 'forlorn damsels' seems to have been omitted. *Travels ...* 374, 383, 389-90, 401.

TO: SARAH BRYDGES WILLYAMS Grosvenor Gate 3555
[Saturday] 9 February 1861

ORIGINAL: RTC [161]
PUBLICATION HISTORY: M&B IV 295, dated at Grosvenor Gate, 9 February 1861, the second and part of the third paragraph; Blake 410, dated 9 February 1861, extract from the third paragraph
EDITORIAL COMMENT: Paper imprinted 'Grosvenor Gate'.

Private Feby. 9 1861

Altho' it is only three weeks since we parted, so much has happened, I have had to see so many persons, write so many letters, settle so many plans & points – that in feeling, & in labor, it is an age!

I think I have got / everything now in good order, & have brought the troops into the field in ample numbers, & in fine condition.

The difficulty is to keep them in: but forbearance & patience are clearly our game, & tho' I could, the first night, have destroyed the government, I was wise enough to refrain.[1] In the meantime, we win every / election, & time is big with great events, which will demand a strong, patriotic, & conservative, government. Her Majesty & the Prince were most gracious at Windsor, where we stayed from Wednesday to Friday: the Court Circle numerous & brilliant. After that, tho' at great inconvenience, we were obliged to pay a visit to Baron Rothschild, at his hunting Castle in Bucks. It was to meet the French Princes whom he feasted, as if / they were still on the throne. On the day of our arrival, there were, after a gorgeous banquet, private theatricals; in the morning of the next day, the Baron's stag hounds met at Mentmore, & it was a most brilliant assemblage; in the evening there was a ball, attended by four hundred persons of the County of Buckingham. So, I had an opportunity of seeing my constituents.

I trust you are well. All the people I meet tell me they understand there was a Siberian winter at Torquay! Slander!

yrs ever, | D.[2]

TO: LORD MALMESBURY House of Lords [Friday] 22 February 1861 3556

ORIGINAL: PS 660
PUBLICATION HISTORY: Malmesbury II 247; Bradford 254, undated altered extract; Sir William Gregory *An Autobiography* (1894) 103, undated altered extract

House of Lords: February 22 1861.

My dear Malmesbury, –

I fear Fitzgerald is shaky about the great battle on Wednesday – Church-rates! Pray write to him *decidedly;* it will never do to have our own men run riot.[1]

1 When Parliament opened on 5 February, D, on an amendment to the address calling for a reform bill, had supported the government's omission and instead focused on foreign policy, an area of the government's strength. *Hansard* CLXI cols 67-81.

2 SBW would reply on 12 February: 'Not being able to get a Torquay paper I write to thank you from my heart for yr kind interesting letter your evolutions are admirable. Her Majesty is amiable and lovable and I am glad dear Mrs Disraeli has made her acquaintance.' RTC [417Q]. SBW must have forgotten that MA had first met the Queen in 1852 (see VI **2268**&n4).

1 At his 4 February dinner (see **3543**n1) D had talked about church rates and having consulted the Bishop of Exeter. Stanley 'thought his ideas very wild: and no two of the party agreed as to what should be done.'

The fact is, in internal politics there is only one question now, the maintenance of the Church. There can be no refraining or false Liberalism on such a subject. They are both out of fashion, too.[2]

Your House of Lords' pens and ink must be my excuse for this miserable scrawl.

Yours ever, | D.

3557 TO: SARAH BRYDGES WILLYAMS

Grosvenor Gate
[Thursday 28] February 1861

ORIGINAL: RTC [162]

EDITORIAL COMMENT: Paper imprinted 'Grosvenor Gate'. *Dating:* by the debate; see n2. *Sic:* Feby. 29 (1861 was not a leap year).

Private Feby. 29 1861

A great personage sent the enclosed to my wife. 'Tis the youngest of the little Princesses, Beatrice;[1] not a pretty child, but droll & clever, an unceasing prattler. She dined one day at table, when we were at Windsor, & amused us, with very fine / hair. We send her to you as a guest to Mount Braddon, & to add to yr collection.

The campaign has been more brisk, than it has appeared on the surface. Yesterday, we had a pitched battle on Church Rates;[2] I am satisfied with the result, & have no doubt of / defeating the bill. A couple of years ago, the enemy used to have 100 majority – it is now only 15: & in a couple of months, may altogether disappear.

We have won the election for the County of Cork – the Yorkshire of Ireland – & for which a Conservative never / before sate![3] But we must not be precipitate. It is, however, very difficult to keep the Government in their places.

Disraeli, Derby 166. The Church Rates Abolition Bill, introduced on 7 February, would pass second reading on Wednesday 27 February 281-266; in his speech opposing it, D declared himself not averse to a just settlement of the Dissenters' grievance, but could not consent to total abolition because that would weaken the union of Church and State. William Seymour Fitzgerald, who had recently been Malmesbury's under-secretary at the foreign office, had voted against the church rates in 1855 but did not vote in this division. *Hansard* CLXI cols 140, 990-1057 (D 1039-45). See further **3563**&n4. Malmesbury would reply on the 25th: 'I cannot find FitzGerald but have written to him. I am beyond measure disgusted at the vote on Hubbards motion [for a select committee on the income and property tax, passed against the government 131-127 on 19 February]. Sir J. Graham told me it was in his opinion the most fatal & democratic one since he has sat in Parlt. – democratic in its principle of course – fatal as shewing how *weak* numerically & morally the landed interest was in the H of C ... With our leaders thus informed, & our men voting so wildly we may well be called an *Opposition* for we are opposed both to the Govt & to ourselves.' H B/XX/HS/108. See further **3573**&n1, **3575**n1, **3581**&n2, **3586**&nn1&2 and **3694**&n3.

2 *Cf* **3551**n3. In an undated note Earle wrote: 'I saw Fitzgerald today & told him to call upon you at 1:30 tomorrow. If this wont do, let me know that I may stop him.' H B/XX/E/201.

---

1 Princess Beatrice Mary Victoria Feodore (1857-1944), Victoria and Albert's fifth daughter and youngest child, would develop other talents (pianist and composer of music; she would also become D's favourite Royal); in 1885 she would marry Prince Henry Maurice of Battenburg. SBW would reply on 1 March: 'Your little chatty Visitor arrived in full spirits and very much amused and delighted me and your brilliant pen still more.' RTC [418Q]. See illustration p liii.

2 See **3556**&n1. Lord Cardigan on 1 March would write: 'I only received your letter of the 26th ult [*not found*] – yesterday morning and an hour afterwards heard ... of the Majority of 15 in favor of Ministers ... I think we can do the work easily for you now in the House of Lords.' H B/XXI/C/46. See further **3560**n1, **3563**n2, **3587**n1 and **3596**n1.

3 In a by-election for co Cork on 28 February, Nicholas P. Leader (first Conservative to stand since he had been soundly defeated there in 1841 and 1847) had defeated the Liberal 6,441-2,352. Evidently the decid-

I have been unceasingly engaged – but well – & I hope you are very so.

'Tis a fine springlike day, & must be enchanting in your bright land of glittering cliffs & waters.

Ever yrs, | D.

TO: MARY ANNE DISRAELI [London] Friday [1 March 1861] 3558

ORIGINAL: H A/I/A/308

EDITORIAL COMMENT: Endorsed by MA on the last page: '1861 March 1st. Dizzy'.

Friday

My dearest love,

I am obliged to receive a *very numerous* deputation tomorrow of all the Scotch members & others about giving / a member to the Scotch Universities. Can we receive them in the Drawing Rooms? as there will be a / great many, perhaps forty or fifty; or more. The hour is three o'ck.[1]

Yrs ever | D.

TO: THE EDITOR OF THE TIMES Grosvenor Gate [Saturday] 2 March [1861] 3559

ORIGINAL: PS 673

PUBLICATION HISTORY: *The Times* (4 March 1861)

TO THE EDITOR OF THE TIMES. Grosvenor-gate, March 2.

Sir, –

In your Parliamentary report of last night there are applied to Sir John Pakington some observations of mine which were addressed to another member.

Far from censuring the comments of Sir John on the charge made against him of "unwarrantable conduct," I expressed my opinion that those comments were justified.[1]

ing factor was the non-interference of the Catholic priesthood. *MP* (16 Feb 1861). Stanley recorded that on 18 February 1861 he 'dined H. of C. with Disraeli: who was full of the expected victory at Cork: he says the union of the R. Catholics with the Conservative party has been his object for twenty years.' *Disraeli, Derby* 167. Cork county is the biggest in Ireland, like Yorkshire in England, and returns 8 MPs (co Cork (2), Cork City (2), Bandon, Kinsale, Mallow and Youghal) compared to Yorkshire's 37. Yorkshire was also largely Liberal.

---

1 The universities of Edinburgh and St Andrews were currently being strongly promoted for at least one of the seats made available by disfranchisement; they would be granted one joint member in 1868. The deputation was currently seeing Palmerston, Gladstone and Granville. *Hansard* CLXI cols 453-4, 908; *The Times, MP* (4 Mar 1861). James Hannay, editor of the *Edinburgh Courant,* had written on 20 February: 'I have the honour to forward you a *Courant* with a leader of mine on the proposed new seat for Scotland. I don't venture to say, that we could bring a Conservative in for it – though we would try: – but a support of the proposal in Parliament by the Party would I think add to its popularity in Scotland.' H B/XXI/H/141.

---

1 Pakington had written from the Carlton on 2 March, 'much annoyed' at a *Times* report that D had censured Pakington instead of Bentinck 'for violence of language, bitterness, &c. ... I think it a serious matter for it to go forth to all England in the Times, that *you had* censured *me* in the terms reported.' H B/XX/P/63. *The Times*'s mistake was in its 2 March report of the 1 March debate on Admiral Duncombe's motion for a select committee on the constitution of the Board of Admiralty. Opening the debate, Dun-

I am, Sir, your faithful servant,

B. DISRAELI.

3560 TO: MARY ANNE DISRAELI [London, Wednesday 6 March 1861]

ORIGINAL: H A/I/A/309

EDITORIAL COMMENT: Addressed by D: 'Mrs. D.' *Dating:* docketed by MA '1861 March 6th.'

7 o'ck

My dearest,

I hardly eat anything – & I don't want to dine very late for other reasons. Taylor persuaded me not to go, as it is a great storm, & other reasons[.][1]

Yours | D.

3561 TO: LORD DERBY Grosvenor Gate [Monday] 11 March 1861

ORIGINAL: DBP Box 146/1

EDITORIAL COMMENT: Paper imprinted 'Grosvenor Gate'.

Confidential Mar 11 1861

Rt Honble | The Earl of Derby | K.G.

My dear Lord,

I will take steps to secure unanimity, & have little doubt of success, as our friends are in good humor, & always remember, right loyally, the cordial manner / in wh: you were supported by Her Majesty, during yr late administration.[1]

combe had remarked on Pakington's lack of courtesy in giving notice of the same motion while Duncombe was ill, knowing that Duncombe intended to renew the motion he had made but withdrawn the previous year. (Pakington on 14 February had asked D whether it was 'good policy for me to take the lead, in calling for an enquiry into the present mode of Admiralty administration. I think the question is now ripe. I was urged to take it up last year – but then it was not ripe ... The Govt, as I hear, will not resist it – Why should not we have the credit of it? – last year Arthur Duncombe moved in it, but I think you will agree that his are not quite the hands it shd be in – It will be a most difficult & laborious affair, but I am screwing myself up to face it. I have seen Lord Derby about it.' H B/XX/P/62. Movers for select committees normally chaired those committees.) When Pakington protested Duncombe's allegation of discourtesy, Bentinck took Pakington to task, for 'unwarrantable, and quite uncalled for' remarks. D, near the end of the debate, had admitted that Pakington had made the motion on his advice, apologized for any offence, and pointed out that Pakington had made things right as soon as the breach of parliamentary etiquette was pointed out. *The Times* then reported D chiding Bentinck for his remarks on Pakington, and addressing him as 'My right hon friend [who] made some observations just now'; only privy councillors such as Pakington are entitled to be thus addressed (*MP* and *MC* both have 'His hon. friend the member for Norfolk'). The matter closed with Duncombe accepting the apology. In *Hansard* the mistake is corrected and the reference made clear: 'My hon. Friend the Member for West Norfolk (Mr. Bentinck)'. *Hansard* CLXI col 1240-1269 (D 1267-9).

---

1 On 6 March 1861, the House had adjourned at 5:45 *pm* after debate in committee on Trelawny's Church Rates Abolition Bill; in the evening the Speaker gave his fourth parliamentary dinner of the season (G.W.P. Bentinck was a guest; see **3559**&n1), followed by a levee. Col Taylor, but not D, is listed among the many who attended. The wind in London on 6 March was recorded as force 5 (on a scale of 1-12). *MP, The Times* (7 Mar 1861); *Hansard* CLXI cols 1489-1525.

---

1 Derby's letter from St James's Square is dated 'Monday': 'I received last night a note from the Queen, informing me, confidentially, that immediately after Easter the Princess Alice's intended marriage would be announced, and application made to Parliament for a provision of £30,000 Dower and £6000 a year

I return you the papers wh: you sent to me yesterday, & will endeavour, if possible, to call on you, in my way to the Committee / on Public Business. We meet for our report to day.[2]

Yrs sincerely, | D.

TO: MARY ANNE DISRAELI House of Commons [Monday 11 March 1861] 3562

ORIGINAL: H A/I/A/310

EDITORIAL COMMENT: House of Commons paper. Endorsed by MA on the second page: '1861 March 11th Dizzy –'.

½ pt 4 o'ck

My dearest Love,

Send me a thick great coat, for it has turned very cold.

I have just left my Committee & presented my petitions.[1]

Your own, | D.

TO: SARAH BRYDGES WILLYAMS Grosvenor Gate 3563
[Saturday] 16 March 1861

ORIGINAL: RTC [163]

PUBLICATION HISTORY: M&B IV 301-2, 326, dated at Grosvenor Gate, 16 March 1861, omitting the third and last paragraphs

EDITORIAL COMMENT: Paper imprinted 'Grosvenor Gate'. There is no salutation.

Private Mar 16 1861

It was most kind of you to write after my health.[1] / *Between ourselves,* I took advantage of a very slight indisposition to absent myself from some debates, where, had I been

Annuity being in each case ¾ of the amount voted for the Princess Royal; and expressing H.M's hope that I would do what I could to secure unanimity, if possible, in favour of "a very moderate demand." I am inclined to concur in opinion with H.M. that the proposed provision is by no means unreasonable, but before replying to Her note, I should be glad to know what you think of the view our friends are likely to take in the H. of Commons. If you can, I wish you would send me an answer which may be shown to the Queen, as it is desirable that H.M. should know that I do not answer such questions without consulting you.' H B/XX/S/288. The Queen's announcement of the Princess's marriage and application for 'full Provision for Her Daughter ... as may be suitable to the Dignity of the Crown' would be made in parliament on 3 May. The bill stipulating the amounts Derby mentions would pass through both Houses without debate or division. *Hansard* CLXII cols 1476, 1488, 1648, 1733, 1854, 1911, 2045-6, 2077, 2191.

2 D was a member of the Commons select committee on facilitating the business of the House, created on 7 February; the committee's report would be tabled in the House on Friday 19 April. Derby was on the equivalent Lords committee, struck on 8 February. *Hansard* CLXII cols 153-79 (D 162-4), 181-92, CLXIII col 899.

---

1 For D's committee, see **3561**&n2. When the House on this day began sitting at 4 *pm,* D presented several dozen petitions against the Church Rates Abolition Bill, the majority from Bucks. *The Times* (12 Mar 1861).

---

1 SBW had written to MA on 11 March grateful for the newspapers MA had sent but concerned at reading in the *Press* that D had been 'prevented by indisposition' from being at a Conservative dinner. MA on 12 March had assured her that D was quite well. RTC [419-20Q]. See also **3560**&n1.

present, more serious consequences might have occurred, than I care, at this moment, to accomplish.[2]

It is difficult, almost impossible, to keep the present Government / in, tho' the sudden death of the Duchess of Kent, which took place last night, will assist that result. The Queen was much attached to her mother, & never would believe in her danger. That, from the terrible nature of her disease, was indubitable, but none believed her state was even critical.[3]

Mrs. Disraeli, & myself, met the Queen & the Prince Consort, yesterday, in Hyde Park, before they had received the summons, & while they / were on their way home. They were full of smiles & bows to us, & so gay & gracious, that it is impossible they cd. have had the ~~sig~~ slightest anticipation of the impending sorrow.

There was a pitched battle in the Commons, last Wednesday, on the County Franchise, & the Conservatives gained a great victory in a full house. This has been our second great effort before Easter; the first being on the Church Rate, when we were only in a minority of *15*!; & after Easter, I think, / we shall win on this also.[4]

An immense suspense in foreign affairs – but what questions! The temporal ex-

2 There is no indication D was in the House on 6,7,8 and 11 March: the main business on the 6th, after the government's Superannuation (Officers of Prisons) Bill was defeated, was the Church Rates Abolition Bill in committee; on the 7th the House resumed its debate on Italian affairs; on the 8th, Trelawny postponed 3rd reading of the Church Rates Abolition Bill until 5 June, and the main business was debate on a motion (against the government) to decrease the duty on fire insurance. On 11 March the major business had been the navy estimates, the focus of debate the importance of maintaining naval superiority over France. *Hansard* CLXI cols 1480-1525, 1542-1627, 1655-75, 1729-92.

3 The official announcement on Monday 18 March stated that the Duchess died at about 9:30 *am* on this day, Saturday 16 March, at Frogmore House, in the presence of the Queen, the Prince Consort and Princess Alice, who had arrived from Buckingham Palace the previous evening at eight. The report in the second edition of *MP* of this day (16th), dated 6 *am* 16 March at Frogmore, was that the duchess's symptoms had '"assumed a very dangerous character."' Palmerston wrote to D on this day to arrange for him to second his (Palmerston's) address of condolence to the Queen on Monday; D would focus on the duchess's unique relationship with her 'Royal child' and conclude: 'She who reigns over us has elected, amid all the splendour of empire, to establish her life on the principle of domestic love. It is this – it is the remembrance and consciousness of this which now sincerely saddens the public spirit, permits a nation to bear its heartfelt sympathy to the foot of a bereaved Throne, and whisper solace even to a Royal heart.' RTC [421Q]; *Hansard* CLXI cols 2155-7 (D 2156-7). For the Queen's excessive grief at her mother's death (of cancer), see Weintraub *Victoria* 289 and *LQV* III 435-9.

4 The House on Wednesday 13 March had heatedly debated second reading of the County Franchise Bill (introduced on 19 February), Locke King's perennial bill for extending the franchise in the counties of England and Wales. D opposed it on the ground that franchise reform had to be done, not by private members, but by Ministers, and in a complete and comprehensive manner. A hostile amendment was passed 248-220, effectively scuttling the bill. *Hansard* CLXI cols 1899-1935 (D 1926-32). Derby had written on 'Monday' (11 March?) asking D to call on him to discuss 'the bit by bit reform bills now in agitation.' H B/XX/S/289. See further **3569**&n4. For the church-rate division, see **3556**&n1.

istence of the Pope:[5] the union of the American states:[6] the dissolution of the Ottoman Empire:[7] the unity of Italy: each of them sufficient for a generation! It is a privilege to live in such an age – to say nothing of "Essays & Reviews" which convulses Christendom,[8] & seems to have shaken down the ~~tower~~ spire of Chichester Cathedral.[9]

Adieu! | D.

TO: N.M. ROTHSCHILD & SONS House of Commons [Monday] 20 March 1861 3564

ORIGINAL: ROTH RAL RFAM C/2/48

EDITORIAL COMMENT: House of Commons paper. Endorsed in another hand on the last page: 'B Disraeli 20 March 1861 Ansd 21st'. *Sic:* Messrs Gordon.

Messrs Rothschild Mar 20 1861

Gentlemen,

Mr. Vance of Bilbao wrote to me, two months ago, to beg, that you wd. have the kindness to pay £100: to his acct, at Messrs Duff Gordon & Co. 79, Gt Tower /

5 The debate of 7 March on the affairs of Italy centred on the perceived ambiguity of Russell's policy in view of his two despatches (see **3526**&n3), on which D had criticized him on 5 February (see **3555**&n1). On 7 March the focus had turned to the invasion of the Papal States by Sardinian forces, several speakers seeing this as presaging the end of the Pope's temporal powers, one even seeing it as the extension of the Reformation to Italy. Russell in clarifying his policy had also expressed approval of this development. *Hansard* CLXI cols 1542-1627. D in his 8 August 1859 speech on Italy (VII **3397**n2) had castigated Gladstone for supporting 'an anti-papal crusade', claiming that it was the same argument Dissenters used against the Church of England. Derby in his letter of 15 January 1860 on France's proposed Congress (see **3443**&n1) had stated his position: 'I should have strenuously resisted any guarantee of any of the new arrangements, and especially any of the temporal Sovereignty of the Pope over any portion of his dominions against his own subjects. This is, in truth, the main difficulty of the Italian question.' H B/XX/S/261. *MP* on 18 March would run a 9 March report from Rome: 'There is here a generally prevalent opinion that after Easter the temporal power of the Pope will be done away with, and that a Sardinian garrison will succeed the French in the Eternal City.'

6 The papers daily carried reports on events in the United States indicating the apparent inevitability of civil war and on 18 March reported Lincoln's inaugural address declaring the Union inviolate, but apart from a few pointed questions in both Houses the matter had not yet been discussed in parliament. According to M&B IV 328, D shared the prevailing English view that the union was falling apart.

7 The idea that the decline of the Ottoman Empire had been reversed by the Treaty of Paris and by Turkey's guarantee of liberalizing reforms had suffered devastating setbacks, most recently by the massacre, evidently with Turkish compliance, of thousands of Christians in Syria in the summer of 1860, prompting the Four Powers in August to send in French troops. Meanwhile, there were regular reports of the deepening financial crisis of the Porte, its treasury having been plundered by a Parisian swindler. *AR* (1860 History) 251-7; *MP* (5, 12 Mar 1861).

8 *Essays and Reviews,* an 1860 collection by seven liberal Oxford and Cambridge scholars and clergymen assailing Biblical literalism, had provoked a storm of controversy and denunciation. D's bookseller would bill him for a copy in December 1861. H A/V/G/[unnumbered]. For a treatment of its impact (rivalling that of Darwin's *Origin of Species* four months earlier), see Victor Shea and William Whitla eds *Essays and Reviews: The 1860 Text and Its Reading* (Charlottesville: U of Virginia Press 2000).

9 The spire of Chichester Cathedral had collapsed during a wind storm on 20 February. *The Times* (23 Feb 1861). Lady Dorothy Nevill had written to MA that its repair was estimated to cost £200,000, the scaffolding alone £8,000: 'You may fancy the county of Sussex will get up this sum when the Queen gives 250 – the prince 100 – I have promised a friend to stand firmer than the spire did – in refusing to give anything.' H D/III/C/1515.

St.[1] – but the letter has only just reached me, having gone by mistake to Mexico[.]

It is probable, that, in consequence of my silence, he may, in the interval, have drawn upon you for the amount: but, if / he have not done so, I shd. feel obliged by yr paying the sum to Messrs Gordon as above, & informing me.[2]

Regretting much to give you this trouble, believe me

Yours faithfully, | *B. Disraeli*

3565 TO: SARAH BRYDGES WILLYAMS

House of Commons [Wednesday] 20 March 1861

ORIGINAL: RTC [164]
PUBLICATION HISTORY: Blake 418, extract dated 20 March 1861
EDITORIAL COMMENT: House of Commons paper. There is no salutation.

March 20 1861

I send you an interesting addition to your collection of autographs. You must keep it to yourself, as it is not etiquette to show these private notes. You will see my / answer to it in the "Times".

Mem: in reading what I said, substitute the word "*tranquillising*" for "*tranquillity*" – a blunder, which makes my words almost nonsense.[1]

I am / in great trouble about a piece of rather good fortune. We have discovered, that a colliery, in wh: Mrs. Disraeli is interested, & which has been represented to us, always, as not being in work, has really, for several years, been profitably producing, without ever paying / to her any royalties. It is a conspiracy of lawyers, & agents & other honest folks, & I have got to go down to Glamorganshire to see after the matter.[2]

Yours ever, | D.

1 See **3542**&n2. The address was that of several wine and spirit merchants and agents, including Duff, Gordon & Co, sherry merchants. *LPOD* (1860).

2 See further **3572**&n1.

---

1 D's enclosure (adjacent in RTC) is Palmerston's letter about seconding the motion on 18 March for an address of condolence to the Queen; see **3563**n3. On 19 March *The Times* and *MP* reported the incorrect word, while *MC* (19 Mar 1861) and *Hansard* (CLXI cols 2156-7) got it right: 'That (*MC* 'This') tranquilizing [*sic in both*] and sustaining memory is the inheritance of our Sovereign.'

2 R.W. Williams, Wyndham Lewis's solicitor, had written to D from Cardiff on 11 March enclosing an account 'shewing the amount just received by Mr. Wyndham Lewis in respect of the Coal under Lyn-y-waun Farm ... I entertain no doubt that the Lyn-y-waun colliery must be the particular colliery which under the arrangement made by Mrs. Disraeli with the late Revd. W.P. Lewis [III **746**n1] entitles that Lady to one half of the Royalties arising from the Coal during the term of her life'. He enclosed a cheque for £539.10.1. Thomas Loftus had written on 12 March about the copies of the account he had received; on 16 March he had written further: 'I was about to draw a cheque for Mrs Disraeli's moiety when I discovered what I conceived to be a mistake ... in dividing the gross amount of Royalties'. H D/II/B/216, 148-9. On 19 March MA recorded receiving £516.8.5 royalties for the coal mine leased to William Booker, after a deduction for the mineral agent's commission and 1 guinea for Loftus: 'N.B. This the above is the first Moiety we have Recd ... (The above to be inquired about)'. See further **3568**&n2.

TO: WILLIAM GLADSTONE Grosvenor Gate [Sunday] 24 March 1861 3566

ORIGINAL: BL ADD MSS 44395 ff221-2

EDITORIAL COMMENT: Paper imprinted 'Grosvenor Gate'. Docketed 'No 3' in the same hand that docketed ff218-19 and 220 (see n1) 'No 1' and 'No 2' respectively; and, in the same hand that marked ff218-19 '(1', it is marked 'Copy | (2'.

The Rt Honble | W.E. Gladstone M.P. March 24 1861

My dear Sir,

I return you the Speaker's letter, & must confess, that I am not surprised at his decision.[1]

I think there are grave objections to extending the original functions / of the "Comm[itt]ee of Selection", & would suggest, in preference, that you should, yourself, propose the Committee; but, on whatever course you may decide, you may count upon any / support, wh: I can give you.[2]

I have the honor to remain | my dear Sir, | faithfully yours, | *B. Disraeli*

TO: HENRY ALMACK Grosvenor Gate [Sunday] 24 March 1861 3567

ORIGINAL: PS 742

PUBLICATION HISTORY: W.V. Daniell's catalogue (July 1905) item 48: 'A.L.s. "B. Disraeli," 3 pp., 8vo. to Dr. Almack, *Grosvenor Gate, March* 24, 1861.'

EDITORIAL COMMENT: *Sic:* Jas.

There is a great crisis in Church Affairs, for the Bill of Sir Jas. Trelawny is only part of a concerted movement, comprising other measures against the union between Church and State, but I am hopeful as to the result and have confidence in the awakened energies of the Country,[1]

1 Gladstone had written twice the previous day (23 March); in the first letter he asked D's opinion on 'the Report of the Committee on Public Monies (1857) which, at p. 6, recommends that the Audited accounts of the Public Expenditure should be "annually submitted to the revision of a committee of the House of Commons, to be nominated by the Speaker." I propose to move for the appointment of such a committee immediately after the recess'. Aware that the Speaker was averse 'needlessly to expose the authority of the Chair to challenge', he discussed having the Speaker appoint the committee before deciding to draft his motion in the form the report recommended. The second letter enclosed one from the Speaker just received: 'I hope his objections may be overcome. The very fact of departure from the recommendation of 1857 would somewhat tend to weaken the basis of the proposed Committee.' BL ADD MSS 44395 ff218-20; H B/XXI/G/102-3. Neither D in 1858 nor Gladstone in 1859 had found a place for the matter in their respective sessions.

2 Gladstone would follow D's advice. As the last item of business on 8 April, he would move the appointment of a committee of public accounts (motion agreed to) and announce that he would at a future date move that such a committee be appointed at the start of each session as a standing order of the House. On 18 April, again as the last item of business, he would announce the government's decision not to have the committee appointed by the Speaker, and move the nomination of a list of members. After brief discussion and defeat 43-15 of a hostile motion to adjourn, the nominations were accepted. *Hansard* CLXII cols 318, 773-4.

---

1 The Rev Dr Henry Almack (1822-1884), BA 1828 (St John's College, Cambridge), DD 1844, was rector 1846-84 of Fawley, Oxfordshire. Sir John Trelawny (1816-1885), 9th Bt, a barrister (Middle Temple 1841), DL for Cornwall 1840, was MP (L) for Tavistock 1843-52, 1857-65, for East Cornwall 1868-74. He moved the bill for total abolition of church rates against which D had spoken on 27 February; see **3556**n1. For the 'other measures' see Bishop Wilberforce's list mentioned in **3551**n3.

3568 TO: SARAH BRYDGES WILLYAMS Cardiff [Saturday 30 March 1861]

ORIGINAL: RTC [165]

EDITORIAL COMMENT: Paper imprinted with an engraving; see n1. There is no salutation. *Dating:* see 3569. *Sic:* Pantgwynlas.

Above are the portraits of some of our new friends, Mrs. Disraeli's former subjects.[1] Cardiff, from wh: I write this, was in her time, a / country town of eight thousand inhabitants: it is now a flourishing seaport of nearly 40,000! Such is the magic of commerce. Its docks are splendid; a little Liverpool; all built by one individual, the late Marquess of Bute, who is rewarded for his patriotism by leaving / to his son, a child – 200,000£ pr annm:![2]

The day before yesterday, we went & paid a visit to Pantgwynlas, the Welch for Greenmeadow, my wife's former residence.[3] It is about five miles from this, a picturesque house, beautifully situate at the gorge of a valley of Welch mountains, / richly wooded, with the river Taff raging through its wild & shaggy bottom[.] I have had so much business to attend to here, that I have not been able to see any of the sights of the neighbourhood; we are leaving this place to day for Tredegar, twelve miles off. Lord Tredegar was Sir Charles Morgan, a great Welch chieftain. I made him a peer,[4] & ~~no~~ he is now going to give me some advice about my colliery.[5] ↑& affairs here.↓

yrs ever, | D.

3569 TO: SARAH BRYDGES WILLYAMS House of Commons [Thursday] 11 April 1861

ORIGINAL: RTC [166]

PUBLICATION HISTORY: M&B IV 326, extract from the last paragraph dated 11 April 1861; Blake 418, extract dated 11 April 1861

EDITORIAL COMMENT: Black-edged House of Commons paper. There is no salutation.

Private April 11 1861

When I wrote to you last, we were going to Lord Tredegars. Our visit there was longer, than I expected. We went on Saturday, & I cd. not bring our business to a

1 The top half of the first page of this letter shows an engraving of 'Welsh Costumes | En[grave]d by Newman & Co 48 Watling St London' showing five rustic women in traditional Welsh attire. *LPOD* (1860) lists John Newman & Co, wholesale stationers, engravers & publishers, at 48 Watling Street EC. The DS left Grosvenor Gate at 9 *am* on 26 March (with £30.5.0 in MA's purse) for Cardiff and Tredegar, passed briefly through London on their way to Hardwicke and arrived back at Grosvenor Gate on 3 April. H acc; *MP* (25, 27 Mar 1861). For the engraving see p liv.

2 John Crichton Stuart (1793-1848), 2nd Marquess of Bute, amassed through inheritance and two marriages land and property that made him the greatest landowner in Britain. Described as 'the maker of modern Cardiff,' he acquired vast mineral and coal interests, the products of which were exported world wide from his Bute West Dock (completed 1839, the year of the DS' marriage). Over 750,000 tons of coal were shipped in 1853 alone. The East Bute Dock opened in 1859. David McLees *Castell Coch* (Cardiff: Cadw 2005) 13-14; *Victorian Travellers' Guide.* The later conversion to Roman Catholicism of the 3rd Marquess, John Patrick Crichton Stuart (1847-1900), would be a main theme in *Lothair.*

3 See III **798**n3. Greenmeadow (Pantgwynlais) has been demolished for a housing estate, though the scene D describes can be seen from nearby Castell Coch, a medieval-style folly built by the 3rd Marquess.

4 See VII **3268**n7.

5 See **3565**&n2.

conclusion until / the following Wednesday. Had I been able to have accomplished it by the Monday, we shd. have paid a brief, & flying, visit to Torquay, wh: we had originally hoped to have accomplished / – but as I was obliged to be in town on Saturday night, the game was hardly worth the candles. I was much disappointed, that we cd. not pass three or four days with you.

Tredegar is a very / fine, old, hall, ~~w~~ built by Inigo Jones, of requisite proportion in all its numerous chambers, & full of admirable oak carving.[1] Ld. Tredegar is quite a Welch Prince with a flowing hospitality, his hall full of his / neighbours, the Welch Squires from their castles; unceasing hunting, & fishing in a thousand torrents! This was not much in my way,[2] but he is an unflinching supporter of mine, with brothers & uncles in the house, returned / for his boroughs, & the two counties in wh: he is paramount.[3] He helped me very much in our private business.

Public business very agitated; & it will be very difficult, not to say impossible, to keep the present Ministry in / their places. I shall however try to do it. Yesterday, they experienced a great & disgraceful defeat – as the papers, which, notwithstanding our many movements, I trust you receive regularly, will tell you.[4]

It is interesting to be / acquainted with the appearance of those of whom we hear a great deal – so I enclose you a portrait of Count Cavour, given to me by an Italian gentleman.[5]

The resemblance is striking, tho' not of the Italian ideal. I can answer for its truth, for when I / was Chancellor of the Exchequer, ten years ago, Cavour was travelling in this country, in order to study the art of taxation, & had letters of introduction to me – & I knew him well.[6]

Adieu! | D.

1 Tredegar Hall, near Newport, Monmouthshire, had belonged to the Morgan family since the early fifteenth century. Originally a medieval stone house, it was completely rebuilt in brick 1664-72, probably by Roger and William Hurlbutt, in the style of Inigo Jones (1573-1652), and was thought one of the finest houses of that period in Britain. Furtado 132; John Newman *Gwent/Monmouthshire* (2000) 562-4.

2 On D as a sportsman, *cf* **3613**&n1, where he catches his first Hughenden trout.

3 Although the Morgans were a long-standing political family, Tredegar currently had only a brother and a son in the House. Charles Octavius Swinnerton Morgan (1803-1888) was MP (C) for Monmouthshire 1841-74, and Major Godfrey Charles Morgan (1830-1913), a Crimean veteran, was MP (C) for Brecknockshire 1858 to 1875, when he would succeed his father as 2nd Baron. He would be created 1st Viscount Tredegar in 1905. The Morgans also had influence at Newport, one of the three boroughs of Monmouth District, and at Brecknock.

4 In the House on 10 April, a bill of Edward Baines (L) calling for a £6 instead of a £10 borough franchise had been defeated on second reading 245-193 after a debate involving no prominent member of either side. *Hansard* CLXII cols 351-413. *The Times* on this day (11 April) thought the bill had had no chance and was therefore an ill-timed self-serving indulgence by Baines and his supporters and an embarrassment to the government.

5 See further **3592**&n2.

6 The 52-year-old Cavour, who would live only until 6 June, is described as 'short, and latterly very stout; his complexion was dark and sallow; his bearing heavy, and his general appearance sluggish and inert.' *AR* (1861 Chronicle) 421. His consultation with D and Gladstone led him to believe that a general income tax would not work in France. Denis Mack Smith *Cavour* (1985) 99-100.

3570 TO: [UNKNOWN] [London, Tuesday 16 April 1861]

ORIGINAL: QUA 64

EDITORIAL COMMENT: A fragment. Endorsed in another hand on the first page: 'The Date of this letter was April 16. 1861.'; and, in another (archivist's?) hand: '[25]'.

~~been silent~~ The only duty of the Opposition has been to watch the Government, &, as the Ministry have been inert, the office of their opponents has been barren. Yet, no doubt, we are encompassed / by impending events of great moment.[1]

Yours very faithfully, | *B. Disraeli*

3571 TO: [OCTAVIAN BLEWITT] House of Commons [Tuesday] 16 April 1861

ORIGINAL: RLF Vol 16 No 2 1861

EDITORIAL COMMENT: Black-edged House of Commons paper. For the recipient, *cf* VII **1405x**n1 and, in this volume, **3577**.

April 16 1861

Mr Disraeli will with pleasure act as Steward on the Anniversary of the "Literary Fund", presided over by H.R.H. the Duc d'Aumale.[1]

3572 TO: N.M. ROTHSCHILD & SONS House of Commons [Tuesday] 16 April 1861

ORIGINAL: ROTH RAL RFAM C/2/49

EDITORIAL COMMENT: Black-edged House of Commons paper. Endorsed in another hand on the last page: 'B Disraeli 16 Apl 1861 ansd 17th'.

Messrs Rothschild April 16 1861

Gentlemen,

I enclose you an extract from a letter of Mr Vance, who seems not to agree with the statement of his acct., contained in yr / last letter to me, & the contents of wh: I transmitted to him.[1] Can you throw any light on the subject?[2]

1 Stanley on 15 April recorded that Gladstone's budget had made D 'angry and annoyed', and on the 19th that he had had a 'Long talk last night with Disraeli about the budget ... we ... discussed the question of tea and sugar as against paper: he ... thought it better to protract the debate as long as possible, and watch the temper of the House.' *Disraeli, Derby* 168-9. For discussion of Gladstone's budget (with his contentious proposal to combine all fiscal measures in one bill) see H.C.G. Matthew 'Disraeli, Gladstone, and the Politics of Mid-Victorian Budgets,' *Historical Journal* 22, 3 (1979) 615-44.

1 See **3577**&n1 and **3578**&n3.

1 See **3564**&n1. The enclosure is a copy in D's hand of part of a Francis Villiers letter dated 31 March at Bilbao: '"Fortunately, I have not drawn on Rothschilds, or there would apparently have been a hitch, tho' by no fault of mine, as the balance of £4., mentioned by them as being in my favor, is quite incorrect. That balance remained, when I drew the last bill on them in July of last year. I have not drawn since for a farthing, & you paid to my acct. in Octr. £95, & in Jany. £80 – so that, deducting the £100 now paid, there ought to be £79 in my favor"'. ROTH RAL RFAM C/2/52.

2 The response (see ec) has not been found; the next extant letter from Villiers is dated 28 May 1861 at Bilbao, sorry to trouble D but reminding him 'that, as yet, I have no authority for you to draw for the £75., which was due on the 1st. April. I say this on the supposition that it has been placed at your disposal, which may perhaps not be the case ... all my endeavours, during [Lord] Villiers's lifetime, to get matters simplified by obtaining an authority to draw at the rate of £300. a year, entirely failed, & I have no other

I am sorry to give you all this trouble, & shd. have called on you / on the matter, were I not much engaged.

Believe me, | Gentlemen, | yours faithfully, | *B. Disraeli*

TO: LADY DOROTHY NEVILL Carlton Club [Wednesday] 24 April 1861 **3573**

ORIGINAL: PS 743

PUBLICATION HISTORY: *Anglo-Saxon Review* IV (1901) 143-4

EDITORIAL COMMENT: *Sic:* Mericia.

Carlton Club, *April* 24, 1861.

Dearest Dorothy, –

There never were such strawberries! They would have gained the prize in any county. But sweeter than the strawberries was your kindness in remembering me.

We are at the commencement of a great struggle. On Monday I executed a reconnaissance in force, which will probably be continued for a week, and during that process I expect to find out the weak point in the enemy's position, and shall in due course give them battle.[1] Every night I come home from a most anxious and exhausting field, I am greeted by the representatives of your faithful affection. They are so large and fragrant that I always expect a fairy will jump out of them – like yourself!

Ever yours, | D.

My love to Mericia, with whom I was delighted.[2]

TO: SARAH BRYDGES WILLYAMS Carlton Club [Wednesday] 24 April 1861 **3574**

ORIGINAL: RTC [167]; H R/II/E/473-4

PUBLICATION HISTORY: M&B IV 302, dated at the Carlton Club, 24 April 1861, extract

EDITORIAL COMMENT: Carlton Club paper. There is no salutation. The RTC copy is incomplete, and the final part as marked has been taken from a fair copy in the Rose papers. *Sic:* reconoissance; aid-de-camps; honour.

April 24 1861

You may be sure, that it will always give me pleasure to assist any friend of yours.[1] I

resource but to apply to you on the subject. I wrote to Madrid & to Rothschild's to try that they wd. consider their letter of Credit of last year annulled, & to the latter to ask them to honour my draft for the said £75. I have had no answer, but suppose it is all right, though I have not in consequence drawn upon them. Duff Gordon & Co. have I believe repaid into their hands the balance of the money overpaid in the £100 – perhaps therefore the simplest & most satisfactory plan wd. be if you wd. desire R. to write me a line to say to what amount they can honour my drafts. I imagine it to be, (including the £75. of April) £170.' H A/IV/J/145. For D's possible response see **3589**.

---

1 On Monday 22 April, the House in committee of ways and means had begun debating Gladstone's budget, the Conservatives arguing that the latest figures vindicated their 1860 predictions and justified their current opposition to reducing revenue (mostly by lowering income tax and tea and sugar duties and abolishing paper duties) without reducing expenditures. The debate would continue for four nights, culminating on 2 May. See further **3574**&n2, **3575**&n1 and **3576**&n1.

2 Meresia Dorothy Augusta Nevill (1849-1918) was the Nevills' second child. The PS includes Lady Dorothy's note: 'Lord Beaconsfield was very fond of my daughter Mericia [*sic*], to whom he alludes in the above postscript.'

---

1 SBW's request has not been found, but *cf* VII **3158**&n1.

do not think, however, that we are as near power as the world imagines – &, for my part, I cd. wish it postponed until next year. / I have endeavoured to keep the Ministry in, but they tempt their fate, & a critical position has occurred.

On Monday, I executed a ~~reno~~ reconoissance in force, which will be continued for some days. I hope, in the interval, / to discover the weak part of the enemy's position, & I count, in about ten days, to give him battle.[2]

This is the real state of affairs. I am quite exhausted in listening to aid-de-camps, instructing / [H R/II/E/473-4:] generals of division, and writing endless despatches – but find time, amid all this turmoil, to tell you I am well, and to hope that you are the same. All honour to Devonia, its blue waters and blushing roses – which latter, I hope, will remember, and reward, me.[3]

Ever yours, | D.

3575 TO: SARAH BRYDGES WILLYAMS Carlton Club [Thursday] 25 April 1861

ORIGINAL: RTC [168]

EDITORIAL COMMENT: Carlton Club paper. There is no salutation.

PRIVATE April 25. 1861

My letter of yesterday was prophetic – for, then, I was only dreaming of the Roses, & they were then / on their journey to me. They arrived, this morning, in all their lustre & fragrance – as fresh as Spring, & / as radiant as Summer!

I received them, as it were, on the field of battle. I don't think the absolute engagement will take place for a / week – &, I think, about Tuesday, I shall be able to foresee the result.[1] In my mind, at present, it depends on the Roman Catholic members.[2]

Yrs ever, | D.

2 See **3573**&n1, **3575**&n1, **3576**&n1, **3578**&nn1&2, **3581**&n2, **3584**&nn2&6, **3586**&nn1&2 and **3588**&nn1&2. Derby on 29 April would ask to see D about the precise form of their amendment on 2 May (to reduce the tax on tea) and 'how far I should refer to it, and to the general position of the Party'. H B/XX/S/282. On 1 May he would use the Lord Mayor's dinner to him and the Conservatives to explain that his party was trying, for the country's good, to keep the government in power to avoid constant changes of weak governments. On the budget, however, they would oppose increasing the tax on tea as a means of offsetting the loss of paper duties. D in his speech would focus on church rates. *The Times* (2 May 1861).

3 SBW would reply the next day (25th): 'I wish my Roses cd reward your fine poetical flowery reception of them but alass [*sic*] to my great annoyance and disappointment my Gardener has not the skill to counter[v]ail the severity of the Winter so that my Roses are not only late in flowering but they are deficient in beauty of appearance and my anxiety and attention to them has not produced better effect. I mention all this as my appology [*sic*] for their late and imperfect appearance.' After recalling D's compliment to a friend's daughter, she concluded: 'How many have I and Devonia to remember?' In a postscript she added: 'On the 18th I voted for Church rates without success at the Townhall'. RTC [422Q].

1 The budget debate (see **3573**&n1) was in its second night on this date. D's next major intervention would occur on the third night, 29 April, when he announced that he would not oppose reducing income tax but would oppose the war tax on tea. *Hansard* CLXII cols 1219-1333 (D 1302-27, 1331). See further **3576**&n1 and **3586**&nn1&2.

2 Earle on the 26th would report a 'satisfactory' interview with Cardinal Wiseman, who promised help, approved of Monsell, Bowyer & Hennessy and discussed the current party situation. The Cardinal thought 'we were quite right in looking to the R.Cs for our majority for they could give it us. If there were any prospect of a Govt. being formed that wd. carry out a respectable foreign policy, the Catholic constituents & their members would all support it.' H B/XX/E/219. Derby on 2 May would write about his fear

TO: SARAH BRYDGES WILLYAMS House of Commons [Friday] 10 May 1861 3576

ORIGINAL: H R/II/E/476-7
PUBLICATION HISTORY: M&B IV 297, undated extract from the second paragraph
EDITORIAL COMMENT: From a fair copy in another hand in the Rose papers.

House of Commons, | May 10. 1861.

I write this in my place in the House – which I can scarcely ever quit.

Since I wrote last, the campaign has been unceasing – constant manoeuvres, and one great battle – almost a drawn one, the majority of the Government being so small – 18! in a house of 600. I said it was not a *majority,* as it was only in its *teens.*[1]

I think the manoeuvres will be yet protracted – and, probably, there will be another pitched fight – but I want to throw it over till after Whitsuntide.[2]

If it were not for your roses, that so frequently greet me, I should think that Spring was a dream. Fogs in May! and almost endless north-east blasts[3] – but I am so absorbed with affairs, that I have no time to quarrel with Nature.

I am quite well – & earnestly hope you are.

Ever yours, | D.

TO: OCTAVIAN BLEWITT Grosvenor Gate [Monday] 13 May 1861 3577

ORIGINAL: RLF Vol 16 No 9 1861
EDITORIAL COMMENT: Paper imprinted 'Grosvenor Gate'. *Sic:* checque.

Oc: Blewitt Esq May 13 1861

Dear Sir,

I hope to dine with the "Lit: Fund" on Wednesday, &, in that case, will have the honor of / proposing the toast you mention.[1]

Let me know *exactly* the desired hour.

Have the kindness to send me, by the bearer, the Report of your last Anniversary, as / I wish to see the list of yr chairmen from the beginning.

that Stanley was 'going wrong. He has been talking with Malins (this I heard from M.) and Walpole. Surely there is no fear of the latter? If any body can keep Stanley right, you can. I presume you know that More O'Ferrall is come over. I presume with orders, but what they may be I know not. Sir George Bowyer's request to be introduced to me last night looks well.' H B/XX/S/283. See further **3579** and **3580**&n3.

1 The budget debate (see **3573**n1 and **3575**n1) had culminated on 2 May (the fourth night), when D had concluded the opposition with a virulent attack on Gladstone himself. After Palmerston's rebuke of D's descent to personalities, the government had won the division (technically on Horsfall's amendment to reduce the tax on tea) by only 18 votes, 299-281 (plus tellers). Palmerston then agreed with D's contention that since 'a Resolution of this great importance has really been carried by a very small majority ... it can hardly be called a majority at all – it would be better ... that we should have time to reflect on what has taken place.' *Hansard* CLXII cols 1379-1474 (D 1456-64, 1473-4, quoted at 1474). See also **3580**&n1.

2 See **3578**&nn1&2.

3 *The Times* next day (11 May) would report that the temperature on this day had been 43°F (6°C), with force 5 east winds, and heavy cloud cover.

1 See **3571** for D's response to the original invitation, and **3578**&n3 for his account of the dinner and his speech.

I enclose, also, a checque for £10.[2] Send the report by the bearer.
Yrs ffly, | D.

3578 TO: SARAH BRYDGES WILLYAMS

House of Commons
[Friday] 17 May 1861

ORIGINAL: RTC [169]
PUBLICATION HISTORY: M&B IV 302, dated at the House of Commons, 17 May 1861, the third and fourth paragraphs
EDITORIAL COMMENT: House of Commons paper. There is no salutation. *Sic:* threw; Chatres.

Private May 17 1861.

The progress of the campaign has been unceasing since I last wrote. I succeeded in my great object, which was to throw the Committee, on the Budget Bill, until / after the Whitsun Recess, which commences tomorrow, & wh: concludes on Thursday.[1]

On Monday week, we shall now go into the Committee, & there will be a great battle. If / the Ministry win, it will be by a slight majority – but there are many combinations on the cards, which may defeat them.[2]

I had a very difficult task on Wednesday, in having to propose the health / of the Duc d'Aumale, as Chairman of the Literary Fund. I could not allude to the most celebrated of his literary compositions – vizt. ~~n~~ the pamphlet, which he has just published on the present state of affairs in France,[3] & / which you have no doubt heard of; perhaps, read. It is a master-piece of composition – of trenchant sarcasm, & incisive logic; not unworthy of Junius, or even Pascal. However, I got threw my task without blundering, &, I may venture to say to / you, with great applause. It was the most brilliant meeting of the kind I ever attended.

The young Princes of France were at different parts of the table, mingling among three-hundred distinguished guests. The youths are ~~always~~ distinguished / in their appearance, with winning manners, & highly educated – bearing wondrous names of historic renown.

2 At the dinner, D's name would be read out among those who had contributed 10 guineas; a total of nearly £900 was raised. *MP* (16 May 1861).

---

1 On 16 May, answering D about the government's proposed business on the first day (Thursday) after the Whitsun recess, Palmerston said that, if the Budget (Customs and Inland Revenue) Bill was given second reading that night as expected, he would postpone going into committee on the bill until the Monday after the recess. He also claimed all financial matters had now been decided. D, concluding the discussion before the bill was read a second time and committed to 27 May, reminded the House that, although some financial resolutions had been passed, the opposition had all along, and especially in light of the close division of 2 May (see **3576**n1), reserved the right to address issues like paper duties on subsequent appropriate occasions. *Hansard* CLXII cols 2100-91 (D 2100, 2184-90).

2 In committee on the Customs and Inland Revenue Bill on Monday 27 May, Newdegate's motion that each tax be treated separately would be defeated and the debate, over D's protest, adjourned. On 30 May, the government would win the division on the clause repealing the paper duty by a margin of only 15, 296-281. *Hansard* CLXIII cols 68-149, 245-345 (D 148-9, 250-66, 275).

3 The 73rd anniversary dinner of the Royal Literary Fund had been held at Freemasons' Tavern on Wednesday 15 May, the duc d'Aumale presiding. D had proposed his health with glowing praise for his lineage, talents and writings, but without mentioning his 1861 book, *Lettre sur l'Histoire de France,* an outspoken attack on the French empire; in France it had already been seized by the police. *MP* (16, 17 Apr 1861).

The Count of Paris
The Duc de Chatres
Gaston of Orleans, }
Count of Eu }
The Prince de Conde
The Duc d'Alencon.[4] /

They are exiles, but they are young, & full of hope & dignity – & favored by nature.

I get to Hughenden tomorrow for three or four days repose,[5] which I begin to want – but the Parliamentary campaign has been brilliant.

Ever Yours, with 1000 thanks for roses & orange blossoms! | D.

TO: WILLIAM STIRLING House of Commons [Thursday] 23 May 1861 **3579**

ORIGINAL: STCL 11/48
EDITORIAL COMMENT: House of Commons paper.

W. Stirling Esqr | M.P.[1] May 23 1861

Dear Stirling,

Writing at this table, I overhear a man saying you are not coming up immediately – &, therefore, send this to say, that there is a great party struggle on Monday next – with no prospect of adjournment[2] – & that, at present, the / chances are about equal – on paper, we seem the best. Elcho, & others, who were against us on the last occasion,[3] are with us now – & the / Catholics will poll stronger than before.[4] Every vote is golden. Pray don't be absent![5]

Yours sincerely, | D.

TO: MONTAGU PEACOCKE Grosvenor Gate [Friday] 24 May 1861 **3580**

ORIGINAL: SPI [10]
EDITORIAL COMMENT: Paper imprinted 'Grosvenor Gate'. *Sic:* G.W.M.; Newdigate's.

---

confidential May 24 1861

G.W.M. Peacocke Esqr | M.P.

4 All five young princes were grandsons of Louis Philippe; see V **1643**n7, **2012**n2 and **1709**n6. Louis Philippe Marie Ferdinand Gaston (1846-1922), Count of Eu, was the eldest son of the Duke of Nemours and on his 1864 marriage to the Princess Imperial of Brazil would be Marshal of the Brazilian army; his younger brother, Ferdinand Philippe Marie (1844-1910), the Duke of Alençon, does not appear in the published reports. *The Times*, MP (16 May 1861).

5 The DS would be at Hughenden 18-22 May. H acc.

---

1 William Stirling (1818-1878), MA (Cambridge) 1843, would succeed his uncle Sir John Maxwell as 9th Bt in 1865 and assume the additional surname of Maxwell. He was Kt and DL for Renfrew, vice-lieut for Perthshire, MP (C) for Perthshire 1852-68, 1874-78, rector of St Andrews University 1862, of Edinburgh University 1872, chancellor of Glasgow University 1876, DCL (Oxford) 1876. In 1877 he would marry, as his second wife, his and D's old friend Caroline Norton.

2 See **3578**&nn1&2.

3 Elcho had voted with the government in the 2 May division, for which see **3576**&n1.

4 See **3575**&n2.

5 Stirling would vote with the opposition on 30 May.

My dear Peacocke,

I intend to fight on Monday night, (not on Newdigate's motion wh: I hope may be withdrawn) & I expect to win.[1]

Do me the favor of looking after / George Lennox.[2]

I expect much greater assistance, this time, from our Catholic friends, than on the previous occasion.[3] What of our friend Fulke? Can you do anything in that quarter?[4] Every vote is golden – & staying away / too – a wonderful ceremony.

I beg my Comp[limen]ts to Mrs. Peacocke & am always

Sincerely yours, | D.

3581 TO: THOMAS BARING [London, Friday] 24 May 1861

ORIGINAL: BAR [8]

Thos: Baring Esqr | M.P. May 24. 1861

My dear Baring,

There will be a real fight on Monday against the clause in the Budget Bill remitting the / Excise on Paper.[1]

Pray look after Hubbard. I should have thought this motion would have exactly suited him, but I hear he is queer, from supposing, that / I threw him over on the Income Tax motion he made the other day, whereas I only spoke, as I understood at his wish, to give him a graceful opportunity of not going to a division. Monday is my Derby day – if all poll, who promise, we shall win.[2]

Do all you can for me.

Yours ever, | D.

1 The debate on Monday would open with Newdegate's motion (see **3578**&nn1&2) that each tax be treated separately; the motion would be defeated 195-34. *Hansard* CLXIII col 92.

2 Lord George Lennox, a new MP (L-C, 1860), would vote with the opposition on 30 May as he had on 2 May.

3 See **3576**&n1 for the 2 May division and **3575**&n2 for the Catholic support.

4 Fulke Southwell Greville (1821-1883), vice-lieut (later LL) of co Westmeath, hon col of the Westmeath militia, was MP (L) for Longford from 1852 until created Baron Greville in 1869 (when he would also assume the additional name of Nugent). He had voted with the government on 2 May, but would vote with the opposition on 30 May. He was Peacocke's kinsman by marriage.

---

1 See **3578**&nn1&2.

2 J.G. Hubbard, who had consulted D in February on the taxation issues, in the 2 May debate (see **3576**&n1) had moved an amendment limiting remittance of tax revenue to the amount of the estimated surplus (it being a central issue whether there was currently a surplus sufficient to offset the effects of the proposed measures). In the ensuing debate, D had advised him to withdraw the motion because it was so important and had such far-reaching implications that it could be accepted by the House only after prolonged discussion. H B/XXI/H/716. In the 30 May division on the paper duties clause he would vote with the opposition. For the equine Derby, see **3582**&n3.

TO: SARAH BRYDGES WILLYAMS Grosvenor Gate 3582
[Saturday] 25 May 1861

ORIGINAL: RTC [170]

EDITORIAL COMMENT: Paper imprinted 'Grosvenor Gate'. There is no salutation.

May 25. 1861

I got three days at Hughenden, where I had not been for nearly six months.[1] Nature was delicious, but estates do not prosper, where their Lords are absentees. / I tried to forget all petty annoyances, however, in the renovated glories of the woods, which were splendid with sunshine, & deep, perfumed, shade.

I was obliged to be in town on Wednesday – & have been / ever since unceasingly engaged. On Monday, there will be a pitched battle – a Magenta or a Solferino – but to whom?[2] I think the Government are in great danger. Whatever the result, it will be a / finer race, than the Derby, which takes place the Wednesday following.[3]

I hope you are well, & enjoying the summer skies.

Yours ever, | D.[4]

TO: MONTAGU PEACOCKE Grosvenor Gate [Sunday] 26 May 1861 3583

ORIGINAL: SPI [11]

EDITORIAL COMMENT: Paper imprinted 'Grosvenor Gate'. *Sic:* G.W.M.; respond on.

Private May 26 1861

G.W.M. Peacocke Esqr | M.P.

My dear Peacocke,

I shd. like you to speak tomorrow.

The main principle of opposition obvious: our financial policy is to remit war taxes in preference to all others. This for reasons / political as well as commercial; the former even stronger. The country will not cheerfully respond on an emergency, when they ↑are↓ called upon to add war taxes to those wh: already exist.[1]

Yours sincerely, | D.

1 See **3532** and **3578**&n5.

2 See **3578**&nn1&2. In these two battles, the French routed the Austrians, who suffered huge casualties each time.

3 The Derby at Epsom Downs on Wednesday 29 May, attended by an unusually large crowd, would be won by Kettledrum, at 16 to 1. *The Times* (30 May 1861).

4 SBW would reply on 27 May: 'I very much fear that you sacrifice too much to Fame and that it may not be done with impunity, however successful and exhilirating [*sic*] [;] what can be hoped from only three days at Hughenden?' She concluded by describing the dreadfully cold weather, with thanks for the many papers and letters sent to her. RTC [423Q].

---

1 Peacocke would not speak until Thursday 30 May, the second night of the debate (see **3578**nn1&2), when he would argue that, if a surplus existed, the war taxes on tea and sugar should be remitted before the duty on paper; see also **3585**.

3584 TO: [SIR WILLIAM HEATHCOTE] [London, Tuesday 28 May 1861]

ORIGINAL: H B/II/60

PUBLICATION HISTORY: M&B IV 298-9, dated [27 May 1861], omitting the eighth and final paragraphs

EDITORIAL COMMENT: A draft in D's hand. *Recipient and dating*: by Heathcote's response written while the servant delivering D's letter waited; see n6.

My dr. Sir W.

~~The great~~ ↑I attribute such↓ importance ~~wh: I attribute~~ to the unity of the Cons[ervativ]e party ~~must be my apology for thus troubling you~~ that I shd. ~~at any time~~, as a general rule, always be ready to waive any course, wh: I ~~thought~~ ↑might think↓ it desirable for ~~them~~ ↑us↓ to pursue, rather than ~~hazard~~ endanger ↑our↓ complete concord.

Under these circ[umstanc]es it is with the utmost pain that I learn / the step you & ~~others~~ Walpole contemplate taking with reference to the question of ~~the paper duties ↑the exchequer↓~~ ↑the↓ pap: dut~~iesy~~. The policy of resisting ~~their~~ its repeal ~~of the paper duties~~ was adopted after ~~council of~~ ↑great deliber[ati]on at↓ wh: Walpole ~~was a member~~ ↑assisted↓ & altho' after that decision I felt it my duty to take every step that I thought likely to effect ~~our~~ ↑the desired↓ result, I / have been ~~so anxious~~ ↑scrupulous↓ not to move again without materially ~~aff~~ advancing our ~~purpose~~ ↑object↓, that I have ~~never sanctioned~~ ↑continually↓ refrained ~~on many occasions~~ from acting ↑tho' ever↓ with a distinct reserv[ati]on of my right ↑to do so↓ & even ↑an↓ assertion of my future purpose.[1]

It was my opinion, that nothing wd. justify our again trying the issue unless we were assured of / the assistance ↑of some of the most eminent members of the Whig party↓ & ~~of~~ even of the course being originated by ~~an eminent member of the Whigs~~ ↑one of yr. body↓.

There was a very ~~strong &~~ general ↑& very urgent↓ disposition in ~~the~~ ↑our↓ party to support the division of the budget bill – but in deference to ~~the course wh: you took on the part of Walpole you f~~ ↑yr. opinions & those of W. on that subject↓ I cd. not sanction ~~it~~ the ↑attempt↓. I inferred however from yr declar[ati]on / in ~~that~~ ↑yr↓ speech, that yr obj[ecti]on to the financial policy was unchanged.[2]

In the midst of the Whitsun week, I received a communic[ati]on that ~~a high[?]: a body of~~ some of the most influential Whig gent: ~~had resolved~~ ↑were prepared↓ to ~~vote &~~ speak ↑& vote↓ agst. the paper clause in Comm[itt]ee, if our party were still prepared to support them and on this I resolved upon ~~the~~ ↑our↓ course.[3]

1 See 3578&nn1&2.

2 In the debate on 16 May, Heathcote (speaking for himself and the indisposed Walpole) had said that, although he had voted against the budget proposals, now that they had passed, he saw the primary issue as the privileges of the two Houses, and therefore would not oppose the bill, as 'he did not view the proposed measure as calculated in any way to trench on the privileges of the House of Lords.' *Hansard* CLXII cols 2112-16.

3 No correspondence fitting this description has been found. In an undated note Earle reported 'a most important conversation with Sir R. Peel. He is violent against paper & certainly intends to speak ... I said that what we wanted was that some influential man on the Whig side, shd. move the rejection of the paper clause, – our own strength being insufficient to succeed & many Whigs, who wd. not vote for an Opposition Amendment, being ready to vote for one emanating from a member on their own side. I suggested that Ramsden or *himself* shd. do this.' H B/XX/E/224. Both Ramsden and Peel would speak against the paper duty clause of the bill on the 27th and vote against it on the 30th. *Hansard* CLXIII cols 131-48, 342.

It was impossible / ↑~~at such~~↓ to consult any ~~one even if consult[ati]ons were possible practicable~~, for everyone was absent, ~~&~~ but with gt deference & with no assumption of arrogance, wh: I hope is foreign ~~to~~ from my nature I wd. observe, that altho' the indiv[idua]l entrusted with the conduct of a parl[iamentar]y party wd. act very unwarrantably / in deciding upon policy witht. consulting his principal friends it is a very different case with respect to the tactics wh: are to carry that policy into effect. These ~~de~~ must necess[aril]y depend ~~upon~~ ↑upon constantly changing circ[umstanc]es & often on↓ the decision of a moment.

If the leader of a parl[iamentar]y party cannot be trusted with deciding on tactics, he really can be entrusted with nothing – & it wd. be very much / like the old aulic councils,[4] wh: full of ~~wisdom~~ prudence & science always conducted the Austrian armies [*changed from* army] to discomfiture.

The course we are now taking is the policy originally decided on. I did not determine on ~~that course~~ ↑the last move↓ until I was assured that Sir Jno. Ramsden & others wd. support ↑it↓ ~~& even vo~~. ~~The~~ / ~~gossip~~ ↑~~huff~~ All↓ about the Galway contract is ↑a↓ mere ↑idle↓ gossip. The ~~course was decided on~~ ↑line was taken↓ before it was ↑even↓ known ↑that↓ the Galway contract was rescinded. Not the slightest communic[atio]n has been held with any person connected with that enterprise & the ~~Irish telegr~~ Irish Telegram of my interview with Father Daly is an ↑utter &↓ impudent fabric[ati]on.[5] /

Believing that I was carrying the wishes of the ↑united↓ party entirely into effect, & by my present course, I view with dismay & the deepest sense of personal ~~annoyance~~ ↑vexation↓ ~~the~~ ↑yr↓ contemplated course ~~of yourself & Walpole~~.

Upon my repres[entati]ons, some hundreds of gentlemen at great trouble & even at great expense have hurried / up to the Ho: of Comm: What must be their irrit[ati]on & their disappointment to find voting agst. them men like y[ou]rs[el]f! ↑the principal personages of the party!↓ [*D has noted that the next sentence (*'Since ... us.'*) is to be placed*] *after next p* [; *ie, after* 'destroyed.' *where it now appears.*] / I entreat

4 *Cf* v **1986**&n1.

5 Gladstone in the House on 16 May had confirmed the cancellation of the mail contract between Galway and the U.S., a blow to Irish aspirations for Galway to become a major seaport; D two years earlier (7 July 1859) had defended the contract which his government had entered into with the Galway company. *Hansard* CLIV cols 800-840; CLXII cols 2094-5. On 23 May, Stanley had talked to D, 'full of some great project of attack for Monday, in which he expected to beat the government: he had been in communication with Lord Normanby, with the Irish Catholics, with the disappointed Whigs; and anticipated great results. The Irish M.P.'s are dissatisfied with the cabinet, because Gladstone, who has always been hostile to the Galway contract scheme, has taken advantage of some failure of duty on the part of the Galway company to cancel the contract.' *Disraeli, Derby* 171&n29. On the 25th the British press had reported a telegram in the *Freeman* stating that D had promised Father Daly in London his utmost support in compelling the postmaster-general to rescind the order. *Times, MP* (25 May 1861). Earle in an undated note advised: 'You do not care about being [*word missing:* beaten] by a majority, purchased by the restoration of the Galway contract, but you do care very much if that majority be swelled by defections such as those of W.H. show that this story about Galway is an impudent calumny [*sic*].' H B/XX/E/194. Palmerston on 28 May would confirm the cancellation, and D on the 30th would denounce the interview as an 'impudent fabrication'. *Hansard* CLXIII col 188, (D 250-66). Stanley (*op cit*) on the 30th would remark on the close division won by the government: 'Many [Conservatives] stayed away; partly because they thought the Irish members had entered into a conspiracy against Lord Palmerston on account of the Galway contract, and did not choose to be mixed up with that'. See further **3594**&n6. The Rev Peter Daly (1784-1868) was a Galway priest active in promoting steam communication between Ireland and the U.S.

you to think of the effect of their ~~disappointed~~ ↑mortified↓ feelings on the mustering of our party on subjects of less exciting, but of far more important interest, than a tax or a duty. The labors of ~~a~~ ↑two↓ Sess: ~~& more than no~~ will be destroyed. Since we have acted together, I have done everything ~~to~~ in my power to meet yr. views & wd. with[ou]t hesit[ati]on have prevented the present movement, had I supposed it cd. have separated us.

/ I write to you with ~~earnestness~~ ↑deep emotion↓, for I know how much is at stake. I expect you to consider well the course you are taking. I feel persuaded that if you will view ~~it~~ ↑the circ[umstanc]es in wh: we are placed↓ deeply & disaff[ected]ly you will not only support me at this moment but use all yr great & just influence / with those who are guided by yr example.

Excuse this most imperfect expression of my feelings. I shd be most happy to confer with you at the House if you like when we can go more into detail.[6]

Believe me

3585 TO: [CONSERVATIVE MPS] Grosvenor Gate [Wednesday] 29 May 1861

ORIGINAL: H B/II/61

PUBLICATION HISTORY: M&B IV 299, to 'others among his followers', an undated paraphrase of the first sentence

EDITORIAL COMMENT: A draft in D's hand, of the fair copy reproduced and sent to any Conservative MPS thought to be wavering on the 30 May division.

Private G.G. May 29. 61

My dear Sir

Ld D is very anx[ious] that the impend[in]g div[ision] shd. prove the unity of the C[onservative] P[art]y. The amount of the Min[isterial] maj[orit]y is of sec[ondar]y imp[ortance], tho', of course, for the sake of our friends in the C[ountr]y, it is des[irabl]e that it shd. not be materially increased.

The pol[icy] in quest[ion] is precisely that, wh: from the first, / we urged upon the House; that in all red[ucti]ons of tax[ati]on *war* taxes shd have the pref[erence] and *that* from cons[iderati]ons of high policy, as well as financial & commercial.

There is nothing in the leg[islati]on, that an acknowledged surplus must be appropriated. It is still open to the Comm[itt]ee on the Bill, when it considers the schedules, to appropriate it either to tea or to / sugar. If you will refer to the clause in the bill, you will observe, that it does not deal with this important point.

6 Heathcote (who in 1857 had declined D's invitation to the party dinner before the opening of parliament, feeling he could be more effective as an independent) would reply hurriedly on 28 May 1861 while D's servant waited that in his speech on privilege he had agreed with D against the government, but thought their own vote prevented them from resisting the reduction of some tax and considered paper doomed. 'In face of my public declaration I feel that *personally* I can hardly vote for retaining the Paper duty as matters now stand ... at the bottom of my objection is that I am not willing to vote for a motion on which I *wish* to be in a minority'. On the 29th, after conferring with Walpole, he would write that much of his difficulty was removed by D's intention to announce next day they would try to preserve the paper duty, so as to ensure 'remission of part of the War Duties on Tea & Sugar, & not in order to pour larger supplies into the Exchequer. – that you are, in fact, trying over again the same issue, on account of the smallness of the majority by which it was decided ... & we shall be able to vote with you & our other friends.' H B/XXI/H/430-2. On the 30th, both he and Walpole would vote with D against repeal of the paper duty. *Hansard* CLXIII col 342.

It must also not be forgotten, that in repealing the excise on paper, we deal with the surplus of next year, as well as of the present.

I earnestly entreat yr presence in the Ho[use] on Thursday when / a division is certain. The majority of the Govt will, probably, exceed that on a late occasion, but if the division prove the complete concord of the Conservatives, the result will be highly advantageous to our cause.

I &c

TO: SIR STAFFORD NORTHCOTE [London, Thursday] 30 May 1861 3586

ORIGINAL: BL ADD MS 50015 f543

EDITORIAL COMMENT: Endorsed in another hand on the first page: 'Mr Disraeli on Horsfall', and on the fourth page: '*May 30 Mr. Disraeli*'.

Sir. S. Northcote | Bart: MP. May 30 1861

My dear N.

In consequence of several things that have occurred, & after consultation with Heathcote & Walpole, I intend to rise myself, immediately after Mellor to night – & state our policy.[1] /

Be so good as to have ready for me in the House when I come down – the figures of yr estimate with respect to the alterations of the tea duties proposed by Horsfall[.] I depend on this, as I / have not them at hand.[2]

Yrs sincerely, | D.

1 Northcote had written on 29 April, 'horribly afraid of moving an amendment in the resolution itself. Gladstone may bring up an array of figures to show that we shall upset the finance of the country, and may carry off a number of votes.' He had worked out for D 'a bit of prospective finance' anticipating a deficiency. He recorded that D was 'in the highest spirits because the battle is to be fought by tactics and not by brute force.' Northcote I 170-2. John Mellor (1809-1887), barrister (Inner Temple 1833, QC 1851), puisne judge Queen's bench 1861, MP (L) for Yarmouth 1857-9, for Nottingham 1859-61, PC 1879, would open the budget debate this night (30 May) by reminding the House of the several times the Conservatives had strongly opposed any tax on paper. D would respond that the issue was whether there indeed was a surplus and, if so, how it should be appropriated; he was not against remitting the paper duty if it could be afforded, but thought a greater benefit would be a reduction in the tea duty. He claimed that it was a principle of their economic system that war taxes such as those on tea and sugar should be remitted at the first opportunity. *Hansard* CLXIII cols 245-345 (D 250-66).

2 Northcote's calculations were evidently the basis of the party's policy on the budget. Derby on 14 April 1861 had written to D: 'According to my promises I return you Northcote's Paper at the appointed hour. I do not myself make out on what data he assumes a diminution of 5,000,000 in the year's expenditure – but I see that the Observer of this morning announces officially that there is to be a surplus – and that there is no question of adding new taxes, but only what are to be taken off. If they attempt the Paper Duties, I think we ought to raise Income Tax, or Tea, or Sugar, against it. But, I do not think Palmerston will give in.' H B/XX/S/281. Earle in an undated note had reported Horsfall's agreement to move the amendment that the tea duty should be reduced a shilling per pound as of 1 October, Northcote's minute calculations having decided this date as a safe proposal: 'an Opposition is at a great disadvantage in dealing with questions of this kind, as the House can only receive authoritative estimates from Ministers, & we know how flexibly Gladstone's will be given ... All we want is an issue that the country may understand.' H B/XX/E/220. For Horsfall's 2 May amendment, see **3576**&n1; he gave detailed estimates of the effect on consumption, and thus on new revenue, of different levels and schedules of remission of the tea duty. Later on 2 May, Northcote had made a speech that evoked from D the remark (col 1456) that 'never since I have had the honour of a seat in this House have I heard a question more completely and more fairly put before the House, supported by ampler knowledge, illustrated in a happier manner, and recommended for our consideration by reasoning more irresistible'. Northcote argued that, 'looking at the

3587 TO: EDGAR BOWRING Grosvenor Gate [Sunday] 2 June 1861

ORIGINAL: PS 693

PUBLICATION HISTORY: Maggs Bros Catalogue 1189 (1995) 32, item 62: 'Autograph Letter Signed ("Yours very faithfully B. Disraeli") to Edgar Bowering [*sic*]. 3 pages 8vo, Grosvenor Gate, 2 June 1861. Gracefully explaining that "[*text given below, including the comment in square brackets*]".

EDITORIAL COMMENT: *Sic:* Trelawnay's; H. Wills.

Wednesday is the third reading of Sir John Trelawnay's bill for the abolition of Church Rates, & I do not think, that any Member of the Ho: of Commons can be absent from his seat on that morning. This is very unfortunate, & I particularly regret it, as it always is a source of satisfaction to me to support H. Wills [? name virtually illegible] in his efforts to refine the public taste.[1]

3588 TO: SARAH BRYDGES WILLYAMS House of Commons Monday 3 June 1861

ORIGINAL: RTC [171]

PUBLICATION HISTORY: M&B IV 302-3, dated at the House of Commons, 3 June 1861, omitting the last paragraph

EDITORIAL COMMENT: House of Commons paper. There is no salutation.

Monday | June 3 1861

The great battle, which commenced this day week, & which, if concluded on that night, would have ended in the defeat of Ministers, terminated on Friday morning / at two o'ck, & later, by their escape – by a slight majority.[1] In the very hour of

demands they had to meet, it was safer to remit part of the duty on tea than to destroy the entire duty on paper. He did not, however, admit that the question then to be argued lay between tea and paper. The question was – Should they or should they not renew those war duties which for so many reasons ought to be remitted.' Whether or not he had Northcote's calculations at hand, D did not cite them in his 30 May speech.

1 'H. Wills' is evidently the cataloguer's rendering of 'H.R.H.'; on Wednesday 5 June at 4:15 *pm*, Prince Albert would formally open the Horticultural Society's new gardens at South Kensington, and in the evening preside at a meeting of the Society of Arts on the 1862 international exhibition. *MP* (6 Jun 1861). Edgar Alfred Bowring (1826-1911) (see ph) was, among other things, précis writer and registrar to the board of trade (1849-64) and secretary to the Royal Commission for the 1851 Exhibition (1850-68), in which latter capacity he had previously corresponded with D as a commissioner. He would be MP (L) for Exeter 1868-74. On 8 September 1859 he had acknowledged D's 40-guinea life membership in the Horticultural Society. He would reply on 3 June from the board of trade that, since twenty-six of the thirty commissioners and members of the government had accepted, he had assumed that an arrangement had been made about the timing of the division. The procession '(not being a full dress one) would not interfere with an early one, say at 3 o'clock, – or with one at 5½ or ¼ to 6. As I believe that the Royal party will arrive punctually at 4½, those in the procession could probably get away in about half an hour. You will however of course know best whether such an arrangement could be made.' H A/IV/N/25-46. Sotheron-Estcourt wrote on this day (2 June) about a meeting next day 'to determine our course with Trelawny.' H B/XXI/E/265. On 3 June Trelawny would agree to postpone his announced motion on third reading of the Church Rate Abolition Bill (see **3556**&n1 and **3567**&n1), also scheduled for 5 June. *Hansard* CLXIII cols 467-8. D would be among the 'many most distinguished personages' who attended the Kensington ceremony; see **3592**&n3. *MP* (6 June 1861).

1 For the budget debate that opened on Monday 27 May and concluded late on Thursday 30 May (*ie* Friday morning) with the close 296-281 division supporting the clause to repeal the paper duty, see **3578**&nn1&2, **3579**, **3580**&nn1,2,4, **3581**&n2, **3583**&n1, **3584**&nn2,5,6, **3585** and **3586**&n1.

victory, when the signal for the last charge was given, I had the mortification, great for a general indeed, to see a division of my own troops, march from the / field of contest.[2] One bears this, however, as one bears many things, when the heat of youth is over, & one ~~had~~ has experienced, in one's time, what is the surest, perhaps the only support, under discomfiture – the memory of former success.

A government, saved by the too prudential forbearance of a section of their foes, is not in a proud, or a strong, position – and, I must say, I look to the future without dismay.[3]

I hope you are well, & you can make out this scrawl, but I am writing in my place, with my hat for a desk.

Yours ever | D.

TO: [FRANCIS VILLIERS?] [London, Wednesday] 5 June 1861 3589

ORIGINAL: H R/IV/D/6e[a]

EDITORIAL COMMENT: A copy among the Rose papers in H. *Recipient*: this copy is adjacent to and similar in kind to **3597**. *Sic:* manouvres.

Extract June 5. 1861

x x x

After a brilliant Campaign we commenced a struggle, some two months ago of prolonged manouvres, which s[h]ou[l]d have resulted on Thursday last in the utter overthrow of the Government, when I had the pleasure of seeing, at the critical moment, nearly twenty of my troops march off the field when the division was called, and the Ministry saved by their want of pluck. I believe it was the fear of an impossible dissolution – a panic! I need not tell you how disgusted I am![1] The curtain has now fallen and a very weak and really unpopular Government have eight months of undisturbed enjoyment of power! At the bottom of all this, I fear, is the utter want of Confidence in the Captain, who has the unhappy talent of depressing his friends every day more developed.

These are my troubles. They are not slight ones but must be borne like others.

Yrs sincerely | D.

2 For Stanley's analysis of the absence of many Conservatives on 30 May, see **3584**n5. On 1 June *The Times* gave a jaded summary of the whole paper duty debate, saying: 'Mr. Disraeli scarcely entered on the merits of the question at all, but confined himself to a somewhat tame defence of his own generalship.'

3 Stanley on this day (3 June) was asked to confirm rumours 'that Disraeli meant to throw up the leadership. I took on myself to deny their truth'. *Disraeli, Derby* 172.

---

1 Theories about the key defections abounded; Malmesbury (II 252) on 2 June had recorded: 'Lord Ossulston [*sic – now Tankerville*] attributes the bad division on the Paper Duty to the stupid dislike of our party to Disraeli, and their wish not to turn out the Government to put him in office; but I think it more probable that they feared a dissolution.' George Beecroft forwarded a letter that contended: 'But are they not Peelites? Did not this little crew of nondescripts always fail us in a pinch?' H B/XXI/B/297. See also **3584**n5. A year later, on 6 June 1862, Henry Edwards would write: 'Am I at liberty to state in the Carlton & elsewhere that last year – after our defeat – you resigned the leadership of the party & were pressed into its service again by Trollope who represented a very influential section of the landed interest in the House of Commons.' H B/XXI/E/49. See further **3590**.

3590 TO: SIR MATTHEW WHITE RIDLEY Grosvenor Gate [Friday] 7 June 1861

ORIGINAL: H B/II/62

PUBLICATION HISTORY: M&B IV 300, dated at Grosvenor Gate, 7 June 1861

EDITORIAL COMMENT: This letter exists in a heavily revised draft and a fair copy of the first four pages on paper imprinted 'Grosvenor Gate', both versions in D's hand; here the draft has been used to complete the fair copy.

Sir M.W. Ridley | Bart: M.P.[1] June 7 1861

My dear Sir Matthew,

I am honored, & deeply gratified, by the invitation, wh: yourself, & others of my friends, have, this morning, brought me from those members of the Carlton Club, / who are also members of the House of Commons, to meet them at dinner "as a testimony of the undiminished value they set upon my services to the Conservative party & of their earnest & friendly / feeling towards myself."[2]

My services are, at all times amply rewarded by the indulgent belief of my friends, that they contribute, however slightly, to the progress & welfare of the party whose interests with / me, I trust, will always be paramount to any personal consideration.

If, therefore, I presume to decline a proposition so flattering as this invitation, it is only because I feel its acceptance at this moment might lead to / misconception, & foster ~~the~~ ↑~~an unfounded~~↓ ~~the notion wh: I hold to be as unfounded, as, if true, it wd. be mischievous that~~ ↑a / notion↓ as unfounded as it might be ~~a~~ mischievous, ~~the unfounded notion, that there is a want of unity in the ranks of~~ that there is any material want of ~~unity~~ concord in the Conservative ranks[.]

3591 TO: SIR JOHN PAKINGTON Grosvenor Gate [Sunday] 9 June 1861

ORIGINAL: H B/II/63

PUBLICATION HISTORY: M&B IV 300-1, undated and recipient unidentified, the last paragraph

EDITORIAL COMMENT: A draft in D's hand on paper imprinted 'Grosvenor Gate'. The following is the most accurate rendition possible.

Private June 9 1861

Rt Honble | Sir J.S. Pakington | G.C.B.

Dear Pakington,

Since ↑–after &↓ we decided on our policy ~~(resistance to the repeal of the Paper Excise)~~ (after ample deliberation at Ld. Derby's,) no question has occurred, on wh: counsel has been / necessary. The tactics by wh: ~~that~~ policy ~~was~~ ↑is↓ to be carried into effect ↑can rarely &c↓, frequently depend upon the information & decision of the moment, & can rarely be made the subject of general ~~deliberation~~ conference.

1 Sir Matthew White Ridley (1807-1877), 4th Bt, sheriff of Northumberland 1841, DL 1852, MP (C) for Northumberland N 1859-68, had written on 6 June to ask for an interview at D's earliest convenience. H B/XXI/R/86.

2 The invitation (if made in written form) has not been found. The dinner evidently was to stave off D's resignation; the 4 June letter forwarded by Beecroft (see **3589**n1) hoped that 'the compliment which the dinner will pay to him will show him that he retains, as he has well deserved, the confidence of all, and, though it serves the renegades right to *threaten them* with a resignation let us hope that the threat will prevent future desertion, & that he will be supported all the more *heartily* now that he has shown that he desires to retain the leadership, so long only as he retains the confidence of the party.'

I ~~was~~ myself, ↑, tho' urged to do so,↓ ~~notwithstanding~~ ↑~~the general view to try another division, but~~ ↑ [*two or three illegible deleted words*] ~~long hesitated before I ventu~~ ↑~~decided~~↓ to↓ was reluctant to try ano[the]r div[isi]on, ~~having~~ / having, received during the W. week a communic[ati]on from Sir R.P. & Sir J.R. I I came up to town, & ↑~~eventually~~↓ decided ~~on an[oth]er venture~~ ↑on our course↓. ~~It was impossible to consult anyone ↑but Taylor↓ for no one was ↑none↓ of my coll[eague]s attended the reassembly of P[arliamen]t & it was ↑absolutely↓ necessary that our resol[uti]on shd be taken on the Thurs first day of our meeting. Instant decision was necessary as none of my coll[eague]s were present for several days~~ /

~~With respe respect to the story you tell me of~~ ↑As for↓ Taylor's message I can make neither head ~~of~~ nor tail of ~~it~~ the story. ~~I may have wished you~~ It must have originated in an *entire* misconception. ~~as~~ I agreed with Graham's view ↑& was opposed to McDs intrusion into the debate↓ ~~I cd. never have wished you to reply to him, tho' I may have wished you to speak on the budget – & as for McDonogh it was agst my wish that he intruded himself into the debate & only on cond[iti]on that he made no motion motion~~ & only gave ↑it↓ a cold assent on cond[iti]on that he moved no amendment.[1] /

It was unfortunate, in yr view, that you shd. have selected a Friday night after a great division to make yr observ[ati]ons on the French navy, when Monday cd. have secured you a good house: but had I been present I cd not have enforced yr represent[ati]ons for ~~I do not think they ought to be made by an opposition~~ ↑generally speaking↓ I think such ~~repres[entati]ons~~ ↑statements↓ on the part of ~~y~~ an oppos[iti]on ~~are~~ ↑to be↓ injudicious – & from what I have since ~~heard~~ ↑learned↓ of the relations / ~~of~~ ↑bet[wee]n↓ the French Govt & our own on the matter, I ~~think~~ ↑deem↓ it fortunate that the demonstration on our part was ~~of so ↑a↓ limited as temperate character rat~~ at least not of a general & violent character.

After all, politics is like war – roughish work. We shd. not be oversensitive. We have enough to do & to bear with[ou]t imaginary grievances. Somebody must lead

1 Pakington had written from Eaton Square on 8 June 1861 to complain about the lack of party support for his Friday 31 May alarmist speech comparing British and French progress in building iron-clad ships; though finding it extremely unpleasant, he told D he had long felt there should be more consultation with former Cabinet members on party policy. He and his colleagues willingly deferred to D as House leader, but he felt they should have a say in and more knowledge of his plans, in particular his request, through Colonel Taylor, that Pakington reply to Graham's rebuttal of Macdonogh's objections to the Supply Bill. Although Pakington agreed with Graham that precedents in 1787 and 1808 discounted the objections, he felt he should have been asked by D himself, and informed on D's policy on the issue. He concluded: 'I will dwell no longer upon anything unpleasant – we have sat together in the House of Coms. for 24 years. I was glad to see yesterday, that you had resumed the seat to which you have so well asserted your claim. I wish to continue the cordial, though humble support which I have long given you as our leader in that House – but I think you will concur with me when I add, that support & confidence can be neither permanent nor useful, unless they are reciprocal.' H B/XX/P/64-5; *Hansard* CLXIII cols 412-27. Macdonogh on 13 May had opened the debate on second reading of the Customs and Inland Revenue Bill (for which see also **3578**&n1), opposing it on constitutional grounds as a measure already rejected by the Lords. Graham had cited precedents for combining remission and imposition of taxes in one bill and denied that it would cause friction with the Lords. Late in the debate, in response to Gladstone's impatience, D confined himself to urging caution and deliberation on the issues in the bill. *Hansard* CLXII cols 1965-2044 (D 2035-40). Francis Macdonogh (1806-1882) of Ballyquin, co Kilkenny, an Irish barrister (1829), QC (1842), JP for Armagh, Kilkenny and Sligo, counsel to inland revenue for Ireland 1858-9, was MP (L-C) for Sligo 1860-65.

but I wish to live with my colleagues on terms of perfect equality – & after reading yr long letter of complaints over again, you will permit me to say that I do not think they are very substantial.

3592 TO: SARAH BRYDGES WILLYAMS Carlton Club [Tuesday] 11 June 1861

ORIGINAL: RTC [172]

PUBLICATION HISTORY: M&B IV 326, dated at the Carlton Club, 11 June 1861, extracts from the first paragraph

EDITORIAL COMMENT: Carlton Club paper. There is no salutation. *Sic:* subtelty.

Private June eleven 1861

The death of Cavour is an immense event![1] It is impossible to see the end of the effects it will produce. I sent you a portrait of him, if I remember right, wh: the Sardinian Minister gave me.[2] It was very like, & you must look at it now / with some interest. He was a thorough Italian statesman of the middle ages; most fertile in device, & utterly unscrupulous; an almost unrivalled ~~specim~~ union of subtelty & vigor.

Last Wednesday, I assisted in a Procession, attending the Royal family, to open the new gardens at Kensington, of which you have read so much. We / wanted Sun. Even Princes & princesses look more brilliant when touched by the inspiring beam; & certainly Italian arcades, American plants, & exotic flowers.[3]

The King of the Belgians, who is on a visit to Her Majesty, has signified that he wishes to see me in a few days, & talk over affairs.[4] He is the wisest Prince in Xdom; / a real statesman; & has seen more of life, in all its varieties, than most other men, & all other Princes, except the Emperor of the French, perhaps.

Tomorrow, I have to take the Chair at a public dinner at the Freemasons' tavern for a great public charity in which the Farmers of England are deeply interested[.][5]

I am glad you like the newspapers, & hope they arrive regularly.[6] It gives great pleasure to Mary Anne to direct them, herself, to you, & occasionally to mark passages.

Ever yours, | D.

1 Cavour had died in Turin on 6 June, the news reaching London in time for the late papers of that day.

2 See **3569**. The Sardinian minister was 'Minimo' Marchese d'Azeglio; *cf* V **2198**&n1.

3 See **3587**&n1. This would be Prince Albert's last public engagement.

4 See **3594**&n3. The Queen, grieving the death of her mother (see **3563**&n3), had asked the King (her mother's brother) to visit and share her reminiscences. *LQV* III 438-9. D may be thinking of Henri IV of France's quip about James VI and I of Britain as 'the wisest fool in Christendom.'

5 On Wednesday 12 June D would preside at the second annual 'festival' of the Agricultural Benevolent Institution ('for the relief of farmers, their widows and orphans') at Freemasons Tavern; a subscription of £1,500 would be raised. In his speech, D would link the Institution to the rapid advances in communication that had effectively raised the farmer's awareness of the world and thus his social consciousness. *The Times* (14 Jun 1861).

6 SBW had written to D on 27 May (see **3582**n4): 'Many thanks for papers I regularly receive and for all your delightful letters they are my greatest comfort I wish I cd give adequate acknowledgment for so much indulgence.' RTC [423Q].

TO: LADY OLLIFFE Grosvenor Gate [Wednesday 19] June 1861 3593

ORIGINAL: PS 744

PUBLICATION HISTORY: Sotheby Parke-Bernet catalogue (Oct 1980) item 12: 'autograph letter signed ("D"), 3 pages 8vo, Grosvenor Gate, 16 June 1861, to Lady Olliffe'. *Dating:* by Mary Anna Morgan's letter (see n1).

[requesting that she invite some friends to her ball] They are people of very ancient family & very great fortune[1]

TO: SARAH BRYDGES WILLYAMS House of Commons Wednesday 19 June [1861] 3594

ORIGINAL: RTC [173]

PUBLICATION HISTORY: M&B IV 326, dated 19 June 1861, extract from the second paragraph

EDITORIAL COMMENT: House of Commons paper. There is no salutation. *Sic:* Sardinia gives up Sardinia.

Private Wednesday – June 19

To day is what is called the Black Drawing Room,[1] but instead of going to Court, I am obliged to be here – the last struggle about Church Rates. The event hangs in the balance – & I do not despair of obtaining a majority, / which will be for me, personally, a very great triumph.[2]

Yesterday, according to Royal appointment, I paid my visit to the King of the Belgians at Buckingham Palace, & had a very interesting audience of an hour.[3] The King, who is a statesman, talked to me very / freely on the present state of affairs, which remain most critical, &, probably, will for several years. This is an age of great & rapid events: their quick succession as remarkable, as their importance; &, to a certain extent, mutually mitigating their exciting consequences. The restless & revolutionary spirits, distracted by the choice / of materials, pause in the selection; not from satiety, but from sheer perplexity to decide where most mischief can be accomplished. Garibaldi does not know where to begin – Venice or Hungary – & talks of going to America! Mazzini says, that he has a copy of the agreement between the Emperor of the French & Cavour, / by wh: Sardinia gives up Sardinia [Savoy?] to

1 Lady Olliffe (d 1898), *née* Laura Cubitt, second daughter and heiress of William Cubitt MP (C, Andover), in 1841 had married Joseph (since 1853 Sir Joseph) Francis Olliffe, a prominent physician. Her wealthy father, a widower, was currently lord mayor of London. On Friday 21 June she would give a lavish entertainment at the Mansion House to nearly 1,000 guests, some of whom danced until 5 *am*. The DS are not listed among the guests. *MP* (24 Jun 1861). Since *The Times*'s report (24 Jun 1861) describes the event as given by the Lady Mayoress, Lady Olliffe presumably acted in that capacity for her father. On 19 June, Mary Anna Morgan, sixth and youngest daughter of 1st Lord Tredegar (see **3569**&n3), would write to MA: 'Do you think you could get Mama & me an invitation to Lady Olliffe's ball ... every body tells me it is to be very good'. H D/III/D/782. *The Times*'s list of guests includes 'Lord and Lady Tredegar and Miss Morgan'.

---

1 The Queen would hold a drawing room at St James's Palace at 2 *pm* on this day (19 June), the first of the season and the first since her mother's death; the royal family would all wear mourning. *MP* (10 Jun 1861); *The Times* (20 Jun 1861).

2 See **3587**&n1 and **3596**&n1.

3 Sylvain Van De Weyer had written to D in French on 16 June asking him to meet the King on 18 June at 12:30 *pm*. H B/XXI/V/2.

France, & which the death of the great Italian for a moment arrests.[4] ↑And Mazzini is generally right in these matters.↓

Yesterday, at Lady Londonderry's, we met the French Princes, the Comte de Paris & the Duc de Chartres at dinner. The first is intelligent, highly educated, & affable – but without charm: the younger brother with a great deal; a / sweet countenance, melancholy & refined – & much grace & graceful talk. You have no doubt received all the papers, & seen that I have been pretty busy of late.

The Agricultural Dinner was very successful, & there was a *precis* of what I said in "the Times" very tolerably accurate.[5] Last Friday, a / very animated Debate on the Galway contract. I think I never spoke more to my satisfaction.[6]

We asked your friend Lady Brownlow to dine with us, & she met Lord & Lady Exeter, & Lord & Lady Normanby, & Lord & Lady Warwick, & some others.[7]

Excuse these hurried notes written / in the House.

I hope you are quite well. Tho' the world is in confusion, England is at least safe; & in addition to all other blessings, we have at least Summer!

Yours ever | D.

3595 TO: WILLIAM W.F. HUME Carlton Club, Saturday [22 June 1861]

ORIGINAL: BRN [29]

EDITORIAL COMMENT: Endorsed in another hand on the first page: 'July 1861 Disraeli'. *Dating:* by context; see n1. *Sic: a la' Inkermann.*

---

confidential Saturday

W.F. Hume Esqr | M.P.

My dear Hume,

The government is in great & unexpected danger from Mr Augustus Smith's motion against a vote on account on Monday.

Mr Henley highly disapproves of / the Government course, & will, probably, support the amendment; at least, he will support me in any course, wh: I may recommend. It is, therefore, of great importance, that you, & all / the friends you can quietly influence, shd. be at their posts, at the meeting of the House on Monday.[1]

4 Garibaldi had lived in the U.S. 1849-54. Victor Emmanuel had sent him to the Balkans to foment insurrections and occupy Austria's attention, leaving Venetia and the Tyrol relatively easy (with French support) to take. Holt *Risorgimento* 275-6. Cavour had signed a secret agreement on 12 March 1861 ceding Nice and Savoy (ruled by Sardinia) to France. Frank J. Coppa *The Origins of the Italian Wars of Independence* (1992) 99-102. Mazzini was currently in London. Denis Mack Smith *Mazzini* (New Haven 1994) 159.

5 See **3592**&n5. The '*precis*' in *The Times* of 14 June is about ¾ of a column of small print in length.

6 See **3584**&n5. In the 14 June debate on a motion for a select committee to investigate cancelling the Galway contract, D had defended the terms he had signed, countering charges of buying political influence by arguing that the alternative to state assistance and direct parliamentary control would have been to award the contract to a company with no Irish connection. *Hansard* CLXIII cols 1142-9.

7 The others were 'Lady Cecil' (the Exeters' eldest daughter, Lady Mary Frances Cecil), Lady Strangford, Lord Hamilton, Lord Jermyn, Lord and Lady Tredegar, Mr Wyndham, Baron Lionel de Rothschild and Col Harvey Bathurst. H acc. Lady Warwick (1829-1903), as Lady Anne Charteris, eldest surviving daughter of 9th (8th in Debrett and Lodge) Earl of Wemyss and March, had married in 1852 Lord Brooke, since 1853 4th Earl of Warwick; see V **1799**n10.

---

1 Augustus John Smith (1804-1872), JP and DL for Cornwall, lessee of the Scilly isles, MP (L) for Truro 1857-65, had given notice of a motion against the supply motion scheduled for Monday 24 June 1861 to vote

I hope you may decypher this product of a Carlton pen!

Yours sincerely, | D. T.O. /

The thing shd. be kept very quiet – & a formal & pressing whip must be avoided. The men must assemble *a la' Inkermann*[.][2]

TO: SARAH BRYDGES WILLYAMS Carlton Club, Thursday 27 June 1861 **3596**

ORIGINAL: H R/II/E/493-4

PUBLICATION HISTORY: M&B IV 359-60, dated at the Carlton Club, 27 June 1861, the first paragraph

EDITORIAL COMMENT: From a fair copy in another hand in the Rose papers.

Carlton Club | Thursday June 27. 1861.

I wrote to you, about a week ago, on the eve of the Church Rate division. I told you how critical it was, and how important success was to me, considering, that the resistance to the bill had been mainly prompted by my counsel. I was not altogether without hope, but not over sanguine. You have seen, in the papers, the strange and wonderful triumph![1] Such a scene has not occurred in the House of Commons, since the impeachment of Lord Melville, in the days of Mr. Pitt.[2]

The Heralds give me some trouble about your arms, which I had hoped to have sent you by this time.[3]

Tomorrow, the Queen gives a State Concert, to which we are invited. It is Her Majesty's first party, since her bereavement, not counting the Drawing Rooms.[4]

The King of the Belgians left us on Tuesday, more hopeful of the peace of Europe, than this time last year.

a sum on account for unspecified civil services; his motion deplored this recurring practice, especially late in the session, and stipulated that sums should be voted only for specific purposes. An undated note from Earle asks: 'Can Heathcote do nothing with Augustus Smith?' H B/XX/E/227. Henley had written to D on this day (22 June), 'quite prepared to follow whatever course you think best on this occasion – the Government I suppose in the hope of getting credit for legislation, have from the beginning of the Session postponed supply ... and so no doubt intend to shove supply over until the hot weather has cleared London.' H B/XXI/H/471. In the House on Monday, debate on Smith's objection (which would be procedurally disallowed) would be delayed by a discussion of whether sending 3,000 troops to Canada was consistent with ministers' announced policy of non-intervention in the American civil war, D doubting the wisdom of the move. When the House returned to supply, D (who had spoken against similar votes on 17 and 24 May 1860) would support Smith, arguing that the government's practice was even more objectionable this year than last: 'By agreeing systematically to vote money on account the Committee could not conceal from itself that practically it was putting an end to all control over the public expenditure.' Smith's attempt to block the supply vote by a motion to report progress would be defeated 148-99, and the motion passed to approve on account a sum not exceeding £811,300. *The Times* (24, 25 Jun 1861); *Hansard* CLVIII cols (D 1422-3, 1670-3), CLXIII cols 1514-16, 1533-44 (D 1541-2).

2 At the Crimean battle of Inkerman, the badly outnumbered allied troops, aided by a concealing mist, had routed the Russians.

---

1 In the 19 June division on third reading of the Church Rates Abolition Bill (see **3594**&n2), the Speaker had broken a tie of 274 in favour of the opposition, defeating the bill. *Hansard* CLXIII cols 1276-1322.

2 Melville was impeached as first lord of the admiralty in 1805, when the Speaker broke the tied division in favour of the motion.

3 See VII **3389**&n2, **3390**&n1, **3435** and, in this volume, **3599**.

4 See **3563**&n3 and **3594**&n1. A second drawing room was held this day (27 June). *The Times* (28 Jun 1861). A state concert of sacred music would be held at Buckingham Palace on 28 June, with more than 200 performers. The Ds are listed among those attending; under the printed 'Full Dress' in their invitation, '(Half Mourning)' has been added by hand. *The Times* (29 Jun 1861); H D/V/A/39.

The Emperor of the French is watching the death of the Pope; and it is believed will get his cousin, who is a Priest and who resides at Rome, elected.[5] This will be a crowning glory for the House of Buonaparte! and will hardly consort with the "Unita Italiana."

I hope you are quite well. I begin to sigh for woods and waters: not for flowers, for my house is sweet with roses.

Adieu! | D.

3597 TO: [FRANCIS VILLIERS] [London, Friday] 28 June 1861

ORIGINAL: H R/IV/D/6e[b]

EDITORIAL COMMENT: An extract copied by Rose. *Recipient:* by context; see n1.

Extract June. 28. 1861

X X X

I am glad to hear that you are about to move a little – change of air – change of scene must do you a great deal of good.[1] There are moments when I envy your repose – especially if you get, as it appears, the Journals. It is a privilege to live in an age of great events, rapidly occurring, especially when we have had sufficient previous experience, as you have, to understand it all. I see no difference in The Queen and I do not believe there was any foundation for the rumours. Her Grief was overwhelming.[2]

Yours | D.

3598 TO: JOHN EVELYN DENISON Grosvenor Gate [Wednesday] 3 July 1861

ORIGINAL: NOT OSC 758

EDITORIAL COMMENT: Paper imprinted 'Grosvenor Gate'.

Rt Honble | The Speaker July 3 1861

5 Lucien Louis Joseph Napoleon (1828-1895), 4th Prince of Canino and Musignano, ordained 1853, cardinal 1868, was the Emperor's second cousin. Pope Pius, on whose frail health (epilepsy) there were regular reports, would live until 1878.

---

1 Francis Villiers had ended his 28 May letter (see **3572**n2): 'I must try & go somewhere for air &c, though I scarcely feel able to move, & have not yet been out of my room. I believe no symptoms precede a paralytic stroke, or I shd imagine I was going to have one.' There evidently was further correspondence (see also n2), which has not been found.

2 For D's correspondence with Villiers on money matters, see **3484**, **3542**, **3564** and **3572**. Villiers would reply on 3 July: 'Many thanks for yrs of 26th [*not found*] & 28th – in accordance with which I have drawn for £245 – & shall make a start in a day or two, (having paid my Bill here,) with £60 in my pocket. I have however not the least idea where I shall go ... I know well how much your time is taken up, & will not bore you now, with any remarks upon what you say about Ceylon, which I do not quite understand, but when Parlt. is up, I will trouble you with a few lines. As you say nothing in answer to my enquiries regarding safety, I suppose I need not trouble my head on the subject – but if you think it necessary to give me any advice, a line addressed P.R. "Perpignan" in the course of the next Fortnight wd. probably find me there ... The Priests here are making a fine harvest ... at the news of H.B.M's conversion to the true faith, which appears in large type with various particulars once or twice a week in the Spanish Papers.' H A/IV/J/148. See further **3621**&nn1&2. For the Queen's bereavement, see **3563**&n3. Weintraub *Victoria* 289 states: 'The Queen's mourning became so excessive that her family and the Court recognized that the hysterical indulgence in sorrow was a sign of serious nervous collapse.' See also Christopher Hibbert *Queen Victoria: A Personal History* (2000) 264-7.

My dear Mr Speaker,

I fear I have abused yr indulgence, which increased the favor, you so kindly conferred on me.

You will think me very / fortunate, or very selfish, when I tell you, that, after all my researches, I have not found a protegé.[1]

Believe me, ever, | Yours sincerely obliged | *B. Disraeli*

TO: SARAH BRYDGES WILLYAMS House of Commons [Monday] 8 July 1861 **3599**

ORIGINAL: RTC [174]

EDITORIAL COMMENT: House of Commons paper. There is no salutation. *Sic:* embarassing.

July 8 1861

I shall send you, in a day or two, the drawing of yr shield of arms, which I settled this morning, after a great deal of dispute with the / Herald. You shall give your opinion before it is engraved, as it will be mortifying to have another failure. The plate is prepared for the engraving, so / we shall lose no time.[1]

Lord Herbert, a Secretary of State, has resigned office, on acct of ill-health;[2] & the consequent re-construction of the government is very embarassing. When a / large brick falls out of a tottering wall, danger is at hand. I am writing this in a full house, fighting about the rival styles of architecture – Italian & Gothic – for the new Foreign Office.[3] I will try to write in a less distracted scene tomorrow.

Ever yrs | D.

TO: SARAH BRYDGES WILLYAMS Carlton Club [Friday] 12 July 1861 **3600**

ORIGINAL: RTC [175]

PUBLICATION HISTORY: Edward M. Kandel, 'Disraeli,' *The Coat of Arms* II (1977) 123-7, undated, extract from the fifth sentence

EDITORIAL COMMENT: Carlton Club paper. There is no salutation. *Sic:* Legh; Caringtons; banquetting.

July 12 1861

The Heralds give me a great deal of trouble[1] – but they are very positive people, & it will not do to make any mistake in their craft. They have promised, this morning, to

1 The 'favor' is presumably the Speaker's tie-breaking vote in D's favour on 19 June; see **3596**&n1. D had gone to him on 20 June to express his 'unqualified admiration' for the way Denison had given his reasons for the vote. J.E. Denison *Notes from My Journal* (1900) 96. Nothing has been found to clarify this paragraph; however, see further **3610**&nn1&4.

---

1 See **3596**&n3 and **3600**&nn1-3.

2 Sidney Herbert, who had just (28 June) been elevated to the Lords, would live only until 2 August.

3 In the last administration Manners had chosen Gilbert Scott's Gothic design for the new foreign office. On Palmerston's return to power, he had made Scott change it to a Palladian design as more appropriate for a public building. On this day (8 July), the House debated (with Palmerston at his most flippant) Elcho's motion to reject the new design in favour of the original; it was defeated 188-95. *Hansard* CLXIV cols 508-40. The original design was later used for St Pancras station. Bell *Palmerston* II 286-8.

---

1 See VII **3390**&n1 and, more recently, **3596**&n3 and **3599**.

give me a correct drawing of your shield on / Tuesday next. They say, that all your previous quarterings have been wrong; that is to say, that the arms of Legh ought never to have been introduced into your shield, your mother not having been an heiress / – but that your own arms of Mendez da Costa ought to have been emblazoned.[2] I did not tell them the reason, why they had not been inserted. They were anxious to know how you had obtained them, as nothing is more difficult, / than correct emblazonments of ancient Spanish arms. I told them that they had been copied from the Queen of Spain's own golden book, which was kept under ↑her↓ own key – which seemed to make their mouths water. I am sorry for these delays, but it will be a / satisfaction to you, that you will now have everything quite correct – the arms of Brydges Willyams & Mendez da Costa ↑in a lozenge↓. They have the arms of Brydges, Willyams, registered, with a Cornish motto – but as Ladies do not use mottoes, or crests, this does not concern us.[3] /

The parliamentary campaign wanes rapidly – it has, on the whole, been a very satisfactory one for the Opposition. The social season is now at its height – banquets & balls, morning festivals in every form, in unceasing flow. On the Queens birthday we went to an Assembly at Apsley House, the Duchess of Wellington, the new Mistress of the Robes, receiving / the great world.[4] Apsley House, is more adapted to reception, than any one in London, even more than Stafford ↑House↓. It has not the splendid hall, wh: is the feature of the latter – but it has more, & finer, rooms on the same floor – the Waterloo Gallery inimitable – & every chamber covered with beautiful, or interesting, pictures – the portraits of all / the sovereigns, statesmen, & heroes, of the Wellesley epoch – the banquetting room gorgeous & glittering with golden shields, & vases, & plateaus – the tribute of grateful monarchs & nations emancipated. Yesterday, we dined at the Duke of Montroses, & to night Mrs. D. is going to a ball at Lady Caringtons, & I to my duties at the House of Commons. I sent you the music of the Royal Concert[5] – it was a sort of requiem for the Duchess of Kent, but very effective.

Adieu! | Yrs ever, | D.

2 SBW's mother was Elizabeth Leigh; her father was Abraham Mendez da Costa (d. 1782). The marriage register of St Margaret's, Westminister records: 'No. 891. Abraham Mendez da Costa of this Parish, Bachelor, and Elizabeth Leigh of this Parish, Spinster, were married by license 29th Dec. 1775 by me J. Mor Curate ...' Lucien Wolf 'Mrs Brydges Willyams and Benjamin Disraeli,' *Miscellanies of the Jewish Historical Society of England* I (1925) xx-xxiii.

3 A lozenge is customary for spinsters and widows. J.H. Pinches *European Nobility and Heraldry* (Ramsbury, Wilts *c* 1994) 254. For the successful conclusion to the arms race, see **3673**.

4 The Duchess of Wellington's assembly at Apsley House in honour of the Queen's birthday (on 24 May, when there were no celebrations because the Queen was in mourning) was originally scheduled for 3 July but changed to the 10th. *The Times* (25 May, 21 Jun 1861); *MP* (11 Jul 1861). The Duchess had been made mistress of the robes on 25 April 1861, replacing the Dowager Duchess of Sutherland (formerly of Stafford House), who had resigned. *The Times* (27 Apr 1861).

5 See **3596**&n4. The program comprised: Mendelssohn, *St Paul* and *Elijah* (selections); Handel, *Israel in Egypt* (chorus); Haydn, *Creation* (selections); Rossini, *Stabat Mater* (selections); Hummel (air and chorus); Mehul *Joseph* (romance). *MP* (29 Jun 1861).

TO: LORD JOHN MANNERS Grosvenor Gate [Monday] 15 July 1861 3601

ORIGINAL: BEA [R1-84]

EDITORIAL COMMENT: Paper imprinted 'Grosvenor Gate'. There is no salutation and no signature. *Sic:* publickly.

Private July 15 1861

Gladstone, early in the Session, accused [the] Duke of Modena[1] of issuing an *ex post facto* edict for the execution of a youth, guilty of homicide.

D of M., thro' Lord Normanby, has proved the statement to / be entirely false; ↑the youth not being executed at all↓. Gladstone, after *six* letters, has been obliged to give in, & promise publickly to retract.

At the last moment, he has written another letter, long & involved, announcing that, while he will retract the false charge, he means, if he means anything, to make a / new one against the Duke. Lord N. has protested against such a course, & holds him to his engagement. Ld. N. says, that the new charge is as false as the old one – but declines to enter into its merits, until the first is disposed of. G. / will probably *explain* to day. I shan't, unfortunately be there.

It is highly desirable, that, while we do not, in any way, mix ourselves up with the D. of Modena, that Lord Normanby shd. not appear in any way to be deserted by our party, which he has greatly served[.][2]

TO: LADY STRANGFORD [London, mid-July 1861] 3602

ORIGINAL: H B/II/64a

EDITORIAL COMMENT: A draft in D's hand. There is no salutation. *Dating:* by Lady Strangford's letter to D (see n1).

~~You have conferred me~~ No act towards me cd be so gracious as giving me the living likeness of one who ~~in~~ ↑rendered↓ the most interesting period of my life more

1 Francesco V (1819-1875), Duke of Modena, had lost his throne when Modena was annexed to the Kingdom of Sardinia on 18 March 1860. *BRF* 336.

2 Gladstone on 7 March 1861 had noted atrocities committed by several Italian regimes. He cited the Duke of Modena's (see VII **3399**&n3) order for execution of a young man convicted of a capital offence but not, being under 21, sentenced to death. Normanby, a former Whig cabinet member, minister at Florence 1854-8, but now hostile to Palmerston, had given notice of motion on 2 July for all papers pertaining to Gladstone's allegations, saying that he had been asked to defend the Duke. On 22 July, he would read out the lengthy correspondence with Gladstone he had started on the 9th; by the 11th, Gladstone had admitted he should have said that Modena had '"issued an edict *ex post facto,* bringing the crime of that youth within the category to which capital punishment was applicable."' On 12 July, Normanby had sent D the correspondence so that D could judge Gladstone's performance. H B/XXI/P/273. Also on the 12th, Gladstone told Normanby that he was '"quite ready to make, or not, as you think fit, an explanation to the effect above described"'. On the 13th Normanby accepted Gladstone's offer to withdraw and apologize for his allegations, but reserved the right to respond to any further ones. On Thursday 18 July, Gladstone would modify his allegations but begin new ones, whereupon D rose on a point of order, that Gladstone was going beyond a statement by introducing controversial issues requiring debate; Gladstone acquiesced and postponed further comment until the next day. On Friday the 19th Normanby would send back the correspondence: 'You have not seen the last two letters ... No 7 will show how disingenuous he was last night.' H B/XXI/P/275. Also on the 19th, Gladstone, citing published documents, would complete his 'explanation' in the debate on the rumoured ceding of Sardinia to France. Only Hennessy would respond, protesting that there had been only five executions because of the edict. *Hansard* CLXI cols 1565-79, CLXIV cols 175-6, 1093-6, (D 1095), 1232-42, 1247-75 (quoted at 1237, 1253, 1256); *Gladstone Diaries* VI 48.

delightful ↑by the splendour of his cultured & imaginative intellect &↓ by his vivid & impassioned friendship. ~~All that He will ever occupy a~~ He ~~occupies~~ ↑absorbs↓ a great part of my memory. All that ~~interests~~ ↑concerns↓ him interests me, & no one & nothing more so / than the Lady who won his heart & who bears his name.[1]

I am her | obliged & ever f[aithfu]l Ser[van]t | D

3603 TO: SARAH BRYDGES WILLYAMS [London] Wednesday 17 July 1861

ORIGINAL: RTC [176]

EDITORIAL COMMENT: There is no salutation.

Wednesday July 17. 61

Let me know, if you approve of the enclosed, or wish any alteration. Would you like, under it, initials?

If so, they must be *S.B.W* – as the arms / denote.[1]

Yrs ever | D.

The Ministry are in a very tottering state – but I hope they may pull over till next Spring.

3604 TO: [GEORGE SCHARF] Grosvenor Gate [Thursday 18] July 1861

ORIGINAL: PS 499

PUBLICATION HISTORY: John Wilson catalogue 65, item 36: 'AL (third person), 1 page 8vo, Grosvenor Gate, 28 July 1861.'

EDITORIAL COMMENT: *Recipient:* see n1. *Dating:* D's '18' often looks like '28'; in this instance (see n1), 18 July is more likely.

[Promising to call at George Street on the following Tuesday to inspect the bust of Lord George Bentinck] as requested by the other Trustees.

1 Lady Strangford had written to D on 12 July 1861: 'I have desired the picture which I promised you last year, to be sent to yr. house. There is no one I am sure who will value it more. Will you accept it'. H B/II/64b. In a later note (on 10 Downing Street paper) D would identify the portrait of George Smythe, 7th Viscount Strangford, by Richard Buckner, in the Hall at Hughenden Manor as that 'by Buckner presented by his widow'. H R/III/D/6; *Hughenden Manor Buckinghamshire* (The National Trust: 1986) 7 (item 6). Lady Strangford (who had already sent portraits of Strangford in 1858) would write to MA on 20 September 1861: 'I was so much gratified by Mr. Disraeli's kind note of thanks, for the Picture, will you tell him that I keep it with all I hold most precious.' H D/III/C/2538a.

1 See **3600**&nn1-3. SBW would reply on 21 July: 'I am extremely sorry that you shd have had any trouble with the Heralds and I fear that the cause is from my not having been sufficiently explicit. The Arms copyed from my Carriage *is correct* with the exception that the Leigh Arms was substituted for that of Mendes da Costa the latter from its antiquity &c being out of reach and but for your high interest wd never have been brought to light. When I have the happiness of seeing you I shall be able to make myself better understood than in writing ...& RTC [427Q]. See further **3647**. MA had also written to SBW on 17 July to thank her for some gifts, and remarked: 'We begin to get quite tired of so much visiting & long for a retreat at Hughenden. We cannot get there before the end of this month. We shall not have to go to Wales again. The newspaper said, we went to see my relations, but like you, I have none, & no friends there except Lord & Lady Tredegar ... We shall now begin to think of our happy meeting again'. RTC [426Q].

1 George Scharf (1820-1895), secretary of the National Portrait Gallery Trust, had written on 16 July as instructed by the trustees at their meeting that day to ask D to inspect the bust of Lord George Bentinck, to decide their purchase of it. D has written on the letter 'Tuesday at 4 o'ck'. H B/XIV/A/140a,b. An 1848 marble bust of Bentinck by Thomas Campbell (see V **1724**n1) is in the gallery's collection.

TO: ALFRED AUSTIN Grosvenor Gate [Sunday] 21 July 1861 3605

ORIGINAL: BRN [28]

EDITORIAL COMMENT: Paper imprinted 'Grosvenor Gate'. Endorsed in another hand on the fourth page: 'Disraeli'.

Alfred Austin | Esqr July 21 1861

Sir,

I thank you for the copy of your poem, & for the honor, wh: you have done me individually.

Your work realises the promise of your earliest production, & I have much hope, & little doubt, that you / will, in time, achieve a position, in the world of letters, wh: y will gratify your just ambition.[1]

Believe me, Sir, | your obliged & faithfl Servt | *B. Disraeli*

TO: MARY ANNE DISRAELI [House of Commons] Thursday [25 July 1861] 3606

ORIGINAL: H A/I/A/311

EDITORIAL COMMENT: *Dating:* by context; see nn1&2.

Mrs Disraeli Thursday

My dearest

I am disappointed about dinner. There is some very important [business] coming on this evening unexpectedly – only just announced.

General Peel had / great success – & the Government much damaged.[1]

The appointment of Sir Robert Peel is very unpopular with the Irish – in consequence of his having advocated the / cause of the Spanish Protestants in the most offensive manner to the Roman Catholics.[2]

Your own, | D.

1 Alfred Austin (1835-1913), the poet, had written to D on 22 June 1861 asking permission to dedicate the second edition of his work *The Season* to him. H B/XXI/A/239. *The Season: a satire* ... had been first published by Robert Hardwicke in 1861; the revised second edition (also 1861) was published by George Manwaring with a dedication: 'To the Right Hon Benjamin Disraeli M.P. by one who reveres his genius and exults in his success, this book is, with permission, dedicated.' Austin's previous publications were *Randolph* (1854), a verse narrative, and *Five Years of It* (1858), a two-volume novel. Austin, an imperialist admirer of Disraeli, in 1877 would publish *England's Policy and Peril: a Letter to the Earl of Beaconsfield,* and in 1896 be made poet laureate.

---

1 On the motion to go into committee of supply at the afternoon sitting of 25 July 1861, Gen Jonathan Peel drew attention to the government's 1860 army expenditure, which he put at over £1 million above the parliamentary grants. When the recess interrupted subsequent discussion in committee of supply, Gladstone announced that Sir Charles Wood would make a statement at 6 o'clock about the East India Loan (whose committee was the first item for the evening sitting), after discussion of which he would propose again going into committee of supply. Wood would detail India's financial situation under the new system before moving to raise another £5 million for railway works (granted after considerable debate). *Hansard* CLXIV cols 1480-1506, 1509-41; *MP* (25, 26 Jul 1861).

2 Sir Robert Peel would become chief secretary for Ireland on 29 July. On 15 March he had urged the government to intervene for persecuted Spanish Protestants: 'I do not accuse the Government of Spain. It is priestcraft and the bigoted Court that are the real agents in this matter.' On 6 June he had criticized the government for not taking action against the British vice-consul (one Gordon) at Seville, a Roman Catholic who was not allowing British citizens there to hold Anglican services even in their own residences. On 7 June, Russell had announced Gordon would be replaced by someone who would not object to Protestant services in private houses. *Hansard* CLXI cols 2053-65, CLXIII cols 676-82, 760-1; *MP* (30 Jul 1861).

3607 TO: WILLIAM FOLLETT SYNGE [London, Friday] 26 July 1861

ORIGINAL: PS 745

PUBLICATION HISTORY: Ifan Kyrle Fletcher catalogue 231 (1968) item 80: 'ALS 3 pp 26 July 1861 to W. Follett Synge, diplomat & author'

[... letter had been in hands of another friend for some time & reception not encouraging. Suggests trying Mr Lindsay before the prorogation] a kind hearted man [with great influence][1]

3608 TO: RICHARD CHENEVIX TRENCH Grosvenor Gate [Sunday] 28 July 1861

ORIGINAL: H B/II/64a

PUBLICATION HISTORY: Maggs catalogue 1144 (1992) item 72, dated 2 July 1861; see EC

EDITORIAL COMMENT: A fair copy (draft?) in D's hand on paper imprinted 'Grosvenor Gate'; a copy in another hand in H H/LIFE is endorsed '*not* Stanley'. As transcribed by the cataloguer (ph), the letter that was sent is slightly different from these two copies: it is dated 'Grosvenor Gate, 2 July 1861'; 'your' in the first sentence is abbreviated as 'yr'; there is no exclamation mark after 'precision'; 'precious' is omitted from the last sentence; there are no paragraph breaks; and the signature begins 'faithfull yours'.

Very Rev: | The Dean of Westminster July 28 1861

Dear Sir,

I have read the journal of your charming parent with infinite zest.[1]

Never were there 100 pages of such vivid grace; / or which conveyed an interesting scene with such picturesque precision!

They will live; & often be referred to.

I am sincerely obliged by your kindness in adding / this precious volume to my library.

Yours obliged & | faithfully, | *B. Disraeli*

1 William Webb Follett Synge (1826-1891), a former *Press* writer now assistant clerk at the foreign office, would be appointed commissioner and consul-general for the Sandwich Islands in December 1861 and, in October 1865, commissary judge in Cuba. On 10 June 1861 he had asked D's help for the widow and extended family of *Press* editor David Coulton; see VI **2551**n2. He asked specifically for D's influence for the eldest nephew, Ambrose Coulton, who had been disappointed of a midshipman's berth and was seeking employment. W.S. Lindsay (VI **2726**n3), of the shipping house W.S. Lindsay and Company, was currently MP (L) for Sunderland. Synge would thank D on 27 July for his letter ('a sore disappointment to the poor Coultons') and ask for letters of introduction to Lindsay and to 'his great friend' Judge Haliburton, who would 'interest himself in the family of a good Tory writer; and if he asked Lindsay to give the lad a berth I should think it would hardly be refused'. Sophia Coulton, David Coulton's sister-in-law, had been seeking D's influence since Coulton's death in May 1857, on 3 January 1858 thanking him for obtaining £100 for them; in December 1862 and January 1863 she would ask his help in applying to the Royal Literary Fund. H B/XXI/S/744-5, B/VI/144, B/XXI/C/464, 467-8, 473, R/II/G/56, A/IV/M/81.

1 Richard Chenevix Trench (1807-1886), dean of Westminster 1856-63, archbishop of Dublin 1864-84, author and poet, in 1861 had edited and published his mother's *Journal kept during a visit to Germany in 1799, 1800* (viii, 97 pages); no correspondence from him to D has been found. Melesina Chenevix St George Trench (1768-1827), poet, daughter and sole heiress of the Rev Richard Chenevix, granddaughter and heiress of the Rt Rev Richard Chenevix, bishop of Waterford, in 1803 as the relict of Col Richard St George had married secondly Richard Trench, a barrister; the dean was their second son. See further **3610**.

TO: SARAH BRYDGES WILLYAMS Carlton Club, Tuesday 30 July [1861] 3609

ORIGINAL: RTC [177]

PUBLICATION HISTORY: M&B IV 303, dated at the Carlton Club, 30 July 1861, the second and last paragraphs

EDITORIAL COMMENT: Carlton Club paper. There is no salutation.

Tuesday July 30.

I have sent you today a haunch of Venison, which ought to be very fine, as it comes from a famous park, Charborough, Mr. Drax, a great supporter of mine, / & the member for Wareham.[1] ~~It~~ ↑The buck↓ was only killed on the 27th: so, that it is too fresh, I should think, even for you – but I give you the date, on wh: you may depend, & you can / decide about keeping it as you like.

The end of the Session, generally so exhausted & insipid, has been, this year, of a peculiarly exciting character: reconstructions of governments,[2] unexpected / elevations to the peerage,[3] unexpected death of young Ministers on whose future much depended[4] – & now a great contested election in the City of London, where there has not been such a thing for twenty years. And a Tory in, or nearly / in. I don't think the Lord Mayor will quite succeed – for, at this hour, *3* o'ck, he is 100 behind – not much when they had polled ten thousand.[5] Such a state of affairs marks a great change in opinion, which has long been occurring[.]

/ Tomorrow, we go to Hatfield, on a visit to Lord & Lady Salisbury, & on Friday from Hatfield to Knebworth, on a visit to Sir Edward Lytton, who is member for the County, & much more famous than that, as you well know. Then we shall pass through / town↑, on Monday or so,↓ to Hughenden,[6] which I long to see again with all its woods & winding streams – & the only fault of which is, that you have unhappily never visited them!

They say, there were never so many marriages, as this year: almost all my unappropriated friends are destined in a few / days, more or less – the Marquess of Bath, Lord John Manners, Lord Mexborough &c. &c.[7] Thus the world wags! Strange

1 John Samuel Wanley Sawbridge Erle Drax (1800-1887), who had assumed the additional surnames of Erle Drax on his marriage in 1827, of Charborough Park, Dorset, Olantigh Towers, Kent, and Ellerton Abbey, Yorkshire, was MP (C) for Wareham 1841-57, 1859-65, 1868-80.

2 For the major government changes at the end of this Session, see *BHF* 22-5; see also the first leader in *The Times* of 25 July 1861.

3 On 28 June Sidney Herbert had been created Baron Herbert and Sir Richard Bethell created Baron Westbury. On this day (30 July) Lord John Russell was created Earl Russell; see further n8.

4 D must be thinking of Lord Herbert, who would die on 2 August aged 50; see **3599**&n2. The elderly Lord Chancellor, Lord Campbell, had died on 23 June.

5 William Cubitt (1791-1863), builder and contractor, sheriff of London and Middlesex 1847-8, MP (C) for Andover 1847-61, 1862-3, lord mayor of London 1860-62, would lose the by-election for the City of London (occasioned by Russell's resignation of his seat) by 5,747 to 5,241 to Western Wood (L). The 3 o'clock poll published in *MP* next day put the margin then at 323.

6 These visits went as planned, the DS returning to Grosvenor Gate on Monday 5 August and to Hughenden on Thursday 8 August. H acc, D/III/C/278, B/XX/LY/132. Stanley recorded a conversation with Bulwer Lytton during the Hatfield visit: 'I find he takes much the same view as I do of the state of politics: not expecting or wishing a Derbyite administration to be formed.' *Disraeli, Derby* 174. For the visit to Knebworth, see **3611**.

7 Mexborough was married on 27 July and Bath would be married on 20 August. Manners would be married again on 15 May 1862. Perhaps D intended the '&c. &c.' to include his brother Ralph, who on 15 August would marry Katharine Trevor.

events every day; the most extraordinary, the retirement of Ld. John Russell from the House of Commons![8]

Adieu! | D.

3610 TO: JOHN EVELYN DENISON Grosvenor Gate [Tuesday] 6 August 1861

ORIGINAL: NOT OSC 775

EDITORIAL COMMENT: Paper imprinted 'Grosvenor Gate'. *Sic:* Phillips.

Rt Honble | The Speaker Augt 6 1861

Dear Mr Speaker

I fear I must have appeared very insensible to yr kindness, but yr letter, about the picture, has followed me, in vain, to several places.[1]

I will / put myself in communication with Mr Phillips[2] whenever I pass thro' town, & I have little doubt his distinguished talent, especially under yr guidance, will do justice to an interesting subject. I take it for granted, / the time of the composition will be before the accession of Ld. John.

Have you seen a little volume of 100 pages or less, privately printed by the Dean of Westminster & consisting of extracts from his mother's journal (1799-1803)?[3] / If not, lose no time in obtaining it. It is one of the most racy contributions to our knowledge, that I can well recollect, & you wd. especially relish it.

And now I can only wish you health & content amid the woods of Ossington![4]

Yours sincerely, | *B. Disraeli*

3611 TO: SARAH BRYDGES WILLYAMS Hughenden [Friday] 16 August 1861

ORIGINAL: RTC [178]

EDITORIAL COMMENT: Paper imprinted 'Hughenden Manor'. There is no salutation. *Sic:* de Lytton.

Private Augt 16 1861

I sent you, the day before yesterday, a curiosity – some grouse wh: had only been killed the day before. I breakfasted off one of their brethren yesterday, & if your

8 Russell's brother, the 7th Duke of Bedford, had died on 14 May and left him his Irish estates. Russell, having left his mark on Italian unification, abandoned further reform measures and become marginalized in cabinet, decided to resign his Commons seat and request elevation to the Lords. Prest *Russell* 392-3. The decision, announced by *The Times* on 15 July, surprised many, who thought it marked the effective end of his political career.

1 Denison had written on 29 July: 'You doubtless know the works of the Artist Phillip who paints the Spanish subjects, and who painted a Picture for the Queen of the marriage of the Princess Royal with such great success. I have asked him, to paint me a Picture of the Interior of the House of Commons, that is, of the Chair, & the Table, and a portion of the Treasury, and the front Opposition Benches. This is to request you to do me the favor to give him one or two Sittings for your Portrait.' H B/XXI/D/156.

2 John Phillip (1817-1867), influenced by Velasquez while in Spain 1851-2, RA 1859, would exhibit his 'House of Commons, 1860, during the Debate on the French Treaty' in 1863. See illustration p lv.

3 See **3608**&n1.

4 Denison replied the same day (6 August) and gave Phillip's address as 'No 1, South Villa Campden Hill ... It is proposed that Ld Palmerston, Ld J. Russell, Mr Gladstone, Sir George Lewis, and perhaps one or two other Members of the Gov. if there shd be room, would be represented on the right hand of the Chair. I shall ask Ld Stanley to allow himself to be placed by your side, on the left. I am not certain, what room may be found on that Bench.' H B/XXI/D/157.

guests were as good, they were an admirable family. I / have just been writing a note of thanks to the Lord of the Yorkshire moors, Mr Edwards, the M.P. for Beverley, who sent them to me, & as he is a very cordial fellow, & one of my strongest supporters, I shd. not be surprised if some more Yorkshire / birds found their way, viâ Bucks, to the West.

We have been here exactly a week – & I have not written a single letter until to day. I feel the stretch of the Session, not at the time, but afterwards. I tried to break the sudden change, this year, by passing a / week in the country among my friends, preparatory to the deep seclusion of our woods, or as the Greek poet has it: "the deep silence of the mighty woods"[.][1]

We were very gay for a few days at Hatfield at Lord Salisbury's, where we met, among others, your friend Lady Brownlow, & afterwards at / Sir Edward Lytton's at Knebworth – an ancient seat of Tudor architecture, amid a deer park, which he has restored like a poet, or an old English Baron, "the last of the Barons", or, perhaps, an imaginative statesman.[2] The hall, wh: is ancient & / grand, is hung with banners from the conquest, illustrating his family, each with an inscription "Siege of Ascalon; Sir Rowland de Lytton" & so on.[3] In the present instance, there is a basis of truth for it all – but banners & armor, which abounds by the bye, shd. be genuine; of the time & persons; & not emblazoned by / modern artists & collected in modern countries. As for ancestry, at this rate, I might put flags up at Hughenden from the invasion of the holy Land; & inscribe on them the title of one of my progenitors; from the siege of Jericho[4] to the siege of Jerusalem;[5] for I dare say they distinguished themselves at both. However Knebworth, / with a great deal of outré taste, is a fine thing; & tho' there wants keeping we can pardon in a feudal domain↑, belonging to a poet,↓ a Roman Garden full of the busts of Horace & his friends, & a lake in the Park with a statued island, rather incongruous with the antlered inhabitants, wh: intimate always a forest.

Two good autographs for you: one *very precious* – of Prince Metternich; the other a very good one just received from Lord Brougham.[6]

Ever Yours | D.[7]

1 *Cf* VII **2958**&n2, where D attributes the phrase to Euripides.

2 *Cf* V **2037**&n1 and **2042** for D's previous descriptions of Knebworth. Lytton, who had published his 3-volume *Last of the Barons* in 1843 (the latest edition was 1860), would himself be made a baron in 1866.

3 Baldwin III, King of Jerusalem, successfully laid siege to the city of Ascalon in 1153. Sir Rowland Lytton was knighted by James I in 1603; at Knebworth his great oak screen is a fine example of the native Jacobean style of the great hall. Furtado 230.

4 See Joshua ch 6 for the late thirteenth-century BCE siege.

5 The siege of Jerusalem by Titus occurred in 70CE.

6 See VII **3236**&n1 for D's last and obviously 'very precious' letter from Prince Metternich; perhaps it was sent and replaced in H after SBW's death. Brougham's most recent letter in H, asking for copies of D's speeches, is dated 1 July 1861. H B/XXI/B/1025.

7 A curious draft in H also contains a description of Knebworth, with some differences. Page 1 is in D's hand. Page 2, in a different hand, has corrections and additions by MA, and includes a reference to *Tannhauser, or, the Battle of the Bards,* a recent poem by Lytton and Julian Fane. The draft was perhaps for an amanuensis to copy for MA. H B/II/134.

3612 TO: SARAH BRYDGES WILLYAMS Hughenden [Thursday] 22 August 1861

ORIGINAL: RTC [179]

EDITORIAL COMMENT: Paper imprinted 'Hughenden Manor'. There is no salutation.

Augt 22 1861

I send you some venison, from Lord Tredegar – & some grouse (a brace) from Lord Orkney. I hope you will keep / them for your own eating, & I wish you a good appetite, now & always.

Yrs ever, | D. /

The venison is quite fresh: only killed the 20th:[1]

3613 TO: SARAH BRYDGES WILLYAMS Hughenden [Wednesday] 4 September 1861

ORIGINAL: RTC [180]

EDITORIAL COMMENT: Paper imprinted 'Hughenden Manor'. There is no salutation.

Septr 4 1861

A clear case of Sympathy: for while, yesterday morning, you were sending us some of our most favorite delicacy, which are so difficult to get good, & which were, in this instance, delicious; we were trying to / catch you a trout in our stream. The morning, however, was so bright, that, after hours, we were unsuccessful; nevertheless the sport, in the bright park, & by the side of rippling waters, was delightful, tho' / fruitless. After the arrival of your case, we determined to try again, a little before sunset, & in the first twilight, landed a gentleman 4¼ lbs in weight! pretty well for our little stream, that was dry for three years. I / packed him up in the flags, among which he was caught last evening, & sent him off instantly from the river side. You ~~hav~~ ought to have had him *early* this morning, so he is as fresh as day – & I told them to put a brace of grouse in the basket.[1]

I hope you are enjoying this fine weather.

Yrs ever, | D.

1 SBW would respond on 25 August: 'Your profuse and delicious presents of Game have all safely arrived. The Haunch of Venison from Charborough [*see* **3609**&n1] was the finest I ever saw not excepting your present of royal Venison [*see* VII **3174**&n1]. I treated the Swetes[?] with a little of it as they are good Conservatives and appreciate what comes from your Domain'. RTC [428Q]. In previous letters SBW had often mentioned people with whom she shared the game D sent. MA was also receiving letters of thanks for grouse sent. H D/III/C/2307, 2880.

1 SBW had written to MA on 3 September: 'I ventured yesterday to send to you some Prawns brought to me by the only Fisherman I cd depend on and who is a great rarity to get a sight of and I hope they have arrived safe'. MA would respond on the 6th: 'The prawns & lobster were a great treat ... You would have laughd to have seen us at the trout stream. The first I think Dizy ever caught, he was anxious to send you, quite fresh ... We shall soon talk about our usual visit, but, at present, we must be here or would be near you.' SBW on the 8th would be ecstatic: 'Your capital sport and the *fruit of it!* and the *description* merit to be recorded in the Temple of Fame'. RTC [429Q, 430Q, 432Q].

TO: [SIR STAFFORD NORTHCOTE] [Hughenden] 3614
[Thursday] 12 September 1861

ORIGINAL: H H/LIFE

PUBLICATION HISTORY: M&B IV 328, dated 12 September 1861, omitting part of the first sentence; Northcote I 181, with minor variations and omitting part of the first sentence

EDITORIAL COMMENT: Taken from a manuscript copy headed: 'D. to S.H.N. Sept 12, 1861'. *Sic*: its.

Our friend Jonathan seems in a pretty state: its like the failure of some immense house; one can hardly realise the enormous results; one of them seems to be that Spain intends to reconquer Mexico![1] It is a privilege to live in such a pantomimic age of glittering illusions & startling surprises.

TO: CHARLES ADDERLEY Hughenden [Thursday] 12 September 1861 3615

ORIGINAL: H H/LIFE

EDITORIAL COMMENT: From a typescript headed 'D. to Rt Hon. C.B. Adderley.'

Rt Honble | C.B. Adderley Hughenden Manor. | Septr. 12. 1861.

Dear Adderley,

I shall feel much honored by having my name associated with yr contemplated labors, & have no doubt, that you will efficiently accomplish them.[1] The Government seems to pause in their policy. What a condition Jonathan is in![2]

Pray make my complimts acceptable to Mrs Adderley,[3] & believe me, always | faithfully yrs. | B. Disraeli.

TO: WILLIAM CARLISLE Hughenden [Monday] 16 September 1861 3616

ORIGINAL: MOPSIK [38]

EDITORIAL COMMENT: Paper imprinted 'Hughenden Manor'. Endorsed in another hand on the last page: '*16 Septr. 1862. Honble B Disraeli*'. A third hand has crossed out '*1862*' and written in '*1861*'.

Private Septr 16 1861

W.T. Carlisle | Esqr

Dear Sir –

I have no confidence, whatever, in Mr Dickson's statements, or designs. The latter

1 On this day (12 September) a *Times* leader on the American civil war had worried 'that the war party in the North is falling from its sovereign ascendancy' and that socialist demands were being made as conditions of supporting it. On 11 September it had reprinted a report from Madrid that '"Spain, in conjunction with England and France, will intervene in Mexico by sending troops into that country from Cuba."' The three powers on 31 October would sign a convention in London to occupy military positions on the Mexican coast; this they would do in 1862, but it was France which in 1863 would conquer Mexico City and place Maximilian on the Mexican throne; see **3791**&n2.

1 Adderley had written from Birmingham on 3 September for permission to address to D a pamphlet on England's colonial relations; *cf* V **1931**n1 and VI **2230**&n3. On 18 December he would thank D for permission and report sending him two copies of his *Letter to the Right Hon. Benjamin Disraeli, M.P., on the present relations of England with the Colonies ... With an appendix of extracts from evidence taken before the Select Committee on Colonial Military Expenditure* (1861, 68pp). H B/XXI/A/76-7.

2 See **3614**&n1. The apparent compromise of official neutrality toward the American Civil War by ordering troops to Canada (see **3595**n1) was seen as having led to temporary suspension of the move. *The Times* (9 Sep 1861).

3 Adderley in 1842 had married Julia Anna Eliza Leigh (1820-1887), eldest child of 1st Baron Leigh.

are fixed, the first vary with circumstances. But what / can we do? We are at his mercy. I authorise you, therefore, on the part of Mr Villiers & his family, to make those arrangements, respecting the reduction of rent, wh:, under the / circumstances, are necessary. But they must be only from year to year, and not expressed in formal leases. In the interval, I will endeavour to obtain accurate information from the / spot.[1]

I wish to have occasionally a statement of the acct bet[wee]n Mr. V. and yr client. I have no communication with Captain Fisher.

Yours faithfully, | *B. Disraeli*

3617 TO: SARAH BRYDGES WILLYAMS [Hughenden, Friday] 20 September 1861

ORIGINAL: RTC [181]; H R/II/E

EDITORIAL COMMENT: There is no salutation. The copy of the MS available to the editors is missing several pages; the text ('Willoughby' to 'given up') has been taken from Rose's copy in H R/II/E.

Septr. 20. 1861.

I send you a black cock (not a grouse, but a much grander bird) that came, with some companions, from Drummond Castle this morning; Lord / Willoughby de Eresby's who is often with his lady at Torquay.

I have put a fish in the basket which was caught only five minutes ago. He is not so gigantic a fellow as his predecessor, but is very handsome, & will just do for your dinner.[1]

I told you that, after the great frost, the microfolia rose was cut down to its very root, & given up / for lost: I forgot to tell you, that it has entirely recovered, with a family of shoots, more than two yards long, & is now trailing over a wire frame. Tho' we had raised largely from the parent stem, I am pleased that the original is spared to us.[2]

Adieu! | D. /

P:S. | The best way to eat a trout is to have it split open, & *broiled* – & eaten with bread – & butter.

D.

3618 TO: WILLIAM FERRAND Hughenden [Sunday] 22 September 1861

ORIGINAL: PS 425

PUBLICATION HISTORY: J.T. Ward 'Correspondence between Disraeli and W.B. Ferrand' *Disraeli Newsletter* 2,1 (Spring 1977) 11-21

Hughenden Manor, | Septr. 22, 1861.

1 See **3520**&nn1&2 for earlier correspondence with Carlisle about Villiers; the letter to which D is responding has not been found. Recent correspondence from Lady Jersey, Padwick, Frederick Villiers and Laurence Peel concerns an aggressive new creditor, Francis Lawley (offering to settle a £12,000 bill for £2,000), a distressing scene for Lady Jersey and D's (unfound) letters of comfort to her, and to Lawley citing illness as D's reason for not seeing him. H A/IV/J/149-51, 154-7, 160-2. See further **3652**. For D's illness see **3621**.

---

1 In her letter of 22 September about D's first trout (see **3613**&n1) SBW would write: 'Your kind comforting note and your splendid present of game arrived safe on Saturday morning in all their beauty and freshness. The black Cock is the first of his grand sort I have seen, the handsome Trout reminded me of young Salmons before they reach the salt sea and the Hughenden Partridge is unrivalled.' RTC [431Q].

2 For the microfolia rose, see VI **2774**&n3 and **2780**, and VII **3186**&n2; for the great frost, see **3547**.

My dear Ferrand,

It gave me great pleasure to be remembered by you. The grouse were worthy of your famous moor. What think you of affairs? It is worth living in an age of such rapid and strange events.

I hope we shall not lose Plymouth – but it looks queer.[1]

We have had a splendid harvest here – in quality, quantity, and time.

I wish you had sent us good accounts of yr. charming wife.[2]

Yours sincerely, | D.

TO: JAMES JOSEPH SHEAHAN [Hughenden, Monday] 23 September 1861 **3619**

ORIGINAL: H B/XXI/S/162

PUBLICATION HISTORY: *Athenaeum* (3 Jan 1863) 9, with minor variations

EDITORIAL COMMENT: A fragment of a letter quoted in Sheahan's letter of 3 January 1863. *Dating:* see n1.

I have made no additions, and have only taken the liberty of correcting and condensing what you have so obligingly said of myself. I have made it a rule through life never to attempt to correct a mis-statement respecting myself, provided it did not impugn my honour; but when utterly erroneous statements are submitted for my sanction, I hope there is no egotism in my presuming to correct them – as, for example, the constantly repeated story of a newspaper called the *Representative,* in which I never wrote a single line, and never was asked to write a single line, and others.[1]

1 Lord Valletort, MP (C) for Plymouth, had succeeded his father on 3 September as 4th Earl of Mount Edgcumbe; at the by-election on 31 October, Walter Morrison (L) would defeat H.W. Addington (C), 1179-984. Sir Lawrence Palk wrote to D on this day (22 September): 'I fear we lose Plymouth, however, I do not grudge the Rads the seat, as it proves that their popularity is so low, & their credit so bad, that none but the very richest Liberals can be returned even for the Government Boroughs.' H B/XXI/P/50.

2 *Cf* **3494**&n2; Ferrand's letter has not been found.

1 In answer to D's request (not found), Sheahan had written from Leeds on 21 September 1861 with a draft of the section on Hughenden from his forthcoming *History and Topography of Buckinghamshire* (1862). On 24 September 1861 he would write to thank D for his corrections: 'They shall have my strictest attention, and your wishes shall be complied with to the letter, in the matter of the paragraph or two connected with yourself ... I shall be most happy to send you the MSS. of Bradenham in a week or ten days hence.' The *History*'s entry on D (p 890) would not mention the *Representative,* but would erroneously give D's birth year as 1805 and the date of his marriage as 1837. After James Hannay's 1862 attempts to refute persistent exaggerations of D's association with the *Representative* (see **3752**&nn1-4 and **3755**&n1) Sheahan would write again; his letter dated 'Saturday evening Dec. 3/63' was evidently written on 3 January 1863, a Saturday. In response to a clipping from the *Leeds Mercury* published in the *Athenaeum* 'of this day week (27th. Ult.)' expressing amused cynicism about Hannay's denial, he published in the *Athenaeum* of '*today*' his quotation from D's 23 September 1861 letter. For having used his letter without permission he begged D's pardon, which D on 12 January 1863 (not found) evidently granted, on 16 January (letter not found) also granting Sheahan's request that he 'subscribe for a copy of my forthcoming History of Hull[.] Your name would be of much service to me here [in Hull] – where the people look at almost everything through political spectacles.' H B/XXI/S/159-64.

3620 TO: WILLIAM PARTRIDGE Hughenden [Tuesday] 1 October 1861

ORIGINAL: GMF [4]

EDITORIAL COMMENT: Paper imprinted 'Hughenden Manor'. *Sic:* checque.

The | Rev. W.E. Partridge | a.m. October 1 1861

My dear Partridge,

I am very sorry, that an engagement prevents my having the pleasure of meeting my Risbro' friends on Thursday, as you obligingly suggest. /

I should be much gratified, if the Committee, next year, would offer a prize, in my name, to the value of five pounds, for some act of meritorious service or labouring skill. I leave / the object, & details, entirely to them, but I do not wish the sum to be divided.

Wishing you a successful meeting, believe me,

Very faithfully yours, | *B. Disraeli*

I enclose a checque.[1]

3621 TO: [FRANCIS VILLIERS] [Hughenden, Wednesday] 2 October 1861

ORIGINAL: H R/IV/D/6e[c]

EDITORIAL COMMENT: A copy by Rose. For the recipient, see n1.

Extract. October 2. 1861.

x x x.

I can't say much for myself.[1] I have been here since the prorogation – but in a low – they say suppressed Gout – sort of state, but one wh: does not favor sanguine views. Howr I am pretty well now. I don't anticipate any Change in public affairs. The Country is thoroughly Conservative, but has little confidence in Conservative statesmen. A mortifying truth! But it is in vain to deceive oneself.

1 Partridge, whose invitation has not been found, on 4 October would respond with gratitude for 'your kind letter and ... the very *substantial* proof of your good wishes'. H B/XXI/P/133. The report of the annual meeting of the Princes Risborough Local Agricultural Association would mention D's prize 'as a proof of the interest he takes in the association'. *BH* (5 Oct 1861). No record of a conflicting engagement has been found.

1 Francis Villiers had written from La Spezia on 24 September: 'You have by this time probably sufficiently recovered from the infliction of stupid speeches in Parlt. not to mind if I bore you for a few moments with an equally stupid Letter.' After reporting at length on his frail health, he continued: 'You said in your last [*not found*] ... there might be a chance of your succeeding in getting me the Ceylon proceeds clear, & that I shd. then be pretty well off – ... but what chance can there be of such a result, except at the end of a very long time? I had imagined that Magenis's claim of principal & Int. would have been completely satisfied some 18 months from now, but by the abstract of the acct. which you sent me last year, it wd. appear ... that nearly another year must elapse, & then there is Hume & Co. to be satisfied'. See **3520**&n2. After describing at length his parsimony, his need for a horse and his thoughts about borrowing money, he continued: 'It is only your marvellous kindness & good nature which could have borne with all the trouble & annoyance which my affairs have given you, & as I shall always implicitly follow your advice, I hope you will not mind giving me some slight sketch of what you may think feasible for the future.' Following several pages about his travels he wrote: 'I have not seen or heard a word of yr. whereabouts since Parlt. broke up, but hope you are flourishing in health & spirits, & that the Political future looks bright'. H A/IV/J/163. Lady Jersey on 4 October would write to D: 'his Birthday is on the 11th ... will you send this Letter to him ... I hope you are better.' H A/IV/J/166.

Dear George Smythe, with characteristic romance, married Miss Lennox on his deathbed, & left her as a legacy to my wife. Mrs. D presented her & launched her in society.[2] She is a woman of ability sufficiently well-looking, & has £8000 pr. annm. This month she marries Charles Hanbury., Bateman's Brother.[3] Her first Husband was all Soul – her second all body. But I believe he is a good fellow, as well as good-looking. Poor dear Smythe! Had he lived, after all, he would have succeeded. Alas! he has gone – & within the last five years – all that I cared for in this world. I am an actor without an audience, & it is not wonderful, that I take refuge in my beech trees, for they are fast becoming my only friends.

Yours sincerely | D.

TO: SARAH BRYDGES WILLYAMS Hughenden [Thursday] 3 October 1861 **3622**

ORIGINAL: RTC [182]

PUBLICATION HISTORY: M&B III 463, dated 3 October 1861; Bradford 221, undated extract

EDITORIAL COMMENT: Paper imprinted 'Hughenden Manor'. There is no salutation. *Sic:* dejeûner.

Octr. 3 1861

Where did you get the lobster – wh: arrived for my dejeûner this morning? From the caves of Amphitrite? It was so fresh!

Tasted of the sweetness – not the salt – of the Ocean – & almost as / ↑creamy, as↓ your picturesque cheese!

We are most obliged, &, most delighted, with your recollection of us. They are most welcome, & most recherché gifts.

I send you by this train – It had gone off, before / your charming packet had arrived – a black cock from Drummond Castle, wh: reached us yesterday – & a brace of grouse from the same good friend, Lord Willoughby de Eresby.

But the magnificent black-cocks / are now robbed of their chief beauty, for such is the demand for their splendid tails, in order to furnish black, & green, & deep dark blue, feathers for the young Ladies' coquettish hats, that the game-keepers retain them for their perquisites!

Adieu, my dear! | D.

2 In his letter (n1) Villiers had written: 'By the bye do tell me something of "Lady Strangford" whom I saw in the list of your Guests, in a Paper some time ago [*see* **3594**n7]. Is she poor George Smythe's widow? the Miss Lennox whose affair with him sounded like a thing in a Novel?' Lady Strangford as Miss Kincaid Lennox had been presented by her mother in 1849. *MP* (27 Apr 1849). On 8 December 1858, almost exactly a year after Strangford's death, MA had written asking to meet her, presented her again (as Viscountess Strangford) on 19 June 1861 and introduced her to current London society (though she drew the line at invitations to Lady Derby's parties). H D/III/C/2531, 2537-8; *MP* (20 June 1861).

3 Lady Strangford on 17 October would marry Charles Spencer Bateman Hanbury (1827-1912), younger brother of 2nd Baron Bateman; Hanbury in 1862 would assume the additional surnames of Kincaid Lennox. He was Fellow of All Souls, Oxford, JP and DL co Hereford, DL co Stirling, MP (C) for co Hereford 1852-7, for Leominster 1858-65. Lady Strangford had written to MA on 20 September (see **3602**n1) to inform her (the first outside her immediate family) of her intended marriage.

3623 TO: THOMAS TAYLOR [Hughenden, Sunday] 6 October 1861

ORIGINAL: H H/LIFE

EDITORIAL COMMENT: From a manuscript page headed 'D. to Colonel Taylor'.

Oct. 6. 1861

We have been here since beginning of August & have literally never been off our own land – & have seen nobody.

The death of dear Eglintoun little disposes me for society. This is a great calamity & even political considerations are forgotten in the social loss. Even his great influence was nothing compared with his engaging & noble disposition.[1]

3624 TO: SIR STAFFORD NORTHCOTE [Hughenden, mid-October 1861]

ORIGINAL: H B/II/119

EDITORIAL COMMENT: A note in D's hand on the fourth page of Block's letter to him; see n1. *Dating:* by Block's letter.

My dear S.

Would this suit you at all? I shall decline the proposal, but say I have submitted it to a distinguished friend.[1]

Yrs ever, | D.

3625 TO: SIR WILLIAM JOLLIFFE Hughenden [Monday] 4 November 1861

ORIGINAL: SCR DD/HY C/2165 [62]

EDITORIAL COMMENT: Paper imprinted 'Hughenden Manor'.

Private Nov. 4 1861

Rt Honble | Sir W.H. Jolliffe Bart | M.P.

My dear Jolliffe,

It gave me great pleasure to hear from you: & I have delayed replying to yr kind letter, in the hope, that some change in our engagements might enable us to pay you a visit.[1] I am sorry to / say, it cannot be. We have been here for three unbroken

1 Lord Eglinton ('Eglintoun' is the older spelling) had died suddenly on 4 October of apoplexy, aged 49. Taylor would reply on 7 October: 'Eglinton was one of my oldest and dearest friends, and as I believe I was principally instrumental in making him a politician, no one knows better than I the irreparable loss he is both politically and socially.' H B/XX/T/20. For D's further comment, see **3627**.

1 Maurice Block, a political economist and compiler of various dictionaries, had written in French from Paris on 10 October 1861 asking D for an article on the finances of Great Britain for his *Dictionnaire général de la politique,* explaining that he was asking only leading members of political parties. H B/II/119. The dictionary would be published in two volumes 1863-4. In volume I, 1124-33, the article on 'Grande-Bretagne (Finances)' is by Northcote.

1 Jolliffe had written from Merstham on 24 October: 'It appears so unnatural to me, never to hear or see anything of you that I must write a line to say that I am alive, and that nothing would please me better than to be able to invent some excuse for a visit from you & Mrs. Disraeli to us here.' He enclosed a 'somewhat political letter' from Newdegate (about replacements for his ailing constituency colleague, Richard Spooner), whom he had also invited to visit: 'I do not think that our Friends influence in the House of Commons is on the increase, but he is useful when he can be kept in any order, and should he name any early time for coming here it might perhaps be possible for you & Mrs. Disraeli to meet him.' H B/XX/J/87, 87a.

months, but have some engagements in the North, wh: we originally made in the view of going, this year, to Scotland – & we cannot extricate ourselves from them.[2] I am detained here, because, on the 14th., there is a County Diocesan meeting / – the Bishop in the Chair, & I have engaged to take a part in it: in these times, a grave & critical duty.[3] Then, we go to Alnwick Castle, & some other places.[4]

We have been quite alone this whole season, but solitude is not very grievous with the rapid events of this wonderful age! How is it all to end? I doubt, whether in our / time – when it begins in earnest, wh: it will very soon.

As we are now breaking up our residence here, & shall be more than once passing thro' town, I count on, some how or other, meeting.

My wife joins me in very kind remembrances to Lady Jolliffe, who, I hope, is quite well, & I am, my dear Comrade,

Ever yours, | D.

3626

TO: JOHN DELANE — Hughenden [Thursday] 7 November 1861

ORIGINAL: H H/LIFE; M&B IV 360

PUBLICATION HISTORY: M&B IV 360, dated autumn 1861, as indicated below

EDITORIAL COMMENT: The following combines a handwritten partial copy in the Monypenny papers with the M&B extract. The two do not overlap but, from Delane's reply, seem to be from the same letter.

[H H/LIFE:] — Hughenden Manor | Nov. 7. 61.

Dear Delane

I suppose you have come back by this time (tho' I don't know where you have been this year) & I hope hearty & happy.

I have been here more than three months – literally in profound solitude. I have not seen a human being, but one does not require society in this age of rapid & great events.

However on the 14th. inst I must come out of my lair. There is a county Diocesan meeting at Aylesbury, one o'ck, the Bishop in the Chair & I have promised him to take some part in the proceedings.

2 On 12 November Derby would write to D, having heard of his plans that morning from Jolliffe. See **3629**&n1.

3 Edward Bickersteth (vicar of Aylesbury and archdeacon of Bucks) had written on 31 July about a county meeting in Aylesbury for the Diocesan Church Building Society with Wilberforce presiding: 'We both feel that it would contribute greatly to the Success of the undertaking, if you would kindly consent to take part in the proceedings.' He closed with congratulations on D's 'vastly improved position as regards Church questions in the House of Commons.' On 23 October he had thanked D for his note (not found), promising a suitably comprehensive Resolution and forwarding papers with information D requested. On the 24th he had written: 'In reference to our conversation last week I take the liberty of enclosing a copy of Dr Wordsworth's Lectures on the Interpretation of Scripture, in the *first* of which you will find views very similar to those which you so well expressed the other morning. This is really what we want v.i.z. refutation of the errors, rather than condemnation of the writers.' H B/XXI/B/486-8. The book was possibly by Christopher Wordsworth (1807-1885), *On the Inspiration of the Holy Scripture: or, On the Canon of the Old and New Testament, and on the Apocrypha: Twelve Lectures, delivered before the University of Cambridge* (1851). See further **3628**&n1.

4 The Ds would be at Alnwick (Northumberland) 22-29 November, at Seaham (Londonderry) 29 November–10 December, at Gunnersbury (Rothschild) 14-16 December, and at Torquay (SBW) 17 December–1 January 1862. H acc. See also **3628**&n2.

Between ourselves I contemplate taking a view of the present position of the Church: a

[M&B:] I will endeavour to make a *précis* of what I intend to say, which I will give your envoy if he will see me before the business. This is rather a difficult thing for me to do, as it is against my grain, being much influenced by my audience and the impromptu; but I must make an effort to entirely control myself, as there must be no mistake.[1]

3627 TO: LADY LONDONDERRY — Hughenden [Saturday] 9 November 1861

ORIGINAL: DUR D/LO/C 530 [125]

PUBLICATION HISTORY: *Lady Londonderry* 184-5, dated at Hughenden, 9 November 1861, and *Frances Anne* 276, undated, the first sentence

EDITORIAL COMMENT: Paper imprinted 'Hughenden Manor'. There is no salutation.

Nov 9 1861

I, generally, know where the Marc[hion]ess of Londonderry is, by the school of oratory, wh: she inspires. I read with great satisfaction, as all the world did, yr own address in Ireland, & now, the Duke's speech informs me you are at Seaham.[1] I hope hearty & happy.

We have been here more, than three months, in profound solitude, / but one does not require society in this age of rapid, & wonderful, events.

What deaths!

Fate seems to pursue the Peelites like the House of Atreus. A series of tragedies! One cannot believe, that Peel, Goulburn, Dalhousie, Herbert, Aberdeen, Graham, should all have departed,[2] & that their senior, Palmerston, should remain, playing

1 Delane would reply on 8 November: 'I am very glad to hear you are about to appear on the platform again and will send my two best reporters to greet you. They are sure to do you justice so that I hope you will not put any restraints on yourself by preparing a *précis* beforehand.' H B/XXI/D/75. On the 9th Bickersteth would send D a copy of the resolution he was anxious that D second. H B/XXI/B/489. On the 15th *The Times* would publish a full report of D's speech seconding the archdeacon's resolution: '"That the efficiency of the work of the Church in this diocese has, under the Divine blessing, been greatly promoted by the action of the three diocesan societies, and that those societies have therefore strong claims to our hearty and zealous support"'; see further **3628**&n1. In a leader it regretted D's call for churchmen to 'unite to force one system of legislation in matters of education and politics ... upon the rest of the country'. Another leader on the 16th would review the 'confession of faith' and comment: 'Let us hope that his audience will not take him too literally; that the clergy, convinced of his intention to "consecrate society and sanctify the State," may believe that in rallying round Mr. Disraeli they are supporting, not an individual, but an institution ... [and] feel it their duty to oppose [a measure on church rates], with results painful, indeed, to the feelings of this self-denying theologian, but not altogether adverse to the interests of his party.'

---

1 Lady Londonderry's annual entertainment for about 300 of her Irish tenants had been held on Thursday 26 September at Carnlough, co Antrim; before handing out prizes she praised their efforts and successes even though the state of their farms and houses was still far from what she wished, regretting only the increased planting of potatoes despite warnings about repeating the famine disaster. *The Times* (1 Oct 1861). On 31 October in the Londonderry Institute at Seaham, the Duke of Marlborough had presided at a meeting for the formation of a Church Defence Association, with Earl Vane and a number of clergymen also on the platform. However, newspaper reports of the Duke's speech defending church establishment do not mention Lady Londonderry. *MP* (6 Nov 1861); *The Times* (5 Nov 1861).

2 Peel had died in 1850, Goulburn in 1856, Dalhousie in 1860, Herbert earlier in 1861, Aberdeen in 1860, and Graham on 25 October 1861.

his tricks with / the volatility of inexperience! I am sorry for Graham, an interesting man with all his errors & indiscretions. I said something kind of him, in a debate last year, & in his absence – & he wrote me a letter, next day, full of fervent thanks.[3] He had a gushing heart, with the affectation of seeming heartless.

But what is all this to the loss / of our own Eglintoun![4] He was the most honest ~~heart,~~ ↑man,↓ & the most straightforward, ~~man,~~ I ever dealt with. He was the only public man I ever knew, who was really beloved.

We have some thoughts, that we may still be in yr part of the world at the early part of next month – &, if so, will ask permission to stay with you a few days.[5]

Ever yours, | D.

TO: SARAH BRYDGES WILLYAMS — Hughenden [Wednesday] 13 November 1861 — 3628

ORIGINAL: RTC [183]

PUBLICATION HISTORY: M&B IV 360, dated at Hughenden, 13 November 1861, the first paragraph and the last sentence

EDITORIAL COMMENT: Paper imprinted 'Hughenden Manor'. There is no salutation.

Most Private — Nov. 13. 1861

The state of the Church is critical – from dissensions & heresy – among its own children. If it were to fall, philosophy would not profit: we should only be handed over to a narrow-minded & ignorant fanaticism. I have been in frequent correspondence of late with the Bp: / of Oxford, the Bp: of this Diocese; as you know, a first-rate man – & I have promised to attend a great ↑Diocesan↓ meeting tomorrow at Aylesbury, & try to give a lead to public opinion in the right direction. It is a nervous business, for what may be said, & done tomorrow, may produce very great effects – like Sacheverell's sermon, wh: was nothing till / it was preached, & then nearly set the Thames on fire. After all, it may end tomorrow in smoke, for a speech is like a play – success seems always a chance.[1]

3 In his speech on 15 May 1861 (see **3578**n1), D had referred to Graham as 'a great authority' on the legal and constitutional question of the Lords' handling of a measure passed in the Commons. *Hansard* CLXII col 2188. The letter from Graham has not been found.

4 See **3623**&n1.

5 Lady Londonderry would reply from Seaham on the 11th: 'I will not delay answering yr interesting letter, & I do so selfishly, because I want to try & pin you & Mrs D'Israeli to coming to me... I have so few friends & I like so few people ... I did not care for Sir James Graham & I hate all the Peelites ... My health is wretched & I am utterly good for nothing but it wd quite revive me to see you. Adolphus is now well & full of America.' H B/XX/V/224. See further **3630**&nn1&2. For the DS' visit, see **3625**n4.

---

1 D's speech would attribute the disunity in the established church's clergy to the existence of two church parties, to *Essays and Reviews* (see **3563**&n8), and to popular disgust at Palmerston's appointments of bishops. He felt there could be a union of all parties within the church, whether Whigs or Tories, essayists or their opponents, on the nation's religious settlement as the best means to serve the people's future needs. He urged churchmen to unite in supporting church rates, when they would be irresistible and prevent church questions from becoming party matters: 'if [churchmen] are only united on Church questions, they will add immensely to the strength of good government and to the general welfare of the people. Then I believe that those admirable institutions, [the church and the monarchy,] the object of which is to ameliorate the whole body of society, will assume that catholic and universal character in their action which is so devoutly to be desired – then the great object of the Church, the education of the people, their perfect spiritual supervision, the completion of our parochial system, and, above all, the free

This business has kept me here somewhat later, than I intended. Immediately after this, we go to Alnwick Castle on a visit to the Duke & Duchess of Northumberland. We shall not get away from the North without a visit to Lady / Londonderry, & perhaps one or two more, but nothing, God willing, will prevent our being at Torquay next month, & dining with you on the 21st. Decr.[2]

The lobsters were delicious – very creamy.[3]

I hope to find you in the highest health & spirits. Think of me tomorrow; a very critical day, I can assure you.

Yours ever, | D.

3629 TO: LORD DERBY Hughenden [Friday] 15 November 1861

ORIGINAL: DBP Box 146/1

PUBLICATION HISTORY: M&B IV 303-4, dated at Hughenden, 15 November 1861, omitting the last sentence

EDITORIAL COMMENT: Paper imprinted 'Hughenden Manor'. Endorsed by Derby on the first page: 'Disraeli B.'

Rt Honble | The Earl of Derby | K.G. Nov 15. 1861

My dear Lord,

We are engaged to be at Alnwick on the day you, so kindly, invite us to Knowsley, & having fixed the time ourselves, after much hesitation, I cannot venture to propose a new arrangement. This I much regret, as it would have given me great pleasure / to have seen, & conversed with, you.[1]

As for public affairs, no difficulty is solved, or even approaching solution. The

and decorous worship of the Almighty, will be securely effected.' *The Times* (15 Nov 1861). For *The Times*'s opinion of the speech, see **3626**n1. Wilberforce thought it a 'Clever electioneering speech to clergy and church'. M&B IV 362. For a fuller treatment of the speech as a religiously orthodox and statesmanlike defence of the established church, especially against the heresies of the essayists derived (he argued) from recent schools of German theology, see M&B IV 360-2. Dr Henry Sacheverell in 1710 was impeached for two 1709 sermons attacking the Whig government for tolerating dissenters; he had previously made the attack in published pamphlets 1701-5, but the sermons had the advantage of his 'striking appearance and energetic delivery'. *DNB*. The trial created a furor, and the lightness of the sentence (forbidden to preach for three years) was seen as a victory for Sacheverell and an embarrassment to the government. The correspondence with Wilberforce mentioned here has not been found. Sotheron-Estcourt would write to D on the 23rd about his 'admirable speech at Aylesbury ... You have entirely surpassed the whole corps ecclesiastique ... in your treatment of the Essays and Reviews ... Everyone, I meet, seems pleased, to find the subject ... put into such a concise nervous and epigrammatic a Form ... our people are at present divided in opinion, and want the voice of a Leader.' H B/XXI/E/266.

2 The DS would go to Torquay on 17 December, in time to celebrate D's 57th birthday with SBW on the 21st. They would return on New Year's Day. H acc.

3 SBW in her letter to MA of 5 November had remarked: 'I have been after my Fisherman repeatedly and I only find that I may as well attempt to get Fish from the Zodiac.' On the 10th she had written letters to both MA and D, in the latter thanking D for his gifts of rare game and 'most brilliant Letter' and wondering whether he might find of interest a title she had come across, '"The life of Cardinal Ximenes by the late Dr Lord"'. RTC [434-6Q].

---

1 On the 12th, having heard that morning from Jolliffe about D's travels, Derby had written to invite D for the time that Jolliffe, Malmesbury and Pakington were going to be at Knowsley, on the 25th or 26th: 'it would give me much pleasure to see you and we might have a little political talk. I do not know whether Mrs. Disraeli will be with you, but if so, Lady Derby begs me to add that she will be very happy to see her also, if she does not mind being the only Lady. I say nothing of politics, which seem to me to be in a more uncertain state than ever: nor of party, which is much in statu quo, though J. Russell, S. Herbert, & Graham will have weakened the Government in your House.' H B/XX/S/287.

recess, hitherto, has advanced nothing, while the general decomposition proceeds. To be, at the same time, head of the Revolution & head of the Latin race, is an inconsistent position; & this is the cause of the perplexities of the Emperor of France – but / the Latin race will carry the day, & the compromise with revolution, sooner or later, must be an European war. Our part in it is another question.[2]

Since the days of the House of Atreus, there has never been a tragedy like the Peelites. Incredible, that, since the fatal act of 1846, Peel, Goulburn, Dalhousie, Aberdeen, Graham, Herbert, have all disappeared – & Lincoln getting as blind as / Œdipus[3] – while Palmn, the senior of all, is rollicking! The Mayor of Oxford[4] told me, yesterday, that Cardwell had been in imminent danger, from dysentery: but this would only have been an affair of the lesser Ajax.[5] Strange, that, after all their loves & hates, Graham & Tom Duncombe shd. die in the same month, & of the same complaint.[6]

Mrs. Disraeli unites with me in kind remembrances to Lady Derby, & I am ever, my dear Lord,

Sincerely Yours, | D.

TO: LORD ADOLPHUS VANE TEMPEST — Hughenden [Monday] 18 November 1861 — 3630

ORIGINAL: DUR D/LO/C 530(19) [203]
EDITORIAL COMMENT: Paper imprinted 'Hughenden Manor'.

The | Lord Adolp: Vane Tempest | M.P — Nov 18 1861

My dear Adolphus,

I was very glad, indeed, to recognise your handwriting.

I had, already, read the letter of "Anglicanus"; & with great satisfaction, as I / saw, at once, it was authentic, & found it most interesting. The "Times" did not publish your postscript as to the resources of the Southern States, or rather the details referred to in your / postscript. I shd much like to have seen these, as the resources of the Confederates are obscure, & much must depend on them.[1]

We are going into the North in a week's time, & propose making a / visit to Sea-

2 The Emperor's dilemma had been summarized by Cowley after a meeting with him in October 1861, and effectively confirmed by Earle's report from Florence of 11 November 1861: 'If, said the Emperor, the Pope were to abandon Rome, it would be said that France was not powerful enough to protect him and, if he remained, France would be accused of being the obstacle to Italian liberty.' Henry Wellesley, 1st Earl Cowley *The Paris Embassy during the Second Empire* (1928) 210; H B/XX/E/234.

3 Lennox on 25 October from Ireland had reported to D: 'The D of Newcastle is really going Blind & means to resign soon.' H B/XX/LX/147.

4 Charles James Sadler (1793-1872), first elected to the Oxford City Common Council in 1823, alderman 1835, was mayor of Oxford in 1836, 1849, 1854, 1860-1. *The Letter-Books of Samuel Wilberforce 1843-68* (Oxford 1970) 186; *The Times* (11 Oct 1861); www.headington.org.uk/oxon/mayors.

5 Presumably the greater Ajax was Gladstone, MP for Oxford University, while Cardwell was MP for Oxford City.

6 Duncombe and Graham had died within a month of each other, the former on 13 November, and the latter on 25 October, both of heart disease. Parker *Graham* 460; *MP* (15, 26 Oct 1861).

---

1 *The Times* on 6 November 1861, under 'The Civil War In America,' had published a letter of 4 November signed 'Anglicanus', responding to a letter from *The Times*'s American correspondent published on 30

ham in the early part of next month. I quite count on the pleasure of seeing you there.

I shall write to your dear Mamma, the moment I see my way a little.[2]

Ever yours | D.

3631 TO: SARAH BRYDGES WILLYAMS — Alnwick Castle
[Sunday] 24 November 1861

ORIGINAL: RTC [184]
PUBLICATION HISTORY: M&B IV 304, dated at Alnwick Castle, 24 November 1861, extracts
EDITORIAL COMMENT: There is no salutation. The letter is written on what appear to be the second and fourth pages of an Alnwick brochure of which the first page has not been photographed in our copy; D has written 'T.O.' on the bottom right-hand corner of the third (printed) page, which offers a view of Alnwick Castle, a poem and a history of the construction of its various parts. The catchword 'magnificence' occurs both as the last word of the first page of D's text and the first of the last page.

Nov 24 1861

Three hundred men, for the last seven years, have been at work daily at this wondrous place, & they are to work for three years more. The result, that the ancient Castle of Hotspur[1] is externally restored in perfect style; while the interior has all the refinement, fancy, & magnificence / of an Italian palace, in the palmiest days of Italian art. But description must be left till our happy meeting, wh: is daily nearer at hand. The Duke has formed a school of carvers in wood, where there are about

October 'which contains so much misrepresentation as to the state of feelings and condition of the people in the Southern States, that I am induced to ask you to insert a refutation of misstatements which, from late personal experience, I am able to afford.' The writer, from a stay with General Johnson, conversations with Generals Beauregard and Smith, and his own observations, refuted allegations that any of the Southern states had been coerced into the confederacy, and insisted that its cause had the people's full support, that abolition was not really what the war was about, and that the South's independence was inevitable: 'Would that this much wished for solution could be brought about. It is in no hostility to the North that I write. I am convinced, as the sun shines, that it is the only possible ending. How much better to arrive at it, if it is inevitable (as all impartial judges know it is), without the further inflictions of this sad and gigantic contest ... P.S. As there is much want of information as to the resources of the South, I enclose you a statement from reliable authority, should you consider it worthy of insertion.' The statement was not inserted.

2 Lord Adolphus would reply from Seaham on the 20th grateful for D's 'kind notice' of the paper on the South's resources he had sent D with his letter on American affairs, especially that D had read the letter and reacted favourably to it before he knew its author. He was annoyed that his paper had not been published, and would pursue the matter. At Lady Londonderry's request, he told D that the inauguration of the late Marquess's monument would take place at Durham on 2 December and invited the Ds to visit from 30 November: 'It would please her to have one like yourself present who appreciated the qualities of him to whose memory the day will be devoted.' H B/XX/V/20. On the 27th Lady Londonderry would respond with pleasure to D's acceptance just received (not found) and give travel directions. H B/XX/V/225. At the event D would make the main speech, praising the Commons and the party system, before paying a long, eloquent tribute to the late Marquess. *The Times* (4 Dec 1861). See further **3633**.

---

1 Sir Henry Percy (1364-1403), eldest son of 1st Earl of Northumberland (4th Lord Percy of Alnwick), was the original of the renowned Hotspur of Shakespeare's *Henry IV*.

thirty men, chiefly youths, working like Gibbons, or Cellini.[2] The frost is here strong & bright: you, no doubt, live in Ausonia.[3]

Adieu, | D.

TO: JAMES VINCENT Alnwick Castle [Wednesday] 27 November 1861 3632

ORIGINAL: QUA 197

EDITORIAL COMMENT: Paper imprinted 'Alnwick Castle'.

The | Rev Canon Vincent Nov 27 1861

Dear Sir,

I feel much honored by your letter, & am gratified you should deem any observations of mine worthy of being translated / into the language of the Principality.[1]

The version, of what I said at the Diocesan Society, is, on the whole, very correct in the "Times".[2] Any one may reprint those / remarks, who wishes, but I, myself, never presume to adopt that course.[3]

Believe me, dear Sir, | faithfully yours, | *B. Disraeli*

TO: SARAH BRYDGES WILLYAMS Seaham Hall [Sunday] 8 December 1861 3633

ORIGINAL: RTC [185]

PUBLICATION HISTORY: M&B IV 304, dated at Seaham Hall, 8 December 1861, the third paragraph, omitting the last sentence; Blake 419, dated 8 December 1861, extract; H. Montgomery Hyde *The Londonderrys* 52-3, dated at Seaham Hall, 8 December 1861, the third paragraph; Meynell II 464, undated extract; Weintraub *Disraeli* 385, dated 8 December 1861, extracts

EDITORIAL COMMENT: There is no salutation.

Seaham Hall | Dec 8 1861

We leave this place on Tuesday morning, for Grosvenor Gate, & after some little stay there, shall proceed to the soft waters of your bay, of wh: I will give you due notice.[1]

What wondrous times are these! Who cd. have supposed, that the U. States of

2 The 4th Duke of Northumberland was currently having the eighteenth-century gothic of Alnwick replaced by Italianate interiors. Grinling Gibbons (1648-1721), wood-carver and sculptor, did much carving for the churches and great houses of his time. Benvenuto Cellini (1500-1571), goldsmith, sculptor, engraver and swordsman, did most of his highly regarded work in Rome; his colourful career is recounted in his famous autobiography.

3 The ancient name for Italy. In her response of 29 November SBW would write a postscript: 'Eloquence ought to predominate in classical Italy and everywhere else'. RTC [437Q].

---

1 James Vincent Vincent (1792-1876), rector since 1834 of Llanfairfechan, Bangor, Wales, BA (Oxf) 1815, MA 1818, Hon Canon of Bangor Cathedral 1851, would be Dean of Bangor 1862-76. He was author of a sermon in Welsh, *Christian Unity, and the Injurious Effects of Division in Preventing the Extension of the Gospel,* as well as various tracts and addresses in Welsh. *Crockford* (1858); Vincent Papers, University of Wales, Bangor. The diocese of Bangor had a lay society to support the Oxford Movement and published a Welsh-language journal, *Baner y Groes* (1855-8). Peter Freeman 'The Response of Welsh Nonconformity to the Oxford Movement' *Welsh History Review* 20,3 (2001)436.

2 See **3628**n1.

3 No reprint of the speech has been found, either in Welsh or English.

---

1 For the DS' itinerary, see **3625**n4 and **3628**n2.

America would / be the scene of an immense revolution! No one can foresee its results. They must, however, tell immensely in favor of aristocracy.[2]

This is a remarkable place, & our hostess is a remarkable woman. Twenty miles hence, she has a palace (Wynyard) in a vast park, with forest rides & antlered deer, & all the splendid / accessories of feudal life. But she prefers living in a hall, on the shores of the German Ocean, surrounded by her collieries, & her blast furnaces, & her rail-roads, & unceasing telegraphs, with a port hewn-out of the solid rock↑, screw steamers↓, & four thousand pitmen under ↑her↓ control. One day, she dined the whole 4000 in / one of her factories.[3] In the town of Seaham Harbour, a mile off, she has a regular office; a fine stone building with her name & arms in front, & her flag flying above; & here she transacts, with innumerable agents, immense business. And I remember her, five & twenty years ↑ago,↓ a mere fine lady; nay, the finest in London! But one must find excitement, if one has brains. 1000 kind thoughts to our next & speedy merry meeting!

Yrs ever, | D.

3634 TO: LADY LONDONDERRY Grosvenor Gate [Wednesday] 11 December 1861

ORIGINAL: DUR D/LO/C 530 [126]

PUBLICATION HISTORY: *Lady Londonderry* 186, dated at Grosvenor Gate, 11 December 1861

EDITORIAL COMMENT: Paper imprinted 'Grosvenor Gate'. There is no salutation. *Sic:* Anglesea.

Dec. 11 1861

We made a good voyage after a happy visit.

I found Sir A. Alison's work here "from the author".[1] My post of two days was so heavy, that I have been unable / to cut a page, but I glanced over the last volume, where it was naturally open, & it appeared to me much hurried.

I should have been pleased to have seen a letter of mine own there, had it not been so incorrectly printed, / that it makes me write insufferable solecisms – but when I ~~gla~~ looked at the Duke's funeral, I found the pall carried by Anglesea, Londony, & other heroes ending with "*Sir Peregrine Pickle*"! *What can / he mean? Why not Sir Roderick Random at once?* I write to Sir Archibald by this post, & have told him, that

2 The *Trent* incident (8 November) had radically changed British perception of the American civil war, with Britain currently in suspense after its ultimatum which made war possible with the Northern Federation. *The Times* on 7 December had found President Davis's recent message to the Southern Congress a convincing prediction of victory; on 10 December it would comment: 'If we are to be dragged into a war, it is now clear that it will be the democracy who will force us into it. It will not be the rich or the educated, but the ignorant and the penniless, who will make a war in which they have nothing to lose, and of the events of which they have no power of perception.' Most commentators (see ph) have taken this passage from Disraeli's letter as an indication of D's sympathies as much as a prediction.

3 *Cf* VI **2830**&n1.

1 Sir Archibald Alison (1792-1867), 1st Bt (created in 1852 by the Derby government), historian, had just published his three-volume *Lives of Lord Castlereagh and Sir Charles Stewart, the Second and Third Marquesses of Londonderry ... From the original papers of the family* (Blackwood & Sons 1861); Lady Londonderry in 1855 had given him access to the papers, and he wrote it at five pages a day for two years. *DNB*.

the work has never reached you. I have addressed him with frankness. I hope he will bear it.[2]

Yours ever | D.

TO: LADY LONDONDERRY Grosvenor Gate [Saturday] 14 December 1861 3635

ORIGINAL: DUR D/LO/C 530 [127]

PUBLICATION HISTORY: *Lady Londonderry* 187-8, dated at Grosvenor Gate, 14 December 1861

EDITORIAL COMMENT: Paper imprinted 'Grosvenor Gate'. There is no salutation.

---

confidl Dec 14 1861

The conspiracy you foresaw has already partially exploded. I have written to Taylor to say, that if he, or any one connected with the party, either directly or indirectly, interfere with / the county, or the City, of Durham, you will withdraw yr. influence from the party, & probably, will ultimately, throw it into the other scale – that without you, the Conservatives can do / nothing, either in County or City, &, therefore, it is no use ~~in~~ kicking against the pricks:[1] that, for the sake of all concerned, the utmost quiet is desirable, &, that as a dissolution of Parlt is / highly improbable, they need not alarm themselves about Sir Hedworth Williamson, or any one else.

This peremptory despatch, wh: goes by this post, will, I hope, keep things tranquil. But great tact & temper on your part are / necessary. It is best to know nothing of all this.

He, who gains time, gains everything. We shall gain time, & the rest depends on / Adolphus.[2]

2 D's letter to Lord Londonderry of 24 July 1839 (III **972**) is reprinted in volume 3, 281-2, with only minor deviations from the original and with altered punctuation and paragraph breaks removed. Evidently there was another printing of the work (perhaps because of D's letter to Alison (not found)), as the surviving edition accurately reads: 'The pall was borne by Viscount Combermere, the Marquess of Londonderry, Sir Peregrine Maitland, Viscount Hardinge, Lord Seaton, Sir Alexander Woodford, Lord Gough, and Sir Charles Napier' (vol 3, 289). See also **3653**&n3. The *Peregrine Pickle* gaffe in the version seen by D, evidently occasioned by Maitland's name, is further intriguing because Smollett's novel includes the chapter contributed by the infamous Countess Vane. *MP*'s reviewer was caustic about the number of errors in Alison's book. *MP* (20 Dec 1861).

---

1 *Cf* Acts 9:5.

2 Evidently the 'conspiracy' had to do with Lord Adolphus's competence as an MP; *eg* in March he had been transferred on medical advice from jail to a lunatic asylum on clear evidence his mind was 'deranged'. *MP* (11 Mar 1861, repr from *The Times*). At Durham earlier in 1861 there had been dissatisfaction with the party line and with Lady Londonderry's influence; before the 8 July unopposed re-election of Sir William Atherton (L, Durham City) after his appointment as attorney-general, there was talk that 'a sort of clerical opposition, or an attempted Conservative reaction on the church-rate question, is threatened; but we understand that the Conservative laity have no great sympathy with the movement'. *The Times* (4 Jul 1861). Also on 4 July, Lord Loughborough had written to D about his brief trip to Durham. John R. Mowbray (C, also Durham City) had either purposely absented himself or had communicated with his constituents without learning Lady Londonderry's wishes or the desires of the party. 'Consequently my arrival caused a bewilderment almost amusing, and using Sir W Atherton's promotion as a pretext for not opposing his return, the friends of Mr Mowbray already sufficiently jealous of Lady Londonderry's influence threw as much cold water as they could upon my project going even as far as to say that if I opposed their wishes on this occasion, they would take care to oppose Lady L's wishes on any future occasion.' To keep the peace Loughborough 'buttered the malignants and extolled their independence & finally obtained a promise that on any future occasion they would cordially unite in *supporting* any man in whom the Party & Lady Londonderry should express confidence. I hope I have acted for the good

In consequence of the critical state of the Prince, I defer my departure for Devon for a day or two. The private accounts, last night, were very black: / I thought almost desperate. What will happen, man knows not. It is a great calamity for this Country. The Prince of Wales, as you probably know, has been perpetrating some / scrapes, & was about to be sent abroad. They say, he has brought about all this: others, that it was the King of Portugal's death, who was a sort of pupil of the Prince Consort, & by whom he man[a]ged to govern Portugal – as well as Engd.[3]

Adieu! | D.[4]

3636 TO: ACHILLE FOULD — Grosvenor Gate [Saturday] 14 December 1861

ORIGINAL: PS 746

PUBLICATION HISTORY: John Wilson catalogue 6 (1972) item 38: 'ALS ('B. Disraeli') to [Achille] Fould ... 2 pages 8vo with blank leaf, Grosvenor Gate, 14 December 1861.'

[Informing Fould, who was the French financial minister, that Lord Henry Lennox] who is a great friend of mine [wanted to consult him on a financial matter of interest to the French government.][1]

of the Conservative cause at Durham & that on any other occasion the return of another Tory Member will be certain.' H B/XXI/R/164. D's 'peremptory despatch' to Col Taylor has not been found. Lady Londonderry would reply on 'Tuesday' (17 December): 'There is a nasty undercurrent of Malignants in this County but I hope we shall defeat them & am gtly obliged by yr firm expression because altho they can all do nothing the buzzing is very disagreeable. I think they can hardly be such Idiots as not to know that only my Son could sit as a Conservative in this Liberal Division & that very much because I am myself so largely embarked in trade & commerce'. H B/XX/V/227. Sir Hedworth Williamson (1827-1900), 8th Bt (since April), of Whitburn Hall, Sunderland, Durham co, previously attaché at St Petersburgh and at Paris (the latter until 1854), JP and DL for Durham co, captain of the Durham volunteer artillery 1860, would win the Durham N seat in 1864 after Lord Adolphus's death, and be MP (L) for Durham N until 1874, high sheriff 1877.

3 Prince Albert would live only until 11 *pm* of this day. The press reports on his health had not become alarmed until earlier this day, and included the news that the Prince of Wales had been summoned overnight from Cambridge to Windsor. *The Times* (13, 14 Dec 1861). Lennox had sent D notes during the previous night, in the last ('Midnight') indicating that the Prince was not expected to live. H B/XX/LX/148, 148a. Albert's cousin (once removed) and favourite, the King of Portugal (for whom see VI **2664**n6), had died on 11 November, like Albert, of typhoid. For Albert's death, its effects and its contributing causes, such as the scandalous behaviour of the Prince of Wales in recent months (*eg*, an incident with a young actress, very poor performance in his military training, riotous behaviour at Cambridge), see *Disraeli, Derby* 179-81 (including an accurate forecast of the effect on Victoria of Albert's death), Longford *Victoria* 367, Weintraub *Victoria* 290-3, Roger Fulford *Prince Consort* (1949) 264-5, and Robert Rhodes James *Albert, Prince Consort* (1983) 267-8.

4 Lady Londonderry's next letter, on 'Sunday', would express her shock at Albert's death and include a promise to write again 'tomorrow on other subjects.' H B/XX/V/226. In her 'Tuesday' letter (n2) she would write: 'I really think in this life every thing happens different to what one expects. Who could have supposed the Queen wd bear this crushing sorrow with so much resignation especially after being so overpowered by a lesser one. It is passing strange.'

---

1 In November 1861 Fould had resumed the post of finance minister in what was regarded as a major restructuring of the French government, the significance of which was being closely watched in Britain. *The Times* (Nov-Dec 1861, *passim*). No relevant correspondence with Lennox has been found.

TO: LORD HENRY LENNOX — Torquay [Thursday] 19 December 1861 — 3637

ORIGINAL: NYM [11]

EDITORIAL COMMENT: Black-edged paper. D has repeated the word 'absorbing' instead of the catchword 'subject' at the top of the second page.

Lord Henry G Lennox | M.P. — Torquay | Dec 19. 1861

My dear Henry,

I can allow nothing to prevent me from thanking you for your most interesting, & authentic, letter.[1] You are, always, my best correspondent, but the absorbing subject / has lent additional color, & vigor, to your animated, & picturesque, pen. I thank you, most cordially, for yr kindness.

It is selfish to wish, even, to hear from ~~yr~~ you again, because your interests, / ever dear to me, command your presence, I apprehend, in another city.[2]

My wife sends you her very kind regards, & I am

Ever your | D.

1 Lennox had written from London on 18 December: 'The Queen still bears up with wonderful calmness & fortitude; although, at times, her bursts of Grief, are grievously distressing. – The Dss Dgr of Sutherland & Lady Augusta Bruce, are with her. – It would seem, that her disposition is returning to what it was, in her girlhood, firm & strong-minded. It now appears, that last Spring, the poor Prince Consort, lectured her severely, on giving way so completely; and told her to remember, that the Blow was dealt by the Hand of the All Wise. – She now remembers all this; & is constantly saying, "Now, you see, I am calm, I am profiting by His advice, I am doing, what He would have wished." – Yesterday, the Queen saw Lord Granville, who brought Palmerstons excuses, and Her M signed several Papers, that were of pressing importance. – The Prince of Wales, seems anxious to take his place, & I hear, behaves with great tact & feeling. – The Funeral, is to be strictly Private; They wish to move the Queen to Osborne, but she puts it off every day, dreading the sight of glaring Day light, & it being impossible, for the Yacht to bring up, under Osborne, after dark. – as matters now stand, she is to go tomorrow morning, the Prince of Wales, escorting her down & returning to Windsor to receive those, who arrive for the Ceremony of Monday. The King Leopold, goes straight to Osborne, being too unwell to go through the Funeral. – The D of Cambridge has not been back to Windsor & I fancy, he is already aware, that his hopes are not to be realized. – It is generally supposed, that he will get the Rifles. – The Prince of Wales, wishes not to have the Grenadier Guards. He told Pr Edward [*sic*], it would be absurd, to give them to him; that they ought to be given to some *old* general officer. – The Pr of Wales, wrote yesterday to Palmerston, by desire of his Mother, to say, that he would always find her, mindful of Her duty & of her People, but that Her worldly career, was at an end. – A rumour was extensively circulated to day, in the City, & the West end, that Palmerston, had had a relapse & was dying, but I called at Cambridge House, on purpose, to know, and he is much better to day. – Here are all the details, I can give you of this dreadful affair. – It is in substance, mere gossip, but every word is true, for I have it from the Fountain Head. – General Grey remains on at the Palace. – The 4 of HRHs Household, who have been with him throughout, continue to receive full salary & are to consider themselves, Honorary Members of the Court; the 3 younger ones, whose salary was, £500 pr ann, are to receive £300 pr ann for life. – You told me to write & I obey: so you must not blame me, although, my news is neither grave, nor of great import. – Four more Ships, put in Commission, & to sail tomorrow, with only 24 hours notice.' H B/XX/LX/149.

2 Lennox's mother, the Duchess of Richmond, had sustained a slight injury in an accident in Chichester on Wednesday 18 December, when her horse was startled and her cart overturned. *The Times* (20 Dec 1861).

3638 TO: LADY LONDONDERRY Torquay [Thursday] 19 December 1861

ORIGINAL: DUR D/LO/C 530 [128]

PUBLICATION HISTORY: M&B IV 382-3, dated at Torquay, 19 December 1861, omitting the fifth and last paragraphs; *Lady Londonderry* 189-90, dated at Torquay, 19 December 1861

EDITORIAL COMMENT: Black-edged paper. There is no salutation. *Sic:* brought Palmerston.

Confidential Torquay | Dec. 19. 61

There is a north post from this place, wh: tempts me to write to you a hurried line as my news, received this morning from the fountain head, may not be stale.[1]

It seems that the departed / Prince had lectured the Queen severely about giving way so completely on the death of her Mother,[2] & told her to remember, that the blow was dealt by the hand of the Allwise. She remembers this now, & / keeps saying "Now you see I am calm; I am profiting by His advice, I am doing what He wished".

The Duchess D of Sutherland & Lady Augusta Bruce with her.[3]

On the 17th. she saw Ld. Granville, who brought / Palmerston, & she signed several papers of pressing importance.[4] The P. of Wales seems anxious to take his place: & I hear behaves with great tact & feeling.[5] The funeral strictly private, wh: I knew before I left town, or shd / have remained.[6] They wish to move the Queen to Osb: but she puts it off every day, dreading the sight of the glaring daylight, it being impossible for the yacht to bring up, under Osborne after dark. As matters now stand she ~~may~~ will go to day, the / P of W. escorting her & returning.[7]

K. Leopold straight to Osborne – too unwell to go to the funeral.[8] The Duke of Cambridge, who forced his first visit, not asked to repeat – & I fancy he is already aware, that his hopes are not to be / realized. It is, howr, generally supposed, that he will get the Rifles.

1 The DS had arrived at Torquay on 17 December. H acc. For Lennox's letter from which D is quoting his 'news', see **3637**n2; Lennox's 'fountain head' presumably was his younger brother, Lord George Lennox, one of Prince Albert's lords in waiting.

2 See **3563**&n3.

3 The recently widowed Dowager Duchess of Sutherland, the Queen's closest confidante in the late 1830s, had been mistress of the robes to the Queen for the fourth time 1859-61; she would later be made a member (second class) of the Royal Order of Victoria and Albert. Weintraub *Victoria* 277. Lady Augusta Frederica Elizabeth Bruce (1822-1876), daughter of the 7th Earl of Elgin, was resident woman of the bedchamber after the Duchess of Kent's death and extra woman of the bedchamber on her marriage to Dean Stanley in 1863.

4 D has miscopied Lennox's letter, according to which Granville had taken (the ill) Palmerston's excuses to the Queen. The papers may have pertained to the *Trent* affair. *AR* (1861 History) 252-5; Malmesbury II 261-3; Weintraub *Victoria* 294-5. See further **3647**&nn1&3.

5 When MA suggested to the Queen that the Prince of Wales must be a great comfort to her, the Queen replied: 'Comfort! Why I caught him smoking a fortnight after his father died!' Weintraub *Edward* 101.

6 The 17 December reports were that it would not be a state funeral; the formal announcement published on the 18th stated that the funeral would be 'private and strictly limited in all that relates to funereal pomp and ceremonial.' The ceremony at Windsor on 23 December would be attended by representatives of every aspect of the Prince's life, including, for example, Lord Derby. *The Times* (17-24 Dec 1861). Evidently the DS left town after realizing that D would not be receiving an invitation.

7 This is what happened. *The Times* (20 Dec 1861).

8 The Queen on 20 December would thank her uncle profusely for his promised visit; he would arrive at Osborne on the 27th. *LQV* III 473-4.

The P of W. wishes not to have the Gren: Gds & says that they ought to be given to some old general officer.[9]

He wrote yesterday ↑to Palmerston↓, by desire of His Mother to say, that Ld P. wd. always find her mindful / of her duty & of her people, but that Her worldly career was at an end.

I find the north post goes off instantly, & I have only just recd. my letters; wh: must excuse this extreme haste: indeed, you must take this scrawl as an act of friendship.[10]

Yrs | D.

TO: HENRY PHILLPOTTS Torquay [Friday] 20 December [1861] 3639
ORIGINAL: BODL MS Autogr c14 f223

The | Ld Bp of Exeter 20: Decr | Torquay

My dear Lord,

On Tuesday next, at 6:30, with very great pleasure.[1]

My wife sends to you, & yours, her kindest / regards.

Ever yr f[aithful] S[ervan]t | *B. Disraeli*

TO: SARAH BRYDGES WILLYAMS [Torquay, Wednesday] 25 December 1861 3640
ORIGINAL: RTC [186]
EDITORIAL COMMENT: There is no salutation.

Xmas Day | 1861

Will you dine with us to day, being Xmas Day? I hope so. We will dine at half / past six. If you will not give us that pleasure, we propose to pay you / a visit, as usual, in the evening.[1]

Yours ever, | D.

9 The Duke of Cambridge (the Queen's cousin, who had inherited his parents' dislike of Albert) had arrived at Windsor early in the morning of Sunday 15 December, and left that afternoon. On the 17th, as commander-in-chief of the army, he had inspected the 1st Battalion of the Grenadier Guards before their departure for Canada; in February 1862, he would succeed Albert as their colonel and in November be made a field marshal. *The Times* (13 Feb 1862). He would not succeed Albert as colonel-in-chief of the Rifle Brigade (later the Prince Consort's Own); in February 1862, the post would go to Lord Seaton. *MP* (15 Feb 1862). Albert's post of constable of Windsor Castle would not be filled until 1867.

10 Lady Londonderry would write on 20 December to reassure D that a fire at Wynyard on 19 December, reported in *The Times* on 20 December, had been confined to the west wing and chapel, both destroyed, but that most of the house had been saved; 'What an ill fated place & what a doomed family'. H B/XX/V/228. For the fire that destroyed Wynyard in 1841, see III **1130**n6.

---

1 Phillpotts, Bishop of Exeter, had written from Bishopstowe, Torquay, on this day (20th): 'I rejoice to hear that you are again at Torquay, and I hope that you will have the charity to gratify an aged friend with your company on some day while you are here. May I propose Tuesday next at *6:30* to you and Mrs D'Israeli – to whom I beg you to offer my kind respects.' H B/XXI/P/268. See further **3645**.

---

1 In a note on monogrammed paper docketed 'Torquay Decr 1861' SBW wrote: 'I shall be most happy to see you and dear Mrs Disraeli as usual in the Evening and thank you many many times for your tempting invitation'. RTC [440Q].

3641 TO: SARAH BRYDGES WILLYAMS [Torquay] Saturday [28 December 1861]

ORIGINAL: RTC [187]

EDITORIAL COMMENT: There is no salutation. *Dating:* by context; see n1.

Saturday

Mrs. Disraeli will call upon you this morning at ½ past three o'ck.

Yours ever, | D.

She does not want / to drive out, as she has no more visits to pay.[1]

3642 TO: SARAH BRYDGES WILLYAMS Torquay [Tuesday] 31 December 1861

ORIGINAL: RTC [188]

EDITORIAL COMMENT: There is no salutation.

Torquay, | Dec 31 1861

We have so many farewell calls to make, this morning, that we propose to pay our visit to you in the evening, especially as we like always to pass our last evening / with you alone.

No reply is necessary, if you can receive us.

Ever yours, | D.

3643 TO: EDWARD KENEALY Torquay [Tuesday] 31 December 1861

ORIGINAL: UO [22]

PUBLICATION HISTORY: James Drake catalogue 225 (1931) item 87: 'AL 1p. 31 Dec 61 to Edw Hyde Kenealy, eccentric barrister & leading counsel in the notorious Tichborne case. D.', the second sentence

EDITORIAL COMMENT: Black-edged paper.

Torquay | Decr 31. 1861

Mr. Disraeli presents his Compliments to Mr. Kenealy, & has received his communication of the 22nd Inst:

Mr. Disraeli is not sanguine as to the result of his interference, but he will make the attempt.[1]

1 SBW replied: 'I shall be most happy to see Mrs Dizzi at ½ past 3, and return you 1000 thanks thanks [*sic*] for the superb mutton'. In another note also docketed December 1861 at Torquay, SBW wrote to MA: 'I can shop today and hope to see you and dear Dizzi when you like ... [P.S.] too cold for my fancy'. RTC [438-9Q]. MA recorded the gift to her this Christmas of a small gold watch from SBW. H acc.

---

1 In his letter of 22 December 1861 forwarded from London, Kenealy had asked for D's help in obtaining an Indian judgeship: 'One word from you to Lord Lyndhurst, or some other such friend, & from him to Sir Erskine Perry would be all powerful ... I think I know more of India & Indian matters than any man in England who has never been there'. D's third-person reply (*cf* **3548** and **3745**) evoked a pained response on 3 January 1862: 'Your note has made me very unhappy. I fear I have incurred your displeasure in some manner ... For twenty years or even longer you have been before my mind as the ideal of writer, orator & statesman, and that your manner should change towards me has affected me very deeply. Thank you for your kindness nevertheless'. On the 14th he would send D a copy of his application and of the glowing testimonials in its support. On the 30th he would acknowledge another letter from D (not found): 'Your letter which I received last night gave me the greatest delight – not indeed for the material benefit which any intervention of yours would be likely to produce ... but because it reassures me by its tone that you ... are unaltered in your generous interest & gracious favour.' On 8 February he would report a promising development: 'Your last note [*not found*] seems to have been speedily followed by this first ray of sunshine. I should be happy if I had your permission to mention to Lord Stanley of Alderley what you have done for me.' H B/XXI/K/88-93. Evidently Kenealy's application was not successful.

TO: SARAH BRYDGES WILLYAMS Torquay [Wednesday] 1 January 1862 3644
ORIGINAL: RTC [189]

For | Mrs. Brydges Willyams Torquay | New Years Day 1862
Many, many, auspicious returns of this interesting day![1]
Yours ever, | D.

TO: HENRY PHILLPOTTS Torquay [Wednesday] 1 January 1862 3645
ORIGINAL: BODL MS Autogr c14 f222
EDITORIAL COMMENT: Black-edged paper.

The | Lord Bp of Exeter Torquay | New Years Day 1862
My dear Lord,
I am grieved, & much disappointed, that I must leave this place without again having the gratification of visiting you.[1]

May / we meet again soon, & may many auspicious returns of this interesting day await you & yours![2]

Ever yr obliged, | & faithful, Servt | *B. Disraeli*

TO: [CONSERVATIVE MPS] Hughenden [Tuesday] 7 January 1862 3646
ORIGINAL: Copy (to William Mitford) in WSRO Mitford Archives MS 1277 f16 f26
PUBLICATION HISTORY: *BH* (1 Feb 1862), addressed to 'the Conservative members' and dated at Hughenden, 7 January 1862
EDITORIAL COMMENT: Black-edged paper. This is another example of the reproduced circular letters from D before the meeting of parliament; *cf* VII **3349**ec and in this volume **3546**ec, **3776**ec and **3889**ec.

Hughenden Manor[1] | Jany. 7. 1862

Sir,
The meeting of Parliament being fixed for Thursday, the 6th. Feby:, I request the favor of yr attendance, in / the House of Commons, on that day when business, of importance, will probably, be brought forward.

I have the honor to remain | Sir, | Your faithful Servant, | *B. Disraeli*

1 SBW replied: 'I gratefully thank you for your new years gift [*unidentified*] and I shall read it with the greatest interest'. RTC [441Q]. The day may have been 'interesting' for reaction to Britain's ultimatum on 23 December 1861 to the North American States for return of the four *Trent* prisoners (see **3633**n2). Despite some pessimistic reports, a *Times* leader on this day (1 January 1862) had 'fair hopes that concessions will be made which will avert the necessity of war. Should this be so, we shall begin the New Year with a fitting subject of congratulation.' See further **3647**&n1.

1 *Cf* **3639**&n1.
2 *Cf* **3644**&n1.

1 The DS were actually at Grosvenor Gate on this day (7 January); they would leave from there for Hatfield on the 22nd. H acc.

3647 TO: SARAH BRYDGES WILLYAMS

Grosvenor Gate
[Thursday] 9 January 1862

ORIGINAL: RTC [190]
EDITORIAL COMMENT: There is no salutation.

Grosvenor Gate | Jany 9. 1862

The news of Peace came yesterday evening, but reached me too late for the post. The Ministry got it about five o'ck[.] During the last two or three days, the Government / had been very gloomy & dispirited; & had lost all hope from the delay of the Americans. *We* were, however, right in our opinion.[1]

It is a great relief.

The Herald was out / of town for his holidays, but I expect he will have returned today, & I shall lose no time in carrying our business through.[2]

Ld Palmerston has had a very long & severe attack, but I am truly glad / to say, that I really believe he has got round again.[3]

Adieu! | D.

3648 TO: N.M. ROTHSCHILD & SONS

Grosvenor Gate
[Saturday] 11 January 1862

ORIGINAL: ROTH RAL 000/848
EDITORIAL COMMENT: Black-edged paper. Endorsed in another hand on the fourth page: '1862 Disraeli Jan 11'; and after the signature in yet another hand: 'Ansd to C. 27 Jan'. *Sic:* Gallagwdwda.

Messrs Rothschild Grosvenor Gate | Jan: 11 1862

Gentlemen,

The estates in Ceylon, respecting wh: you were so kind, as to say, yr agents shd. enquire, are Middleton, & / Gallagwdwda. They belong to Hon: Francis Villiers, & are let, & heavily mortgaged. I am anxious to know what is their general character & condition, & if possible, their probable value. I have no confidence, whatever, / in the persons in the Colony, who are connected with these properties, & who, I believe, are anxious to force sales to their own advantage, & not that of the mortgagee & proprietor. Otherwise, I / would not venture to give you all this trouble.[1]

Yours sincerely, | *B. Disraeli*

1 The news that the Federal (Northern) States had consented on 27 December to deliver the four *Trent* prisoners to Lord Lyons in Washington, thereby avoiding war with Britain, had reached London on 8 January; Lyons had delayed delivering the British ultimatum until 23 December to allow for a cooling off period, and lack of a response as late as the 26th had caused much anxiety. *The Times* (8, 9 Jan 1862). See **3644** and **3645** for the DS' confidence of peace.

2 See **3600**&nn1-3 and **3650**.

3 Although Palmerston had been so ill that rumours arose of his death, it was in fact a severe attack of gout. Bell *Palmerston* II 297. Malmesbury had noted on 28 December: 'Lord Palmerston has been dangerously ill, but is better. His death at this moment would be a national misfortune, when we consider who the men are who are likely to succeed him among the Whig party.' Malmesbury II 266.

---

1 For the continuing Villiers affair see **3616**&n1, **3652**&n1 and especially **3714**&n1. No reply from Messrs Rothschild has been found. One estate evidently was named after the Jerseys' seat in Oxfordshire, Middleton Park; the other estate's name is spelled 'Gallageddera' in Thomas Dickson's letter to D of 17 July 1862 (see **3714**&nn1&2). For a contemporary account of Ceylon that treats estate ownership, see Sir James Emerson Tennent *Ceylon: An Account of the Island Physical, Historical, and Topographical* (1859), which had reached a fourth edition by 1860.

TO: PHILIP ROSE [London] Sunday 12 January 1862 3649

ORIGINAL: H R/I/A/146

P. Rose Esq Sunday night | Jan. 12. 62

My dr Rose,

I did not get yr. note until yesterday. I shd be obliged, if you wd, for the / moment, attend to the interest; I will make, very shortly, a fresh payment to yr Cashier.

I hope Peacocke will / take a sensible view of the matter, as, I agree with you, the consolidation is the basis of everything, &, if effected quickly, may / have the happiest results.[1]

Yrs sincerely, | D.

Colonel Fane writes to me, that he is all right, tho' it does not appear that Dashwood has resigned.[2]

TO: SARAH BRYDGES WILLYAMS [London] Tuesday 14 January [1862] 3650

ORIGINAL: RTC [191]

EDITORIAL COMMENT: There is no salutation. *Sic:* Legh.

Tuesday 14 Jany.

I saw the Herald on Saturday – but he was very busy, having just returned to town. He, however, called on me, by appointment to day, & went over the whole business. There / are to be two shields, & he will send me a drawing, which I shall forward for your consideration, in a few days.

He says, however, that you cannot impale the Legh arms, your mother / not having been an heiress, & that your shield must be that of the Mendez da Costas, pure & simple, in the form you wished.[1]

1 See VII **3290**&n1 for the business with Peacocke that in February 1859 was supposed then to be settled by 'the end of the month'. Rose's 'note' has not been found. For discussion of D's evidently improving financial situation (his pension and help from Andrew Montagu and Lionel de Rothschild) see M&B V 77-9 and Blake 421-4. In the summary list of Hughenden estate papers the following item is dated '1st January 1858[:] Transfer of Mortgage from Mr Richard Durant the younger and Mr. W. Enoch Durant Cumming with the concurrence of Benjamin Disraeli Esqre. to George Montagu Warren Peacocke Esqre. endorsed on above mentioned Indenture 15th December 1853.' The previous two items are of 1 November 1848 and 15 December 1853, and the items before that step it back to 28 June 1847, the second item of the list being for the 5 Sept 1848 mortgage of £25,000 by Rose to D. Bucks Record Office, Aylesbury. See further **3683**&n2.

2 At a by-election for Oxfordshire on 31 January after the death on 19 December 1861 of George Harcourt (L), Lt-Col J.W. Fane (C) would defeat Sir H. Dashwood (L) 1909-1722; see **3660**. On 'Monday' it would be reported from Oxford that 'The rumour prevalent on Saturday relative to Sir Henry Dashwood's retirement was unfounded.' *The Times* (14 Jan 1862). On 12 January (this day), Victoria Fane had acknowledged D's letter (not found) on behalf of her husband and reported no doubt that he would win. H B/XXI/F/48. Lady Jersey had been anxious since December that Dashwood be opposed and, once Fane was requisitioned, offered support from herself (£100) and her agents, who would tell her Oxfordshire tenants not to vote for Dashwood; she had heard that 'if people vote *from Party* Dashwood has not *a chance*'. H A/IV/J/175, 185, 364. *MP* on 27 January reported the same and saw Dashwood's second address (declaring himself a Liberal after at first announcing himself independent) as having made the election a party struggle and overturned his otherwise almost certain success. Sir Henry William Dashwood (1816-1889), 5th Bt (since September 1861), of Kirtlington Park, Oxon, was JP and DL for Oxon, high sheriff 1866, LL 1883.

1 See **3647**&n2.

The men are calling great news about the / streets, & on enquiry, I find, that the American packet has just come in with the news, that the American Banks have suspended cash payments![2]

I am glad your securities are not Trans-atlantic.

Yours ever, | D.

3651 TO: SARAH BRYDGES WILLYAMS — Grosvenor Gate [Saturday] 18 January 1862

ORIGINAL: RTC [192]
EDITORIAL COMMENT: There is no salutation.

CONFIDENTIAL — G. Gate. Jany. 18. 62

The King of the Belgians is in town on matters of grave import, & I am obliged to place myself at the command of His Majesty,[1] wh: has prevented my pushing on / the herald, as much as I could have wished – but, yesterday, he left the enclosed here, with a note, saying, that "the arms of Willyams are drawn too much aslant, but did not think it worth while, it / being only a rough sketch, & I in a hurry, to detain it for alteration"[.]

The two shields ought to be a little aslant, he said.[2]

Yours ever, | D.

3652 TO: WILLIAM CARLISLE — Grosvenor Gate [Monday] 20 January 1862

ORIGINAL: MOPSIK [39]
EDITORIAL COMMENT: Black-edged paper. Endorsed in another hand on the fourth page: '*20th Jany 1862* | HONBLE B DISRAELI | Magenis & Villiers'. *Sic:* T. Carlisle; Magenis'; Dixon.

T. Carlisle Esq — Grosvenor Gate | Jan 20. 1862

Dear Sir –

I am disappointed at not receiving from you a note of Mr. Magenis' acct. with Mr. Villiers. I have heard from that gentleman, / who seems much annoyed at the reduction of the Ceylon rents, observing, that, if the representations of Mr. Dixon, & his friend, are correct, the reduction proposed would be quite inadequate. It is useless, / however, to take any decided step in this matter, until we can act with effect. I trust, however, I may yet, ↑& soon,↓ be able to do that. In the meantime, the first consideration is / the liquidation of the claim of yr client.[1]

Yours faithfully, | *B. Disraeli*

2 The news of Federal banks' suspension of specie payments had reached London on Tuesday evening; it was regarded as evidence that the North would be unable to continue the war and be compelled to reach some peaceful settlement with the South. *The Times* (15 Jan 1862).

---

1 Palmerston and the Queen had appealed to the King to facilitate their interaction after the death of Albert, who had acted as a buffer between them, and thus avoid holding up crucial public business such as the response to the Federalist answer in the *Trent* affair. Bell *Palmerston* II 297-9; *LQV* I 11-15. There is no evidence that D's services were called upon.

2 See **3654**&n1 for SBW's reply.

---

1 For D's last correspondence with Carlisle, see **3616**&n1; for Villiers's most recent extant letter to D, see **3621**n1. On 29 January Dickson in London would send D a lengthy statement on the Ceylon estates he

TO: LORD DERBY Grosvenor Gate [Wednesday] 22 January 1862 **3653**

ORIGINAL: DBP Box 146/1

EDITORIAL COMMENT: Black-edged paper. Endorsed by Derby on the fourth page: 'Disraeli B.' *Sic:* Hennessey.

Rt Honble | The Earl of Derby K.G. Grosvenor Gate | Jany 22. 62

My dear Lord,

I send you

1. Adderleys Pampht[1]

2. Observer – article marked. I understand, tho' I have not seen them, these views have been followed up in the / "Globe" yesterday & the day before[.]

See, also, City article in "Times" today on this subject.[2]

3. I enclose confidential mem: respecting men in Parliament as to new talent &c. I made / it, reflecting on the late Session during the Recess.

If you have Alisons Lives of the two Stewarts – vide – 3. Vol: p. 289. Pall-bearers of the Duke of Wellington.[3] As / you were the Prime Minister of the Country at the time, it is well you shd know for what Posterity will hold you responsible.

Yours sincerely, | D. /

CONFIDENTIAL

Men of mark in the New Parliament

Hubbard

and others had held under Villiers's lease. After complications with Magenis, Burley and Carlisle (apparently acting for both Villiers and Magenis) had begun negotiations for sale of the two estates, subject to their ten-year leases. After several years, £6,000 was decided on, but Burley and Carlisle were unable to obtain the deeds necessary for the sale. Meanwhile the districts in which the estates were situated had suffered so much that the lessee of Gallageddera was in serious difficulties and the other thousands of pounds in debt. Burley and Carlisle had suggested reducing the rent, to which D had agreed verbally, but Dickson needed written authorization. He had Captain Fisher's letters corroborating his statement and suggesting reductions of £100 & £70 respectively, without which the estates would fall into ruin and become worthless. On 6 February Carlisle would write enclosing a statement (not found) showing £1,818.2.10 due to Magenis 'on the 1st. Septr last' and copies of Dickson's two last accounts for the rents up to 1 July 1861: 'You will observe that Mr Magenis has given credit for the £792.14.10 remitted to him by Bill as the Exchange for the balance of £776.17.9 and he has only charged the discount he paid to Messrs Hoare in Decr last for cashing this Bill.' H A/IV/J/182, 186. See further **3714**&nn1&2.

---

1 See **3615**&n1 for Adderley's latest publication in his program espousing colonial self-government; see further **3655**&n1.

2 The City column in *The Times* of this day (22 January) had commented that British markets were responding adversely to the partial blockade of Southern American ports by Federal forces. The dearth of Southern cotton was affecting France more severely than Britain, which had an alternative supply from India, and France was eager to break the blockade. Although it would be difficult for Britain to refuse to join with France on the issue, the general feeling in London was that Washington should be left to work out its own anarchy and bankruptcy. Information kindly supplied by Zachary W. Elder, Duke University Libraries, RBMSCL Research Services. The *Observer* of 19 January 1862 under 'Aspect of Affairs In America' had reported that 'Mr Seward has informed Lord Lyons that the Government will offer no objection to the conveyance of our troops and military stores through the territory of the United States, from Portland to the Canadian frontier ... If this statement be correct, it must be regarded as indicating feelings by no means so unfriendly towards this country as many persons supposed to have existed in the Northern States.' D and Derby are evidently working on their responses to the Address when they will endorse government neutrality on North America. *Hansard* CLXV cols 30-1 (Derby) and 64-6 (D).

3 See **3634**&nn1&2. In his reply later this day, Derby would remark: 'I had not seen, but I had heard of the "Pickle" Alison has got into.' H B/XX/S/309.

Cave[4]
Hennessey[5]
Fergusson[6]
Holmesdale[7]
Farquhar
Alg. Egerton (from his position ↑&c↓, tho' himself rather a stick)[8]

T O. /

Old hands, but who have never been in office.
Ker Seymer
Du Cane
Elphinstone
Cecil
Gregory
Stirling
Knightley

3654 TO: SARAH BRYDGES WILLYAMS

Grosvenor Gate
[Wednesday] 22 January 1862

ORIGINAL: RTC [193]
EDITORIAL COMMENT: The postscript is written on a small slip of paper. There is no salutation.

PRIVATE Grosvenor Gate | Jan 22 1862

I think all your criticisms are quite just, & that there may be no mistake, ~~ske~~ he shall make another & more complete sketch, wh:, when approved, the engraver shall identically reproduce.[1] /

4 Stephen Cave (1820-1880), of Cleve Hill, Bristol, a barrister (Inner Temple 1846), MP (C) for Shoreham 1859-80, would be paymaster-general and vice-president of the board of trade 1866-8, PC 1866, judge advocate general 1874-5, paymaster-general 1875-80, GCB 1880.

5 John Pope Hennessy (1834-1891), of Cork, JP for co Cork, a barrister (Inner Temple 1861), MP (C) for King's co 1859-65, would be governor of Labuan 1867-71, governor of Hong Kong 1877-82, KCMG 1880.

6 Sir James Fergusson (1832-1907), 6th Bt, of Edinburgh, wounded at Inkerman while serving with the Grenadier Guards, captain Royal Scottish Archers, DP and JP for Ayrshire, MP (C) for Ayrshire 1854-7, 1859-68, for Manchester NE 1885-1906, would be under-secretary for India 1866-7, for the home office 1867-8, PC 1868, governor of South Australia 1868-73, of New Zealand 1873-5, KCMG 1874, LLD (Glasgow) 1879, governor of Bombay 1880-5, CIE 1884, GCSI 1885, under-secretary for foreign affairs 1886-91, postmaster-general 1891-2.

7 William Archer Amherst (1836-1910), Viscount Holmesdale, late captain Coldstream Guards (severely wounded at Inkerman 1854), JP and DL for Kent, MP (C) for W Kent 1859-68, for mid-Kent 1868-80, would be elevated to the Lords 1880, and succeed as 3rd Earl Amherst 1886.

8 Algernon Fulke Egerton (1825-1891), younger son of 1st Earl of Ellesmere, lieut-col commandant of two Lancashire regiments, MP (C) for S Lancashire 1859-68, for SE Lancashire 1868-80, for Wigan 1882-5, would be 1st secretary of the admiralty 1874-80; since 1855 he had been superintendent trustee of the Bridgewater Trust.

---

1 SBW had responded on 20 January to **3651**: 'The sketch at first sight appears handsome yet I fancy it requires a little alteration. I do not admire the shield of the Willyams being larger at the Base than at the Top and the Crest shd be a little higher above the top of the Shield. The Coronet of Mendez Da Costa is *too large* and it *shd just touch the top of the Shield,* an impression of a Seal of som[e] antiquity may be some guide'. At the top of the next page appears the impression of a seal on wax underscribed by SBW: 'Coronet of Daniel Mendez da Costa'. The letter continues: 'It is with the greatest reluctance that I intrude

We have also had a fall of snow, but it has vanished, & we have a springlike morning.

We go to day to Hatfield, on a visit to Lord & Lady Salisbury, & shall stay there until Friday, when I must be in town again.[2]

Lord Derby has come up unusually early this year, in consequence of the expected accouchement of his daughter, Lady Emma Talbot.[3]

The Queen insists upon the Prince of Wales accomplishing those travels in the East, & especially in Syria & Palestine, wh: his father planned / for him. The Ministers have strongly resisted this, & the King of the Belgians disapproves of the Prince leaving England under the altered circumstances of the case. But the Queen is firm: everything her husband planned is to be executed.[4] The King is not well, & is detained here with bronchitis.[5] I hope the change of weather may cure him & that nothing may happen to complete the tragedy of the Royal Family.[6]

Ever yours, | D. /

My paper was so full, that I put this in to express my hope, that your domestic troubles may have vanished like the Snow.

D.

TO: CHARLES ADDERLEY Grosvenor Gate [Sunday] 26 January 1862 **3655**

ORIGINAL: PS 1439

PUBLICATION HISTORY: M&B IV 329, dated at Grosvenor Gate, 26 January 1862

... You have placed your views before the country in a clear and complete light,

these trifling details in your precious happy time[.] Addio'. She had written again (dated 24 January in the H copy but obviously before D's reply): 'It is with great reluctance I write again about the Shields just to say that I prefer both Shields to be upright not the least aslant. Last night there was a beautifying fall of snow the first of the season – it is now melting away. The Thermometer at 64.' RTC [442Q]; H R/II/E/523. The engravings would be done by the firm of John and Richard Longman (see **3455**n3), of Waterloo Place, who on 12 March would submit a statement for £5.5.0 for 'Engraving Bookplate, Arms, 2 Shields, Crest, Coronet & Motto'. H A/V/G/(unnumbered).

2 The DS left for Hatfield on this day, Wednesday, but did not return until Saturday the 25th. H acc. See **3658**.

3 Lady Emma Talbot, Derby's only daughter, would give birth on 31 January to her first child, a son, at Derby's town residence, 23 St James's Square. *MP* (1 Feb 1862).

4 The Prince of Wales would go on the planned tour of the Holy Land. Longford *Victoria R.I.* 314.

5 By the following week the King of the Belgians had fully recovered from his 'severe cold'. *MP* (28 Jan 1862).

6 On 11 January, Vitzthum had recorded D's views on Albert's death: 'With Prince Albert we have buried our Sovereign. This German Prince has governed England for twenty-one years with a wisdom and energy such as none of our kings have ever shown. He was the permanent Private Secretary, the permanent Prime Minister of the Queen. If he had outlived some of our "old stagers," he would have given us, while retaining all constitutional guarantees, the blessings of absolute government. Of us younger men who are qualified to enter the Cabinet, there is not one who would not willingly have bowed to his experience. We are now in the midst of a change of government. What to-morrow will bring forth no man can tell. To-day we are sailing in the deepest gloom, with night and darkness all around us.' Vitzthum II 176. On the 23rd, Stanley also recorded D's remarks: 'He considers Albert's death as the commencement of a new reign: it is the destruction of that long-mediated plan of establishing court-influence on ruins of political party which the late Prince had for years been working out with perseverance equal to that of George the Third, and talent infinitely greater.' On 23 February he recorded D's further remarks: '"A few years more, and we should have had, in practice, an absolute monarchy: now all that is changed and we shall go back to the old thing – the Venetian constitution – a Doge."' *Disraeli, Derby* 182-3.

but what is taking place convinces me that the theme is beyond the domain of mere reasoning, however just and wise. The passions of the people are very high at the present moment, and if the Ministry chose to send 50,000 men to Canada they would be supported.

When our Colonial System was reconstructed, either the Colonies should have had direct representation, or the military prerogatives of the Crown should have been so secured that the faculty of self-defence in the Colonies should always have been considerable....[1]

3656 TO: SAMUEL WILBERFORCE Grosvenor Gate [Monday] 27 January 1862
ORIGINAL: BODL MS Wilberforce c13 ff124-5
EDITORIAL COMMENT: Black-edged paper.

The | Ld Bishop of Oxon Grosvenor Gate | Jan: 27. 1862

My dear Lord,

Your letter of the 21st. Inst.[1] only reached me last Saturday, at Hatfield.

I hope the banquet was successful, & can only regret, / that I had not the honor of being your guest.

I shall be glad to see you, & as soon as you like, about the Education Minute.[2]

Yours, my dear Lord, | sincerely, | *B. Disraeli*

1 For Adderley's pamphlet (*Letter to ... Disraeli ... on the Present Relations of England with the Colonies* ...), dedicated to D and sent to him in mid-December 1861, see **3615**n1 and **3653**&nn1&2. On Monday 20 January, Adderley had given a lecture on the value of the colonies in light of £4 million extra taxation for defence of Canada against possible North American aggression. He reviewed the evolution of colonial policy which had resulted in the colonies' governing themselves but being defended by British troops (Canada had recently refused to pass a militia bill). He argued that the colonies should be responsible for their own peacetime security, and that Britain and her colonies should assist each other militarily only in times of war. *The Times* (24 Jan 1862). Adderley would reply on 28 January: 'I am quite satisfied with the Pamphlet, as you consider it states the case clearly ... There is not a word in my Letter to you against sending 50,000 men to Canada when threatened, if we have them to spare: & getting men from Canada when we want help: but only that each should keep the peace for themselves in ordinary times. The Country certainly has not yet opened its eyes to the existing state of things, but by the Press all over the kingdom one sees the subject is being taken up.' He would write again on 4 February: 'E. Ellice requests me to forward the enclosed letter to you ... He hopes you will talk over its contents with Lord Derby, as he thinks instant action necessary. His chief fear relates to the growing colonial appetite for loans & debts & taxing our trade to meet them. His proposition to use the Crown veto more largely seems to me mad: and his idea that there is no alternative but separation.' H B/XXI/A/78-9a. See further **3700**&n2.

---

1 Wilberforce had written on 21 January: 'The Mayor & Corporation of Oxford dine with me on Thursday – the 23rd at 6. PM. They are as you probably know generally radicals – But we have this year a good Tory Mayor. If you could & would honour them by meeting (as some of our magnates generally do) I should be delighted'. H B/XXI/W/355.

2 Wilberforce (n1) had asked for 'a confidential conversation' on the implications of the new minute on Education. The former Conservative government's commission on education had submitted a report in 1861 on which the privy council committee on education had based a minute tabled by the current government in the previous session. The minute proposed that government grants to schools be more equitably distributed (for example, by number and attendance of students rather than quality of performance), and teachers be more stringently certified. The leading clergy opposed the minute, thinking it would damage elementary schools, training schools, and the pupil-teacher relationship. *The Times* (2, 17 Sept 1861). See further **3664**&n1, **3665**&n1 and **3666**&n1. On 4 March Wilberforce would lead the Lords' opposition to the code. *Hansard* CLXV cols 990-1007.

TO: EMILY CLUBBE Grosvenor Gate [Tuesday] 28 January 1862 3656A

ORIGINAL: RIC [014]
COVER: Mrs. Clubbe, | Vicarage, | Hughenden, | High Wycomb | *B Disraeli*
POSTMARKS: in circle: LONDON | 2 | JA 28 | 62; a cancelled one-penny stamp
EDITORIAL COMMENT: Black-edged envelope and paper. *Sic:* Wycomb.

Dear Mrs Clubbe, Grosvenor Gate | Jan: 28 1862

I fear you have embarked in a rather difficult undertaking, when I recollect the result of yr subscription for the amendment of / the Organ.[1] I doubt, whether an Harmonium of £25 even will fill our Church, from what people tell me. However, if you will forward me, at yr. convenience, your subscription list, when it is closed, I will give / it my best consideration.

We have been wandering about in extreme parts of the Kingdom, from Alnwick Castle to the Land's End, but are, at length, settled here for the season.[2] It will be / a sad one.[3]

Mrs Disraeli unites with me, in every kind wish to yourself, & Mr Clubbe.

Yours sincerely, | *B. Disraeli*

TO: GEORGE POTTS Grosvenor Gate [Wednesday] 29 January 1862 3657

ORIGINAL: QUA 111
EDITORIAL COMMENT: Black-edged paper. *Sic:* I. Potts.

I. Potts Esq | M.P. Grosvenor Gate | Jany. 29. 1862

Dear Sir,

I regret, that from my various movements, your letter, of the 31st. Ulto:, has not received a reply. I / conclude you have, ere this, forwarded the address, as is customary, to the Secretary of State.[1]

Believe me, dear Sir, | Very faithfully yours, | *B. Disraeli*

TO: SARAH BRYDGES WILLYAMS Grosvenor Gate [Wednesday] 29 January 1862 3658

ORIGINAL: RTC [194]
EDITORIAL COMMENT: There is no salutation.

Private Grosvenor Gate | Jan 29 1862

We were detained at Hatfield a day longer, than I expected, as Lord Derby came down on Friday, & I could not well leave the day he arrived. We had an agreeable

1 Mrs Clubbe had written on January 18 requesting D's financial support for the acquisition of a Harmonium 'to try & get our singing better which we find is impossible with a Barrel Organ ... we think of trying to get one of £20 or £25 as a small one would not be heard in our Church.' H B/XXI/C/286.
2 See **3625**&n4, **3628**&n2, **3633**&n1 and **3654**&n2.
3 Prince Albert had died on 14 December 1861.

1 George Potts (1807-1863), MP (L-C) for Barnstaple 1859-63, whose 31 December letter has not been found, would reply from Trafalgar House, Barnstaple, on 1 February: 'Your conjecture is quite right relative to the Address to Her Majesty – on receiving no reply from you and having occasion to go to Town, I left it with the Secretary of State.' H B/XIX/B/ADD [unnumbered]. Presumably the address was one of condolence to the Queen; Sir George Grey was secretary of state for the home department at this time.

party: Lord & Lady Verulam,[1] (he is the Ld. Lieutenant of Herts) Lord & Lady Edwin Hill,[2] / Sir William & Lady Jolliffe, & their daughters,[3] Lord Stanley, the Master of Lovat, the eldest son of Lord Lovat, a Roman Catholic & old Jacobite Peer, & whose eldest son bears this picturesque title:[4] a very handsome young man, tall, with a flowing beard, & a great sportsman. /

There was doubt, for some time, whether the Leaders of the Two Houses, & of the Opposition, were to give their parliamentary dinners at the opening, as usual; but the Queen has expressed her wish, that they shd. be given: so I have sent out my cards.[5]

I / saw the Herald on Monday, & gave him all yr criticisms, & expect every day a new & corrected drawing. He made a stand for the two shields being aslant, but I was firm.[6]

I hope yr domestic affairs are more tranquil; my public labors are commencing.

Yrs ever, | D.

3659 TO: SIR HENRY STRACEY — Grosvenor Gate [Friday] 31 January 1862

ORIGINAL: BUL L ADD 2555 f15s

EDITORIAL COMMENT: Black-edged paper; all the names in the letter have been partially cut out, but then superadded in another hand.

Sir Henry Stracey | Bart. M.P. — Grosvenor Gate | Jany. 31. 1862

Dear Sir Henry,

You have sent me a most welcome, & a most graceful, present; & I beg you will accept, for it, my / gratified thanks.

Great events have happened since we last met, & greater await us.

I hope Lady Stracey[1] is quite well. Pray, have the kindness to present my compliments to / her, & believe me,

Sincerely yours, | *B. Disraeli* /

1 Elizabeth Joanna Weyland (d 1886), daughter of Major Richard Weyland, in 1844 had married James Walter Grimston, since 1845 2nd Earl of Verulam.

2 Lord Arthur Edwin Hill (1819-1894), second surviving son of 3rd Marquess of Downshire, in 1858 had married secondly Hon Mary Catherine Curzon (1837-1911), daughter of Hon and Rev Alfred Curzon and sister of 4th Baron Scarsdale. Lord Edwin, who would add the surname of Trevor this year, was JP and DL for counties Denbigh, Down, Notts and Salop, major N Salop cavalry 1863, MP (C) for co Down 1845-80; he would be created Baron Trevor in 1880.

3 The Jolliffes had five surviving daughters, of whom the youngest two at this time were unmarried: Cecil Emily Jolliffe (d 1899), who in 1866 would marry 4th Earl of Sefton, and Mary Augusta Jolliffe (d 1925), who in 1865 would marry Edward Birkbeck, 1st baronet 1886.

4 Thomas Alexander Fraser (1802-1875), LL of Inverness-shire, Kt 1864, a descendant of 4th Baron Lovat, was nominally 12th Baron Lovat. Simon Fraser (1667?-1747), 11th Baron, had been executed for his part in the Jacobite rebellion of 1745-6 and the title forfeited until the death of his last attainted son in 1815; otherwise, the 12th Lord would have been 16th Baron Lovat. His eldest son and heir, Simon Fraser (1828-1887), styled Master of Lovat, would succeed his father as 13th Baron Lovat 1875, and be LL of Inverness-shire 1873, hon col 2nd battalion Queen's Own Cameron Highlanders, and ADC to Queen Victoria.

5 Derby in an undated note had written: 'Granville writes me word that the Parliamentary Dinners are to be given as usual.' H B/XX/S/310. See further **3661**&n2.

6 See **3654**&n1.

---

1 Charlotte Denne (d 1884), only daughter and heiress of George Denne, The Paddock, Canterbury, had married Sir Henry Stracey in 1835.

I proposed gold crowns to M of M five months ago – but he objected on the score of attrition, but surely anything is better than the present state of constant complaints.[2]

TO: JOHN FANE Grosvenor Gate [Saturday] 1 February 1862 3660

ORIGINAL: BODL MS Top Oxon b217 f114
EDITORIAL COMMENT: Black-edged paper.

Lt Col Fane | M.P. Grosvenor Gate | Feb 1. 1862

Dear Colonel Fane –

We heartily congratulate yourself, & Mrs. Fane, on your glorious victory![1] It will re-animate our friends / throughout the country.

I conclude you will take your seat on Thursday.

Yours very faithfully, | B. DISRAELI

TO: SARAH BRYDGES WILLYAMS [London, Tuesday] 4 February 1862 3661

ORIGINAL: RTC [195]
EDITORIAL COMMENT: There is no salutation.

I. Feb 4. 1862

Altho' I am at this moment very much engaged, I will not neglect our Herald. He protests against the ~~shi~~ coronet touching the shield, & does not value the authority of the seal, as, he says, the arrangement, there, arises from the contracted space, wh: rendered it necessary. However, as I can't understand, that any heraldic *principle* is / involved in the question, I shall leave you to decide; only, for the sake of symmetry, the coronet shd. perhaps balance the crest.[1]

I am now going to Lord Derby for a long conference, & have to see many other people: tomorrow is my parliamentary dinner, & on Thursday, the great game begins![2]

Yrs ever, | D.

2 The letter to which D is responding has not been found; Stracey presumably had an interest in currency matters, and 'M of M' is an abbreviation of 'Master of the Mint'. Thomas Graham (1805-1869), a chemist, FRS 1836, DCL (Oxford) 1853, FGS, was master of the mint 1855-69. On 31 August 1861, *The Times* had reprinted from the *Mechanics' Magazine* an item (often very funny) about Mint experiments on deterioration rates of different coins; gold coinage deteriorated much more slowly than the others. A crown = 5 shillings.

---

1 See **3649**&n2; Fane would take the oath on the opening of parliament, Thursday 6 February. *MP* (7 Feb 1862).

---

1 See **3658**&n6. SBW would reply on 5 February: 'I write gratefully to thank you for your most kind Letter enclosing an improved sketch. If our Herald "protests against Coronets touching the shield" he protests against all the precedents without exception in Lodge's Peerage and Elements of Heraldry[.] Perhaps it may be a heraldic distinction that when a Coronet touches the shield it denotes the side the shield belongs to and when otherwise that it is a meer Crest[.] The arms are beautifully sketched I shd be very glad for the Engraver to define in the best manner the *winged arm* that holds the sword. I shall look out for all your fine speeches!' RTC [444Q]. See further **3666**&n2.

2 D's parliamentary dinner on 5 February before the opening of parliament on the 6th is described by MA on the 3rd: 'Eighten only are invited, as the larger dinners, when we have them in the drawing rooms, give me so much trouble & makes the house so uncomfortable & every thing must be moved to make room for 40

3662 TO: SIR CHARLES PHIPPS Grosvenor Gate [Sunday] 9 February 1862

ORIGINAL: RAC R2 105

PUBLICATION HISTORY: M&B IV 385, dated at Grosvenor Gate, 9 February 1862, with minor alterations; Weintraub *Disraeli* 388, dated 9 February 1862, the second paragraph

EDITORIAL COMMENT: Black-edged paper.

Grosvenor Gate | Feby. 9. 1862

The Honble | Sir Charles Phipps | K.C.B.

Dear Sir Charles,

Lord Derby has communicated to me the gracious expressions of Her Majesty, & I should feel, obliged to you, if the opportunity offer, to lay, before / Her Majesty, my humble & dutiful acknowledgements.

What I attempted to express on Thursday night, I deeply felt. During those conversations, with which, of late years, the Prince occasionally honored / me, I acquired much, both in knowledge & in feeling, wh: will ever influence my life.[1]

Believe me, | dear Sir Charles, | Very faithfully Yours | *B. Disraeli*

3663 TO: SIR WILLIAM JOLLIFFE [London, Wednesday] 12 February 1862

ORIGINAL: ATM [1]

PUBLICATION HISTORY: *Autographic Mirror* I (1864) 4 (MS facsimile).

The Right Honble | Sir Wm. Jolliffe. M.P Feb: 12 1862

My dear Jolliffe,

Be so kind as to call on me before the House meets today.[1]

Yours sincerely, | *B. Disraeli*

people at dinner.' RTC [443Q]. Sir John Trollope and Col Taylor were prevented by illness from attending. H acc; *MP* (6 Feb 1862). Northcote would comment on 6 February: 'Dizzy has set up a small peaked beard. He was in high spirits. The Queen's speech has less in it than usual, and I suppose there will be scarcely anything said tonight except in the way of condolence.' Northcote I 185. See further **3662**n1.

1 On Thursday 6 February in the debate on the address in response to the speech from the throne (it having been decided from precedent not to have a separate address of condolence to the Queen), D had concluded his speech with an eloquent panegyric to the late Prince: 'this, at least, posterity must admit, that he heightened the intellectual and moral standard of this country; that he extended and expanded the sympathies of classes; and that he most beneficially and intimately adapted to the productive powers of England the inexhaustible resources of science and art ... the country is as heart-stricken as its Queen. Yet in the mutual sensibility of a Sovereign and a people there is something ennobling – something which elevates the spirit beyond the level of mere earthly sorrow.' *Hansard* CLXV cols 64-71. Derby had written on 'Saturday night' about a letter from Phipps that ended: '"The Queen would be glad that Mr. Disraeli should ... be made aware of H.M's grateful sense of his testimony to the worth and character of the Prince ..." I think you had better send to Phipps, as I shall do, your acknowledgements for H.M's gracious acceptance'. H B/XX/S/294. See further **3667**&n2. Sir Charles Beaumont Phipps (1801-1866), second son of 1st Earl of Mulgrave, lieut-col Scots fusilier guards 1837, CB 1853, KCB 1858, equerry to the Queen 1846, private secretary (subsequently treasurer) to the Prince Consort 1847, keeper of the Queen's privy purse and cofferer to the Prince of Wales 1849, would be made receiver-general of the duchy of Cornwall in May 1862, one of the council to the Prince of Wales 1863, secretary to the Prince of Wales 1864. On 10 February, MA would send SBW clippings of D's speech from the *Evening Star and Dial* (7 Feb 1862) and the *Observer* (9 Feb 1862). RTC [455-457Q].

1 The House on this day met for only half an hour, at noon. *Hansard* CLXV col 169. There is no extant response from Jolliffe. Incidentally, D on this day (12 February) was elected a governor of Wellington College, as Talbot would inform him the next day. H B/XXI/T/39.

TO: SIR EDWARD BULWER LYTTON — Grosvenor Gate [Wednesday] 12 February [1862] 3664

ORIGINAL: HCR D/EK C5 [21]
EDITORIAL COMMENT: *Dating:* see n1. *Sic:* 1863.

Rt Honble | Sir Ed: Lytton — Grosvenor Gate | Feb 12 1863

Dear Bulwer,

There is a Council, on the Education Min:, at Ld. Derby's on / Friday morning, at 12 o'ck – wh: you should attend, if you be in town.[1]

Yours ever, | D.

TO: SIR WILLIAM JOLLIFFE — [London] Monday 17 February 1862 3665

ORIGINAL: SCR DD/HY C/2165 [63]
EDITORIAL COMMENT: Black-edged paper.

Rt Honble | Sir W.H. Jolliffe — Monday. Feb. 17 | 62

My dear Jolliffe,

There is a council at Ld. Derby's on Wednesday at eleven o'ck. If, by any chance, you are in town, / it would be most desirable you should attend it. Again on Education, on wh: we met the other day, when, from an inadvertence, you were / unfortunately absent.[1]

Yrs ever | D.

TO: SARAH BRYDGES WILLYAMS — House of Commons [Monday] 24 February 1862 3666

ORIGINAL: RTC [196]
EDITORIAL COMMENT: House of Commons paper. There is no salutation.

Feby. 24 1862

I have been so much engaged with the new Education Code, & all the debates & divisions to wh: it will lead,[1] that I only cd. find time this morning to see how the / engraving was going on. It progresses very satisfactorily, & the *coronet rests upon the*

1 The '1863' in the text is unusually clear, but evidently should be 1862; the 'Friday morning' of Derby's council on the education minute was that of 14 February 1862; see **3665**n1. On 12 February 1863 D knew that Bulwer Lytton was at Nice; see **3784**n1.

1 Derby had written to D on 10 February to arrange a noon meeting on Friday the 14th, if Lowe presented the revised education code (see **3656**n2) on the 13th as scheduled. When Lowe did present the education minute and tabled the papers pertaining to the revised code (printed copies would be presented to parliament on the 18th), D protested that such a presentation precluded adequate scrutiny of what was in effect a revision of the revised code of the previous year. *Hansard* CLXV cols 191-257 (D 242-9); *MP* (19 Feb 1862). Derby would write again, on 18 February, about 'the Education question ... it strikes me that a motion, or a notice, limited to a single point, will have more the effect of an attempt to obtain a party division, than to co-operate in improving the government measure ... I have therefore drawn up five resolutions, including that on which we agreed, which I shall be prepared to submit to the meeting tomorrow.' H B/XX/S/295-6. See further **3668**&n2.

1 See **3656**&n2 and **3665**&n1. The education code would next be debated on 27 February; see **3668**&n2.

shield, as you wished. I found no principle of sound heraldry offended by the arrangement, but the reverse, & so was positive in my orders. /

We agreed, when we talked over the matter last, that there shd. be no name or initials under the arms. But you are quite in time to have them inserted, if you wish.[2]

Confidential

~~The~~ I have received a most gracious communication / from Her Majesty, expressing her "*grateful sense*" of what I said in the House of Commons respecting the Prince – & with many compliments.[3]

I hope you are quite well[.] We have not received any Torquay telegrams of late.[4] I hope you will be able to decypher this – but it is written in my place, on my hat: not a very good desk.

Yrs ever, | D.

3667 TO: [SIR CHARLES PHIPPS] [Grosvenor Gate, Tuesday] 25 February 1862

ORIGINAL: H B/XIX/A/22[a]

EDITORIAL COMMENT: A draft in D's hand.

---

another[1] in reply to receiving the portraits.[2] Feb. 25. 1862

Dr Sir Chas –

I have received the hallowed gift.

The portraits will be placed in the room in wh: I am now writing, & amid the turmoils of pol[itica]l life, they will sustain, & elevate, my sense of duty.

Yrs &c.

2 See **3661**&n1; see further **3669**&n2.

3 See **3662**n1.

4 MA on the 26th would write to SBW: 'I hope you are well, quite well, and have not the Influenza ... We have escaped as yet'. She invited SBW to visit: 'I will take such care of you, as much as I do of Dizzy'. SBW would reply on the 28th: 'I have been confined to my Room a long time by the effects of a horrid cold though I am convalescent my Head is unfit to guide my pen to express my grateful thanks for all your kindness and your tempting invitation with all its attractions I must not think of but I always keep in view the delight of seeing you and dear Dizzi some future happy day.' RTC [445-6Q].

---

1 See **3662**&n1.

2 MA next day (26th) would write to SBW: 'The Queen has sent Dizzy two engravings from the famous portraits, of herself & the Prince, by Winterhalter, as large as life.' On 3 March she would write again: 'I am going to look for some pretty frames, for the 2 beautiful, interesting engraving[s] her Majesty has given Dizzy. I shall order the frames – oval and with a Crown on the top.' RTC [445Q, 447Q]. On 27 May she would pay John and William Vokins, carvers and gilders, 14 Great Portland Street, £7 for '2 frames, with true lovers knot The Queen & late Prince Consort Given by her Majesty to Dizy.' H acc. Winterhalter had painted portraits of the royal family at regular intervals since 1842; his 1843 portrait of the Queen was Albert's favourite; his 1859 portrait shows the Prince in uniform as colonel of the Rifle Brigade. The two copies presented by the Queen are now in the South Bedroom at Hughenden, shoulder-length signed lithographs, 35" by 52", in twin oval frames joined by a gilt ribbon and surmounted by crowns. Hughenden Inventory number NT/HUG/D/110. Information kindly supplied by Jessie Binns, Community Learning Officer, Hughenden Manor. See illustration p lvi.

TO: LORD JOHN MANNERS Grosvenor Gate [Wednesday] 5 March 1862 3668

ORIGINAL: BEA [085]

EDITORIAL COMMENT: Black-edged paper. *Sic:* Kaye; cadeaus.

Rt Honble | Lord John Manners Grosvenor Gate | March 5 1862

My dear J.M.

It was very considerate in you to send me a line about our dear friend.[1] Pray offer him / my kind regards & best wishes.

At four o'ck today, we have a council on the Resolutions.[2] Kaye Shuttleworth is to be there.[3] We shall miss you. I hope they will confine them to / the critical & condemnatory character.

Our friend, Lady Jersey, has returned: I have not seen her. Yesterday, was her birthday, & Henry Lennox says she was sitting / before a table covered with cadeaus & bouquets! Pleasant in her 77th. year! H.L. wisely confined himself to a letter of congratulation, eno' in an age of war taxes.[4]

Yrs ever, | D.

TO: SARAH BRYDGES WILLYAMS Grosvenor Gate [Thursday] 6 March 1862 3669

ORIGINAL: RTC [197]

EDITORIAL COMMENT: There is no salutation. *Sic:* Wycomb [*twice*]; Carington.

Grosvenor Gate | Mar: 6. 1862

It gave me great pleasure to see your hand-writing again.[1]

1 Manners's brother, the Duke of Rutland, had been severely injured when his horse fell on him, 'causing concussion of the brain, and, it was feared, injury to the spine.' *BH* (8 Mar 1862). Manners had written on 3 March from Belvoir Castle: 'You will, I know, be glad to hear that although my brother is now suffering from a severe attack of gout, consequent upon the fall, the doctors are confident that no permanent mischief will result from the accident ... It was a most providential escape. I propose remaining here till Monday next.' H B/XX/M/120.

2 See **3665**&n1. On 11 March in the House, Walpole would table eleven resolutions critical of the government's proposed changes to the education code (*eg,* opposition to payments based exclusively on tests of reading, writing and arithmetic, and to grouping by age, detrimental to those with poor early education). These would be debated on 25 and 27 March on Walpole's motion that the House go into committee to consider the best distribution of education grants. After Easter the government announced the concessions it was willing to make (*eg,* grants based on attendance as well as tests); on 5 May Walpole declared himself satisfied, and withdrew the resolutions. *Hansard* CLXVI cols 21-106, 137-250, 323, 1204-77. See further **3678**&n1.

3 Sir James Phillips Kay-Shuttleworth (1804-1877), 1st Bt (1849), who had assumed the additional name of Shuttleworth on his marriage in 1842, MD (Edinburgh) 1827, JP and DL for Lancashire, high sheriff 1863, was the 'founder of the English system of popular education' (*DNB*); first secretary to the privy council committee on education 1839-49; joint-founder of Battersea training college for pupil-teachers 1839-40; novelist and writer on medical and education topics; in 1862 he published *Four Periods of Public Education, as reviewed in 1832, 1839, 1846, and 1862.* He would write to D on 25 and 31 March with advice and information to assist in opposing the code. H B/XXI/S/200-1.

4 On 7 April D would attack the government's expenditure, notably the continuation of war taxes on income, sugar and tea. See **3674**n2 and **3675**&n1. For treatments of the attack, see Blake 428 and M&B IV 305*ff.* In January Count Vitzthum had commented that the outlay for arms in preparation for war with America was estimated at £5 million. Vitzthum II 177.

---

1 For SBW's most recent letter, to MA on 28 February, see **3666**n4; MA had acknowledged it on 3 March: 'It made me very happy to see your hand writing again'. RTC [446-7Q].

I enclose a proof. It seems well done. You are, however, yet in time to make observations. How many / impressions shall I send you?[2]

The day before yesterday, I sent you a leash of golden plovers – the greatest delicacy of this season. They suit the palate after a bad cold / – as well as Oliver's biscuits, wh: are famous.[3]

I am going down today to Wycomb Abbey, to dine with my Lord Lieutenant, ~~at Wycomb Abbey~~ ↑Lord Carington↓, to meet Her Majesty's Judges of Assize.[4] I shall / sleep at the Abbey, & return to town early tomorrow morning, not even seeing Hughenden, tho' I am in sight of its woods & the House is only two miles from the Abbey.

Yours ever, | D.

3670 TO: LORD DERBY House of Commons, Thursday [13 March 1862]

ORIGINAL: DBP Box 146/1

EDITORIAL COMMENT: Black-edged House of Commons paper. There is no salutation. Endorsed by Derby at the top of the first page: 'Disraeli B.' *Dating:* by context; see n1. *Sic:* Wycomb; Carington; *330* votes.

Private Thursday

My agent has just come up from Wycomb with *very good accounts.*[1]

Lord / Carington's tenants are all for Lochiel, & actively working for him – & every person, that I / can influence, responded instantly. Our man is the popular candidate, &, at the end of the first days canvass, had 127 promises. / There are

2 See **3666**&n2. SBW would reply next day (7 March): 'How much I have always to be thankful and grateful to you I can never express I must therefore trust to your own fine fertile imagination[.] The Proofs inclosed in your Letter are beautiful I may observe on the Crest of the Willyamses shield whether the Bird intended to be a Martin is not more like an Eagle and I *particularly prefer the shield without scroll and motto,* this is easily omitted. The M. D C's shield is complete infinite thanks to you for its restoration I shd like about 40 impressions of Bookplates'. RTC [448Q]. See further **3673**.

3 SBW (n2) would acknowledge receiving 'a Leash of most delicious golden Plovers they were a feast for days to me and a Box of most delicate Biscuits. I ventured to send in the returned Hamper a taste of ~~Oliver~~ Osborne biscuits and Devonshire Cream for Coffee this you may laugh at[.] I am very sorry I have been obliged to give up gardening and have no longer the pleasure of cultivating early moss roses to send to Grosvenor Gate'. MA recorded the 'Hamper to Torquay, biscuits & 3 golden plovers 1/8d'. H acc. Bath Olivers, easily digested biscuits developed at Bath for his patients by Dr William Oliver in the eighteenth century, are still sold. Osborne biscuits were first made in 1860.

4 The Bucks Lent Assizes were opened this day (6 March) by Chief Baron Pollock, Baron Martin also presiding. *BH* (8, 15 Mar 1862).

---

1 At the Wycombe by-election on 18 March 1862 after the death of Sir George Dashwood (L), John R. Mills (L) would defeat Donald Cameron of Lochiel (C) 220-150; an independent candidate would receive one vote. George Vernon, the Hughenden estate agent (see V **1776**&n1), had evidently reported to D as he had to Rose, who on this day (the 13th) wrote: 'Vernon has been here this morning and tells me that Cameron is going ahead most surprisingly – that Lord C[arrington]'s interest is being openly exerted for him that is to say, that all Lord Cs tenants are in his favor and are actively working for him – which has proved to the Wycombe people that neutrality at the Abbey is all moonshine ... Would it do good for you to see Lord C. and talk over matters with him. A little money would make the result *quite secure.*' H R/I/B/83. Also on this day, James Disraeli wrote to MA with astonished approval of Cameron's letter just received, thinking he could 'win the election or nearly so if the abbey will come out.' H/D/III/B/65. However, on 17 March Rose would write from Wycombe: 'I have just completed *my* examination of the lists and am satisfied that Cameron cannot win & will probably lose by from 30 to 50 votes – but I will do my best to reduce this majority.' H R/I/B/84.

only *330* votes – & there are many yet to visit. I have sent a man down this evening, & everything is put in action, wh: is possible, or impossible.

Yrs ever | D.

TO: LORD DERBY Grosvenor Gate [Sunday] 16 March 1862 **3671**

ORIGINAL: DBP Box 146/1

EDITORIAL COMMENT: Paper imprinted 'Grosvenor Gate'. Endorsed by Derby on the last page: 'Disraeli B.'

Private March 16 1862

Rt Honble | The Earl of Derby | K.G

My dear Lord,

If the issue were as clear & simple, as you have placed it – one between the maintenance of our naval power or our commercial interests, I don't / think, with the exception of some quakers, there cd. be two opinions among those worthy of being Englishmen. But, alas! I don't find it so simple, tho' I have thought of nothing else, since our last conversation.[1]

The / Paris Declaration has changed everything. Our mercantile naval service will follow the carrying trade, & if we are belligerent, will leave our shores. What becomes of our royal navy unless it is fed by the mercantile service? /

I shd. venture to come on to you, if I could – but I shall feel much obliged if you will see the bearer of this, Northcote, with whom I have considered the case in every way. By conferring with you, we may be able to shape something for tomorrow.[2]

Yrs ever | D.

1 On 11 March Horsfall had moved a resolution calling for the government to consider the unsatisfactory state of international maritime law; he thought the 1856 Paris declaration (prohibiting privateering and declaring blockades legal only if maintained by force) disadvantageous to British shipping and commerce, and argued that the prohibition should be extended to ships as well as to cargoes, that is, to all private property. Palmerston declared that the proposal would be fatal to the country's naval power, an act of political suicide. Further debate was postponed until 17 March. *Hansard* CLXV cols 1359-92. Derby had written to D from St James's Square on 15 March: 'Since I saw you, I have reflected much on Horsfall's motion; and the result is an earnest hope that you will not, in the debate, give any countenance whatever, not to the motion, which may be objected to on other grounds, but to the principle, which is sought to be inferred, of conceding what is left of our belligerent rights by the admission of the immunity of Enemies' Merchant Vessels. Palmerston did not use too strong an expression when he said that such a course would be suicidal to us as a maritime power ... True it is that the unhappy Paris conference has greatly weakened our Naval preponderance; but the country which has to trust for its commercial transactions exclusively to the intervention of neutrals, must be placed under a great disadvantage, and *some* at least of its interests must suffer to the extent of utter ruin. If we have allowed our arm to be weakened, that is no argument for cutting it off. No doubt, those who look *only* to the extension of Commerce, and whose private interests are directly involved, naturally desire to see removed every obstacle whether in peace or in war; but we are bound to look to higher objects still; and I earnestly entreat you, not, in deference to the short sighted views of interested parties, to do, or consent to, or encourage, any thing which may tend to lower the position, and diminish the Power of the Country, or to reduce the relative importance of that arm in which we are the strongest ... I write earnestly, because plausible arguments will no doubt be brought forward in quarters commanding considerable influence, and because I thought, when we talked the matter over, you were rather taken with the ad captandum [*for the sake of pleasing*] case. I hope, and believe, from his language the other day, that Palmerston will speak out – if he does, I hope you will stoutly support him, but whether he does or not, that *we* shall strenuously support the line which is in perfect consistency with our own course in 1856, and maintain the Naval power, even in preference to the Commercial interests of the Country.' H B/XX/S/297.

2 Derby replied on 'Sunday Night ... I am sorry to hear that you are suffering from incipient Influenza which however I hope may not keep you from the House tomorrow. I have had a long talk with North-

3672 TO: LORD DERBY Grosvenor Gate [Monday] 17 March 1862

ORIGINAL: DBP Box 146/1

EDITORIAL COMMENT: Paper imprinted 'Grosvenor Gate'. Endorsed by Derby on the last page: 'Disraeli B'.

Rt Honble | The Earl of Derby | K G. March 17 1862

My dear Lord,

I am going down to the House, & you may rely upon it – that I will do my best to effect your wishes.[1] It is difficult, however, to / take a high tone, when one is in a low position – as we have been placed by the Declaration of Paris.

I have got Palm'ns speech at Liverpool,[2] wh: he travelled 200 miles to deliver, & will / do my best to pull his skin off, if he indulges in a leonine bray.

I will impress upon Northcote not even contingently to contemplate the possibility of having to adopt the / Horsfall policy.[3]

Yours ever sincerely, | D.

cote today, which however ended, I fear, in neither of us being convinced by the arguments of the other. I have acquiesced in the line he proposes to take, in following Cobden, and urging the withdrawal of the motion; but I own I greatly regret that a higher line should not be taken, and I hope that too much encouragement may not be given to the principle involved in Horsfall's motion, even if the objection to it be confined to the ulterior consequences into which it may lead us. The more I reflect upon it, the more I feel the injury done to our highest interests by the insane concessions made at the conference of Paris; and it *is* a trial to political patience to hear the Minister who was the Head of the Government when they were made, and who in a Speech at (or a letter to?) Liverpool expressed a hope that they might be carried farther, and even go beyond the scope of Horsfall's motion, now coming forward to shout "Rule Britannia," and talking of the "political suicide" which he, of all men, had most to do with originating, and in part perpetrating. Still I hold to my doctrine, concede no more! Northcote was obliged to admit that if Horsfall's principle was carried, the Naval Service would be powerless for aggression, and useful only for defence. If so, what would be our position if engaged in a war with a merely continental power? we might, at great expense, defend ourselves; but we should be powerless to strike a single blow! Can this be a position in which England should be placed, by the act of her own Government!' H B/XX/S/304. See further **3672**&n3.

1 See **3671**n2.

2 At Liverpool Town Hall on 7 November 1856, Palmerston had conveyed the government's gratitude for Liverpool's supportive role with shipping and commerce in the recent war: 'It has been a subject of great satisfaction to us to reflect that, at the commencement of the conflict, we, the Government of England, in concert with that of France, made changes and relaxations in the existing laws of war, which, without in any degree impairing the power of opponents – the power of belligerents against their opponents – humanised the course of hostilities, and tended to mitigate the pressure which hostilities inevitably produce upon the commercial transactions of the countries that are at war. (Hear, hear.) I cannot help hoping that these relaxations of former doctrines which were established in the beginning of the war in practice, and which have been consigned at the peace to formal engagements, may perhaps still further be extended, and that in the course of time those principles of war which are applied to hostilities by land may be extended, without exception, to hostilities by sea, and that private property may no longer be an object of aggression on either side. (Hear, hear.)' *MP* (8 Nov 1856).

3 In the resumed debate on this day (the 17th), Northcote would vaguely oppose Horsfall's motion while hoping that a full discussion of the Paris Declaration would not be swept aside; D would conclude the discussion with a strong rejection of the motion, using Derby's argument that it would reduce the navy's role solely to a defensive one. In response to Palmerston's claim that he supported the Paris Declaration but not Horsfall's motion, he cited the Liverpool speech in which, he said, Palmerston had recommended the policy that he now called suicidal. Horsfall then withdrew the motion. *Hansard* CLXV cols 1599-1706.

TO: SARAH BRYDGES WILLYAMS — Grosvenor Gate [Thursday] 20 March 1862 — 3673

ORIGINAL: RTC [198]
PUBLICATION HISTORY: Blake 417, mentioned, dated 20 March 1862
EDITORIAL COMMENT: There is no salutation. *Sic:* belted [*for 'belled'*]; this matters.

Grosvenor Gate | Mar. 20 1862

By this post, you will receive a packet of impressions of your arms, now completed.[1]

I trust they will please you. They appear to me to be as beautifully, as they are accurately, represented.

In consequence of your startling announcement respecting the supposed error in the B.W. crest, I / went, myself, to the Earl Marshal's Office, & made a research in the College as to the point.[2] I found there the arms of

Willyams of Carnanton

duly registered, & the *crest* is thus described

"on a ducal Coronet *or*, a falcon cl: ppr: belted *or*"[3] /

There can be no doubt, therefore of the perfect accuracy of the emblazonment. Had there been an error, I shd. have ordered another plate to be engraved, for, ~~th~~ after the immense care & trouble, which have [been] taken in this matters, ambassadors & ministers of State having interfered in the business, & the private cabinet of the / Queen of Spain having been laid under contribution; & considering the great personal interest, which you take in the matter, an imperfect, or inaccurate, representation would have been highly mortifying to me.

I hope you continue gaining health & strength after your cold, wh: is very prevalent in London, & I have a touch myself of Influenza.[4]

Ever yrs, | D.

1 See **3669**&n2.

2 The Office of the Earl Marshal (since 1860 the 15th Duke of Norfolk (1847-1917), hereditary holder), College of Arms, at Bennet's Hill, Doctors' Commons EC, was open daily 10-4. *LPOD* (1860).

3 The current Willyams of Carnanton was SBW's brother-in-law, Humphry Willyams (1792-1872), JP and DL for Cornwall, deputy-warden of the Stannaries of Devon and Cornwall, major of the Cornwall Miners' Militia, Liberal MP for Truro 1849-52.

4 For D's 'incipient Influenza' see **3671**n2. MA had received two recent reports from an acquaintance of SBW, first said to have '"*a horrid cold & her first attack of Bronchitis*"', but later to be '*better* tho' immovable on the subject of a doctor – her theory I believe is that nobody need die before *100* provided they take care of themselves & *avoid* doctors'. RTC [491-2Q]. In an undated fragment, she would enclose the menu for D's political dinner on 22 March, and an invitation from Mr and Mrs Samuel Gurney for 26 March to mark the telegraph line between Ireland and Newfoundland which promised telegraph communications throughout the evening between England and Egypt, Africa, etc.: 'Tea and Coffee at 9 o'clock. Conversation and Electric Correspondence from 10 to 12 o'clock.' For SBW's amusement she also enclosed a card from an American, Cyrus W. Field of New York, which she thought looked 'so American'. RTC [451-2Q]. SBW would respond on 23 March: 'I never can sufficiently express my sense of your great kindness and the advantage of your great interest and researches for the beautiful and accurate completion of the Arms for my Book plates and which has highly enhanced their value. I hope you defeat the uncomfortable effect of this prolonged winter. I am trying what I can do. In this day of wonders I wish some one would invent a machine to expel the carbonic acid from ones residence and introduce charming oxygen gas I am so fond of. You may laugh at the idea but I am really in earnest and would be glad indeed to contribute to a prize for such a blessing.' H R/II/E/539.

3674 TO: SIR JOHN PAKINGTON Grosvenor Gate [Tuesday] 6 April 1862

ORIGINAL: WRC 705:349 BA 3835/7(ii)16

EDITORIAL COMMENT: Paper imprinted 'Grosvenor Gate'. Endorsed in another hand on the fourth page: '1862 Disraeli'.

Rt Honble | Sir J. Pakington | G.C.B. April 6 1862

My dear Pn.

Did I understand you correctly, that we did not lay down any keel when we were in office 58-9, & / that the only ships we built were the iron ones – or one, I fear, as it turned out afterwards.[1]

Let me know tomorrow morning, as / I propose speaking on the Budget, the moment the Ho: meets.[2]

Yours sincerely, | D.

3675 TO: SARAH BRYDGES WILLYAMS Grosvenor Gate [Monday] 14 April 1862

ORIGINAL: RTC [199]

PUBLICATION HISTORY: M&B IV 307, dated at Grosvenor Gate, 14 April 1862, the first two paragraphs

EDITORIAL COMMENT: Paper imprinted 'Grosvenor Gate'. There is no salutation.

Private April 14 1862

The first portion of our Parliamentary campaign has closed, & it ended with a great financial duel.[1] I believe there is no doubt who was the conqueror. In fact, the circumstances were so grave & strong, that they had only to be put powerfully, / & *clearly*, before the country to carry conviction.

Nevertheless, it has taken both the House of Commons & the kingdom by surprise. They had heard so much, & so long, of financial skill & prosperity, that when the balance sheet was fairly put before them, all were as surprised & startled, as / if

1 See VII **3213**nn1&8.

2 Pakington would reply on 7 April: 'You must not infer from what I told you the other evening, that we were in /59 so convinced of the importance of iron cased ships (then wholly untried except as batteries) that we did not contemplate any more wooden ships ... As a fact, I do not think any keel was laid while we were in Office, though I am not quite sure about the "Royal Oak" – now being converted into an iron frigate ... We may fairly claim *both* the Iron ships (Warrior & Black Prince) although I resigned before I had contracted for building the latter.' H B/XX/P/66. That evening in the House, contending that Gladstone's budget misrepresented the country's critical financial position, D would refer to Sir S.M. Peto's 3 April charge that, after France had decided to build no more wooden ships, Britain had spent £11 million on new wooden ships: 'All I have to say is, that though the expenditure which was recommended by the late Government with respect to the navy, and which was entirely sanctioned by the House and by the public opinon of the country, was so great, if I am not mistaken, that charge does not apply to us. If I am not mistaken, during that great process not a single new keel was laid down by the late administration. They built new ships: for they built two iron ships, the money for defraying the cost of which appeared in the Estimates.' *Hansard* CLXVI cols 639-55 (quoted at 643). See further **3682**&n4.

---

1 On 3 April Gladstone had made his financial statement for 1862, in effect admitting a substantial deficit although trying to present it as a slight surplus, for which he primarily blamed the American civil war. D on 7 April (see **3674**&n2) called Gladstone's figures miscalculations based on incorrect projections coupled with various manipulations (such as the continued war taxes on income, tea and sugar) to disguise the alarming financial position of the country. *Hansard* CLXVI cols 446-92, 512-16, 639-55. For a discussion of the debate, with an extract from D's speech, see M&B IV 305ff. The debate on the budget details had continued in committee until the House adjourned on 11 April until 28 April for the Easter recess.

Baring, or Rothschild, had failed. It was a *coup* d'etat – & nobody talks of anything else. ~~Itw~~ It will influence events, tho,' myself, I trust the tottering government will still totter on.

I have not seen the Sun this year – & yesterday, the 13th. April, we had snow! I am very well, & content – still, / I can't help fancying the want of Sun must affect mind & body. The Italians say of a house, that "if the Sun does not enter it, death will" – & I feel↑, sometimes,↓ that our planet is changed, & that we are really dwellers in Saturn.

You, I hope, are well & bright in your bright & healthy scene.[2]

Ever, | D.

TO: THOMAS HANSARD Grosvenor Gate [Saturday] 19 April 1862 3676

ORIGINAL: ILLU XB B365b1 Cards 1,2
PUBLICATION HISTORY: Meynell II 452, dated at Grosvenor Gate, 19 April 1862
EDITORIAL COMMENT: Paper imprinted 'Grosvenor Gate'.

April 19. 1862

Mr Disraeli has received from Mr Hansard a proof of Debate of Mar: 18 on "Science, Art &c"[1] but he has not received any proof / of his speech in the preceding debate on Mr Horsfalls motion on Belligerent rights.[2]

Why is this?

This is important & must be immediately attended to.

TO: SARAH BRYDGES WILLYAMS House of Commons [Tuesday] 29 April 1862 3677

ORIGINAL: RTC [200]
EDITORIAL COMMENT: Black-edged House of Commons paper. There is no salutation.

Confidential 29 Apl. :62

I am much pleased with your idea.[1] I am not myself on the ~~Memorial~~ ↑Monument↓

2 SBW on 16 April would reply with good reports on her health, and continue: 'I am glad the stupid Government must see the impolasy of repealing the paper duty every one must see the selfish malignancy of the Times [leader on D's speech]. As to the Income Tax it is carried on in the most vexatious manner as I have proved to my annoyance perhaps you can enlighten me whether an Assessor has any right to assess my small House and garden at 130£ per an. when I pay annually a ground rent to Mr Cave so that I pay doubly and the duty demanded in advance'. RTC [459Q].

---

1 Lennox on 18 March had moved a resolution that a minister of the crown be responsible to the House for estimates for and expenditures by institutions promoting education, science, and art such as the British Museum and National Gallery. D argued that, in light of Gladstone's protests against allegations of mismanagement while admitting problems, it would be imprudent to press for a division even though he concurred generally with the resolution except for the British Museum. Lennox then withdrew the resolution. *Hansard* CLXV cols 1750-1802 (D 1795-1801).

2 See **3672**&n3. Earle on 9 April had compared press reports of D's 'magnificent' budget speech (see **3675**n1), finding *The Times* less than perfect but the *Daily News* & *Morning Post* 'better, – especially as regards yr. interruptions. It is so important that we must correct it carefully for Hansard.' H B/XX/E/245.

---

1 In a 'Confidential' letter of 27 April SBW had written: 'I have just thought of a memorial to our lamented Prince Consort which I believe he wd approve of, it is a grand impregnable Fortress or Fortification against invasion, may it not be popular and enlist support to a great extent? Will you give it your prescience and yr eloquence?' RTC [460Q].

Committee, but I shall mention it to Lord Derby.[2] He comes up to town this evening, but, so weak & unwell, that, I fear, he will not be able / to open the Exhibition on Thursday next: for opened it certainly will be, tho' in a very chaotic state. The French Court, for example, will not be ready for inspection, until the 1st. of June.[3] /

Yesterday, there was a great banquet at the Mansion House to the Foreign & Home Commissioners, & I was invited & attended. You will see about it in the "Times".[4]

This morning, we went to the rehearsal of the / Exhibition music, wh: took place at Exeter Hall.

There was a grand composition by Meyerbeer, wh: struck me as very fine.[5] At least, to my unlearned ears, it was very effective. This great genius was himself present, standing on the platform by the side of Costa, / who directed. Amid the crash of 600 Instruments, Costa, stamping, gesticulating, correcting &c. it was interesting to observe the *gran maestro* himself. He was quite unmovable, absorbed in the realisation of his wondrous ideas! A little man, very spare, but with a profound face. / He, like most celebrated composers, & even singers & musicians, is a child of the great House of Israel.[6]

I have got to walk in the opening procession on Thursday, which takes from me at this moment a precious morning, for great financial debates are / at hand, &, probably, will commence that very day.[7]

The Sun has also put out all our fires, but we defy carbonic acid gas,[8] for Hyde

2 Derby, along with Clarendon, Lord Mayor Cubitt and Sir Charles Eastlake, president of the Royal Academy, had been nominated by the Queen to an advisory committee for the Albert memorial; on 14 March they had heard reports on a monumental obelisk for which the Queen had expressed a desire. Donations to the Memorial Fund had been decreasing (total of £40,500 as of 14 March), the general opinion being that an obelisk would cost comparatively little. *MP* (10, 15 Mar 1862). See Weintraub *Victoria* 314.

3 On this day (the 29th) *The Times* reported on the International Exhibition, to open on Thursday 1 May: 'Already the arrangements, or rather disarrangements, in the order of the opening ceremonial, have begun'. Having on 23 April bemoaned the unpreparedness of the Austrian and French courts, it now disputed rumours that the Exhibition would be closed for a fortnight after the official opening for completion: 'The French Court is making immense progress towards final adjustment, and the other foreign countries are almost ready. The Roman Court is quite complete'. In the event, Derby did attend the opening, the French court was complete, but the Exhibition was declared open by the Queen's representative, the Duke of Cambridge. *The Times* (2 May 1862).

4 At the Lord Mayor's grand banquet at the Mansion House on 28 April, D had been the last speaker. In response to the toast to the commissioners of the 1851 Exhibition, he echoed the earlier speakers' regret at Albert's death and called the upcoming exhibition 'perhaps the best memorial' to him: 'Industry stimulated, invention refined, taste elevated are the due offerings we make to the memory of that serene and sagacious spirit.' *The Times* (29 Apr 1862).

5 The German composer Giacomo Meyerbeer (1791-1863), born Jakob, or Yaakov, Liebmann Beer, son of a Jewish banker, had written his *Ouverture en forme de Marche pour l'Inauguration de l'Exposition Universelle à Londres en 1862* in response to a request for a march; it comprised a 'Marche Triomphale', a 'Marche Religieuse' and a 'Pas Redoublé', this last incorporating strains of 'Rule Britannia' in a fugal treatment. *The Times* (30 Apr 1862).

6 Michael Costa (1810-1884), Kt 1869, conductor and composer born in Naples of Spanish ancestry, active in England since 1830, director of music at Covent Garden since 1846 and prominent in many musical endeavours, had conducted the 408-piece orchestra (148 violins!) with Meyerbeer himself superintending the rehearsal of his grand overture. *The Times* (30 Apr 1862).

7 The debate in committee on supply would resume on 2 May. *Hansard* CLXVI col 1188.

8 SBW (n1) had written: 'Thanks to the Sun for putting out my Fire I hope your fire has received the same attention and that you and dear Mrs Dizzi have with impunity braved the atmosphere of London, without

Park is bright with foliage, & Kensington Gardens gleam, in / the distance, like an enchanted forest.

Adieu! | D.

TO: LORD DERBY House of Commons [Friday] 2 May 1862 3678

ORIGINAL: DBP Box 146/1

EDITORIAL COMMENT: House of Commons paper.

Rt Honble | Earl of Derby | KG May 2. 1862

My dear Lord,

We have had our Council here on "Education" – & have come to, I / might say, a unanimous resolution, that it is impossible to move any further in the business:[1] so it will be quite unnecessary to trouble you / tomorrow, wh: I am glad of for yr sake.

I trust yesterday's exertion has done no harm.[2] I called to enquire, but would / not trespass on you.

They say Paris is much agitated about the Roman question:[3] the Empress of the French talks of leaving France with all the women of / distinction of all parties, if the Emperor yields: on the other hand, the Jacobinical quarter has offered the Emperor to massacre all the priests / in France, if he will give the word. The Emperor does not appear to have made up his mind.

This is the Bear's account – just returned.[4]

Yrs sincerely | D.

Leaves to absorb its carbonic acid gas.' Carbonic acid gas is more commonly known as carbon dioxide, absorbed by plants for nutrition.

---

1 Pakington had written to D on 1 May that he, Manners, Walpole, Henley and Estcourt had conferred 'behind the chair' that day on education and decided he should notify Palmerston next day of his request to postpone the debate scheduled for the 5th. 'I read my resolutions, but we did not, of course, in your & Lord Derby's absence, arrive at any final opinion upon them. We found however, that Henley & I have formed very much the same opinion as to the principal *objects* to which our attention should now be directed.' H B/XX/P/68. Evidently a second consultation decided them not to press the government for further changes to the revised education code (see **3665**n1 and **3666**&n1); on the 5th in committee on the bill, Walpole would open debate by declaring himself satisfied with the existing changes, and move a resolution (that tests not be the sole basis of funding), but that, to allow for other opinions to be expressed, he would not press to a division. Before the topic was dropped, both Henley and Pakington would ask how the scheme would reach the many poor children for whom there were no current provisions. *Hansard* CLXV cols 1204-77.

2 See **3677**&n3.

3 In the budget debate on 8 May (see **3680**&n3) D would analyse France's dilemma, what to do with the Pope if French troops were withdrawn from Rome in suppport of Italian unity. One prospect was to move the papacy to France or another Catholic country. D thought that what was important was not the Pope's temporal power, but his independence: 'the Emperor of the French ... knows that, whatever may happen, England and the world will never agree that the Pope should be permanently settled in France ... and he is also aware, that if the Pope were to be resident in any other Catholic State, great embarrassments to himself might be the result. His own influence ... might as a consequence be lessened, while that of another Sovereign might be proportionately increased.' *Hansard* CLXVII col 1419.

4 Edward 'Bear' Ellice's regular correspondent Prosper Merimée had written on 6 April to him in Paris: 'Le clergé catholique y a plus de dispositions qu'aucun autre, et notre église ci devant gallicane est devenue plus romaine que les Romains. Il est hors de doute que sans les excitations du clergé français la cour de Rome aurait transigé déjà avec Victor Emmanuel. Ici les masses sont violemment irritées contre les prêtres, et s'il y avait un mouvement je ne doute pas qu'il ne tournât contre eux.' Prosper Merimée *Lettres à Edward Ellice 1857–63* (Paris 1963) 67-70.

3679 TO: LORD ELMLEY [London, Friday] 9 May 1862

ORIGINAL: BCP [6]
EDITORIAL COMMENT: *Sic:* d'ouvre.

Visct Elmley | M.P. May 9 1862

My dearest Elmley,

I am glad to hear from Fred[1] good accounts of you – & continued good accounts. Be sure nothing / can give me greater happiness. How do you like Renan? No one ever touched the Semitic mysteries with a finer & deeper / appreciation, I think.

His "Etude" on the "Song of Solomon" is the most fascinating, & the most complete interpretation, in the world. It is a / chef d'ouvre.[2]

Yours ever, | D.

3680 TO: SARAH BRYDGES WILLYAMS House of Commons [Friday] 9 May 1862

ORIGINAL: RTC [201]
PUBLICATION HISTORY: Meynell II 461, undated extract; Weintraub *Disraeli* 394, undated extract
EDITORIAL COMMENT: House of Commons paper. There is no salutation. *Sic:* Chrystal.

May 9 1862

The papers have told you, that my life has not been inactive of late. What with opening the Exhibition, attending rehearsals of Meyerbeer & Auber & Sterndale Bennett,[1]

1 Frederick Lygon was Elmley's younger brother; both were Conservative MPS.

2 Ernest Renan (1823-1892), French philologist influenced by the German Higher Critics and best known for his *Vie de Jésus* (1863) (a copy of the 1864 eleventh edition is in the Hughenden Library), the first in his series on the *Histoire des origines du Christianisme* (1863-85) (copies of several in HL), and his five-volume *History of Israel* (1887-94). He had already published *Histoire générale et systèmes comparés des langues sémitiques* (1845) (copy of the second edition in HL), *De l'origine du langage* (1858), *Essais de morale et de critique* (1859), *Histoire générale des langues sémitiques* (1854), *Le livre de Job* (1858) (HL), and of Solomon (HL). Elmley would reply on 21 May from Madresfield: 'I have been laying [*sic*] in a most weak & prostrate state & really too unwell to write, or I should not have allowed so long a time to intervene without thanking you for yr kind remembrance of me. I cannot but feel much gratified in thinking that your thoughts should be diverted if only for a moment from yr. engrossing schemes of future empire to a sick, & absent friend ... Renan is charming – you must tell me when I see you in town some of his other works. I thought the 2nd essay in the vol you lent me much the best. I hope another week will enable me to get to town.' H B/XXI/L/425. Elmley may be referring to Renan's *Études d'histoire religieuse* (1857); the second essay examines the history of the Jewish people as recorded in Biblical sources, and argues its primacy as the source of monotheism. Renan's *Le Cantique des Cantiques traduit de l'hébreu, avec une étude sur le plan, l'age et le caractère du poème* (1860) argues (contrary to earlier studies) for the *Cantique*'s literary unity, as a dialogue divided into parts equivalent to scenes in a play and marked by recurring refrains.

---

1 See **3677**&nn5&6. The Exhibition commissioners had invited four composers, each regarded as the best from his respective country, to write for the exhibition: Meyerbeer for Germany, Auber (see III **1006n6**) for France, Verdi (Rossini having declined) for Italy, and William Sterndale Bennett (1816-1875, Kt 1871) for England. Verdi's *Inno Delle Nazioni,* for tenor, chorus and orchestra, arrived too late, the commissioners decided, for the opening and would be first performed on 24 May 1862. Auber's 'Grand Overture', *Marche triomphale pour l'Exposition universelle de Londres,* left Meyerbeer 'disheartened by the fact that Auber's *Exhibition March* is being played in many London concerts, and yet my overture [*Overture in the Form of a March*] is not.' Robert Ignatius Letellier, trans, ed, ann *Diaries of Giacomo Meyerbeer, Volume 4, The Last Years, 1857-1864* (Madison, WI 2004) 263 (9 June 1862). Bennett contributed his 'Ode for the Opening of the International Exhibition', a cantata setting of Tennyson's 'Ode ... Uplift a thousand voices' for choir

making speeches at / the Mansion House,[2] & carrying on a financial campaign in the House of Commons,[3] I have not been quite as idle, as I generally am at Mr Webbs Hotel.

The great Exhibition is not as fascinating a one, as that you remember; when / you made me an assignation by the Chrystal fountain, wh: I was ungallant enough ~~to~~ not to keep, being far away when it arrived at Grosvenor Gate. But tho' not so charming, it is even more wonderful. One was a woman; this is a man![4]

I / write this amidst the din of the House of Commons – but I thought you wd. like to hear I was alive, & I am delighted to have the opportunity of hoping you are quite well.

Yrs ever, | D.

TO: THOMAS HAMBER Grosvenor Gate, Tuesday 13 May [1862] 3681

ORIGINAL: BRN [68]
COVER: Mr. Hamber Esq | The Standard Office | 129 Fleet Street | D. | [*in another hand:*] M.P.
POSTMARK: LONDON | 5 | MY [*paper torn*] | 6 [*paper torn*]
EDITORIAL COMMENT: Paper imprinted 'Grosvenor Gate'. *Dating:* see n2. *Sic:* –61.

Private Tuesday May 13.

Thos: Hamber Esq[1]

My dr Sir,

I thought the notice very effective – & the retrenchment articles, both in H[*erald*] & S[*tandard*], very effective & apropos. Sir Stafford Northcote also / mentioned them to me, in the same feeling.

and orchestra of 2,400 (nearly 2,500 at the rehearsal D attended), also specially written and amended after Albert's death to include the lines 'O silent father of our Kings to be / ... For this, for all, we weep our thanks to thee!' *The Times* (30 Apr 1862).

2 See **3677**&n4. MA on 12 May would write to SBW: 'Dizzys reception at the Mansion House was enthusiastic, both before & after he spoke. You would be amused at the peoples anxiety to see him, when we walk about at the Exibition. Great numbers take off their hats.' RTC [461Q].

3 D had made his latest major speech in the budget debate (see also **3675**&n1) the night before (8 May) despite Derby's wishes; Derby had written on 'Sunday ... I find there is an expectation, I know not on what foundation, that there is to be another financial passage of arms between you and Gladstone on Thursday next. I hope you will find some means of postponing it, as it is really of consequence that the discussion (probably not a long one) on the Lancashire distress should not be postponed.' H B/XX/S/307. On 2 May Palmerston, replying to questions, said he was not sure of Gladstone's arrangements for proceeding with his budget, but promised that Lancashire distress would be discussed on the following Thursday or Friday; D and Gladstone had their encounter on Thursday 8 May, while distress in the manufacturing districts was discussed on this day, Friday 9 May. D had argued that the 'councils of Europe' consisted of England and France alone, and that, since their European objectives were the same, relations between the two were better served by co-operation than by immensely expensive increases in armaments ('the exercise of moral power'); he urged the government to adopt a policy of conciliation towards France, which would afford the taxpayer substantial relief. *Hansard* CLXVI cols 1130, 1361-1446 (D 1403-28, quoted at 1409-10, 1421), 1490-1522.

4 *Cf* VII **2883**&n2. Evidently D again recycled the trope; MA in her letter to SBW (n2) would write: 'There are some wonderful & most interesting things in the Exibition. D. says this one is the gentleman, the other the lady.'

---

1 Thomas Hamber (1828-1890?), of Islington, Middlesex, BA (Oriel College, Oxford) 1851, Lincoln's Inn 1854, was editor of the *Standard* 1857-70 (*MH* was a subsidiary of the *Standard*), and of the *Morning Advertiser* 1877-82. Foster; Koss *Political Press* 135, 183.

I shall be at your service tomorrow at 12. as you propose.[2]

Very flly. yrs. | D. /

The rumor, that there is to be an alliance, offensive & defensive, betn. France & Italy will, if realised, turn my speech of –61 into a prophecy![3]

3682 TO: LORD DERBY Grosvenor Gate [Wednesday] 21 May 1862

ORIGINAL: DBP Box 146/1

PUBLICATION HISTORY: M&B IV 308, dated at Grosvenor Gate, 21 May 1862, omitting the first two and the last paragraphs

EDITORIAL COMMENT: Paper imprinted 'Grosvenor Gate'. Endorsed by Derby on the last page: 'Disraeli B *Ansd'*. The catchword at the bottom of the first page is 'Navy', but on the next page the text resumes with 'Naval'; the former is given here.

Confidential May 21 1862

Rt Honble | The Earl of Derby | K G

My dear Lord,

Northcote finished his analysis of the Navy Estimates last night. He will, in due time, prepare a paper for you, wh: will place all the details at yr command.

This is the result of the analysis of the Military & Navy / estimates, that, witht. the slightest reduction of force, "you may be sure, that we can cut off a million & a half without any fear."

There is a Committee on Public accounts now sitting of wh: N. is a member.[1] This has greatly assisted him. The revelations before it are frightful, & prove that "the outlay on stores, during the last two or three years, has been perfectly reckless." / This Committee will of course report: Cobden is on it.

"Money voted for iron ships has been applied to all kinds of purposes"[.]

2 Hamber had written on 12 May: 'Perhaps you may like to see the Pamphlet in its complete form. I had a notice of it this morning which I trust you will like. I should be very glad to see you for a few minutes on Thursday morning and will take my chance by calling at about 12 oclock.' Presumably the notice was similar to that in *The Times* on 15 May: 'Now ready, price 1s ... Mr. Gladstone's Finance, from his accession to office in 1853 to his Budget of 1862. Reviewed by the Rt. Hon. B. Disraeli, M.P. London, Saunders, Otley, and Co'. On 27 May Hamber would write: 'I am still working the question of retrenchment in each paper by turns; I shall have a possible leader in tomorrow's Herald & two leaders in Friday's papers leading up to the discussion on Friday night.' On 4 June he would write again: 'My present intention is to proceed in the same track in both papers, still holding up retrenchment as the principle of the party.' H B/XX/A/82, 109, 110. A note from Earle dated only 'Wednesday' and referring to D's speech of '*Thursday*' states: 'I have found a line for reconciling our own swollen estimates with the policy of retrenchment, we are now to profess.' H B/XX/E/249.

3 D is presumably thinking of the interventions and speeches he made on 9 and 13 March 1860 on France's annexation of Savoy and Nice; he then identified France's motivation as the doctrine of empires having natural boundaries, countenancing which would be disastrous: 'if that principle of natural boundaries of empires now to be countenanced by, as I believe, the certain annexation of Savoy and Nice be realized; if distrust and despair be spread throughout Europe; if there be scenes of horror and sanguinary war; if empires be overthrown and dynasties subverted – then I say it is the Minister, it is the Government, who assisted that policy who will be responsible to their country and to history for those calamitous results.' *Hansard* CLVII cols 289-309, 490-504 (quoted at 503-4).

---

1 Northcote, along with Cobden and Walpole, was on the committee on public accounts appointed on 3 April, it having been decided earlier in the session that it would henceforth be a standing committee with nine members appointed at the start of each session. *Hansard* CLXV cols 1025-7, CLXVI cols 528-31. D is presumably quoting from Northcote's preliminary report (not found) to him; *cf* **3684**.

The general conclusion is, that the "enormous expenditure has outgrown all control".[2] The report of this Committee will in all probability greatly affect public opinion, & will prove the wisdom, I think, especially / when connected with a falling revenue, of the position wh: we have assumed, & wh: Gladstone had his eye on.[3]

I do not mean by these, somewhat hurried, observations to say, that I think the amount of our force ought not to be considered – but that is too grave a question for this sort of communication.[4]

Yrs sincerely, | D.

TO: PHILIP ROSE | Grosvenor Gate [Wednesday] 21 May 1862 | 3683

ORIGINAL: H R/I/A/147

EDITORIAL COMMENT: Paper imprinted 'Grosvenor Gate'.

Private & C. May 21 1862

My dear Rose,

Enclosed is a letter for Mr Montagu,[1] informing him, that I have proposed, & Mr Ernest Duncombe seconded, him for the Carlton. Will you forward it?

With reference to the point you mentioned yesterday in regard to the 20., what was wanted was 19 – for *two* businesses – the first *10* is of old date, guarded by insurances, on wh: the premiums for the year are now paid. Any delay in their respect is of no importance, comparatively speaking. The *9* is modern, & not secured except by a high rate, / & as well as for that, & for other reasons, it wd be of importance to conclude it.

Would it be practicable to get a temporary advance, in this respect, in anticipation of the larger, & permanent, arrangement?[2]

You see the point?

Yours ever | D.

2 This had been one of D's themes in the speech on 19 May in which he argued that increased expenditure did not necessarily mean increased security. *Hansard* CLXVI cols 1863-84.

3 The first report (No. 220) was ordered to be printed 8 May, the second (No. 414) 16 July, the third (No. 467) 29 July. *JHC* CXVII (1862-3) 186, 338, 378.

4 Derby would reply immediately: 'The note which I have just received from you is most important and if the report of the Committee on Public Accounts should be such as you expect, the course which you have taken in your last two speeches will be more than justified. My only fear has been, and would be, that of holding out expectations (and especially if they were to lead to our assumption of Office) which we could not practically realize without endangering the defences of the Country, and especially those connected with the Navy, which we gained so much credit for strengthening, and with which I am sure you would be as unwilling to interfere as I should. I cannot forget that we entered on our examination of the state of the Navy and its expenditure, with the hope, and intention, of effecting considerable reductions, and that hope founded also on what seemed very good authority and that the result was an enormous increase, and the beginning of the "reconstruction." I shall however expect with great interest Northcote's analysis, and I need not say shall be most happy to find that his anticipations can be realized.' H B/XX/S/298. See further **3684**.

---

1 Andrew Montagu (1815-1895), of Melton Park and Ingmanthorpe Hall, Yorks, and Papplewick, Notts, was DL for Yorks, high sheriff 1853. In 1868 he would decline D's offer of a peerage. M&B V 79. See further **3740**&n2.

2 Rose in 1862 was consolidating D's debts (see VII **2895** for D's 1857 account of them) by transferring them to Montagu. Eventually, with the cooperation of Lionel de Rothschild, Montagu would buy up the debts

3684 TO: LORD DERBY House of Commons [Thursday] 22 May 1862

ORIGINAL: DBP Box 146/1

EDITORIAL COMMENT: House of Commons paper.

Rt Honble | The Earl of Derby | K.G. May 22 1862

My dear Lord,

I have been obliged to expand, & a little remodel, the list. I have told Northcote to ask you to see him tomorrow, as his papers may not formally be / ready, but with some mems, & vivâ voce, he may be able to put the case clearly before you – so that you may open the subject generally.

Yrs sincerely, | D. /

Naas
Bankes Stanhope
T. Baring
Sir M.W. Ridley
Sir W. Heathcote
Ld. Robt Cecil
Col. W. Patten
Ld. Lovaine[1] /
Stanley
Walpole
Henley

in return for a mortgage on Hughenden for which he charged only 3% interest instead of the 10% D had been paying. In 1868 an anonymous correspondent would put Montagu's loan at £50,000, interest-free. H R/I/C/44 and see M&B V 78-9 and Blake 421-4, who estimates it at £60,000. With consolidation, D's annual payment of £6,000 was reduced to £1,800, an amount he could pay out of his £2,000 pension. *Norton Rose* 55. Rose on 5 March had written to D: 'I am very pleased to hear from Spofforth of the meeting with Montagu yesterday which was very apropos.' H R/I/B/82. Montagu had written to D in March reluctantly declining, because of North Riding election affairs, D's invitation to dinner on the 22nd (not found). H B/XXI/M/407. Item 19 (*Deeds of Personal Estate*) of the summary list of Hughenden Manor Estate Title Deeds reads: 'B. Disraeli to Andrew Mountague [*sic*]: items relating to mortgage assignments of life assurance policies, etc., to secure £20,000. [*Date:*] 1863-1869'. Many of the assignments and transfers to Montagu listed in the 'Schedule of Deeds and Documents deposited with Messrs. Rothschild ... in 1881' are dated 14 March 1862. An entry in the section for the Hughenden Vicarage dated 28 August 1871 reads: 'Indenture between Benjamin Disraeli of the one part and Andrew Montagu of the other part whereby lands purchased at Hughenden were added to Security of 14th. March 1862.' One of the 14 March 1862 items is the assignment to Montagu of the mortgage transferred on 14 April 1858 from Peacocke to C.C.F. Greville 'and another.' Bucks Record Office, Aylesbury. See also **3649**&n1, **3692**&n2, **3737**&n1, **3740**&nn1&2 and **3748**&n1. No correspondence from Rose at this time has been found.

1 There are extant notes of acceptance from Heathcote and Cecil. Lovaine would write from Alnwick on 25 May: 'Your letter of the 22nd [*not found*] did not reach me till yesterday ... I cannot say that I think that we have always done our duty as an Opposition in checking the expenditure of the country; nay, we have some times done the reverse – and it will require very great caution to retrace our steps so as not to incur the charge of popularity hunting & inconsistency. The war expenditure in time of peace is a source of profit to so many influential persons & bodies in & out of the House, that an attempt will certainly be made to connect us in public opinion with the Manchester party, hateful as it is to 9/10ths of the nation, the moment we make an effort to reduce the estimates – naval & military – which are the two great leaks in the coffers of the state – nor is the idea of reposing confidence in the Emperor one whit more palatable. Beware of these two rocks ahead! The second, perhaps, even more fatal than the first!' H B/XXI/H/433, XX/CE/2, XXI/L/345.

Pakington
Peel
Estcourt
Trollope
Ker Seymer
Jolliffe
Stirling
Taylor
Northcote
Fitzgerald[2]

TO: SIR WILLIAM JOLLIFFE House of Commons [Thursday] 22 May 1862 **3685**
ORIGINAL: SCR DD/HY C/2165 [64]
EDITORIAL COMMENT: House of Commons paper.

Confidential May 22 1862

Rt Hon. | Sir W.H. Jolliffe

My dear Jolliffe,

There is a Council at Ld. Derby's on Saturday next, at twelve o'ck – to consider the subject of national expenditure. Let us / count on your being present![1]

Yours ever, | D.

TO: WILLIAM STIRLING House of Commons [Thursday] 22 May 1862 **3686**
ORIGINAL: STCL 29/30/19/1
EDITORIAL COMMENT: House of Commons paper.

Confidential May 22 1862

W. Stirling Esqr | M.P.

My dear Stirling,

There is a Council at Ld. Derby's on Saturday next, at twelve o'ck to consider the subject of our national expenditure – & I should / be very glad, if you could make it convenient to be present on that occasion.

The meeting is very limited.[1] | Yrs sincerely, | D.

2 Stanley noted in his diary entry for 24 May 1862: 'Meeting at Lord D.'s of twenty members of the H.C. to consider how far reduction of expenditure might be possible. The general feeling, elicited by nearly three hours discussion, appeared to be in favour of reduced estimates, but against any vote that might seem to censure ministers for the largeness of theirs ... Peel and Pakington were for keeping the expenditure at its present amount: Disraeli opened the case: I spoke strongly for reduction: Lord D. appeared not to disapprove, but he expressed no opinion. Sir M. Ridley talked sensibly, as indeed did most, except Banks Stanhope: and he was only asked in order to mollify him by the compliment of being consulted.' *Disraeli, Derby* 185.

1 See **3684**n2. No response from Jolliffe has been found.

1 See **3684**n2. No response from Stirling has been found.

3687 TO: SIR EDWARD BULWER LYTTON [London, Friday] 23 May 1862

ORIGINAL: HCR D/EK C5 [18]

Rt Hon: Sir Ed. Lytton | Bt. MP May 23. 1862

My dear Sir Edward,

There is a meeting tomorrow (Saturday) morning, at Lord Derby's *on matters of great import.* / Pray come – at twelve o'ck.

You ought to have had this sooner.[1]

Yrs ever, | D.

3688 TO: LORD DERBY Grosvenor Gate [Sunday] 25 May 1862

ORIGINAL: DBP Box 146/1

EDITORIAL COMMENT: Paper imprinted 'Grosvenor Gate'. Endorsed by Derby on the first page: 'Disraeli B.' There is no salutation. *Sic:* Stansfield's.

Confidential May 25 1862

Rt Honble | The Earl of Derby | K.G.

The Government is much disturbed about the financial position.

It has been stated to them, that, even with a good harvest, they must contemplate the possibility of a deficit of *three millions.* This estimate, so / early in the year, must be very speculative, but the fact of such an hypothesis being put before a government, proves we were not a day too soon in taking up our position.[1]

Palmerston would evade the subject at present, & decide when the evil day arrives, but Gladstone & / Gibson, looking to their future position, are very troublesome. They do not like, in the face of such a prospect, to vote against Stansfield's resolution, or anything of the kind. Their retirement even is on the cards.[2]

You may rely upon all this, as it comes from the fountain-head,[3] / but it refers to a state of affairs anterior to the meeting of the Cabinet yesterday, of the results of wh: I know nothing.

As you will be engaged tomorrow I send ↑this↓, but cd. call if you wished.

We drifted once into war. To drift into chronic deficits is not less dangerous. If you said this tomorrow, from so unusual, & so high, a place as the Ho: of Lords, it would sink into the public mind, & affect opinion.[4]

Yrs sincy, | D.

1 Lytton would reply from Buxton on 25 May that D's note had reached him only that morning. H B/XX/LY/135.

---

1 See **3684**&n2.

2 James Stansfeld (1820-1898), barrister (Middle Temple) 1849, was Liberal (Radical) MP for Halifax 1859-95 and would be a junior lord of the admiralty 1863-4, of the treasury 1868-9, financial secretary to the treasury 1869-71, PC 1869, president of the poor law board 1871, of the local government board 1871-4, 1886, GCB 1895. On 13 May notice had been given that in three weeks he would move a resolution to reduce public expenditure. On 30 May Palmerston would give notice of an amendment to Stansfeld's motion to allow reductions as conditions might warrant. *The Times* (14 May 1862); *MP* (31 May 1862). In the event, Palmerston would declare the issue to be one of confidence; see further **3690**&n2.

3 Cf VII **2971**&n1 and **2972**&n5.

4 For D's specific views on how the country had 'drifted' into the Crimean War, see VI **2642**&n1 and **2644**&nn1-3. On 30 May in the Lords' debate on third reading of the Customs and Inland Revenue Bill

TO: SARAH BRYDGES WILLYAMS House of Commons [Tuesday] 27 May 1862 3689

ORIGINAL: RTC [202]

PUBLICATION HISTORY: M&B IV 311-12, dated at the House of Commons, 27 May 1862, most of the first paragraph

EDITORIAL COMMENT: House of Commons paper. There is no salutation. *Sic:* manouvres.

Confidential May 27 1862

The newspapers have made you aware of the change, that has taken place in public affairs. I have been, as it were, bringing large bodies of troops in to the field during the month,[1] & the Government / have suddenly found themselves, almost without notice, surrounded, surprised, & endangered. The state of the finances gave this opening, & I have entirely availed myself of it. It will, ultimately, produce their fall, but I wish, myself, rather to discredit, than to / defeat, them. It shd. go on for eight or ten months more, if possible, when the state of the country, the decline of the revenue, the want of employment in Lancashire,[2] & their profuse & extravagant foreign policy, will combine for their permanent / discomfiture. So, you see, I have had much to do – constant observation of the enemy, & thought as to the necessary manouvres; wh: is the reason I have not written – for the time glides away in these absorbing pursuits, wh: unfit one for everything else, either of business or pleasure.

Your letter yesterday was most gay & graceful![3]

Yours ever, | D.

TO: LORD DERBY Grosvenor Gate [Saturday] 31 May 1862 3690

ORIGINAL: DBP Box 146/1

EDITORIAL COMMENT: Paper imprinted 'Grosvenor Gate'. Endorsed by Derby on the last page: 'Disraeli B *Ansd*'.

Rt Honble | The Earl of Derby | K.G. May 31 1862

My dear Lord,

I am very sorry indeed, that I cannot personally thank you, this morning, for the

(given second reading on 26 May without debate) Derby would explain and endorse D's position on the budget and use D's suggestion to describe 'the real condition in which we stand ... that at the present moment we are incurring habitually a deficit to a very large amount. We are, to use an expression that was applied to the Crimean war, gradually "drifting" not into war, but into a state of chronic deficiency.' *Hansard* CLXVII cols 176-85 (quoted at 178-9). See **3690** for D's response.

1 See **3684** for D's list, all of whom (except Baring) had recently spoken in the House.

2 A.F. Egerton (C, S Lancs) on 9 May had raised the matter of distress in the cotton manufacturing districts, principally Lancashire, because the American civil war had cut off the cotton supply; he claimed that one-seventh of England's working class was dependent on cotton. *Hansard* CLXV cols 1490-4. A relief subscription was advertised in the papers. See further **3694**&n5.

3 SBW had written to MA on the 25th with profuse thanks for the DS' letters, their invitation to the exhibition (declined), and 'some of yr beautiful Trout but I wd rather think of them flourishing in their own element in Hughenden Manor than on my lonely table'. She mentioned that 'yr Fr[ien]d' the Bishop of Jamaica [Spencer Aubrey] was likely to move to Braddon Toor and asked: 'Have you read "Sursum Corda by E[lla] L[ouisa] H[arvey] with Preface by the Bishop of Jamaica Father of the Authoress?"' On the 31st she would send thanks for more trout and report that the bishop had taken Braddon Toor for seven years. RTC [462-3Q].

kind, & cordial, manner in wh: you supported me last night. I am very sensible / indeed of it.[1]

The notice, that Palmn. has placed on the paper,[2] requires a council before the general meeting – I mean a council of Henley, Pakn, & one or two others only. The resolutions are very flabby – / especially the last – wh: might, I think, refer to the present critical state of the finances.

An amendment ↑in this sense↓ moved by Henley, & seconded by Trollope wd do.[3] I think it worth considering / whether there shd. not be a third Resolution referring to the Volunteers.[4]

Is it impossible for you to see four or five of yr friends after Church tomorrow?[5]

Yours siny, | D.

1 See **3688**&n4. Derby would reply the same day (31st) from St James's Square: 'I am very glad to find that the language I held last night, after the two Dukes [Newcastle and Argyll] had given me the opportunity, of referring to the "bloated armaments" was satisfactory to you; and that you do not look upon it as the Morning Post is ingenious enough to do, as "throwing you over." Carnarvon's speech was excellent, and followed up as it was by Overstone & Grey (Monteagle was ill) cannot but be damaging.' H B/XX/S/299. *MP* in a leader on this day had stated: 'Last night the Conservative leader in the House of Lords distinctly disavowed the Conservative leader in the House of Commons. Lord Derby's disavowal of Mr. Disraeli took the form of absolutely denying that [D] meant what he said ... [Derby] has thrown the shield of his eloquence over his former colleague, but only on the condition that the new war-cry against "bloated armaments" shall be heard no more'.

2 See **3688**n2. The amendment read: '"That this house, deeply impressed with the necessity of economy in every department of the state, is at the same time mindful of its obligation to provide for the security of the country at home and the protection of its interests abroad. That this house observes with satisfaction the decrease which has already been effected in the national expenditure, and trusts that such further diminution may be made therein as the future state of things may warrant."' *MP* (31 May 1862).

3 It would be Walpole who on Monday 2 June would give notice that he proposed to move an amendment to Palmerston's amendment if Stansfeld's resolution was defeated and Palmerston's became thereby a substantive motion; its second paragraph would be replaced by the following: '"And this House trusts that the attention of the Government will be earnestly directed to the accomplishment of such further reductions, due regard being had to the defence of the country, as may not only equalize the revenue and expenditure but may also afford the means of diminishing the burden of those taxes which are confessedly of a temporary and exceptional character."' *The Times* (3 Jun 1862). See further **3691**&nn1&2.

4 Lord Elcho on 2 May in the Lords had asked 'when the Royal Commission will be issued which is to inquire into the position and prospects of the Volunteer force'; answer: 'shortly.' On 29 July Lord Truro in the Lords would state: 'some time ago the Government were made aware that the funds of several corps of the Volunteer Force were not by any means in a sound state, and that unless they received some aid from Government there was little hope of those corps remaining in their present strength or condition of efficiency.' He asked when the commission's report would be received; answer: 'within the next few days'. The only money voted for volunteers in this session would be £6,500 for the Volunteer Corps (Yeomanry) on 21 July. *Hansard* CLXVI col 1126; CLXVIII cols 625, 976.

5 Derby (n1) would reply: 'I have already seen Taylor this morning, and desired him to ask you if you could come here with Northcote at ½ past 4 or 5 tomorrow. I am glad that Palmerston has shown his card. It will greatly assist us. I own I have some doubt as to asking anybody here tomorrow except yourself and Northcote. I think those who were at our last Council might not like our having a further distillation – a crême de la crême – but do about this as you think best. Taylor will ascertain what course the Speaker will take – but I conclude he will call on Palmerston. We could take his Amendment without difficulty were it not for the expression of our "*satisfaction* at the present decrease". If there be any, which I doubt if we look to actual expenditure and not estimate, it is so small as hardly to warrant a distinct vote of approval. We must consider whether we cannot move an Amendment on his Amendment – but it must be very carefully worded. I do not think the Volunteers could be dragged into a resolution. The course of our debate last night afforded no opportunity for a reference to them.' An *Observer* item reprinted in *MP* on 2 June would state: 'Lord Derby has called a meeting of his supporters in special reference to the motion of Mr. Stansfeld on Tuesday night. A very special circular was issued on Saturday by Col. Taylor'.

TO: SIR STAFFORD NORTHCOTE Grosvenor Gate [Sunday] 1 June 1862 3691

ORIGINAL: BL ADD MS 50015 f572
EDITORIAL COMMENT: Paper imprinted 'Grosvenor Gate'.

Confdl June 1 1862

Sir Stafford Northcote | Bt: MP

My dear N,

The objection to my doing it, is that I mayn't *reply* on an amendment, wh: will be a great advantage to Palmerston, on whom / I meant to have waited, howr. late the hour.[1]

Would he have the reply, if his amendment becomes a substantive motion? I am not sure. That would remove all difficulties. /

Otherwise, he wd. triumphantly contrast the narrow financial issue, on wh: I now placed it, with the broad basis of my former speech.

I shall be at your service any time tomorrow / after ten o'ck.[2]

Yrs sincerely, | D.

TO: PHILIP ROSE Grosvenor Gate [Friday] 6 June 1862 3692

ORIGINAL: H R/I/A/148
EDITORIAL COMMENT: Paper imprinted 'Grosvenor Gate'. Endorsed in another hand on the second page: 'B.D.'

Private June 6 1862

Philip Rose | Esqr

My dear Rose,

I am going to Mentmore tomorrow – but shall return on Wednesday, at latest.[1]

If you could give me, by that time, any *opinion*, whether the arrangement, ~~could~~ wh: we talked about, / could be made or not, it would be of importance in guiding me at this moment. A word would do – *yes* or *no*.

1 See **3688**&n2 and **3690**&nn1-3&5. Northcote had written on this day (1 June) from 42 Harley Street: 'I will see Sir J. Trollope either tonight or early in the morning. If he will take the amendment I think it will do. If not, I think you ought to take it yourself, and I am by no means sure that you ought not to do so rather than give it to anybody. I keep Mr Henley's note.' BL ADD MS 50015 f572.

2 Stanley noted a strategy meeting (*cf* **3690**&n5) at the Duke of Marlborough's next day (2 June): 'it was agreed that in order to avoid voting with Stansfeld, a resolution in the same sense as his should be voted as an amendment to Palmerston's. This was drawn up, I believe, by Lord D., was entrusted to Walpole, who agreed to move it.' Stanley would also record the 3 June debate on Stansfeld's motion: 'The House began by an irregular conversation ... which ended in a sort of agreement to withdraw all amendments except Palmerston's and Walpole's, so that the debate and division might proceed without impediment. But Palmerston at the outset took an opportunity of declaring that he should consider the motion as one of confidence: and Walpole, either acting in concert with him, or seized with a sudden panic, intimated that under those circs he must ask time to consider whether he should bring on his amendment: which was in effect equivalent to giving it up ... Disraeli spoke, though under the mortification, not only of defeat, but of desertion, with more tact, skill, and power, than I have known him show since 1852 ... Stansfeld's resolution was negatived by an immense majority ... Walpole's conduct is blamed by all parties.' *Disraeli, Derby* 186. See also M&B IV 310-12 and **3693**&nn1&3.

---

1 The DS would be at Mentmore (the Mayer de Rothschilds) 7-10 June 1862. H acc.

With regard to the larger, & more permanent, arrangement, I think the enclosed is very favorable / in its tone, tho' I agree with you, it shd. not be forced.[2]

Yours ever, | D.

3693 TO: LORD DERBY Grosvenor Gate [Saturday] 7 June 1862

ORIGINAL: DBP Box 146/1

EDITORIAL COMMENT: Paper imprinted 'Grosvenor Gate'. Endorsed by Derby on the last page: 'Disraeli B. *Ansd*'.

Rt Honble | The Earl of Derby K.G. June 7 1862

My dear Lord,

This arrived last night.[1]

I have answered it very kindly,[2] but declined correspondence on such matters – & entreating him not to take any precipitate step without fully conferring together on / my return, as his secession from our benches might lead to other, if not more important, changes.

Until I received his letter, I fancied, rather, I was the injured person, & especially by Walpole's last remarks.[3]

I forward Estcourts letter to you, because, if / he be in town, you might see him, if you thought proper. At any rate, as I understand from Taylor, he ↑(Taylor)↓ is to

2 See **3683**&n2. Neither the 'enclosed' nor any relevant correspondence from Rose has been found.

---

1 Sotheron-Estcourt had written to D on 6 June in 'great Pain, and ... Anxiety' after the events of 3 June (see n3). He felt Walpole had not been given sufficient instructions in case the Government resisted his amendment, since he understood Derby's policy was not to 'shake the Ministry'. He conceded that Walpole's behaviour would be unpopular with Conservatives but was 'greatly pained by the Terms and Tone in which you spoke of him in your second short speech, for it seemed to me ungenerous to sacrifice the Man who had been pressed into the service, and placed in an embarassing [*sic*] Position, by ourselves.' He feared the incident would alienate Walpole and other Conservatives and generally discredit themselves. Recent *Standard* and *Herald* articles made the matter worse because they seemed at variance with Derby's intentions at their meeting. Since he could not see how to reconcile the discordant elements in the party and his own inclinations were towards the reactionaries, he felt he ought to retire to the back benches. 'Do not infer,' he concluded, 'that I am at all less attached to our Cause, or to the Colleagues with whom I have had the Honour of being associated.' H B/XXI/E/270.

2 This letter has not been found.

3 See **3691**n2. D in his first, long speech of the evening had mocked the idea of regarding Stansfeld's motion as a non-confidence measure, and had declared that, 'if this Resolution, therefore, is one of want of confidence, it is one which I could not support.' He expressed sympathy for Walpole's discomfited reaction, but admitted he felt as if his favourite for the Derby had bolted. After the division, Walpole announced that, in light of Palmerston's statement, he would not proceed with his amendment; he assumed full responsibility for a decision that would be unpopular with some colleagues, but concluded that his course was best for the country, 'for I think it not desirable to attempt to disturb the Government at such a moment as the present, when I have no reason myself to say that the Government do not deserve the confidence of the country.' When Palmerston rebuffed yet another amendment as identical to Walpole's, D suggested that, as the matter was sure to recur, they should simply pass the resolution so they could all go home: 'I think the best thing is always to put a good face upon a disagreeable state of affairs, and take that sensible view which may be taken even of the most distressing and adverse occurrences, if you have a command over your temper and your head ... I will not impugn the conduct of my right hon. Friend. I certainly did expect that one who has so many real claims to the name and character of a statesman, and whose Parliamentary knowledge is so great that I have always willingly and readily bowed to it, might have contemplated the possible issue, that the Government might choose to raise, however unwarrantably. There has been a discussion to-night whether it was a question of want of confidence

be with you this morning, it was desirable, you shd. be aware of all that takes place.[4]

Yours sincerely, | D.

TO: SARAH BRYDGES WILLYAMS Grosvenor Gate [Friday] 13 June 1862 **3694**

ORIGINAL: RTC [203]

PUBLICATION HISTORY: M&B IV 312, dated at Grosvenor Gate, 13 June 1862, most of the first paragraph; Blake 428, extract from M&B

EDITORIAL COMMENT: Paper imprinted 'Grosvenor Gate'. There is no salutation.

Confidential June 13 1862

When I wrote to you last, I hinted at the financial crisis, that was slowly gathering. The House of Lords followed up the movement ~~in~~ ↑of↓ the Commons – & a resolution, then unwisely announced by a Radical member, precipitated affairs.[1] The papers will have told you the result. My second in command lost his head & heart, the moment the trumpets sounded for battle.[2] Such / an incident never before happened in the House of Commons, & I hope may never happen again. They say you should see everything once. I did what I could to cover the retreat, & mitigate the humiliation, of ~~the~~ my troops. Between ourselves, as you well know, I had no wish whatever to disturb Ld. Palmerston, but you cannot keep a large army in order without letting them, sometimes, smell gunpowder.[3] The question, however, cannot be disposed of in / this manner. It is a growing question – & when Parliament meets next Spring, & it is proposed to increase the Income tax to one shilling in the pound, retrenchment will become fashionable.[4]

or not. I think, no doubt, on the part of my right hon. Friend there was a want of confidence.' Shortly thereafter Palmerston's motion was agreed to without a division, and the House adjourned at 1:15 *am*. *Hansard* CLXVII cols 292-394 (D 333-55, 391-2). The *Hansard* version does not include a passage reported in *The Times* (following 'possible issue'): 'that the Government might have been defeated, and the probable, not possible, consequences that might ensue. (Cheers). But my right hon. friend has told us tonight publicly that of which I was privately aware, that he was in attendance on a committee, and I have no doubt exhausted and fatigued by the labours of the committee - and every one will, I am sure, admit that a more valuable member of a committee could not be found. He had not, therefore, an opportunity of giving all the consideration which was necessary to the question, and, perhaps, those who requested him to undertake the office did not think consideration essential. (Laughter.)'

4 Derby replied the same day (7 June): 'I am very sorry to see in what light Estcourt views the unfortunate proceedings of Tuesday night; and if I have an opportunity I will do my best to smooth matters; but I fear it will require time to reunite the party. My own opinion is that you were the person who had the most reason to complain; but I know that Walpole himself (though I have had no communication with him) is very sore, and thinks himself aggrieved by your language respecting him; and some of his personal friends may probably take the same line. As to what Estcourt says about the tone of the Morning Herald, I quite agree with him – there was an article on Tuesday morning so injudicious, that on my way down with Jolliffe I could not help calling his attention to it, as placing upon the motion the very construction which I was most anxious to avoid, and treating it as a motion which, if carried, must lead to the overthrow of the Government. I think the tone of your answer to Estcourt quite the right one.' H B/XX/S/300.

---

1 See **3688**&n2 for Stansfeld's motion.

2 See **3691**&n2 and **3693**&n3.

3 On 6 June, Henry Edwards had told D he thought they would have lost the division on Walpole's amendment if he had not backed off. For the sake of party unity, he advised D to tell everyone they could have won by 20-30 votes. 'Our object now should be to widen the breach as much as possible between the Whigs & Rads' in preparation for next session. H B/XXI/E/49.

4 In his budget presented on 16 April 1863, Gladstone would propose to reduce the income tax by 2*d* on the pound. *Hansard* CLXX col 230.

Public affairs are gloomy. The civil war in America is impoverishing Europe. Lancashire & Lyons are both distressed;[5] the trade returns fall off, the revenue declines, & the rain never ceases.

The world is trying to be gay, & give the foreigners a hospitable reception / without the Court; but it is difficult to succeed in this.[6] A little while ago, Lord Granville gave us a magnificent fête at Chiswick House,[7] & today another of the Royal Commissioners of the Great Exhibition has engaged the Crystal Palace for the occasion, & invited all the foreign guests, & all the great world. The fountains are to play, & Blondin to ascend to a private party of two thousand persons. It requires the wealth of a Baring to accomplish this.[8] But alas! under a grey, if not humid, sky! His Highness the great Pacha will sigh for the sunshine of the Nile!

Adieu! | D.

3695 TO: SIR GEORGE BOWYER — House of Commons [Monday] 23 June 1862

ORIGINAL: PS 748

PUBLICATION HISTORY: Maggs Bros catalogue 299 (Nov 1912) item 3743: 'A.L.S. "B. Disraeli" to Sir George Bowyer. 1 page, 8vo. House of Commons, June 23rd, 1862.'

May I *depend* upon your bringing forward the .... Court Bill on Wednesday?[1]

3696 TO: SIR STAFFORD NORTHCOTE — Grosvenor Gate [Thursday] 26 June 1862

ORIGINAL: MOPSIK [235]

EDITORIAL COMMENT: Paper imprinted: 'Grosvenor Gate'. Endorsed in another hand: '(D'Israeli)'.

Sir Stafford Northcote | Bart: M P — June 26 1862

My dear Northcote

I entirely approve of your suggestion, & much admire the epigram.[1]

Yours sincerely, | D.

5 For concise summaries of the effects of the American civil war on cotton manufacturing and the switch by English and French businesses to Indian and Egyptian cotton, see Clapham II 220-3 and *NCMH* X 638.

6 As recently as 11 June the Queen had told Russell that, following Albert's death, her mind was 'much occupied with leaving this world' and she was anxious to put her own affairs in order. *LQV* 2nd series I 34.

7 Lord Granville had given an afternoon fête at Chiswick on Saturday 31 May for 'nearly 2,000 persons'. *MP* (2 Jun 1862).

8 Jean François Gravelet (1824-1897), 'Blondin', the French rope walker and acrobat who first crossed Niagara Falls in 1859, performed at the Crystal Palace 1861-2. On this day (13 June) he would do his stunts over the heads of the numerous guests at the Crystal Palace at an afternoon fête given by Thomas Baring to the jurors and foreign visitors to the Exhibition. *The Times* (14 Jun 1862).

1 On Wednesday 25 June Bowyer would move second reading of his Inns of Court Government Bill to regulate the constitution and administration of the Inns of Court. He argued that benchers currently operated on an irresponsible and secret system of self-election and arbitrary exclusion. After discussion, a hostile amendment was agreed to and the bill lost, with Bowyer promising to bring forward another measure before the close of the session. *Hansard* CLXVII cols 1030-73.

1 Northcote had written to D on this day (26 June): 'How will the epigram do? "*Aeratos muros cum condimus aere alieno / Fronte tua magnum est, Bernale noster, opus.*"' (We build bronze-covered defences with foreign money, Great is the work of your brow, our Bernal). Northcote I 204. On 31 March 1862 in debate on national fortifications, Bernal Osborne had heatedly called on the government to suspend expenditure on forts and iron-clad ships 'until we are in a position to know they will be able to hold their own against the

TO: SARAH BRYDGES WILLYAMS Grosvenor Gate **3697**

[Tuesday] 8 July 1862

ORIGINAL: RTC [204]

PUBLICATION HISTORY: M&B IV 330, dated at Grosvenor Gate, 8 July 1862; Weintraub *Disraeli* 395, undated extract

EDITORIAL COMMENT: Paper imprinted 'Grosvenor Gate'. There is no salutation.

Private July 8 1862

If it had not been for the Court being in deep mourning, & the unceasing summer rain, London, this season, would have been a Carnival! There are so many great sights, & such gatherings of innumerable thousands! Of all these, however, I think the most remarkable was the Show of / the Royal Agricultural society.[1] It gave me an idea of one of those great Tâtar hordes of which we read; of Genghis Khan & Attila. It was so vast, so busy, & so bovine!

The Pacha of Egypt, who speaks very good French, is the Royalty who most exhibits himself. The newspapers have told you of the Banquet, wh: the Lord Mayor gave him[2] – & we, also, met / His Highness at a state dinner given to him by the Speaker of the House of Commons & Lady Charlotte Denison, tho' that was a very small, & very select, party.[3]

That happened to me, which, a year ago, many would have betted 100 to 1 would not have happened to any Englishman in the year of grace 1862. I was asked to dine, on the same day, by the two rival French Princes: the Duke d'Aumale, & / the

monsters of the deep which are now being constructed.' *Hansard* CLXVI col 282. In the House on this day, 26 June, Northcote, critical of the government's bill to raise money for fortifications by a loan instead of taxation, would give notice 'that in Committee of the Fortifications Bill he should move the insertion of a clause or clauses to restrict the application of money which might be raised under the authority of the Act to the completion of such contracts for works as were already made, or such as might hereafter be made, subject to the previous approval of Parliament.' *Hansard* CLXVII col 1105. An altered form of the proviso would be accepted.

---

1 The annual Royal Agricultural Society show had opened at Battersea Park on 23 June, with cattle judging and prize-giving before many distinguished guests on 25 June; daily attendance figures ran as high as 38,000. *The Times* (7, 21 Jun, 1, 2 Jul 1862). The DS attended on opening day and purchased the guide book for 10*d*. On 16 July they paid 4*s* for James Foote (footman) and Mrs Cripps (housekeeper) to attend, plus another 8*s* for their omnibuses to the Exhibition and other city sights. H acc.

2 At the banquet in, appropriately, the Egyptian Hall of the Mansion House on Saturday 5 July, D had responded to the toast to the House of Commons with an encomium on the Viceroy of Egypt, Said Pasha: 'I am happy to inform your illustrious guest that nowhere is his government viewed with more interest than in the assembly on whose behalf I speak (cheers); and that it is with admiring satisfaction they have seen under his rule, the energies of his country developed, the elements of its prosperity increased, and have observed on many occasions the happy results of a wise and temperate administration. (Cheers.) Above all, I may say, that it is with peculiar pleasure we have witnessed under his sway that admission of the rights of labour which forms the best foundation of the wealth of nations. (Loud cheers.)' *The Times* (7 Jul 1862).

3 A state dinner and 'grand entertainment' for the Viceroy of Egypt had been given by the Speaker and Lady Charlotte Denison at their residence in the House of Commons on 2 July; the DS are listed among the select guests. *MP* (3 Jul 1862). Their invitation is dated 23 June. H B/XXI/D/159. Lady Charlotte Scott Bentinck (1806-1889), third daughter of 4th Duke of Portland, in 1827 had married John Evelyn Denison, current Speaker of the House of Commons.

Prince Napoleon![4] I fulfilled my previous engagement with his *Royal* Highness, but, two days after, I had a long, & interesting, audience with His *Imperial* Highness, who conversed very frankly, & very confidentially, on great affairs. The Prince is a true Bonaparte: in mind & visage – a very striking likeness of the great Emperor, & all his charlatanry of manner & expression – for he is picturesque & eloquent. On the other hand, the Bourbon Prince is thought to resemble, both in character & physically, his great ancestor, Henry the 4th.

Yours ever, | D.

3698 TO: LADY HARRY VANE — Grosvenor Gate [Tuesday] 15 July 1862

ORIGINAL: KCR U1590 C502/7 [6]

EDITORIAL COMMENT: Black-edged paper imprinted 'Grosvenor Gate'.

Dear Lady Harry, July 15 1862

An old acquaintance of mine, now a reigning Prince, has just sent a message, that H.R.H. proposes to dine at Grosvenor Gate on Sunday next, the 20th. / Inst.

It would give us very great pleasure indeed, if you, & Lord Harry, would honor us with yr presence that day, at ¼ to 8 o'ck, & meet the Grand / Duke of Weimar.[1]

Ever, dear Lady Harry, | Yours sincerely, | *B. Disraeli*

3699 TO: LADY HOLLAND — Grosvenor Gate [Wednesday] 16 July 1862

ORIGINAL: BL ADD MS 37502 f130, 131

COVER: [*a Grosvenor Gate envelope:*] The | Lady Holland, | Holland House. | *B Disraeli* [*No postmarks, ie hand-delivered*]

EDITORIAL COMMENT: Paper imprinted 'Grosvenor Gate'.

July 16 1862

My dear Lady,

An old acquaintance of mine, who is now a Sovereign Prince, has just deigned to propose, that H.R.H. shd. dine at Grosvenor Gate on Sunday next, the 20th Inst:

It would give Mrs Disraeli, / & myself, very great pleasure, indeed, if you would

4 The equerry to His Imperial Highness Prince Napoleon ('Plonplon') had asked D to meet the Prince at 1 *pm* on 5 July at the Clarendon Hotel. H D/III/D/429. The Ds are listed among the numerous guests at a 'grand *fête*' given by their Royal Highnesses the Duke and Duchess d'Aumale at Orleans House in the afternoon of Friday 4 July. *MP* (5 Jul 1862).

1 The Ds would give a dinner at Grosvenor Gate on Sunday 20 July to Karl Alexander August Johann (1818-1901), Grand Duke of Saxe-Weimar-Eisenach 1853-1901. The other guests were the Russian ambassador (Baron Brunnow, who arrived after dinner to avoid breaching diplomatic etiquette), Duke of Hamilton, Marchioness of Ely, the Derbys, the Hardwickes, Countess of Glengall, Lord and Lady Harry Vane, Lord Forester, the Alphonse de Rothschilds (of Paris), and Baron von Zedlitz. *MP* (22 July 1862). Regrets were received from Lord Bath (Lady Bath's health), Duke of Rutland, Lady Malmesbury ('I make it a rule never to dine out on Sundays'), Lady Carrington, Duke of Richmond (leaving town), Lady Cowley (illness in the family), and Lady Holland (see **3699**&n1). Lady Chesterfield had been expected but was prevented when Lady Carnarvon (her daughter) went into labour with a dead child. H acc. On the 21st, Hardwicke would send thanks: 'Your dinner was excellent, & in Company the *great* guest must have felt honor'd.' H B/XXI/B/1095, 170, D/III/C/1031, B/XXI/R/340, XX/HS/109, XXI/C/84, XX/LE/6, D/III/C/1043, B/XXI/C/552, B/XXI/F/203, B/XXI/H/186. See further **3702**&nn1-4.

honor us with your presence on that day, & meet the Grand Duke of Weimar at ¼ to 8 o'ck:[1]

Ever, yr much attached, | D.

TO: CHARLES ADDERLEY Grosvenor Gate [Tuesday] 22 July 1862 **3700**

ORIGINAL: HARV Houghton Library [41]

EDITORIAL COMMENT: Paper imprinted 'Grosvenor Gate'. *Sic:* J.C. Adderley.

Rt Honble. | J.C. Adderley M.P. July 22 1862

Dear Adderley,

I found yr note, enclosed from Jolliffe, on my return from the House last night. He is in great sorrow, Lady Jolliffe being quite despaired of.[1]

I quite approve of / your moving in the Canada question: the Appropriation bill, in all its stages, will give you a choice of opportunities. I will not undertake to be present – but I will endeavour to be there, & support you[.][2]

Pray make my / compliments acceptable to Mrs. Adderley, who is, I hope, quite well, & believe me ever

Sincerely yours, | D.

1 See **3698**&n1. Lady Holland would send her regrets the same day (16th): 'I go nowhere & have refused all invitations, not having spirits for it ... Again thank you – let me see you sometimes – it reminds me of happier times!' H D/III/C/1043. Lord Holland had died in December 1859; see VII **3386**n1.

---

1 On the 21st Jolliffe had forwarded Adderley's letter of the 19th asking for D's verbal opinion (to save D the trouble of writing) about raising a question in the House (see n2): 'I have told Adderley that under the sad affliction caused by the extreme danger of my poor Wife, I can only forward it to you, feeling sure, that notwithstanding the difficulty of the question, you would at once give him the benefit of your advice.' H B/XX/J/89. Lady Jolliffe would die on 23 July. See further **3701**.

2 Adderley had recently written twice (see also **3655**&n1) to D (D's response, if any, not found) on protecting Canada from American invasion, since the Canadian government relied totally on British troops instead of adequately developing their own militia. On 19 June he had written that 'the Canadian Government will never induce their Legislature to pass an efficient Militia Bill on the present understanding with this Country'; he advised simply announcing a date for British withdrawal. On 9 July he had offered, subject to D's approval, to ask the Government: '1. Now that the Canadian Parliament is about to separate without passing any Militia or Volunteer Bill, whether the 12,000 British Troops there are to remain so wholly unaided and 2nd. on another subject, whether we may have a copy of the Duke of Newcastle's letter to the Canadian Government offering on certain conditions the security of the British Treasury to a loan of £3,000,000 for a Railway got up by private speculation – & which, as far as we are concerned, can only be of use to bring the invaders for our 12,000 men to fight with.' On 11 and 15 July, he had asked these questions in the House, and on 19 July had written his letter to Jolliffe, after the Lords on 18 July had discussed and passed Carnarvon's motion for the government's correspondence with the governor general of Canada regarding the militia bills passed in the Canadian parliament. 'Only imagine us at war with the North & Canada invaded as she is.' The Consolidated Fund (Appropriation) Bill would pass committee without discussion on 25 July and be debated and given third reading on 28 July. On the 25th Adderley would raise the Canadian matter by rising before G.C. Lewis could respond to a question about an award for a military cooking apparatus; he argued that Canada was in imminent danger and that Britain either must increase its forces there or induce Canada to take adequate defence measures. In the ensuing discussion, D would trace the background of the current relationship between Canada and Britain and fault the government for damping Canada's independence by sending troops there after the *Trent* affair; though he praised Adderley's speech, he trusted to the sense and spirit of the Canadians and their governors to enact whatever measures were needed: 'I am anxious to maintain our colonial empire; but that I feel can be done only on principles of freedom and equality.' After further discussion the matter was dropped. H B/XXI/A/80, 81, XX/J/89a; *Hansard* CLXVIII cols 241-2, 349, 479-98, 779, 843-76 (D 867-72; quoted at 871), 909-31.

3701 TO: SIR WILLIAM JOLLIFFE Grosvenor Gate [Wednesday] 23 July 1862

ORIGINAL: SCR DD/HY C/2165 [65]
EDITORIAL COMMENT: Paper imprinted 'Grosvenor Gate'.

Rt Honble | Sir W.H. Jolliffe July 23 1862

My dear Jolliffe –

All that concerns you – either in joy or sorrow – must ever interest me, – & rest assured, that, at this moment, you have my deepest sympathy. I wrote / to Adderley.[1]

Ever yours, | D.

3702 TO: SARAH BRYDGES WILLYAMS Grosvenor Gate [Saturday] 26 July 1862

ORIGINAL: H R/II/E/551-2
PUBLICATION HISTORY: M&B IV 330-1, dated at Grosvenor Gate, 26 July 1862, with minor variation and omitting part of the first and all the last paragraph; Blake 419, mentioned
EDITORIAL COMMENT: From a fair copy in another hand in the Rose papers.

Private Grosvenor Gate | July 26. 1862

The whirl – political & civil – begins a little to slacken its fascinating velocity – and the sudden burst of sunshine & blue skies begins to make people remember that there is another & a better world "*out of town.*" We have never been home for eight months, tho' from the occasional direction of a newspaper, I observe that you, sometimes, think we are at Hughenden. The trout, that occasionally reach you, are caught in the morning, & sent off by the fisherman the moment that he gets them out of the stream, by the G.W. Railway, so that they may travel by night & reach you quite fresh.

Nothwithstanding the Court being in seclusion, London has been full of Royal blood this season. The Prince of Carignan,[1] the Prince of Orange,[2] the Princes of Saxony,[3] cum multis aliis – all Royal Highnesses – & one *crowned* head – the Grand Duke of Saxe Weimar. Strange to say this, tho' the greatest, was my guest – a great honor. I knew him in early years, when he was Crown Prince only; very literary & accomplished – & proud of the German Athens – over which his father ruled, & where Wieland, & Herder, & Goethe & Schiller, blazed at the same time.[4] He deigns to be an admirer of my writings & has often asked me to Weimar, which, unfortunately, I have never visited. So instead of my being H.R.H's guest, he deigned to honor my roof – & met a very choice party – among them Lord & Lady Derby, the Duke of

1 See **3700**&n1 and **3703**&nn1&2.

1 Eugenio Emanuele (1816-1888), Prince of Carignano 1834, HRH 1849, was lieut-gen of the Kingdom of Italy.

2 Willem (1840-1879), Prince of Orange, was the eldest son of King Willem III of the Netherlands.

3 There were two Princes of Saxony: Albert (1828-1902), eldest son of King Johann I of Saxony whom he would succeed as King Albert I in 1873; and Georg (1832-1904), who would succeed his brother as King Georg I in 1902.

4 The life dates of these luminaries are: Christoph Martin Wieland (1733-1813); Johann Gottfried von Herder (1744-1803); Johann Wolfgang von Goethe (1749-1832); and Johann Christoph Friedrich von Schiller (1759-1805). The Grand Duke's grandfather, Grand Duke Karl August, ruled 1758-1828, and his father, Grand Duke Karl Friedrich, 1828-53.

Hamilton, the Russian Ambassador &c.[5] I shall enclose you the bill of fare, if I can find it. It may amuse a moment.[6]

What immense events! The Italian & the American revolutions not only in one age – but in one year. I hope you are well. I am very – but yearn for my woods.[7]

Ever yours | D.

TO: SIR WILLIAM JOLLIFFE Grosvenor Gate [Friday] 8 August 1862 3703

ORIGINAL: SCR DD/HY C/2165 [66]

EDITORIAL COMMENT: Black-edged paper.

Grosvenor Gate | Augt. 8 1862

The Rt Honble | Sir W.H. Jolliffe | Bart: M.P.

My dear Jolliffe –

Now that the inexpressible pang may be somewhat mitigated by the only softener of sorrow, I would approach you with that sympathy, wh:, even from the truest / friends, is, at first, almost an intrusion.[1]

You, & yours, have deeply engaged our thoughts & feelings.

Tomorrow, we are going to Hughenden, & shall remain there some time. You know our sort of life, & the extreme seclusion, in wh: we live; with very / few companions except books & trees. But, if the fancy touch you, at any moment, to come & join us, my wife unites with me in saying, that, at all times, & under all circumstances, you will be welcome; / & you will be received with that affection, wh: we both have long felt for you.[2]

Ever, my dear Jolliffe, | Yours, | *B. Disraeli*

TO: RALPH DISRAELI Grosvenor Gate [Friday] 8 August 1862 3704

ORIGINAL: BL ADD MS 59887 ff 91-2

COVER: [*recto:*] *Private* | Ralph Disraeli Esqr | Gloucester Place | Hyde Park. | Aug. 8. [*verso:*] a wax seal

---

R. Disraeli Esqr G.G. Augt 8. 1862

As I do not hear, notwithstanding several interferences on my part, that the mat-

5 See **3698**n1.

6 See illustration p lvii.

7 On 28 July SBW would gratefully acknowledge D's letter, five trout and the bill of fare: 'I delight in imagining that you and dear Mrs Disraeli enjoy all the dissipation of the day.' On 8 August she would apparently acknowledge another D letter (not found): 'How good and kind you are to find time to think of one and to tell me you are well! though day and night hard at work in London atmosphere[.] How glad I shall be to hear of you and dear Mrs Disraeli coming Westward[.] Never ending thanks to dear Mrs D. for a profusion of interesting newspapers.' RTC [464-5Q].

---

1 Lady Jolliffe had died on 23 July.

2 Jolliffe at Merstham would reply next day (9 August): 'I was well aware of the sympathy you felt for us all, when this bitter calamity was impending, and now I have to thank you for a demonstration of regard, which I feel to be particularly soothing, since it comes from One, who under so many changeful circumstances, I have never for a moment thought of, but with the most sincere attachment & respect ... I trust there is a chance of my seeing the autumn tints upon your Beech Woods, and perhaps, on some quiet Sunday, hearing one of Mr. Clubb's [*sic*] sermons which have heretofore given me so much satisfaction.' H B/XX/J/90. The Ds would be at Hughenden 9 August to 6 November, but evidently Jolliffe did not visit them during this period. H acc.

ter of the Tedesco annuity is arranged, &, as I feel the great injustice of its being left in this condition / as regards yourself, I now redeem my portion of the liability as I at first suggested, & wh: I only delayed, in order, that the settlement might be complete.[1]

Yrs, | D.

3705 TO: WILLIAM FERRAND Hughenden [Tuesday] 19 August 1862

ORIGINAL: PS 426

PUBLICATION HISTORY: J.T. Ward 'Correspondence between Disraeli and W.B. Ferrand' in *Disraeli Newsletter* 2, 1 (Spring 1977) 11-21

EDITORIAL COMMENT: *Sic:* Wycomb.

Hughenden Manor, | High Wycomb, | Aug. 19/62

My dear Ferrand,

The Yorkshire moors for my money! I hope you have good sport, as you are so bountiful. I assure you I am very much touched by yr. constant remembrance of me.[1]

I won't write politics in August – but towards the decline of the year, or indeed whenever you be at leisure, I shall be glad to have the advantage of yr. observation and experience on public matters, and especially in your district.[2]

Very kind remembrances to Mrs Ferrand, I beg, if she will accept them from Yrs sincerely, | D.

3706 TO: THE DUKE OF BUCKINGHAM AND CHANDOS Hughenden [Thursday] 21 August 1862

ORIGINAL: BUC AR 30/63(L) 42 [2]

EDITORIAL COMMENT: Paper imprinted 'Hughenden Manor'. *Sic:* burthern; checque.

Private Augt 21 1862

His Grace | The Duke of B[uckin]gham & Chandos

My dear Duke,

Altho' Lowndes placed himself in the serious & critical position in wh: he now finds himself, without, I believe, conferring with a single friend, I quite / agree with you, that his motive, his character, & his name, alike render it imperative on our part, to assist him. I shall, therefore, be quite prepared to combine with yr Grace, & others, with that object.

I should hope, also, that / Parrott would find no difficulty in securing the continuance of the Journal, provided it is freed from debt, & that the stock is gratuitous

1 No relevant correspondence or documentation has been found. Isaac D'Israeli's half-sister Rachel (see IV **1395**n1) in 1792 had married secondly Angiolo Tedesco and died in 1807. John McLeod 'Genealogy of the Disraeli Family' in *Genealogists' Magazine* 24,8 (Dec 1993) 673-85. Perhaps relevant is that in July MA's Taynton estate at Gloucester was offered for sale. H D/II/B/301-17, 373-5. See further **3737**&n1.

1 MA on this day (19th) recorded '4 birds' received from Ferrand. H acc.

2 Ferrand had written on 2 June enclosing an unidentified correspondent's critique of Gladstone's financial policy that concluded: 'Whiggery is based upon corruption – the country is made to pay – but the Tories used to pay their bribes out of their own pockets.' On 24 September he would write about the worsening crisis in the weaving districts. H B/XXI/F/138-9.

– tho' all this shd. be done on conditions, wh: will secure, on the part of / the new undertaker, prudent conduct, & discreet management, for the future.[1]

With regard to the still more important matter of Registration,[2] affairs stand thus.

In 1858, it was generally deemed desirable, that a comprehensive & complete / revision of the Registration shd. take place – the cost was estimated as at between

1 The Duke of Buckingham and Chandos had written from Wotton on 19 August about an interview with Joseph Parrott of Powell and Parrott, the Conservatives' Bucks agents, on Lowndes's involvement in the critical state of *BH*. He was concerned for the Conservative interest in Bucks if the paper folded, and suggested that, although Lowndes had taken it on without consultation, the party contribute some help. H B/XX/A/27. He enclosed a copy of Parrott's 9 August 1862 letter to Lowndes detailing *BH*'s position – debt of £3,100, accounts mostly uncollectable, type virtually worthless, and no buyer to be found; 'the concern under the present management must be closed although I cannot help thinking under good and economical management it ought to pay.' Parrott regretfully warned that creditors would soon proceed against Lowndes for £2,500, and advised him to raise the money with a mortgage. On 28 August Lowndes would write to D distressed that the paper supplier was threatening to stop delivery. H B/XX/A/16, 17. On 20 August Rose had reported receiving enclosures from D and expressed his concern about *BH* and Lowndes; winding the paper up would be politically unfortunate and he disliked Lowndes's implications that D and the party were somehow responsible. '*Personally* I never knew that he had thus involved himself and was entirely ignorant of the basis upon which the Paper was proceeding after our last crisis – and no one that I know of ever asked or expected Lowndes to step into the gap in the way he has done.' H R/I/B/86a. For some of the background, see V **1723**&n1, **1865**&nn1-3, **1866**&n1 and **2025**&n1. As far back as 11 November 1855 Lowndes had written to D after their 'very satisfactory' London meeting the previous week about *BH*, a Committee to implement their decisions and a £25 cheque D had promised in Aylesbury. H B/XX/A/14. On 2 June 1857 E.R. Baynes, clerk to the Aylesbury commissioners of property and income tax, had written to D from Aylesbury about further negotiation between D, Lowndes and Richard Rose (like Parrott, a lawyer with the Aylesbury firm of T. White & Sons): 'I ... have in conjunction with Mr.↑R.↓ Rose & Mr. Parrott done all in my power to assist matters, & by this day's post have written to Mr. Philip Rose urging him to assist ... by procuring, as a temporary Loan, a sum of £200, which will enable Mr Lowndes to make arrangements for having the Paper properly carried on, *whilst more permanent measures* are being taken for insuring the Paper being firmly established, & supported.' He suggested that the leading Bucks Conservatives establish a capital fund for the paper. H B/XX/A/24. Parrott on 15 January 1858 had reported that *BH* was being kept solvent by Lowndes's guarantee of £1,000, and on 13 February 1858 that a subscription had been established. H B/XX/A/25-6. On 27 April 1862, Lowndes had written to D asking to meet him and Parrott at Rose's office to discuss the situation. H B/XX/A/15.

2 The Duke (n1) had written: 'What is the present state or position of registration arrangements for the County – I hear of claims &c by the other side but of nothing doing on ours?' On 23 June 1862 William Powell had responded to D's letter (not found): 'You are quite correct in your understanding that a County subscription was to form the basis of expenditure in the Revision of the Register in 1858 and applications were made to Conservative Proprietors and other friends throughout the County ... In June 1858 Mr P. Rose in reply to a letter I addressed to him on the subject of the Revision sent to me as follows "I hope you fully understand that subscription or no subscription the matter is to be done and done well, as regards Mr DuPre's contribution that had better be arranged between him and Mr Disraeli. I am instructed by the latter to see that the arrangements progress and at once." In consequence of this letter I refrained from making any further application to Mr. DuPre who had promised £50 only. I concluded he would, in being again appealed to, contribute £100 the amount you had then proposed to subscribe.' On 8 August at Newport Pagnell he had acknowledged receipt of D's £200 cheque: 'I have seen that all our friends in this quarter have been properly registered and Mr. Parrott promised me that he would attend to the Aylesbury district.' On 13 September he would acknowledge receipt of D's letter of 3 September (not found) and report that he had written for an Eton district list of objections. He would make partial reports on the registration process (conducted locally from 25 September to 4 October), on 9 November acknowledging D's letter of the 5th (not found): 'I have not yet been able to work out satisfactorily the result of the late Registration[.] I hope to get a copy of the new Register this week when I shall be able by comparing it with the old Register to see where the changes have occurred'. On 2 June 1863 he would acknowledge receipt of D's £160 cheque 'in payment of the balance due on Registration account for the year 1858'. H B/I/D/37a-43; *BH* (13, 20 Sep 1862); H A/V/G/[unnumbered].

5 & 600 £. It was represented to me, that it was deemed by influential persons as a matter wh: properly concerned the County itself; that a County subscription would undoubtedly be made; but, altho the members would / not be called upon, in their character of Representatives, to bear the burthern, still, in their character of landlords, contributions would be gratifying, & could not be considered unreasonable. I subscribed £100.

The County subscription turned out to be moonshine – & after long & great dissatisfaction on the part of the agents, I was informed, this year, that Powell of Newport was about to throw up the general agency, if the matter were left any longer unsettled.

Under these circumstances, always having a horror of unsettled Election claims, & feeling the probable injury to the party, if any scandal occurred, I took upon myself the balance due, little less than £400, & forwarded a checque to Powell.

Dupré is absent, & I do not intend to make any appeal / to him, further than to make him acquainted with the result, & to express my hope, that when affairs change favorably for him, he will, in his turn, support the Registration.[3]

Its present state is a source to me of great anxiety, & the total want of any concert or cordiality on the subject among those, / whose interests it, after all, mainly concerns, I should be happy to have yr Grace's views of this subject generally.

All this does not render me less anxious to combine in assisting Lowndes, but it, necessarily, diminishes my power.

I hope / Her Grace, is quite well. I beg my Compliments to her, & remain, as ever, | my dear Duke, | Sincerely yours, | D.

3707 TO: SARAH BRYDGES WILLYAMS Hughenden [Thursday] 21 August 1862

ORIGINAL: RTC [205]

PUBLICATION HISTORY: M&B III 470, dated 21 August 1862, omitting part of the third paragraph and the fifth; Blake 417, extract from M&B

EDITORIAL COMMENT: Paper imprinted 'Hughenden Manor'. There is no salutation.

Aug 21 1862

Here I have been ten days, & meant to have written to you the very first. And yet, I have done nothing; but have remained in a state of complete languor & apathy. It is always so. The sudden change & contrast from a life of unceasing excitement acts most strangely on the nervous system, & it takes / me some time to acclimatise.

Not that it is *ennui*. For here is a great deal to do. No one could have been absent eight months from his estate, & find *ennui* on his arrival – but I am incapable of performing what awaits me, & which, in its sort & manner, is also urgent, as much as affairs of State. /

I begin, however, to thaw. It is so long since I was here, that even my ancient trees seem to have grown, & the modern conifers have wondrously shot up. This morning we launched some cygnets on our lake; & as for flowers, all Hughenden sparkles

3 Rose on 5 July 1859 had reported: 'My last attempt at informing [Du Pré] of the intended subscription to the Registration was not a happy one, and I doubt if I am the best channel for communicating with him.' H R/I/B/57a.

with the Microfolia rose, the numerous & brilliant offspring of the colony you sent from Mt. Braddon.[1] Thus you see, how races are propagated, / & how empires are formed!

But our public buildings are still more striking: a new school nearly finished,[2] & a monument to my father, raised, in my absence, by my wife, & which, both for design, execution, & even material, is one of the most beautiful things not only in the County of Buckingham, but in England![3]

I hope you are well. This sun must make you happy. I will write soon again.[4]

Ever yours | D.

TO: BARONESS LIONEL DE ROTHSCHILD [Hughenden, late August 1862] **3708**

ORIGINAL: PS 1516
PUBLICATION HISTORY: Weintraub *Disraeli* 395-6, undated extract
EDITORIAL COMMENT: Weintraub *Disraeli* 679, citing 'the Rothschild Family Archive', quotes an 'August' letter from Charlotte de Rothschild to Leonora and Leopold de Rothschild 'about "the great Disraeli, who rhapsodizes about the enchantments of his dear country home, the silver river, where rose-coloured trout disport themselves, the ever-growing, ever-improving and really beautiful trees, and '[*the extract given below*].' How pleased Mrs Dis must be with the success of the secretly planned monument."' *Dating: cf* **3707**&n3.

... though last not least a monument to my father, raised by my wife, and in my absence. It is quite finished and really, whether I consider the design, the execution or even the material – I think it one of the most beautiful things in England.

1 See VI **2609**&n2, **2651**, **2774**, **2780** and VII **3186**. See further **3709**.

2 See VI **2519**&n1, **2792**n1 and, in this volume, **3723**&n1 and **3725**&n3.

3 Rose in 1881 would record: 'In the spring of 1862, Mrs. Disraeli ... consulted me as to her wish to erect a Memorial at Hughenden to the late Isaac Disraeli, to whom she was much attached, of which her husband was to know nothing until it was completed ... truth compels me to say that he had received some inkling of it before that time, tho' he would on no account let her suspect it; and she frequently recalled to me the "clever" way in which "we" had kept the secret.' H R/III/C/2. *BH* on 20 September would report on the fifty-foot Bath stone Ionic monument designed by E.B. Lamb and placed on a hill with a view of Windsor Castle: 'On the northern entablature is a basso relievo bust of the elder Disraeli, and the following inscription: – In Memory | of Isaac Disraeli, | of Bradenham, in this County, | Esq., and Hon. D.C.L. of the | University of Oxford, | Who, by his happy genius, diffused | among the multitude that | elevating taste for literature, | which, before his time, was the | privilege only of the learned, | This monument was raised, | in affectionate remembrance, by | Mary-Ann, the wife of his eldest son, | The Right Hon. Benjamin Disraeli, | Lord of this Manor, Chancellor of the Exchequer 1852-8 | and 9, and now, for the sixth time, Knight of this shire. | June, 1862.' On 3 June, MA had recorded paying Lamb £200 for the monument, which had cost a total of £500. H acc. On 4 August Thomas Coates had written to D from High Wycombe: 'Received of the Right Honourable Benjamin Disraeli, by the hand of Mr. Vernon, the sum of Twenty Pounds, being a sum I agree to accept for all my Interest in the Land at Hughenden used for erecting a Monument and for a road-way thereto'. H A/V/G/[unnumbered]. See illustration p lviii.

4 On 24 August SBW would thank D for his letter and some game, and give a remedy for his condition: 'As nerves indicate they are not to be trifled with I venture to recommend for their benefit a good plain delicate Broth'. RTC [466Q]. See further **3709**&n1.

3709 TO: SARAH BRYDGES WILLYAMS Hughenden [Monday] 1 September 1862

ORIGINAL: RTC [206]

PUBLICATION HISTORY: Meynell II 464-5, dated at Hughenden, 2 September 1862

EDITORIAL COMMENT: Paper imprinted 'Hughenden Manor'. There is no salutation. *Sic:* Shalot.

Private September 1. 1862

I am quite myself again – &, as I have been drinking your magic beverage for a week, & intend to pursue it, you may fairly claim all the glory of my recovery – as a fairy cures a Knight after a tournament or a battle. I have a great weakness for / mutton broth, especially with that magical sprinkle, wh: you did not forget. I shall call you in future after an old legend, & a modern poem,

"The Lady of Shalot"![1]

I think the water, of wh: it was made, would have satisfied *even you.*[2] For it was taken, every day, from / our stream, wh: rises among the chalk hills, glitters in the sun over a very pretty cascade, & then spreads↑, & sparkles,↓ into a little lake, in wh: is a natural island. Since I wrote to you last, we have launched in this lake, two most beautiful cygnets, to whom we have / given the name of Hero & Leander. They are a source to us of unceasing interest & amusement. They are very handsome & very large – tho↑, as↓ yet, dove-colored.[3]

I can no longer write to you of Cabinet Councils or Parliamentary struggles: here, I see nothing but trees & books, so you must not despise this news of my Swans!

Adieu! | D.

3710 TO: JOHN HUBBARD Hughenden [Wednesday] 3 September 1862

ORIGINAL: QUA 105

EDITORIAL COMMENT: Paper imprinted 'Hughenden Manor'.

J.G. Hubbard Esqr | M.P. Septr 3 1862

My dear Hubbard,

I was unable to reply to yr kind letter[1] yesterday, as my prospect of attending the dinner at Buckingham was uncertain. / I am happy to say, now, that I can have that pleasure, & the still greater one, of being your guest.

My wife begs, that Mrs. Hubbard will not think of giving herself / the trouble of sending her a formal invitation to Addington, where, however, she proposes to ac-

1 On 24 August (**3707**n4), SBW had given her recipe: 'Cut a lb of fresh prime mutton into very thin slices *simmer* with a qt. of sparkling rock water *20 minutes* after it has been *once* boiled and been skimmed, season with shalot and a little salt when settled it will appear clear as crystal.' Tennyson's 'The Lady of Shalott' had been published in 1832, revised in 1842, and much expanded in 1859 as *Elaine*, later 'Lancelot and Elaine', in *Idylls of the King*.

2 *Cf* VI **2556**&n3 and **2560**&n9.

3 On 20 August MA had recorded: 'Two Sygnets arrived a present from Mr. Hussey, taken to the Island'; presumably the donor was John Hussey, one of D's tenants at Naphill. H acc; V **1929**n1. At the International Exhibition, D would purchase a statue of 'Hero expecting Leander' by Ignazio Villa, a Milanese sculptor who also designed buildings. *BH* (15 Nov 1862).

1 On 31 August Hubbard had invited D to stay when he attended the North Bucks Agricultural meeting at Buckingham on 17 September. H B/XXI/H/717.

company me, on the *16*th. Inst:, &, in person, thanking you / both for your obliging invitation.[2]

Believe me, always, | sincerely yours, | *B. Disraeli*

TO: FREDERICK LYGON Hughenden [Thursday] 4 September 1862 3711

ORIGINAL: BCP [9]

EDITORIAL COMMENT: Paper imprinted 'Hughenden Manor'.

Hon: F. Lygon | M.P. Septr. 4 1862

My dear Lygon,

I hope you may be disengaged on the 25th. Inst – & that you may be able to quit the Malvern, & visit the Chiltern, Hills – & stay with us till the / following Monday, the 29th:

Pray give my kindest regards to yr. father: my first, & my best, ↑H of Commons↓ critic.[1]

Yours sincerely, | D.

R.S.V.P.

TO: RALPH EARLE Hughenden [Monday] 8 September 1862 3712

ORIGINAL: H H/LIFE

EDITORIAL COMMENT: From a typescript headed: 'D. to Mr. R.A. Earle, Hughenden, Sept. 8. '62.'

... you have youth, which is better than fortune; for youth can bring fortune, but fortune cannot bring youth ...[1]

2 Hubbard (n1) had added that, if MA was to accompany D, Mrs Hubbard would invite her too. On 9 September Mrs Hubbard would ask MA whether the DS were coming by road or if they could meet them at Winslow station. H D/III/D/311. Hubbard in 1837 had married Hon. Maria Margaret Napier (1817-1896), eldest daughter of 9th Baron Napier. D had once considered buying the Addington estate (see IV **1597**&n3), which instead was bought by Hubbard, who would be created Baron Addington in 1887. See further **3715**&n2.

1 On 6 September Lygon would write from Madresfield Court, Great Malvern: 'It will give me great pleasure to come to you on the 26th & stay till the Monday following. A meeting ... will unfortunately detain me here on the 25th. My father desires me to thank you for your message & sighs after the old days when he had the pleasure of sitting near you in the House of Commons.' H B/XX/LN/14. For Lygon's father (since 1853 4th Earl Beauchamp) see II **690**&n4. Other guests on 26 September would be Ralph Earle and Sir William and Lady Georgiana Codrington. H acc, B/XXI/C/302.

1 Earle had written from Grosvenor Square on 6 September to report his return from Germany, retail political gossip and make suggestions for D's speech, including a draft outline, at the Bucks agricultural meeting. Possibly D is responding to Earle's complaint: 'Lady Egerton was at Ems, (with the wrong daughter).' On 13 September Earle would write again: 'Chère Excellence, I am very grateful for yr sympathetic letter. Altho' I could report no accomplished fact, I think I have succeeded in establishing a new & hopeful basis for future operations. This is perhaps a little enigmatic but I shall explain, some day or other.' He then discussed information he had gathered on the continent and at home. H B/XX/E/255-7.

3713 TO: LORD ST ASAPH Hughenden [Wednesday] 10 September 1862

ORIGINAL: PS 750

PUBLICATION HISTORY: Unidentified catalogue (Christmas 1922) item 2962: 'ALS to Viscount St. Asaph. 3 pp., 8vo., Hughenden, Sept. 10, 1862'

Where are you? and how are you? Mrs. Disraeli says that the air of the Chiltern Hills will invigorate you and hopes that you may be disengaged on the 25th inst., and meet one or two of our friends here, who are going to stay with us till the following Monday.[1]

It is a land of beechwoods and trout streams, and you may visit some old houses in the hills in which the English constitution was invented; like Hampden.

3714 TO: MESSRS BURLEY & CARLISLE Hughenden [Friday] 12 September 1862

ORIGINAL: MOPSIK [40]

EDITORIAL COMMENT: Paper imprinted 'Hughenden Manor'. Endorsed in another hand on the last page: '*12 Septr 1862* Honble B. Disraeli.' *Sic:* accounts ... varies; Magenis'; Villiers'.

Private Septr 12 1862

Messrs | Burley & Carlisle

Dear Sir

In consequence of the communication you made me at the beginning of the year, I consented to the deductions in question, but I don't understand, why they are made at the commencement of the year, instead / of being calculated pro ratâ. The point is, however, of, comparatively, little importance, as my consent to the deduction was *limited to one year.*[1]

I have no confidence, whatever, in any of the parties, with whom we have to deal in this matter. My private accounts / of the value, & condition, of the estates varies from theirs, & the motives of their present behaviour are too obvious.

I conclude, that Mr Magenis' claim is now reduced to nearly ⅓rd. of its original amount, &, if it were not for the / difficulties of the Dutch law, I shd. be disposed to recommend Mr Villiers' family to pay off the balance at once, & effect a sale, wh: would not be difficult, so far as candidates for purchase are concerned, at once.[2]

Believe me, | Yrs faithfully | *B. Disraeli*

1 See **3711**&n1. St Asaph would reply on the 15th from Taymouth Castle, Perthshire, where D's invitation had just reached him, regretfully declining because of Scottish engagements. H B/XXI/A/219. Bertram Ashburnham (1840-1913), Viscount St Asaph, would succeed his father as 5th Earl of Ashburnham in 1878.

---

1 See **3652**n1 for Carlisle's letter of 6 February 1862. Villiers had died on 8 May, from 'exhaustion', as D was informed by telegram and a letter of 9 May. On 28 March 1863 Burley & Carlisle would send a 'Statement of Principal & Interest due to F R Magenis Esqre from The Honorable Francis ... Villiers under the mortgage of the Ceylon Plantations dated 29th. August 1861'. H A/IV/J/191, 238, 238a. See further **3800**&n1.

2 The lessee of the Gallageddera estate, E. Ormiston, had written to D on 12 June that he was returning to London and wished to see him before any final disposition of the estate. Thomas Dickson, acting for Ormiston, had written twice, on 13 June that Ormiston was ill and financially embarrassed, and on 17 July that he was now in London and that Dickson had referred him to D. H A/IV/J/203, 204, 209.

TO: SARAH BRYDGES WILLYAMS — Hughenden [Monday] 15 September [1862] — **3715**

ORIGINAL: RTC [207]
PUBLICATION HISTORY: Blake 410, extract dated 15 September 1862
EDITORIAL COMMENT: There is no salutation. *Sic:* Paulets.

Private Hughenden. Septr 15

Tomorrow we are going to the North of the County, to Addington Manor, the seat of Mr Hubbard, the member for the Borough of Buckingham, preliminary to the Agricultural dinner, wh: I have to attend in that town on the 17th. Inst.[1] I never was at Addington, but I understand a very fine place, recently built by the architect, Hardwick, on the ancient site of the manor house of / the Paulets, to whom the estate belonged, when I was a boy.[2] The Hubbards are immensely rich; a new family – Russian merchants. He is a man of great ability; a capital speaker, who has the ear of the House of Commons; Mrs. Hubbard, a daughter of the late, & sister of the present, Lord Napier.[3] Tremendous Puseyites; with an ancient Church in the park restored in a very frenzy / of ecclesiological lore;[4] priests in every chamber, & gliding about! But, I suppose, it amuses her.

The whole of the North of the County, the Duke of Buckingham, the Fremantles, Barringtons, Verneys,[5] Cavendishes &c &c. are invited to meet us. As there may be a general election next year, this visit to the North, wh: is very distant from me; between 30 & 40 miles, is opportune.

We must return on the 18th: as next week, beginning the / 22nd, we receive the world at Hughenden, & for ten days successively. Lord & Lady Salisbury are coming, Sir Wm. & Lady Georgiana Codrington, Lord & Lady Godolphin Osborne,[6]

1 See **3710**&nn1&2. Responding to the toast to Bucks MPs, D would celebrate the increase and influence of agricultural associations over the past 30 years, and vindicate their practice of prize-giving; he would himself contribute a prize for the best-kept cottage and garden, challenging the north to meet the standard set in the south: 'In South Bucks, I will venture to say that a cottage with a thatched roof is probably not to be found'. He would conclude by contrasting Bucks prosperity to the textile districts' poverty because of the American civil war. That, he thought, might last a long time, and their countrymen would soon need their substantial help. *MP* (18 Sep 1862).

2 In 1857 J.G. Hubbard had demolished part of Addington House (owned by kinsmen of the Earls of Paulett until 1830) and had built Addington Manor, designed by Philip Hardwick in the style of a French chateau, on a new site; it has since been demolished and replaced by a neo-classical manor. *VH-B* IV 138; Sheahan 253. Philip Hardwick (1792-1870), FSA 1824, FRS 1831, RA 1841, designed St Katharine's Docks and Euston Station in London; he was vice-president of the Institute of British Architects 1839 and 1841, and treasurer of the Royal Academy 1850-61.

3 The father of Maria Hubbard and her brother Lord Napier was William John Napier (1786-1834), 9th Baron Napier, captain RN, ardent and published sheep farmer, chief superintendent of trade in China 1833-4.

4 The Church of St Mary in 1858 had been largely rebuilt by the high-church architect G.E. Street totally at Hubbard's expense; it had been reconsecrated in 1859. Sheahan 253-4.

5 Frances Parthenope Nightingale (d 1890), daughter of William and Frances Nightingale, of Embley, Hants, and Lea Hurst, Derbyshire, and sister of Florence Nightingale, in 1858 had married Sir Harry Verney (see II **377**n2).

6 There were at this time several couples styled Lord and Lady Godolphin Osborne, the senior of which was Lord William Godolphin Osborne (1804-1888), a younger son of 5th Duke of Leeds, and his wife, Caroline, Lady Godolphin Osborne (see III **1067**n2).

Lord & Lady Curzon,[7] Lord Elmley, Lord Stanley, Lord St Asaph, Colonel & Mrs. Fane, Baron Rothschild of Paris[8] – & many others. ~~Its~~ Its as hard work as having a playhouse – or keeping an Inn.[9]

Thanks to mutton broth[10] & dame nature, I am very well. I hope, & conclude, you are so – & send you from Mrs Disi. a great many kind words.

Ever yours, | D.

3716 TO: ROBERT HARVEY [Hughenden, Thursday] 18 September 1862

ORIGINAL: PS 751

PUBLICATION HISTORY: Sophie Dupré catalogue 2/2 (1983) item 50: 'ALS to R.R.[*sic*] Harvey, signed in full ... 3 sides 8vo, n.p., 18th September 1862, the printed crest at the head of the letter has been cut out without any loss of text, repaired.'

[asking him to] induce Mrs Harvey to pay us a visit here. It would give Mrs Disraeli and myself very great pleasure ... [suggesting a date when they could come and meet some agreeable friends][1]

3717 TO: PHILIP ROSE Hughenden [Saturday] 20 September 1862

ORIGINAL: H R/I/A/149

EDITORIAL COMMENT: Paper imprinted 'Hughenden Manor'.

Philip Rose Esq Septr 20 1862

My dear Rose,

Will you, & Mrs. Rose, give us the pleasure of your company at dinner on ~~W~~ Thursday next the 25th. Inst., at 7 / o'ck:?

7 Lord Curzon (see IV **1434**n5) in 1846 had married Harriet Mary Sturt (d 1877), daughter of Henry Charles Sturt, of Critchill, Dorset.

8 Baron James Mayer de Rothschild (1792-1868), youngest son of Mayer Amschel Rothschild and reputedly the richest man in France, was founder and head of the family's Paris house, Rothschild Frères, and owner of the Lafite vineyards. Frederic Morton *The Rothschilds* (New York 1983) 73.

9 MA recorded 'Receptions in September from 22d Monday till Monday 29th', a total of 62 dinners served by 8 servants. On the 22nd the Salisburys, Elmley, William Peel and Drummond Wolff would arrive, joined at dinner on the 23rd by Lady Curzon and Rev and Mrs King, and on the 24th by Lady and Miss Vere Cameron and Rev John Graves. On the 25th the Salisburys, Peel and Wolff would depart, Earle arrive, and with Elmley be joined at dinner by the Roses and the Clubbes. On the 26th Elmley would depart and Sir William and Lady Georgiana Codrington and Frederick Lygon arrive. On the 27th Mr and Mrs Robert Bateson Harvey and George Cameron would arrive, joined at dinner by the Roses and Mr Newman. All the guests would leave by the 29th. The following sent regrets: Stanley, St Asaph, Fanes, Rothschilds, Lady Dashwood, Hardwickes, Count Wimpffen, Col and Lady Mary Hood, Mrs and Miss Drake, Lennox, James Macdonald and Delane. H acc, B/XX/S/709, XXI/A/219, B/419, 933, C/299-301, 607, D/76, 632, F/47, H/191, L/126, M/32, D/III/C/287. See further **3719**&n2.

10 See **3709**&n1.

---

1 R.B. Harvey would reply on 20 September: 'If Mrs Disraeli and you would kindly permit us to come over on *Saturday*, we will gladly avail ourselves of your invitation to Hughenden, till the following Monday. I am very sorry just now that we must be deprived of the pleasure of the longer stay, your hospitality offers us, but we shall much enjoy the short time I am only able to propose.' MA on the 27th would record 'Mr & Mrs Bateson Harvey' as dinner guests. H B/XXI/H/274, acc. See also **3715**n9. Robert Bateson Harvey in 1855 had married Diana Jane Creyke (d 1866), daughter of the Ven Stephen Creyke, archdeacon of York.

At least, I hope you are at Rayners, & may be able, & that Malvern has done a great deal of good.[1]

Ever yrs sincerely, | *B. Disraeli.*

TO: SARAH BRYDGES WILLYAMS Hughenden [Friday] 26 September 1862 3718

ORIGINAL: RTC [208]

EDITORIAL COMMENT: Paper imprinted 'Hughenden Manor'. There is no salutation. *Sic:* a ... a present.

Septr 26 1862

There never was a more choice, or more acceptable, a present! It came, exactly, at the right time.

A great delicacy, delicately appreciated.

Have you seen Lord Normanby's / letter, from the winter villa at Plymouth – to the Editor of the "Western Times"? Somebody sent me the two numbers – in one of which was the attack, & in the other Lord Normanby's answer.

My "annual visit" to Torquay, & my possible visit to Lord Normanby, the subject of leading articles – & of a correspondence with a K.G. & an Ex-Ambassador![1] They arrived the same day / as the prawns – & I read them out loud at breakfast, introducing the prawns as "annual visitors *from* Torquay."

I hope you are quite well.

Yours ever, | D.

TO: BARONESS LIONEL DE ROTHSCHILD Hughenden [Tuesday] 30 September 1862 3719

ORIGINAL: ROTH RAL 000/848

PUBLICATION HISTORY: Weintraub *Disraeli* 396 and *Charlotte and Lionel* 170, undated extract

EDITORIAL COMMENT: Paper imprinted 'Hughenden Manor'. *Sic:* Folkstone; Bredalbane.

Septr 30 1862

Dear Baroness,

The month shall not close without a gentle hint, from Hughenden, not to forget, entirely, yr friends. I should, indeed, have ventured to trouble you before, but we

1 Rose had written on 20 August that he and Mrs Rose were taking their daughter to Malvern for the water cure. The Roses would dine at Hughenden on 25 and 27 September. H R/I/B/86a, acc.

1 Lord Normanby, ambassador at Paris 1848-52 and at Florence 1854-8, KG 1851, had written from the Winter Villa, Stonehouse, Plymouth, on 24 September about a local zealot of D's, Samuel Triscott (see VII **3214n1**), whom Normanby had dissuaded from asking D to make a public appearance while at Torquay. On 22 September a leader had appeared in the widely read *Western Morning News,* implying political discussions between Normanby and D during D's 'annual visit to Torquay.' Normanby attributed the article to Triscott and enclosed a clipping of his own rebuttal in the *Western Morning News* of 23 September: 'I am at a loss to conceive how you can consider yourself justified in requiring Mr. Disraeli to say "if his relations with the Marquis of Normanby are merely those of a guest and host, or those of disciple and teacher in the school of retrograde politics at home, and restored despotism abroad." ... The Roman question, which has caused this unexpected personal attack, and which excites so much popular feeling, is well known to me in all its bearings, and can only be settled permanently and peaceably by giving satisfaction to the religious interests and convictions of two-thirds of the Christians upon earth. My opinion as a Protestant could have no influence on its decision, nor, allow me to add, will the most impassioned articles in our metropolitan or provincial press.' H B/XXI/P/281, 281a; Bourne II 258.

received, indirectly, information from Folkstone, wh:, on the whole, was / satisfactory. I hope Alfred continues advancing, & that the Baron is himself again.[1]

Hughenden has been quite full, the last ten days,[2] & our friends have been very agreeable. The only fault of our party was, that it contained no Rothschilds – but that was not our fault, for we tried not only the English, but the French & Austrian, dynasties, but in vain! Lord & Lady Salisbury / were here – but he was not well, & I thought him, I grieve to say, changed. On the contrary, Lord Elmley, who, we thought, was dying, was full of life, & most delightful. He is going to Egypt on the 1st. Novr., & it is thought, that, if the Duchess do not follow him – she did, last year, to Spain – ~~that~~ he may recover.[3]

They said, that marriage was out of fashion. It may be / among youth – but, certainly, not among those, whose judgment is matured.

The Duke of Leinster!

The Marq: of Bredalbane!

The Earl of Essex![4]

&, I dare say, every other grade of the peerage, if we knew all the impassioned vows, that are whispering, or mumbling.

The carriage is at the door, & we are going to Aston Clinton, where we shall hear some news of you, & support Sir Anthony at Aylesbury tomorrow[.][5]

Ever yrs, | D.

1 Baron Lionel de Rothschild suffered from, among other afflictions, severe rheumatoid arthritis, and was now often confined to a wheelchair. The Rothschilds' second son, Alfred, had taken ill (a '"stoppage"' requiring surgery) during the past summer at Cambridge. Weintraub *Charlotte and Lionel* 77, 169-70. *MP* on 3 October would report: 'Baron Lionel de Rothschild, who has been suffering from indisposition for some time past at Folkestone, is now much better. The baron and baroness and family will shortly leave Folkestone for Gunnersbury Park.'

2 See **3715**n9.

3 The 33-year-old unmarried Elmley would live only until March 1866. The Duchess may have been the Duchess of Montrose, whose character and movements fit observations made by Earle. On 19 September he had written: 'I saw Elmley the other day looking wretchedly ill – The Duchess was in town – He is evidently *au plus mal* with his own people.' On 'Thursday' (docketed March or April 1863) he would write: 'I think very poorly of Elmley – He is, or was 2 days ago – at Paris with the Duchess.' H B/XXI/E/258, 287. *MP* on 13 April 1863 reported that the Duchess of Montrose was expected in London that week from Paris after Egypt, and on 27 April that she had arrived on 'Friday last.' Caroline Agnes (1818-1894), *née* Beresford, third daughter of Lord Decies, in 1836 had married 4th Duke of Montrose, lord steward of the household (1852) and chancellor of the Duchy of Lancaster (1858) in the Derby administrations. She was a prominent society hostess, with 'a grand disregard for the opinions of others,' and a successful racehorse owner, known in racing circles as 'Carrie Red' for her hair. After the Duke's death she married William Crawfurd, another racehorse owner, had after his death a close relationship with the jockey Fred Archer, and married again in 1888 when she was 70, 46 years older than her new husband, Marcus Henry Milner. *ODNB*.

4 Leinster, Breadalbane and Essex were all recently widowed, Leinster in 1859 after 41 years of marriage, Breadalbane in 1861 after 40, and Essex in August 1862 after 37; only Essex would marry again, on 3 June 1863, although two of Leinster's sons had married within the past year. John Campbell (1796-1862), 2nd Marquess of Breadalbane, lord-lieutenant of Argyllshire, was MP for Okehampton 1820-6, for Perthshire 1832-4, rector of Glasgow University 1841, Lord Chamberlain 1848-52 and 1853-8.

5 The DS left Hughenden for Aston Clinton at 2 *pm* on this day (30th) and on 1 October would attend the annual meeting of the Central Bucks Agricultural Association of which Sir Anthony de Rothschild was president. In his toast to the association, D would point out how, since the inception of agricultural associations, various breeds of stock had been improved and the moral and physical condition of the agricultural labourer advanced. H acc; *BH* (4 Oct 1862).

TO: CHARLES CLUBBE Hughenden [Tuesday] 30 September 1862 3719A

ORIGINAL: RIC [015]

EDITORIAL COMMENT: Hughenden paper. *Sic:* W.W.

Rev. W.W. Clubbe Sept 30 1862

Dear Mr Clubbe

It is the Q: Sess: 13th. & 14th. &, therefore, neither of these days would suit / me.

Wednesday, the 15th:, would do very well. I will try to see the Arch[deaco]n at Aylesbury, but can't undertake / to do so. You had better write at all events.[1]

Yrs ffly. | D.

TO: SAMUEL WILBERFORCE Hughenden [Friday] 3 October 1862 3720

ORIGINAL: BODL MS Wilberforce c13 ff185-6

EDITORIAL COMMENT: Paper imprinted 'Hughenden Manor'. *Sic:* Wycomb [*twice*].

The | Ld Bp of Oxford Octr 3 1862

My dear Lord,

I have hesitated, very much, about yr request,[1] but I feel, as a matter of duty, I ought to endeavour to comply with it.

Octr. 30 wd suit me. I am inclined to / recommend Wycomb; it has some disadvantages in its population, but it is central, easy of access both from Berks & Oxon, & the gentry of the South, if they can be roused, more numerous & wealthy, than in the other parts of Bucks.

If / you decide on Wycomb, I hope you will give Mrs Disraeli, & myself, the great pleasure of being our guest, & I will endeavour to get the Drakes,[2] & people of that calibre, to meet you, & support us at the meeting.

The / town-hall belongs to a radical corporation, but would, of course, not be refused. Or would the National School-room be sufficiently capacious?[3]

Yours very faithfully, | *B. Disraeli*

1 D would attend the Quarter Sessions in Aylesbury on the 13th only. Edward Bickersteth, the Archdeacon of Aylesbury, would open the National school at Hughenden on the 16th. See **3723**&n1 and **3725**&n3.

1 Bishop Wilberforce had written on 27 September anxious to establish a Bucks Diocesan Society that autumn so as to increase the endowments of the poorest benefices. 'We shall succeed if we have you with us: and I venture to hope it may not be unpleasant to you to give us another such lecture on Sound Church Principles as you gave us at Aylesbury [*see* **3628**n1]. We think that Newport Pagnell or Buckingham or Wycombe as you may elect would be the best & would Oct *29* or *30* be days likely to suit you?' H B/XXI/W/356.

2 Thomas Tyrwhitt Drake (1817-1888), of Shardeloes, Bucks, JP, DL, high sheriff of Bucks 1859, in 1843 had married Elizabeth Julia Wedderburn (d 1885), daughter of John Stratton and widow of Col Wedderburn. On 18 October, she would accept MA's invitation for 'ladies without their husbands.' MA recorded that the event was attended by 'Mrs & Miss Drake,' presumably the eldest daughter, Elizabeth Caroline (d 1901), who in 1865 would marry William Hicks Beach. H D/III/C/608, acc.

3 On 6 October the Bishop would accept D's invitation and suggestions. H B/XXI/W/357. The meeting would be held on 30 October in the town hall; see further **3732**&n1 and **3734**&n1. The Wycombe National Schools for boys, girls and infants were built in 1855, and were attended on average by 270 pupils. Sheahan 924.

3721 TO: GEORGE FELL [Hughenden, Saturday 4?] October 1862

ORIGINAL: H B/II/121

EDITORIAL COMMENT: A draft in D's hand on the *verso* of a letter from George Fell dated '3rd. October 1862'; see n1. Endorsed in another hand on the first page of Fell's letter: 'A letter from the Secretary of the Agric. Associ[ati]on'. *Dating:* response by return post to Fell's 3 October letter; see n1.

Sir,

I lose not a post in removing from yr mind the unauthorized impression that ~~I~~ on Wedy. last I used any observ[ati]on ~~justly~~ ↑wh: cd with justice be construed as↓ personally offensive to yrself.[1]

To ~~say~~ ↑have sd↓ that "you were a disgrace to the Society" wd not ↑have been thought↓ only ~~but~~ a↑n↓ ~~violent~~ unjustifiable, but a silly, observa[tio]n. What I stated was, that the manner in wh: the lists were drawn up was a disgrace / to the Society. This was an opinion ~~given on~~ ↑of↓ a matter of business not ~~upon~~ ↑of↓ an indiv[idua]l.

As I ~~have now lea~~ have now learned who is the Secy. of the Socy. I beg leave to take this opport[unit]y of enclosing my subscription &c &c &c[.]

I am Sir, | Yr fa ser

3722 TO: LORD JOHN MANNERS Hughenden [Monday] 6 October 1862

ORIGINAL: NOT MY BD 2378

EDITORIAL COMMENT: Paper imprinted 'Hughenden Manor'.

Rt Honble | Lord Jno. Manners Oct 6. 1862

My dear JM.

Are you in England? I hope so; & that you will induce Lady John to pay us a visit on Friday the 17th. Octr. wh: will give / Mrs Disraeli, & myself, the greatest pleasure.[1]

Yrs ever, | D.

1 George Fell, secretary of the Central Bucks Agricultural Association, had written on 3 October from Aylesbury, offended by a conversation with D at the association meeting (see **3719**&n5), where D and Du Pré were listed under London, not Bucks, addresses: 'You stated that "I was a disgrace to the Society," and when I attempted to explain the matter to you, & mentioned that the list of Members published in the catalogue had been handed to me by my predecessors Messrs Acton Tindal and Edward Stone, you pronounced them to be "as bad as myself – and no excuse could be made for such a mistake" – Many of the Members of the Association to whom I have given the details of my interview with you, think it only due to the Society and to my own position as a Solicitor practising in the Town of Aylesbury, that I should request an explanation; and as the charge "of being a disgrace to the association" is as unbecoming in me to submit to, as it was in a Gentleman of your high position to make I trust you will on a calm consideration of the case do me the justice which I am entitled to demand.' H B/II/121. George Fell, an Aylesbury attorney, deputy coroner of the Aylesbury division of Bucks and a member of the London firm of Torr, Janeway, Tagart & Janeway, was admitted to practice in 1850. *Law List* (1870). Since he is not listed under Aylesbury in the 1860 *Law List,* he was presumably a recent arrival in the town.

1 Lord John Manners would reply from 6 Cumberland Terrace on 7 October that they regretted other engagements prevented acceptance. H B/XX/M/121. Lord John on 15 May 1862 had married Janetta Hughan (d 1899), eldest daughter of Thomas Hughan, of Airds, Kirkcudbright, and Lady Louisa Hughan, daughter of 8th Duke of St Albans.

TO: JOHN GRAVES Hughenden [Saturday] 11 October 1862 **3723**

ORIGINAL: CUL MS Coll Disraeli [6]
EDITORIAL COMMENT: Paper imprinted 'Hughenden Manor'.

The Rev: J. Graves | A.M. Octr 11 1862

Dear Mr Graves,

The Archdeacon is going to honor us by opening our school on Thursday next the 16th. Inst: & by previously preaching a / sermon.[1]

Divine service commences at two o'ck:, but if you could make it convenient to lunch here at one o'ck:, I am sure it would give much / pleasure to the Archdeacon, as well as to

Yours sincerely, *B. Disraeli*

TO: CALEDON DU PRE Hughenden [Saturday] 11 October 1862 **3724**

ORIGINAL: PML [8]
EDITORIAL COMMENT: Paper imprinted 'Hughenden Manor'. *Sic:* Wycomb.

C.G. Dupré Esq | M.P. Octr. 11 1862

Dear Dupré,

The Bishop comes to us on Wednesday the 29th. Inst:, & stays over Thursday. It will give Mrs Disraeli, & myself, very great pleasure, / if you will be one of his companions at Hughenden during his visit. I hear from him, that the meeting is to be on the 30th, Thursday, & / at Wycomb.[1]

Yours sincerely, | D.

TO: SARAH BRYDGES WILLYAMS Hughenden [Tuesday] 14 October 1862 **3725**

ORIGINAL: RTC [209]
PUBLICATION HISTORY: Blake 413, undated extract
EDITORIAL COMMENT: Paper imprinted 'Hughenden Manor'. There is no salutation. *Sic:* Sarcophagus'; close bye.

Oct 14 1862

Thank you for remembering your dear friends – & in so agreeable a manner!

Last night, I returned from Quarter Sessions, always a busy scene in our provincial life. It is, in fact, the old assembling of the estates of a Province, with the Governor, or Ld. Lieutenant, in the chair, & all the notables / around him: great debates about little things. In this County, there is a regular Magistrates mess, so we don't

1 Archdeacon Bickersteth had corresponded with Clubbe about postponing the opening of the National school at Hughenden, and whether 16 October would be as convenient for D as the 15th. On the 4th he had accepted D's invitation (not found) to Hughenden on the 16th and to stay with the Ds that night. No correspondence from Graves has been found, but he attended the lunch. H B/XXI/C/287-8, B/491, acc. See further **3725**&n3.

1 See **3720**&nn1&3. No response from Du Pre has been found, nor is he mentioned in the report of the event or H acc. He seems to have been abroad, as on 16 February 1863 he would write from Nice saying he would be back in London in time to dine with D on 4 March and attend a registration meeting. *BH* (1 Nov 1862); H D/III/C/910. See further **3732**.

dine together ~~not~~ at an hotel, or a pothouse, as in many other counties, but under our own roof, sitting on our own furniture, & drinking our own wines out of our own cellar; all which makes us a little pompous; especially the Wine Committee, who, you would think, / were a Council of State.

On Thursday next, we open our new school.[1] It is built by the same architect ↑who↓ restored the crypt, designed the two Sarcophagus', & also my father's monument,[2] wh: latter erection is much admired by all the world. It is fifty feet high, & of that Italian style of the renaissance period, which is, at the same time, rich & graceful.

The Archdeacon of Buckingham comes / from Aylesbury to open the school. There is a luncheon at the Manor at one o'ck, to wh: all the neighbourhood, & all the Clergy of the district, are invited: then we walk to the Church, wh: is close bye in the Park, & the Archdeacon, after the morning prayers, preaches a sermon. Then we are to walk to the school, wh: is in the village, one mile & a half away; a sort of procession – but alas! what weather! 'Tis the middle of the equinoctial gales, wh: are a fortnight after their time. Think of us on Thursday – & pity me – addressing the infant generation under their new roof, probably wet to the skin.[3]

Ever yours, | D.

3726 TO: MARY ANNE DYCE SOMBRE — Hughenden [Tuesday] 14 October 1862

ORIGINAL: QUA [159]

COVER: (Imprinted 'Hughenden Manor') The | Hon: Mrs. Dyce Sombre, | Willey Park, | Broseley | *B. Disraeli*

POSTMARK: (1) a cancelled one-penny stamp; (2) in circle: BROSELEY | B | OC15 | 62; *verso* (3) in circle: HIGH WYCOMBE | B | OC14 | 62; (4) in circle: WELLINGTON SALOP | B | OC15 | 62

EDITORIAL COMMENT: Paper imprinted 'Hughenden Manor'.

The | Hon: Mrs. Dyce Sombre — Octr 14 1862

My dear friend,

I have seldom read a letter, wh: gave me more satisfaction, than that, wh: greeted me on my return home, last night, from Quarter Sessions.[1]

1 See VI **2519**&n1 for the Hughenden National school built at D's expense.

2 The architect was E.B. Lamb; see VI **2792**n1 and, in this volume, **3707**&nn2&3 and **3723**&n1. Edward Buckton Lamb (1805?-1869), Gothic revivalist architect, designed over a hundred country houses, churches and schools.

3 In the event it would be a clear day. In his address on 'one of the highest and holiest purposes that can influence man', D would contend that, in the past twenty years, education had gone from being an advantage to being a necessity, even for agricultural workers: 'There is no longer a choice between ignorance and knowledge. Such is the progress of improvement in all the conduct of men in the present day, that the time is rapidly approaching when what was formerly the rudest labour of this parish will be conducted with men of intelligence, and this consideration should influence you all.' He acknowledged the difficulty facing young men deferring wages to remain in school, and hoped that this might be overcome by night school, at least in the summer. The Archdeacon would thank D for his speech and for 'the great aid which he has rendered to the erection of this school' and hope 'that the sun which now shines so brightly on our work is an emblem that we have the smile of our God in this undertaking.' The event would end at 5, with the children staying on for tea. H acc; *BH* (25 Oct 1862).

---

1 D's long-time friend since at least 1834, G.C.W. (Cis) Forester (see II **608n1**), had written from Willey Park, Broseley, on 12 October: 'I write you one line to announce my marriage to Mrs Dyce Sombre whom I know you appreciate[.] I am very happy and so I hope she is, at least I will do my best to make her so.

Those, who, like myself, / have always been interested by your character, & have recognised your talents, originality of mind, & affectionateness of disposition; have ever felt, how great might be your happiness, if united to one worthy of your companionship, & / devotion.

I have known Forester for the greater part of my life, & a better-hearted, or more honorable, man never existed. He has excellent sense, & thoroughly knows the world; while his sweet temper completes the / domestic spell.

My wife, who, probably will be writing to you by this post, is as charmed, as I am, with all this, & augurs, for your union, almost as much happiness, as has accompanied our own.[2]

Ever yours sincerely, | *B. Disraeli*

TO: CECIL FORESTER Hughenden [Tuesday] 14 October 1862 3727

ORIGINAL: QUA [158]

EDITORIAL COMMENT: Paper imprinted 'Hughenden Manor'.

Col: | The Rt Hon: C. Forester | M.P. Oct 14 1862

My dear Forester,

I am quite delighted; & have taken the liberty, without asking your permission, of telling the Lady so.[1]

I have always had a very sincere regard for her, & recognised, at an early period, / that union of lively, & original, talents with affectionateness of disposition, wh: deserved a partner for life worthy of her companionship & her devotion.[2]

If honor, sweet temper, excellent sense, thorough knowledge of the / world, are qualities, wh: conduce to domestic happiness, she has made a right good choice; & after having known you, & sometimes intimately, for the greater part of my life, I think it is scarcely presumption, in my giving this opinion. /

She begs me to remember her kindly to you, and to request you to tell Mrs Disraeli with her love that at last she has found the right man.' H B/XXI/F/194. See further **3727**. For Mrs Dyce Sombre, separated from her first husband in 1843 and widowed since 1851, see I **279n4** and V **1861**&n3. The wedding would take place on 8 November.

2 MA would write on the 15th: 'Believe in my cordial congratulations – I know not which will be the happiest. My husband admires you more, than ever. "Forester is an honourable, sensible, and good temperd man – Mrs Dyce Sombre, like you, thats me, will have her way in all things"[.] Marriage with the right "man" & woman is the only happy state. When shall you be in town, & when do you change your name, pray let us hear from you?' QUA 160. Mrs Dyce Sombre would reply to MA on the 18th: 'I this day recd. yr. most kind felicitations, & most especially gratifying it is to find that this marriage appears to be so universally approved of by friends & Relatives of both families ... I am *quite* sure WE shall be happy ... I believe we are to have a yacht & pass the Winter in the Mediterranean'. H D/III/C/625. She would also reply to D on the 18th: 'May I call you "my dear Friend" in return? Your letters to Cecil & myself will be kept & treasured for ever – *thank you* for what you say about him – every word is true – your delineation of his character is an additional proof of penetration. He is much attached to you, at wh. I rejoice, for you have ever been a kind friend to me ... I find I have not replied to Mrs. Disraelis question. I shall be in Town the *beginning* of Novr., as our marriage takes place early in that month.' H B/XXI/F/212.

---

1 See **3726**&n1.

2 In 1833, D himself had thought of courting her as '*Miss Jervis* ... a great heiress and clever ... She is pretty also.' I **279**.

Few things have ever happened, wh: did not immediately concern myself, that have given me greater pleasure, & satisfaction, than the announcement in yr letter.

Ever | Very sincerely yours | *B. Disraeli*

3728 TO: THOMAS TAYLOR Hughenden [Monday] 20 October 1862

ORIGINAL: H H/LIFE

EDITORIAL COMMENT: Taken from a handwritten copy in the Monypenny papers. *Sic:* Taylour (three times).

Col Taylour, M.P. Hughenden Manor | Oct 20, 1862

My dear Taylour

If an union with an honourable & intelligent man, with a kind disposition & a thorough knowledge of the world, be a good foundation for happiness[,] I think Miss Tollemache is much to be congratulated, but as, altho' I have not yet the great pleasure of her acquaintance, I have little doubt she will bring to the alliance every other quality, necessary to complete the domestic spell, I will venture to congratulate Colonel Taylour, & with all my heart.

I am sure Miss Tollemache will not counsel you to quit public life: all the great whips have been married men; & therefore I trust I shall not lose the services of one in whose energy & fidelity I have from experience, the utmost confidence.

My wife sends you her best regards & warmest congratulations[.][1]

Yours sincerely | B. Disraeli

3729 TO: SIR WILLIAM JOLLIFFE Hughenden [Tuesday] 21 October 1862

ORIGINAL: SCR DD/HY C/2165 [68]

EDITORIAL COMMENT: Paper imprinted 'Hughenden Manor'. *Sic:* very great indeed.

Rt Hble. | Sir W.H. Jolliffe Octr 21 1862

My dear Jolliffe,

The Bp of Oxd. comes to us on Wedy the 29th. Inst:, & stays till Friday.[1]

It wd. give Mrs Disraeli, & myself, very great [pleasure] indeed, if you cd. meet him. /

I venture to ask you as a bachelor on this occasion, wh:, otherwise, I shd not have done, but we are obliged to ask some county families, & cannot befittingly receive / yr daughters, wh:, otherwise, we shd. have delighted to do.

Yours ever, | D.

R.S.V.P.[2]

1 Col Taylor had written from Ardgillan, Balbriggan, on 15 October with an interim report on Dublin registration and to announce his forthcoming marriage. 'I fully intend to continue my services, such as they are, to the "Party" next session, if you & Lord Derby care to have them – as I see no reason why a gentleman should become a drone because he passes from a Bachelor to the condition of a Benedict.' On 13 November he would marry Louisa Harrington Tollemache (1833-1928), fourth child of the Rev Hugh Francis Tollemache (brother of 8th Earl of Dysart) and Matilda (Hume) Tollemache. He would write again, on the 24th from 16 Carlton House Terrace, to thank D and MA for their respective congratulations; he would be in town the following week and available if D wished to see him. H B/XX/T/30, 31.

---

1 See **3720**&n3 and **3732**&n1.

2 On the 23rd Jolliffe would decline because of a conflicting engagement and suggest instead visiting in two weeks; see further **3735**. H B/XX/J/91. For his unmarried daughters, see **3658**&n3.

TO: LADY VERE CAMERON Hughenden [Wednesday] 22 October 1862 3730

ORIGINAL: TEXU [31]
EDITORIAL COMMENT: Paper imprinted 'Hughenden Manor'.

Octr 22 1862

Dear Lady Vere,
I hope we may be so fortunate as to find you, & Miss Cameron, disengaged for Wednesday the 29th. Inst, & that you will give us the pleasure of your company at dinner on that / day, & meet the Bp of Oxford, & one or two other friends, at seven o'ck.[1]

Yours sincerely, | *B. Disraeli*

TO: SPENCER WALPOLE Hughenden [Friday] 24 October 1862 3731

ORIGINAL: QUA [36]
EDITORIAL COMMENT: Paper imprinted 'Hughenden Manor'.

The Rt Honble | Spencer Walpole. Octr 24. 1862

My dear Walpole,
The Bishop of Oxford comes to me on Wednesday, the 29th. Inst:, & stays over the following Thursday. It will give me very great pleasure, indeed, / if you will be his companion during his visit.

I much regret, that I am obliged to offer you, on this occasion, only a bachelors invitation; but it is necessary, that I shd. ask some County families to meet the Bishop, / & we could not, therefore, receive Mrs, & Miss, Walpole befittingly.[1] We hope, however, that their visit to Hughenden is only a gratification postponed to us, &, perhaps, to a more alluring season.

Mrs. Disraeli unites / with me in kind remembrances to Mrs. Walpole & yr hearth.[2]

Yours sincerely, | *B. Disraeli*

TO: SAMUEL WILBERFORCE Hughenden, [Tuesday] 28 October 1862 3732

ORIGINAL: BODL MS Wilberforce c13 ff189-90
PUBLICATION HISTORY: M&B IV 158n1, dated only 1862, extract from the last paragraph; Morley *Gladstone* I 591n1, extract dated only 1862
EDITORIAL COMMENT: Paper imprinted 'Hughenden Manor'.

The | Lord Bp of Oxford Octr 28 1862

My dear Lord,
I quite count on yr staying with us over Thursday.[1]

1 No response has been found, but the two would be dinner guests at Hughenden on 29 October. H acc. According to a catalogue entry (see Chronological List), D had sent a similar invitation on 14 October.

1 For the Walpoles' eldest daughter see VI **2692**&n4; their younger daughter, Isabella Margaretta Elizabeth Walpole (1840-1938), in 1869 would marry Capt George Parker Heathcote.

2 Walpole would accept next day (25th) and convey his wife's regards to the DS. H B/XXI/W/53.

1 Wilberforce had written on 25 October: 'I hope to be at the High Wycombe Station at 6:20 on Wednesday – with bag & baggage. May I ask you to order if order is needed a conveyance to be ready. I have written

I have got a good Bucks party for you in the house:[2] the Drakes,[3] Sir Chas Young,[4] Hubbard:[5] / Walpole will also be here, &, I think, you must get him to take a part in the proceedings. He has a locus standi; University M.Ps belong to the nation; certainly to the Church. I have given Evetts a hint to prepare him a / resolution.[6]

You will find everything prepared for you at the Station.

I hope you may have a good meeting. It is now, or never, with the Laity. If they move, all will be right; but we have troublous times before us. / I wish you cd. have induced Gladstone to have joined Ld Derby's government, when Ld Ellenboro resigned in –58.[7] It was not my fault, he did not. I almost went on my knees to him. Had he done so, the Church, & everything else, would have been in a very different position.[8]

Yrs sincerely, | D.

3733 TO: JAMES FARRER [Hughenden, late October? 1862]

ORIGINAL: H B/II/120

EDITORIAL COMMENT: Written in pencil in an almost illegible scrawl on the back of a letter from James Farrer. *Dating:* see n2.

Dr Mr Farrer,[1]

Accept my cordial thanks for the interesting add[iti]on wh: you have made to my library ~~w~~ ↑by ~~sending~~ a↓ copy of your privately printed &c ~~I highly prize it~~ acct of

to many of our Squires to ask them to support us on Thursday. Some I hope will. Lord Taunton, *cannot* be with us or he would: Lord Chesham does not attend in *the body* – but tenders his support. I am very thankful to you for your help. I hope to remain with you if you wish to keep me until Friday morning.' H B/XXI/W/358.

2 On 29 and 30 October, the following stayed over: Wilberforce, Mrs and Miss Drake, Hubbard, Walpole and Sir Charles Young. Regrets came from Stanley, Jolliffe, Malmesbury and Bickersteth. Additional dinner guests were, on the 29th, Lady and Miss Vere Cameron, Rev Clubbe and Mr Crew, and on the 30th, Rev and Mrs Evetts, Rev Clubbe and Rev Partridge. H B/XX/S/710, J/91, M/121, XXI/B/492, acc.

3 See **3720**&n2.

4 Sir Charles Lawrence Young (1839-1887), 7th Bart, of Delaford, Bucks (son of a former holder of D's Bucks seat and grandson of John Norris, former owner of Hughenden) was a future barrister (Inner Temple 1865). At the meeting he would second the resolution '"That the Diocesan Society for the Augmentation of the Endowments of Small Livings has strong claims upon our sympathy and support."' *BH* (1 Nov 1862). *MP* on 1 November would report his return to town.

5 J.G. Hubbard, MP (C) for Buckingham, would make one of the supporting speeches at the meeting. *BH* (1 Nov 1862).

6 Calling D 'one of the most brilliant, if not the most brilliant geniuses that [the House of Commons] ever possessed', Walpole (MP for Cambridge University) would not move a resolution but support that moved by Archdeacon Bickersteth and seconded by D: '"That the poverty of a large number of the livings of this diocese is a subject which demands the careful consideration of all those who are interested in the welfare of the National Church."' See further **3734**n1). Evetts, the rural dean, on 23 October had accepted D's dinner invitation (not found) and added: 'As soon as things seem to be in shape, I will either send or bring the Resolution, which the Archdeacon has suggested for your kind & able advocacy.' *BH* (1 Nov 1862); H B/XXI/E/287. *MP* of 3 November would report Walpole's return from his visit.

7 See VII **3111**&n1, **3113**&n1, **3127**&nn2&3 and especially **3128**&n7.

8 Presumably D is lamenting the loss of Gladstone as a potentially powerful ally against the threat of disestablishment.

---

1 James Farrer (1812-1879), of Ingleborough, WR Yorks, a barrister (Lincoln's Inn) 1837, JP for Yorks, Westmorland and Durham, DL for WR Yorks and Durham, was MP (C) for S Durham 1847-57, 1859-65.

yr observs in Orkney.[2] I highly prize it. It is a ~~serious~~[?] choice add[iti]on to the cat[alogu]e of privately printed books & is interesting for its subject & treatment [*illegible word*] admirably got up. The Runic [*illegible word*] has now taken its place in our collection.

TO: SARAH BRYDGES WILLYAMS Hughenden [Sunday] 2 November 1862 3734
ORIGINAL: RTC [210]
EDITORIAL COMMENT: Paper imprinted 'Hughenden Manor'. There is no salutation.

Private Nov 2 1862
Nothing could be more successful, than the Episcopal Re-union – both publickly & privately. My speech has given great satisfaction to the Country, & I am told / by great authorities, & I venture to believe it, that it was the speech of a statesman, without cant.[1]

Your fishmonger faithfully remembered yr orders, & never were offerings better timed. / Prelates, however bright & spiritual, & our Diocesan is a man of eloquence

2 Farrer's letter to D (see EC) is dated 'Ingleborough[,] Lancaster October 23': 'I have recently published for private circulation only a short account of my discoveries in Orkney during the Summer of 1861, & I have given instructions to the Publishers to forward a copy to you, hoping you will do me the honour to accept it.' H B/II/120. Farrer's *Notice of Runic Inscriptions Discovered during recent Excavations in the Orkneys* (40 pp, illustrated) was 'Printed for private circulation, 1862'. National Library of Canada.

---

1 *BH* on 1 November had begun its report of the 30 October meeting of the Society for Augmenting Small Benefices in the Diocese of Oxford (see **3720**&nn1&3) by declaring that D's, Walpole's and Wilberforce's 'statesmanlike ... addresses on the nationality of the Established Church will be read throughout the length and breadth of the land with feelings of delight by every true Churchman.' D had argued that, 'if you wish to engage the highest education and the highest sense of duty in the performance of the sacred office, it is most inexpedient that you should offer to those from whom you expect such a high fulfilment, rewards and remunerations which no class of society out of that service would accept.' Because the Church of England had been despoiled, its clergy were not rich; however, the 'estimable descendants of the original appropriators ... must feel an impulse that will make them apply a portion of that property ... to purposes of character which society will recognize, and by its approbation reward.' Despite the examples of Lord Howe and the Duke of Bedford, the laity could not be expected to exert themselves 'unless the Church itself takes a more definite and determined position [on being the established national church] than it has occupied during the last twenty-five years.' He then developed at length a defence of the national church: that disestablishment would give the civil power religious dominance and revolutionize the national character currently based on deep feelings for industry, liberty and religion. Church nationality should be asserted by educating the people, extending the episcopate, transferring non-spiritual matters to the laity, maintaining the parochial system and, finally, increasing clerical efficiency through adequate remuneration and support staff. Four of the measures could be effected without appeal to the legislature. After challenging his listeners to perform their duty courageously, he concluded: 'I hold [the church] hallowed, not merely because it is the sanctuary of divine truth but because I verily believe it is our best security for that civil and religious liberty of which we hear so much, and which we are told are opposed to its institution.' The speech was widely reported, e.g., *MH* (31 Oct), *Standard* (31 Oct), *MP* (1 Nov), *The Times* (3 Nov 1862); *BH* (8 Nov) also quotes a laudatory letter from the *Standard*. Archdeacon Bickersteth on 1 November had written about having the speech printed for general distribution, and on 6 November would thank D for his 'kind answer' (not found) and ask for a corrected copy, as he would 'gladly undertake to have it printed.' H B/XXI/B/493-4. A copy of the printed text is in H B/XV/7. It would be published as *Speech delivered by the Right Hon. B. Disraeli at a Public Meeting in Aid of the Oxford Diocesan Society for the Augmentation of Small Benefices, held at High Wycombe on Thursday, October 30, 1862* (London 1862). See also **3973**n5.

& almost genius, are by no means insensible to creature comforts, & I assure you the delicate prawns / of your lovely bay were duly appreciated.[2]

Ever yrs, | D.

3735 TO: SIR WILLIAM JOLLIFFE Hughenden [Tuesday] 4 November 1862

ORIGINAL: SCR DD/HY C/2165 [69]

EDITORIAL COMMENT: Paper imprinted 'Hughenden Manor'.

Private Nov. 4 1862

Rt Honble. | Sir Wm. Jolliffe Bart | M.P.

My dear Jolliffe,

I think you said, there was a chance of yr paying me a morning visit, in the early part of this month:[1] therefore, I send you a line to say, that we are going to town / tomorrow, & shall, probably, be absent a week or ten days.[2]

The French Ambassador is recalled, because "he is an old Whig Dandy" &, I believe, the Emperor &, our government are poles asunder ~~both~~ alike on / Italy, America, & the East.[3]

You may safely bet 100/1 that Napoleon will not desert the Pope.[4]

Yrs ever, | D.

2 On 31 October SBW had expressed delight at the DS' promised visit and hoped that her fisherman had not disappointed. On 5 November, MA would guess they would visit Torquay in mid-November: 'Dizzy is quite well & keeps out in the air as much as possible, but there are so many trees here it is very damp, and the owls make such a noise as soon as it gets dark, you might hear them at dear Mount Braddon.' RTC [467-8Q].

1 See **3729**n2.

2 The DS would be in London 6-17 November. H acc.

3 Auguste Charles Joseph, comte de Flahaut de la Billarderie (1785-1870), Napoleonic general, was ambassador at Berlin 1831, Vienna 1841-8, London 1860-2. Acknowledged as Talleyrand's natural son, he was famous for gallantry and elegant manners; in 1817 he had married Margaret Mercer Elphinstone, subsequently Baroness Keith and Nairne in her own right; their eldest daughter was Countess of Shelburne, after 1863 Marchioness of Lansdowne (second wife of the Earl of Shelburne, after 1863 4th Marquess of Lansdowne) and in 1867 would succeed as Baroness Nairne in her own right. Earle had written on 1 November: 'H Lennox was here yesterday – he says that Flahaut is really going, wh:, after your conv[ersa] tion last summer with Prince N, is significant.' H B/XX/E/266. On 2 November Malmesbury had written from London that Flahaut had been superseded. He would be officially replaced by Baron Gros later in the month. H B/XX/HS/111. Malmesbury II 286. By 'the East' D possibly refers to Russian ambitions for Montenegro, and/or to the situation in Greece (currently under the protection of England, France and Russia), where a military revolt had just deposed King Otto (who had left the country on 24 October). Derby on 31 October had written to Malmesbury: '[Russian] intrigues, I have no doubt, have led to the revolution which has broken out in Greece; though I should be sorry to swear that our ubiquitous friend Louis Napoleon has not thought that a little *imbroglio* in the East might serve to distract attention from the difficulties and embarrassments of the Italian question.' Malmesbury II 285.

4 Malmesbury on 2 November (n3) had written: 'You may safely bet 100/1 that L.N will not abandon the Pope.'

TO: ANNE GILCHRIST — Hughenden [Wednesday] 5 November 1862 — 3736

ORIGINAL: LIS [1]
PUBLICATION HISTORY: Raymond Lister 'A letter from Benjamin Disraeli to Anne Gilchrist' in *Blake: An Illustrated Quarterly* 14,1 (Summer 1980) 99
EDITORIAL COMMENT: Paper imprinted 'Hughenden Manor'.

Mrs. Gilchrist[1] Nov 5 1862

Madame,

There are some drawings, I believe a considerable number, by Blake, in this collection. It is many years, since I have seen them, but my impression / is, that they are, in a great degree, rather his own etchings, colored by himself, than, strictly speaking, drawings.

I leave this place tomorrow, for a fortnight, but, on my return, if Mr. Rossetti care to examine them, I will give / orders, that they shall be prepared for his inspection.

I am sorry to say, there is not the slightest foundation for any of the statements, contained in the letter, to wh: you refer. My father was not acquainted with / Mr Blake, nor is there a single volume, in the Hughenden ~~collection~~ library, enriched by his drawings.[2]

I have the honor to be | Madam, | your faithful Servt: | *B. Disraeli*

TO: PHILIP ROSE — [London, Friday] 14 November 1862 — 3737

ORIGINAL: H R/I/A/151
COVER: *Immediate* | Philip Rose Esq | 59 Rutland Gate | Hyde Park | London | *B. Disraeli*

Private Nov 14: 1862

Phil: Rose Esq

My dear Rose,

I am sure it will give you sincere pleasure to hear, that, after immense difficulties, we completed the sale of Taynton yesterday, & that Lovegrove carried out, successfully, all his views & expectations.

1 Anne Burrows Gilchrist (1828-1885) was currently completing the biography of William Blake (1757-1827) left unfinished by her husband, Alexander Gilchrist, at his death in 1861, and was being assisted by the brothers Rossetti, Dante Gabriel Rossetti (1828-1882), the Pre-Raphaelite poet and painter, and William Michael Rossetti (1829-1919), art critic, man of letters, and bibliographer. Her letter to D has not been found.

2 On 8 December 1862, W.M. Rossetti would tell Mrs Gilchrist that a 'very civil note from Mr Disraeli [*not found*] reached me this morning. He encloses a list of his Blakes, & offers to bring them to town for me if I do not know them. The list is headed "170 Drawings &c by W. Blake," followed by the names of various books, Urizen, Los, &c &c. The list (tho' not clear in this respect) & letter combined satisfy me that the "170 Drawings" are the *same* thing as the engraved books. I have written to say that, *in that case,* I know them, & need trouble him no further.' C. Ghodes and P.F. Baúm eds *Letters of William Michael Rossetti ... to Anne Gilchrist ...* (Durham, NC 1934) 5-6. In her memoirs Mrs Gilchrist would write: 'Only think of Mr. Disraeli's collection turning out such a mare's nest, and [T.F.] Dibdin's whole account a mere fabrication. [The antiquarian said that Disraeli (Beaconsfield) possessed original drawings by Blake; so W.M. Rossetti wrote to Disraeli, and he replied in the most courteous spirit, showing that he possessed only some of the published books.]' H.H. Gilchrist *Anne Gilchrist: Her Life and Writings* (1887) 132 (square-bracketed text in the original). The Gilchrists' *Life of William Blake, 'Pictor Ignotus'*, would be published by Macmillan in two volumes in October 1863. Isaac D'Israeli's will had left the prints to MA. H G/V/2.

We / have invested the mortgage money in E. India 5 pr Cts., wh: makes a considerable addition to the Income, & he has handed over to me a balance of £2,200.[1]

This is a great year, commencing, as it did, with yr. masterly consolidation;[2] in private affairs, / it has been successful throughout, & it is on the cards, that it may be a conclusive one.

We shall leave town for Hughenden on Monday, & in about a month, or less, shall be again passing thro' for / Torquay.

Yours ever, | D.

3738 TO: LORD DERBY Carlton Club, Sunday 16 November [1862]

ORIGINAL: DBP Box 146/1

EDITORIAL COMMENT: Carlton Club paper. Endorsed by Derby on the first page: 'Disraeli B. *Ansd*' and in another hand: 'Pol [P&C?]'. *Dating:* by context; see n1.

Rt Honble | The Earl of Derby | K.G. Sunday Nov 16

My dear Lord,

We have been in town for a couple of days, & return to Hughenden tomorrow.

Yesterday, I heard a piece of information, wh: astonished me, but wh: / you may rely upon, as if it occurred in yr own Council.

Lord John is in favor of mediation.

1 See **3704**&n1 and **3741**&nn1&2. On 16 April 1862 Lovegrove had acknowledged D's letter of the 14th (not found): 'I feel much obliged to you for placing the Taynton affair so unreservedly in my hands'. Subsequent correspondence deals with the complexities of the case (obtaining the mortgage deeds from Loftus, MA's London solicitor and trustee of the estate, handling outstanding claims against the estate, recovering the value, £467.13.2, of outstanding insurance on D's life, having the Ds certify facts such as the date and place of their marriage and the pedigree of Wyndham Lewis's entire family complete with a copy of his will and evidence that he left no issue, and obtaining an evaluation of the estate's timber). On 27 July Lovegrove had happily reported that, despite difficulties with the title, 'we are at last in a fair way to offer the Taynton estates for sale' and that enquiries had already been made. On 11 August he had requested information about the death and will of William Price Lewis and on 13 August sent 'an extract of our Counsels opinion on the question I put when placing the conditions of sale before him to settle as to Mrs Disraeli's right to have the full interest made up to her out of the sale proceeds. I must confess I am not at all satisfied with it and still think if the estates sell all above £11500 the mortgage due thereon will be applicable to make good Mrs Disraeli's past income 5 per cent' (the enclosed opinion stated that MA was not entitled to the deficiency between the mortgage interest and the rent received); he proposed to make 'a careful case' after the sale. On 21 August he had reported that the successful bidder at the auction was William Laslett, a former MP, at £12,650. Obtaining the evidence to complete documentation of the descent of the legal estate continued to be a problem, according to Lovegrove's 31 October letter (D's letters of 20 and 22 October therein acknowledged have not been found), but a new opinion stated that MA was entitled to the full balance of the purchase money after the capital due on the mortgage was invested; Lovegrove thought Loftus would be satisfied if she paid him £11,000 and retained the difference: 'I gave him distinctly to understand we should only deposit £11000, upon his undertaking to invest it in Mrs Disraeli's name alone in East India Stock, and upon this point he promised to communicate with his Co Trustee, and endeavor to get his sanction to it.' Lovegrove also said that the conveyance would have to be acknowledged by MA before two commissioners. On 6 November he reported having met with the trustees' representatives, who were still not satisfied that all outstanding claims had been settled. He suggested D nevertheless try to get the deeds from Loftus by directly offering him the £11,000, as otherwise the matter could drag on for months. On 9 November he acknowledged D's telegram (not found) and reported having got Laslett to go along with this arrangement, proposing the following Wednesday for the final transaction. H D/II/B/301-315, 373-7. Evidently the scheme worked.

2 See **3683**&n2 and **3740**&n2 for Rose's successful efforts in consolidating D's debts.

The Cabinet, that was put off, so mysteriously, some three weeks ago, was called by him to submit a proposition similar to the French one. /

Lord P. in the country, when informed of the object, refused to attend, & insisted, that the Cabinet shd. not meet.

Ld. John urged his views again the other day, but the Premier thundered, & the Secy. of State finally indited a recommendation of the policy, wh: he disapproved.

I / am not surprised, that you raise yr eyebrows, & are incredulous.

You may entirely rely on this.

It throws light on Gladstone's escapade.[1]

1 In the American civil war, the South in early September appeared to be winning, and was on the point of invading the North. The Confederate emissary in Paris, Slidell, had persuaded the Emperor, already strongly favouring the South, to propose a joint mediation to Britain with the alternative (as the North would almost certainly reject it) of recognizing and supporting the South. In cabinet, Palmerston had wavered, deciding to await the invasion of the North and suggesting that meanwhile Russia be invited to join the mediation; Russell and Gladstone had strongly favoured immediate action on the French offer, while Argyll, Milner Gibson and others had opposed it altogether. News of the horrendous but crucial battle at Antietam Creek on 17 September (when the Confederate advance was repelled) and Lincoln's subsequent Declaration of Emancipation on 22 September had reached London on 1 and 6 October respectively, deciding Palmerston against mediation. However, on 7 October Gladstone had made a statement at Newcastle that he later regarded as one of the worst blunders of his career; still convinced of a South victory and appalled at the carnage, he suggested the North accept the international view that Jefferson Davis had succeeded in forming a nation, and that Europe should offer 'friendly aid towards composing the quarrel.' Despite his later attempts at explanation, his remarks were generally regarded (*eg* by the outraged American minister, Adams) as indicating a switch in the government's declared neutrality, and were even seen by some as an endorsement of slavery. On 14 October at Hereford, War Secretary Cornewall Lewis had refuted any change in the strict neutrality policy and declared that, while the war remained undecided, recognition of the South was premature. An item in *The Times* of 27 October (reprinted from the *Observer*) reported: 'A Cabinet Council was appointed to meet on Thursday last [23rd], but on Wednesday afternoon, by direction of the Foreign Secretary, Earl Russell, the meeting was countermanded. The postponement, however, was notified too late to prevent several of the Ministers travelling ... Lord Palmerston did not leave his country seat'. Earle on the 26th had told D of the *Observer* item, adding that he had not yet heard any explanation, but thought 'there *must* be something up'. Cabinet Councils had subsequently been held on 11 and 14 November, and on the 15th the papers had published Russell's instruction (dated 13 November) to Cowley to decline the French proposal; Russia had not yet been heard from and in any case Ministers thought the North would at this point decline, and that it was therefore better to wait for a more promising time. Derby would reply on the 22nd: 'If I did not know how good your sources of information generally are, I confess I should have been incredulous as to the respective parts which you assign to Johnny and Palmerston with reference to the French proposals; and had I known of a difference of opinion between them, I should have reversed the quarters from which the assent and the objection proceeded. But I confess that if Johnny entertained the views you ascribe to him, and let it be known in Paris what his opinions were, it goes far to explain what otherwise I did not understand, what was the Emperor's object in making the offer, and exposing himself to the chance of a snub. That he contemplated an offer of mediation, I heard from Malmesbury, on his own authority, as long ago as the first of this month; but he did not say whether he had received any encouragement from hence. If he had, he will have good reason to complain of having been misled by our Foreign Minister; but if he had not, I should not be disposed to find much fault with the decision, especially if Russia held back, as she seems to have done. If she had assented, our refusal would have placed us in a very unpleasant position; but her rejection of the offer of co-operation deprived the proposal of any chance of being accepted, as the Armistice at this moment, would have been altogether in favour of the South, and the North could not have assented to it.' H B/XX/E/264, S/303; *The Times* (1-6, 17, 27 Oct, 12, 15 Nov 1862); *MP* (9 Oct 1862); Ridley *Palmerston* 558-9; Morley *Gladstone* II 78-83.

I hope you are well, & Lady Derby, to whom I beg my Complim[en]ts.[2]
Yrs sincerely, | D.

3739 TO: CHARLES PYNE Hughenden [Friday] 21 November 1862

ORIGINAL: PS 752

PUBLICATION HISTORY: Christie's catalogue (22 Oct 1980) item 32: 'A.L.S. to Charles Pyne, Hughenden Manor, 21 November 1862 ... 3 pp., 8vo, with envelope signed by Disraeli'.

Unfortunately I don't know Mr. Commissioner Jay, except, of course, by his high reputation.[1] If I had any claim upon his kindness, I would, willingly, exercise it for one, in whose fortunes I feel ever interested ...[2]

3740 TO: PHILIP ROSE Hughenden, Sunday 23 November 1862

ORIGINAL: H R/I/A/150

EDITORIAL COMMENT: Paper imprinted 'Hughenden Manor'.

Phil: Rose Esq Sunday | Nov 23 1862

My dear Rose,

This arrived this morning: tone not bad – but it is unfortunate that he avoids, or has escaped, seeing you.

I / trusted much to your happy address.[1] Written communications & written answers, on such questions, are "cold meat".

I lose not a moment in sending this over to / Penn, on the chance, that you may contrive to see him tomorrow.

If you are not at Penn, my servant will post it for Rutland Gate.[2]

Yrs ever, | D.

2 D's inquiry may be more than a formality. On 27 October Earle had written that he had heard 'Lord Derby's health is more than ever precarious. As far as I could follow the mysterious communication, some new symptom has shown itself, of an alarming character. The fact is kept very secret & is supposed to have been divulged to three persons only. On the whole, I am disposed to believe this account to be substantially true.' H B/XX/E/265.

---

1 Samuel John Jay, a London commissioner to administer oaths in Chancery, had an office at 1 Montague Terrace, Islington. *Law List* (1860).

2 D's former financial adviser William Pyne had died in 1849. There is, however, a Henry Pyne, assistant commissioner in the Tithe Office, 3 St James's Square. *LPOD* (1860). If it is he, he was still an assistant commissioner in 1864. The same Christie's catalogue (see ph) lists 'a letter from [D's] clerk James Daly to Pyne on Disraeli's behalf concerning a customs appointment' in 1874.

---

1 D is presumably referring to one of Rose's London addresses, his office at 6 Victoria Street or his residence, Rutland Gate, 59 Kensington Road. On 2 November 1862, Rose, who had earlier been travelling outside London, had told D he would be permanently in town after the 10th, making him available to meet D's unnamed 'friend' (see n2). H R/I/B/87.

2 Penn is the address of Rose's Bucks house, Rayners. Rose would reply next day (24th) from 6 Victoria Street: 'I find our friend left London yesterday, but he had some conversation with Baxter [*Rose's partner*] and will be here again in a day or two. I have written to Melton to ask for an appointment. Baxter has great influence with him and is now quite prepared to cooperate[.] I am almost glad that I did not see him today for I am still so prostrated with the effects of the Influenza that I should have been hardly able to talk to him.' H R/I/B/88. Melton Park, Doncaster, was one of the seats of D's future benefactor Andrew Montagu, with whom Rose was negotiating to take over D's consolidated debts (see **3683**nn1&2 and **3748**&n1). Baxter's influence may be due to his ownership of the *Doncaster Chronicle*, his other law office in Doncaster or his involvement in railway companies. *Norton Rose* 29-30.

3741[1]

TO: SARAH BRYDGES WILLYAMS Hughenden [Sunday] 23 November 1862

ORIGINAL: RTC [211]

PUBLICATION HISTORY: M&B IV 366, dated at Hughenden, 23 November 1862, the last paragraph

EDITORIAL COMMENT: There is no salutation. *Sic: sergens de ville.*

Hughenden Manor | Nov. 23. 1862

Since I wrote to you last, we have been in London & for some time. We went on account of some business connected with Mrs Disraeli's Gloucestershire estate, for two days, but we were kept by the lawyers two weeks.[1] However, after a Chancery suit, that has lasted a quarter of a century, it is all happily finished. The estate belonged to my wife's uncle, / the late General Sir James Viney, & after paying off some mortgages he left upon it, the remainder was hers.[2] But we never could effect a sale until this year, & now we are clear of it, with something in our pockets. This is the property, to visit wh: we approached the West in years gone by, & then extended our ~~visit~~ ↑travels↓ to Torquay, where we paid you our first happy visit, wh: has led to so much, that has increased the interest & pleasure of life, I hope, to all of us.

We came back here to superintend our annual planting, which has / now become a considerable affair. We have planted, in the course of years, our walks for some ~~man~~[?] miles in the woods, with evergreens, & the effect, especially in winter, is most animated & refined.

A private letter from Paris, from a great source, assures me, that the recent plot against the Emperor, wh: was to have transpired beginning of the next month, on the inauguration of the Boulevard Prince Eugene, was of a most serious character, tho' orders are given to all the journals to suppress all details, & ↑indeed↓ not to mention the subject. Three hundred conspirators were to have been dressed as *sergens de ville,* or municipal police; & to have surrounded the Imperial carriage, under pretence / of guarding the Emperor & Empress, & then to have assassinated them. They are equally violent against both. All the conspirators are Italians; obeying the orders of the secret societies.[3]

The Church is much agitated by a book disputing the authenticity of the Pentateuch, & written by a Bishop – one Dr Colenso, a colonial Bishop. 'Tis a great scandal, & is almost as bad, as Kings becoming Republicans. An indignant clerical critic says, it is "a queer name, Colenso; he supposes Italian, probably a Jesuit." I

1 See **3737**&n1 for the sale of the Taynton property including the requirement that MA be in town to acknowledge conveyance of the property before two commissioners. D had last written to SBW on 2 November (**3734**) and the Ds had been in London 6-17 November; see **3735**&n2 for D's earlier estimate of their stay in London.

2 See III **806**n1, IV **1329**&n1, **1479**&n1, **1599**&n1, V **2001**&n1 and VI **2540**&n1.

3 The Boulevard du Prince Eugène would be officially opened by the Emperor and Empress on 7 December 1862; the *MP* correspondent's report of the previous night was sanguine about 'reported plots': 'When criminal acts are so much talked about they seldom occur.' *The Times, MP* (8, 9 Dec 1862). The 'private letter' is Earle's of 18 November from Paris, which D quotes here virtually word for word. On 20 November Earle added: 'The Rothschilds believe in the plot, wh: is almost a sign of disaffection.' H B/XX/E/268-9. When the Emperor visited James de Rothschild in France in December 1862, they were so nervous of assassination attempts that '"there were police agents in every corner."' Weintraub *Charlotte and Lionel* 175-6. For more on the conspiracy, see **3904**n1.

believe, on the contrary, 'tis good Cornish, & ~~I believe~~ ↑that↓ you Western people, are answerable for the heresy, so we must leave the Doctor to yr friend, the Bishop of Exeter.[4]

Yours ever, | D.

3742 TO: SAMUEL WILBERFORCE Hughenden [Sunday] 30 November 1862

ORIGINAL: BODL MS Wilberforce c13 ff207-8

EDITORIAL COMMENT: Paper imprinted 'Hughenden Manor'.

Private Nov 30 1862

The | Lord Bp of Oxford

My dear Lord,

Your letter marked "secret"[1] was duly attended to by me – but I did not think it expedient to write to the individual on the matter, tho' a gentleman, &, I believe, an / Oxford man.[2] I saw him, however, a few days back, in London.

I find, that there is no absolute personal feeling, but an association of yr Lordship with the "Guardian" newspaper, wh:, I am told, is peculiarly distasteful to / the great body of the Tory party.

This is one of the unhappy consequences of the unfortunate disruption of 1846 – but, like many others equally inconvenient, time will cure it.[3]

I said upon this matter everything wh:, I / thought expedient, pointing out the difference of times & circumstances: &, I have no doubt the result will be, if not instantly, in due course, satisfactory.[4]

Believe me | my dear Lord, | Ever sincerely yrs | *B. Disraeli*

4 John William Colenso (1814-1883), born at St Austell, Cornwall, the first Anglican bishop of Natal since 1853, in 1862 published the first volume of *The Pentateuch and Book of Joshua Critically Examined* (1862-79), arguing that these Old Testament books are not factual but largely derived from myth and legend. This forerunner of modern liberal theology incurred a torrent of church protest and abuse including an attempted excommunication, not upheld by the law courts. The elderly ritualist Bishop of Exeter (Phillpotts), who built Bishopstowe at Torquay rather than live in Exeter and was famous for his defence of orthodox doctrine in the Gorham affair (see V **1995**n3), seems to have contented himself at this point with sermons against infidels. In failing health, he conducted his last visitation this year (1862).

---

1 Wilberforce had written on 1 November 1862: 'I am convinced from his frequent snarls sneers insinuations, and omissions, that the Editor of the Standard has some personal grudge against me. One word from you would change this tone & it would I think be useful that it should be changed.' H B/XXI/W/359.

2 The editor was Thomas Hamber (an Oxonian); see **3681**n1.

3 In Palmerston's continuing policy of preferring Evangelical or Low Church clerics to high ecclesiastical offices, Archbishop Longley on 20 October had been translated from York to Canterbury, and Wilberforce's former curate at Cuddesdon, Bishop Thomson, was about to be translated to the archbishopric of York. The Tractarian *Guardian* had recommended the High-Church Peelite Wilberforce, widely regarded as Gladstone's ally, for York. Meacham, *Lord Bishop* 271, 281; Chadwick I 238.

4 Wilberforce would reply on 4 December: 'Many thanks for your kind attention to my wish. Certainly *that* particular ground of offence was unreal. For the tone taken of late by the Guardian has been so offensive to me & to those who for the most part think with me that there have been most serious movements towards substituting for it another paper which should more accurately express our views.' H B/XXI/W/360.

TO: LORD CARRINGTON Hughenden [Sunday] 30 November 1862 3743

ORIGINAL: CARR [16]

EDITORIAL COMMENT: Paper imprinted 'Hughenden Manor'. *Sic:* Carington.

The | Lord Carington Nov 30 1862

My dear Lord,

We are quite delighted at the prospect of paying you, & Lady Carington, a visit.[1]

As to time, we await her suggestions; but / our plans at present, wh:, however, we would modify to suit yr convenience, are something like this:

In the middle of the month, (Decr), to pay our annual visit to Torquay.[2] Our stay in / the West will be a little prolonged this year, as we are engaged to pass a few days with Lord & Lady Normanby, who are now residing at Ld. Mt Edgcumbe's winter villa.[3] This, if accomplished, would bring us back to Hughenden towards the middle of Jany, or perhaps even earlier.

Our petty Sess: have not yet met, but ~~I will~~, I believe, will on Tuesday. I suppose the world is waiting to see, what the Lancashire landlords give on the 2nd. Decr[.][4]

Yrs sincerely, *B. Disraeli*

TO: EDITOR OF THE *BUCKS HERALD* Hughenden [Tuesday] 2 December 1862 3744

ORIGINAL: PS 753

PUBLICATION HISTORY: *BH* (6 Dec 1862); Bernard Halliday catalogue 178 (1934) item 135: 'A.L.S., 2 pp., 40, Hughenden, Dec. 2, 1862, to the "Editor of the Aylesbury News"', part of the first and second paragraphs with minor alterations

EDITORIAL COMMENT: D evidently sent this letter to more than one newspaper; see PH. The following is the *BH* version; the catalogue partial version has 'Country' instead of 'County' and omits the phrase 'in reference to this subject'. The *BH* version appears under the heading 'THE LACASHIRE [*sic*] DISTRESS.'

TO THE EDITOR OF THE BUCKS HERALD. Hughenden Manor, Dec. 2, 1862.

SIR, –

There is a subscription now taking place throughout the County in aid of our suffer-

1 Carrington had written from Gayhurst (N Bucks) on 25 November to invite the DS for a few days in January. On 9 December he would suggest 27-30 January; see further **3751**. H B/XXI/C/71-2.

2 See **3759**.

3 William Henry Edgcumbe (1833-1917), 4th Earl of Mount Edgcumbe, MP (C) for Plymouth 1859-61, was currently equerry to the Prince of Wales and would hold various royal household posts, including ADC to the Queen 1887-97. MA would record that the DS left Torquay on 5 January 1863 for the Normanbys 'at Winter Villa, Plymouth.' H acc. See further **3766**&n3.

4 The Lancashire textile industry was devastated by the lack of cotton due to the American civil war. On 2 December a county meeting would be held in Manchester at which £70,000 would be subscribed, including £5,000 by Derby, for relief of distressed workers. *MP* (3 Dec 1862). Carrington on 25 November (n1) had written: 'I ought to have written to you to say I had addressed each bench of Petty Session recommending the Justices to use their local influence in promoting a County Fund in aid of Lancashire distress & naming the Banks where an account would be opened. Forgive my apparent inattention – I am sure you will not think it prompted by intentional discourtesy, or by any diminution of long standing most friendly feelings.' See further **3744**.

ing fellow subjects in Lancashire,[1] and I heartily hope that its amount may be worthy of this community and adequate to the critical occasion.

There is, however, in reference to this subject, one special point, which I am anxious to bring before your consideration. In our dark period of 1835-6, many of our people, with the encouragement, and at the instigation, of the local authorities, emigrated to Lancashire. Their sufferings and struggles were at first severe. Some returned home; some sank before small-pox and fever; but some remained and prospered. In one town of Lancashire, at this moment, is a little Buckinghamshire colony, of thirty-three persons. They have sustained themselves for nearly a year on the property which they had realised by their industry, but that is now exhausted. In their dire necessity, they have appealed to their ancient home. I hope not in vain. The local sentiment is the strongest that influences man, and is the foundation of many virtues.

A fund has been formed here to afford them immediate relief; but it is most desirable that they should be supported for the next twenty weeks. Any contributions with this object, addressed to me, or the Vicar of Hughenden, will be acknowledged in your columns.[2]

I have the honour to remain, Sir, | Your faithful servant, | B. DISRAELI.

3745 TO: EDWARD KENEALY — Hughenden [Tuesday] 2 December 1862

ORIGINAL: MOPSIK [204]
EDITORIAL COMMENT: Paper imprinted 'Hughenden Manor'.

E.V. Kenealy Esqr[1] — Dec 2 1862

1 See **3743**&n4. In one of many local subscriptions, the Aylesbury drive (for clothes and money) established on 14 November had decided that house-to-house and parish-by-parish canvassing was 'the best means to be adopted for collecting subscriptions in aid of the funds now being raised throughout the country for alleviating the distress in the cotton districts in the north.' It was stated that at least a quarter of the two million people engaged in the cotton trade in the north were already desperately dependent on relief, and that £1,000,000 would be needed over the next three months to sustain them through the winter, by which time it was hoped that cotton could be obtained from other sources or the American civil war would be over. *BH* (15 Nov 1862).

2 By 13 December, D's 'fund for the relief of the Buckinghamshire families who emigrated to Lancashire in 1835-6 in consequence of the agricultural distress' had raised a total of £29.7*s* from six subscribers (£20 from D himself) and £40.5*s* by 20 December. *BH* (13, 20 Dec 1862). As well as Charles Clubbe, vicar of Hughenden, Philip Dauncey and W.E. Partridge were evidently also canvassers to whom D had forwarded pleading letters from Lancs, and who sent donations; Dauncey on 19 December would thank D for his note (not found) and ask for another letter to use (not found, if written). H B/XXI/D/33-4, P/130-1, A/VII/E/16. See further **3756**&n1 and **3762**.

---

1 Kenealy in an undated note had asked if he could dedicate a new edition of his *Goethe, A New Pantomime* to D (see V **2004**&n4). D, who in January 1862 had supported Kenealy's unsuccessful attempts to procure an Indian Judgeship (D's letters not found; see **3643**n1), had replied (letter not found), as Kenealy on 28 October thanked him for his 'kind permission' and included the proposed dedication: 'To the Rt Hon B Disraeli M.P. &c &c &c To you the first and most kind of Critics on this Poem in its fragmentary shape it is now dedicated in its complete form.' On 22 November he had written that he had sent a copy to Hughenden, but as D might be in town, he was also leaving one with his note at Grosvenor Gate. D evidently thanked him (letter not found) as Kenealy wrote on 27 November to say 'how highly honoured & delighted' he was with D's note: 'As to any "prejudice" arising from my opinion as expressed in print, of such a man as you I need not say how little I should regard it ... if there be prejudice in me, it will be more

My dear Sir,

I return you his Lordships letter happy & just.[2]

I have the pleasure of his acquaintance, & knew him thirty years / ago. He was, always, a very brightminded man.

I am curious to know what the critics will say, or whether they have honesty, or nous, enough, / to say anything.[3]

Ever, dear Sir, | Sincerely yrs, | *B. Disraeli*

I am not "devouring" but, intentionally, reading it slowly.[4]

TO: LADY GEORGIANA CODRINGTON Hughenden [Tuesday] 2 December 1862 3746

ORIGINAL: QUA [428]
EDITORIAL COMMENT: Paper imprinted 'Hughenden Manor'.

Decr 2 1862

Dear Lady Georgiana,

You, & Sir William, are most kind to remember our wishes. We have obtained a truffle dog; only a week ago; but he has not yet arrived. He comes / from Hampshire.[1]

Hughenden is a chaos, but I hope the garden will be achieved in time for your next visit; & then it will be an / Eden.[2]

Ever yrs | D.

TO: LADY DOROTHY NEVILL Hughenden [Friday] 5 December 1862 3747

ORIGINAL: EJM [24]
PUBLICATION HISTORY: *Anglo-Saxon Review* IV (1901) 144-5; Weintraub *Disraeli* 395, undated extract
EDITORIAL COMMENT: Paper imprinted 'Hughenden Manor'. *Sic:* Edgecombe; wheras.

The | Lady Dorothy Nevill Decr. 5 1862

than counterbalanced by good feeling on the other by those who enthusiastically admire you personally, politically & in your literary capacity.' H B/XXI/K/88-98.

2 On 29 November Kenealy had written again, enclosing a letter from Sir Alexander Cockburn (see V **2132**&n2): 'After you he is about the only person in England for whose good opinion of it I would care ... because there are very few more perfectly accomplished men in England than he, & there certainly never sat in Westminster Hall, a man who makes *justice* more thoroughly his guiding star in all that he adjudicates upon.' H B/XXI/K/99. Cockburn called it 'a marvellous production, the like of which has not appeared in modern days. You have passed Dante, Spencer [*sic*], Goethe, Byron and Aristophanes in the alembic of your own mind, and given us the quintessence of their genius in one united whole.' Kenealy 208.

3 The *Times* review was not kind. Kenealy's own preface had described the poem as 'an enigma to the many and [it] will always remain so.' The reviewer remarked darkly: 'A conundrum is all very well for those who are lazily cracking nuts after dinner; but a riddle involved in nearly 20,000 lines of verse and spread over nearly 600 pages is a bad job.' *The Times* (3 Feb 1863).

4 Cockburn (n2) wrote that he had '*devoured*' the work.

---

1 Evidently the DS had let it be known that they wanted a truffle dog; Lady Georgiana (see **3715**n9) had written from Chippenham on 29 November 1862 that one was available for £5 through William Palmer, head keeper at Goodwood, and that Sir William would transact all the necessary business if they wished. H B/XXI/C/303.

2 See **3747**&n2.

Dear Dorothy,

Maryanne has requested me to be her Secretary, &, tho' I am a bad letter writer, it is always agreeable to write to you.

In your last letter, wh: had no date, you talk of being in town the beginning of November, & speculate on the / chance of meeting us there – but the postmark of yr letter is Nov. 17, & it reached us, of course, two days afterwards.[1] Is it possible that it was mislaid?

Hughenden is now a chaos, for Mary Anne is making a new garden. She never loved her old one: &, now, she has more than twenty *navvies* at work, levelling & making terraces.

We / have as many workmen inside of the House, for altho' I always thought, that, both from form, & situation, I was safe from architects, it turns out that I was wrong, & Hughenden House will soon assume a new form & character.[2]

In a week, we go to Devonshire – & you will justly say, full time to do so. After a fortnight at Torquay, we are going on for a few days to the Normanbys, who / are dwelling in Lord Mt Edgecombe's winter villa.[3] Then, we shall pay a visit to our Ld Lieutenant, who lives at Gayhurst, fifty miles, & more, from this; a very different country – the land of Cowper & lowing ~~kind~~ kine, & pastoral meads,[4] wheras we dwell in beechclad hills, & among trout streams & water cresses – & then, will come Parliament! Adieu dearest Dorothy. Nevill I hope is well. Kiss, for me, Meresia, who will be beautiful at the right time[5] – & believe me,

Yr affectionate, | Dis.

3748 TO: PHILIP ROSE — Hughenden [Saturday] 6 December 1862

ORIGINAL: H R/I/A/152

PUBLICATION HISTORY: Bradford 246, 247, extracts

EDITORIAL COMMENT: Paper imprinted 'Hughenden Manor'. There is a copy in another hand at H R/IV/C/28 (possibly the letter to Rutland Gate).

Private Dec 6 1862

Philip Rose Esq

My dear Rose,

There is no difficulty on either point. I have written to you, thereon, to Rutland

1 Lady Dorothy's letter to MA, addressed to Grosvenor Gate, is full of gossip on society scandals, her breeding of silk worms and her unwanted pregnancy. (No child was born in 1863.) H D/III/C/1520a,b.

2 This was the early phase of the extensive renovation of the house and gardens of Hughenden under the architect E.B. Lamb; *eg* on 18 November he and a Mr Roberts had 'commenced height[en]ing the rooms,' presumably the vaulted and ribbed ceilings. In early December MA planted four dozen 'fine Scotch firs ... in the Ladys walk at 1/6d each.' H acc; Pevsner 173. For a treatment of the changes see Weintraub *Disraeli* 395-6. See also Introduction pp xv-xvi, Appendix VIII, and illustration p lix.

3 See **3743**&n3.

4 See **3743**&n1 and **3780**&n9. Gayhurst House was Lord Carrington's Elizabethan seat near Newport Pagnell; Cowper, who lived at nearby Olney, said of it: '"The situation is happy, the gardens elegantly disposed, the hot-house in the most flourishing state, and the orange-trees the most captivating creatures of the kind I ever saw."' Sheahan 538.

5 Lady Dorothy (n1) had written of her 13-year-old daughter: 'Meresia is ~~very~~ ↑pretty↓well but growing so nosy and lanky and armmy not a trace of good looks left – all her goodness is gone internally – poor little thing – we hope some of it may appear outwardly – hereafter but she is a dear little thing'. Meresia (who never became beautiful) was afflicted with St Vitus Dance (chorea), which in children may initially manifest itself as awkwardness.

Gate, as I am not sure, whether you are at Rayners, & I wish to secure your having the / answer on Monday.[1]

I could not, however, resist congratulating you on Southampton. It is very great.[2] Pam's own Liverpool! Where he has been making speeches, & tom-fooling, the whole of the Recess. He has dined there twice, & got off his horse, & hobnobbed with / an Austrian mercantile traveller, on another occasion.[3]

I will not be too sanguine about the great affair. It is too great. The figures come out thus: £35,000 to be raised by a charge of £800 pr ann: & after deducting the amount of that charge, the encrease to the Income / is £4,200 pr ann:![4]

This really beats the diggings.[5]

Yours ever, | D.

TO: PHILIP ROSE   Hughenden [Sunday] 7 December 1862   3749

ORIGINAL: H R/I/A/153

PUBLICATION HISTORY: Bradford 247, dated December 1862, extract

EDITORIAL COMMENT: A copy in Rose's hand is adjacent to this letter at H R/I/A/154a; in it the word 'lending' (para. 1) is followed by Rose's initialled insertion: '(Diz meant giving PR.).'

SECRET   Hughenden Manor | Dec. 7. 1862.

Philip Rose Esqr

1 See **3683**&n2, **3737**&n2 and **3740**&n2 for Rose's consolidation of D's debts. Rose had written on 5 December: 'We are proceeding satisfactorily but not *conclusively*. I anticipate that I shall be required to mention the *name* of the person willing to come in at the end and make the clearance. Can this be done? and even would it be possible IF insisted on for the two to be brought together and mutually understand that the success is to be a clear one. I wish for information on these two points by Monday. I look upon the *first* as of essential importance – the name –. the next if it can be volunteered very desirable indeed, but you know how far it would be practicable or useful.' H R/I/B/89. See further **3749**&n1.

2 On 20 November 1862, Spofforth had written to D: 'I am happy to tell you that the Lord Mayor's canvass at Southampton is of the most satisfactory character but he is in great fear the election is going to cost more than £1200 and is unwilling to go to the poll unless he can be assured he will not be mulcted in a larger amount. I am going down to Southampton tomorrow night to endeavour to get a guarantee from the leaders of the party, that they will return him for that sum ... We have hopes that at last we shall be enabled to induce Mr [John] Dent the great Tea Merchant to go and contest the seat at Totnes, the difficulty hitherto has been to find any one willing to spend between three and four thousand pounds, the sum required to win the election.' H B/XXI/S/393. Rose (n1) had written: 'I sent you a telegram of our victory at Southampton. I have reasons for believing that Totnes is equally safe.' In the Southampton by-election on 5 December, a constituency which had not returned a Conservative since 1842, William A. Rose, lord mayor of London, had defeated the Liberal 1,715-1,647. At the Totnes by-election on 9 December, Dent, the Conservative, would be disgraced by the Liberal victor 171-5.

3 Palmerston had spoken at a public dinner at Winchester on Monday 13 October, and been the main speaker at Southampton on 15 October on the opening of the Hartley Institution, as well as at the banquet following. On Monday 27 October, he had been spotted riding past the Southampton chamber of commerce where officials were at a civic *déjeuner* with Baron Thierry, who was inspecting the docks as part of his mission to increase communication and trade between Austria and England. Palmerston was induced to join the party, where he made a free-trade-extolling speech that concluded with an invitation for Thierry to dine that evening at Broadlands; he then returned to his horse. *The Times* (16, 17 Oct, 8 Dec 1862); *MP* (28-9 Oct 1862).

4 See **3749**&n4.

5 Reports from the Australian goldfields, while not up to those of 1861, continued very favourable, with new fields opening up in Australia and a new 'rush' at Otago, New Zealand. Reports in mid-November had noted the *Great Britain* had sailed from Australia with a cargo of 100,721½ ounces of gold and 50,000 sovereigns, worth in total nearly £500,000. *The Times* (14, 15 Nov 1862).

My dear Rose,

My second friend is Rothschild.[1] He is not eager in this matter. It is against his system. He likes to give to his friends, not lend. This sum is beyond lending [*corrected in Rose's hand:* Diz giving], & as he never takes interest, from me at least, it is a post obit without any return, & great risk – but he has yielded to the urgency of the case, & the great result for me at stake, wh: cannot be exaggerated. When he promised first, the aspect of the money world was very blooming, & his health was good, wh:, at present, it is far from being.[2] Whatever he has promised, however, he will rigidly perform, tho' not more: he / is as certain, as the payment of the dividends.

He would require no evidence of the affair being consummated beyond my word, but, if the great result be accomplished, then I had intended to have asked you to have written me a letter, referring to the circumstances, & informing me, that the second mtge was ready for execution, or some statement virtually to that effect.

This would be unnecessary if he saw our friend & conferred with him, to wh: on my part, if desired, there could possibly be no objection – all you would have to do, would be to take care, that the application to ~~him~~ ↑R↓ sho[ul]d not be abrupt. Tho' really one of the best men alive, his manners are not always fascinating, & if not prepared by some little ceremony or attention, he / is apt to put his back up. I think, he ought to be spoken to ~~me~~ ↑by me↓ first, & his permission, or rather assent, requested.

You can settle all this when you see me. I shall be in town probably on Thursday, & for some days, preparatory to going to Torquay.[3] Will you have the kindness to let me know, whether I shall find you, or if your circuit at all interferes, for it would be very annoying not to see you at such a moment. I could make my visit to London square with your movements.

The epithet at the top of this sheet means that it shd. not be about your office – not that it contains anything, wh: I wish not to be communicated to our friend.

Your telegram was really glorious. I / wrote to you, to thank you, at Rayners – my letter has by this time, I doubt not reached you, if you happened not to be there.

The private matter, that we have in hand, would, if achieved, make a difference to me of more than 4000£ pr annm.[4]

Ever yours, | D.

1 See **3748**&n1. The first friend was Andrew Montagu; see **3683**&nn1&2, **3737**&n2 and **3740**&n2.

2 For Rothschild's health see **3719**&n1.

3 The DS would go on the 20th; see **3757**.

4 Rose would reply next day that he was committed for the coming week to his circuit (presumably in connection with his post as county court treasurer; see VII **3184**&n4) and would not return until Saturday night: 'The great affair is working steadily. I am expecting his most Confidential Agent immediately. I have received your letters which give me all the information I wish. I dont think a personal meeting between the two will be needed. Of course none would take place without all due preliminaries – but it is a great thing to be able to make use of such a name as the person willing to come last in the arrangement. It will inspire confidence'. H R/I/B/90. From the Hughenden deeds file, it seems that Montagu gave only £20,000 at this time, with Rothschild lending the rest, about £40,000, on a second mortgage.

TO: SARAH BRYDGES WILLYAMS Hughenden [Tuesday] 9 December 1862 3750

ORIGINAL: RTC [212]

PUBLICATION HISTORY: M&B IV 331, dated at Hughenden, 9 December 1862, omitting the first paragraph; Blake 414, 419, dated 9 December 1862, extracts; Meynell II 465, dated 9 December 1862, omitting the first paragraph; Ellen Moers *The Dandy* (1960) 326, undated extract

EDITORIAL COMMENT: Paper imprinted 'Hughenden Manor'. There is no salutation.

Decr. 9 1862

It gave us great pleasure to receive your letter this morning.[1] Here we are entirely absorbed in preparing for our Western tour, by trying to finish all the business, very various, wh: claims our attention on quitting home, & / quitting it for many months. An estate is a little Kingdom, & there is almost as great a variety of interests, & characters, & parties, & passions, on these acres, as in Her Majesty's realm.

They say, that the Greeks, resolved to have an English King, in consequence of the refusal of Prince Alfred to be their monarch, intend to / elect Lord Stanley. If he accepts the charge, I shall lose a powerful friend & colleague. It is a dazzling adventure for the House of Stanley, but they are not an imaginative race, &, I fancy, they will prefer Knowsley to the Parthenon, & Lancashire to the Attic plain.[2]

It is a privilege to live in / this age of rapid & brilliant events. What an error to consider it an Utilitarian age! It is one of infinite Romance. Thrones tumble down, & crowns are offered, like a fairy tale, & the most powerful people in the world, ↑male & female,↓ a few years back, were adventurers, exiles, & demireps.

Vive la bagatelle!

Adieu! | D.

TO: LORD CARRINGTON Hughenden [Thursday] 11 December 1862 3751

ORIGINAL: CARR [17]

EDITORIAL COMMENT: Paper imprinted 'Hughenden Manor'. *Sic:* Carington.

The | Lord Carington Decr 11 1862

My dear Lord,

We shall keep ourselves disengaged for the 27th. Jany, & anticipate very great pleasure from a visit / to Gayhurst.[1]

Our united kind regards to its Lady.

Ever yours, | *B. Disraeli*

1 SBW had written to MA on 2 December: 'I am quite charmed with the idea of soon seeing you and dear Dizzi and in the best Health[;] time has made inroads in mine which I wish may be restored before we meet'. RTC [470Q].

2 Following the military deposition of King Otto in Greece (since 1832 an independent kingdom under the joint protection of Russia, France and Great Britain), its throne, by a virtually unanimous plebiscite currently in the news, was offered to Prince Alfred, who however was declared ineligible by the terms of the protectorate. Stanley on 7 December had recorded: 'Much laughing at Frederick and me, because a newspaper (the *Post* I think) quotes the resolution come to by some Greek club somewhere, that if they cannot have an English prince, they will vote for "a son of Lord Derby."' On the 19th he would record: 'There has been some talk of my name being suggested as a candidate for the Greek throne: I have never treated it otherwise than as a joke'. *Disraeli, Derby* 192-3. In 1863, Prince William George of Schleswig-Holstein would be elected George I, King of the Hellenes. See further **3783**, **3784**&n2 and **3791**.

1 See **3743**&n1.

3752 TO: JAMES HANNAY [London, Monday] 15 December 1862

ORIGINAL: PRIN Parrish Coll AM 17749

EDITORIAL COMMENT: In the fourth paragraph, 'principle' has been corrected from 'principal'. *Sic:* this morning. (The DS had left Hughenden by train for London on 13 December. H acc).

Private Dec 15 1862

Jas. Hannay Esq[1]

My dear Sir,

At the Taplow station, this morning, I took up a vol: of Cr. North. Look at Vol. 1 – 150p.[2]

It is a matter of little importance whether I were, or not, editor of a Newspr., wh: expired nearly forty years / ago – but truth, even on slight affairs, is not without value.

I never was the Editor of the Repres[entativ]e paper; I never wrote a single line in it, on any subject, nor was I ever asked, nor did I ever ask, to do so.[3]

I have frequently at times, & often recently, seen ~~a d~~ this statement in question in ephemeral organs – but / I have made it a rule never to embark in any self-vindicating controversy, where the principle of personal honor was not concerned. This is, however, in a more substantial form, & there is a spice of extra malice in it, I suspect – from the quarter whence it comes.

The Editor of the Repres[entat]ive / paper was Mr Lockhart. When it was given up, I was abroad, & one of those mystifications; in wh: Mr Lockhart excelled, was invented to cover his retreat & confusion.

He fixed upon the name, of an absent youth, perfectly unknown, but who, during the projection of the paper, had been used, by those interested in the future, as / a competent & convenient means of communication with various parties & interests – as the scapegoat for his own inefficiency.

I feel a disrelish, in the position wh: I now, however unworthily, occupy, to rush into print on such a matter, but I feel also somewhat indignant at this prolonged, & / insistent, injustice.

If you can make out these lines, written with a frozen hand, & in a London twilight, I would venture to ask you, as a Journalist, a man of letters, one acquainted

1 James Hannay (1827-1873), in addition to the attributes D lists, was editor of the *Edinburgh Evening Courant* 1860-4; for D's previous brief exposure to Hannay's poetic talent, see VI **2632**n4.

2 'Christopher North' was the pseudonym of John Wilson (1785-1854), a prolific writer for *Blackwood's*. In 1862 his daughter Mary Gordon had published her *Christopher North; a Memoir of John Wilson, late Professor of Moral Philosophy in the University of Edinburgh. Compiled from Family Papers and Other Sources* (2 vols, Edinburgh). The passage to which D refers is actually in volume 2 p 105 to which is appended a footnote taken from 'Histories of Publishing Houses,' *Critic* (21 Jan 1860): 'With Mr. Benjamin Disraeli for editor, and witty Dr. Maginn for Paris Correspondent, John Murray's new daily paper, *The Representative* (price 7d.), began its inauspicious career on the 25th January 1826. It is needless to rake up the history of a dead and buried disaster. After a short and unhappy career of six months, *The Representative* expired of debility on the subsequent 29th of July. The Thames was not on fire, and Printing House Square stood calmly where it had stood. When, in after years, sanguine and speculative projectors enlarged to John Murray on the excellent opening for a new daily paper, he of Albemarle Street would shake his head, and with rather a melancholy expression of countenance, pointing to a thin folio on his shelves, would say, "Twenty thousand pounds are buried there."'

3 For D's youthful adventure with the *Representative,* see the entries under that name in the index of I p 461. For recent examples of D's version of events, see **3460** and **3619**.

with politics, & as an honorable gentleman, to give me your opinion upon the circumstances wh: will be calmer than my own – & advise me as to what I shd do, or whether, I shd. do anything.[4]

Believe me, | my dear Sir | sincerely yrs | *B. Disraeli*

My best direction will be Grosr. Gate. I am en route for Devon.

TO: CHARLES CLUBBE London [Monday] 15 December 1862 **3752A**

ORIGINAL: RIC [016]

COVER: The | Revd. C.W. Clubbe, | A.M. | Hughenden Vicarage, | High Wycomb. | *B. Disraeli*

POSTMARKS: in circle: LONDON | 6 | DE 1[?] | 62; the stamp and part of the postmark have been cut out

EDITORIAL COMMENT: *Sic:* Wycomb.

Rev. C.W. Clubbe | A.M. Decr: 15 1862

My dear Clubbe,

Many thanks.

The emigrants will be very gratified.[1]

I have written a line of acknowledgmt.[2]

With my kindest remem: to Mrs. Clubbe[.]

Yrs sincerely, | D.

TO: SAMUEL WILBERFORCE Grosvenor Gate [Tuesday] 16 December 1862 **3753**

ORIGINAL: BODL MS Wilberforce c13 ff217-18

EDITORIAL COMMENT: Paper imprinted 'Grosvenor Gate'. In another hand at the top of the first page: 'Read'.

The | Lord Bp of Oxford. Decr 16 1862

My dear Lord,

Let me cordially thank you for yr kind, & most liberal, donation to our fund.[1] I am

4 Hannay replied next day from 28 Buccleuch Place, Edinburgh: 'I have read your obliging letter with great interest, and not without some astonishment. I must honestly say that I always believed that *Representative*-myth, myself, – since it would not interfere with my belief in any man's genius that he had failed to establish a new London newspaper. As far as I know, my generation generally believe the story; and it ought assuredly to be dispelled by a Niebuhrian process at once and for ever. The indirect effect even would be good, as it would show the impartial credulous wide public that other loose floating stories about public men like yourself, are very likely to be lies also. – The story having been last circulated here, the *Courant* would be, I venture to think, a proper organ for its' [*sic*] extinction. If you can trust me to write a quiet goodnatured exposure of the error, I shall be only too happy and will be very discreet in the mode. Without pretending to contradict the tale, *officially,* I would indicate that we were not guessing merely at the facts, and the correction would soon disseminate itself. It were well, if Lockhart's memory needed to be charged with nothing worse than *a mystification* –, and that if you are sure *he* first spread the tale, there was no malignity of a serious kind in his doing so. The reserve which I believe the family maintain about his papers, looks as if they did not like too close a discussion of his literary history. But as he is the latest type of a Scotch literary Tory, t'were well to make his delinquencies as pardonable as possible. – Not that I think you are seriously bound to suffer absurd & false gossip in his cause, of course. – For, in any case, I think the nonsense should be exploded. – I will by no means, of course, take any step in the matter till I have heard from you again.' H B/XXI/H/143. See further **3755**&n1.

---

1 See **3744**&nn1&2, **3753**&n1, **3762** and **3765A**n1.

2 This letter has not been found.

---

1 Bishop Wilberforce had written on 15 December: 'I see that you are willing to take charge of small sums

sure our poor emigrants, when they learn, wh: they will do by this days post, / that they have been remembered, in their adversity, by their Bishop, will be cheered, & deeply gratified.

I have sent for the person acquainted with the circumstances mentioned in the other part of yr letter.[2] These deplorable effusions / are the result, I am convinced, of ignorance, & not of ill-intention. There has been nobody, of the adequate knowledge & position on these matters, to guide these popular scribes. They require educating. The Ch: organs, are, generally speaking, written by the clergy, / & read only by the Clergy. But the chance, wh: the "Standard" gives us, of influencing the opinion of the million must not be lightly relinquished. It has really a sale of some 50,000 daily.

I will write to you further anent.

Yrs ever, | D.

3754 TO: SARAH BRYDGES WILLYAMS

Grosvenor Gate
[Wednesday] 17 December 1862

ORIGINAL: RTC [213]
EDITORIAL COMMENT: Paper imprinted 'Grosvenor Gate'. There is no salutation.

Decr. 17 1862

We hope to reach Torquay on Saturday – & I shall inform you immediately of my arrival.[1]

I trust to find you quite well, & / look forward to a most happy visit.

I am oppressed with business of all kinds; particularly the Kent Election[2] – & I / shall be very glad to get into Devon.

Yours ever, | D.

for our Bucks Emigrants ... May I send you the inclosed five pounds for them.' H B/XXI/W/361. For the fund, see **3744**&nn1&2.

2 The Bishop's letter (n1) had continued: 'SECRET I have read today not without indignation the article in the Standard on Church affairs. How is it possible that with one organ venting such things the Church can ever heartily support us. Mr Jarvis & his miserable "friend of the Clergy" called into being for his own *percentage* may appeal by apocryphal stories to the low radicalism which festers in the poorest part of our clergy. But the body of them hate to have their Archdeacons & their Bishops indiscriminately libelled. What can the Church do without its leaders & what can the leaders do if they are the base wretches that article over & over states every one of them to be in its long tissue of falsehoods: e.g. I have been 17 years a Bishop & never gave but one Perpetual Curacy of 30 pound a year to relation or connexion. Then you will see that it tries to link all this onto your speech at Wycombe [*see* **3734**&n1]. I hope you will interfere: for the mischief one such article does is incalculable'. The Friend of the Clergy Corporation was established in 1849 to provide pensions of up to £40 per annum to needy clergymen of the Established Church and their widows, unmarried daughters and orphans.

---

1 See **3759**.

2 On 9 January 1863, in a by-election at E Kent after the death of William Deedes (C), Sir Edward Dering (L) would defeat 2,775-2,687 Sir Norton Knatchbull (C), 10th Bt, whose late father had held the seat until 1845; in his election address, Sir Norton had declared his principles to be the same as his father's, and that he was '"prepared to uphold our Protestant religion as established in Church and State"'. *The Times* (15 Dec 1862). On 10 January 1863 *The Times* would deplore the absence of significant differences between parties: 'what would Sir N. Knatchbull have done that Sir E. Dering will not do? ... there is nothing ... between Conservative and Liberal.'

TO: JAMES HANNAY Grosvenor Gate [Wednesday] 17 December 1862 **3755**

ORIGINAL: PS 754

PUBLICATION HISTORY: W.V. Daniell's catalogue 7 [1911] item 493: 'A.L.s. (initial), 12 pp. 8vo. *Grosvenor Gate, Dec.* 17, 1862, *marked private and confidential* to J. Hanney [*sic*].'

[respecting the "Representative" and his first ideas of entering politics when a youth of 19] .... I caught hold of the secret – anything political and wh. concerned Mr. Canning interested me. I rather I dare say very intrusively pushed myself into their affairs, but boys are pardoned and often encouraged. I saw some opening to public life and some connection with an eminent leader, with whom I sympathised. It is not very easy now to get into Parliament; in those days it was still more difficult. I managed, in many things, to make myself the medium of communication with some persons of influence connected with this undertaking; among others, Lockhart. [He then details the cause of the quarrel between himself and Lockhart, whom he charges with misrepresentation.][1]

TO: [MILFORD] REED Grosvenor Gate [Friday] 19 December 1862 **3756**

ORIGINAL: PS 1453

PUBLICATION HISTORY: Julian Browning Autographs & Manuscripts, Advanced Book Exchange Internet site (March 1999), item 277: 'Autograph Letter Signed "B. Disraeli," to Jn. [*sic*] Reed Esq. ... 4 pp. ... Grosvenor Gate, 19 December 1862.'

[looking forward to success] in effecting my main object, wh. is to carry the Buckinghurst Colony through the winter months. ... They inhabit Staley Bridge, & form seven families & 35 individuals – & were in the enjoyment of the highest class of wages, before the catastrophe occurred. I was obliged to omit the name of their whereabouts, as they, probably, would have been deprived of parochial aid, if our special assistance were known.[1]

1 See **3752**&n4. *BH* on 3 January 1863 would publish the following under the heading 'MR. DISRAELI, M.P., AND THE "REPRESENTATIVE" NEWSPAPER': 'The *Edinburgh Courant,* in an article in which we trace the "fine Roman hand" of Mr. James Hannay, alluding to the *Representative,* says:– "When such a fable begins to be solemnly recognised in our literature, it is time that its real character should be pointed out. And the latest recognition of it having appeared in a Scottish book, we venture to think that the exposure will most properly come from the *Courant.*"' After showing the absurdity of a youth of 19 being appointed to edit a new newspaper by a man of John Murray's stature and experience, the article concludes: 'If [*Lockhart*] made the young Disraeli the scapegoat of the *Representative*'s failure, it was a "mystification," not perhaps malignant in intention, but certainly more mischievous than other performances of his in a line in which he excelled ... people may take our word for it that the widely-spread statement that the *Representative* failed under the conduct of Mr. Disraeli is purely and entirely a popular delusion.'

1 See **3744**&nn1-3. 'Buckinghurst' is probably the cataloguer's mistranscription of Buckinghamshire, perhaps abbreviated by D. The cataloguer probably also misread the recipient's first initial. The 27 December list of subscribers to D's distress fund includes 'Mr. Milford Reed, *Bucks Herald* office,' who contributed 1 guinea. *BH* (27 Dec 1862). His letter to D has not been found. For the success of the fund, see **3762**.

3757 TO: PHILIP ROSE Grosvenor Gate [Friday] 19 December 1862

ORIGINAL: H R/I/A/155

EDITORIAL COMMENT: Paper imprinted: 'Grosvenor Gate'. Endorsed in Rose's hand on the second page: Montagu'.

Private Decr 19 1862

Philip Rose Esq

My dear Rose,

We are off tomorrow morning, by express, to Torquay – & shall be in the same hotel as Rothschild! It must be fate.[1]

Write / to me *under cover* to

Mr. Webb

Royal Hotel

Torquay

Yrs ever, | D.

3758 TO: HENRY PADWICK Grosvenor Gate [Friday] 19 December 1862

ORIGINAL: LCC LC.1 Item 6; Frame C4

EDITORIAL COMMENT: Paper imprinted 'Grosvenor Gate'. There is no salutation.

Private Decr 19 1862

I forgot to say, that my address will be *under cover* to

Mr. Webb

Royal Hotel

Torquay.

The ~~y~~ chances are, however, / that I shall have to write to you first.[1]

Yours sincerely | D.

3759 TO: SARAH BRYDGES WILLYAMS [Torquay] Saturday 20 December 1862

ORIGINAL: RTC [215]

EDITORIAL COMMENT: Docketed by SBW 'Decr 20 1862'. There is no salutation.

Saturday

We have just arrived; train very late;[1] & shall be delighted to see you again.

I fear it will be too late to night. If so, at what time may I call tomorrow?

Maryanne's love[.]

Yrs ever | D.

1 Charlotte de Rothschild had written to MA on 5 December from Webb's Royal Hotel in Torquay where the Rothschilds were passing the season. H D/III/C/1831a; *MP* (8 Dec 1862); Weintraub *Charlotte and Lionel* 172-3. MA recorded that the DS left for Torquay on 20 December, with £60.17.5 in her purse. H acc. For Rothschild's part in Rose's current efforts to consolidate D's debts, see **3749**&n1 and **3767**&n2.

1 For D's next letters to Padwick, see **3761** and **3766**. Padwick's most recent extant letter to D, of 22 November 1862, concerned the Villiers affair; he enclosed an 'irregular application' from a Mr Ronaldson but recommended they not comply with it. H A/IV/J/230.

1 On 19 and 20 December severe gales had done much damage along the South Coast, disrupted the telegraph to London and wrecked at least one railway line. Harriet Semper wrote to MA on this day (20th) that they 'must have had *a rough passage* to Torquay.' *The Times*, *MP* (22 Dec 1862); H D/III/C/2314.

TO: SARAH BRYDGES WILLYAMS Torquay, Saturday 20 December 1862 3760

ORIGINAL: RTC [214]

EDITORIAL COMMENT: Docketed by SBW: 'Torquay Decr. 20 1862'. There is no salutation.

It is now nearly half past seven, & there is no prospect of getting any dinner for an hour yet. I am much vexed – but it is no use coming / to you so late tonight.

A verbal message at what time may I call tomorrow?

Yrs ever, | D.

TO: HENRY PADWICK Torquay [Thursday] 25 December 1862 3761

ORIGINAL: LCC LC.1 Item 7; Frame C7

EDITORIAL COMMENT: Endorsed in another hand on the fourth page: '*Disraeli*'.

Confidential Torquay: Dec. 25: 62

H. Padwick Esq

My dear Sir,

I found my dear, kind, friend in such a state, that it would be mockery to send her that annual offering, wh: you used so kindly to forward here, & wh: always gave her so much pleasure.[1]

She / no longer receives her friends, or ever leaves her house, & is much changed.[2]

Not in mind or memory, wh: are as commanding & as complete, as ever. I had no difficulty on the subject of our last conversation, for she herself originated it yesterday. The conversation was / satisfactory – but not conclusive – &, to use her own expression, is to be *resumed*.

I shall write to you & report immediately afterwards.[3]

Yours sincerely, | D.

TO: CONTRIBUTORS TO FUND FOR BUCKS EMIGRANTS [Torquay] [Wednesday] 31 December 1862 3762

ORIGINAL: PS 1540

PUBLICATION HISTORY: *BH* (3 Jan 1863)

EDITORIAL COMMENT: The following text is taken from a *BH* article headed 'LANCASHIRE DISTRESS. FUND FOR THE RELIEF OF THE BUCKINGHAMSHIRE FAMILIES WHO EMIGRATED TO LANCASHIRE IN 1835-6 IN CONSEQUENCE OF THE AGRICULTURAL DISTRESS.' It lists the 19 donations made totalling *£61.9s.7d.*, and concludes with D's third-person letter. A clipping of this notice, with minor differences, taken from an unidentified newspaper, is in H B/II/131.

Dec. 31, 1862.

Mr. Disraeli has the gratification to inform the inhabitants of the County, who have

1 Padwick had previously sent gifts of game and mutton to Torquay; on 31 Dec 1860: 'It has been impossible to get any Pheasants for you ... I trust however the little Basket I have sent you may prove acceptable'; and on 20 Dec 1861: 'I have sent you by freight train a brace of Grouse (the very last of the Season) & a Haunch of Mutton ... belonging to the Duke of Richmond.' H B/XXI/P/6, 9.

2 On 3 December 1862 Rev W. Parks Smith, vicar of St John's, Torquay, had written in confidence to D from Belvidere House, Torquay, that SBW was now confined to the house; he suggested that, as SBW was stubborn, the DS might be able to persuade her to accept a nurse: 'would she object to a sister of mercy?' RTC [495Q].

3 See **3766**.

kindly responded to his appeal on behalf of the Buckinghamshire Emigrants to Lancashire,[1] that the object he contemplated, which was to secure the Emigrants such an amount of continuous assistance as, in addition to other sources of relief, would prevent the breaking up of their homes during the winter months, has been effected.

The "colony" to which he particularly referred is secured aid, varying according to its necessities, as indicated by a trustworthy weekly report, for the next three or four months, while some isolated cases of Bucks people in Lancashire and Cheshire have been investigated and dealt with.

Under these circumstances Mr. Disraeli has taken the liberty of closing the list of contributions.

3763 TO: CHARLES CLUBBE [Torquay, late December 1862?]

ORIGINAL: QUA [338]

EDITORIAL COMMENT: *Dating:* The following snippet may be from a letter containing a contribution to D's emigrant fund (see **3744**&nn1-2 and **3765A**&n1), and is tentatively dated on that basis.

---

missed it, & a Welsh Lady has sent me a contribution, & I don't know whom to give it to.

Try to find out for me.

How do you get on? Let us know.

Ever yours, | D.

3764 TO: JOHN SKELTON [London, early-January 1863?]

ORIGINAL: H B/II/122

EDITORIAL COMMENT: Draft on the back of a letter from John Skelton dated 'December 1862'; see n1.

Sir,

I am honored, & I am gratified, by the dedication of "Thalatta".[1]

I entirely sympathise with the object of yr work, wh: gracefully developes a tone of thought ↑& sentiment↓ on the prevalence of wh: the continued greatness of this country depends.

1 See **3744**&nn1-3 and **3756**.

1 John Skelton (1831-1897), author of, among other titles, *Thalatta, or the Great Commoner* (1862), and *Benjamin Disraeli: The Past and the Future* (1868), had written from 20 Alva Street, Edinburgh (letter dated only 'December 1862'): 'May I ask you to accept the little work entitled *Thalatta!* ... inscribed ... to you, & ... an attempt – however inadequate – to associate Toryism with some of the more liberal & advanced habits of thought which at present influence our younger men.' H B/II/122. D is supposedly the model for the hero, George Mowbray. Stewart *Writings* '1673; *MP* (28 Jan 1863). The work, a political romance also involving Scottish seafaring life, took its title from the shout of the journeying Greeks in Xenophon's *Anabasis,* 'Θαλαττα! Θαλαττα!' [the sea! the sea!]. It had been previously published in six parts in *Fraser's Magazine* Vol 65 (January to June, 1862) and first advertised in *MP* on 9 January 1863. In a prefatory note, Skelton wrote: 'Had [dedications] been still in fashion, I should have ventured to inscribe a political story to Mr. Disraeli,' out of loyalty to his leadership, respect for his handling of social and religious controversies and 'a breadth of aim and generosity of sentiment ... which comprise the best and most sterling elements of "Liberalism" ... Tories alone, it would seem, are prepared to resist the fanatical legislation of the modern puritan; and – when the National Church is menaced by the intemperance of Prelates, and the rancour of a partisan theology – to utter words of warning, reproof, and moderation.'

TO: PHILIP ROSE — Torquay [Thursday] 1 January 1863 — 3765

ORIGINAL: H R/I/A/157
EDITORIAL COMMENT: Endorsed by Rose on the first page: 'Friday R. G.'

Phil: Rose Esqr — Torquay. Jan 1. 1863

My dear Rose,

We leave this place, on Monday next, for Lord Normanby's Plymouth, where we shall stay a couple of / days, arriving in town (D.V) on Thursday night.[1]

It is of great importance, that, if you be in town, I shd. see you on Friday morning, before I see anybody else. I propose, therefore, to call on / you, at Rutland Gate, on Friday morning, not later than ten o'ck.

On Monday, 12th, we go to High Clere, Lord Carnarvons, for a couple of days.[2]

I hope this year will / bring to you & yours all that yr warmest friends desire.

Yours ever, | D.

TO: CHARLES CLUBBE — Torquay [Thursday] 1 January 1863 — 3765A

ORIGINAL: RIC [017]

The | Rev. C.W. Clubbe | A.M — Torquay. Jan. 1 1863

My dear Clubbe,

I had not an opportunity, yesterday, to acknowledge the receipt of yr letter, & its munificent enclosure – the amount of wh: I mainly attribute to yr acknowledged influence in / the Pulpit. It enables me, not only to effect all I originally contemplated, but no longer to trespass on the liberality of the County; & I have, consequently, written to the Papers to close their lists.

I hope they will publish a / complete catalogue of our contributors. It will be rather a curious one, & contains, among others, a Whig Cabinet Minister. Hughenden, however, eclipses all in liberality, even Little Horwood, wh: must have a great heart, since it sent us a second donation of / £5.[1]

Here, we have the scenery, & more than the climate, of Nice!

I am glad, now, that I cd not write yesterday, since I have the opportunity of hoping, that the New Year may bring to you & yours nothing but satisfaction & content.

Ever yrs sincerely, | *B. Disraeli*

1 The DS kept to this schedule. MA would record on 10 January their Torquay hotel bill of £33.18*s*, '4£ less than last time.' H acc. See **3770**.

2 This visit would be postponed; see **3772**&n1.

---

1 Clubbe had written from Hughenden Vicarage on 29 December with 'another contribution to the emigrant fund. £11 is the amount of our collection in Church on Xmas Day; which I told the people would be applied to this purpose, and 10s/– has been sent me by Mr King (Bradenham) for the same object.' H A/VII/E/16. See **3744**&nn1-2. The list of donations published in *BH* on 3 January 1863 includes £1 by Lord Granville, currently lord president, two of £5 each by the parish of Little Horwood and £11.0*s*.1*d* by the parish of Hughenden 'after a sermon by the Vicar on Christmas Day'. D's donation of £20 heads the list that totals £61.9*s*.7*d*.

3766 TO: HENRY PADWICK Torquay [Saturday] 3 January 1863

ORIGINAL: LCC (LC.1 Item 8; Frame C10)

EDITORIAL COMMENT: D has drawn a line after the Plymouth address. There is no signature. *Sic:* tomorrow; Foot; embarass.

Confidential Torquay, Jan 3 1863

H. Padwick Esqr

It is all right.

I leave this place tomorrow,[1] & shall be in town on Thursday night.

I shall call on you on Friday morning – about noon, or earlier.

If I can't, then, fix the / day, or hour, for the general settlement, we must make a temporary, & provisional, arrangement, as I can't have you worried, but I won't anticipate difficulties.[2]

Don't suppose, that I am insensible to your devotion, at this critical juncture of / my life.

I appreciate, & shall never forget, it.

Yours most sincerely, | D.

My direction is Tuesday, & Wednesday, in case anything presses, under cover to / Mr. James Foot,[3]

Marquess of Normanby K.G.
Winter Villa[4]
Plymouth

If I came up to town direct, it would not expedite affairs, wh: are taking their course, & would otherwise greatly *embarass* me.

3767 TO: PHILIP ROSE Torquay [Sunday] 4 January 1863

ORIGINAL: H R/I/A/158

PUBLICATION HISTORY: Bradford 247, undated, part of the second last sentence

EDITORIAL COMMENT: Paper imprinted with a crest illegible in our copy (Webb's Hotel?).

Confidential Torquay. Jany. 4 1863

Phil: Rose Esqr

My dear Rose,

Your letter[1] was inspiriting. I had concluded you had received some severe check, but, great as is the stake, I could have borne it with fortitude, because I felt, that

1 The DS would leave Torquay on Monday 5 January. H acc.

2 See VII **2895**&nn1-4. No letter by Padwick during this period has been found.

3 James Foote had entered the DS' service on 6 July 1857 as a footman. H acc. See VII **3283n1**.

4 The Mount Edgcumbes' Winter Villa was in Stonehouse, Plymouth, near the south end of Durnford Street, overlooking Firestone Bay. It was a 'lavish mid-nineteenth-century Italianate creation with glazed arcaded loggias, replaced, alas, in 1978 with the more prosaic buildings of Nazareth House.' Bridget Cherry and Nikolaus Pevsner *The Buildings of England: Devon* (1989) 672. MA on 17 January would record the gift of 'a coverlid pink & white' made by Lady Normanby. H acc.

---

1 This letter has not been found, perhaps destroyed by Rose or his son, Frederick. See H R/IV/A/6 and R/I/C/1b.

everything / had been done, that firstrate talent, & devoted friendship, could suggest & enforce.

As to the other individual, your dream was quite authentic. I shd., indeed, have been a blunderer, to have lost the marvellous opportunity of the last / fortnight![2] It is to say the least, that I have converted an unwilling into a zealous, & even eager, ally.

I shall be with you on Friday morning, at ten o'ck (D.V.)

Yours ever, | D.

TO: RALPH EARLE Torquay [Sunday] 4 January 1863 **3768**

ORIGINAL: H H/LIFE

EDITORIAL COMMENT: From a typescript completed in manuscript and headed 'D. to Mr. R.A. Earle, Torquay, Jan. 4. '63.'

..... What of the "Essay on a Patriot King"? I quite forget, though I have read it very often .....[1]

2 For the DS' and Rothschilds' stay at the same Torquay hotel, see **3757**&n1. See further **3770**&n2, **3773**&n1, **3778**, **3782**, **3786**. The following transactions of this time in the summary list of Hughenden estate documents (excluding those transferred to Montagu in March 62) appear in the 'Schedule of Deeds and Documents deposited with Messrs. Rothschild at New Court, E.C. Box No.1 containing Deeds received from Mr Saunders on Reconveyance from Mr Montagu in 1881'.
20 January 1863: a 'Further Charge' on a mortgage of 14 March 1862 from D to Montagu; a 'Deed of Covenant Same to Same' and 'Assignment of Policies', also from D to Montagu; a 'Covenant for Assignment of Pension Same to Same' and a 'Power of Attorney – Benjamin Disraeli to G.M. Saunders.'
27 January 1863: (under 'Brock Street Bath') an 'Indenture of Mortgage to secure £1,500 – Benjamin Disraeli to Robert Ranking [Rose's father-in-law]', transferred to Messrs Carter on 20 April 1864; an 'Indenture of Mortgage to secure £2,500 The Right Honble. Benjamin Disraeli to Philip Rose.'
30 January 1863: 'Notice to Eagle Insurance Company of Assignment of Policies accepted.'
According to the summary list, the assignment of mortgages, life insurance policies, 'etc', by D to Montagu from 1863 to 1869 totalled £20,000.

1 Earle had been working on a pamphlet critical of British foreign policy since September 1862, when he told D he had collected abundant material and suggested the format of a correspondence between two party members. On 20 October 1862 he had asked if *Church and State* might publish a political summary, and on 4 November had requested figures on peacetime armament expenditure which would allow him to show that British policy, far from checking France, had allowed her to increase her power. On 'Saturday' (docketed in another hand '3 Jany 1863') he had written from Brighton to 'My dear Excellency': 'The work expands & assumes the proportion of a book – an "avant propos" & 4 chapters are its' [*sic*] present divisions. The 1st. treats of party Govt[;] the 2nd. – your measures[;] – 3rd. – your Parliamentary conduct[;] – 4th. – general considerations, explaining the decline of party spirit. Is the contemplated title still applicable; – to a book, I mean, as well as to the pamphlet, for wh: it was originally intended? or do you prefer either of these: 1 [*brace*] Mr. D & the Tories[:] an essay in contemporary history. 2 [*brace*] Disraeli judged[:] or The Truth about the Tory Party. Can an "*essay*" have Chapters? ... [P.S.] Ld George Manners declares for Retrenchment! "*Disraeli Unmasked*" – or "Disraelism unveiled, or exposed" – best perhaps'. H B/XX/E/257, 262, 267, 280. Bolingbroke's *Letters on the Spirit of Patriotism; on the Idea of a Patriot King; and on the State of Parties, at the Accession of King George the First,* was first published in 1749. It is in three sections: Letter I: On the Spirit of Patriotism. Letter II: Introduction; The Idea of a Patriot King. Letter III: Of the State of Parties at the Accession of King George I. For its influence on D, see Richard Faber *Beaconsfield and Bolingbroke* (1961). Earle's pamphlet, if published with or without any of the suggested titles, has not been identified.

3769 TO: SIR JOHN NEELD [Torquay, Monday 5 January 1863?]

ORIGINAL: PS 891

PUBLICATION HISTORY: Winifred A. Myers Autographs catalogue No 7 (Spring 1969) item 290: to 'Sir John (after Sir J.) Neild [*sic*], M.P.'

EDITORIAL COMMENT: The '(?)' after 'Benett' is the cataloguer's. *Dating:* see n1. *Sic:* pilgramage.

[going to stay with Normanbys in Plymouth, must be back at Grosvenor Gate] to receive our Parlty. friends, [sorry cannot now visit him at Grittleton.][1] My wife is a Wiltshire woman, and with the blood of Scrope and Benett (?) in her veins,[2] I tell her she ought to make a pilgramage to her native Cy.

3770 TO: PHILIP ROSE Plymouth [Monday] 5 January 1863

ORIGINAL: H R/I/A/159

EDITORIAL COMMENT: Paper imprinted 'Winter Villa | Stonehouse | Plymouth'.

Private Jan 5. 1863

P. Rose Esqr

My dear Rose,

I received yours[1] this morning, &, I need not say, read it with great relief.

R. wd., I am sure, from what he said, very much like to make the / acquaintance of our friend on his return to town. Far from entertaining the impression, wh: our friend seemed to apprehend was possible, R. congratulated me on / possessing such a generous & powerful ~~an~~ ally, & dwelt on the satisfaction, it must be to me, that we were, also, politically connected.[2]

I think, indeed, *R.* / has been greatly influenced in his own conduct by the inspiriting example, that has been set him – tho' this is between ourselves.

Yours ever, | D.

Shall be in town Thursday night & call as arranged.

3771 TO: SARAH BRYDGES WILLYAMS Plymouth, Thursday 8 [January 1863]

ORIGINAL: RTC [216]

EDITORIAL COMMENT: D has crossed out the imprint 'Winter Villa | Stonehouse | Plymouth'. Docketed (evidently by SBW) 'Jan 8 1863'. There is no salutation.

Thursday 8 –

Arrived safe in London.

yrs ever | D

I write this at Plymouth to post on my arrival.

1 On 4 January 1863 Sir John Neeld had written from his seat at Grittleton, near Chippenham, Wilts, to invite the DS there for a few days, having seen in the papers that they were in 'the "far West"'. H B/XXI/N/43. Presumably D had time to reply before leaving for Plymouth on this day (the 5th). For the reception of D's friends, see **3781**&n2.

2 For Scrope see III **801**n6; for Wilts Benetts in the DS' acquaintance, see III **917**&n3 and **1006**&n3; Lucy Benett, wife of John Benett of Pythouse, Wilts, was a cousin of MA's. H D/I/F/1 *ff.* For MA as 'a Devonshire woman,' see VI **2540**&n1.

1 This letter has not been found.

2 'R' is evidently Rothschild, and 'our friend' presumably Montagu (see **3683**&nn1&2, **3737**, **3740**&n2 and **3749**&n4. See further **3786**.

TO: SARAH BRYDGES WILLYAMS Grosvenor Gate **3772**

Saturday 10 January [1863]

ORIGINAL: RTC [217]

EDITORIAL COMMENT: Inserted in another hand after the date: '1863' There is no salutation.

Grosvenor Gate, Park Lane | Saturday, Jan. 10.

The party, at High Clere Castle, is postponed: Lady Carnarvon being unwell – a delicate cause.[1] We remain here for a few days, & then go to Hatfield[2] – perhaps, if business, wh: begins / to thicken, ↑permits,↓ to Mentmore, previously, for a couple of days.[3]

Parliament is to meet on the 5th. Feb: my dinner on the 4th.[4]

The loss of the Kent Election,[5] wh: was entirely counted on by my friends, is / a check to them.

It was a very hard battle, to the last moment.

Lord Derby has recovered – the attack lighter, than usual.

Adieu! | D.

TO: [PHILIP ROSE] Carlton Club [Wednesday] 14 January 1863 **3773**

ORIGINAL: H R/I/A/160

EDITORIAL COMMENT: Carlton Club paper. There is no salutation.

Jan 14 1863

Lovegrove writes, by this post, that the policy shall be forwarded to me by return, whenever instructions are received from me to / that effect.

I am surprised at what you tell me, having heard of this for the first time – & have written to him this moment. Whatever may be the state of the case, / the policy must of course be produced.

I am awaiting a definite answer respecting the Westminster & hope to have it this evening.[1]

Yrs | D.

1 See **3765** for the planned visit. Lord Carnarvon in 1861 had married Lady Evelyn Stanhope (1834-1875), only daughter of 6th Earl of Chesterfield. Carnarvon had written to MA on 4 January that his wife had been 'so very far from well' the previous week that they must postpone the DS' visit; she would not be able to receive company for some time. H D/III/C/1027.

2 See **3777**&n1.

3 Baroness Juliana de Rothschild had invited the DS to visit Mentmore after 10 January. In the event they would not go, but MA would later record a birthday gift from the Rothschilds of 'six yards & ¾ fine wide black lace 10 inches very beautiful.' H acc.

4 See **3781**&n2 and **3783**&n2.

5 See **3754**&n2. According to Hamber's 2 January report attempting to reassure D, the election had been lost not because of '"Palmerstonism"' but because the local Liberals had been better organized and had had 'the better man'. H B/XXI/P/285a.

1 See **3767**&n2 for the available evidence on the deeds and policies being transferred to Montagu during this period. The letters by Lovegrove and Rose here mentioned have not been found. See further **3782**.

3774 TO: SARAH BRYDGES WILLYAMS Grosvenor Gate
[Wednesday] 14 January 1863

ORIGINAL: RTC [218]
PUBLICATION HISTORY: M&B IV 396, dated at Grosvenor Gate, 14 January 1863
EDITORIAL COMMENT: Docketed on the last page by SBW: 'Jany 14 1863'. There is no salutation. *Sic:* Vitzhum (twice); St. James.

Grosvenor Gate | Jan. 14. 1863

The Saxon Minister at this Court, Comte Vitzhum,[1] told me on Sunday, that he was ↑at↓ Dresden in the autumn, on leave of absence from St. James, when the Prince of Wales arrived there, & the King of Saxony[2] consigned His Royal Highness to his care. He was the Prince's / companion for three days, making Dresden (& Saxony too, for they went several excursions), agreeable to him.

He says the Prince has good talents – not of the high class of the Princess Royal & Princess Alice – but good. He is gay, extremely amiable, well informed, & altho' simple & unaffected, quite *Grand Seigneur.*

The King of Saxony told the Prince / not to waste time in paying state visits of compliment, & wearing uniforms – but to go about, in plain clothes, & see all that was worth looking at in Dresden – "& in the evening, we will dine at a Palace in the Country, where there will be no form, & you can wear a plain coat."

After Cte. Vitzhum & the Prince had examined the Museums, Galleries &c. the Prince said to him "Don't you think, now, we / might have a little shopping?" Agreed: & they went to a great Jewellers, & the Prince ~~brou~~ bought some bracelets for his future bride[3] – & ↑to↓ some porcelain shops, where he purchased many objects for his brothers & sisters – but he never asked the price of anything – which quite delighted the Saxons, who look upon that as quite "grand seigneur".

Yours ever, | D.

3775 TO: SIR WILLIAM JOLLIFFE Grosvenor Gate
[Thursday] 15 January 1863

ORIGINAL: SCR DD/HY/C/2165 [67]
EDITORIAL COMMENT: Black-edged paper.

Grosvenor Gate | Jan. 15. 1863

Rt Honble | Sir W.H. Jolliffe | Bart. M.P.

1 Count Carl Friedrich Vitzthum von Eckstaedt (1819-1895) was the Saxon minister in London 1852-66. On 12 January 1863 he recorded a long conversation with D (presumably on Sunday the 11th), in which D confirmed that the Conservatives would continue their political waiting game: 'We shall not form a weak Ministry a third time.' Vitzthum thought D ill-informed on Greece and wrong to see Russell's mediation in the Danish question as interference. Vitzthum II 228-31.

2 Johann I (1801-1873), King of Saxony 1854-73. For the Prince of Wales's travels, see Weintraub *Edward* 104-14.

3 The Queen had officially announced on 1 November 1862 the engagement of the Prince of Wales to Princess Alexandra (1844-1925), eldest daughter of the Prince of Denmark (after November 1863 Christian IX of Denmark), and of his wife, Princess Louise. *The Times* (5 Nov 1862). The marriage would take place on 10 March 1863. See **3792**&n4, **3794**&n1, **3795**&nn1-6, **3797**&nn2-6.

My dearest Jolliffe,

I have not had heart to write to you – &, now, only sympathise – & do not presume to condole.[1]

I know, from my own great sorrows, in / this province of affliction, that the distraction of public life is one of the surest, & most enduring, courses of support – & it is only with a strong impression, on this head, that I venture to say, that you will meet only a few / friends here on the 4th., when the Queen's Speech will be read – & when we shall all listen, with confidence & ~~fr~~ affection, to the suggestions of one, whom we all regard & respect.[2]

Ever Yrs | *B. Disraeli*

TO: [CONSERVATIVE MPS] Hughenden [Thursday] 15 January 1863 3776

ORIGINAL: Copy (to William Mitford) in WSRO Mitford Archives MS 1277 f23

PUBLICATION HISTORY: *MP* (22 Jan 1863), addressed to 'the Conservative members of the House of Commons' and dated at Hughenden, 15 January 1863; *BH* (24 Jan 1863), similarly addressed and dated

EDITORIAL COMMENT: This is another example of a reproduced circular letter; *cf* VII **3349**ec and in this volume **3546**ec&n1, **3646**ec and **3889**ec. For a reference to the 'apparatus' for circulating the letter, see Taylor to D, 24 January 1865, H B/XX/T/45.

Hughenden Manor | Jany. 15th. 1863

Sir,

I have the honor to inform you, that Parliament will meet on the 5th. Feby., & to express my hope, that you may find it convenient to be in your / place on that day, as business of importance will, probably, be brought forward.

I remain, Sir, | Your faithful Servant, | *B. Disraeli*

TO: SARAH BRYDGES WILLYAMS Grosvenor Gate 3777
Wednesday 21 January [1863]

ORIGINAL: RTC [219]

PUBLICATION HISTORY: M&B IV 331, dated at Grosvenor Gate, 21 January 1863

EDITORIAL COMMENT: Paper imprinted 'Grosvenor Gate'. Inserted in another hand after the date: '1863'. There is no salutation.

Wednesday Jan: 21.

We are now going to Hatfield, where we shall make a rather longer visit, than usual,[1]

1 Jolliffe's daughter Julia (Mrs Howard Vyse) had died on 30 December 1862.

2 Jolliffe would reply next day (16th) from Heath House, Petersfield, thanking D for his kindness but declining the invitation as on the 28th or 29th he would be taking his 'girls' to their sister Allada Wells, who was at Cannes for the winter: 'I am persuaded to take this winter journey in the hope of relief, which I feel certain I shall not experience, but it may distract from the grief of my fellow sufferers, & particularly of the poor absent Daughter.' H B/XX/J/92.

---

1 The visit would be interrupted; see **3780**&n9. Before they left on this day (21st), MA had an accident in a Regent Street shop that required a doctor at Hatfield 'for the b[ruise?] on my eyes & face' and on the 27th a call from Dr Fergusson. On Friday [30?] January, her cousin Emma Poulett Scrope would hope that MA was over her shock and that her face and eyes were resuming their normal colour. MA asked her hostess, Lady Salisbury, not to tell D about her accident, since he was preparing a speech (presumably the one of 5 February on the Answer to the Address) and must not be upset: '"He has lost his eyeglass, and if you put me a long way from him at dinner he will never see what a condition I am in."' D learned of the accident only two days later, presumably when the DS had to return to London. H acc, D/III/C/2187; Sykes 79.

as I have a great deal to do, & Ld. & Lady Salisbury, who are real friends, let me do what I like, & not come down to breakfast, & / all that sort of thing, so that I can work, & prepare for the coming campaign. A week of quiet mornings is what I now require, in order to digest all I have heard, & planned, during the last fortnight. I could not well go to Hughenden, as it is full of workmen,[2] & I have this advantage at / Hatfield, that it is a palace, full of company, changing every day, & all the most distinguished persons in the country, especially of my own party, in turn appearing. I meet & converse with all these, after the solitude of the morning, every day at dinner & / in the evening, which is very advantageous & suggestive. It allows me to feel the pulse of the ablest on all the questions of the day.

God bless you!

Yours ever, | D.

3778 TO: PHILIP ROSE Hatfield, Friday 23 January 1863

ORIGINAL: H R/I/A/161

Philip Rose Esqr Hatfield | Friday Jan 23. /63

My dear Rose,

If I hear, to that effect,[1] by tomorrows post, I shall come up directly: if not, I shall call upon you on Monday, about 12 o'ck: I / should think. We leave by an early train, & I shall come on to you at once from Kings X.

Yrs ever, | D.

3779 TO: MARY ANNE DISRAELI [Eaton Terrace] Monday 26 January 1863

ORIGINAL: H A/I/A/313

EDITORIAL COMMENT: Docketed by MA on the first page: '1863 Jan 26th Dizzy'.

Monday

Favorable bulletin.[1]

~~Conscious~~ Sensibility to the affected parts continues to return.

Dr Basham[2] thinks very well of the case in consequence, & thinks he may entirely recover[.] Does / not consider it a regular stroke, or fit – but a paroxysmal affection – of course, not nearly so serious.

When I arrived, they told me he was much worse – having had so bad a night, & having / been in so much pain, that they sent for Mr Brown[3] in the middle of the

2 On 16 January MA had recorded a cheque paid by D to Roberts the builder for £200 on account. H acc. On 1 April she would tell SBW that Hughenden was now a 'very noisy place, for we are restoring the house inside & out.' RTC [475Q]. For the extensive renovations see Appendix VIII and Introduction pp xv-xvi.

1 Rose's letter has not been found. For the context, see **3773**&n1.

1 James Disraeli had suffered 'an attack of paralysis' on 24 January; see **3780**&n9.

2 William Richard Basham (1804-1877), MD (Edinburgh) 1834, since 1843 physician to the Westminster Hospital, was a published expert on dropsy and renal disease.

3 There are too many medical men with this name listed to enable a plausible identification.

night. In the midst of this account, Dr Basham arrived. It is, therefore, of no use to send before his / arrival, as we are liable, either way, to be misled.[4]

Adieu! dear Wife | D.

TO: SARAH BRYDGES WILLYAMS Grosvenor Gate **3780**

[Monday] 26 January 1863

ORIGINAL: RTC [220]

EDITORIAL COMMENT: Paper imprinted 'Grosvenor Gate'. Docketed by SBW on the fourth page: 'Jany 26 1863'. There is no salutation. *Sic:* Marquess'es; Buccleugh; Edgecombe; Carington.

Jany. 26 1863

We met at Hatfield, the Marquess & Marchioness of Abercorn, & their very pretty daughter, Lady Georgiana Hamilton;[1] Lord & Lady Enfield;[2] Earl Cowper;[3] the Prussian Ambassador, & Countess Bernstorff; General Peel & his daughter,[4] & some others: a / brilliant circle: our host & hostess most friendly & hospitable.

We dined at a brilliant round table: with the Marquess'es band playing in the long gallery adjoining. Lord Abercorn has thirteen children, & looks as young as his son, ↑who is an M.P. & in Egypt.↓[5] His daughters are so singularly pretty, that they always marry during / their first season, & always make the most splendid matches. One is Lady Dalkeith, & will be the future Duchess of Buccleugh;[6] another is the wife of your neighbour, the Earl of Mt Edgecombe, Lady Brownlow's nephew;[7] another is Countess of Lichfield.[8] Whether Lord Cowper, who is a young man, just come to

4 MA would send for Dr Fergusson on 28 January. H acc. See further **3787**.

---

1 The 2nd Marquess of Abercorn in 1832 had married Lady Louisa Jane Russell (1812-1905), second daughter of 6th Duke of Bedford; their fifth daughter, Lady Georgiana Susan Hamilton (1841-1913), would marry 5th Earl Winterton in 1882.

2 Lord Enfield in 1854 had married Lady Alice Harriet Frederica Egerton (1830-1928), eldest daughter of 1st Earl of Ellesmere.

3 Francis Thomas de Grey Cowper (1834-1905) had succeeded as 7th (and last) Earl Cowper in 1856; he would not marry until 1870. He would be KG 1865, PC 1871, captain of HM's corps of gentlemen-at-arms 1871-4, viceroy of Ireland 1880-2.

4 The Peels' eldest daughter was Margaret Peel (1831-1890), who would die unmarried.

5 James Hamilton (1838-1913), Viscount Hamilton (Marquess of Hamilton 1868 on his father's dukedom), who would succeed his father as 2nd Duke of Abercorn in 1885, was MP (C) for Donegal 1860-80, lord of the bedchamber to the Prince of Wales 1866-86, groom of the stole 1886-1901, special envoy to several foreign courts, KG 1892.

6 William Henry Walter Montagu Douglas Scott (1831-1914), Earl of Dalkeith, who would succeed his father as 6th Duke of Buccleuch and 8th Duke of Queensberry in 1884, in 1859 had married Lady Louisa Jane Hamilton (1836-1912), the Abercorns' third daughter. Dalkeith was MP (C) for Edinburgh (Midlothian) 1853-68, 1874-80; Lady Dalkeith as Duchess of Buccleuch would be mistress of the robes to the Queen 1885-92, 1895-1901.

7 William Henry Edgcumbe (1833-1917), 4th Earl of Mount Edgcumbe, in 1858 as Lord Valletort had married Lady Katherine Elizabeth Hamilton (1840-1874), the Abercorns' fourth daughter; he had been MP (C) for Plymouth 1859 until his succession in 1861, extra equerry to the Prince of Wales 1858. He would be lord chamberlain to the household 1879-80, lord steward 1885-92, ADC to the Queen 1887-97, and special envoy to several foreign courts. Mount Edgcumbe House is located near Plymouth.

8 Thomas George Anson (1825-1892), 2nd Earl of Lichfield, in 1855 had married Lady Harriett Georgiana Louisa Hamilton (1834-1913), the Abercorns' eldest daughter. Lord Lichfield as Viscount Anson had been MP (L) for Lichfield from 1847 until his succession in 1854.

his / title, very rich & clever, will yield to the charms of Lady Georgiana, time & fate must decide.

On Saturday morning, amid all this splendid gaiety, a telegram arrived, that my brother, the Commissioner, was seized with an attack of paralysis. We were in town in less than two hours, & from that moment have scarcely left his bedside. I *think* he is out of immediate danger, but we have, of course, sent to Lord Carington, to say we cannot come to Gayhurst, & I can only write this line to you.[9]

Ever Yrs | D.

3780A TO: CHARLES CLUBBE Grosvenor Gate [Tuesday] 27 January 1863

ORIGINAL: RIC [018]

COVER: The | Revd. C.W. Clubbe | A.M. | Hughenden Vicarage | High Wycomb. | *B. Disraeli*

POSTMARKS: in circle: LONDON W. | 6 | JA 27 | 63 ; a cancelled one-penny stamp; on verso, in circle: HIGH WYCOMBE | JA 29 | 63

EDITORIAL COMMENT: Paper imprinted 'Grosvenor Gate.' *Sic:* Wycomb; C.C.

The | Rev. C.C. Clubbe | A.M Jan 27 1863

My dear Clubbe,

I have never acknowledged the receipt of yr last enclosures. I will write a line to James Price.[1]

We were due, to day, at Gayhurst, but are detained in / town by the sudden, & alarming, illness of my brother, the Commissioner.[2]

Yours sincerely, | D.

3781 TO: HENRY BRAND [London, Tuesday] 3 February 1863

ORIGINAL: UO [26]

Hon: H. Brand | M. P.[1] Feb. 3 1863

Dear Mr Brand,

My chief of the Staff has not turned up, as I expected, to day, &, therefore, I hope you / will excuse me for troubling you, & saying, that I count on your usual courtesy

9 For the proposed visit to Gayhurst, see **3743**&n1. For James's illness, see **3779**. MA would record a payment of £10 on 26 January to James's 'housekeeper,' Mrs Bassett, 'on account for her master,' and on the 28th £1 to Dr Fergusson for James. On 16 April she would receive from D £1 'due from James Disraeli for one of the Doctors.' H acc.

---

1 Price was presumably a late donor to the emigrant fund; see **3765**An1. D's letter to him has not been found.

2 See **3780**&n9.

---

1 Henry Bouverie William Brand (1814-1892), second son of 21st Baron Dacre, MP (L) for Lewes 1852-68, for Cambridgeshire 1868 until created Viscount Hampden in 1884, was private secretary to Sir George Grey and keeper of the privy seal to the Prince of Wales 1858, a lord of the treasury 1855-8, and parliamentary secretary to the treasury 1859-66 (Palmerston's chief aide). He would be Speaker of the House 1872-84.

respecting the Speech, & shall feel obliged, if you / will send me a copy, in fair time, tomorrow, at Grosvenor Gate.[2]

Yours very truly, | *B. Disraeli*

TO: PHILIP ROSE 6 Victoria Street, Westminster Abbey, S.W. [Wednesday] 4 February [1863] **3781A**

ORIGINAL: H R/I/A/189

EDITORIAL COMMENT: Paper imprinted: '6, Victoria Street, Westminster Abbey, S.W. _____ 186__.' Docketed '1866?'. *Dating:* the year is established by context; see nn1,2&4. *Sic:* checque.

P. Rose Esqr Feb 4

My dear Rose,

I called to day, as I did before, to give you a checque for the Montagu Insurance[1] – & also the Syndicate affair.[2]

In my way, I found yr letter, wh: I read at this desk.[3]

I don't want their / acceptances, but I wish to have the opportunity of making some corrections in one of the volumes.[4]

I will send you the agreement after tomorrow[.]

Yrs ever | D.

TO: PHILIP ROSE House of Commons [Friday] 6 February 1863 **3782**

ORIGINAL: H R/I/A/162

EDITORIAL COMMENT: House of Commons paper.

P. Rose Esqr Feby. 6 1863

My dear Rose,

Will you, on Monday morning next, pay £1561:12:6. into Messrs. Williams Deacon & Co. to Mr Lovegrove's credit at / the Glo[uce]ster Bank, & forward the receipt to me at the Carlton.[1]

Yours sincerely, | B. Disraeli

TO: SARAH BRYDGES WILLYAMS [London, Saturday] 7 February 1863 **3783**

ORIGINAL: RTC [221]

PUBLICATION HISTORY: M&B IV 331-2, dated 7 February 1863, omitting the first and fourth paragraphs and last sentence; Blake 419, undated extract; Weintraub *Disraeli* 397, undated extract

EDITORIAL COMMENT: There is no salutation. *Sic:* ill-breding.

Feb. 7. 1863

On Tuesday last, when I returned home, they told me, before I went up stairs, I was

2 The parliamentary session would open on 5 February, and D's dinner to see the Throne Speech beforehand, a customary government courtesy to the opposition, was scheduled for the 4th. Jolliffe, D's chief of staff, was out of the country; see **3775**&n2.

1 See **3683**n2.
2 See **3855**&n1 and **3856**.
3 Rose's letter has not been found. D is writing from Victoria Street on Rose's office stationery (see ec).
4 See **3855**n2.

1 *Cf* **3773**&n1.

to look at a wonderful dish of fish, wh: had arrived from Torquay. It was brought up, & I beheld a group, wh: only a Dutch painter could do justice to – a colossal Turbot, prismatic mullets, & a lobster splendid in color & proportions. But the next day? How did they eat? I can truly say, from my own experience, & from general criticism, that a superior / fish to the turbot was never placed on any table. In flavor, & in consistency, it was of the highest class – & as it was given to me I cd. without ill-breding, dilate upon its merits. It was a most happy, a most acceptable, & a most successful, offering at the commencement of the campaign.[1]

My party was distinguished & brilliant – and I am going to give a series of dinners to my parliamentary friends of both Houses.[2] The members of the House of Commons like, very much, ↑to meet↓ members of the House of Lords, who have themselves, in their time, sate in the House of Commons[.] It is / like old schoolfellows meeting; the ~~associations~~ [?] ↑memories↓ of the past are interesting, & from old experience, they understand all the fun of the present. The Duke of Buckingham,[3] the Earl of Shrewsbury,[4] & the Marquess of Normanby,[5] who were, all of them, a long time in the House of Commons, dine with me on Wednesday, & meet a number of the lower House.

Lord Derby seems very well, & in good spirits. His conduct during the Lancashire Distress appears to have gained him golden opinions / from all parties. His subscription of many thousands was munificent, but his administrative talent in managing the vast sums entrusted to the Central Committee by the nation, not less admirable.[6]

The external public world is more interesting & active than the internal political life.

The Greeks really want to make my friend, Lord Stanley, their King.[7] This beats any novel. I think he ought to take the Crown, but he will not. Had I his youth, I would not hesitate, even with the Earldom of Derby in the distance.

Ever yrs | D.

Mary-Anne sent the enclosed.[8]

1 The turbot figured prominently in the fish course for the 4 February parliamentary dinner before the opening of parliament next day; on 5 February MA had also written to SBW to thank her for her gifts and to say that SBW's watch that they had had repaired in London would be sent to her that day. SBW on 'Monday' wrote that, though she could not get fine fresh fish until next day, if she sent them then they should arrive on Wednesday. RTC [471Q, 472Q].

2 MA in her 5 February letter (n1) had reported that the previous night's dinner ('all came 18 with D') had gone off well: 'instead of having them in the drawing rooms 40 at a time, D. will ask his political friends oftener from the upper & lower House.' She added: 'I take Dizzy to the latter today.' For D's eight political dinners and guest lists 4 February-9 May, see Appendix II.

3 The former Lord Chandos had succeeded as 3rd Duke of Buckingham and Chandos on 29 July 1861; he had been MP (C) for Buckingham 1846-57.

4 The 18th Earl of Shrewsbury as Henry John Chetwynd-Talbot and then as Viscount Ingestre had been Tory MP for Hertford 1830-31, 1832-4, for Armagh 1831, for Dublin 1831-2, for Staffordshire S 1837-49.

5 Lord Normanby, who would live only until 28 July 1863, as Constantine Henry Phipps had been MP for Scarborough 1818-20, Higham Ferrers 1822-6, Malton 1826-30.

6 Derby in 1862 had been named chairman of the central relief committee for the Lancashire distress caused by the American civil war cutting off the supply of cotton for the textile industries. He himself donated £10,000, at the time considered to be the largest contribution by an individual to a charity. He continued to work hard in this capacity until 1865. See also **3743**n4.

7 See **3750**&n2.

8 Probably the 4 February menu (see n1), which SBW preserved alongside MA's letter of 5 February (n2).

TO: EDWARD BULWER LYTTON Grosvenor Gate [Sunday] 8 February 1863 **3784**

ORIGINAL: HCR D/E C22 [2]

EDITORIAL COMMENT: Paper imprinted 'Grosvenor Gate'.

Feb 8 1863

My dear Bulwer,[1]

The definitive refusal of the D. of S.C. has removed the Ionian Isles out of the class of living questions. The contingencies & conditions, wh: are to lead to their surrender, appear to all persons so remote, & / shadowy, that there is a general opinion, on all sides, that nothing will be done.[2]

We therefore breathe. It won't do to have these questions taken up by free lances – the mass of the party will vote on national questions – the debate / & division assume a party character, & the latter, with a free lance leader, is always bad. It was the fear of this, that made me consider our best course, in case we were forced to act: but I am now clearly of opinion, that we can be silent with dignity, / & with safety.[3]

Everything is dead in the House; dangerously dead – one cannot conceive, how a popular assembly can exist for six months in such inertness & apathy.[4]

You need not disturb yourself – & I hope, when we meet, that I shall find you quite well.[5]

Yrs ever, | D.

1 Bulwer Lytton had written to D from Nice on 3 and 4 February in response to an Earle letter evidently about the party's position on the Ionian Isles in the coming session. (See VII **3209**&n1.) He asked if debate could be postponed until March, the earliest he could be back. In the second letter he wondered if they could 'get up much interest about them, or provoke much indignation agst the cession. And if, as the Papers report, the Duke of Coburgh [*sic*] accepts Greece it will be a help to the Govt ... and, to a certain extent, an embarassment [*sic*] to the opposition. I had thought therefore, that it would be more prudent to leave the disscussion [*sic*], which must ensue, to be opened by any free lance, & not commit the party to the issue of a motion raised by any member of Lord Derbys Cabinet.' H B/XX/LY/138-9.

2 In the complex interactions on replacing the deposed King Otto (see **3750**&n2 and **3783**), Palmerston proposed that England cede the Ionian Isles to Greece on condition that Greece establish a constitutional monarchy with an Anglophile king acceptable to the other three protecting powers. The latest candidate approved by England was Prince Albert's elder brother, Ernst II (1818-1893), Duke of Saxe-Coburg and Gotha since 1844, who had initially accepted the throne only to have it virtually withdrawn when he stipulated that he keep Coburg. When Greek negotiations with another candidate failed, the offer had again been made to the Duke, who accepted on four conditions: that the matter be explained to the Bavarian dynasty; that the Diet of Gotha give its consent; that Greece be made materially stronger; and that he remain a German sovereign, occupying the Greek throne only until his nephew, the Prince of Coburg-Kohary, came of age. When Gotha reminded him of his constitutional obligation to reside there, he revoked his acceptance. The news had reached London by telegram in time for the late editions of Thursday 5 February; in that night's debate on the Address, D had attacked the government's foreign policy and declared himself opposed to ceding the Ionian Isles to Greece as it would encourage Greek designs on Turkish territory and diminish British power. Bell *Palmerston* 332-6; *MP* (6-9 Feb 1863); *Hansard* CLXIX cols 91-5. See further **3785**&n1.

3 Christopher Darby Griffith, nominally a Liberal-Conservative but a declared independent, would be the first to raise the issue as a question on 9 February. *Hansard* CLXIX cols 227-8.

4 *MP* in a leader on 10 February would gloat over 'the existing disorganisation of the Conservative party in any attempt to bring about a faction fight in the House of Commons. The truth is that real Conservatism flourishes already without any support from Conservative leaders ... [because] at this moment there is no great party question in dispute ... There is really nothing, in respect of broad legislative principles, left to quarrel over.'

5 Bulwer Lytton would reply on 15 February in full agreement with D's views. H B/XX/LY/140.

3785 TO: SARAH BRYDGES WILLYAMS

House of Commons
Tuesday [10 February 1863]

ORIGINAL: RTC [222]
EDITORIAL COMMENT: Docketed in another hand on the first page: 'Feb 10 1863'. There is no salutation.

Tuesday

A line from the House of Commons. The Ionian Question seems to vanish, as we approach it. Conditions, alike precedent, & impossible, are not very promising of a / practical result.[1]

In fact, it is a hoax. This is the age of Burlesque, & Lord Palmerston has embarked in a career of comic diplomacy. I ought to have told him this just now, but it has only / occurred to me, while I was writing to you.

Yesterday, news arrived, that the Duke of Rutland had had a fatal fall in the hunting field, & it was generally supposed – that my friend, John / Manners, was a Duke – but, today, I hear from Belvoir Castle, that tho' his Grace is paralysed, he has rallied, & will, probably, recover.[2] My friend John Manners must reconcile himself, therefore, to remaining a Cadet, &, in due time, being again a Cabinet Minister.

Yours ever, | D.

3786 TO: PHILIP ROSE

6 Victoria Street, Westminster Abbey, S.W.
[Wednesday] 11 February 1863

ORIGINAL: H R/I/A/163
EDITORIAL COMMENT: Paper imprinted '6, Victoria Street, Westminster Abbey, S.W. _____ 186_.' This is Rose's office address. The date has been completed in a clerk's hand to read 'Feby 11 1863'.

Private

Philip Rose Esq

My dear Rose

R. sent for me yesterday. What passed was very satisfactory. He was quite astonished, when he found, that I thought the interview was a failure. He seems to like M. very much, & said he was very clever.[1]

The matter may rest for / the moment – at any rate, until we can hold council on it. M. certainly made the most favorable impression, & R. evidently wishes to cultivate him.

1 See **3784**&nn1&2. In a brief afternoon sitting on 10 February 1863, Palmerston, responding to questions and attempted parallels with other cases, explained that, as the Ionian Islands were a protectorate and not a possession, the government could cede them without consulting parliament. *Hansard* CLXIX cols 226-33.

2 Rutland's accident had occurred on Saturday 7 February while he was out with his hounds near Grantham; after regaining consciousness, he appeared to have lost the use of his left side. *MP* (10 Feb 1863). The report of 'a fatal fall' has not been found. Manners had written from the George Hotel, Grantham, on the 9th that his brother was recovering there, sensation had returned to the left arm, and they hoped to move him soon to Belvoir. On the 11th he would write again to report continued improvement and to convey the Duke's thanks for D's 'kind message' (not found). He would report further progress on the 19th, and on the 24th from Belvoir describe the Duke's successful removal there, with 'Many thanks for your amusing letter [*see* **3790**&n7], which exactly answered it's [*sic*] object.' H B/XX/M/122-5. Lord John would again be a cabinet minister in 1866 and succeed his brother as 7th Duke in 1888.

---

1 For the prelude to Rothschild's meeting with Montagu see **3770**&n2.

I have settled with Boyds office, & brought you the bond &c. here, but / as you are not within, I shall put them in your fire, as I did Lovegroves documents.[2]

Be so good as to forward to Mr Montagu a packet wh: you will find on your desk.

Yours ever, | D.

TO: MARY ANNE DISRAELI Eaton Terrace [Thursday 12] February 1863 3787

ORIGINAL: H A/I/A/314

EDITORIAL COMMENT: Docketed by MA on the last page: '1863 Feby Dizzy'. *Dating:* by the election.

My dearest Wife, Eaton Terrace

It is now past three, & I have only just got here, & I must be at the H: of Comm: at ½ past four o'ck – so I have sent the Carriage home, that you / may use it. I don't think from what I hear, I shall dine at home – there is to be something important in the House about Lancashire.[1]

Ferrand / was *68* ahead at 12 o'ck but all agree his bad time is coming.[2]

Yr affec husband | D.

James has just come down: but very weak & shattered.[3]

I shall try to dine at home; even as late as 8 o'ck or ½ past.[4]

TO: SARAH BRYDGES WILLYAMS House of Commons 3788

Friday [13 February 1863]

ORIGINAL: RTC [223]

EDITORIAL COMMENT: House of Commons paper. Docketed in another hand on the first page: 'Feb 13 1863'. There is no salutation. *Sic:* [*opening lower-case*] a.

Friday.

a very bad account of the Duke of Rutland – arrived this morning.[1]

The turbot very fine & fat. But, I think, at / this munificent rate, we shall exhaust the waters of Torbay, gifted as they are. You are too generous: I fear, it was some very

2 No basis for identifying Boyd has been found. Two possible candidates are: James Boyd, solicitor and Scotch law agent at 3 Furnivall's Inn; and Edward Lennox Boyd, FRGS, FSA, trustee and resident director of the United Kingdom Life Assurance Co, 8 Waterloo Place, Pall Mall. *LPOD* (1856, 1859, 1860, 1864). For Lovegrove, see **3773**&n1 and **3782**.

---

1 After brief discussion on this day (12th), the Commons would give first reading to the Union Relief Aid Act (1862) Continuance Bill to extend the act guaranteeing resources for adequate relief of the Lancashire distress; D did not speak. *Hansard* CLXIX cols 267-92.

2 In a by-election at Devonport on this day (12th), Ferrand would win the seat that had eluded him several times since 1859 in very close polls, this time beating his Liberal opponent 1234-1204.

3 See **3780**&n9 and **3779**&nn1-4.

4 The House would adjourn at a quarter to eight.

---

1 See **3785**&n2; Manners's account of 11 February was hardly 'very bad'; the doctors had just seen the Duke and issued a bulletin: '"The Duke's symptoms have been gradually improving for the last twenty four hours – and there is every probability of his Grace progressing favourably"'. Manners added: 'He had become depressed, and nervous about himself, but the result of the consultation has been to cheer him.' H B/XXI/M/123.

awkward, & inadvertent phrase, / of mine, wh: put you in the secret of my second dinner.[2] You will feed, & feast, the whole Tory party!

I enclose you, from Mrs. Di., a wonderful / little almanack. It only cost one penny, but is marvellously full of information. She has turned down a page on the comparative nutriment of food, wh:, she thinks, worthy of yr attention.

Yours ever, | D.

3789 TO: LORD SYDNEY [London, Friday] 20 February 1863

ORIGINAL: FIT Ashcombe MS I.47

EDITORIAL COMMENT: In the date, the '3' has been written over a '2'.

Rt. Honble | The Lord Chamberlain Feb 20 1863

My Lord,

I beg to say, that it is my intention to attend the Levée on Wednesday next, & to have the honor of / presenting Mr Cubitt, M.P. for the County of Surrey.[1]

I beg leave to remain, | my Lord, | Yr faithful Servt | *B. Disraeli*

3790 TO: LORD JOHN MANNERS House of Commons [Friday] 20 February 1863

ORIGINAL: BEA [86]

EDITORIAL COMMENT: House of Commons paper.

Rt Honble | Lord John Manners | M.P. Feb 20 1863

My dear J.M.

Politics, at least internally – are dead. The only event is the return to his old scene of the "intrepid Ferrand".[1]

There is nothing, wh: requires yr attendance on Tuesday – as Pakington intends / to advise Sir Jno. Hay not to divide. Sir John will, probably, not follow the advice – but we can't support him in his resolutions, tho' we may sympathise in the general policy they indicate.[2]

2 See **3783**&n1; possibly SBW's 'Monday' letter was written on 9 February, the Monday before D's dinner on the 14th. For the dinner and guests see Appendix II. SBW would write again, to MA, on the 18th: 'I have always so much more to thank you and dear Dizzi than I can express that I must give it up.' She was much taken by an account of the Imperial Fancy Dress Ball at the Tuileries, which 'must have been very amusing to see and talk about but very tiresome to prepare for'. RTC [474Q].

---

1 On behalf of the Queen, the Prince of Wales would hold a levee for about 1,700 people on Wednesday 25 February at St James's Palace. In the published list headed 'The following presentations at the Levee on Wednesday took place, the names having been previously left at the Lord Chamberlain's office, and submitted for her Majesty's approval', D is entered as having presented Cubitt. *MP* (26-7 Feb 1863). See further **3792**. George Cubitt (1828-1917), three-time prizeman at Trinity College, Cambridge (MA 1854), was MP (C) for Surrey W 1860-85, Mid-Surrey 1885-92 (when he was elevated to the Lords as Baron Ashcombe), second church estates commissioner 1874-9. In an undated letter (docketed by the archivist '?Jany 1863') Earle had suggested that D encourage 'those candidates for town constituencies, of whom we are in great need' by inviting (presumably to a dinner) either the current Lord Mayor of London, William Rose, or Cubitt, 'a very suitable guest.' H B/XXI/E/281. 'Mr Cubitt' had been a dinner guest on 11 February; see **3783**&n2.

---

1 See **3787**&n2 for Ferrand's recent election; he had been sworn on Tuesday 17 February. *Hansard* CLXIX col 393.

2 Sir John Hay on 24 February would move for an address to the Queen requesting a review of navy poli-

Dillwyn's motion is postponed sine die – like Ch: rates.[3] In fact, there is nothing on the paper before Easter, wh: would make / a House, except estimates.

Externally – the French Minister, at Washington, I learn today, has not yet delivered the Emperor's offer at Seward's own suggestion. There is a pause, wh: may portend something.[4]

The Empress gave Lady Royston a bracelet of great magnificence, wh cost 25,000 francs. The bride / & bridegroom are to loiter about, & to get to Florence, at last.[5]

The Emperor had a long political conversation with James Rothschild[6] & said "You talk to me about Russia & all these powers. I tell you what it is. I look upon England as my wife, & treat her as such; I look upon all these other powers as my mistresses, & treat *them* as such."

My kind regards to our dear friend & to Lady John.[7]

Yrs ever | D.

cies on promotion, pay and retirement of officers. The motion as amended (to include a call for a select committee) received strong support from Pakington and was agreed to after discussion but without a division. *Hansard* CLXIX cols 731-85. Sir John Charles Dalrymple-Hay (1821-1912), 3rd Bt, JP and DL for Wigtownshire, a seasoned RN veteran since 1834, captain 1850, was MP (L-C) for Wakefield 1862-5, Stamford 1866-80, Wigtown Burghs 1880-5, a public works loan commissioner 1862-74, rear-admiral RN 1866, a lord of the admiralty 1866-9, DCL Oxford 1872, FRS, FRGS, PC 1874, KCB 1885, GCB 1886, LLD Glasgow 1904.

3 The Church Rates Abolition Bill(2) and Dillwyn's Endowed Schools Bill(3) had been given *pro forma* first reading on 6 February. The former bill would be killed after discussion on second reading on 29 April by a division of 285-275, and Dillwyn would withdraw his bill after brief discussion on 17 June. *Hansard* CLXIX col 146, CLXX cols 926-78, CLXXI cols 1004-8.

4 See **3738**&n1. The French minister at Washington since 1859 was Baltimore-born Henri Mercier (1816-1886), later Baron Mercier de Lostende. William Henry Seward (1801-1872) was the Federal secretary of state 1861-9. The Emperor's offer of French mediation in a meeting of North and South on neutral ground had been sent to Mercier on 9 January 1863; Seward had sent his administration's polite rejection on 6 February. *The Times*'s New York correspondent had reported on 14 February that Mercier's despatch of 13 April 1862 (stating that Mercier had visited Richmond because Seward had expressed his administration's desire for peace) had just been received in America *via* publication in France. On 12 and 13 February, at Senate request, Seward had shown President Lincoln his correspondence with Mercier and others, refuting Mercier's account and showing that he had specifically declined France's offer of mediation. *The Times* (25-7 Feb 1863). On 6 March, Malmesbury would record: 'The French are very sore at the refusal of the American Government to accept their mediation, and at the peremptory contradiction by Mr. Seward of M. Mercier's despatch.' Malmesbury II 293.

5 Charles Philip Yorke (1836-1897), Viscount Royston, eldest son of 4th Earl of Hardwicke, on 16 February 1863 in Paris had married Lady Sophia Wellesley (see **3547**n1), the Cowleys' second daughter. Royston would be MP (C) for Cambridgeshire 1865-73 (when he would succeed as 5th Earl of Hardwicke), and (thanks to his friendship with the Prince of Wales) comptroller of the Queen's household 1866-8, master of the buckhounds 1874-80. Stanley had recorded on 20 September 1862 that the marriage hung fire because Royston (known as 'Champagne Charlie') had incurred so many gambling debts. *Disraeli, Derby* 191.

6 Baron James Rothschild (1792-1868), head of the Paris Rothschild branch, was the youngest child of Mayer Amschel Rothschild and his wife, Gutele.

7 Lord John would acknowledge D's 'amusing letter' (presumably this one) on the 24th; see **3785**&n2.

3791 TO: SARAH BRYDGES WILLYAMS House of Commons

Monday [23 February 1863]

ORIGINAL: RTC [224]

PUBLICATION HISTORY: M&B IV 335-6, dated at House of Commons, 23 February 1863; Weintraub *Disraeli* 397, undated extract

EDITORIAL COMMENT: House of Commons paper. Docketed in another hand on the first page: 'Feb 23 1863'. There is no salutation.

Monday

Nothing thought of, but Poland. It recalls the days of Thaddeus of Warsaw, wh:, I dare say, you read with a flashing eye, & a flushing cheek.[1]

The cards seem, most / unexpectedly, to throw the Rhine into the grasp of Napoleon. How he must regret the disciplined troops, that he has sent, upon a Quixote adventure, to the land of yellow / fever, & black vomit –![2]

Who is to be King of Poland? Thats the question now. Poor Greece has not yet been furnished with a Crown.[3] Life becomes like a fairy tale, & our / intimate acquaintances turn into ~~Sovr~~ Sovereign Princes, who, the day before, were M.Ps, & guardsmen, & foxhunters.

I am content with being leader of the Opposition: at present, an office more of thought than action – but the Spring will return.

Adieu! | D.

3792 TO: SARAH BRYDGES WILLYAMS [Carlton Club]

[Wednesday] 25 February 1863

ORIGINAL: RTC [225]

PUBLICATION HISTORY: M&B IV 397, dated at the Carlton Club, 25 February 1863, omitting the second paragraph

EDITORIAL COMMENT: There is no salutation. *Sic:* St. James'; Princess'es.

Feb 25 1863

I went to the Prince of Wales' first Levée today.[1] He received me very cordially, &

1 The Polish insurrection of 1863-4, the latest unsuccessful attempt to throw off Russian (and this time Prussian) occupation, had broken out on 21 January when Russian troops had arrested for military service all Polish men suspected of unacceptable political opinions. There was currently much speculation about the European nations' alignment, the risk of general war, and the reassignment of disputed European territories. In the Lords on 20 February, Ellenborough had called for support for the Poles, hoping that a constitutional kingdom might arise in a free Poland. The first major debate on Poland in the Commons on 27 February would focus on England's Treaty of Vienna obligations, D contending that the main object of the discussion was to gain a sense of House opinion. *Hansard* CLXIX cols 560-70, 879-943 (D at 939-43). Tadeusz Kosciusko (1746-1817), who had risen to brigadier-general on the colonists' side in the American War of Independence, in 1784 had returned to his native Poland and become a nationalist hero. He rose to power briefly at Warsaw before his defeat in 1794. After regaining liberty in 1796, he lived for a year in England. In 1803 the Scottish novelist Jane Porter had published her popular 4-volume historical novel *Thaddeus of Warsaw* based on eye-witness accounts of the Polish uprising in the previous decade.

2 The French were currently fighting in Mexico to restore it to a monarchy and in May would offer the crown to Archduke Maximilian of Austria.

3 See **3783**&n7.

1 See **3789**&n1.

shook hands with me. I had not seen His Royal Hss for / two years.[2] He looked well, & has grown. Sir Henry Holland says, that he is $5^f..8^i$. high – but then Sir Henry is not only a physician, but a Courtier.[3] However, the Prince certainly looks taller, than I / ever expected he would turn out to be.

Having the Entrée, it was very easy work – for I went a little before two o'ck, &, in less than an hour, was at home again: but for those, who have not the entrée, the crowd was enormous; it is now *½ past five,* & / Pall-Mall, & St. James' Sqre. are still full of carriages. There were more than a 1000 [*illegible deletion*] presentations, besides those, who attended without that ceremony: still more numerous.

Nobody talks of anything, but of the Princess'es entrance into London.[4]

Adieu! | D.

TO: MARY ANNE DISRAELI [Carlton Club] 3793
[Wednesday] 25 February 1863

ORIGINAL: H A/I/A/312
EDITORIAL COMMENT: Docketed by MA on the last page: '1863 Febry 25th Dizzy'.

7 o'ck

I am kept here my dearest[.][1]

Yrs | D.

TO: QUEEN VICTORIA Grosvenor Gate [Saturday] 28 February 1863 3794

ORIGINAL: QUA [144]
EDITORIAL COMMENT: Paper imprinted 'Grosvenor Gate'. Endorsed on *verso* in another hand: 'Mr. Disraeli *accepts* P. of Wales's Marriage March 10.'

Feby. 28 1863

Mr Disraeli will obey Her Majestys command, & have the honor of attending the ceremony of the marriage of H.R.H. the Prince of Wales with H.R.H. the Princess Alexandra of Denmark, on Tuesday the 10th March.[1]

2 See VII **3237**&n3, when D sat next him at dinner in 1858. For comment on the Prince's height, see **3456**. D's last sighting of the Prince was likely at the opening of the Royal Horticultural Society gardens at South Kensington in June 1861 (see **3587**n1 and **3592**&n3). *MP* (6 June 1861).

3 Sir Henry Holland (I **24n7**), 1st Bt, MD (Edinburgh 1811), FRS 1816, FRCP 1828, was physician in ordinary to Prince Albert from 1840, and to Queen Victoria from 1852.

4 For the Prince of Wales's approaching marriage to Princess Alexandra, see **3774**&n3. For weeks the papers had been full of the elaborate preparations along the Princess's route for her reception. She would arrive on the royal yacht off Margate on 5 March and in procession at London on 7 March. *The Times* of 9 March would begin its 20-column account of the arrival: 'We to-day lay before our readers a full and faithful record of one of the most remarkable receptions accorded to Royalty in modern times.'

1 For the place of origin, see **3792**.

1 The invitation ('The Lord Chamberlain has received Her Majesty's Commands to invite ...'), addressed to D alone, is dated 27 February. Another, addressed to both Ds, is dated 28 February, with a cover letter of the same date signed 'Spencer Ponsonby', the Lord Chamberlain's cousin who worked in his office: 'By a mistake of the Invitation Clerk your invitation to the Prince of Wales's marriage did not include the name of Mrs. DIsraeli. I now send a corrected card with many apologies for the error.' The seating plan for the choir of St George's Chapel, Windsor, shows the Ds in the first two seats in the third row on

3795 TO: SARAH BRYDGES WILLYAMS

Grosvenor Gate
[Wednesday] 4 March 1863

ORIGINAL: RTC [226]

PUBLICATION HISTORY: M&B IV 397, dated at Grosvenor Gate, 4 March 1863, the third to seventh sentences; Blake 431-2, part of the fourth and fifth paragraphs

EDITORIAL COMMENT: Paper imprinted 'Grosvenor Gate'. Although not mentioned, a menu for D's 14 February parliamentary dinner was included with this letter.

Quite private March 4 1863.

I have sent you half a dozen of golden Plovers: I think, I remembering your once admiring them. They are my favorite bird. Summer weather, & the world quite mad! All London is encased with tapestried scaffolding, & carpeted galleries – & the streets already swarm.

The / Lord Mayor[1] has invited us to view the procession from the Mansion House; Baron Rothschild from Piccadilly, & there are many intermediate invitations between these extremes of East & West.[2]

This is for Saturday, the seventh. Monday the 10th. is the bridal day. Fancy all the invited guests going down, in full dress, by an express train to St. Georges Chapel & Windsor Castle! / Decolleté at ten o'ck in the morning, standing on the Paddington platform in flashing tiaras![3]

The chapel being very limited, the invitations are still more so. There never was anything so *recherché*. I listen hourly to the lamentations of the great ladies, who are not asked. The Duchess of Marlboro' in despair! The Duchess of Manchester, who was once Mistress of the Robes!!! Madame de / Flahault, only a month ago Ambassadress of France,[4] & a host of others – as eminent. None of my ↑late↓ colleagues are invited except Lord Derby, & he would go, as a matter of course, as a Knight of the Garter.[5]

But I am invited!

the left side nearest the nave. They would be among the last to arrive, D in his Windsor uniform and MA 'radiant with diamonds'. On 5 March, she would record her dissatisfaction with Andrew Barrett of 63 and 64 Piccadilly for a comb to support the feathers ladies were permitted to wear. H D/V/B/3a-e, 4, acc; Weintraub *Victoria* 555; *The Times* (11 Mar 1863). See further **3795**&nn2&6 and **3797**&n2.

1 William Anderson Rose (1820-1881), a London merchant, as lord mayor 1862-3 would welcome Princess Alexandra to London; he was MP (C) for Southampton 1862-5; Kt 1867, FRSL, FRGS.

2 The Ds would also be offered 'a window' at Northumberland House, but they would have their own procession-watching party on top of Grosvenor Gate, with guests both invited (*eg*, the Clubbes and the Poulett Scropes) and self-invited (*eg*, Lord De La Warr). On 17 March MA would pay £3 to Timberlake & Priestley, wax and tallow chandlers of 107 New Bond Street, 'for Illumination on the 10th... a Star of Love'. H B/XXI/N/90, D/III/C/389, 551, 2188, acc.

3 On 8 March Malmesbury would record the confusion at Paddington: 'The Duchess [*sic;* Marchioness until 1874] of Westminster, who had on half a million's worth of diamonds, could only find place in a third-class carriage, and Lady Palmerston was equally unfortunate. Count Lavradio had his diamond star torn off and stolen by the roughs.' Malmesbury II 294.

4 Margaret Elphinstone Mercer Keith (1788-1867), Baroness Nairne and Keith in her own right, in 1817 had married Comte de Flahault de la Billarderie, French ambassador at London 1860-2.

5 Derby had received his KG in 1859.

and what is still more marked, Mrs. D. too: and this by the Queens particular command.[6]

Yours ever, | D.

TO: ROBERT J. NEWMAN Grosvenor Gate [Friday] 13 March 1863 3796

ORIGINAL: BRN [31]

EDITORIAL COMMENT: Paper imprinted 'Grosvenor Gate'. Endorsed in another hand on the third page: 'Right Hon. B. Disraeli.' and in a third hand on the fourth page: '1863 Right Hon: B. Disraeli Recd 13th March.'

March 13 1863.

Mr Disraeli presents his Compliments to Mr Newman, & much regrets the trouble he has taken in calling at Grosvenor Gate.

Mr Disraeli is very sensible of the honor of presiding at the anniversary dinner of St. John's Foundation School, / & it is with regret, that he feels obliged to say, that he cannot undertake to fulfil that distinguished duty.[1]

TO: SARAH BRYDGES WILLYAMS Grosvenor Gate 3797
[Saturday] 21 March 1863

ORIGINAL: RTC [227]

PUBLICATION HISTORY: M&B IV 397-8, dated 21 March 1863, omitting part of the second paragraph and the last

EDITORIAL COMMENT: Paper imprinted 'Grosvenor Gate'. There is no salutation. *Sic:* St. James' (twice); dejeûner.

Mar. 21. 1863

I hope you have not had the Influenza: if any of your friends have, avoid them; 'tis infectious. It has raged in London:[1] half the House of Commons are absent from their posts: Gladstone ill; Lord Russell *very*. I have escaped comparatively lightly: that is to say, I have not absolutely knocked up, & during / the Court festivities, have managed to make my appearance, but that was all. Very weak, & witht. energy, & quite unable to write even a letter, which is the reason, I have not troubled you.

The wedding was a fine ↑affair, a↓ thing to remember. A perfect pageant with that ↑sufficient↓ foundation of sentiment, wh: elevates a mere show. The bridal of a young heir to the Throne would have / been enough in this sense, but the presence of the imperial & widowed mother, in her Gothic pavilion, watching everything with

6 See **3794**&n1. D was unaware that Palmerston had asked he be invited as Conservative leader in the Commons and one who had supported funding the Prince of Wales's household. Weintraub *Disraeli* 397. For D's description of the wedding, see Appendix III.

1 St John's Foundation School for the free education and maintenance of the sons of poor clergy, Robert J. Newman secretary, would hold its anniversary dinner at the London Tavern on Thursday, 28 May 1863, with Lord Carnarvon in the chair. *The Times* (21 May 1863).

1 The weekly report on London's health published on 20 March showed an increase in deaths of 9% over the ten-year average for the week ending on 14 March, 'caused principally by pulmonary diseases.' For the week ending on this day (21st) the death rate was almost 15% above average, with 366 deaths attributed to 'pulmonary complaints' compared to the average of 315. *The Times* (20, 25 Mar 1863).

intense interest, seeing everything, tho' herself almost unseen, was deeply dramatic, & ↑even↓ affecting.[2]

For the rest, the various & ↑brilliant↓ costumes – the knights of the Garter in their purple robes, the gorgeous heralds, the flashing diadems of the ladies, / the beautiful antique chamber, filled, witht. being crowded, in every nook with beauty of color & of form, ~~&~~ ↑the frequent ↑brilliant↓ & well ordered processions, &↓ the marvellous music – made a whole, wh: satisfied the most exquisite taste.

After the ceremony, there was a splendid dejeûner at Windsor Castle.

The Queen was very anxious, that an old shoe shd. be thrown at the Royal pair on their departure, & the Lord Chamberlain showed me, in confidence, the weapon with / wh: he had furnished himself. He took out of his pocket a beautiful white satin slipper, which had been given him, for the occasion, by the Duchess of Brabant.[3] Alas! when the hour arrived, his courage failed him – & he hustled the fairy slipper into the carriage! This is a genuine anecdote, wh: you will not find in the Illustrated News.

On the Friday following, the Duchess / of Cambridge gave a grand entertainment to the Danish Royal family at her rooms at St. James'. The Danish ↑Minister,↓[4] ~~introdu~~ presented me to the father of the Princess of Wales, the Prince Christian; still a very young man, or looking so. 5 & 20 years ago, he came over to Queen Victoria's coronation, as one of her suitors.

Later in the evening, the Duke of Cambridge presented me to the mother of the bride, the Princess Christian: / a woman of great vivacity & grace; still pretty, & once famously so.[5]

Last evening, the Prince & Princess of Wales, having returned from Osborne, gave their first evening party at St. James' Palace, wh: had not been used for such an occasion since the reign of George III.[6]

It was a very brilliant affair, limited to 500 guests of the diplomacy, & the haute noblesse: all the Dukes & Duchesses with scarcely an / exception. The Prince & Princess looked like a young couple in a fairy tale. She had on a crown of diamonds, & walked in procession thro' the illumined saloons, while the Queen's private band, of the choicest musicians, played triumphantly.

2 The Queen, in 'the simplest and plainest of widow's weeds' and accompanied by Albert's look-alike brother the Duke of Saxe-Cobourg and Gotha, had taken her place in the enclosed royal pew high above the altar and appeared only briefly at its window. *The Times* (11 Mar 1863). See illustration p lx.

3 Marie Henriette Anne (1836-1902), youngest daughter of Archduke Joseph of Austria, in 1853 had married the Duke of Brabant, who in 1865 would succeed as Leopold II, King of the Belgians.

4 The Danish minister to London at this time was Baron Thorben de Bille, envoy extraordinary and minister plenipotentiary. *MP* (26 Feb 1863); *BA* (1863).

5 Prince Christian (1818-1906), a younger son of William, Duke of Schleswig-Holstein-Sonderburg-Glücksburg, and a direct descendant of King Christian III of Denmark and his wife Louise (a granddaughter of King Frederick V of Denmark), designated Prince Christian of Denmark 1852, on 15 November 1863 would succeed as Christian IX, King of Denmark; his contentious succession would lead in 1864 to the war by which Denmark would lose to Prussia the duchies of Schleswig, Holstein and Lauenburg. In 1842 he had married Louise Wilhelmine Friederike Caroline Auguste Julie (1817-1898), in 1852 designated Princess Christian, third daughter of Landgrave William of Hesse-Cassel and his wife, Princess Louise Charlotte of Denmark (Princess Christian being thus a cousin of Frederick VII).

6 George III reigned 1760-1820.

In the meantime, politics are very idle. In a week, commence Easter holidays.[7] We go for a week to Hughenden, & then to Wotton ↑on↓ a visit to the Duke & Dcss of Buckingham.[8]

Adieu! my dear friend | D.

TO: LORD CARRINGTON Grosvenor Gate [Monday] 23 March 1863 **3798**

ORIGINAL: CARR [18]

EDITORIAL COMMENT: Paper imprinted 'Grosvenor Gate'. *Sic:* Carington.

March 23 1863

The | Lord Carington

My dear Lord,

I highly approve of a County Meeting to address the Prince of Wales, & feel obliged, & honored, by your proposal / to add my name to the Requisition.[1]

I trust Lady Carington & all the family are quite well.

Yours sincerely, | *B. Disraeli*

TO: SARAH BRYDGES WILLYAMS [House of Commons?] [Wednesday] 25 March 1863 **3799**

ORIGINAL: RTC [228]

EDITORIAL COMMENT: House of Commons[?] paper. There is no salutation.

Mar. 25 1863

We propose going to Hughenden on Monday next – & on the following Monday, going to Wotton, on a visit, for a few days, to the Duke & Duchess of Buckingham, where we shall meet the Duke & Duchess of / Marlboro'.

I hope this fine weather has been enjoyed by you in some rides in the little carriage, which so much pleased Mary Anne last year, when you, & she, went on your daily visits.

I / wrote to you on Saturday, pretty fully, about our Court festivities. The Danish family have now returned home, so everything is quiet again.

Adieu! | D.

TO: MESSRS BURLEY AND CARLISLE [London] [Wednesday] 25 March 1863 **3800**

ORIGINAL: MOPSIK [41]

EDITORIAL COMMENT: Endorsed in another hand on the last page: '*25 March 1863 Rt. Honble. B Disraeli Magenis & Villiers*'. *Sic:* Magenis'; Dixon.

Messr | Burley and Carlisle Mar: 25 1863

7 On Friday 27 March the House would adjourn for Easter (5 April) until Monday 13 April. *Hansard* CLXX col 110.

8 See further **3804**.

1 Carrington had written from Gayhurst on 22 March about the meeting: 'Will you authorize me to have your name added to those who sign the requisition to the Sheriff.' H B/XXI/C/73. At the Aylesbury meeting on 6 April, chaired by the high sheriff Philips Cosby Lovett, D would second Carrington's motion proposing congratulatory addresses to the Queen and the Prince on the royal marriage, and express great confidence in the Prince as a future king. *BH* (11 Apr 1863).

Gentlemen,

I shd. like to receive the annual statement of Mr Magenis' acct. with the estate of the late Hon: Fras Villiers: have / you heard anything of Mr Dixon, and his colleague? I expected to have received some offers from them.[1]

Yours faithfully, | *B. Disraeli*

3801 TO: LORD PALMERSTON Grosvenor Gate [Thursday] 26 March 1863

ORIGINAL: PP GC/DI/141

PUBLICATION HISTORY: M&B IV 400, dated March 1863, with minor variants

EDITORIAL COMMENT: Paper imprinted 'Grosvenor Gate'.

Rt Honble | The Viscount Palmerston | K.G. March 26 1863

My dear Lord,

There are few distinctions I should more highly value, than to become a Trustee of the British Museum.[1]

My father was the first man of letters who, much more than half a century ago, began to turn its / MS. wealth to account; in the illustration of our history; & I have been brought up in a due appreciation of its treasures, & a due reverence for its authorities.

But what I most esteem, in the present matter, are the mode, & medium, by wh: my election has been communicated to me.

I hope yr Lordship is / not quite unaware of the sincere regard, wh: I have always personally entertained for you; since our first acquaintance; &, notwithstanding the inevitable collisions of public life, I can truly say, that, perhaps, no one grudges yr greatness less, than

Your obliged, & very faithfl Servt, | *B. Disraeli*

1 For D's previous letter to Burley and Carlisle after Villiers's death, see **3714**&nn1&2. They would reply to D's letter of this day (25 March) from Lincoln's Inn on 28 March enclosing a statement of £1,174.8.8 owed to Magenis under the 1861 mortgage of Villiers's Ceylon estates after payments due 5 March (£379.18.11) and 13 May (£363.2.9) 1863 were credited: 'From what we hear we consider that the Lessees of the Plantations will endeavour to retain possession of them after Mr Magenis' debt is paid, as they are evidently under the conviction that no member of the Villiers family will undertake the burden of representation to him on account of his debts, and the Lessees expect from this circumstance that they will have an undisturbed possession after Mr Magenis is paid off. The family of Mr Villiers should therefore consider the position of the matter, which we some time since brought to the notice of Mr Richard Hall the Land Agent of Lady Jersey.' H A/IV/J/238. For the prospect in 1857 of selling the Ceylon estates through Thomas Dickson, of Dawson, Dickson & Co, Colombo, Ceylon, see VII **3012**&n1. Dickson had written to D from 73 Gloucester Terrace, Hyde Park, on 17 July 1862 offering to see him about Villiers's affairs and mentioning a man returned to England and interested in the Gallageddera estate. H A/IV/J/209. The Burley & Carlisle response makes no mention of Dickson.

---

1 Palmerston had written from 94 Piccadilly on 25 March: 'You will of Course receive from the Secretary to the Trustees of the British Museum the official notification that at a meeting held by them this afternoon you were elected a Trustee in the Room of the late Lord Lansdowne; but it may be agreable to you to know the grounds upon which the choice of the Trustees was made. The Trustees were of opinion that in making Choice of a new Colleague they ought to Select a Person distinguished by literary Eminence; That it would be useful to the Interests of the Museum that he should be in a prominent Position in the House of Commons, so as to be able when occasions might arise, to explain with authority to the House any Matters connected with the Museum which might be brought under Discussion, and lastly it was felt

TO: LORD STANHOPE Hughenden [Saturday] 4 April 1863 3802

ORIGINAL: KCR Stanhope MSS 681(7)
EDITORIAL COMMENT: Paper imprinted 'Hughenden Manor'.

The | Earl Stanhope April 4 1863

My dear Lord,

My friends, in the Lower House, like, very much, to meet Peers, who have been regular House of Commons men.[1] It is a habit, wh: keeps the party together, fosters a / good understanding between the two Houses, & enlarges the sympathies of political connection. At least, they think so: I wish, I could induce yr Lordship to be of their opinion; & give me the pleasure, & very great honor, / of yr company, at dinner, on Saturday, the 18th. Inst:. You would meet many, who would be very much pleased to meet you.[2]

With my complimts to Lady Stanhope, believe me,
sincerely yours, | *B. Disraeli*

TO: LORD CAMPDEN Hughenden [Friday] 10 April 1863 3803

ORIGINAL: PS [1541]
PUBLICATION HISTORY: M&B IV 367, dated at Hughenden, 10 April 1863
EDITORIAL COMMENT: A manuscript copy in H H/LIFE, headed 'To Viscount Campden (Campton?)', gives the signature as 'Yours sincerely | D.'

Private Hughenden Manor, April 10, 1863

My dear Lord,

I shall certainly support the Prison Ministers bill which is conceived in the spirit of the policy of the late Government, and I shall do all I can to induce friends to act with me.[1] I anticipate, however, in that respect, no little difficulty. What neutralises

that Whereas many of the existing Trustees belong more or less to one political Party, it was desirable that the Choice to be made should shew that Party Politics are not to be permitted to enter within the Gates of a Building dedicated to Learning and to the Arts. All these Considerations seemed to point to you as the proper object of choice, and accordingly you were unanimously Elected.' H B/XXI/P/92. Lansdowne had died on 31 January 1863. The deputy principal librarian, J. Winter Jones, would send the official announcement on this day (26 March). H B/XIV/A/10. On 31 March Walpole, also a trustee, would forward to D a letter from Panizzi, the principal librarian, who had written to him from Italy on the morning of 25 March, before the afternoon election: 'I must congratulate you & the Museum on the election of Mr d'Israeli to be a Trustee. I know how much you had it at heart, and you know that I was not less desirous of it than you were.' He asked that D be told his opinion that 'this election will prove of the greatest advantage to the Museum.' H B/XXI/P/110, 110a. MA on 1 April would convey the news and newspaper clippings about it to SBW: 'It is considered one of our greatest honor's, as it is never given but to first rate abilities'. RTC [475Q].

1 Stanhope (I **91**n7) had been in the Commons as Lord Mahon until 1852.

2 Stanhope would accept the invitation on 7 April from Chevening, agreeing on the benefit of meetings between members of the two Houses. H B/XXI/S/487. In this latest of D's House-bridging dinners, 17 guests would dine at Grosvenor Gate on Saturday 18 April. H acc; *MP* (21 Apr 1863). For the guests, see Appendix II.

1 The Prison Ministers Bill (allowing prisoners to be served by ministers of their own faiths) would come up for second reading on 20 April; as a mostly pro-Catholic measure, it was heavily opposed by D's party. Lord Campden (for whom see V **1745**&n4), a former Liberal MP and unsuccessful Liberal candidate in

my efforts in these matters is the systematic hostility always shown by the Catholic members of the House of Commons to the Church of England. This is most unwise. We live in times when Churches should act together.

I do not expect Catholic members, generally, to vote, for instance, for Church rates, though were I a Catholic I would do so, but at least they might keep away from such divisions. There would be no difficulty about Prison Ministers bills, and many other measures of that description, if men of the position of Mr. Monsell would only act in church affairs as Montalembert recommended.[2] I mention Mr. Monsell; both by position and talents he is a leading man, and might exercise even a more considerable influence. If the Churches drew more together, the following of the Newdegates and the Whalleys would sink into insignificance.[3]

Peto's bill comes on next Wednesday; most offensive to the English clergy.[4] It

a recent co Cork by-election, on 9 April had asked D to support the bill: 'It proposes to accomplish what I hoped & trusted would have been done three years ago, if Lord Derby's Administration had not been factiously overturned; as both Lord Derby and yourself had expressed yourselves favourably as to giving equal religious provision to R Catholic Prisoners ... As is the case with other Government measures, owing to the strength of the Conservative party in the House, you probably have the fate of the bill in your hands ... And as the R. Catholic body are anxious for its passing, and are aware of the good dispositions of the leaders of that party to do them justice, they anxiously look for their aid in support of the bill ... But supposing the Conservatives generally followed the lead of Mr Newdegate and Mr Whalley, still the support of the measure by the leaders of the party would counteract that influence'. H B/XXI/G/10. In the debate on second reading, D would support the bill as simple justice, pooh-poohing the alleged threat to the established Church, which he thought adequately protected by the discretion of magistrates allowed by the bill: 'It is the interest of the Church of England – it is the interest of all ecclesiastical institutions, and, indeed, of all religious bodies – to favour the development of the religious principle – to cherish, encourage, and nurture those spiritual influences which hitherto have controlled and regulated man'. Despite strong speeches against it by Newdegate and Whalley (see n3), the bill would pass second reading 152-122, D voting with the majority. *Hansard* CLXX cols 401-48 (D 429-34). After much turmoil in both Houses, the bill eventually passed.

2 Charles Forbes René (1810-1870), comte de Montalembert, was an English-born advocate of liberalism within the French Catholic Church. William Monsell, educated at Winchester and Oriel College, Oxford (no degree), was a popular landlord and MP (L) for co Limerick 1847-74, when he would be created Baron Emly. He had converted to Catholicism in 1850 and, as a friend of such eminent Catholics as Wiseman, Newman, Montalembert and Ward, took a leading part in church affairs in parliament. He did not speak at any stage of the Prison Ministers Bill's passage through the House. D in his speech on the Bill remarked that there was only one Roman Catholic in the Commons, *ie,* Monsell. It would be Newdegate who in the 20 April debate would cite 'the advice ... given to the Roman Catholics of this country ... by Count Montalembert ... in 1856 to his co-religionists in this kingdom – "What remains to them (English Roman Catholics) now is to obtain in practice a more sincere and equitable observation of the principle of equality in all that refers to the nomination of employments, an equal share in public grants, the intervention of ecclesiastics paid by the State in the army, in the prisons, and in the hospitals, and this they will attain – slowly, perhaps, but they will attain it – their rights, their rapidly increasing numbers, the necessities of the time in which we live, everything is for them."' *Hansard* CLXX col 442.

3 The anti-Catholic Newdegate and Whalley spoke offensively against the Prison Ministers Bill on 17 February during debate on first reading. Whalley declared that the 'acts which brought [the prisoners] within the walls of a prison were directly taught in the books of Roman Catholic writers', while Newdegate hoped that on second reading 'the House would prevent the forcing into the cells of the unwilling prisoners the representatives of a priesthood whose success in moral instruction was illustrated by the enormous preponderance of Roman Catholic prisoners in our gaols.' *Hansard* CLXIX cols 464-7. George Hampden Whalley (1813-1878), a barrister (Gray's Inn 1836), assistant tithe commissioner 1836-47, was MP (L) for Peterborough 1852-3, 1859-78.

4 Sir Samuel Morton Peto (VII **3360n3**) on 5 March had introduced a Burials Bill, one he had been proposing since 1861, to allow Dissenters to hold burial services in churchyards of the established Church. The

would be wise in the Catholic members, and would greatly assist me in my conscientious efforts on their behalf, if they did not mix themselves up with these Pedo or Peto Baptists, or whatever they may be.[5]

TO: SARAH BRYDGES WILLYAMS Hughenden [Friday] 10 April 1863 3804

ORIGINAL: RTC [229]

EDITORIAL COMMENT: Paper imprinted 'Hughenden Manor'. There is no salutation. *Sic:* embarassed; comparitive; Chandos'.

April 10 1863

We went to Wotton last Monday, to stay a few days with the Duke & Duchess of Buckingham. It was the first time he had opened his house since his accession to his title & since he got his / long embarassed estate in comparitive order & comfort.[1] The Duke is made to be the restorer of a family – an acute, & indefatigable, man of business: very intelligent, but very hard. More like an American, than an English Duke, the lord of two duchies, & / the heir & representative of the Grenvilles & the Chandos'. He dwells on the most ancient estate in England, with nothing of the old world about himself. He has drained 14,000 acres of the finest land in England, & wh: have been in his family, in a direct line, since the Plantagenets. Among / others, the Duke & Duchess of Marlboro,' very agreeable people, were here – but on Tuesday night, or rather morning, the Duchess was taken ill: a premature confinement! Alas! the addition to the House of Churchill was lifeless! But they have ten children: tho' only two sons.[2] Conceive the confusion! No town nearer than eleven miles, & the oracle of that town away!

yrs ever, | D.

issue was burial of unbaptized children of adult-baptizing Baptists (*ie,* 'Pedo' Baptists); the bill proposed that dissenting ministers require a parish incumbent to allow services in the churchyard or to report to his bishop his reasons for not allowing it. The bill would come up for second reading on Wednesday 15 April, when D would oppose it as another threat to the established Church, arguing that Dissenters who did not wish to be buried by established Church rites had the freedom of their own cemeteries. The bill would be defeated 221-96. *Hansard* CLXIX cols 1120-21, CLXX cols 139-67 (D 163-6).

5 Lord Campden would write again, from Paris on 6 May, to thank D for his letter and his 'effective speech': 'It is quite understood, even by ... Whigs, that the success of the measure on the 2nd reading was owing to the support of yourself, and the Conservative leaders, and the abstention of many of our party from voting ... I cannot but hope that in time a better *political* feeling will exist between Protestants & Catholics in the Legislature. And I look to the time when the Conservative Party will come into office upon its own strength, receiving the additional support of a large section of the Catholic members. The chief obstacle is the distribution of Patronage in Ireland when Conservatives are in power.' H B/XXI/G/11.

---

1 See IV **1579**&n1 and V **1678**&n2. The former Lord Chandos had succeeded as 3rd Duke of Buckingham and Chandos on 29 July 1861 on the death of his improvident father, the 2nd Duke.

2 The Marlboroughs at this time had eight children, having lost three sons in infancy or childhood; they would have one more daughter, in 1865. The two surviving sons were: George Charles Spencer Churchill (1844-1892), Marquess of Blandford, who would succeed his father as 8th Duke of Marlborough in 1883; and Lord Randolph Henry Spencer Churchill (1849-1895), the future secretary for India 1885-6, Commons leader and chancellor of the exchequer 1886.

3805 TO: SARAH BRYDGES WILLYAMS

House of Commons [Wednesday] 15 April 1863

ORIGINAL: RTC [230]
EDITORIAL COMMENT: House of Commons paper. For a note filed with this letter, see **3810**ec. There is no salutation.

April 15 1863

A great division in the House of Commons, & a great triumph. I write to you while the cheers are still ringing in my ~~year~~ ↑ears↓. Gladstone, to the astonishment of his friends, deserted the Church, & I replied to / him, & closed the debate.[1]

The unexpected death of Sir George Lewis greatly weakens the Government,[2] but I hope, myself, that they will totter on.

You will be glad to hear, that my strict injunctions / ~~to~~ not to destroy small birds, at Hughenden, have been successfully carried out – & that we found, during our late visit, a most grateful chorus from our groves every morning, when we woke, & all day long. /

I hope you are quite well. I am particularly so[.]

Sir John Pakington was at Torquay during the Easter Recess, & gave me some account of the place, & my friends. He had not been there for thirty years, & is as astonished, as delighted with your English Nice.

Ever yrs | D.

3806 TO: SIR HENRY STRACEY

[London, Friday] 17 April 1863

ORIGINAL: PS 794
PUBLICATION HISTORY: Christie's catalogue (4 Nov 1981) item 44: 'to Sir Henry Stracey, sometime M.P. for Norwich' and dated '17 April 1863'
EDITORIAL COMMENT: See **3489**; the following extract is among the topics that 'Disraeli communes [with Stracey] on'.

[the state of their own party] The division of Wednesday was most gratifying, as proving the consolidating conservative feeling of the Kingdom[1]

3807 TO: HENRY WHITMORE

[London, Monday, 20 April 1863]

ORIGINAL: PS 749
PUBLICATION HISTORY: P.J. and A.E. Dobell catalogue 64 (Mar 1927) item 8: 'A.L.s. (initial), 2½ pp., 8vo, August 29th, 1862,' quoted and paraphrased in square brackets as shown below, '*with franked and stamped envelope*'
EDITORIAL COMMENT: *Dating:* by context; see n1. This paraphrased extract is evidently from the '"hasty line" of last night' to which Whitmore responds on 21 April 1863.

My dear Whitmore,
[respecting a misunderstanding with regard to the sending out of a Parliamentary] Whip[1]

1 See **3803**&n4 for the Burials Bill that D helped to kill on this day.
2 Sir George (V **1801**n2), war secretary in the cabinet, had died suddenly and unexpectedly on 13 April.

1 See **3803**&n4 and **3805**&n1.

1 This snippet preserves just enough of the original letter to allow dating and annotation of an interesting correspondence. Thomas Collins on 'Monday night' (docketed 20 April 1863) had written to D: 'I

TO: QUEEN VICTORIA [London, Friday 24 April 1863] 3808

ORIGINAL: H B/XIX/A/28

PUBLICATION HISTORY: M&B IV 392n1, the second paragraph, with minor variations

EDITORIAL COMMENT: A draft in D's hand. Docketed '1866'. *Dating:* by context; see n1.

Mr Disraeli, with his humble duty to Your Majesty, trusts that he may not be deemed, by Yr Majesty, presumptuous or egotistical, if he ventures to enclose a memorandum of what he really said on the 23rd. Inst. in the House of Commons.

Ld. P. had judiciously arranged that the Memorial ~~Deb.~~ ↑vote↓ shd take precedence ↑of o[the]r bus:↓ & there were skilled reporters ↑ready↓ who wd. have faithfully represented what was said on that occasion. But ~~an~~ ↑~~a fiery~~↓ ↑a fiery↓ American Debate was ↑irresistibly↓ forced on & the skilled reporters ~~expended~~ ↑exhausted↓ their energies on its grey proceedings, so that those who spoke aftds. ↑, on the gentler theme,↓ fell to very rude & uncouth hands.[1]

find the enemy are aware of the importance of the Borough Residence Bill & mean to oppose it[;] still I feel confident that with the Liberal aid I have got I can carry it with a good party whip on our side.' He explained that the absent (chief whip) Taylor had instructed Henry Whitmore to issue a strong whip for the bill on Wednesday morning. Collins would write to D again, on 'Tuesday 10 am': 'I gave your note to Whitmore[;] he is indirectly much out of sorts about it because he may be personally injured in Bridgnorth [*Whitmore's constituency*] but in this matter he clearly is only doing Taylors part who if present would as a matter of course have issued the order.' H B/XXI/C/321. Also on 'Tuesday', Whitmore would write, evidently in response to D's '"hasty line"': 'I have obeyed your orders & put out a strong Whip for Collins, – I should not have hesitated on the subject but knowing Collins's extreme views whenever he has a Bill before the House, I thought he had waylaid you & that the "hasty line" of last night had been written to pacify him. The Bill will I believe be injurious to me, should it become Law, but I can assure you that my *sole motive* for refusing "The Whip" was an objection on my part to make it a Party question & asking men to come down & vote for a Bill brought in by Messrs. Collins, *Paget & Ayrton,* the names of those individuals being on its back.' H B/XXI/W/326. Thomas Collins was a Liberal Conservative, Charles Paget (the only 'Mr Paget' currently in the House) was a Liberal, and Acton Smee Ayrton was a Radical. Their bill was the Borough Residence Uniform Measurement Bill to remove anomalies in measuring distances of residences from boroughs to determine voting eligibility. To opposition cheers it would pass second reading 171-135 on Wednesday 22 April 1863, but on 30 April would die at the committee stage. *Hansard* CLXX cols 536-44, 1036-42.

---

1 Presumably D wrote this on 24 April after he saw the morning newspaper reports of his 23 April speech and before he received the Queen's response to it; see **3809**&n1. Next to this draft is a 4-page MS in D's hand of that speech, beginning 'I cannot agree with the hon gent: as to the causes he alleges for the inadequacy of the pub: cont: for this monument nor with the prin: on wh: he thinks that mon: shd be erected.' In *The Times* and in *Hansard* this sentence reads: 'I cannot agree with the hon. gentleman as to the causes he alleges for the inadequacy of the public contributions for this object; nor can I agree with him as to the principle upon which the monument should be elevated.' *MP* has a similarly stilted, but different, version. Early in the speech, after the sentence in all the accounts ending 'not altogether satisfactory', the MS, *The Times* and *MP* have an extra passage that does not occur in *Hansard;* MS: 'Nor can I agree with the Hon gent: that in their desire to raise a memorial to the illus: Prince the country became dissatisfied with the nature of the propos[iti]ons for carrying it into effect.' *The Times:* 'As to the original feeling when that sad event occurred, some time ago, I cannot agree with the hon. gentleman in the inference he draws, that, in the desire to raise a memorial to the illustrious Prince, the country became dissatisfied with the nature of the propositions that were made.' *MP:* 'With regard to the original feeling when this sad event occurred, some time ago, I cannot agree with the hon. gentleman in the inference which he has drawn, that in the desire to raise to the memory of that illustrious person whom the country lost there was any dissatisfaction with the nature of the appeal that was made to them.' H B/XIX/A/28a. Before Palmerston's motion on the memorial, there had been heated discussion about response to the American North's interference with British shipping; Roebuck, for example, called for action that might lead to war. There had also been an acrimonious exchange between Roebuck, who had forced the discussion, and Bentinck on a point of order and parliamentary courtesy. *Hansard* CLXX cols 576-600.

3809 TO: QUEEN VICTORIA Grosvenor Gate [Sunday] 26 April 1863

ORIGINAL: RAC R4 79

PUBLICATION HISTORY: M&B IV 394, dated at Grosvenor Gate, 25 April 1863; Blake 431, extracts from M&B; Weintraub *Disraeli* 400, *Victoria* 317, extracts from M&B; Bradford 251-2, extracts

EDITORIAL COMMENT: Black-edged paper. Two copies in D's hand in H B/XIX/A/24a,b are dated 25 April 1863. M&B, Blake and Weintraub (see ph) use b, apparently the earlier; apart from the date, the main differences from the version D sent are: (paragraph 3, first sentence) 'the Prince is *one of* the most'; (paragraph 3, second-last word) 'exalting' instead of 'elevating' (this also in the other copy); (paragraph 4, first sentence) 'has *ever* known'; (paragraph 4, second sentence) 'None *with whom he is acquainted* have ever'; (paragraph 6, last sentence) 'master-type of *a generation* of'. The version sent has 'vaster' (last sentence) messily written over 'wider', while both copies have 'vaster'. *Sic:* None have.

Grosvenor Gate | April 26. 1863

Mr. Disraeli, with his humble duty to Your Majesty, begs permission to express his gratitude to Yr Majesty, for Yr Majesty's gracious, & affecting, condescension, & for the inestimable volume, which Your Majesty has deigned to present to him.[1]

If, in venturing to touch upon a sacred theme, Mr. Disraeli may have, occasionally, used expressions, which Your Majesty has been graciously pleased to deem not altogether / inadequate to the subject, he has been enabled to do so, only because, on that subject, he speaks from the heart; & from long, & frequent, musing over its ever-living interest.

His acquaintance with the Prince is the most satisfactory incident of his life: full of refined & beautiful memories, & exercising, as he hopes, over his remaining existence, a soothing & elevating influence.

The Prince is the only person, whom Mr Disraeli has known, who realized the Ideal. None have ever approached it.

There was / in him an union of the manly grace, & sublime simplicity, of chivalry with the intellectual splendor of the Attic Academe. The only character in English history, that would, in some respects, draw near to him, is Sir Philip Sidney: the

1 On 23 April D had supported Palmerston's motion in a supply debate to add up to £50,000 to the public subscription of a similar amount for a memorial to Prince Albert. He had referred to Albert as 'The peerless husband, the perfect father, the master whose yoke was gentleness – the wise and faithful counsellor of the Sovereign' who 'united the faculty of contemplation with the talent of action ... [and added] to these qualities all the virtues of the heart ... The task which the Prince proposed to himself was to extend the knowledge, refine the taste, and enlarge the sympathies of a proud and ancient people. Had he not been gifted with deep thought and a singular facility and happiness of applying and mastering details, he could not have succeeded so fully as he did in those efforts, the results of which we shall find so much the greater as time goes on.' He called for a monument that would 'represent the character of the Prince himself; in the harmony of its proportions, in the beauty of its ornament, and in its enduring nature. It should be something direct, significant, and choice; so that those who come after us may say, this is the type and testimony of a sublime life and a transcendent career, and thus they were recognised by a grateful and admiring people!' *Hansard* CLXX cols 601-12 (D 607-10). The Queen had written from Windsor on 24 April: '[*copy in the hand of Gen Charles Grey, the Queen's private secretary*] The Queen cannot resist from expressing, personally, to Mr Disraeli her deep gratification at the tribute he paid to her adored, beloved, & great, Husband. The perusal of it made her shed many tears, – but it was very soothing to her broken heart, to see such true appreciation of that spotless, & unequalled, character. The Queen asks Mr Disraeli to accept the accompanying book.' The copy continues on a separate page: 'The book was a copy of the Prince's speeches &c., richly bound in white morocco, with this inscription, in Her Majestys handwriting[:] To | the Right Honorable Benjamin Disraeli; | In recollection of the best | & greatest of Men; | from the beloved Prince's | broken-hearted Widow | Victoria R. | Windsor Castle | April 24. 1863'. H B/XIX/A/23.

same high tone, the same universal accomplishment, the same blended tenderness & vigor, the same rare combination of romantic energy & classic repose.

Both left us in their youth.[2] But there is no person in our history, who has established such a permanent, & almost mystic, / ascendancy over national feeling, as Sir Philip Sidney; & the writer of these lines is much mistaken, if, as time advances, the thought & sentiment of a progressive age will not cluster round the Prince; his plans will become systems, his suggestions dogmas; & the name of Albert will be accepted as the master-type of an age of profounder feeling, & vaster range, than that, wh: he formed, & guided, with benignant power.[3]

TO: SARAH BRYDGES WILLYAMS | Grosvenor Gate [Monday] 27 April 1863 | 3810

ORIGINAL: RTC [231]
EDITORIAL COMMENT: Paper imprinted 'Grosvenor Gate'. A note in SBW's hand is with **3805**: 'Envelope & Crest dated April 27 1863 given to Janet Wilmot Chetwode at her request.' There is no salutation.

Confidential April 27 1863

A great deal has happened, since I wrote to you last.

On Wednesday, I was invited to Windsor Castle – & on Thursday, I had my first audience of the Queen since the death of the Prince, or, to use her Majesty's own words, ↑in a *subsequent* letter to me↓ since she became "*a broken-hearted widow*".[1]

Her Majesty received me in the Prince's private room. Nothing in it changed: it is just, as if he were alive & now inhabiting it, only on his accustomed chair, there is / a brass plate saying "This is the chair used by the Prince Consort from to – ." mentioning the dates.

The Queen looks well: still in weeds; & seems stouter, tho' that I think arises from her mourning dress, wh: is stiff & heavy. She was calm, &, after speaking of several matters, touched naturally on the Prince, but witht. any reference to her calamity. Afterwards, she seemed to take more courage, & spoke to me of her "forlorn condition" – but with entire self command. She told me she had seen with great / pleasure, that I had been chosen to succeed Lord Lansdowne as a trustee of the British Museum,[2] & spoke of its general management, & of the Prince's-views about it – then she conversed very freely about America & Poland, & after twenty minutes or a little more, asked after my wife, & then bowed, & vanished, thro' a door hardly perceived.

The banquet on Wednesday was the same as in old days, except that she was not present, & there was no military band at dinner, & no "God save the Queen" when they rose. The / Prince & Princess of Wales, Prince Alfred & Princess Helena,[3] now

2 Sir Philip Sidney was not quite 32 when he died in 1586, while Prince Albert was 42.

3 The Queen would have extracts of this, 'the most striking and beautiful letter that Her Majesty has received,' sent to Arthur Helps, the editor of the book of Albert's speeches she had sent to D. M&B IV 395. See **3813**&n1.

---

1 See **3809**n1.

2 See **3801**&n1.

3 Princess Helena Augusta Victoria (1846-1923), third daughter in the royal family, in 1866 would marry Prince Christian of Schleswig-Holstein-Sonderburg-Augustenburg.

quite a woman, were at the dinner, & a crowd of courtiers in the Windsor uniform: the only guests being myself, & Lord John Russell. In the evening, I was presented to the Princess of Wales, & conversed with her for some little time. She is natural, animated, & evidently very happy. The Prince has grown fat: too soon. The younger Prince, Alfred, whom I had not seen for three years,[4] is not only a man, but manly: & full of intelligence & information. Both in look & voice, he resembles his father.[5]

Adieu! *till tomorrow;* for there is more to say.[6] | D.

3811 TO: BENJAMIN LUMLEY — Grosvenor Gate [Monday] 27 April 1863

ORIGINAL: MOPSIK [99]
COVER: B. Lumley Esqr, | Hon: H Stanhope, | 23 Spring Gardns | *B. Disraeli*
POSTMARK: (1) In circle: LONDON S.W. | 6 | AP27 | 63 (2) a cancelled one-penny stamp (3) *verso* [*not photographed in our copy*]
EDITORIAL COMMENT: Paper imprinted 'Grosvenor Gate'.

B. Lumley Esqr — April 27 1863

Dear Sir,

I recognised yr handwriting with pleasure, &, I trust, you may yet live to surmount yr undeserved / misfortunes.[1]

I am sorry I cannot comply with yr request; but, I think, the "Memorial" system has been carried to an inexpedient extent, & is defeating its own / purpose.[2]

Yrs very faithfully, | *B. Disraeli*

3812 TO: JOHN GRAVES — [London, late-April 1863]

ORIGINAL: PS [529]
PUBLICATION HISTORY: Sotheby catalogue (13 Dec 1990) item 379
EDITORIAL COMMENT: *Dating:* by context; see n1.

...I leave everything with confidence to your good taste & good feeling – all that I desire is to preserve the link, wh: connects my name with a place I so much regard, as Bradenham...[1]

4 See **3456**&n1.
5 For another account by D of this visit to Windsor, see Appendix III.
6 For the continuation see **3814**.

1 For Lumley's illustrious but failed career as lessee of Her Majesty's Theatre, see IV **1422**&n1. His letter has not been found. Perhaps relevant to his unidentified request is that on 22 January he had received an unconditional discharge in the court of bankruptcy, and that on 25 and 29 May and 3 and 8 June there would be benefit concerts for him at Drury Lane Theatre.
2 For the technicalities of 'memorial' applications for public funds, see **3831**&n2.

1 D is presumably responding to a letter from the Reverend John Graves (current lord of the manor of Bradenham) at Bradenham House on 18 April 1863: 'We shall soon commence the restoration of Bradenham Church. The North wall of the Chancel, according to Mr Street's Plan, must be removed, that a 2nd arch may be built into the Mortuary Chapel. Would you kindly allow me to transfer the Tablet to your family to one of the walls of the Mortuary Chapel. I will see that [it] is removed with great care.' H A/VII/E/9. Bradenham Church would undergo extensive conversion to Victorian Gothic in 1863, when the Norman chancel arch and windows were replaced according to current fashion, resulting in the loss of many antiquities. Kenneth Glass *Bradenham Manor Past and Present* (Thornton Baker/Grant Thornton, 1985) 18.

TO: ARTHUR HELPS [London, Tuesday 5 May 1863] 3813

ORIGINAL: H B/XIX/A/26a

EDITORIAL COMMENT: A draft in D's hand.

Mr D. thanks Mr Helps for his obliging note & for its interesting inclosure.[1]

Mr. D. ~~perused~~ ↑read↓ the Introduction to the ~~speeches Vol.~~ ↑Albertine vol., on its appearance,↓ with critical anxiety & concluded its ↑perusal↓ with ~~perfect~~ complete satisfaction. ~~The pen was then unknown to him, but~~ The general conception of the character is strong & true; ~~it is~~ ↑the details are↓ full of just & fine ~~delicate~~ discrimin[ati]on; & all is conveyed in a style – pensive & gracious – like the subject. –

TO: SARAH BRYDGES WILLYAMS Grosvenor Gate [Tuesday] 5 May 1863 3814

ORIGINAL: RTC [232]

PUBLICATION HISTORY: M&B IV 393, dated at Grosvenor Gate, 5 May 1863; Bradford 251, extract

EDITORIAL COMMENT: Paper imprinted 'Grosvenor Gate'. A menu for the 9 May 1863 political dinner at Grosvenor Gate is enclosed. There is no salutation.

Confidential May 5 1863

I must continue, & conclude, my Windsor adventures.[1] When I came up to town on the Thursday, from the Castle, there was a debate in the House of Commons on the vote for a Monument to Prince Albert.[2] The Queen, with great delicacy, had not / mentioned the subject to me – &, of course, I did not allude to it.

You, probably, read the observations, which I made on the question in the Ho: of Commons.[3]

That was on Thursday night, & on Saturday morning I received from the Queen her own copy of the speeches of the Prince (the same work wh: I gave you when first / published). The copy was bound in White morocco, & on the fly leaf, in the Queens own handwriting, was this inscription

1 Arthur Helps (1813-1875), clerk of the privy council 1860-75 and reviser of several of the Queen's works, KCB 1872, had at her request edited the volume of Albert's speeches of which she had sent D a copy; see **3809**&nn1&3. Helps had written on this day (5 May) from the council office, Downing Street, enclosing a 4 May letter to him from Lady Augusta Bruce (extra woman of the bedchamber to Her Majesty) at Osborne; she had written: 'The Queen ... has been anxious that you should have an opportunity of perusing the most striking & beautiful letter that Her Majesty has received, and has therefore directed me to send you the enclosed Extracts from that in which Mr. Disraeli acknowledges the Volume sent to him by the Queen. I need not tell you how Her Majesty has been affected by the depth & delicacy of these touches, or how soothing it is to the Queen to have this inexhaustible theme so treated. I had the great enjoyment of hearing Mr Disraeli speak on the character of the Prince the other evening at Windsor, & what added much to the interest & satisfaction with which I listened, was the hope I conceived, from something Mr. Disraeli said, that he would one day give to the world his full conception of the Prince's character.' Helps wrote (3rd person): 'Nothing more worthy to be said, has, in Mr Helps's judgment, been said, in few words, of the Prince Consort's great nature and character, than the description of him contained in the extracts from Mr Disraeli's letter, which the Queen has honoured and gratified Mr Helps by allowing him to see.' H B/XIX/25-6.

1 See **3810**.

2 See **3809**&n1.

3 See **3808**&n1. MA regularly sent SBW newspapers with D's parliamentary activities.

To
the Rt. Honorable Benjn. Disraeli,
in memory of the best & greatest of men,
from the beloved Prince's
broken-hearted Widow,
Victoria
R.
Windsor Castle
April 24

I / think you will agree with me, that this is the most remarkable inscription, wh: a Sovereign ever placed in a volume, graciously presented to a subject!

But there was also a packet tied with black silk – & that contained a letter! But I must stop, like the Sultana in the Arabian ↑nights↓, & find I cannot conclude, as I intended.

Yrs ever, | D.

3815 TO: SARAH BRYDGES WILLYAMS Grosvenor Gate [Thursday] 14 May 1863

ORIGINAL: RTC [233]
EDITORIAL COMMENT: Paper imprinted 'Grosvenor Gate'. There is no salutation.

May 14 1863

The telegraph from Torquay is silent[1] – but, I hope, you have not got the Influenza, like most people in London.[2] Nothing but the Prince & Princess of Wales. They are everywhere, & do everything!

We have / got an invitation, from the University of Oxford, to meet them on the 14th. June[3] – from the City of London to meet them at a Great Ball at Guildhall. From the Merchant Taylors, to meet the Prince at a Great Banquet.[4]

On Saturday, we go / to the Drawing Room.[5]

We dined, yesterday, with Lord & Lady Derby:

on Saturday ↑next↓, with Lord & Lady Stanhope:

on Wednesday next, with the Duke & Duchess of Northumberland, & then we

1 For the 'telegram' see **3817**. Though D may be only joking here, he had on 14 September 1862 (letter not found) asked Elliott Bros, 30 Strand, for a quotation on installing the telegraph at Hughenden. On 16 September Elliott had quoted £60 for two telegraph instruments with a bell, £40 per mile for wires and poles or £5 per mile for wires installed on convenient trees. Instruction in use was included. H A/V/G/233.

2 For influenza in London, see **3797**&n1. The metropolitan health report published on this day (14 May) makes no mention of any respiratory diseases. *The Times* (14 May 1863).

3 At Oxford, 14 June began Commemoration Week, the highlight of which this year would be the conferring of honorary DCL degrees on the Prince and Princess. The Ds would be guests of Dean and Mrs Liddell at the grand state banquet in honour of the Prince and Princess in the hall of Christ Church on Tuesday 16 June; on Wednesday, D would be in the procession to the Sheldonian for the presentation of honorary degrees; both Ds would be at a banquet at Exeter College that evening, and at the ball at Christ Church on Thursday concluding festivities. *The Times* (15-20 Jun 1863). See further **3824**.

4 See D's account of these events in **3821**.

5 The Princess of Wales would hold a drawing room on behalf of the Queen at St James's Palace on Saturday, 16 May; about 2,000 nobility and gentry, including the Ds, would attend, and over 500 ladies be presented, equivalent to presentation to the Queen. By prior press announcement gentlemen would not be expected to appear 'except as accompanying the ladies of their families.' *The Times* (15, 18 May 1863).

shall go to Hughenden for a week – to pass the Whitsun / holidays – see our chestnuts & pink May in bloom, & taste our May trout.

I hope to send you some, & that they will bring you a good appetite.

Ever yours, | D.

TO: CHARLES GREY — Grosvenor Gate [Friday] 15 May 1863 — 3816

ORIGINAL: RAC F28 32

EDITORIAL COMMENT: Paper imprinted 'Grosvenor Gate'.

M Genl. | The Hon: Chas Grey — May 15 1863

My dear General,

You may always rely, upon my utmost exertions, as a Royal Commissioner of 1851, to carry into effect the plans of our beloved, & / illustrious, chief.[1]

Ever yours sincerely, | *B. Disraeli*

TO: SARAH BRYDGES WILLYAMS — House of Commons [Thursday] 21 May 1863 — 3817

ORIGINAL: RTC [234]

EDITORIAL COMMENT: House of Commons paper. There is no salutation.

May 21 1863

I was very much pleased to receive a Torquay Telegram again in the right handwriting – so well known – & so much loved![1]

We are going to Hughenden to day for one week. Yesterday, we dined with the Duke & Duchess of Northumberland in their old / palace at Charing Cross. It is almost the only great house left, with its porte cochere, & court yard, &c.[2]

The Duke is a man of great science; a complete philosopher; his knowledge is immense, & he has travelled all over the world. He is now much excited by the discovery of the / sources of the Nile; having himself selected Captain Speke for that object, & having furnished the funds for a discovery wh: baffled the ancients.[3] We met there the Prussian Ambassador & his Countess & the French Ambassador,[4] & other distinguished & agreeable people.

1 On 13 May Grey had written from Buckingham Palace at considerable length, and on his own initiative, to ask D, as the most enthusiastic of the 1851 commissioners supporting Prince Albert's 'Kensington schemes', and in view of further proposals coming before parliament, to 'give the subject all the attention it deserves'. H B/XIX/D/1; copy in RAC F28 31. See further **3825**&n1.

---

1 SBW's letter has not been found.

2 The portal of the Jacobean Northumberland House, Charing Cross, was by this time almost the only part of it that was mostly old. Cunningham 361-3.

3 John Hanning Speke (1827-1864), who served in the Indian army 1844-54 and with a Turkish regiment in the Crimean War, had devoted himself to African exploration since 1856. In his latest expedition (1860-3) with J.A. Grant, on 2 July 1862 he had established Lake Victoria as the source of the Nile; Speke's telegram that the question was '"settled"' had reached the foreign office on 6 May 1863. *The Times* (7 May 1863). The claim, however, would not be confirmed for another twelve years. Northumberland, a noted patron of science and learning, had himself been in Africa in the 1820s and 1830s, mostly Egypt and the Cape.

4 Baron Jean-Baptiste Louis Gros (1793-1870) was French ambassador to London 1852-63.

The state of the Continent is / very alarming – & if a general struggle comes, Prussia will be the Kingdom most in danger.[5]

There are hopes, that the recent successes of the Southerns in America are so striking, that some settlement may now take place.[6] The arrival of the next news, hourly expected, from the United States, is awaited with much anxiety.

Ever yours, | D.

3818

TO: SARAH BRYDGES WILLYAMS Hughenden [Wednesday] 27 May 1863

ORIGINAL: RTC [235]

EDITORIAL COMMENT: Paper imprinted 'Hughenden Manor'. There is no salutation.

Private May 27 1863

Mr Butler Johnstone's speech was the best first speech I recollect. As Mr Canning said of Ld Derby's first speech in the Ho: of Comm:, when he was Mr Stanley – "It is not so much the speech, as the speaker, that I admire." As you say of riders, Mr Johnstone went / well to his subject. He will mount. He knows well my opinion of his effort, for I did not content myself with private praise, but congratulated him publickly, in the course of the evening, wh: shows that Mrs Butler, tho' she naturally reads her nephew's speeches, does not / do me the honor of reading mine.

I return her letter.[1]

Alas! we go back to town tomorrow. Our hills are covered with fresh woods; the park, wh: is full of ancient thorns in bloom, looks illuminated; the trout stream sparkles; & the birds repay me for my ceaseless efforts / to prevent their destruction, with a chorus of joyous gratitude!

5 In the long-standing disputes over the duchies of Schleswig and Holstein, the latest significant event had been Denmark's royal proclamation repudiating previous compacts, defining Holstein's separate position as part of Denmark and negating all German claims on Schleswig. In the Lords on 15 May Ellenborough had raised the Schleswig-Holstein matter, which he saw as a serious threat to European peace when conditions in Poland (see **3791**&n1) allowed the German powers to turn their attention to it. The ensuing debate showed considerable support for Denmark despite Russell's critical stance towards it. *Hansard* CLXX cols 1738-65. *The Times* in a leader on 16 May feared that Russell's remarks might mislead Germany as to feeling in England and Europe and encourage it to violence against Denmark.

6 A *Times* leader on 19 May had rehearsed 'overwhelming' Confederate victories in early May repulsing Federal attacks east of Fredericksburg.

---

1 SBW had written on the 23rd to thank D for an offer of trout (**3815**); she continued: 'To save writing I enclose Mrs B's note the Irish one so energetic it is always best to please them'. Emily Mary Butler had written to SBW from Dublin on the 11th about 'the Maiden Speech of our nephew Butler Johnstone who has realized the anticipations we had of his Success. All parties came forward to congratulate him & even the prime Minister who no doubt would like to grasp him for his Party. I am sure your clever friend Mr. Disraeli has approved of the young Orator.' RTC [476-7Q]. Henry Alexander Butler-Johnstone (1837-1902), BA (Christ Church, Oxford) 1861, MA 1862, MP (C) for Canterbury (his father's former seat) 1862-78, had made his 'very promising' maiden speech on 8 May defending the Italian government's handling of serious problems in Neapolitan prisons. *The Times* (9 May 1863). Later in the same discussion, D had begun by remarking that 'three speeches were delivered to-night, to which everybody who heard them must have listened with the utmost pleasure and satisfaction,' *ie,* the substantial speeches by his junior colleagues George Cavendish Bentinck, Henry Lennox and Butler-Johnstone. Later he had referred specifically to 'the sensible observations made by my hon. Friend the Member for Canterbury, in his admirable speech – a speech great in performance, greater still in promise, and from which it may be hoped that the hon. Member will contribute much to the interest of our future debates.' *Hansard* CLXX cols 1397-1499 (D 1482-90). See further **3823**&n2. Derby had made his maiden speech (as Mr Stanley) on 30 March 1824.

You take in the "Illustrated News". In page (I think) 350 of this week, you will find the Hughenden Monument.[2] The architect sent us the No: here; & I shd. have forwarded it to Torquay, did I not recollect it was always on yr table. He (Mr Lamb) was down here yesterday, & said with glee, that he had had, in consequence, an order for a monument from Devonshire!

Yrs ever, | D.

TO: SIR THOMAS [unknown] Carlton Club [Saturday] 30 May 1863 **3819**

ORIGINAL: UO 18

EDITORIAL COMMENT: Carlton Club paper.

30 May 1863

My dear Sir Thomas,

Is this what you want?

Yours sincerely, | B Disraeli

TO: [ANTHONY PANIZZI] [London, Saturday] 13 June 1863 **3820**

ORIGINAL: MOPSIK [185]

EDITORIAL COMMENT: Endorsed in another hand below D's signature: 'The above is the signature of the Rt. Honle. Benjamin d'Israeli [*sic*], a Trustee of the Brit Museum[.] June 13th. 1863[.] A Panizzi'. In another hand: [*paper torn*] '15 June 1863. AES'.

This is my signature as a Trustee of the British Museum.[1]

B. Disraeli

TO: SARAH BRYDGES WILLYAMS Grosvenor Gate [Sunday] 14 June 1863 **3821**

ORIGINAL: RTC [236]

PUBLICATION HISTORY: M&B IV 398-9, dated 14 June 1863; Blake 433, undated fragment; Bradford 252, extract from fifth paragraph

EDITORIAL COMMENT: Paper imprinted 'Grosvenor Gate'. There is no salutation. *Sic:* Tuilleries.

June 14 1863

This royal honeymoon, of many months, is perfectly distracting. Nothing but balls & banquets, & receptions, & inaugurations, & processions, so that one has not ~~to~~ a moment to oneself, & lives only in a glittering bustle. This has been a remarkably busy week. On Monday, a marvellous fête given in the Guildhall by the Corporation / of London. A very great success, & in its splendor & fine taste quite equalling the similar displays at Paris, which hitherto we have not approached; for tho' the Hotel de Ville may yield to us in turtle soup, it has always surpassed our citi-

2 See **3707**&n3. The engraving of the monument had appeared in the *Illustrated London News* of 23 May on p 560.

1 As a newly appointed trustee (see ec and **3801**&n1), D is probably providing his signature to Anthony Panizzi (1797-1879), principal librarian of the British Museum 1856-66, KCB 1869. He is perhaps best remembered for his design of the great domed reading room and library of the British Museum. For D's admiring description of him see M&B IV 400-1 and *DR* 114-15.

zens in the elegance & invention of their festivals. But on Monday, Gog & Magog triumphed.[1]

On Tuesday, I was taken up with the "Act of the Uniformity" & / the House of Commons,[2] but tho' kept up late, I was in time, on Wednesday, to take my place in a procession, when the Prince of Wales inaugurated the uncovering of the statue of his father at Kensington.[3]

Thursday was a tremendous banquet given to the Prince by the Merchant Taylors Company, where I had to return thanks for the House of Commons: a very grand affair with four Royal Princes ~~of the~~ & six dukes present.[4]

But / everything yielded in splendor, in brilliancy, in gorgeous magnificence to the fête wh: the Duke & Duchess of Northumberland gave to the Prince & Princess of Wales on Friday last!

We dined, sixty guests, of the high nobility, in a magnificent gallery, as fine in dimensions, & far more splendid, than the Galerie de Diane of the Tuilleries. Such plate, such diamonds, so many Duchesses, & Knights of the Garter, were never ↑before↓ assembled together![5]

Tomorrow, we go to the glories of Oxford.[6]

Yrs ever, | D.

3822 TO: DUKE OF NORTHUMBERLAND

Grosvenor Gate
[Sunday] 14 June 1863

ORIGINAL: CUL [6]
EDITORIAL COMMENT: Paper imprinted 'Grosvenor Gate'.

His Grace. | The Duke of Northumberland | K.G. June 14 1863

My dear Lord Duke,

It occurred to me, that, in the temporary retirement, the cause of wh: we all so

1 Gog and Magog were legendary British giants made to act as royal porters in London and for centuries represented by 14-foot effigies at the Guildhall.

2 On Tuesday 9 June the Commons defeated a motion to relax Church of England clergy's subscription to the Thirty-Nine Articles and the Prayer Book required by the Act of Uniformity, as this prevented many university graduates from entering holy orders. D spoke against the motion, protesting that it was not possible to have a church without a creed, formularies and articles; however, if the act must be revised, he suggested that this be done by a royal commission. The House adjourned at 15 minutes to 2. *Hansard* CLXXI cols 574-657 (D 642-55).

3 The statue of Prince Albert replaced, by the Queen's wish, one of herself as Britannia presiding over the four quarters of the globe, a design chosen in 1858 to memorialize the Great Exhibition. Sculpted by Joseph Durham in copper electroplate, it was ten feet high on a decorated base thirty-two feet high and eighteen feet across, and depicted Albert in the regalia of Master of the Order of the Garter. It was unveiled in the Royal Horticultural Society gardens in Kensington, but would be moved in 1899 to its present site outside the Albert Hall. *The Times* next day was amused to observe, near the designated time of 4 *pm*, 'in how affectionate a manner the rivals of public life fraternized with each other within the neutral ground of the enclosure – how Mr. Gladstone and Mr. Disraeli had a friendly gossip'. In the procession, D's place was with the 1851 Exhibition commissioners.

4 In his response to the toast to the House of Commons, D had pointed out that the Prince was, among all his exalted positions, also a member of parliament, having taken his seat in the Lords on 5 February. *The Times* (12 Jun 1863).

5 See **3822**&n4.

6 See **3815**&n3 and **3824**.

deeply regret,[1] you might find some interest in the accompanying / volume, "Atlantis".

The article, in reply to Sir George Lewis, is evidently from a master, & there are other contributions, of an analogous character, which seem first-rate.[2]

I was sorry to hear at the Museum yesterday, that poor / Poole continues ill.[3]

The banquet, at Northumberland House on Friday, will always remain in my memory, as the most gorgeous, & radiant, I remember. The gallery blazed with color, but all in harmony.

There was only one drawback, on wh: I will not dwell. To / a certain degree, it must have depressed all hearts; at least, it did mine. But the Duchess bore up against the great difficulty with a quite imperial spirit, & ~~lork~~ looked more brilliant, even, than her tiara.[4]

Ever, my dear Lord Duke, | yr faithful, & truly obliged, | *B. Disraeli*

TO: LORD CAMPDEN Grosvenor Gate [Monday] 22 June 1863 3823

ORIGINAL: BL ADD MS 37502 f132

EDITORIAL COMMENT: Paper imprinted 'Grosvenor Gate'.

Visct Campden June 22 1863

My dear Lord,

The House of Commons (both sides) now that the Kingdom of Italy is acknowledged,[1] is very unwilling to listen to details of its internal condition. They deem

1 The Duke was suffering from gout, but would be pronounced much better on Thursday, the 18th. *MP* (19 Jun 1863).

2 Cornewall Lewis in 1862 had published *Suggestions for the Application of Egyptological Method to Modern History; Illustrated by Examples,* suggesting that Egyptian science was of poor quality; he particularly challenged the idea that the pyramids were relevant to British units of measurement. On 21 February 1862 the Duke had written from Alnwick: 'Many thanks for Sir George Lewis revival of the [Richard Doyle work] Jones Brown & Robinson [*sic*] of ancient renown ... If Sir George Lewis will give up his false ideas about Egyptology, & take the Office of Chancellor of the Exchequer while his Party remain in the Government, it will be better for his credit, & more to the advantage of the Country.' Peter (later Sir Peter) Le Page Renouf, professor of ancient history and eastern languages (1858-64) at the Roman Catholic University of Ireland, had responded to Lewis in the current issue of the university's journal *The Atlantis* (Vol IV:1863) pp 23-56. On 24 July 1863 the Duke would respond from Syon House: 'The Atlantis has been of very great interest to me, and especially the article by Mr Renouf. The life of Sir G. Lewis [*he had died on 13 April 1863*] was not only valuable to himself & his country for ordinary & political affairs, but was highly valuable to Egyptologists as offering a hope, that all which could be brought forward from Classical writings against the truth of Hieroglyphs would be ably handled ... Mr Renouf pleads his first point well; pointing out Sir G Lewis' disadvantages in being ignorant of Hieroglyphics and the manner in which Egyptologists have studied them: but the truth is that the study is so new, & crude that a beginner finding that the Cesars [*sic*] followed each other (as we know they did) accepted such a result, as a proof of the truth of hieroglyphics.' H B/XXI/N/184-5.

3 Reginald Stuart Poole (1832-1895), archaeologist, orientalist and egyptologist, was at this time assistant in the British Museum department of antiquities; he would become keeper of coins 1870, be sent by the Museum to report on antiquities in Cyprus and Alexandria 1869, lecture to Royal Academy students 1883-5. The Duke in his July letter (n2) would praise Poole's erudition highly.

4 See **3821**. On Friday 12 June the Duke and Duchess had given a lavish entertainment at Northumberland House to the Prince and Princess of Wales, but the Duke at the last minute had absented himself because of an attack of gout (see also n1). D, but not MA, is listed among the 60 guests at the banquet that began the evening, the numerous other guests arriving after 9:30 *pm. The Times, MP* (13 Jun 1863).

---

1 Britain had recognized the Kingdom in February 1861.

these matters for the Italian / Parliament. I think, on the whole, Cavendish Bentinck is the best person for you to communicate with, but I doubt, whether your friend will succeed in his object. There were peculiar circumstances, wh: assisted the late Italian / debate in our house, but it was floated with great difficulty.[2]

John M. is in the country, & will not return before tomorrow at the earliest. He has written to me on your letter, as time pressed.[3] It wd. be quite impossible for him to undertake the / office in question.

I am sorry to hear about Lady Campden.[4] Pray offer to her my very kindest remembrances & regards.

Yrs sincerely, | D.

3824 TO: SARAH BRYDGES WILLYAMS [London, Thursday] 25 June 1863

ORIGINAL: RTC [237]

PUBLICATION HISTORY: M&B IV 399, dated 25 June 1863, omitting the second paragraph and postscript

EDITORIAL COMMENT: The postscript is at the top of the first page. There is no salutation. *Sic:* functions; fetê; Ri'dottos.

June 25. 1863

Oxford was a Carnival.[1] There was too much crowded into every day. That was the only fault. Every day there were five or six "*functions*" as the Spaniards call them. On Wednesday, for example, there was Grand Commemoration; a collation in the Library of All-Souls Coll: wh: is more / than 300 feet long: the noblest of apartments; a Bazaar for the Radcliffe Infirmary; a garden fetê; a boat race, worthy of the Regat-

2 Campden had written from Rome on 12 June on behalf of a member of the chamber of deputies at Turin, who wished contact with a British MP to whom he would supply for presentation to the House the 'official information and positive facts [regarding] the real feeling of the people of South Italy towards their present rulers, & the real nature of the Piedmontese occupation'. Campden deferred to D's judgement, but suggested Baillie Cochrane, Cavendish Bentinck, Lord Henry Lennox and Lord John Manners. H B/XXI/G/12. For the 8 May Italian debate to which D is referring, see **3818**&n1. When the House was about to go into committee of supply, Pope Hennessy, through a motion for papers on commerce with Naples, had opened a discussion on the appalling conditions in Southern Italy (which Cavendish Bentinck had tried unsuccessfully to raise on 12 March. *Hansard* CLXIX col 1332). Hennessy had referred to a previously refused consular despatch on commerce, now laid on the table but, he claimed, inaccurate. Seconding the motion, Bentinck addressed Italy's sovereignty, arguing that her 'gross infractions of the law of nations' warranted intervention in her internal affairs, if only because leaving her actions unchallenged might set a precedent for the Federal Americans to invade Canada. Lennox, just back from Italy, cited specific gross violations of Italy's official policy of liberty, but Butler Johnstone returned to the position that the Italian government should be trusted to manage their own internal affairs. On 20 November, Campden, about to leave for Rome, would tell D that he had been keeping Earle informed about Naples and had sent Earle papers and pamphlets for the use of Lennox or anyone else; he added that his wife in Rome had been authoritatively told of 'the fearful misgovernment of the Piedmontese'. H B/XXI/G/13.

3 Manners had written on 20 June as he was about to leave for the country: 'As Campden seems anxious for a prompt answer will you kindly read the enclosed, and let me know ... what you would advise. My own feeling is rather against becoming the lion's mouth, and I am inclined to think that duty had better be discharged by some back-bencher'. Campden's enclosed letter, dated at Rome on 12 June, mentions that he is writing to D with the same request. H B/XX/M/126, 126a.

4 Campden had mentioned (n2) that his wife had been ill, but was now recovering. The Viscountess as Lady Ida Harriet Augusta Hay (1821-1867), eldest daughter of 18th Earl of Erroll, one of the Queen's bridesmaids, had married Campden in 1841.

---

1 See **3815**&n3. MA sent SBW reports of the occasion from *MH* and *MP*. She also recorded expenditure of £3.17.0 for railway tickets to and from Oxford for themselves and two servants. RTC [478Q, 479Q]; H acc.

tas & Ri'dottos of Venice; a banquet ~~of~~ at Exeter Coll:, & a Christchurch Ball[2] – & the Prince & Princess went to all! – and all this amid endless cheering, & music, & shouts.[3] Too much even for Youth & Beauty. We had three / days of it – & this holiday made such an arrear of business, that I have never been able to get right since my return. As Lord Chesterfield said of the old Duke of Newcastle, who was Minister in his time, I am always running after the three days I have lost.[4]

This morning we assisted at the wedding of Miss Copley, the daughter, & / only child of Lord Lyndhurst by his second wife. She has married Mr. DuCane a young M.P. & follower of mine; of good fortune.[5]

Tomorrow the Conservative Association give me a public dinner[6] – & in the evening the Brigade of Guards are to give the Princess of Wales ~~are to give~~ the most gorgeous ball ever produced in any age or any country. Mrs Disraeli will be there, & I, if possible.[7]

Yrs ever | D. /

I have sent you some trout[.]

2 Some of these events in fact took place on Monday 15 and Tuesday 16 June. The Exeter College ball was on the 15th; the St John's College bazaar, Christ Church Hall banquet and Freemasons' ball on the 16th. Despite *MP*'s report, the garden fête, the Oxford Horticultural Society show in Trinity gardens, was rained off on the 15th and took place on the 16th. The boat race in Christ Church meadows was also on the 16th. *MH, MP* (17 June 1863).

3 Both *MH* and *MP* (n2) made much of D's reception at the Sheldonian Theatre on the 16th. 'In a moment he was seen, recognised, and cheered with a deafening shouting that sorely tried the ears. Nor one, two, or three cheers, but many – cheers never allowed to drop, but taken up and kept up for full five minutes ... In fact it was – the Royal party's apart – the ovation [of] the day.' *MP* recorded that D 'bore the weight of honour shouted down upon him like a Stoic. Even the familiar name "Dizzy" – "three cheers for Dizzy," left him unmoved.'

4 Thomas Pelham-Holles (1693-1768), 1st Duke of Newcastle, was prime minister 1754-6, 1757-62. Chesterfield's bon mot that D is here adapting is usually given as '"His Grace loses an hour in the morning, and is looking for it all the rest of the day."'

5 The Ds were among the over 100 guests at the wedding at St George's Church, Hanover Square, and the breakfast at the Lyndhurst residence in George Street. *MP* (26 Jun 1863).

6 The National Conservative Registration Association would hold its annual banquet on Friday 26 June at Willis's Rooms; D would make the major speech of the evening in response to the toast to the Conservative leaders. He confronted the government's repeated taunt that there were now no substantial issues on which the Conservatives opposed them by attributing this to the Liberals' failure currently to put into practice their principles, which he then distinguished from the Conservative ones: '"The Liberal party are of opinion that the electoral franchise should be democratic; we are not ... [They] think the mode of exercising the suffrage should be so conducted that property should be deprived of its legitimate influence; we do not ... [They] are of opinion that the union between Church and State should be abolished; we are not ... Our colonial empire, which is the national estate which assures to every subject of her Majesty as it were a freehold, and which gives to the energy and enterprise of Englishmen an inexhaustible theatre, the Liberal party are of opinion that the relations between the metropolis and the colonies should be abrogated; we do not ... [They] are opposed to the ancient rights of corporations and privilege of endowments, and think they ought to be terminated; we do not."' He predicted that the Conservatives would soon come into power, as the Liberals held power only by forming coalitions, in 1852 with '"the pupils of Sir R. Peel"' and in 1859 with those of Mr Bright: '"In the purgatory in which the Liberal party found themselves they first applied to celestial archangels, and then in their despair to the lowest abyss of hell." (Cheers and laughter.) "But a lower abyss there is not – their means are exhausted."' *MP* (27 Jun 1863).

7 The Ds would both be among the approximately 2,000 guests who on Friday 26 June attended the Guards' ball for the Prince and Princess in the former picture galleries of the exhibition building; guests were asked to arrive before 10 *pm*, when the royal couple was expected. *MP* (27 June) also thought 'that no preceding event has equalled the brilliant ball of last night'.

3825 TO: CHARLES GREY Grosvenor Gate [Tuesday] 30 June [1863]

ORIGINAL: RAC F28 40

EDITORIAL COMMENT: Black-edged paper.

Private June 30. Grosvenor Gate

M Genl. | Hon: Chas Grey

My dear General,

I begin to think we may win. I can only act by a personal canvass, wh: renders it, of course, difficult, & slow, to form calculations – but I shall keep / some, I hope many, away, who were violent & some I have converted.[1]

Yours ever, | D.

3826 TO: CHARLES GREY [Grosvenor Gate] Friday [3 July 1863]

ORIGINAL: RAC F28 44

PUBLICATION HISTORY: *LQV* 2nd series I 96-7, dated [3 July 1863], with minor differences

EDITORIAL COMMENT: Black-edged paper. *Dating:* The letter's date reflects the passing of midnight; the events described took place on 2 July, the House adjourning at 1.45 *am*. Cf VII **3140**. *Sic:* looked badly; aide de camps.

M Gl. | Hon C. Grey one o'ck. Friday | morning

My dear General

Before I go to bed –

A crashing defeat![1] The House was really mad, or drunk.

It began badly – Gladstone / made much too clever a speech – sarcastic instead of conciliatory – & sent them all to dinner in a bad humor.[2]

At ½ pt. 10, hearing that affairs looked badly, / I put up Northcote with an amendment, wh: wd. have reduced the vote 25000£ & bought the building & then referred the matter to a Committee.[3] But they wd. not hear him / after 10 minutes. The legions returned from dinner, & then a din quite demoniac.

1 See **3816**&n1. The House on 15 June had begun considering the government's proposal to buy the 1862 Exhibition building and related property for Prince Albert's Kensington scheme; the land purchase was agreed to, but the vote for the building was postponed until 2 July. *Hansard* CLXXI cols 903-37. On 25 June, Col Grey had written: 'I think it right to keep you acquainted with all I hear respecting the vote for purchasing the Building – Elcho, as you know moves its rejection, & calculates I am told on large support from your side of the House. In which expectation I trust he will be defeated.' He had heard that the government had a majority in favour, but he could not understand those opposed to it. On 1 July he would write that he had shown D's note to the Queen: 'it is this moment returned to me with a charge from H.M. to say how sensibly she appreciates your zealous support. It is indeed impossible to overstate H.M's anxiety on the subject – for She sees, as every one must see, that, to refuse the purchase of the building, is to postpone indefinitely any progress whatever towards even the partial realization of the Prince's plans.' H B/XIX/D/3-4. See further **3826**&n1.

1 See **3825**&n1. On 2 July the House in committee of supply, after the discussion D describes here, had rejected 121-287 the government proposal to allocate £105,000 to buy the 1862 Exhibition building. *Hansard* CLXXII cols 74-135 (D 130-1, 131).

2 Malmesbury would record on 5 July how Gladstone's speech had infuriated the House, who thought the government was trying to force them into buying the building, at great expense according to Lord Elcho. Malmesbury II 300.

3 Lennox had written to Grey at 11 *pm* during the debate that D, who had 'done his best by personal communion with the various members of our Party', would probably not speak 'on account of the cry of a conspiracy between the front Benches but will put up Stafford Northcote.' RAC F28 42.

I tried to stem the tide & stay the storm, but in vain.[4]

Then there was a / regular panic on both sides of the House.

I sent to Gladstone not to divide – but he insisted.

I, of course, supported him with a few aide de camps. My marshals / even deserted me.

'Tis most vexatious. I kept away nearly 70 men.

However we have got the land![5]

Thats something, & / we may yet accomplish all we wish – & more than we had hoped.[6]

Yrs ever | D.

TO: FREDERICK LYGON [Friday] 3 July 1863 3827

ORIGINAL: BCP [10]

EDITORIAL COMMENT: Paper imprinted 'Grosvenor Gate'.

Hon: Fred. Lygon | M.P. July 3 1863

My dearest Lygon,

I return the book – signed by the dwellers in this house, & in memory of our delightful visit to yr famous University.[1]

I sent a most urgent appeal, last night, / to Gladstone not to divide.[2] It was insanity.

Yours ever, | D.

TO: SARAH BRYDGES WILLYAMS Grosvenor Gate [Monday] 6 July 1863 3828

ORIGINAL: RTC [238]

PUBLICATION HISTORY: Blake 419, dated 6 July 1863, extract

EDITORIAL COMMENT: There is no salutation.

Grosvenor Gate | July 6. 1863.

Amidst a blazing season, morally & materially, I bid you "good morning"[.]

There is to be a very fine, & a very early, harvest, wh:, with cargoes of Australian nuggets,[1] & European peace, will bring us a swinging prosperity.

4 Malmesbury (n2) would also record: 'Disraeli had canvassed his supporters, telling them that he had a letter in his pocket from the Queen. This had a disastrous effect, and when he got up the hooting was so terrific that he could not be heard.'

5 In the supply committee of 15 June, the 1851 commissioners' very special price of £67,000 (on condition the land be used for the arts and sciences) had been agreed to.

6 Col Grey from Windsor Castle on this day (3 July) would thank D for his note, although bitterly disappointed at the result: 'Elcho [*n2*] shd. be condemned to ride along the Cromwell road every day for the rest of his life.' H B/XIX/D/5.

---

1 Lygon, a Fellow of All Souls College, Oxford (see **3824** for the DS' visit), had written on this day, 3 July: 'I send the book for your signature & I hope you will persuade Mrs Disraeli to add hers also.' Several other signatures were wanted, presumably in the official commemoration guest book. H B/XX/LN/17.

2 See **3826**&n1. Lygon had written (n1) that he never thought he would 'regret the absence (even temporary) from the House of Commons of Lord Palmerston. He never would have taken that very foolish division last night.'

---

1 The arrival of 'a quarter of a million of gold ... from Australia' had just been announced, but with

I understand there is *not* to / be a Russian war, in spite of the general apprehension.[2]

The papers have given you some news of the great Conservative banquets, in the East & in the West End: at the Guildhall, & at Willis' rooms. It was poetical justice to meet at the latter, for, there, the last Coalition was arranged, / wh: turned out the Derby Government.[3]

I long to see my woods & waters: but it is some consolation, in this refulgent summer, that I live in a Park, even in London – & that one wakes in the morning with eyes refreshed by the green shadow of stately trees.

Adieu! | D.

3829 TO: PHILIP ROSE — House of Commons [Thursday] 9 July 1863

ORIGINAL: H R/I/A/164
COVER: *Private* | Philip Rose Esq | *B. Disraeli*
EDITORIAL COMMENT: House of Commons paper.

Private July 9 1863

Philip Rose Esqr

My dear Rose,

1000 thanks for this – & all yr constant kindness.[1]

Yrs sin[cerel]y, | D.

3830 TO: LORD DERBY — Grosvenor Gate [Monday] 20 July 1863

ORIGINAL: DBP Box 146/1
EDITORIAL COMMENT: Paper imprinted 'Grosvenor Gate'.

Confidential July 20 1863

Rt Honble | The Earl of Derby | K.G.

My dear Lord,

The Cabinet on Saturday was, I am told, decidedly anti-gallic.

The Austrian note does not include the armistice proposition, because Austria deemed / it impracticable; I shd. think Lord Russell's assurance, on that head, therefore, founded on a misapprehension.

The Russian note to Paris is very different from that to our Court: "tres tran-

minimal effect on the funds. A report two weeks later would tell of 'an extraordinary early harvest and splendid crops.' *The Times* (6, 22 Jul 1863).

2 For the current Polish insurrection against Russian occupation, see **3791**&n1. On this day (6 July) *The Times* reprinted a Paris newspaper's confidence that Russia would accept the proposals of Britain (by Russell), France and Austria for an eight-power peace conference. The optimism was premature; see further **3830**&n1.

3 For the recent Guildhall dinner attended by the DS see **3821**, but it was not a Conservative affair; for the one at Willis's Rooms (Almack's) in the west end, see **3824**&n6. The rooms had been the site of the meeting on 6 June 1859 when the Whigs, Peelites and Radicals united as the Liberal party to defeat the Conservative government. See VII Introduction x. The other recent Conservative dinner was the Lord Mayor's dinner to Lord Derby on 1 July, at the Mansion House (east end), when D had responded to the toast to the Commons. *The Times*, MP (2 Jul 1863).

---

1 For possible illumination of this note, see **3767**n2 and **3786**.

chante". It more than intimates, that / all the insurrections – not merely in Poland – but in the eastern portions of the Empire – have been concocted at Paris.

Many thanks for your letter.[1]

Yrs ever sinc[ere]ly, | D.

TO: FREDERICK FURNIVALL Grosvenor Gate [Monday] 20 July 1863 3831

ORIGINAL: HUNT FU 271

COVER: F.J. Furnivall Esqr | 3 Old Square | Lin: Inn. | *B. Disraeli*

EDITORIAL COMMENT: Paper imprinted 'Grosvenor Gate'.

July 20 1863

F.J. Furnivall | Esqr[1]

Mr Disraeli presents his Compliments to Mr Furnivall, & regrets, that he cannot sign the Memorial, in favor of Miss Watts, & addressed to / Lord Palmerston.[2] The Prime Minister has no power to grant pensions. That is the prerogative of Her Majesty.

1 Derby had written from St James's Square on 'Sunday': 'Brunnow has just left me after a conversation of an hour, in the course of which he showed me the Russian answer [*to Russell's proposal; see* **3828**&n2].' Russell's proposal consisted of three propositions, the first with six points for negotiation, the second for a provisional armistice, and the third for a conference of the eight signatories of the Treaty of Vienna. *AR* (1863) 287. Derby continued: 'It is moderate in tone, but contains an absolute refusal of the "conférence à huit" and substitutes for it a proposal for a conference at Petersburgh – between Russia, Austria and Prussia on the basis of the six points, the results to be communicated for the assent or refusal of England & France. Of course he knows that this will not be accepted by the two latter; & Russell has told him that he has reason to know it would not be accepted by Austria. He is evidently very uneasy as to the possible course of events, and very distrustful of Palmerston, who, he thinks, will so conduct matters that his colleagues, against their wishes, when Parliament is up, will be drawn into a position in which they will of necessity follow at the heels of France. I own I do not think his apprehensions unfounded. The dispatch farther declares the impossibility of adopting the Armistice; and in this respect Russell expressed himself to him yesterday as "much disappointed." I own I do not see what other answer he could have expected. Brunnow is afraid of Austria being induced to join France & England in declaring the armistice to be a sine quâ non: but I do not think it likely. I am inclined to think that Russia would not decline a conference of the *five* powers, if it were proposed; but the real difficulty is that if we were asked to say what we wished Russia to do, and she were to place herself unreservedly in our hands, we should not know what advice to give her. Brunnow is very anxious about the language to be held in the House of Commons tomorrow, and alarmed at the probability of some violent language on Palmerston's part. He describes Russell as having been very reserved in his interview yesterday and as having only said that he must consult his colleagues as to the present state of affairs. Have you had any information as to what passed in the Cabinet?' H B/XX/S/318. *The Times* on this day, 20 July, published Paris reports of the negative Russian responses to the notes from Great Britain, France and Austria, and of French insistence on an armistice. In the House later this day, Gladstone and Palmerston resisted a challenge that England, having encouraged the Poles to revolt, now had a responsibility to assist them, by insisting that recourse to the Treaty of Vienna was the only way to solve the Polish question without war, and that the government would communicate with France and Austria to that end. *Hansard* CLXXII cols 1058-1136. See further **3832**.

---

1 Frederick James Furnivall (1825-1910), textual editor and scholar, responsible for much of the groundwork for the *OED*, was founder of a number of literary and philological societies such as the Early English Text Society.

2 Neither Furnivall's request, nor the identity of Miss Watts, has been found. Earlier in July Furnivall had also applied to Dickens on behalf of a candidate for a civil list pension and been similarly refused. *Dickens Letters* X 272.

3832 TO: SARAH BRYDGES WILLYAMS — Grosvenor Gate [Tuesday] 21 July 1863

ORIGINAL: RTC [239]
PUBLICATION HISTORY: M&B IV 339, dated at Grosvenor Gate, 21 July 1863, omitting the last sentence
EDITORIAL COMMENT: Paper imprinted 'Grosvenor Gate'. There is no salutation.

Confidential July 21. 1863

Just when I was anticipating tranquillity & repose, the affairs of the Continent have assumed so serious a character, that the worst may be anticipated.[1] For the last fortnight, we have received accounts of the most alarming nature, & they have entirely absorbed the / attention both of Lord Derby, & myself. Lord Napier, our Ambassador at St. Petersburg, says we are again "drifting into war"[.]

A war in the centre of Europe, on the pretext of restoring Poland, is a general war, & a long one. The map of Europe will be / much changed, when it is concluded, but I doubt, whether the name of Poland will appear in it.

All the great questions of the day are still unsolved, & the materials for the infernal cauldron are plentiful.

The Rothschilds, who have contracted two loans, this / year; one to Russia & the other to Italy – the latter the largest on record, more than thirty millions – & the Russian fifteen – are naturally very nervous.

The state of affairs is enough to shake any one, who has any degree of responsibility. It is the reason I have not written to you – & why my letter now is so little gay.

I hope you are well.

Yrs ever, | D.

3833 TO: SARAH BRYDGES WILLYAMS — Hatfield [Wednesday] 29 July 1863

ORIGINAL: RTC [240]
EDITORIAL COMMENT: There is no salutation. *Sic:* Fontainbleau; Edgecombe.

Hatfield | July 29. 63

I write you a line from this beautiful place, wh: we shall leave this morning.[1] It never looks so well as in the heat, & heart, of a refulgent summer. A stately Elizabethan palace in a vast old English park: in parts as wild & as / agrestic, as Fontainbleau; huge trees, glades & innumerable green roads; & colossal fern – in breadth of acres.

Here we found Lady Brownlow, Lord Clanwilliam,[2] Lady Mildred Hope,[3] Lord & Lady Eustace Cecil[4] & some others – agreeable people – but our pleasure dimmed

1 See **3830**&n1. On 20 July Horsman had brought a motion that, since the Treaty of Vienna had proved inadequate for Poland's security, further negotiations on that basis would lead only to turmoil. It was in effect a call for war against Russia, but was eventually withdrawn. *Hansard* CLXXII cols 1058-1135.

---

1 The DS had been at Hatfield (Salisbury's) since 27 July. H acc.

2 Richard Charles Francis Meade (1795-1879), 3rd Earl of Clanwilliam, was under-secretary for foreign affairs 1822-3, ambassador at Berlin 1823-7, GCH 1826, captain of Deal Castle.

3 Lady Mildred Gascoyne Cecil (1822-1881), elder daughter of Lord Salisbury and his first wife, Frances Gascoyne, had married Alexander Beresford Hope in 1842.

4 Lord Eustace Cecil (1834-1921), Salisbury's younger son by his first wife (n3), lieut-col Coldstream Guards, JP for Dorset, Essex and Middlesex, would be MP (C) for S Essex 1865-8, for W Essex 1868-85,

/ yesterday morning by the news of the sudden death of Lord Normanby, who was just on his return to the Winter Villa of Ld. Mt. Edgecombe at Plymouth, wh: he had rented of late years, & where we visited him at the commencement of this.[5] Altho' some years ago he had suffered a paralytic stroke, / such was his sanguine temperament, & the exuberance of his still remaining vital ↑power,↓ that he not only thoroughly enjoyed life & entered into all its pleasures with unceasing relish – but ↑still↓ pursued a public career with fire & energy.

He was an amiable man, with captivating manners, & had been everything except Prime Minister. He had been Ld. Lt. of Ireland, Ambassador to France, Secy. of State, K.G. &c. &c. &c. His wife, ↑who watched over him like a guardian angel,↓ will feel it much.

Ever yrs | D.

TO: REES HOWELL GRONOW Grosvenor Gate [Friday] 31 July 1863 3834

ORIGINAL: GLA [2]

EDITORIAL COMMENT: Paper imprinted 'Grosvenor Gate'.

July 31 1863

Mr Disraeli presents his Compliments to Captain Gronow, & thanks Captain Gronow for the copy of his "Recollections", wh: Mr Disraeli has read with much interest.[1]

TO: [LADY NORMANBY?] [August 1863?] 3835

ORIGINAL: H B/II/070

EDITORIAL COMMENT: A draft in D's hand. The recipient is almost certainly Lady Normanby; *cf* D's description in **3833** of Lord Normanby, who died on 28 July 1863. *Dating:* 'even now' suggests that it was written later than within the week observed in Victorian convention.

It is even now with reluctance that I intrude upon your sorrow, but a feeling wh: I cannot resist impels me to express to you my sympathy.

His vital principle seemed so strong, & your angelic care so constant, that I looked upon him as one, who might be the / friend of many years, & the only circumstance I regretted in our intimacy was, that I had not, sooner in life, enjoyed an acquaintance with such amiable & such high, qualities.

His engaging manners, his sweet disposition, his chivalric spirit, & bright / intelligence, formed a rare combination, that we shall not again easily encounter.

↑I will↓ I will not presume to console – but some alleviation may be found in ~~your sweet~~ ↑the tender↓ recollection of your own unrivalled devotion, in the manifold / resources of your intellect, & in the love of your many friends, among whom, the humblest, but not the least affectionate, is

D. D. D. D. D. D. D. D. D. D. D.

surveyor general of the ordnance 1874-80. In 1860 he had married Gertrude Louisa Scott (1841-1919), fourth daughter of 2nd Earl of Eldon.

5 See **3765**, **3769**, **3770** and **3771**. Lord Normanby had died on 28 July.

1 Rees Howell Gronow (1794-1865), the famous dandy, captain 1st foot guards (retired 1821), MP (L) for Stafford 1832-3, in 1863 published *Recollections and Anecdotes, being a Second Series of Reminiscences by Captain R.H. Gronow,* the second of what would be a four-volume series.

3836 TO: BARON LIONEL DE ROTHSCHILD

Grosvenor Gate
[Sunday] 2 August 1863

ORIGINAL: ROTH RAL 000/848
EDITORIAL COMMENT: Paper imprinted 'Grosvenor Gate'.

The | Baron de Rothschild | M.P. Augt 2 1863

My dear Lionel,

France has received a great check from England & Austria, & all fear of immediate war has ceased.[1]

But, / doubtless, you know all this, or will before my letter can reach you, there being no post today.

Tomorrow, we are off for our woods.

I / hope to hear that Buxton will prove a Bethesda for you.[2]

My kindest remembrances to the Baroness.

Ever yrs, | D.

3837 TO: LORD DERBY

Grosvenor Gate [Wednesday 5?] August 1863

ORIGINAL: DBP Box 146/1
EDITORIAL COMMENT: Paper imprinted 'Grosvenor Gate'. Docketed by Derby on the blank last page: 'Disraeli B. *Ansd*'. *Sic:* Blackburne; *Dating:* by Derby's reply; see n14.

Confidential Mem: | 1863. Augt.

With reference to your last observation as to numbers, I have always thought that what we wanted was an addition to our force of about forty men.[1]

The two general Elections of 1852 & 9 proved that sheer Derbyism could produce about 300 members. We never got beyond that tether.

Since the election of 1859, three causes have been, gradually, at work, the tendency of wh: is to increase the area of our electoral power.

1°: The severance between Liberalism & / the R. Cathc. party.

2°: The organisation of a Church party, wh:, previously, the intimate & subtle relations of Gladstone with the clergy had always frustrated.

3°: The confirmed disrelish, among the influential town electors, to a degradation of their franchise.

It appears to me, that if there be no haste on our side, & the present Government fall from internal causes, these three influences may conjointly supply the requisite increase of force. /

1 D's source has not been determined, but he presumably refers to rumours of successful negotiations between Britain, Austria and France to produce a moderate common reply to Russia's rejection of their previous separate notes on the Polish rebellion, France's having been the most confrontational in demanding an armistice; see **3830**&n1 and **3832**. *The Times* (3 Aug 1863).

2 The next extant Rothschild letter is a long, chatty one on 26 August from Charlotte at Buxton, a North Derbyshire spa where they had gone for Lionel's health. She was, however, 'unable to see much improvement[;] the aches & pains are as obstinately faithful as they were in London[,] walking remains out of the question but, thank God! the sufferer is more than patient, he is quite cheerful and greatly enjoys homeopathic baths in the morning and immense drives in the afternoon'. H B/XXI/R/234. For the healing pool Bethesda, see John 5:2ff. See further **3843**.

1 *Cf* the list in **3653**.

M P.s.
Northcote
Hardy
Fitzgerald
Taylor
Whitmore
H. Lennox
Blackburne
Baillie
Lygon
Knight
Sir H. Leeke[2]
Dunne[3]
Kelly — Whiteside
Cairns — Mure[4] — George[5] /
House of Commons
In office 1858-9.
Cabinet
D.
Stanley
Peel
Pakington
Manners
Estcourt
Walpole
Henley
Lytton /
P. C's out of the Cabinet
Naas
March
Jolliffe
Lovaine
Adderley
Corry
Mowbray
Forester
Newport

2 Sir Henry John Leeke (1794-1870), who entered the navy 1803, vice-admiral 1860, admiral 1864, Kt 1835, KH 1836, KCB 1858, DL of Hampshire, was MP (L-C) for Dover 1859-65.

3 Francis Plunkett Dunne (c1802-1874), entered the army 1823, lieut-col 1851, major-general 1866, DL of Queen's co, was MP (L-C) for Portarlington 1847-57, for Queen's co 1859-68, clerk of the ordnance 1852.

4 David Mure (1810-1891), a barrister (Scotland) 1831, sheriff of Perthshire 1853-8, solicitor-general for Scotland 1858-9, lord advocate of Scotland 1859, was MP (L-C) for Bute 1859-65, as Lord Mure judge of court of session 1865-89.

5 John George (1804-1871), a barrister (King's Inns, Dublin) 1826, (Gray's Inn) 1827, QC 1844, bencher (King's Inns) 1849, was MP (C) for co Wexford 1852-7, 1859-66, solicitor-general for Ireland 1859, PC (Ireland) 1866, judge of Queen's Bench, Ireland, 1866-71.

Claud Hamilton /
1st. List of New-Men

Cecil – Bovill[6] –

Cave

Seymer

Elphinstone

Hay

Noel[7]

Fergusson

DuCane

Hunt[8]

Ingestre

Alg: Egerton

Hennessy[9]

S. Booth[10]

B. Johnstone /

2nd. Class of New Men

Holmesdale[11]

Ld. W. Graham[12]

Ld. R. Montagu[13]

6 William Bovill (1814-1873), a barrister (Middle Temple) 1841, QC 1855, was MP (L) for Guildford 1857-9, MP (C) for Guildford 1859-66, solicitor-general July-November 1866, Kt 1866, chief justice of the common pleas 1866, DCL (Oxford) 1870, FRS.

7 Gerard James Noel (1823-1911), second son of 1st Earl of Gainsborough, captain 11th Hussars (retired 1851), JP, DL, CA of Rutland, was MP (C) for Rutland 1847-83, a lord of the treasury 1866-8, parliamentary secretary to the treasury 1868, PC 1874, chief commissioner of works and public buildings 1876-80.

8 George Ward Hunt (1825-1877), a barrister (Inner Temple) 1851, JP and DL for Northamptonshire, was MP (C) for Northamptonshire 1857-77, financial secretary to the treasury 1866-8, chancellor of the exchequer February to December 1868, PC 1868, DCL (Oxford) 1870, bencher 1873, 1st lord of the admiralty 1874-77.

9 Algernon Fulke Egerton (1825-1891), third son of 1st Earl of Ellesmere, DL for Lancashire 1860, was MP (C) for S Lancashire 1859-68, for SE Lancashire 1868-80, for Wigan 1882-5, 1st secretary of the admiralty 1874-80, Lancashire alderman 1888-91.

John Pope Hennessy (1834-1891), the first Roman Catholic Conservative MP and a barrister (Inner Temple) 1861, was MP (C) for King's county 1859-65, Kilkenny N 1890-1; he would be governor of various British colonies (including Hong Kong) 1867-86 and be made KCMG 1880.

10 George Sclater-Booth (1826-1894), a barrister (Inner Temple) 1851, JP for Hants, DL for Southampton, was MP (C) for N Hants 1857-87, parliamentary secretary to the poor law board 1867-8, financial secretary to the treasury 1868, chairman of the committee of public accounts 1868-74, president of the local government board 1874-80, PC 1874, chairman of the Commons grand committees 1880, created 1st Baron Basing 1887, LLD, FRS.

11 William Archer Amherst (1836-1910), Viscount Holmesdale, eldest son of 2nd Earl Amherst (whom he would succeed as 3rd Earl in 1886), captain Coldstream Guards (severely wounded in Crimea), retired 1862, DL, JP for Kent, was MP (C) for W Kent 1859-68, for Mid Kent 1868-80, called to the Lords as Baron Amherst 1880.

12 Lord Montagu William Graham (1807-1878), youngest son of 3rd Duke of Montrose, captain Coldstream Guards (retired), was MP (L-C) for Grantham 1852-7, for Herefordshire 1858-65.

13 Lord Robert Montagu (1825-1902), second son of 6th Duke of Manchester, JP, DL for co Antrim (high sheriff 1855), JP for Londonderry, former captain Huntingdonshire Militia, was MP (C) for Huntingdonshire 1859-74, MP (Home Rule) for co Westmeath 1874-80, vice-president of council of education 1867-8, PC 1867.

Liddell
Farquhar
Cav. Bentinck
Cochrane
Peacocke[14]

TO: SARAH BRYDGES WILLYAMS Hughenden [Friday] 7 August 1863 3838

ORIGINAL: RTC [241]

PUBLICATION HISTORY: M&B III 463, dated 7 August 1863, omitting the first sentence and last paragraph; M&B IV 339, dated at Hughenden, 7 August 1863, the last three sentences

EDITORIAL COMMENT: Paper imprinted 'Hughenden Manor'. There is no salutation.

Augt 7 1863

The Torquay telegraph has worked admirably, & its arrival always gives us great satisfaction. Yesterday a party of Torquay visitors ↑also↓ arrived, & were most hospitably received. There was a great entertainment given in their / honor, at which no less a personage, than our distinguished County member, the Rt. Honble: B. Disraeli, ~~at~~ was, what the Reporters call, "observed" & his Lady. The rest of the Buckinghamshire guests must be discreetly described by an &c., but the Devonshire party attracted much attention. We are unable to state, whether the most conspicuous was an Italian / nobleman, Count Janitore, or ↑a member of↓ the famous French family Jean Doré, or the representative of the ancient English house of Dory,[1] settled for centuries in several of our counties, tho, certainly no branch of it in Bucks. Several members of the highly fashionable family of the Mulletts were present; & we were charmed at the tender graces, & fascinating / freshness, of some of the junior members of the highly popular family of Prawn.

Here, we are living in two rooms; Hughenden House being still full of architects, builders &c &c.[2] We have made an Italian Terrace, which would delight you, & which, in time, is entirely to be dressed up with statues & vases, like Isola Bella.[3] Our government, frightened, seems to be leaving France in the lurch. There will be no war this year.[4] That's something[.]

Adieu, dear friend! | D.

14 Derby's letter of 6 August 1863 from Knowsley is evidently his response to D's undated letter: 'Many thanks for your lists, especially for that of your new men. Whenever we are called upon, one of our great difficulties will be, not the selection of new ones, but the discarding of the old. It does not however seem to me that our time is very near at hand; as, even if any thing were to happen to Palmerston, some one of his present colleagues would probably be sent for, and accept, if only to secure the dissolution in his own hands; in which case it seems to me a sanguine view to suppose that even with the operation of the three causes you mention, we could obtain such an accession of strength as you consider, and I think rightly, to be necessary.' H B/XX/S/314. See further **3840**&n1.

---

1 The fish called John Dory in English and Jean-doré (jaune dorée, or golden yellow) in French is called janitore (gatekeeper) in Italian, an allusion to Matthew 17:24-7; the fish in which St Peter found the tribute money was, according to legend, a janitore, as it bears the traces of his thumb and forefinger in the markings on its sides.

2 For MA's current renovations at Hughenden, see Appendix VIII.

3 The small island in Lake Maggiore wholly occupied by a villa and its famous garden. For D's opinion of it on his visit in 1826, see I **52**.

4 See **3836**&n1.

3839 TO: RALPH EARLE [Hughenden, Friday] 7 August 1863

ORIGINAL: H H/LIFE

EDITORIAL COMMENT: From a typescript headed: 'D. to Mr. R.A. Earle, Aug. 7. '63.'

My dear Earle,

Would you have the kindness to answer this man. I have a recollection of some astrological insanity, in which I was mixed up, being sent to me, and throwing it into the waste basket. It can't be recovered, but if not answered, he will write to me for ever.

Be civil to him, as he is insane. Say no MS. can be found – at least, in my absence, which will be for many months: dissuade publishing pamphlets, which never sell under any circumstances &c.

Yours sincerely, | D.

You might perhaps venture to say, like the newspapers, that I don't undertake to return communications.[1]

3840 TO: LORD DERBY Hughenden [Friday] 7 August 1863

ORIGINAL: DBP Box 146/1

EDITORIAL COMMENT: Paper imprinted 'Hughenden Manor'. Endorsed by Derby on the fourth page: 'Disraeli B.' *Sic:* Entres.

Augt 7 1863

Rt. Honble | The Earl of Derby K G.

My dear Lord,

I return you the letter, having myself received not exactly, what the diplomats call, an identic note, but one to the same effect, tho' more terse & rough.[1] I had / not

1 Earle on 1 October 1863, just returned from Germany, would write: 'I hope you have not been troubled by your madman, the Astrologist, – I did not admit that you had recd. the MS. but I said that, at your request, I had looked for it, but in vain.' H B/XX/E/293.

1 Derby had written on 6 August (see **3837**n14): 'I send you confidentially a letter which I received a day or two ago from "Frances Anne," to which I have sent an apologetic letter, excusing the somewhat indiscreet zeal of Mr. Spofforth. She is too important a personage for us to go against her wishes even for the chance of gaining a seat, and especially when it is evident that she apprehends the consequence might be the loss of another. If you agree with me, perhaps you would write either to Taylor or to Spofforth to discourage any over activity in the City of Durham, unless Lady L's sanction can be obtained. I will ask you to return me her letter, and tell me what you think of the case.' Sir William Atherton, MP (L) for Durham City, was very ill, and would live only until 13 January 1864: his seat would be won by another Liberal, John Henderson, without a contest. Lady Londonderry's letter to D is dated '*Private* Seaham Monday' and docketed '3 August 1863'; it has no salutation: 'The Carlton Club are at their old tricks meddling here. Mr Spofforth is writing to all the D[urha]m people who are obliged to remind him that it must depend on me. Now he too knows nothing of matters here & the different ramifications & I thought poor Ld Eg[linto]n had impressed upon them not to interfere. I write you this line because if they go on meddling they will repent it & I will not be answerable for results. I consider it wd. be the worst policy in the world to provoke a contest & I dont believe any one wishes it but a few drunken firemen who of course wd like the uproar. It is very provoking.' She would write again on 12 August: 'I was afraid my letter had not reached you but I find fm Ld. Derby you recd it. The attempts to get up a contest are perseveringly persisted in & can only end in complete failure. Meanwhile an infinite deal of mischief is done in producing very bad feeling'. On 16 August she would write again, evidently in reply to D (not found): 'I see no reason for appearing to believe what one knows is false. I *saw* a letter of Mr S's to a Gentleman (not "a local Agent") & ... more have been written asking people to come forward. One marvels at the folly & impertinence of this meddling after being told nothing cd be done without me who have never been

replied to it, but ↑now↓ write to Taylor, who is in town, in consequence of your letter.

Entres nous, I much doubt, whether any forbearance will be able to save the County seat for Adolphus,[2] wh: is the main spring of all his mother's movements, but / she must be humored, as we can do nothing without her, & time may mitigate, or even entirely remove, the perplexing difficulties, in wh: the misconduct of her younger sons[3] has involved Lady Londonderrys election influence.

The Pomfret election will not encourage a premature / dissolution. A ludicrous & appropriate end to Dicky's H of Commons' career![4]

I am here, &, I hope, for an indefinite period.

Ever yours sincerely, | D.

TO: LORD DERBY Hughenden [Friday] 14 August 1863 3841

ORIGINAL: DBP Box 146/1

EDITORIAL COMMENT: Paper imprinted 'Hughenden Manor'. Endorsed by Derby on the fourth page: 'Disraeli B. *Ansd*'. *Sic:* forcus.

Private Aug 14 1863

Rt Honble | The Earl of Derby | K. G

My dear Lord,

The Carlton & Cons[ervativ]e Clubs are filled to overflowing, & hundreds of candidates are waiting their turn for a ballot, wh: will not, in some cases, come on for years.

They are also necessarily so exclusive, that the working corpus of our party never can / be admitted. The Carlton will rarely admit a professional candidate, & the Cons[er]v[at]ive a small pr Centage only.

Our strength is great in country attorneys & agents, who want a political ↑& social↓ forcus in London. As Henry Drummond used to say "of all powers in the 19th. Century, the power of Attorney is the greatest"[.]

They want to form a new political Club: to be called the / Junior Conservative ↑or something of that sort, &c ↓ – but to effect the purpose aimed at, it must be started under powerful, & unmistakeable, auspices. Taylor says it will organise, strengthen,

even consulted except by my own friends who being on the spot can judge the *tendency* & possible *results* of Mr S's mischievous attempts better than people at a distance. We have none of the heat you complain of[;] there has been a frost that did the flowers no good.' H B/XX/V/236-8.

2 Lord Adolphus, still MP for N Durham despite his deterioration to total madness, would live only until 11 June 1864. *Londonderrys* 56. In the subsequent by-election, the seat would be won by a Liberal without a contest.

3 Lord Ernest, after an 1855 incident when he had forced himself on actresses at a theatre, had been transferred to the 4th dragoon guards. Shortly after his return from the Crimea, he had been dismissed from the army, after being involved 'in a disgraceful "ragging" of another cornet'. He was currently living abroad, his mother paying him an allowance on condition that he stay there. *Londonderrys* 56-7.

4 Richard (Dicky) Monckton Milnes, MP (L) for Pontefract (Pomfret) since January 1837, had been elevated to the Lords as Baron Houghton. Despite expectations of a hotly contested election, Sir Edmund Head (L), former governor of New Brunswick and of the united provinces of Upper and Lower Canada, had surprised his supporters at the 3 August nomination by withdrawing, after five days canvassing convinced him he had no chance of victory. This left Samuel Waterhouse (C) to take the seat without a contest. *The Times* (29 Jul, 1, 4 Aug 1863).

& encourage, our party greatly, & has written to me very strongly on the matter, with an unreasonable wish, that I shd. communicate with you anent.[1]

What he wishes is, that the five trustees of the new Club / shd. be yr Lordship, Ld. Malmesbury, Ld Colville,[2] Colonel Taylor, & myself.

I believe the affair has been long maturing, is needed, & will be successful – but, of course, I await your wishes & opinion, on wh: all must depend.[3]

It is hard work to write letters on business in August, but I hope you may catch the drift of this. Taylor is kept in town.

Yours sincerely, | D.

3842 TO: SARAH BRYDGES WILLYAMS   Hughenden [Saturday] 15 August 1863

ORIGINAL: RTC [242]

EDITORIAL COMMENT: There is no salutation.

Hughenden Manor | Augt 15 1863

We have sent you, by this train, the finest trout that has been caught in Hughenden Waters for years. It weighs nearly six pounds, & was alive a quarter of an hour ago. / Don't be alarmed at its size, for it ↑is↓ the most delicate eating cold, with bread & butter, & will last, in that way, for days.

I have sent you also a leash of grouse, the freshest, the tenderest, & / the youngest, that ever paid you a visit. They came from a Yorkshire moor this morning.

1 Taylor's letter has not been found, but it presumably accompanied the circular dated 8 August that he sent to D from 6 Victoria Street, Rose's and Spofforth's London office. D has used some of the circular's wording. H A/IV/M/32, 34.

2 Charles John Colville (1818-1903), 10th Baron Colville of Culross, a representative peer of Scotland 1850-85, former captain 11th Hussars, chief equerry and clerk marshal to Queen Victoria 1852-8, master of the buckhounds 1866-8, PC 1866, lord chamberlain to Queen Alexandra 1873-1903, Kt 1874, would be created Baron Colville of Culross (U.K.) 1885, Viscount Colville of Culross (U.K.) 1902.

3 Derby would reply from Knowsley on 18 August: 'I should, I own, have thought it doubtful whether there were room for the establishment of a third professedly Conservative and Political Club in London; and also whether it might not have the effect either of placing the new Club in a position of avowed inferiority, or of creating jealousies and differences which might lead to embarrassment in reference to Election matters; and, more especially if a large proportion of the new Club were, as you seem to intimate, Country Attornies, et id genus. You appear however to have considered the first point, and to concur with Taylor in opinion that there is ample room for the proposed Institution; and if you and he are of opinion that there is no danger to be apprehended from the second, I shall be happy to aid in promoting the success of the undertaking. But, before agreeing to undertake the office of one of five Trustees, I should like to know clearly what liabilities we should thereby incur. If it be merely intended that our names should be a guarantee for the political character of the Club, and that our duties were merely formal and ministerial, I should of course have no difficulty, if the other four whom you name were also willing to act; but I should not wish to make myself (nor, I should think, would you) personally and pecuniarily responsible for the Club's success or failure'. H A/IV/M/33. Taylor on 'Friday' would ask D to write to Colville, would write to D on the 22nd that Derby's requirements would be seen to, and on the 24th that he had obtained Colville's consent. H A/IV/M/34-7. See further **3844**&n2 and **3847**&n1. The Junior Carlton Club (the name eventually chosen), with the five trustees named here, would be formed at a meeting on 11 February 1864, and by 1 July be open in the former premises of the Parthenon Club in Waterloo Place, capable of accommodating 1,200 members, pending the purchase of a site and construction of the Club's permanent facility at 14 Regent Street. H A/IV/M/40-3; *LPOD*.

I hope you are quite well, & will have a capital appetite for your visitors. I wrote / to you yesterday, & therefore have nothing further to say.[1]

Yrs ever, | D.

TO: BARONESS LIONEL DE ROTHSCHILD Hughenden **3843**
[Friday] 21 August 1863

ORIGINAL: ROTH RFAM C/2/5
PUBLICATION HISTORY: Weintraub *Disraeli* 365, dated 21 August 1863, part of the fourth paragraph
EDITORIAL COMMENT: Paper imprinted 'Hughenden Manor'.

Augt. 21 1863

Dearest Baroness,

I want to know how you are, & all that belong to you. Harrogate, I trust, is a success, even a great one.[1] We always hope what we wish.

I can / tell you little of ourselves, tho' we have passed two or three weeks here most happily: my wife in an infinity of creation,[2] & I seeing only books & trees, but both good of their kind.

I want / to know, how you like the volume I gave you when we parted. Some friends of the author have been consulting me about its translation, & wishing me to recommend a pen equal / to the office.[3] Not easy; the professional translators from the French are miserable. It should be an amateur. Miss Evans, the author of "Adam Bede", was the translator of "Strauss".[4] It is a masterpiece; superior / to the original. But from the language, the style of the writer, & the general treatment of the theme, that was a much harder nut to crack. Renan is fruit, indeed, of quite a different kind; a melting peach, plucked in a / sunny hour, & digested with ambrosial facility!

1 D's letter of the previous day has not been found. SBW in her 17 August letter of thanks for the trout and grouse would conclude: 'Your incomparable Letters are my admiration and my comfort.' RTC [480Q]. The grouse had been sent to the DS on the 14th by Sir James Fergusson. H acc.

---

1 Harrogate in North Yorkshire is a major watering place, but it was Buxton to which the Rothschilds had gone for Lionel's health; see **3836**&n2. Harrogate may have been on D's mind from Col Edwards's letter of this day (21 August): 'Many thanks for your very kind letter [*not found*] of congratulation on the sensation produced by my regiment at Harrogate also for your short but most expressive note [*also not found*] a day or two ago.' Edwards however then describes the sensation made by the regiment in Halifax during a visit by the Prince of Wales. H B/XXI/E/55. In the Baroness's reply (**3836**n2), she would joke that D's letter had 'been a great traveller, or to have tarried long on the road,' suggesting it was misaddressed. H XXI/R/234.

2 For MA's current renovations at Hughenden, see Introduction pp xv-xvi and Appendix VIII.

3 Lady Salisbury had written from Bournemouth on 17 August: 'Renan is casting about for a translator of his book; Sir John Bowring wants to do it; Renan has written to England to ask advice, & Arthur Russell is consulted. Arthur is here with us; he is anxious to find some more fit person. It occurs to me that you might feel some interest in there being a good translation, & that you might know some one & might be able to offer a suggestion.' H B/XX/S/1420. Ernest Renan (see **3679**n2) in 1863 published his famous *Vie de Jésus,* which would be published in an English translation (no translator named) by Trübner in London in 1864. Henri Girard and Henri Moncel *Bibliographie des Oeuvres de Ernest Renan* (Paris 1923) 89.

4 Mary Ann (later Marian) Evans (1819-1880), the eminent intellectual and novelist George Eliot, had published anonymously in 1846 her translation of the highly controversial *Leben Jesu* (1835) by David Friedrich Strauss (1808-1874). *Adam Bede* (1858), her first full-fledged novel, had been warmly received; her most recent publication was *Romola* (1862-3).

I shd. like very much to know, from your bright mind & glowing pen, what you think of this work.[5]

Here we hope to conclude by the end of this month, the / finest harvest in the record of the Chilterns. Not only magnificent crops of wheat, & golden barley, & exuberant oats, but matchless turnips; wh:, as the astrologers used to say, seldom come into a conjuncture. Never was such prosperity. I hope Yorkshire is as fortunate. /

I am sure not a day passes in our solitude, that we do not think, or speak, of some of you. What are terraces, & gardens of delight without dear friends like you!

Pray, therefore do not forget us, & write to

Your faithful | D.

3844 TO: LORD MALMESBURY Hughenden [Saturday] 22 August 1863

ORIGINAL: HCC 9M73/460/19/1

PUBLICATION HISTORY: Malmesbury II 302, dated at Hughenden, 22 August 1863

EDITORIAL COMMENT: Paper imprinted 'Hughenden Manor'.

Confidential Aug 22 1863

Rt Honorable | The Earl of Malmesbury

My dear Malmesbury,

The Carlton & the Conserv[ativ]e Clubs are overflowing, & years must elapse before some men can enter them. They are also very exclusive. The Carlton rarely admits professional persons, & the Conservative only an insufficient pr Centage.

Taylor impresses on me the absolute necessity of a Junior / Conservative, wh: shall be a Central point for those Country attorneys, & Land Agents, &c. who are winning, & are to win, our Elections. He thinks, that it will powerfully organise, & encourage, our friends.

But there must be no mistake ~~on~~ about the politics & he wants for trustees

Ld. Derby

Ld. Malmesbury

5 In her reply (n1), the Baroness would write: 'How delightful is the volume which you so kindly gave me. It reads like a beautiful poem, written by an ardent poet inspired to reveal the truth & to reveal it with tenderness, with reverence & with glowing zeal. For enlightened Jews there will not, I believe, be any novelty of appreciation in the book as regards the principal figure, the great founder of Christianity, of the religion which has ruled the world these eighteen hundred years; but many of our co-religionists will be deeply pained at having been painted by Renan in colours so dark & so repelling. When prejudices are believed to be waning it is doubly distressing to see a long persecuted nation held up to the scorn of calm readers & earnest thinkers, as incorrigibly sordid, cold, cunning[,] cruel, – *ever* stubborn[,] hard-hearted & narrow-minded. A great writer, apparently so fair & just in the enunciation of his opinions – one whose judgment is so correct, whose feelings seem so pure & noble, should not have condescended to heighten the dazzling brilliance of his grand picture by introducing such deep shadows – as if he had felt it requisite to calumniate the Jews in order to atone to the religious world for the liberties taken with the greatest & highest of all subjects of human interest[.] But such considerations regard merely, or chiefly the Jewish community and are mere spots on the disk of the Sun. I do not think any foreigner could translate the book into English, and no Jew should attempt it.' Lady Salisbury would write again, from Hatfield, on 7 September: 'If Renan be not entangled with his publishers, there seems just a chance that he may be persuaded to refuse to allow his book to be translated; I have seen several letters from him, he is perplexed & unhappy; he neither knows England, nor the language, & was not prepared for the noise he has made in this country.' H B/XX/S/1421.

Mr. Dis[rael]i
Ld Colville
Col. Taylor

I have, at his suggestion, communicated with Lord Derby, who is favorable to the suggestion, if no liability is incurred by the Trustees. This, of course, must be a sine qua non.[1]

What do you say to it?[2]

Yours sincerely, | D.

TO: SARAH BRYDGES WILLYAMS Hughenden [Saturday] 22 August 1863 3845

ORIGINAL: RTC [243]

PUBLICATION HISTORY: M&B III 463, dated 22 August 1863, the last paragraph; Blake 417, the last sentence from M&B

EDITORIAL COMMENT: Paper imprinted 'Hughenden Manor'. There is no salutation. *Sic:* Wycomb; Carington.

Augt 22 1863

I forgot to tell you, that, about a week ago, coming from Wycomb Abbey, where we had been dining with Lord & Lady Carington, we were struck by sparks of light dancing about the glasses of our carriage. It was eleven o'ck. For some little time, we thought it must be some illusion, produced / by the refraction of the carriage lamps upon the windows – the carriage being a Brougham. But on putting down the window, lo! & behold! they were fire-flies! Not merely softly luminous, like glowworms, but sparkling as you have seen them in Italy, & as they glitter in their native land of S. America. I don't expect you to believe it, / & will pardon general incredulity, for which I am prepared. I never heard of fire-flies in England. Have you?[1]

We now very much regret, that we did not stop the carriage, & examine the affair more minutely, but we were in our own park, ascending the hill, wh: is steep, & rather critical for London horses. The servants saw nothing, but they never do see / anything. We resolved to repair to the same scene, at the same hour, the next night, & every night, until we had satisfied ourselves. But the next day, the weather ↑changed,↓ & since then, we have had a temperature fatal, I fear, to fire-flies, & all exotics.

I sent you the other day some grouse from Drummond Castle.[2] These birds travel so fast in the 19th. Centy., that they are always fresh.

1 See **3841**&n3.

2 Malmesbury would reply on the 27th from Torquay (where he had had the loan of Lord Willoughby's yacht for the last month) in full agreement with the proposal 'on the condition that I incur no liability. The fate of the Trustees of the Piccadilly & Young Crockfords is a warning.' H B/XX/HS/112.

---

1 SBW would reply on 30 August: 'The only time I ever [saw] any thing like fireflies was long ago on my returning from dining at Dundridge house near Totness about 12 o clock at night in Decr. in going up a Hill the Horses backed and I had to wait a long time for others in a storm of snow which had the appearance all around the Carriage and Lamps of glittering Fireflies in rapid motion[.] These are the only sort of Fireflies I ever have remarked.' RTC [481Q].

2 Drummond Castle in Perthshire was a seat of Lord Willoughby de Eresby.

We thank you much for your kind recollection.[3] Turbots visiting trout, are patricians noticing country cousins.

Ever yrs, | D.

3846 TO: BARON LIONEL DE ROTHSCHILD Hughenden [Thursday] 29 August 1863

ORIGINAL: ROTH RAL 000/848

EDITORIAL COMMENT: Paper imprinted 'Hughenden Manor'. *Sic:* Wycomb.

The | Bn. de Rothschild | M.P. Augt 29 1863

My dear Lionel,

I have sent you some grouse by this train: they arrived, this morning, from a Yorkshire moor, & I ~~as~~ send them to you, because they are all picked / birds.[1]

Thank the Baroness for her charming letter. I am sorry you have found such a savage clime in Derbyshire.[2] About ten days ago, returning from Wycomb Abbey, where we had been dining, it being about / eleven o'ck, we were struck by some perplexing sparks about the windows of our carriage, & thought at first it was the reflection of the lamps on some marks in the windows. On putting down the windows, we found they / were fire-flies! I don't expect you to believe it.

Mary Anne sends her best love to the Baroness, yourself, & all. Tell Evelina, I have a beautiful book about Haddon Hall, full of wondrous drawings by Cattermole[3] – but, alas! it is in town. I will lend it her some day.

Ever yrs. | D.

3847 TO: LORD DERBY Hughenden [Wednesday] 2 September 1863

ORIGINAL: DBP Box 146/1

PUBLICATION HISTORY: M&B IV 399, dated at Hughenden, 2 September 1863, the sixth and seventh paragraphs

EDITORIAL COMMENT: Paper imprinted 'Hughenden Manor'. Endorsed by Derby at the top of the first page: 'Disraeli B.'

Rt Honble | The Earl of Derby | K.G. Septr. 2 1863

My dear Lord,

I hate to bore you with business – from wh: I shrink myself – but the enclosed, wh: was sent me a week ago, was intended, I apprehend, for your eye as well.[1]

3 See **3842**n1.

---

1 In his 21 August letter (**3843**n1) Col Edwards had promised the DS a hamper of grouse.

2 In her 26 August letter (**3836**n2 and **3843**nn1&5), the Baroness had written: 'Here it has been intensely cold, and no day has passed without bringing a torrent of rain, and obliging us to light blazing fires.'

3 George Cattermole (1800-1868), watercolour painter and illustrator, had done 24 illustrations for *Evenings at Haddon Hall; a series of romantic tales of the olden time* (1832), edited by Baroness E.C. de Calabrella. Haddon Hall was a seat of the Manners family (Dukes of Rutland).

---

1 Derby would respond from Knowsley on 6 September: 'I return Spofforth's letters. From what he says, I should think the prospects of the proposed Club [*see* **3841**&n3] are sufficiently fair, and the risk slight enough, to justify us in accepting the office of Trustees, and Members, though I should certainly decline acting as a Committee man; and if you are prepared to give your consent, I shall be ready to join you.

Taylor remains in town / – from a domestic cause,
"Torquatus volo parvulus",
but all the others are scattered.[2]

I have heard from Malmy., who is in favor of the move, provided no risk &c.[3]

There is no hurry about the business: the house should be full before the piece is announced.

Here, we have just closed the / most wondrous harvest in the records of the Chiltern Hills: an exuberant harvest of all crops; turnips coming, as the astrologists used to say, in a conjuncture with grain – wh: is rare.

The Queen returns from a not uneventful German campaign, for not only is Princess Helena to be married; but Prince Alfred, & that too in the early spring: the / Princess not inferior to the Princess of Wales! But you know all this.[4]

For my part, I think that even Princes shd. sow their wild oats, & not step out paterfamilias from the nursery, or the middy's berth.

The war-cry seems nearly over.[5]

Yrs sincerely, | D.

TO: SIR ANDREW BUCHANAN Hughenden [Thursday] 3 September 1863 **3848**

ORIGINAL: NOT BU 18/49/1

EDITORIAL COMMENT: Paper imprinted 'Hughenden Manor'. *Sic:* G.C.B.

His Excellency | Sir Andrew Buchanan | G.C.B.[1] Sept 3 1863

My dear Ambassador,

A son of Colonel Edwards, the M.P. for Beverley, is now at Berlin. He has been travelling with a young Yorkshire friend, still his companion, for some time on the Continent, & neglected to be presented at / our Court before his departure. If any notice by Yr Excellency could mitigate the inconvenience, wh: he will, consequently, experience, I shd. feel personally obliged to you.[2]

Probably we shall neither of us ever set foot in the Club.' H A/IV/M/38. Taylor on 26 August had forwarded to D Spofforth's letters on Derby's position, asking that they be returned: 'I trust what Spofforth writes is to the point, & meets Lord Derby's objections.' H A/IV/M/34, 36.

2 The quotation from Catullus's poem LXI ('I wish a little Torquatus') involves an older man anticipating the birth of a son. The 52-year-old Taylor, married on 13 November 1862, would become father to a son on 21 September.

3 See **3844**&n2.

4 Derby (n1) would reply that D's letter was the first he had heard of these weddings. D had got the news from Charlotte de Rothschild's letter of 26 August (**3843**nn1&5). The 17-year-old Princess Helena would not marry Prince Christian of Schleswig Holstein until 1866. 19-year-old Prince Alfred would not marry until 1874, to Grand Duchess Marie Alexandrovna, only daughter of Czar Alexander II. The Queen had been in Germany in an unsuccessful attempt to reconcile the monarchs of Prussia and Austria. Longford 318.

5 See **3836**n1 on the diminishing threat of war with Russia. .

---

1 Sir Andrew, the career diplomat whom D had met in Constantinople in 1831 (see I **109**n6), had been British ambassador to Prussia since 1862. He had been made KCB in 1860, would become GCB in 1866 and be created 1st Bt in 1878.

2 On behalf of her husband, Maria Churchill Edwards had written on 1 September from Pye Nest, near Halifax, to ask for an introduction to Buchanan for their eldest son (Henry Coster Lea Edwards, 1840-1896) and a friend, R. Brown, who were in Berlin. 'A letter from you stating that my son is residing at

His father is a man of great wealth & influence, & one of my most devoted supporters, & I should be glad to oblige, & serve, him.

We / were extremely vexed, that, thro' the inconceivable carelessness of our servants, we were deprived of the pleasure of seeing Lady Buchanan[3] when she was in England. I hope she is quite well, & that you will offer her our kind remembrances.

Here, we have concluded the finest harvest known in / the records of the Chiltern Hills, &, I believe, it is generally the same. This, & the prospect of the maintenance of peace, make everybody, & everything, prosperous.

We hear also, that Prince Alfred is to be married, & in the early spring – but you know more about this matter than I do.

Yours sincerely, | *B. Disraeli*

3849 TO: SARAH BRYDGES WILLYAMS

Hughenden
[Saturday] 12 September [1863]

ORIGINAL: RTC [244]

EDITORIAL COMMENT: Endorsed in another hand on the first page: '1863'. There is no salutation. *Sic:* chaf.

Hughenden Sept 12.

I send you some birds (two brace) & a hare – not from Scotch Castles or Yorkshire moors, but from an old English Manor: nut-brown partridges. I hope you will eat them for the sake of Hughenden.[1]

Here we pass our lives; & / have no company, but book & trees.[2]

Except owls, wh: abound here; they hoot all night, & even tap at our windows. In the day time, they roost in the woods, & sometimes in yew-trees, of wh: they are very fond, in the pleasure-grounds.

My woodman,[3] yesterday, offered / to shew me one, & I asked him, how he found

Berlin and unfortunately neglected to be presented before leaving England will suffice.' She enclosed Brown's 28 August 1863 letter to Col Edwards from Berlin, asking for the introduction so that they could be admitted to privileged places for reviews beginning on 9 September and for British functions likely to be attended by Prince Alfred and the Duke of Cambridge. 'Unless you are introduced [to the ambassador] you are kept off the ground among the thousands who cannot see to any advantage ... The Ambassador's wife – (Lady Buchanan) is, I understand a Yorkshire lady, & formerly a Miss Busfield.' H B/XXI/E/81, 81a; www.angeltowns.com/town/peerage/baronetse.htm.

3 Sir Andrew in 1857 had married secondly Georgiana Eliza Stuart (1821-1904), third daughter of 11th Baron Blantyre. Her elder sister, Fanny Mary (see V **1945n3**), had married in 1847 D's friend William Busfeild Ferrand (*né* Busfeild).

---

1 MA recorded expenditure of 1*s* 8*d* for sending the game to Torquay, but left blank the name of the donor. H acc.

2 D does not mention several recent engagements, on 1 September to the Dowager Duchess of Sutherland at Cliveden, where they tipped the servants (including the gardener and housekeeper) 7*s* 7*d*, and on the 4th to the Jerseys at Osterley Park by rail (16*s* 6*d*) and carriage (9*s* 6*d*). On the 18th they would entertain at dinner an interesting assortment of Rothschilds and clergy: Charlotte, Evelina and Emma de Rothschild, 'Madam' [Louisa?] and Miss [Constance?] de Rothschild, Mr and Mrs Clubbe and her brother Mr Barlee, Mr Evetts, Mr Coling and Mr Barker, about to be confirmed as a clergyman. In the following year, Charlotte de Rothschild was pleased with her welcome by 'the great man and his shrewd, good-natured wife' and was impressed with the renovations to the house. H acc; Charlotte de Rothschild to Leopold de Rothschild, 13 September 1864, MS ROTH.

3 The woodman at Hughenden was named Lovet. H acc (15, 22 Sept 1863).

out their resting place. He replied, "By the number of little birds, who, in the day time, gather about them, chiefly chaff-finches, & an occasional black-bird, & chatter, & chaf, & mock them!"

And, sure enough, he took me / to a thick bushy acacia, & introduced me to a very handsome blue owl. His f head & face were like a great cat's; he was asleep. The blue owl is a handsome bird; very preferable to the old-barn door owl. ↑He is in your Gould:[4] we found him last night.↓

What a queer letter about birds & ugly ones, instead of Dukes & Marchionesses! But it comes from a sylvan, a faun, or a satyr.

Yours ever, | D.

TO: CHARLES CLUBBE Hughenden [Thursday] 17 September 1863 3849A

ORIGINAL: RIC [019]

COVER: The | Revd. C.W. Clubbe | A.M. | The Vicarage | *B Disraeli*

EDITORIAL COMMENT: Envelope and paper imprinted 'Hughenden Manor'. *Sic:* C.C.

The | Rev. C.C. Clubbe | A.M. Septr 17 1863

My dear Mr Clubbe,

I think on reflection, that, as yr gathering is an experiment, & we are so near a large town, that it would be / expedient, that the meeting should not be held in the grove, but in some part of the park as remote from our house as is convenient. / This, I hope, & shd think, wd. be consistent with yr other arrangements.[1]

Yrs sincerely, | D.

TO: WILLIAM ROSE Hughenden [Friday] 18 September 1863 3850

ORIGINAL: DA [1]

Private Hughenden, Septe 18, 1863

William Rose Esq[1]

My dear Sir,

I returned yesterday from Bulstrode:[2] I tried the champagne remedy, but found its effects too active: otherwise I can't help feeling that / some good tonic & stomachic remedy might put me right.[3]

Perhaps you will call, or if engaged to day, send me something by the bearer as you contemplated.

Yrs flly | D.

4 See VI **2745**&n3 for the bird book illustrated by Gould that SBW gave the DS in 1855.

1 For the Harvest Home at Hughenden, see **3851**&nn3&4.

1 William Rose (for whom see IV **1521n1**), Philip Rose's elder brother, was a physician in High Wycombe.

2 Bulstrode Park, Gerrard's Cross, was the seat of the Duke of Somerset. No information has been found on D's visit there.

3 According to W.A.N. Dorland *Illustrated Medical Dictionary* (1951), champagne is a 'diffusible stimulant, used to soothe an irritable stomach.' Perhaps D preferred to tell people that he had suffered a leg injury rather than an internal problem to avoid the public anxiety that nevertheless did arise. See further **3851**nn2&4. D's urgency to Rose may be because on this day (18th) the DS were scheduled to entertain several Rothschilds and assorted clergy to dinner; see **3849**n2.

3851 TO: SARAH BRYDGES WILLYAMS

Hughenden
[Sunday] 20 September 1863

ORIGINAL: RTC [245]
PUBLICATION HISTORY: M&B III 471-2, dated 20 September 1863, omitting the first paragraph
EDITORIAL COMMENT: Paper imprinted 'Hughenden Manor'. There is no salutation.

Septr 20 1863

On Friday, there arrived here a basket of the most delicious fish, that ever were furnished by the beautiful waters of yr famous bay.[1] All the specimens were perfect. The soles worthy of Torbay; the Janitore of St. Peter himself; but the Prawns!! In size, color, flavor, sweetness / & tenderness, I have only known them equalled, & never surpassed, at Naples. And I have always, thought that the waters of Parthenope should count them among their most precious treasures; beyond even their boasted beds of coral.

Here, we are full of Harvest homes! A novel feature, as now / practised, of our English country life. In old days, or rather two or three years ago, every farmer, after the harvest, gave a supper to his hinds, where they guzzled & got tipsey, & resumed their work in the morning, with aching heads, after a rural debauch.

Now, instead of an isolated nocturnal revel in a ↑farmhouse↓ kitchen ~~of a farmhouse~~, all the farmers of the parish unite together, & give to their collected labourers a / festival in a tent, wh: will hold hundreds, with banners & a band. A day is set apart – all go in procession to the Church, wh: is adorned with flowers & sheaves, the children sing chorales, & every one has a favor, & a stalk of corn in his buttonhole.[2]

The Clergy are at the bottom of this movement:[3] it connects the harvest with religion, & the Church. Even a *dissenting* farmer can scarcely refuse to walk in the procession on such an occasion.

Unconsciously, all are reviving pagan rites, & restoring the Dionysian festivals![4]

Yours ever, | D.

1 On 22 September MA would record paying 3*s* 1*d* for carriage of the fish from Torquay. H acc.

2 A Harvest Home of this sort had been held on 16 September at Rose's Bucks home, Rayners, with Rose presiding and D giving the first toast, to the landlords of the parish, and Lord Howe in particular. He praised Harvest Homes because they 'cause all classes in the agricultural world to mix and meet together.' Between that festival, however, and the Royal and Central Bucks Agricultural Association's meeting at Aylesbury on Wednesday 23 September, D injured his leg (see **3858**&n1), preventing him from attending. *BH* (26 Sept 1863).

3 On 17 September, Rev Clubbe had sent D a notice to be circulated in the parish for Harvest Home 'as an experiment' on 24 September (n4), and invited D to chair and MA to attend a service at St Michael's Church, Hughenden, and a following dinner in a tent in D's park. H B/XXI/C/289.

4 *BH* (n2) also reported: 'One of the "Harvest Homes" which are gradually usurping the place of those rough and ready gatherings with which the labouring population were wont to celebrate the garnering of the fruits of the earth, took place at Hughenden on Thursday [24 September]. It was a first attempt in this parish, and as such it may be regarded as the successful precursor of many others. It had the approval of Mr. Disraeli, the lord of the manor ... The service having concluded, a procession of the farmers and their labourers, headed by the drum and fife band of the 2nd Bucks Volunteers, marched up to the Manor House, and some hopes were entertained that Mr. Disraeli, who was prevented by indisposition from taking any active part in the day's proceedings, would address a few words to the men. The right hon. gentleman, however, did not appear, but Mrs. Disraeli bowed her acknowledgments from one of the windows.' At the subsequent dinner (2*s* a head) to about 200 people including MA, the first toast after those to royalty would be to D's health. On 6 October, MA would record expenditure of 6*s* for the dinners of the DS' gardener, another called Anderson and Lovet, the woodman. H acc.

TO: CHARLES CLUBBE [Hughenden, Friday 25 September 1863?] 3852

ORIGINAL: PS 719

PUBLICATION HISTORY: Myers catalogue 381 (1955) item 342

EDITORIAL COMMENT: The undated catalogue extract originally placed here has now been superseded by the text of the dated whole letter discovered after the letters were assigned final numbers; see **3896A**.

TO: SARAH BRYDGES WILLYAMS Hughenden [Monday] 28 September 1863 3853

ORIGINAL: RTC [246]

PUBLICATION HISTORY: M&B III 472, dated 28 September 1863; Blake 416, dated 28 September 1863, the first paragraph from M&B

EDITORIAL COMMENT: There is no salutation.

Hughenden Manor | Septr 28. 1863

You live in the world [compared] to what I do – who never see anything but books & trees. When we left Hughenden last year we sent in an architect & suite, & tho' ten months have elapsed, some workmen still linger about. We have realised a romance we had been many years meditating: we have restored / the House to what it was before the civil wars, & we have made a garden of terraces, in wh: cavaliers might roam, & saunter, with their ladye-loves![1] The only thing wanting is, that you sho[ul]d see it – but I am going to have, in due time, a competent artist down, who will photograph the House, gardens, terraces, monument, &c &c, in every aspect, & these shall / be sent, or, I hope, brought to you, for the time is approaching, when we must turn our thoughts to the western ocean; the classic waves of gigantic soles, & colossal prawns!

All these alterations have prevented our receiving our friends this year, so I have been like a man on a desert island – beautiful tho' lonely, & free from the despair of a Robinson Crusoe, or / an Alexander Selkirk, for I have a future – at Mount Braddon!

In making the alterations here, a great number of owls have been disturbed among the yew trees, but they have been religiously cared for, as if I were the priest of Minerva, & now they have resumed their haunts. Their hooting at night is wilder & louder, than the South-West wind, wh:, indeed, is only the accompaniment to their weirdish arias. And they tap at the windows with their fell beaks!

Yrs ever, | D.

TO: LORD BEAUCHAMP Hughenden [Monday] 28 September 1863 3854

ORIGINAL: BCP [11]

PUBLICATION HISTORY: Bradford 248, dated 9 June 1864, extract

EDITORIAL COMMENT: Black-edged paper.

The | Earl Beauchamp Hughenden Manor | Septr 28: 1863

1 On 3 September MA recorded the dimensions of 'the terrace walk 125 feet by 12-20 feet with the grass from one side to the other.' On the 22nd she noted expenditure of 1*s* 1*d* for grass seed. H acc.

My dearest Elmley,

I did not like to intrude on you in the midst of sorrow, cares, & business – but I don't like to be altogether silent, / lest you shd. deem me insensible.[1]

He, whom you have lost, was, strange to say, one of my earliest encouragers, when encouragement was most rare. He was the last person, from whom I could have expected sympathy, for / he was a patrician cynic – but he proffered it, & not scantily; I have always felt grateful to him, & duly appreciated his quick perception & fine taste.

What I want to know is, how, amid the inevitable excitement of / your new life, you find yourself. It is a life precious to me. I have lost D'Orsay, & George Smythe, who were the delights of my existence, & I cannot afford to lose you, who alone remain.[2]

We are living here in profound solitude. A / few days after you left us last year, the architects & suite took possession of Hughenden, & a troop of workmen still lingers about it. We have realised a romance we had talked of for many years, for we have restored the place / to what it was before the civil wars, & have made a garden of terraces, in wh: cavaliers might have wandered with their ladye-loves.

We don't receive our friends this year, for the house internally is still much in the hands of / artisans, but, if the humor hits you, you will find, here, your usual welcome, & yr favorite library, wh: is, I think, enriched & improved.[3]

My wife sends you her kind regards, & I am, ever yrs | D.

3855 TO: PHILIP ROSE — Hughenden [Wednesday] 7 October 1863

ORIGINAL: H R/I/A/165

EDITORIAL COMMENT: Paper imprinted 'Hughenden Manor'.

Private — Octr 7 1863

Phil: Rose Esqr

My dear Rose,

I have got a notification, in reply to my letter, that 200: will be allotted to me; but not the allotment, wh: I will, as you suggest, immediately forward / to you.[1] Probably, in

1 The 4th Earl Beauchamp (II **690n4**) had died on 8 September and been succeeded by his son, formerly styled Viscount Elmley.

2 The new (5th) Earl would live only until 4 March 1866.

3 Beauchamp would reply from Madresfield on 30 September: 'Your letter was truly welcome perhaps all the more so as I had begun to think that in this my time of cares & sorrow you had forsaken me. Certainly the change my father's death makes in my life is very great and a more modest position would better suit my tastes & habits, the pomp & vanities of the world far from giving me pleasure oppress me. You seem fortunate in being satisfied with the work of yr. architects. I shall certainly take advantage of yr. invitation & shall look forward to passing a day or so at Hughenden & strolling on your new terraces.' He closed 'With many thanks for yr. expressions of regard & esteem which I highly value'. H B/XXI/L/428.

---

1 Rose's response is evidently an unsigned, undated fragment in his hand to which D responds next day (**3856**). It reads: '*Private.* I have received Laings note and find I was correct. He says "I have kept 200 for Mr Disraeli". Mine are to be in the Syndicate which locks them up for *3* months or perhaps *6* months, but I understand yours to be free. So that I have sent instructions to my Broker to sell *100* at 4 pm. if they reach that amount, thinking you will approve of this in any case. In fact now that you are sure of your allotment it will be for you to determine at what price you will realize. There are only *25,000* shares

person, as, I think, I shall be in town in a few days. I am quite mindful of the 14th.

I think, Routledge's lease expires at the commencement of next / year.[2]

Yours ever, | D.

TO: PHILIP ROSE [Hughenden, Thursday] 8 October 1863 3856

ORIGINAL: H R/I/A/166

Private Octr. 8. 1863

P. Rose Esqr

My dear Rose,

I am syndicated for three months, & I am sorry to hear, from you, what are the consequences of that situation. Instead of receiving money, I shall have to lock up £400.

This is most vexatious, but / it must be borne. It wd. be infra dig., & rather gross, to notice the matter.

If foreign affairs go right, we shall survive.

I hope you will not get into any difficulty by your premature offer of the 100 shares. I have / not received any formal allotment.[1]

I wrote to you, yesterday.

Yours ever | D.

TO: PHILIP ROSE Hughenden [Thursday] 8 October 1863 3857

ORIGINAL: BODL MS Wilberforce c25 ff221-2

EDITORIAL COMMENT: Paper imprinted 'Hughenden Manor'.

Philip Rose Esqr Octr 8 1863

My dear Rose,

I am very glad to hear, that you think of asking the Bishop to Rayners for the Visitation, for I was rather nervous about the hospitality of this District. It had been /

for *public* allotment, & the applications yesterday exceeded a *million*. I am thinking of starting a Credit Foncier [*a mortgage fund*] for Australia under the auspices of the General Credit if the market continues as it is now. It will be as great a success [*end of fragment*]'. H R/I/B/94. On 23 May 1864, S[amuel] Laing (VI **2734n2**), writing from 6 Kensington Gardens Terrace, would invite D and offer to drive him to a 4 June dinner the Directors of the General Credit Co. were giving him, as D had 'taken an interest in our undertaking'. H B/XXI/L/6. *The Times*'s 'Money-Market' column of 6 October 1863 had reported: 'The General Credit Company have to-day issued the prospectus of the Land Mortgage Bank of India (*Crédit Foncier Indien*) with a capital of 2,000,000£, in shares of 20£. The functions of the company will be strictly limited to making advances on landed estates – the highest form of security in India; and as the margin between which they can borrow money in this country on debentures and lend it on real property in India is stated to be at least 3 per cent., the field for profit is both legitimate and extensive.' An advertisement the same day for the Land Mortgage Bank of India identifies its chairman as 'S. Laing, Esq., late Finance Minister of India' (*ie* Samuel Laing, MP (L) for Wick 1859-60, 1865-8) and states that the shares may be obtained for a deposit of £3 each. At the end of October (a date chosen at random) the Indian Land Mortgage Bank was trading at 3 to 3¼ premium. *The Times* (31 Oct 1863). For Laing's financial career and connection with Rose, see *Norton Rose* 93-5.

2 See VII **3063**n1. According to the listings in Stewart *Writings* 106-7 (items 651 and 656), the Routledge 10-volume uniform shilling edition of D's works published in 1862-3 was the last to be published by Routledge in D's lifetime. See further **3903**&nn1-3.

---

1 See **3855**&n1. Earle's letter of this day concludes: 'Laing's crédit foncier of India a great success.' H B/XX/E/294.

my intention to have requested the pleasure, & honor, of receiving him, but I see, now, no chance of getting the workmen out of Hughenden this year. I have got rid of them externally, but I have only one bedroom finished, / & I see a prospect of increased internal paint, wh: will soon drive me into Devonshire.[1]

With my best Complimts. to Mrs Rose,

Yours sincerely, | D.

3858 TO: LORD CAMPDEN Hughenden [Saturday] 10 October 1863

ORIGINAL: PS 795, 654

PUBLICATION HISTORY: Reginald Atkinson catalogue 92 (1932) item 60: 'AL.s "D" to Viscount Campden 3pp Hughenden Oct. 10, 1863', and catalogue 56 (1924) item 75: 'item previously quoted to Visc Campden, but adding in n.p.'

EDITORIAL COMMENT: The text combines the two catalogue snippets. *Dating:* by Earle's return from Germany (n2); see also n3.

[*1932*] I ... hoped to have had the pleasure of seeing you – but I am detained here by a stupid accident to my leg, which I have neglected, and wh. imprisons me.[1]

[*1924*] Earle is in town, and just returned from Germany.[2] Have the kindness to see him and tell him everything ...[3]

1 Rose had written on 7 October enclosing a 6 October letter to him from Rev Charles Lloyd thanking him for inviting Bishop Wilberforce to stay at Rayners. As Lloyd had conveyed Rose's invitation, he now conveyed the Bishop's reply: 'Whenever [the Bishop] has been at "the visitation" of late years He has been asked by Disraeli to Hughenden and he does not wish so to engage himself as to prevent his accepting the Invitation if it comes as usual – because he feels Disraeli's civility to him in entertaining on many occasions & coming forward to help him – I hope you understand! But failing this he will be very pleased to come to you – and I suppose that you are on such terms with Disraeli that you can arrange this with him'. Rose explained at length the history of his contacts with the Bishop and the circumstances of his invitation, adding that he had assumed that Hughenden would not be in condition to receive visitors this year: 'Now I am sure you will understand me and let me know what your intention HAD been if you had heard nothing from me.' H R/I/B/91a,b.

---

1 See **3851**n2 for dating of D's leg injury. *BH* on 26 September had reported that, at the Royal and Central Bucks Agricultural Association meeting at Aylesbury on 23 September, 'Much regret was expressed at the absence of the... Right Hon. Mr. Disraeli, who, it was stated, had met with an accident which prevented him from leaving the house.' Rose would write on 14 October: 'I received your letter with its enclosure [*not found, but see* **3855**&n1] this morning and am sorry to find that you are still in the Doctor's hands. I enclose a letter to which I have been able to send from personal observation a very satisfactory reply.' The enclosure was from Henry Edwards at Pye Nest, written on 13 October to Rose so as not to disturb D: 'It is utterly impossible for me to describe how shocked I felt on reading the enclosed paragraph [reprinted] from the Court Journal ... I dread the consequences to the country should his precious life be prematurely cut short for besides being the life & soul of the party in this country representing its wealth & influence he is undoubtedly the most rising statesman in Europe.' The cutting stated that D was in a state of failing health that was causing his friends much anxiety. H R/I/B/92a,b.

2 Earle had written to D on 1 October that he had returned from Germany on 28 September and had information from Frankfurt for him on European affairs. H/B/XX/E/293.

3 D's business with Campden was probably on Italian affairs. On 12 October Earle would write, evidently in response to this letter: 'I will look up Campden, altho' to say truth, I have been avoiding him at the Carlton, dreading intrigues, in public, with that degree of surdity.' H B/XX/E/295. On 20 November, Campden would write to D that he had discussed Neapolitan affairs with Earle and sent him papers for use in a Commons speech, perhaps by Lennox. He hoped D was quite recovered. H B/XXI/G/13.

TO: SARAH BRYDGES WILLYAMS Hughenden [Saturday] 17 October 1863 3859

ORIGINAL: RTC [247]

PUBLICATION HISTORY: M&B IV 339, dated 17 October 1863, omitting the first and last paragraphs; Blake 430, dated 21 July 1863, extract from the fourth paragraph; Weintraub *Disrael* 400, dated 17 October 1863, extracts from the third and fourth paragraphs

EDITORIAL COMMENT: Paper imprinted 'Hughenden Manor'. *Sic:* to heard; Phillippe; pogniard. There is no salutation.

Octr 17 1863

The number of elections lost by the government, especially their defeat at Coventry & Tamworth,[1] has revived political passions, & I receive a great many letters from those who, I had hoped, not to heard of, or from, for some months yet. You know, how little desirous I am to precipitate any change, & how anxious, that the next administration should be / an enduring one. Everyone says, the pear is ripe: I wish, that it should deserve a stronger, scarcely a more refined, epithet, before it is introduced to the political dessert.

The troubles & designs of the French Emperor are aggravated, & disturbed, by the death of Billault, his only parliamentary debater, & a first-rate one. With, for the first time, a real opposition to encounter, & formed of the old trained speakers of Louis Phillippe's reign, in addition to the young democracy of oratory, wh: / the last revolution has itself produced, the inconveniences, perhaps the injuries, of this untimely decease are incalculable. It may even force, by way of distraction, the Emperor into war.[2]

Our own ministry have managed these affairs very badly, according to their friends. The Polish question is a diplomatic Frankenstein, created, out of cadaverous remnants, by the mystic blundering of Lord Russell.[3]

1 At by-elections between 1860 and 1863, the Conservatives had won or retained over 30 seats. For the vacancy at Coventry after the death of 'Bear' Ellice, Morgan D. Treherne (C), who had unsuccessfully contested it twice before, on 8 October had defeated Arthur Peel (L) 2,263-2,129. *The Times* on 10 October had called the election of the self-described '"unmitigated Tory"' of the Col Sibthorp school over the late prime minister's son a disgrace to the constituency, and predicted that Treherne would be unable to 'submit to the leadership of so advanced a thinker' as D. At Tamworth, on 12 October, John Peel (L-C, no relation to Sir Robert Peel) had defeated Henry Cowper (L) 224-167 for the seat left vacant by Lord Raynham's succession to the peerage as 5th Marquess Townshend. Sir Robert Peel, the other member for Tamworth, had canvassed and predicted victory for Cowper, and had been so chagrined by his defeat that, according to Earle, he had 'knocked over 2 men at the polling booth!!' *The Times* (15 Oct 1863); H B/XX/E/295. See also **3863**&n2.

2 Adolphe Augustin Marie Billault (1805-1863), president of the legislative assembly 1852-4, Legion d'Honneur 1855, minister of the interior 1854-8, 1859-60, minister without portfolio 1860-3 (*ie* minister obliged to defend against such orators as Thiers and Berryer governmental acts with which he often did not agree), also since June Walewski's replacement as minister of state and chief exponent of the Emperor's foreign policy, had died of overwork on 13 October. The Emperor expressed his deep regret at Billault's death by ordering a state funeral.

3 See **3830**&n1. Russell as foreign secretary had exacerbated the Polish insurrection, implying earlier that Britain would intervene militarily on Poland's behalf against Russia, but now declaring that Britain would offer only moral support. He called instead for a year's armistice during which Poland would be restored to its (unsuccessful) post-1815 constitutional status. See further Bell *Palmerston* II 343-53. Earle had written on 8 October: 'Hardy ... thinks badly of the state of foreign affairs, – condemns the ministerial Polish policy & says it's very awkward doing nothing after so many words.' On 12 October Earle had reported that Baron de Rothschild, 'very ill, – apparently – condemned the Polish policy.' H B/XX/E/294-5.

At present, the peace of the world has been preserved not by / statesmen, but by capitalists. For the last three months, it has been a struggle between the secret societies & the European millionaires. Rothschild, hitherto, has won; but the death of Billault may be as fatal for him, as the pogniard of a Polish patriot: for, I believe, in that part of the world, they are called patriots, tho,' in Naples, only brigands.

I am shocked, that the earthquake[4] has not elicited a single religious sentiment. Even those, who confess they knew it was an earthquake at the time, did not fall to their prayers. This seems lamentably to prove, that the religious principle is rather in abeyance: but / [*to top of first page:*] what can you expect from an earthquake, that even did not crack a china jar?

Ever yrs | D.

3860 TO: EDWARD KENEALY Hughenden [Monday] 19 October 1863

ORIGINAL: PS 1448; H H/LIFE

PUBLICATION HISTORY: Michael Silverman Manuscripts (Dec 1998): 'Fine Autograph Letter Signed to ... E.V.H. Kenealy ... 3 pages 8vo. Hughenden Manor, October 19, 1863.'; Kenealy 210, extract from the first paragraph

EDITORIAL COMMENT: A copy of the first page was kindly provided by Michael Silverman. Paper imprinted 'Hughenden Manor'. There is a typescript of the whole letter in H H/LIFE, from which the rest of the text has been taken.

E.V. Kenealy Esq | LLD Oct 19 1863

My dear Sir,

You have, kindly, sent me a volume distinguished by all the flow, & fine scholarship, for wh: yr writings are / remarkable.[1]

You are not the first lawyer who has bid adieu to the House,[2] and I hope you will not be less successful than Blackstone.[3]

Believe me, yours faithfully, | B. DISRAELI.

4 An earthquake centred in Hereford had struck at 3:20 *am* on 6 October. Charles Dickens was one of many who reported their experience of it to the press: 'I was awakened by a violent swaying of my bedstead from side to side, accompanied by a singular heaving motion. It was exactly as if some great beast had been crouching asleep under the bedstead and were now shaking itself and trying to rise.' *The Times* (8 Oct 1863). *The Times* on 9 October observed: 'It is surely a sign of the times that, amid all the fright and trepidation which such a phenomenon could not fail to excite, no one seems to have been prostrated by the dread of a supernatural visitation.'

---

1 Kenealy in 1863 published *Poems and Translations,* professedly to '"bid a final farewell to the Muse"' (*MP* 8 Oct 1863), and presumably the book he had sent D.

2 'House' is obviously a mistranscription (see ec) of 'Muse'. D quotes Byron's 'First Kiss of Love': 'If Apollo should e'er his assistance refuse, / Or the Nine be dispos'd from your service to rove, / Invoke them no more, bid adieu to the muse, / and try the effect, of the first kiss of love.'

3 Sir William Blackstone (1723-1780), the eminent jurist and author of the highly influential *Commentaries on the Laws of England* first published in four volumes in 1765-9, MP for Hindon 1761-68, for Westbury 1768-70, Kt 1770, had also dabbled in minor writing. D knew his grandson; see III **800** and **891**&n3.

TO: BARONESS LIONEL DE ROTHSCHILD — Hughenden — 3861

[Wednesday] 21 October 1863

ORIGINAL: ROTH RAL RFAM C/2/56

PUBLICATION HISTORY: Weintraub *Disraeli* 401, dated 21 October [1863], part of the fifth paragraph; Weintraub *Charlotte and Lionel* 170, extract from the fifth paragraph, and 185, a mention of the letter

EDITORIAL COMMENT: Paper imprinted 'Hughenden Manor'. *Sic:* Waleski.

Octr 21 1863

Dearest Baroness,

I was in hopes to have had the gratification of seeing you before this, but nothing happens as one expects. I hope, still, that it will be a pleasure not long delayed, & that we shall find Lionel improved – / I must add in health, or it would not be English: he cannot be improved in any other respect.[1]

Lord Lyndhurst's death was a shock to me: I had quite counted on his completing his century. He seems to me quite prematurely cut off. I / remember his mother; a fine old lady, who must have been nearly a hundred years old; & then he has living sisters who are his seniors;[2] & males, they tell us, are more enduring, than yr softer sex. When I first knew him, he was a very / handsome man, with a particularly fine presence, but, of late years, he had shrunk into nothing. I have observed the same result in another member of the heroic age of politics – Metternich, who was not as old as Lord Lyndhurst, but who, / originally, had as grand a mien.[3]

Pray can you tell me, or find out for me, who wrote the memoir of him in the "Times".[4]

1 See **3843**&nn1&5 for Charlotte de Rothschild's 26 August letter while at a spa for her husband's health. On 26 October she would write from Kingston House: 'Lionel begs me to thank you a thousand times for all your kind words & good wishes. I should be the happiest of women could I send satisfactory accounts of his health[;] unfortunately I am unable to discern the slightest improvement; but he is often cheerful, and always delighted to be remembered by his friends.' H B/XXI/R/235. She would also use D's letter to scold her son Leopold: 'I only wish you could see it, and notice, and remember that a great man, while lavishing the pearls of thought and the gems of style, does not disregard the graces of penmanship.' Weintraub *Charlotte and Lionel* 185.

2 Lyndhurst had died in the early morning of 12 October. Both he and his mother, Susannah Farnum Copley (see II **466**n3), died aged 91. Lyndhurst had only one surviving elder sister, Elizabeth Greene (1770-1865), another sister having died in 1785. His other sister, Mary Copley (*contra* II **410**n1 born in 1773 and thus one year his junior), would live until 1868. Sir Theodore Martin *A Life of Lord Lyndhurst* (1884) 14n1; Dennis Lee *Lord Lyndhurst: The Flexible Tory* (Niwot, Colorado: UP of Colorado 1994) 24; http://freepages.genealogy.rootsweb.com.

3 For D's last letter to Metternich, who had died in 1859 aged 86, see VII **3236**&nn1&2.

4 *The Times* had printed a brief announcement of Lyndhurst's death on the 12th, and a leader and a full-page article on the 13th, the latter including several references to D. In recounting the events of 1834 after the fall of the Whig government, the article reads: 'On that occasion Sir Robert [Peel] was found to be quite indispensable; but Sir Robert was only to be had at his own price, and that price, it has been said in a work of fiction more authentic than most history, he had sufficiently indicated "when he declared to his late colleagues, after the overthrow of 1830, that he would never again accept a *secondary* position in office."' The quotation is from *Coningsby* Bk 2, Chap 1 (World's Classics ed p 72). The article further states that, when the Whig government was tottering during the Reform Bill debates, Lyndhurst made an arrangement with the King to form a government if Melbourne resigned and Peel refused to form one: 'He was to have 12 seats placed at his disposal in the Commons for young aspirants of his party capable of rendering him service in debate ... [and] the first on the list was Mr. Disraeli, then a young man not yet recognized by the public as a statesman.' And, finally, the following: 'It is singular, indeed, that [Lyndhurst's] greatest efforts in [the Upper Assembly], his famous sessional reviews, at first fell coldly

The earthquake has not shocked me so much, as its total failure in eliciting any religious feeling in the country. Even those, who recognised it, & did not / suppose it was an affair of burglary, never seem to have thought of falling on their knees. I fear, this is significant of an infidel age. But, perhaps, one ought not to expect too much from an earthquake, that did not even break one of yr china jars.[5]

We live here in perfect / solitude, & were it not for newspapers, who come, by the train, like pleasant visitors to a country house, we should forget not only the day of the month, but the date of the year. It is only the golden limes & the scarlet creepers, that keep us au fait to the seasons. But the / deciduous glories are fast departing, & like those, who comfort themselves with respectability after romance, we are preparing to fall back on our evergreens, & find comfort & consolation in yews & conifers. Mary Anne has been very busy the whole year, & still remains so. / She has nearly finished some rooms, wh: are named after you, so that, now, that you have a vested interest in Hughenden, I trust, that yr visits will be more frequent, & not so brief. For my part, were it not, that it deprives me of seeing you, & yr hearth, I should not much / care, if I always remained here. I don't think one is much wanted now in the House of Commons. Parliamentary government, indeed, seems, after all, at a higher premium at Paris, than at Westminster, notwithstanding all the Emperor's efforts & contrivance. / What a great man is M. Billault, since his decease! Fancy an imperial car arrested in its fiery course, from the want of a debater! I knew him at Paris: Waleski introduced him to me. A very sharp man, but I had no idea I was conversing with one, on whose words / the destinies of France depended.[6]

My wife is in the woods, or she would send you her love. You must, therefore, accept mine instead, & pray share it with Lionel & Evelina.[7]

Yours ever, | D.

3862 TO: RALPH EARLE — Hughenden [Wednesday] 21 October 1863

ORIGINAL: H H/LIFE

EDITORIAL COMMENT: From a typescript headed: 'D. to Mr. R.A. Earle, Hughenden, Oct. 21. '63.'

R.A. Earle, Esq.

My dear Earle,

Enclosed is a dispatch, which, I think, I have had nearly three months. I have begun

on his fastidious audience. The idea of his first summary, suggested to him by Mr. Disraeli, then acting in amateur as his private secretary, was seized upon by his keen perception as the right thing at the right moment. It was, in fact, the first body blow, and was electrical in the country, though it was not in the first instance so effective in the House.' The extant Earle letters (see **3862**) do not mention Lyndhurst. As Dennis Lee writes (*op cit* 265), 'Disraeli was believed to have been the author of Lyndhurst's obituary in the *Times* ... The best evidence in support of this claim is a memorandum Disraeli prepared on October 13, 1863... Disraeli's notations contained parallels to the *Times* obituary in both subject matter and language.' See n7 and Appendix IV.

5 See **3859**&n4 for a prior instance of this witticism.

6 See **3859**&n2.

7 In her reply (n1) the Baroness would recount at length her attempts to get Delane to say who had written the Lyndhurst obituary; he finally admitted he had written three-fourths of it, and that the other fourth was '"the contribution of another pen."' She said she had not pressed him further, thinking it futile to do so, and offered a few guesses.

to read it more than once, but it produced upon me a mesmeric effect of a peculiar nature, I dare say not the fault of the writer, but rather of the unsuitableness of the season to such studies. I fancy, he has got hold of our old friend, voting papers, which he seems to think he has invented: but I may be wrong. What I want you to do, is to write him a courteous line or so: you need not return the paper to me.[1]

Who wrote the Lyndhurst biog: in the "Times"?[2]

I am quite well.[3]

Barnstaple is a bore, but, I suppose, the seat may be regained at a dissolution. The moral effect is nothing compared with Coventry and Truro. What of Windsor? Oxford, of course, nothing.[4]

Make my compliments to Lady Buchan,[5] and believe me,

Ever yours, D.

TO: W.W. FITZWILLIAM HUME Hughenden [Wednesday] 21 October 1863 **3863**

ORIGINAL: BRN [32]

EDITORIAL COMMENT: Paper imprinted 'Hughenden Manor'.

W.W. Fitzwilliam Hume | Esq. M.P. Octr. 21 1863

My dear Hume,

I was very glad to hear from you, & to learn, that your time, since our separation, has been so agreeably employed.[1]

As for myself, I think, I / was never better in my life. I have heard of, tho' not seen, some paragraphs about myself, wh: seemed, as if they were going to precede bulletins, but as I am perfectly insensible to what people say or write, I have never taken any notice of / them: trusting, that I shall be at my post, at the right time, & in good condition.

1 The enclosure has not been found or identified, and Earle's correspondence at this time makes no mention of it.

2 See **3861**&n4.

3 Earle on 12 October had written: 'I am sorry to hear of your leg – I wonder whether you require a little sea air to set you up'. H B/XX/E/295. See **3858**&n1.

4 Earle on 8 October had written: 'Coventry getting on well – I wish I cd. say the same of Barnstaple.' H B/XX/E/294. On 20 October at Barnstaple, Thomas Lloyd (L) had defeated Richard Bembridge (C) 305-285 in the vacancy left by the death of George Potts (L-C). For the 8 October Conservative win at Coventry see **3859**&n1. On 14 June at Truro, F.M. Williams (C) had defeated J.C.W. Vivian (L) 302-251 for the vacancy left by the appointment of Montague Smith (C) to the bench. At Windsor on 4 November, Col R.H.H. Vyse (C) would defeat Capt A.D. Hayter (L) in the vacancy left by the death of G.W. Hope (L-C). At Oxford on 7 November, Charles Neate (L) would be unopposed for the seat left vacant by the death of James Langston (L). Earle would respond from Himley Hall, Dudley (a seat of the Earl of Dudley), on the 29th: 'Barnstaple is a bore, but if we gain Windsor, it will be the substitution of a good Tory for a Peelite & Neate, who comes in for Oxford, will be better than Langston. But nothing avails, unless we are able to put before the country new names & a new government.' H B/XX/E/296.

5 Earle's aunt, the Dowager Countess of Buchan (d 1893), as Caroline Rose Maxwell, youngest daughter of James Primrose Maxwell, had married the late 12th Earl of Buchan in 1839, his third marriage. Earle on 12 October had written (n3): 'Lady B thanks you for your kind inquiries. She has returned & is well.'

---

1 Hume had written from Curzon Street on 18 October that, on his return from Holland and Germany, he had heard that D was unwell. He hoped the report was either untrue or exaggerated, and protested his interest in D's wellbeing. H B/XXI/H/757.

What fun is Sir Robert Peel! better than any of the good old farces – of the days of Liston & Keeley.[2]

We have had, here, the finest harvest, known / in the records of the Chiltern Hills. I hope you have been equally favored in Wicklow.[3]

We shall be passing thro' town in our way to Devon in a month or so – & I hope we shall meet there.

Yours, my dear Hume, | sincerely, | D.

3864 TO: FREDERICK LYGON Hughenden [Thursday] 29 October 1863

ORIGINAL: BCP [12]

EDITORIAL COMMENT: Paper imprinted 'Hughenden Manor'.

Hon: | Fred: Lygon | M.P. Octr 29 1863

My dear Lygon,

Let me cordially congratulate a brother County member, & one, whom I greatly regard.[1]

Yrs ever, | D.

3865 TO: LADY LONDONDERRY Hughenden [Thursday] 29 October 1863

ORIGINAL: DUR D/LO/C 530 [129]

EDITORIAL COMMENT: Paper imprinted 'Hughenden Manor'. Endorsed by Lady Londonderry on the first page: 'Mr D'Israeli'. This is the last extant D letter to Lady Londonderry.

Octr 29 1863

I see by the papers you are at Seaham & surrounded by yr friends:[1] therefore, I hope, & conclude, you are well.

We have remained here since the Prorogation.

What do you think of the great escapade? I dare say, he thinks, he will be / more popular, than ever, & has perhaps, got up the whole thing, that he may dissolve on it. They wanted a cry.

2 Hume's next letter, also dated 21 October (postmarked 22nd in Dublin and 23rd in High Wycombe), told of his conversation with Peel in which Peel denied having knocked a man down at Tamworth (see **3859**&n1). In response to Peel's praise of D, Hume had declared that over fifty MPs would follow him even if he 'went below the gangway ... that we recognised you as a power in the state – and no Conservative ministry could be formed in which you were not a *principle* – and that if it were attempted – in the house – you would soon be found to be simply a *dictator*.' He added that reports of D's ill health were even more prominent in Dublin than in London. H B/XXI/H/758, 758a. See further **3866**&nn9-10. John Liston (*c*1776-1846), the famous actor and comedian, had retired in 1837. Robert Keeley (1793-1869), also an actor and comedian, had retired in 1857.

3 Hume's Irish estate was Humewood, co Wicklow.

1 In the by-election on 26 October for the W Worcestershire seat left vacant by Lord Elmley's succession as Earl Beauchamp (see **3854**&n1), Frederick Lygon (C), Elmley's younger brother, had been elected without opposition. In his election speech reported at length in *The Times* on 27 October, he had concurred with D's position on such issues as the constitution, church-rates, and Poland, while strongly castigating Palmerston as a political opportunist.

1 *MP* on 26 October had reported Lady Londonderry to be 'surrounded by a large family circle at Seaham Hall, Durham'.

It is a pity, that the Low Church party had recognised him as "the man of God." But so was King David, & he behaved even worse.

If she be really Kane, he, / all must confess, is Able: a pun more atrocious, than his conduct.[2]

I hear the young Duchess of Beaufort[3] is using her utmost endeavours to stop the other divorce; I hope she may be more successful, than Mr Osborne in stopping the duel.[4] Colonel Armytage seems quite a Valmont.[5]

I hear the Cte. de Paris marries the beautiful daughter of the Montpensiers, & that the Empress Eugenie's visit, wh: was to prevent it, has entirely failed.[6]

Yours ever, | D.

TO: LORD DERBY Hughenden [Friday] 30 October 1863 3866

ORIGINAL: DBP Box 146/1

PUBLICATION HISTORY: M&B IV 340, dated at Hughenden, 30 October 1863, the first sentence and seventh and ninth paragraphs; Blake 434, dated 30 October 1863, the second and third paragraphs

EDITORIAL COMMENT: Paper imprinted 'Hughenden Manor'. Endorsed by Derby at the top of the first page: 'Disraeli B *Ansd*'. *Sic:* Gortschakoff; Castiliogne; Stovor.

Rt Honble | The Earl of Derby | K. G. Octr 30 1863

My dear Lord,

I am very sorry to hear of the gout,[1] but I hope only a light cavalry attack, & that you will be even better, when it has departed. I thought, perhaps, as you could not get about, it might not bore / you to receive a few lines.

2 In October 1863 Palmerston was named co-respondent in divorce proceedings. Mrs Margaret O'Kane had visited the 78-year-old premier at his Piccadilly home, Cambridge House, in June and later claimed that they had committed adultery. Her husband, Timothy O'Kane, a radical journalist, claimed £20,000 in damages as part of the suit. The O'Kanes being unable to prove that they were married, the case was dismissed, but, as D here predicts, the allegation and publicity increased Palmerston's popularity. *Eg*, an *MP* leader on 5 February 1864 strongly supported Palmerston. Ridley *Palmerston* 531; *MP* (27 Jan, 3, 5 Feb 1864). For Palmerston's Low Church sympathies and appointment of bishops, see Bell *Palmerston* 302-4 and Ridley *Palmerston* 499 ff.

3 Lady Georgiana Charlotte Curzon (1825-1906) in 1845 had married Lord Worcester, since 1853 8th Duke of Beaufort; D is distinguishing her from her mother-in-law, the Dowager Duchess.

4 On 8 October Earle had told D of gossip that 'Mrs. Dick Bulkeley has been surprised at B[e]aumaris with Armytage, – *rem in re*.' H B/XX/E/294. Richard L.M. Williams-Bulkeley (1833-1884), of Baron's Hill, Beaumaris, captain Royal Horse Guards, in November 1864 would divorce his wife, Mary Emily, daughter of Sir Henry Bingham Baring. The suit was granted on grounds of adultery with Henry Armytage (1828-1901), of Broomhill, Kent, Lieut-Col Coldstream Guards, brother of Sir George Armytage, 5th Bt, and son-in-law of 1st Lord Fitz-Hardinge, the former Francis Berkeley. On 23 September 1863, Bulkeley, obviously suspicious, had gone to the Beauforts,' leaving Baring, Armytage and Mrs Bulkeley at Baron's Hill, where he had servants watch Armytage enter Mrs Bulkeley's bedroom on five successive nights. *MP* (12 Nov 1864). The Beauforts had two homes in Wales, one at Monmouth and the other in Brecon, both some distance from Beaumaris.

5 The Vicomte de Valmont is a villainous seducer in the 1782 epistolary novel *Liaisons Dangereuses* by Pierre Ambroise Choderlos de Laclos, the basis of several modern films.

6 Prince Antoine of Orléans (1824-1890), duc de Montpensier, Infant of Spain 1859, in 1846 had married Maria Luisa Fernanda (1832-1897), Infanta of Spain, daughter of King Fernando VII; their eldest daughter, Maria Isabel (1848-1919), Infanta of Spain, on 30 May 1864, at Kingston-on-Thames, would marry her first cousin, the comte de Paris, head of the royal house of France.

---

1 Earle on 29 October had written: '*The Chief has a bad gout.*' H B/XX/E/296.

The Palmerston escapade! It should make him, at least, ridiculous; perhaps, it may make him even more popular. How do we know, that the affair has not been got up to dissolve on? They wanted a cry.

It is a little annoying for the Low Church party, wh:/ had acknowledged him as "the Man of God" – but so was King David, & he behaved even worse.[2]

I hear the young Duchess of Beaufort is using her most earnest efforts to prevent the other divorce. I hope she may be more successful, than Mr Osborne in his attempt to hinder the / duel. Colonel Armytage is a regular Valmont.[3]

The elections have been very favorable, tho' we may not have gained much in numbers: but the places we have lost are, as every-body knows, seats, that will be regained, whereas our victories are not only important, but permanent. I / hope, from what I hear from my Eton agent, who is also Colonel Vyse's, that we may retain the Royal Boro,' wh: is a triumph in itself for an Opposition. It will be close.[4]

I think the Registrations, however, are more important than the elections. I have gained 436 in my County.[5] It is a curious thing, that the / Registration cost me exactly 436£; so I count the expenditure as head money.

From what I hear, the Polish affair is virtually extinct. So much for recognising the rights of the insurrectionists as belligerents. The only result of the Polish Insurrection has been, that Gortschakoff, who, a little more than a year ago, was to / have been displaced, in order to secure England & Austria, has become the most popular & powerful Minister of the day. I think John Russell has exposed himself throughout this. Very priggish & pedantic; a policy, wh: was neither flesh, fish, nor fowl, nor &c.[6]

2 See **3865**&n2.

3 See **3865**&n3. Derby on 5 November would reply from Knowsley: 'I was inclined at first to think the Palmerston esclandre a canard; but I see the papers are taking it up, and insisting on full publicity; and I see a letter from the Solicitor to the Plaintiff, repudiating all idea of compromise. On the other hand I hear that the said Solicitor is rather a disreputable person (I don't know his name) who is notorious for getting up cases of this kind with the object of making money. The affair, however it may end, will not increase H.M's affection for Her Minister.' H B/XX/S/315.

4 At the 4 November by-election for the New Windsor seat left vacant by the death of G.W. Hope (L), Col R.H.H. Vyse (C) would defeat Capt A.D. Hayter (L) 287-236. The 'Eton agent' may have been Charles Stuart Voules, a Windsor solicitor at whose offices the Conservatives held meetings and who as Vyse's solicitor accompanied him on his canvass. *The Times* (24, 27 Oct 1863); *Law List* (1860). Derby (n3) would write: 'This morning we hear of the Windsor success ... It is satisfactory in every way: if the Castle influence was used against us, the triumph is the greater; if it was neutral while we are in opposition, we need not fear its being turned against us if we were in power.'

5 William Powell had sent a report to this effect from Newport Pagnell on 23 October. On 2 June 1863 he had acknowledged, with receipt, D's cheque for £160 'in payment of the balance due on Registration accounts for the year 1858'. H B/I/D/47,43.

6 Gorchakov throughout 1863 had defied attempts by Austria, France and England to intervene on behalf of the Polish nationalists, who, however, had been misled by what they saw as promises of material support. See **3859**&n3. Napier had reported to Russell on 27 October from St Petersburg that Gorchakov was pleased with Russell's 20 October despatch declaring the British government satisfied with Russia's assurances on Poland, thus effectively backing off from the confrontation. *AR* (1863, Chronicle) 330-51. Derby (n3) would write: 'Johnny seems to me to have got into such a muddle in every part of the world, that I do not see how we are to keep our hands off him. The Japanese affair is a very unfortunate one; but I do not think that the chief blame attaches to him; but his dealings with Denmark, Poland, and America have been such as to disgust all parties with whom he has had to do; while in the matter of the Ionian Islands, he has been positively out-manoeuvered by their Legislature'.

French finance seems, at last, blowing up; I hear very / serious.[7] It must alone prevent war. They say, the real object of the Empress' visit to Madrid was to prevent, if possible, the marriage of the Cte. de Paris with the daughter of the D. of Montpensier. If so, it has failed, for the Spanish match is to take place.[8] They say, that the Princess is of such dazzling & transcendent beauty, that / even the fires of Made. Castiliogne will pale before her.

Sir Henry Holland, who has just returned from a visit of six weeks to the Disunited States, speaks, with wonder, of the splendor & magnificence of life in New York. It is alike glaring & incomprehensible. He has seen nothing like it in any European capital. He was received with equal / hospitality.

What fun is Sir Robert Peel! Better than any farce in the good old days of Liston & Keeley. He met a friend of mine, the other day, at a Railway station, & complained very much of the manner in wh: he had been treated, especially by the "Times"[.][9] He had *not* knocked any voter / down; had *not* given orders to bonnet any elector; & when he drove thro' the town with Mrs Stovor,[10] it was only to fetch a lady from the Station, who had come down to them on a visit. He consulted Palmerston what he was to do, who told him it was useless to attempt to put himself right / with the public – & also, wh: is more important – gave it as his opinion to Sir Robert, that a general election wd. not mend matters for the Ministry.

I hope to hear, that you are better, or rather well – & I trust, that Lady Derby is quite so.[11]

Yours sincerely, | D.

TO: RALPH EARLE Hughenden [Sunday] 1 November 1863 3867

ORIGINAL: H H/LIFE

EDITORIAL COMMENT: From a typescript headed: 'D. to Mr. R.A. Earle, Hughenden, Nov. 1. '63.'

R.A. Earle, Esq.

7 Fould's financial statement in early December would predict that the 1863 deficit, although substantial (from the war in Mexico), would not turn out as bad as feared, because of an excellent harvest. He would warn, however, that the 1862 and 1863 deficits required prudence in all financial matters. *AR* (1860) 227-30.

8 See **3865**&n6.

9 See **3863**&n2. The report complained of was in *The Times* of 13 October 1863, augmented by a leader on the 15th.

10 According to *The Times* leader (n9), Peel had disappeared after the jostling incident in the morning, but then 'at twelve o'clock he returned, no longer to fight on foot in the *mêlée,* but, after the manner of one of HOMER's heroes, in a chariot and four, in which he drove through the town with one of his sisters, as if he was afraid he had not sufficiently identified his family with the election.' Evidently other gestures had been seen as significant, such as Peel pointing his stick at his father's statue. Peel's younger sister, Eliza (1832-1883), in 1855 had married Francis Stonor, second son of 5th Baron Camoys.

11 Derby would reply (n3): 'Many thanks for your gossiping letter of the 30th. for which at the time I was hardly in a condition to write my acknowledgments, my hand being still very weak after an attack of gout in *every* limb, which kept me in my bed for a fortnight. I am now however recovering'. After touching at length on aspects of the political situation he concluded: 'On the whole, it looks like a stormy Session, and the position of the Government seems very precarious: but how far are we prepared to take the responsibility of the consequences of success? I wish I saw my way more clearly, and were better prepared to meet a *danger* which appears growing more imminent. We must discuss this *very* seriously when we meet'.

My dear Earle,

"I hear, that Austria is certainly going to war about Poland" – you say in your letter of yesterday.[1]

Be so good as to let me know, and immediately, your authority for this.

Everything – the position of the Government, our own course, the future of Europe, depends upon such an event.

Pray let me hear, if possible, by return.[2]

Yours ever, D.

3868 TO: BARON LIONEL DE ROTHSCHILD Hughenden
[Sunday] 1 November 1863

ORIGINAL: ROTH RAL 000/848
EDITORIAL COMMENT: Paper imprinted 'Hughenden Manor'.

Confidential Nov. 1 1863

Baron de Rothschild | M.P.

Dear L.

Since we last met, I have heard, now & then, perplexing things about Austria, but having left London with an assurance, from authority, that she was resolved to act entirely with England, I have dismissed them from my mind.

They wrote to me from Frankfort, at the end of Septr, that positively, there had been communications betn. France & Austria; / that France had suggested, that, in the event of an European war, & the breaking-up of the Kingdom of Prussia, that Silesia sho[ul]d be restored to Austria, & that the latter had listened, with great interest, to this suggestion – no longer caring, in comparison with increased German influence, about her Italian possessions & position. Yesterday, I received a letter from the same quarter, no despicable one, in wh:, witht. any details, or reasons, were these words. "*I hear that Austria ~~will~~ is certainly going to war about Poland*"[.][1] /

1 See **3868**&n1 for the letter to Rothschild in which D quotes Earle's line before receiving Earle's reply.

2 Earle on 2 November would write that his source had been Somerset Beaumont, a banker and MP (L) for Newcastle-on-Tyne, recently involved in Austrian bank negotiations and on intimate terms with Austrian ministers. He had forewarned Earle of Austria's rejection of France, as well as of the Frankfort Congress. Cautious about the possibility of war, he cited an *Observer* article of 25 October (reprinted from the Vienna *Press*), that summed up Austrian intentions, more hostile to Russia than friendly to Poland, and proposing little reconstruction other than the cession of Gallicia and perhaps Posen in return for Silesia. Earle continued: 'The two last numbers of the Memorial diplomatic seem to confirm Beaumont's news, for the attempt to establish a close alliance last summer, between Austria & France, would hardly have been disclosed, after so many months, if it had no bearing upon the present phase, the change wh: Francis-Joseph's sentiments have undergone upon the Mexican Empire (to wh: he was originally most averse) seems to indicate a decided reaction, in favor of France. This is all I know. There is nothing positive & the policy of Austria is so vacillating, that it wd. be difficult to accept the appearances of the moment, as safely guiding us to the right interpretation of her intentions. Nevertheless, I am disposed, on the whole, to believe that the question of war against Russia & alliance with France, is at present very seriously entertained at Vienna.' H B/XX/E/297. See further **3869**&nn8&11 and **3870**&n2.

---

1 D's source is Earle (see **3867**&n2), who on 1 October, on his return from Germany, had written: 'I was at Frankfort during the Congress & have one or two things to tell you, of what I there learnt. The elements of confusion in Europe seem rather to increase.' In a postscript to his 8 October letter (**3859**n3), he had written: 'It is inconceivable that the Govt. shd. have failed to stay the Holstein business. When I arrived at

What can all this mean? I take it for granted, that you know much more about it, than I do; but thought it better to send this line.[2]

England is in such a commanding position, now, compared with all other states, that a British Minister ought to dictate the policy of Europe. But I, really, from what has passed, have no confidence in your late colleague,[3] & the present state of Prussia would / facilitate the Silesian project.

I hope it is a *canard,* but it does not come from a duck catcher.

Yrs ever, | D.

TO: LORD STANLEY   Hughenden [Wednesday] 4 November 1863   3869

ORIGINAL: DBP Box 42/7

PUBLICATION HISTORY: Weintraub *Disraeli* 400, a sentence fragment

EDITORIAL COMMENT: Paper imprinted 'Hughenden Manor'. Endorsed by Stanley on the last page: 'Disraeli. Nov. 63'. *Sic:* terrors; Kane.

---

confidl., except, of course, to the Captain

Rt Honble | Lord Stanley, M. P.   Nov 4 1863

Dear Stanley.

Knowsley & Hughn must have awakened from their lethargy about the same time, for a letter of mine, to the Captain, must have almost crossed yrs.[1]

I am glad to hear, that you are well, & to hear it / from yourself. I never was better. I have not seen the paragraph about my approaching dissolution, tho,' of course, I have heard of it.[2] It did not frighten me. Death, perhaps, has less terrors for me, than for most men, as my biography has been written in my lifetime.[3]

I was going to tell you, that the Pam: scandal[4] was / not compromised, but the "Star", this morning, has anticipated me. When writs are once issued in such matters, they are never compromised. The Plaintiff is a clergyman. Ld. P's friends treat it, as a case of conspiracy & extortion. Of course; life is conspiracy and extortion. If the Revd. Mr. Kane really contemplated getting a good round sum / out of a man, who is distrained on even for his taxes, & has an action brought against him by his

Frankfort, a German Plenipo: told me it was "très *Krave* (grave)" & that they were really going to act.' On 29 October he had written: 'I hear that Austria is certainly going to war about Poland.' H B/XX/E/293-6.

2 Rothschild's reply (if any) has not been found.

3 Russell had been Rothschild's constituency colleague for the city of London until 30 July 1861, when he had been elevated to the Lords as Earl Russell.

---

1 See **3866**. Stanley had written from Knowsley on 31 October: 'I have not troubled you for these three months, politics being dead; indeed it seems as if we were all subsiding into country squires, in default of more exciting pursuits.' H B/XX/S/713.

2 See **3858**&n1. Stanley (n1) had written: 'How are you? reports of your being invalided have reached me, but knowing how little liable you are to illness, I treated them as inventions of the enemy. I hope they are so.'

3 A third book-length biography of D was published in 1863, *Disraeli, the author, orator, and statesman* (Darton and Hodge), by John Mill. Stewart *Writings* 123 (#753).

4 See **3865**&n2 and **3866**&nn2-3. Stanley (n1) had written: 'The Palmerston scandal seems to have passed off – was it ever more than an attempt to extort money? It is lucky, that none of what are called our newspapers have taken it up.'

trainer,[5] he did not know his [*illegible deletion*] ↑*terrain.*↓ Ready money never was Pam's forte. But why didn't Kane ask for a Bishoprick?[6]

To make affairs on this subject more supremely ludicrous, & perhaps, ultimately, something serious, Mr. U.S. Layard is also a co-rrespondent ↑in the same Court↓; of course, in another case.[7] / The Queen will have enough to do, if she conducts the F. O. from all, that reaches me.[8] It is curious, that, having got rid of Hanover, we still experience the inconveniences of not having indigenous sovereigns. It's a pity, that yr house couldn't have managed the affair, thro' old Lady Margaret,[9] or somehow. But I dare say, yr father wd. prefer being Premier to Sovereign.

Did Lord Clarendon tell / you of any approaches made betn. France & Austria? They wrote to me, from Frankfort, to that effect, but I treated it as a canard, tho' the news did not come from duck catchers. From what I heard a few days back, I believe the matter is grave. What think you of an alliance betn. France, Italy, & Austria – & the partition of Prussia? Be sure, that the proposition has been made, & not rejected. / Austria is to obtain the restoration of Silesia after having lost it for more than a century, & to become a great German power. Posen, & Gallicia, to be both relinquished. What France will have, we all know. As the war is to commence for Polish independence, England, at least, Ld Russell, will be checkmated from any interference.[10]

If this combination takes place, the whole politics of / Europe will be changed. Who is to ride this whirlwind, & direct this storm?

In this debacle of the Prussian Monarchy, wh: has no nationality, Saxony will want her old provinces ↑back,↓ wh: we have guaranteed to Prussia, but, perhaps, the Elector of Brandenburgh will not insist upon the remnant of his rights.[11]

5 The trainer of Palmerston's racehorses was John Day, whose stable was at Danebury, twelve miles from Palmerston's country home at Broadlands. Ridley *Palmerston* 282.

6 BH on 31 October had run a précis of an earlier *Star* piece (see **3872**n3), which had not actually named names, but given hints broad enough to identify Palmerston as co-respondent in a divorce case, 'a clergyman's wife being the respondent'. On 7 November it would publish an update naming names, and a 'Thursday' report from its own correspondent: 'The "great divorce case" was too delicate a matter to be touched seriously last week, but now that ... the solicitors for the Petitioner and Respondent have written letters to the *Star* and *Morning Herald* on the subject, there is no reason why I should pretend ignorance of the matter. Mr. Horsley, the solicitor for the respondent, declares that no compromise has been or will be attempted, and says that all his client desires is the appearance of the Petitioner in court, in order that he may be thoroughly exposed. He is not a clergyman, never was a clergyman, but is a person of inferior position'. It pointed out (as Derby had done earlier – see **3866**n3) that the lawyers for the plaintiff were notorious for making money from divorce cases and actually advertised for business.

7 Earle on 2 November had mentioned that 'Layard is also to be a co-respondent in the Divorce Court.' H B/XX/E/297. The unmarried A.H. Layard had been under-secretary in the foreign office since 15 August 1861. The divorce case in which he was involved has not been found.

8 Stanley (n1) had written: 'Ld Clarendon was here about a month back: he spoke of the Queen as very hard to manage, especially in foreign affairs: bent on making her personal influence felt, but not knowing how to set about it. This is just what one might have expected.'

9 Lady Margaret Beaufort (1443-1509), mother of King Henry VII, in 1472 had married fourthly 2nd Baron Stanley (his second marriage), created Earl of Derby 1485.

10 See **3867**&n2 and *cf* **3868**&n1.

11 D is presumably imagining that the reversion of Prussia to something like its status before the creation of Prussian royalty in 1701 could also involve a reversion to the earlier titles of Elector (and Margrave) of Brandenburg held by the Dukes of Prussia, even though the Holy Roman Empire had ended in 1806.

Let me know, whether Ld Clarendon hinted at anything of this kind. In 8 & 40 hours, the words, or the silence, of the great Imperial [*illegible deletion*] Sphinx may throw some light on it. ↑All my hope is in the proverbial vacillation of Austria.↓[12]

Yrs ever | D.

TO: RALPH EARLE Hughenden [Thursday] 5 November 1863 3870

ORIGINAL: H H/LIFE

EDITORIAL COMMENT: From a typescript headed: 'D. to Mr. R.A. Earle, Hughenden, Nov. 5. '63.'

My dear Earle,

Many thanks for your letter.[1] The Imperial Sphinx is now speaking, but I shall know nothing of it until tomorrow. Write me a line, if you have time.[2] I have heard from Knowsley. I don't think the gout is very severe.[3]

I never, myself, was better, and therefore won't show. If I were really indisposed, I would come up directly, and well made up.[4]

I can't tear myself away from this place. This is my great planting time; and I have got a new batch of workmen in the dining room, putting down a new floor.[5] I feel, if I leave any workmen here, they never will go out.

Is there any real foundation for the P. scandal?[6] ....

12 Napoleon would make a speech at the opening of chambers on 5 November; see **3870**n2 for Earle's sinister reading of it.

---

1 See **3867**n2.

2 On 6 November Earle would reply from the Anglo-Austrian Bank, 10 Birching Lane, Lombard Street: 'The [Emperor's 5 November Chambers-opening] speech seems to me most alarming. En resúmé [*sic*], it amounts to this, – that there is nothing but a Congress, (wh. we know to be impracticable,) between our present position & a European war. The Congress he wants is the CONSTITUENT assembly, wh: he has been trying to convene, ever since Villafranca, to ratify annexations & rectify frontiers. By this overture, it seems to me that England, far more than Russia, is placed in dilemma, for it is by *us* & *not* by Russia, that this Congress, wh: is announced as the means to the maintenance of peace & to a general disarmament, has been perseveringly opposed ... I shd. like to know your impression of the speech. That it was considered pacific here did not surprise me, for they were foolish enough to suppose that the Emperor was going to announce war. As if he wd. declare in November, a war wh: he need not commence before April or May!' H B/XX/E/298. See further **3874**&nn2-3.

3 Stanley (see **3869**n1) had written to D from Knowsley: 'My father is still and for a fortnight has been in the gout; the attack was at no time severe, and is now passing off. On the whole, his health and spirits have been better this year than for many seasons past. He is not keen about politics, but that will come again.'

4 Earle (n1) had asked: 'When are you coming up? Is not Hughenden a little damp & leafy for you, at this season? The world has taken it into it's [*sic*] head that you are ill & so it wd. be perhaps advisable to put in an appearance ere very long.' On 6 November (n2) he would be 'delighted to hear yr. flourishing bulletin.' *BH* on 7 November would reprint an item from the *Standard,* 'in reply to numerous inquiries, that there is no foundation for the reports that have appeared in the columns of some of our contemporaries respecting the indisposition of Mr. Disraeli. We are happy to say that the right hon. gentleman was never in better health.'

5 On 13 October MA recorded paying 3*s* 9*d* for carriage of an Axminster dining room carpet, which had cost £33 10*s*, repaid to her by D on 30 November. H acc. See also Appendix VIII.

6 See **3869**n6. Earle (n2) would reply: 'I dont know *what* to think of Pam's business[;] the solicitor [Thomas Wells] & the petitioner his client [O'Kane], are both loose fish, so I fear it may be a plant. They say *she* [Mrs O'Kane] was Nursery Governess at Lady Jocelyn's.' *BH* on 7 November would identify the firm acting for the O'Kanes as Weston and Wells, of 47 Moorgate Street; *ie,* Thomas Wells, solicitor, and Henry Weston, merchant. *LPOD* (1864).

3871 TO: PHILIP ROSE [Hughenden] Thursday 5 November 1863

ORIGINAL: H R/I/A/167
COVER: Philip Rose Esqr | D.
EDITORIAL COMMENT: There is no salutation.

Thursday Nov 5. 63

Is there any real foundation for the P. scandal![1]

Windsor – glorious![2]

Yrs ever | D.

3872 TO: SARAH BRYDGES WILLYAMS Hughenden [Thursday] 5 November 1863

ORIGINAL: RTC [248]
PUBLICATION HISTORY: M&B IV 340, dated at Hughenden, 5 November 1863, omitting the first, fifth and sixth paragraphs; Blake 420, 434, dated 5 November 1863, extracts from the second and fifth paragraphs
EDITORIAL COMMENT: Paper imprinted 'Hughenden Manor'. There is no salutation. *Sic:* transcendant; Castiliogne. This is D's last letter to SBW.

Nov. 5. 1863

I had the pleasure of sending you a Hughenden hare yesterday, & a cock pheasant, of which my keeper was very proud. I hope you kept them for yourself.

The "great Imperial Sphinx" is at this moment speaking.[1] I shall not know the mysterious utterances until tomorrow, & shall judge of his conduct, as much by his silence, as his words. The world is very alarmed, & very restless. Altho' England appears to have backed out of the possible war, / there are fears, that the French Ruler has outwitted us, & that by an alliance with Austria, & the aid of the Italian armies, he may cure the partition of Poland by a partition of Prussia!

Austria, in that case, to regain Silesia, wh: Frederick the Great won, a century ago, from Maria Theresa;[2] France to have the Rhine; & Gallicia & Posen to be restored to Poland. If this happen, it will give altogether a new form & color to European politics. The Queen is / much alarmed for the future throne of her daughter, the Princess Royal of Prussia, but as the war will be waged for the relief of Poland, of wh: England has unwisely approved, & to wh:, in theory, she is pledged, we shall really be checkmated, & scarcely could find an excuse to interfere, even if the nation wished.

1 Rose would respond from Victoria Street next day (6 November) with thanks for D's cheque for £500: 'Everyone believes that there is substantial foundation for the Scandal tho' the parties are disreputable and the object no doubt was extortion. There are fifty different rumours afloat but I shall know all particulars that the Plaintiffs attorney can supply in a day or two as a person we know is acquainted with [Thomas] Wells [solicitor for the plaintiff] and has promised to let me know. I am rather sorry that Hamber [editor of the *Standard*] touches the subject so soon & in such a vulgar way. He ought merely to have copied the Star paragraphs.' H B/XX/R/16. See **3869**n6.

2 For the victory at Windsor, see **3866**n4.

1 See **3870**n2.

2 Frederick II (1712-1786), The Great, King of Prussia 1740-86, in 1740-2 conquered and in 1756-63 (the Seven Years' War) confirmed possession of Silesia, after the succession in 1740 of Empress Maria Theresa (1717-1780), Queen of Hungary and Bohemia and Archduchess of Austria, instigated several foreign claims to her dominions.

So, you see, there is a good deal on the cards.

Lord Palmerston's almost absurd escapade, of wh:, I believe Mrs D. informed you,[3] is probably a case of extortion founded on some slight / imprudence – &, it is to be hoped, will evaporate.

They say the real cause of the Empress of the French going to Madrid, was to prevent a marriage between the Comte de Paris & the daughter of the Duc de Montpensier. If so, the mission failed, for the marriage is to take place, & the Montpensier Princess is described of such a transcendant & dazzling beauty, that even the splendor of Made. de Castiliogne will pale before it.[4]

Adieu! We shall soon meet.

Yrs ever, | D.

TO: LORD CARRINGTON Hughenden [Saturday] 7 November 1863 **3873**

ORIGINAL: CARR [19]

EDITORIAL COMMENT: Endorsed in another hand on the fourth page: 'Copy of letter from Right Honble B. Disraeli to *Lord Carington* on subject of C. Carington coming forward as member for Bucks – *Nov 7. 1863*.' *Sic:* Carington; seems; Dupré; realy.

Confidential Hughenden Manor | Novemr 7. 1863

The Lord Carington

My dear Lord

I hope Lord Chesham may flicker on,[1] but we ought to be prepared for all contingencies.

If Charley were of age there would be a natural solution of our difficulties which I know would be hailed by all persons & parties, & although I had always cherished the hope that he might have entered public life under my auspices, & not have identified himself with what I hold to be an exhausted party, still mere personal disappointments, though in this instance, great, must be endured.[2]

But what are we to do, in case he is not of age, when the crisis arrives?

At present there seems to me only two courses, either that you should produce a warming pan, always a difficult, sometimes a hazardous proceeding or that some Conservative of high county standing should come in, & Charley at the impending General Election should take the Seat of Dupré who insists on retiring.[3]

3 MA on 30 October had written to SBW: 'I send you the Evening Star of Oct. 27th., because there is a Paragraph in it, which causes the greatest possible excitement. Page 4. Dizzys letters from Town say *on authority*, that the persons alluded to are Lord Palmerston & a Mrs. Cane, in June 1863 at Cambridge House. How improbable – but it is believed – as the worst is taken out'. RTC [484Q].

4 See **3865**&n6.

---

1 Lord Chesham would live only three more days, until 10 November, when he would be succeeded by his son, W.G. Cavendish, currently D's Liberal colleague for Bucks.

2 Lord Carrington's eldest surviving son, Charles Robert Carrington (1843-1928), would not be 21 until 16 May 1864. He would be MP (L) for Wycombe 1865-8, when he would succeed his father as 3rd Baron Carrington, governor of New South Wales 1885-90, president of the board of agriculture and fisheries 1905-11, lord privy seal 1911-12, created Earl Carrington 1895, Marquess of Lincolnshire 1912.

3 On 29 December, Robert Bateson Harvey would win the vacant seat for the Conservatives with an overwhelming majority; see **3879**&n1, **3880**&n2 and **3881**&nn1&3. In the event, Du Pre would not retire until 1874.

I give you my impressions with entire frankness, but I realy wish to know your Lordships views & wishes. Believe me I shall receive them with that perfect confidence & real friendship which I always hope to cherish with you & your house[.][4]

Sincerely yours | B. Disraeli

3874 TO: RALPH EARLE Hughenden [Monday] 8 November 1863

ORIGINAL: H H/LIFE

PUBLICATION HISTORY: M&B IV 341, dated November [1863], the fourth paragraph; Blake 430, dated November [1863], the fourth paragraph

EDITORIAL COMMENT: From a typescript headed: 'D. to Mr. R.A. Earle, Hughenden, Nov. 8. '63.'

My dear Earle,

Thanks for your notes.[1] Write when you have time.[2]

The whole thing seems to me a masterpiece: he has muzzled the faction of the Chambers: checkmated the English Government: and gained time.

If he make his book with Austria, there will be war in the Spring, and backed by the Italian armies, the combination must be irresistible.

Prussia, without Nationality, the principle of the day, is clearly the subject for partition.

The restoration of Silesia, mainly Catholic, to Austria, will be in harmony with that principle.[3]

4 Carrington would acknowledge D's letter from Whitehall on 10 November and write more fully on the 12th: 'You may suppose how painful it would have been to me to discuss a subject contingent on the death of one of the oldest & most valued of my friends, but the crisis having arrived I assure you that I received your communication with a full sense of the friendly feelings which have prompted it. I agree with you in thinking a temporary substitute is not desirable, & if I could assure my friends that Mr Dupré would in fact make the Vacancy at the next Election they would I think be satisfied to raise no contest at the present time, & I would endeavour to persuade them to take this course. There is an impression that Mr Duprés course may be influenced by future events, but if you can enable me to assure my friends that Mr Dupré would, under any contingency, make the Vacancy I would lose no time in obtaining their sentiments. Could not a communication to this effect be obtained from Mr Dupré by Monday? I understand that he is abroad. Let me add that I have not yet mentioned the subject to my friends without whose sanction & knowledge of the facts I am sure you will agree I ought not to pledge myself.' H B/XXI/C/74; CARR 39 [a copy]. See further **3878**.

---

1 See **3870**&nn1-6.

2 Earle had written on 7 November (postmarked at High Wycombe on the 8th): 'Everything seems to confirm the view, wh: in the very first instance, I was disposed to take of the Emperor's speech, altho' the opposite opinion was so general that I could not but doubt whether I had read it aright. The fall at the French bourse can no longer be explained, as it was last Thursday, as the consequence of the increase in the rate of discount here, – for it continued throughout yesterday. At Vienna, too, the french policy is looked upon as warlike. Lord Clarendon does not concur in this view. It seems the Prussian family are in great alarm. The Princess said to Lord C the other day – "I begin to fear I shall live to see my children beggars & outcasts on the face of the earth".' H B/XX/E/299.

3 Earle would respond on 9 November: 'Many thanks for the interesting despatch. All seems to depend upon Austria's attitude. Supposing her to decline the partition, the Emperor wd. hardly venture with Italy alone to make war upon all Germany & Russia. The ~~alliance~~ cooperation of Italy, seems to render the neutrality of Austria out of the question. What will happen, if Russia accept the congress & we decline? All the french papers speak of our policy with the greatest contempt.' H B/XX/E/300.

TO: SIR JOHN PAKINGTON — Hughenden [Sunday] 8 November 1863 — 3875

ORIGINAL: WRC 705:349 BA 3835/7(ii)17
EDITORIAL COMMENT: Paper imprinted 'Hughenden Manor'. *Sic:* less terrors; conveniencies.

Private Nov. 8 1863

Rt Honble | Sir Jno. S. Pakington Bart | G.C.B.

My dear Pakington,

I was glad to hear from you.[1]

I was never better, & have not, for a moment, been unwell. I heard of, but have not seen, the paragraph announcing my approaching dissolution. It did not frighten me: perhaps / death has less terrors for a man, whose biography has been written in his life-time.[2]

I heard from Ld Derby on the 5th. Inst. He was then weak, but wrote in excellent spirits. Indeed, I think he might well be. A leader of Opposition must be a glutton, who is not satisfied with what has occurred during the / recess.[3]

You must have enjoyed Paris.[4] We have never left this place for 4 & 20 hours. You may just, perhaps, remember Mrs Disraeli showing you some drawings of what we were doing, or proposing to do, here. The workmen have been here now, more than a year, & they have not yet / entirely disappeared. She has been very much amused, wh: is something for your money.[5] As Xmas approaches, I get more gloomy.

I hope, however, that you & Lady Pakington will come & see us next year, wh: will go a great way to compensate for all my conveniencies.

Our kind remembrances to her.

Yours sincerely, | D.

TO: ROBERT E. ROBERTS — Hughenden [Monday] 9 November 1863 — 3876

ORIGINAL: MOPSIK [144]

Hughenden Manor | Nov. 9. 1863

Mr Disraeli has only received Mr Roberts' accts. within a few days, & has not yet been able to examine them.[1]

There are some points respecting the works, performed at Hughenden, wh: will require observation. Mr Disraeli is leaving this place to day, for Devonshire, sud-

1 Pakington had written from Westwood Park on 6 November to ask D to confirm reports that he was healthy: 'No regiment can afford to have *both* the Field Officers sick, & Lord Derby has only just recovered, if he has recovered, from a bad attack of gout!' H B/XX/P/72.

2 *Cf* **3869**&n3.

3 See **3866**nn3,4,6,11 for Derby's 5 November letter. Pakington (n1) had remarked: 'I think there seems at last, to be a favourable turn in our affairs. Surely Pam in the Divorce Court, Peel at Tamworth, & Johnny's Foreign policy, must have some effect on the political future!'

4 Pakington (n1) had written: 'After six weeks in France, during which I was charmed with L.N's doings in Paris, I have been quietly here, & my life varied only by local engagements.'

5 See Introduction pp xv-xvi.

---

1 There is in H a very rough sheet of names and figures totalling £3,156.12.3 that includes sums for Roberts in 1863, the first undated (£500), others dated 18 February (£200), 24 June (£200), 13 August (£300) and 11 November (£400), and one for Lamb dated 8 May (£200). H A/V/F/41.

denly,[2] but, / in consequence of Mr Roberts' urgent letter, has written him a further order, on other side, for £400.[3]

Mr Disraeli expects to see Mr Lamb in town very shortly, when he will balance & settle all accts.

3876A TO: CHARLES CLUBBE — Torquay [Thursday] 12 November 1863

ORIGINAL: RIC [020]

COVER: The | Revd. C. W. Clubbe | A.M. | Hughenden | High Wycomb | *B. Disraeli*

POSTMARKS: in circle: C | TORQUAY | NO 12 | 63; the stamp has been cut out; on verso, in circle: HIGH WYCOMBE | A | NO 13 | 63

EDITORIAL COMMENT: Black-edged envelope and paper. *Dating:* by context and postmarks. *Sic:* C.C.; Lègatee; Wycomb (twice); Simmons.

The | Rev: C.C. Clubbe | A.M. — Royal Hotel | Torquay

My dear Mr Clubbe,

Mrs. Brydges Willyams of Mount Braddon, who has appointed me her residuary Lègatee & Executor, has expressed, in her will, her desire to / be buried in my vault at Hughenden[.]

Would you have the great kindness to give the necessary directions in this matter, & also generally as regards her funeral.

I propose, that the corpse, attended by my servant, should be moved from / this place by a night train, wh:, I am told, is the custom; that it shd. be met, at the Wycomb station, by a hearse, & carried to Hughenden House, where it shd. rest, until interment, in the saloon. /

I wish the funeral to be as quiet, & simple, as possible: I shall be the only mourner.

Would you have the kindness to give instructions to Simmons in this matter.[1]

I only require the hearse / to take up the body to Hughenden: not to be mixed up with the funeral. Will you let me know, by return if possible, when you think you will be prepared.

Mrs. Brydges Willyams died yesterday morning, at / five o'ck:

I will then let you know exactly, & in more detail, when, & how, the body will arrive, so that you may order Simmons accordingly.

Mrs Disraeli will remain / here at present.

2 See **3877**&n1.

3 R.E. Roberts, builder, had written from 32 Rheidol Terrace, Islington N, on 7 November, to ask D for immediate payment of the balance owing him, explaining that he was approaching D directly because he had a heavy amount to meet on Thursday (12th) and had just learned that Lamb was out of town for nine or ten days. H B/XX/R/17a. On 10 November Roberts would send D a receipt for £400 'on account of work done at Hughenden Manor' with a note on the other side that he was 'greatly obliged'. H A/VII/E/10; *LPOD* (1864).

---

1 Future invoices (see **3883A**n2) would be drawn on stationery dated at High Wycombe and headed 'Herbert Simmonds. Undertaker. Appraiser. Auctioneer. and Estate Agent.' (*Cf* V **1877**&n3.) The one dated 18 November itemized a 'crape hatband scarf & gloves for mourner' at £1.9.9, 'Silk hatband scarf & gloves for Clergyman' at £1.17.3, and further hatbands and gloves, plus the use of the pall and his own fee for attendance 'at interment and previously' for a subtotal of £12.13.3. The 'removal to Hughenden, and Interment' is listed at £4, with another £2.2.0 for refreshments for the 'Bearers and assistant attendance'. The funeral carriage with a pair of horses cost £1.10.0, and the coachman £0.3.0. H A/V/G/148ad,ag. See further **3878A**&n1.

She joins me in hopes, that Mrs Clubbe is going on quite well, & in kind remembrances to you both.

Yrs faithfully, | *B. Disraeli*

TO: JAMES BUTLER Torquay [Friday] 13 November 1863 **3877**

ORIGINAL: PRIN Parrish Collection AM 21169

PUBLICATION HISTORY: Weintraub *Disraeli* 402, dated 13 November [1863], parts of the fourth and sixth paragraphs; Weintraub *Charlotte and Lionel* 189, undated, part of the fourth paragraph

EDITORIAL COMMENT: Black-edged paper. In the seventh paragraph, D has altered '12th' to read '11th'. *Sic:* I have I have.

Hon: James Butler Torquay | Nov. 13. 1863

Dear Mr Butler,

We were summoned here to attend the last hour of our kind & dear old friend – but were too late.[1]

Her illness was short & sudden. A few days before, she was about paying visits, & a few weeks before, / she actually walked to the Post Office, & walked back up that steep hill!

I had also received a letter from her, about a week before her decease, written with great liveliness, & in her usual decided handwriting.[2]

She has left many legacies; chiefly to her god-children – & from the death of my / co-executor,[3] I am obliged to undertake the whole management of her affairs.

She has, in her will, expressed her wish to be buried in my vault at Hughenden, & the moment I have I have fulfilled her intentions, I shall ↑place↓ that documentation in the hands of my lawyer to do all that is proper.[4]

I could not, however, refrain from writing myself to / an old acquaintance, & to inform you, that your daughter is left a legacy of 500: Consols.[5]

Mrs Brydges Willyams died on ↑Wednesday↓ the 11th:, the morning of our arrival.

1 SBW's doctor, I.B. Toogood (see n6), had written at 4 o'clock on Sunday 8 November: 'Yr old Friend Mrs B Willyams is very ill, so ill indeed that her recovery is very improbable. There is no one about her, but her Maid Servants & therefore I think it BEST to inform you of her state. I will write again, & telegraph if necessary.' On the 10th he had written again: 'Mrs Willyams was so ill last night, that I thought it impossible for her to go on many hours. She was quite unconscious, & had taken no sustenance for many days. This morning she has rallied a little, but she is still very incoherent, & takes little, or no food. She may live still a day, or two. I have visited her regularly, – & seen that she is well attended to. I will telegram to you when necessary & I suppose you will be in touch.' RTC [496-7Q]. MA recorded that SBW had died at 5 *am* on the 11th. H acc. On the 18th, Lady Janet Wilmot Chetwode would write to D that SBW 'would not have you sent for till too late because "you were a Statesman & must not be disturbed."' H A/V/G/144.

2 This letter has not been found; the last from SBW in the Rothschild collection is dated 14 October 1863, with no salutation, and merely expresses thanks for 'an airy Basket of delicious Game.' RTC [483Q].

3 See **3487**&n1. This list of eleven monetary legacies in D's hand totals £6,450. RTC [489Q]. SBW's will (proved 10 December 1863) lists additional bequests of personal items, *eg*, to her brother-in-law Humphry. H R/II/D/8. For D's share, see VI **2493**&n1 and, in this volume, **3887**&n1.

4 See illustration p lxi and **3884**&nn1&2.

5 The list of bequests (n3) includes one of £500 to Emily Sarah Fitzgerald Butler (1838-1925), the James Butlers' eldest daughter, who in 1865 would marry Walter Harvey Thursby Pelham. For her relationship with her godmother see VII **3007**n2.

Mr. Toogood[6] has reported her age to the Registrar as 102 completed. I cannot find in her papers the slightest clue to this matter, & will not take the responsibility of sanctioning the statement.[7]

Mrs. Disraeli unites with me in kind remembrances to Mrs Butler.

very faithfully yrs | *B. Disraeli*[8]

3878 TO: LORD CARRINGTON Torquay, 13 November 1863

ORIGINAL: CARR [20, 44, 45]

COVER: *Private & Immediate* | The | Lord Carington | Whitehall | *B Disraeli*

EDITORIAL COMMENT: There are two copies of this letter (CARR20) and the last page of the MS letter (CARR44) with the address (CARR45) on its verso. Endorsed in another hand on the fourth page of the first copy: 'Copy of letter from Right Honble B Disraeli to Lord *Carington* Nov *13. 1863*'; and on the second copy: 'The R. Honble B Disraeli to Lord Carington Nov. 13, 1863.' There are minor differences between the two copies, the first of which has been used here for the part missing from the MS. *Sic:* Carington.

[CARR20:] Torquay Nov 13 1863

My dear Lord,

Your letter[1] only reached me this morning & so far as the Telegraph will aid, I have moved in every necessary quarter to bring about a result, which wisdom & friendship alike prompt.

I was summoned here to attend the last hour of a kind & faithful friend, but arrived too late. Being the sole Executor, I have much to do & am prevented from doing as much as I could wish in the matter on which your Lord[shi]p has done me the [CARR44:] honor of writing to me. But I am sanguine, that all will be right.[2]

Ever, dear Ld Carington, | faithfully yours | *B. Disraeli*[3]

6 Dr Isaac Baruch Toogood, of Torquay, MRCS (Eng) 1833, Lic. Soc. Apoth. (Lond) 1833, registered 1 January 1859. *Medical Register* (1879).

7 In the Hughenden burial register (an 1874 copy) her age is given as 94. RTC [500Q].

8 On 18 November from Baden Baden Butler would acknowledge D's 'considerate and thoughtful letter': 'she had been to me and mine for seven & twenty years too staunch a friend not to sadden at her loss ... My daughter begs me to assure you that she is grateful for the handsome legacy left to her by her God Mother and feels as I do that Mrs. Willyams could not have chosen a more efficient person than yourself to undertake the disposal of all her wordly goods. May I still hope that you will comply with her kind request to provide for me when you are in power. I have a large family to provide for.' H A/V/G/145.

---

1 See **3873**n4.

2 Carrington would reply from Whitehall next day (14 November): 'I collect from your letter that the old Lady is no more & things are as they ought to be. With all respect to her memory, with a just appreciation of her society when amongst us, no one of yr friends is more pleased to think that she has kept the word she gave.' H B/XXI/C/75. See **3877**&n3, **3885**n2 and **3887**&n1.

3 The following epitaph to the recently deceased Lord Chesham appears after D's signature in both copies, but not in the MS letter, and it is not clear why the copyist added it to the letter: [CARR20:]

Here lies Charles Cavendish of honor clear
He lived a Gentleman, & died a Peer.

TO: CHARLES CLUBBE Torquay [Saturday] 14 November 1863 3878A

ORIGINAL: RIC [021]
COVER: The | Revd. C.W. Clubbe | A.M. | Hughenden Vicarage | High Wycomb | *B. Disraeli*
POSTMARKS: in circle: C | TORQUAY | NO 14 | 63; stamp removed
EDITORIAL COMMENT: Black-edged envelope and paper. *Sic:* Simmons; Wycomb (twice).

The | Rev. C.W. Clubbe | A.M. Torquay, Nov 14/ 63

My dear Mr Clubbe,

Many thanks for yr letter received this morning.

I decide on a new vault, &, with that view, will arrange for the burial on Thursday next.

It is / a leaden coffin, hermetically sealed, the Railway requiring this security – so the Burials Act cd. not touch us, but the Burials Act, tho' that is of no consequence now, does not apply to our Country churches.[1]

Unless I hear from you to the contrary, I will / write to Simmons to let him know when a hearse shall be in attendance at Wycomb Station, to bring the body to Hughenden.[2]

Our very kind remembrances to Mrs. Clubbe.

Yrs sincerely, | D.

TO: RALPH EARLE Torquay [Sunday] 15 November 1863 3879

ORIGINAL: H H/LIFE
EDITORIAL COMMENT: From a typescript headed 'D. to Mr. R.A. Earle, Torquay, Nov. 15. '63.'

My dear Earle,

I am here, summoned to the last hour of a kind, and faithful, friend, but arrived too late. Being her sole executor, I cannot personally interfere about the County at present, but I have written all letters that are necessary.....[1]

TO: PHILIP ROSE Torquay [Tuesday] 17 November 1863 3880

ORIGINAL: H R/I/A/168
PUBLICATION HISTORY: Bradford 247, dated 17 November 1863, extract from the first paragraph

Private Torquay. Nov 17. 63

P. Rose Esq

My dear Rose,

I have been remiss in not writing before to so faithful a friend, to say, that what has

1 See **3884**&nn1&2 for Clubbe's correspondence at this time.
2 D's letter, if written, has not been found.

---

1 Earle had written on 13 November about the Bucks vacancy (for which see **3873**&nn1-4): 'Spofforth wishes you to be informed that he has heard from H. Bull of Aylesbury ... that they have agreed to contest the seat, in the event even of the leaders declining to do so, & that Harvey of Langley Park is spoken of as a probable candidate. I ... have told S that you were quite prepared for Lord C's death & for an attack upon the seat.' Earle would write again to D at Torquay on 23 and 25 November, first of all reporting that there would be a contest at Bucks, and then at great length making suggestions for D's speech on the hustings and for possible appointments if the Conservatives were asked to form a government, taking it for granted that D would be going to the India office. H B/XX/E/301-3.

happened here is all that we could have wished, & that my kind & faithful friend has never / swerved from her purpose.[1]

I have, however, been inundated with business, & the County vacancy occurring in the midst, – altho' I had foreseen the contingency, &, so far as I cd., provided for it – has really nearly distracted me. I think the telegraph between Torquay / & Stowe has not stopped for the last four days. All is right in that matter, & I only hope there may be a contest.[2]

Mrs Brydges Willyams is to be buried at Hughenden on Thursday, but I must return here immediately after the funeral.

I / was very sorry I was obliged to give up dining with you to meet the Bishop.[3] I hope Mrs Rose got my letter. Hers ~~le~~ came to me by the very post that summoned me here.

Yrs ever, | D.

3881 TO: LORD DERBY — Torquay [Tuesday] 17 November 1863

ORIGINAL: DBP Box 146/1

EDITORIAL COMMENT: Black-edged paper. Endorsed by Derby upside down at the bottom of the fourth page: '*Ansd* Disraeli B'. *Sic:* Caringtons.

Rt Honble. | The Earl of Derby | K. G. — Torquay Novr. 17. 63

My dear Lord,

Mr Harvey, of Langley Park, has agreed to stand for our County, & his address will be out on Wednesday.[1]

He will win: to clutch the third seat of an undivided / county from such potentates, as the Cavendishes & the Caringtons, is very important, &, at this moment, very significant.

1 See **3877**&n3 and **3887**&n1. Rose had written from Victoria Street on 16 November: 'Your note to Mrs. Rose [*not found*] made me aware of the cause of your journey to Torquay. I trust the result will be all that can be desired. If it should be so I wish you would consider at the fitting time whether some paragraph might not be advantagiously [*sic*] inserted in the newspapers alluding to the bequest and the grounds for it. These things are catching and the great probability is that the example would be followed if properly made known.' H B/XX/R/18.

2 Rose (n1) had written: 'Spofforth went to Langley yesterday & saw *Mrs* Harvey. He had gone to Stowe and Mrs H thought the Duke [of Buckingham and Chandos] would succeed in persuading him to stand. Humphrey Bull writes to tell me that the Farmers are determined to have a Candidate & that they have a Tenant farmer ready if the heads of the party fail them as "*they will never consent to the plan of one Whig & two Tories merely to save the expense of a contested Election*".'

3 See **3857**&n1.

---

1 See **3873**&nn1-4 and **3880**n2. Derby had written from Knowsley on 16 November (but see n3) about John Peel, elected at Tamworth as a Conservative (see **3859**n1) but now ambivalent about party affiliation: 'I think it better to let you know what is going on, and you will judge if anything can, and ought, to be done.' He continued: 'I hope you are going to fight Buckinghamshire. Spofforth says you are in favour of it; that after the 30th. Inst. there will be a Conservative majority of 1000, and that you have the prospect of a good Candidate.' H B/XX/S/316. Harvey's address would profess 'Conservative principles,' and promise, if elected, policies '"calculated to maintain the dignity of our country, prosperity at home, and peace abroad; to promote and develope the agricultural and industrial resources of the land, and to maintain in their integrity those institutions under which, by the blessing of God, this country has so long flourished."' In response to farmers' questioning at Aylesbury, Harvey favoured the *status quo. The Times* (23 Nov 1863). See further **3890**&n2.

It will be an example to similar constituencies. We are fortunate in this affair: our new registration, of wh:, I believe, I wrote to you,[2] comes into / play, & Carington's eldest son, who might have been a formidable competitor, is not of age till the Spring.

It is unfortunate, that I am absent from the County at this moment, but I am summoned here by domestic circumstances of an urgent nature. I had, luckily, foreseen the / possible contingency, & arranged, as far as I could, everything, a month ago. The telegraph betn. Torquay & Stowe, however, has scarcely ceased working during the last four or five days.

I hope you are quite well.[3]

Yours sincerely, | D.

TO: MARKHAM SPOFFORTH   Torquay [Saturday] 21 November 1863   3882

ORIGINAL: ILLU [27] f184

PUBLICATION HISTORY: See ec

EDITORIAL COMMENT: From an undated newspaper clipping among others from the British *World* in ILLU, with the recipient identified as Markham Spofforth.

Private.   Torquay, Nov. 21, 1863.

My dear Sir,[1] –

Passing thro' town, I saw Mr. Earle, & sent you a message, by him, respecting the new member for Tamworth wh[ich] requires your attention. He seems a slippery fellow, like all the Peelites, & contemplates sitting on the Ministerial side. As he was brought in by the Tories at Tamworth, our friends there should look after this.[2]

If it be true, as I hear, that the New Club is to be managed in an aristocratic spirit & not to fulfil the purpose contemplated, I beg to withdraw my name from any connection with it.[3] I require on this matter precise information, as I am resolved, so far

2 See **3866**&n5.

3 Derby would reply on the 19th: 'Your letter of the 17th must have crossed one which I wrote to you a few days ago (but directed to Hughenden) on the subject of our(?) new Member for Tamworth, whom I am afraid we shall find a very slippery Gentleman, like most of the Peelites ... Your satisfactory intelligence respecting Bucks is confirmed by a letter I have received this morning from the Duke of Buckingham, who is very confident as to this Election, but doubts our being able to keep the three seats. Even if we cannot, a victory now will be very important. There was a meeting yesterday at Lord Carrington's, to consider the question of opposition; from which I rather infer that there will be no contest now, but that they will bring forward his Son at a general Election. If such is their intention, they will be wise not to embarrass themselves with another Candidate on the present occasion.' H B/XX/S/317.

---

1 Markham Spofforth (1825-1907), solicitor 1850, was the second son of Samuel Spofforth of Newfields, Yorkshire, and his wife, Anne (*née* Richardson). In 1853 he joined Rose as assistant Conservative agent and, after Rose resigned in 1859 (see VII **3393**n1), was principal agent until replaced by J.E. Gorst in 1870. He was the principal founder of the Junior Carlton Club, would help form the National Union of Conservative Associations 1867 and involve Rose in the case of the Tichborne Claimant before D made him taxing master in chancery 1876.

2 See **3881**&nn1&3. In his 16 November letter, Derby had passed along the suggestion that, since 'Mr. Peel had been brought in by the Conservatives, ... perhaps Taylor might give a hint to his Tamworth friends to put the screw on him.' Taylor however was in Ireland.

3 See **3841**&nn1&3 and **3844**&n2. Derby on the 19th had written (**3881**n3): 'From what I hear, the projected new Club is likely to be very successful in obtaining Members; but I am inclined to doubt whether it will largely admit the Class for which it was mainly intended. Spofforth says "it will be another Carlton, and just as exclusive." This I am sorry to learn.'

as my influence can operate, to sanction no exclusive political society. What we want is a rallying point for our working friends in the country, & not a gilded receptacle for town loungers.

Yours faithfully, | D.

3883 TO: LORD DERBY Torquay [Saturday] 21 November 1863

ORIGINAL: DBP Box 146/1

PUBLICATION HISTORY: M&B III 473, undated, the fourth paragraph

EDITORIAL COMMENT: Black-edged paper. Endorsed by Derby upside down on the fourth page: 'Disraeli B'.

Torquay Nov. 21. 1863

Rt Honble | The Earl of Derby | K. G

My dear Lord,

Your letter addressed to me at Hughenden,[1] reached me here on Wednesday morning on my way to that place to attend a funeral, & as I slept in town, I had an opportunity to put Mr Peel's affair in / train – & I shall probably hear something about it.[2]

If the club is not to fulfil its purpose, why shd. you lend yr name? I think it ought to be withdrawn.[3]

I am here, I think, for some little time. I dislike always to talk about myself, but it would hardly be frank to let yr assumption, that the business, that keeps me / here is "unpleasant", pass over in silence.

I have lost a kind & faithful friend, but I have lost her in the fullness of years, & she has made me the heir to her not inconsiderable fortune.[4]

Your letter of this morning, dated the 19th Inst:, came *open:* by no means, the first time. The / adhesive matter to your covers requires strengthening. If the matter of the communication is secret, as well as important, I believe wax is wisest.

I hope Stanley will not give a policy to the Govermt; they seem to be on the watch for one.[5]

I am, my dear Lord, | sincerely Yrs | D.

3883A TO: CHARLES CLUBBE Torquay [Saturday] 21 November 1863

ORIGINAL: RIC [023]

COVER: The | Revd. C.W. Clubbe, | A.M. | Hughenden Vicarage, | High Wycomb. | *B. Disraeli*

POSTMARKS: in circle: C | TORQUAY | NO 21 | 63; stamp removed

EDITORIAL COMMENT: Black-edged envelope and paper. *Sic:* Wycomb.

The | Rev. C.W. Clubbe | A.M. Torquay, Nov. 21. 63

1 See **3881**n1.

2 See **3882**&n2.

3 See **3882**&n3.

4 Derby on the 19th (**3881**n3) had written: 'I fear, from what you say, that the circumstances which keep you at Torquay, are of an unpleasant nature. When you write, if you write, let me know if you can, how long you are likely to be there, that I may know where to address you.' For SBW's 'fortune' see **3887**n1. The DS would return from Torquay on 28 November. H acc.

5 Derby on the 19th had written: 'Stanley is going, or gone, down to Lynn: I am always rather apprehensive as to what he may say on those occasions, but I hope he may not commit himself imprudently.'

My dear Mr Clubbe,
I was obliged to leave Hughenden so quickly, that I had not the satisfaction of seeing the vault closed, & / I feel somewhat uneasy on the point.[1]

Has it been substantially closed, & if not, will you see that all, that is requisite in this sense, be accomplished – & let me know? It will not / be opened again, until it receives myself, or my wife.[2]

With my kindest regards to Mrs. Clubbe,
Yours faithfully, | D.

TO: PHILIP ROSE 6 Victoria Street, London **3884**
[Tuesday] 1 December 1863

ORIGINAL: H R/I/A/169
PUBLICATION HISTORY: M&B III 473, dated 1 December 1863, omitting the fifth paragraph; Bradford 247, most of the fourth paragraph
EDITORIAL COMMENT: Paper imprinted '6, Victoria Street, Westminster Abbey, S.W. 186_'. D has added the '3' to the date. Endorsed in Rose's clerk's hand (see n2) on the fourth page: '15 & 16 Vict 17 & 18 Vict 22 Vict'.

Decr. 1 [186]3

My dr R.
What are my rights as to [the] vault in Hughenden Church?

My benefactress was to have been buried in my vault there.

Mr Clubbe wrote to me, that [the] Interment act prevented burials / in a Church, & that the vault in the Chancel (wh: I called, & believed to be, *my* vault) was closed accordingly.[1]

I told him, that [the] Burials Act, in my belief, did not apply to country churches, & that the vault ought not to have been closed. It / was impossible, howr., at such a moment, to have a controversy, & I was obliged, by great exertions, to have a vault made in the Church Yard, contrary to the express wishes of the deceased, & where neither my wife, nor myself, will be buried: preferring / even Kensal Green to anything so unprotected.

1 Among the Clubbe papers (RIC [022]) is a note dated 19 November 1863 at Hughenden: 'With Mr Disraeli's thanks & kind regards.' Presumably this enclosed Clubbe's honorarium for conducting the funeral service.

2 Clubbe would reply on 23 November: 'The vault has been substantially closed up with masonry, and the whole has been covered over with earth in the usual way ... and then it may remain until you have time to consider what more you wish to be done. I will see to this'. On 25 November Simmonds would submit his bill for £47.18.3, which included £21 for the vault 'securely closed'; he added that, with D's permission, he would see to it that a problem of water dripping on the vault and possibly causing problems would be attended to. H A/V/G/146, 148aa.

---

1 On 13 November Clubbe had replied to D's letter (**3876A**) on SBW's funeral. D had wanted the Norris vault in the church, but Clubbe thought it was solely for that family, and, since the Burials Act banned church burial, preferred to have a new vault made: 'there is plenty of space for the purpose in the Churchyard just beneath the East Window which we call your window.' A new vault would delay the funeral a day until Thursday the 19th. On the 15th, in response to the letter (**3878A**) he had requested by return of post, he would write that he had ordered a new vault to be made, and a hearse to be at the station at the time D specified. RTC [498-9Q]. On the 16th he would reply to another D letter (not found): 'Twelve o'ck. on Thursday will do very well ... I have told [the undertaker] to provide a hatband &c for your servant as well as for yourself.' H A/V/G/142.

Before I take any further steps in this matter, wh: I cannot neglect, I ~~will~~ wish to ascertain, from you, what are my rights under my title.[2]

Yrs sincerely, | D.

3885 TO: LORD STANLEY Carlton Club, Wednesday [2? December 1863]

ORIGINAL: DBP Box 42/7

EDITORIAL COMMENT: Black-edged paper. Docketed by Stanley on the last page: 'Disraeli. Dec. 63.' *Sic:* St. James'. *Dating:* by context; see n1.

The | Lord Stanley Carlton | Wednesday

Dear S.

I wrote you a line, this morning, to ask you to dine with us on Friday next ½ pt. 7 o'ck. precisely / – sans façon, to meet one or two – but I found my note on your table at St. James' – & therefore, / send this.

I hope you may come: if not, send me a telegram at once.[1]

Yrs ever | D.

My kindest remembrances to the / Lady of Hatfield.[2]

3886 TO: LORD JOHN MANNERS Grosvenor Gate [Sunday] 13 December 1863

ORIGINAL: NOT MY BD 2379

EDITORIAL COMMENT: Black-edged paper.

Grosvenor Gate | Dec: 13. 1863

My dear J.M.

Should we be so fortunate, as to find you disengaged & in / town, we hope, that

2 Rose's 5 December reply from Victoria Street (in a clerk's hand but signed by Rose) stated that D's purchase of Hughenden did not include a vault, although the chancel did belong to him, as 'Lay Impropriator'; even if a vault had been included, Clubbe was correct that under the Interment Act it would now be closed. The researching clerk (see ec) had extreme difficulty in finding an exception to the act. H R/I/B/93. D's exasperation is understandable, as on 20 December 1861 (presumably at D's request in anticipation of SBW's death), Lovell had reported that under the 1848 Public Health Act and the 1857 Burial Act, D as owner could use the Hughenden vault, provided 'no Certificate has been made by a Local Board of Health, being a Burial Board, and published in the Gazette stating that it is dangerous to health to bury within the walls of the Church or in the Churchyard & no order in Council has been made prohibiting burials within the walls of the Church or in the Churchyard.' H A/V/G/193. Despite D's assertion, both he and MA are buried with SBW in the vault Clubbe suggested outside the east window of the church. Kensal Green Cemetery in London was begun by a joint-stock company as a public burial ground in 1832. Cunningham 269-70.

---

1 According to MA's accounts, the DS gave only two dinners in December 1863, on Thursday 3rd and Thursday 17th. On the 3rd the guests were Count Vitzthum, Lords Lonsdale and Exmouth, Sir Henry Bulwer, Samuel Laing and Sir Emerson Tennent. D's request for an immediate telegram suggests a date more imminent than 'Friday', *ie,* he has given the wrong day. At 12.30 on 'Thursday' (3 December? [docketed '?Novr or Decr 1863']) Stanley would write from St James's Square: 'I am sorry to have missed your note yesterday, and still more so that I cannot come tomorrow, as I shall be out of town. I send this off at once.' H B/XX/S/714.

2 Stanley was one of a large party at Hatfield on 30 November and 1 December 1863, staying 'a few days longer' than most of the others. *MP* (5 Dec 1863). In his diary entry for 1 December 1863, in London, Stanley noted calling on D, who told him of SBW leaving him '£40,000'; they also discussed cabinet prospects. *Disraeli, Derby* 202-3.

Lady John, & yrself, will give us the great pleasure of your / company at dinner on Thursday next, 17th. Inst., at ½ past 7 o'ck precisely, / & sans façon.[1]

Yours ever | D.

TO: JOHN DELANE Grosvenor Gate [Sunday] 13 December 1863 3887

ORIGINAL: TIA Vol 12/124

EDITORIAL COMMENT: Black-edged paper.

J.T. Delane | Esqr Grosvenor Gate | Dec. 13. 63

Dear Delane,

If it be not very much against yr rules, I shd. be personally obliged by the insertion of the accompanying mem: / of a will I proved yesterday, & wh: by a brief & quiet notice wo[ul]d anticipate the routine diffuseness of the "Illustrated News" &c. a week / hence.[1]

Yrs sincerely, | D.

TO: CATHERINE BERNAL OSBORNE Hughenden [Sunday] 3 January 1864 3888

ORIGINAL: SIL [5], Osborne Papers, Hatfield House, Herts

EDITORIAL COMMENT: Paper imprinted 'Hughenden Manor'.

Jany 3. 1864

Dear Mrs Osborne,

Let me thank you for your books, & still more for your letter, wh: I highly appreciate, coming, as it does, from / one, whom I always remember with esteem & regard.[1]

Yours sincerely, | *B. Disraeli*

1 Manners on 'Sunday', the same day, would accept the invitation for Thursday, though his wife would be out of town. H B/XX/M/127 (however dated 2 November 1863 by AES). MA would record the other guests as the Earl and Countess of Donoughmore, Beauchamp, Hardwicke and an unidentified 'Count C'; they drank 3 bottles of sherry, 1 of champagne and 2 of claret. H acc.

1 Delane, who on 2 December had declined a dinner invitation, would insert the notice on the 14th under the heading 'WILLS AND BEQUESTS. - The will of Mrs. Sarah Brydges Willyams, of Mount Braddon, Torquay, widow of James Brydges Willyams, of Carnanton, in the county of Cornwall, Esq., and Colonel of the Royal Cornwall Militia, has been proved in the Prerogative Court by her sole surviving executor, the Right Hon. B. Disraeli. The testatrix by this instrument, dated November, 1857, after some legacies to her godchildren, bequeaths the whole of her estate to the said Right Hon. B. Disraeli, "in testimony of her affection and of her approval and admiration of his efforts to vindicate the race of Israel." Personalty sworn under 40,000*l*.' For Rose's advice about this notice, see **3880**n1. H B/XXI/D/77; *The Times* (14 Dec 1863). A similar notice would appear in the *Illustrated London News* of 26 December (655).

1 The letter has not been found. Mrs Osborne was author of at least two romances, the second of which would be 'most unmercifully cut up' in the *Saturday Review* in May 1864. Charlotte de Rothschild to Leopold de Rothschild, 8 May 1864, MS ROTH. For Mrs Osborne's possible previous interest in D, see IV **1367**n1.

3889 TO: [CONSERVATIVE MPS] Hughenden
[Tuesday] 12 January 1864

ORIGINAL: Copies in WSRO Mitford Archives MS 1277 f27-8 (to William Mitford) and BCP [13] (to Frederick Lygon)

PUBLICATION HISTORY: *MP* (26 Jan 1864), 'addressed ... to the members who usually act with him in the House of Commons' and dated at Hughenden, 12 January 1864; *BH* (30 Jan 1864) 'addressed ... to the members of the Opposition' and dated at Hughenden, 22 [*sic*] January 1864

EDITORIAL COMMENT: This letter is another example of a reproduced circular letter; *cf* VII **3349**ec, **3546**ec&n1, **3646**ec and **3776**ec. H B/II/76d is a draft.

Hughenden Manor | Jany. 12. 1864

Sir,

I have the honor to inform you, that Parliament will reassemble on Thursday, the 4th. February, & I would express my hope, that you may find / it convenient to be in your place on that day, as business of importance may be expected.

I am, Sir, | Your faithful Servt, | *B. Disraeli*

3890 TO: LORD JOHN MANNERS Grosvenor Gate [Monday] 18 January 1864

ORIGINAL: BEA [87]

EDITORIAL COMMENT: Black-edged paper.

Grosvenor Gate | Jan: 18. 1864

Rt Honble | Lord John Manners | M. P.

My dear J. M.[1]

Harvey, in Bucks, pledged himself to the farmers to vote for the repeal of the Malt-Tax, if brought in by a Government.[2] Very safe!

You must put the question to the farmers in this form. Do / you prefer repeal of the Malt-Tax & one shilling Income Tax, or the present rate of Income Tax, & probable reduction, & the existing Malt-Tax?

Your drawback suggestion is very much opposed by the Inland Revenue, & has never stood the fire of Debate. /

The agitation comes from a Committee in London.[3] I, sometimes, think, it has been started by the liberal party to disorganise the country ranks.

1 Manners had written from Beaumanor Park, Loughborough (William Herrick), on 14 January 1864 that Leicestershire was so concerned about the malt tax that he and E.B. Hartopp, his Leicestershire colleague, would attend a meeting on it at Leicester on the 23rd: 'I propose to take no part till the close of the proceedings, and then to be as guarded as possible; but I understand the feeling in favour of abolition to be strong and general ... I should much like to know what you think on the subject. Parliament seems to me pledged to Sugar, Fire Insurance, & Income Tax, and if so to talk of Malt Tax repeal is absurd; but would it be possible to meet the justice of the farmer's case by a drawback upon malt for feeding purposes?' H B/XX/M/128.

2 See **3873**&n3, **3880**&n2 and **3881**&nn1&3. In a speech at Aylesbury on 21 November, Harvey had said that, though he thought the tax could be decreased, it would be unfair to his party for him to pledge himself to repeal. It might have been done if the paper duty had not been repealed, but now they must 'be content to know that Gladstone's claret was cheaper in some quarters.' *The Times* (23 Nov 1863); *BH* (28 Nov 1863).

3 In the 1863 session duties had been reduced on several articles but not on malt. Gladstone had explained that it was the residual indirect duty on beer, itself not taxed directly, and that the revenue could not afford a reduction. Nevertheless, he agreed to the appointment on 23 June of a select committee '"To

You might remind yr friend, that you were a member of a Government, who proposed a reduction of half the duty, & laid the way for total repeal.[4]

We / came from Burghley on Saturday, & are here only for two days.[5] I have not yet seen the Captain, who is in town, but hope to do so today.[6]

Our kindest regards to Lady John,

Yours ever, | D.

TO: SIR JOHN PAKINGTON Grosvenor Gate [Monday] 18 January 1864 **3891**

ORIGINAL: WRC 705:349 BA 3835/7 (ii) 18

PUBLICATION HISTORY: M&B IV 42, dated at Grosvenor Gate, 18 January 1864, omitting the last paragraph; Blake 365, extract dated 1864

EDITORIAL COMMENT: Docketed in another hand on the first page: '*1864 Disraeli*'. *Sic:* expence.

Grosvenor Gate | Jan: 18. 1864

Rt Hon | Sir John Pakington | G.C.B.

My dear Pakington,

I should keep very shy of B.[1]

Nothing can ever satisfy his ravenous egotism. He used to send me, some years ago, many plans of administrative, &, especially, / admiralty, reform[2] – but I found out, that the object of all his changes was to advance the permanent, at the expence of the parliamentary, officials. Such reform is / not our "metier," as the Emperor Joseph said to the first French republicans.[3]

B. wants to turn clerks into Privy-councillors. He had energy & organising ability, but he has been over-rewarded & / over-promoted, & tho' still restless is, I think, used up.[4]

consider whether, compatibly with the interests of the Revenue, the Laws relating to the Excise Duty upon Malt can be amended so as to operate more advantageously with reference to the cultivation and price of Barley, to the manufacture and price of Malt and Malt Liquor, and to the use of Malt in the feeding of Cattle and Sheep."' *Hansard* CLXXI cols 1379-82. The committee of nineteen would be appointed on 13 July and its report tabled by Sir Fitzroy Kelly on 20 July. *JHC* 118 (1863-4) 360, 376.

4 Manners would go even further; *The Times* in a leader on 27 January reported: 'At Leicester Lord John Manners, admitting the difficulty and confessing to a slight fellow-feeling with Governments, had the modesty and the courage to suggest reducing the duty by half.' For the Derby government's proposal to reduce the malt tax in 1852, see VI **2455**&nn1&3. During the session attempts to reduce the tax on malt would fail but a bill to reduce the tax on malt made for cattle would eventually pass in both Houses.

5 The DS had just returned from a visit, 13-16 January, to the Marquis and Marchioness of Exeter at Burghley, Northants. From 20 to 22 January they would visit Lord Broughton at Tedworth House, Hants, and leave again on the 27th for the Anthony de Rothschilds at Aston Clinton. *MP* (14, 21 Jan 1864); H acc.

6 Derby had returned to London from Knowsley on the 15th. *MP* (16 Jan 1864).

---

1 Pakington's letter (not found) evidently asked about using Sir Richard Bromley in parliament's continuing attempts to reform the royal dockyards' administration. On 25 February, opening discussion on the 1861 report of the latest (1860) commission on the matter, W.S. Lindsay would rehearse the record since Pakington, as first lord of the admiralty, appointed a committee of inquiry in 1858. This would lead to another committee being nominated on 26 February, with Pakington reluctantly agreeing to be a member, as he thought the matter best handled by the admiralty itself. *Hansard* CLXXIII cols 1073-81, 1235-40.

2 See VI **2431**&n1, VII **3010**&n1, **3025**n2, **3213**&n6, **3239**n2 and **3260**.

3 Joseph II (1741-1790), Holy Roman Emperor 1765-90, instituted far-reaching reforms during his reign; in fiscal matters he was influenced by the French economists known as 'physiocrats', with unsuccessful results.

4 D's opinion of Bromley had obviously changed since his 1852 endorsement (see VI **2431**&n1) and his recommendation of Bromley for his KCB in 1858. M&B IV 42.

I came to town on Saturday evening from Burghley, & am only here for two days.[5] The Captain is in town, &, I hope, to see him today. When we meet, I shall be glad to hear yr plans.

Yours sincerely, | D.

3892 TO: SIR GEORGE SINCLAIR [London, Wednesday] 20 January 1864

ORIGINAL: H B/XXI/S/265

PUBLICATION HISTORY: M&B IV 343-4, dated 20 January 1864, the second sentence

EDITORIAL COMMENT: From a D letter dated 20 January 1864, as quoted by Sinclair in a letter of 17 June 1864 (see n2).

I think its hero will obtain all his objects without further effort.[1] AN ENGLISH GOVT. THAT, IN ITS WISDOM, GOES TO WAR WITH GERMANY, MUST MAKE FRANCE THE MISTRESS OF EUROPE.[2]

3893 TO: GEORGE FREDERICK SMITH Grosvenor Gate [Tuesday] 26 January 1864

ORIGINAL: H A/V/B/26

EDITORIAL COMMENT: Paper imprinted 'Grosvenor Gate'. *Sic:* G.S. Smith (see n1).

G.S. Smith Esq Jan 26 1864

My d[ea]r Sir,

I approve of your proposals – & have been ready, on my part, several days, to carry them into effect – but it is absolutely impossible for me at this moment, to / attend to private business.

Nevertheless, as, from your letter, I conclude it is of importance to you to close the business, I will endeavour to call on you on Wednesday next, / between four & five o'ck: & do so.

Yours faithfully, | D.

Write, if necessary, to C as usual.[1]

5 See **3890**n5.

1 Sinclair had written to D from his son's home, The Mount, Upper Norwood, on 14 January 1864, asking if he had received a copy of Sinclair's book, probably his *Reflections on the anniversary of the coup d'etat: [A] letter addressed to Monsieur le comte de Chambord* (London: G.J. Stevenson 1859). H B/XXI/S/261. Chambord was a pretender to the French throne.

2 In his letter of 17 June (see ec), Sinclair would refer to their party 'being anxious to involve Gt. Britain in a preposterous war with Germany' and suggest that D use the quoted material in debate. H B/XXI/S/265. For D's opinion on Britain's role in the Schleswig-Holstein situation, see **3872**&nn1-2 and see further **3895**&n1.

1 The recipient is presumably George Frederick Smith of Wright & Smith, solicitors, in whose correspondence with D this letter is located in H; see IV **1298**&n1. Neither his letter nor his business has been found, although D's letter bears a striking resemblance to his letters to Smith of the 1840s. However, there is a scrawled note from Smith to D dated 29 July 1869: 'I will be ready at ½ p 2 on Wednesday. The amount payable will be [*listed*] In Consideration 4200 | Annuity to date 158 | costs [*illegible*] 12 | [*totalling*] 4370 | Value of Policy 1070 | [*totalling*] 3300.' H A/V/F/32. 'C' is presumably the Carlton Club, where D preferred to have his business mail addressed.

TO: DUKE OF WELLINGTON Grosvenor Gate [Friday] 29 January 1864 3894

ORIGINAL: ADM [1]

EDITORIAL COMMENT: Black-edged paper. Half of the sheet (normally pp 3&4) has apparently been torn off.

Grosvenor Gate | Jany. 29. 1864

His Grace | The Duke of Wellington | K.G.

Dear Duke of Wellington,

It was truly kind of Your Grace to remember me.

Altho' I cannot, as I ought to do, provide my friends with loaves & fishes, they will, I am sure, appreciate delicious game from / the heroic groves of Strathfieldsaye.[1]

Believe me, | Yours sincerely, | & obliged, | *B. Disraeli*

TO: LADY ELY [London, Tuesday] 2 February 1864 3895

ORIGINAL: RAC I94 13

EDITORIAL COMMENT: A copy, not in D's hand, endorsed, in yet another hand, 'Mr. Disraeli to the Marchioness of Ely.' *Dating:* the date number in the copy can be read as either '9' or '2', but the context (see n1) indicates that it is the latter.

Feb: 2. 1864.

Passions are very high here about the S-Holstein Question, but I do not anticipate anything inconvenient in Parliament on Thursday. After the mover & seconder of the Address, Ld: Derby & myself will rise, and our words must commit our party to such a degree, that no man of mark or expectation, in either House, on the Opposition side, will set the firebrand.[1]

1 On 2 February MA would record paying 2*s* 7*d* for carriage of game, as well as 2*s* 9*d* for woodcock from Lady Dorothy Nevill. H acc. D would give his first parliamentary dinner of the season on 3 February; see Appendix II. *The Times* (25 Jan 1864); *MP* (4 Feb 1864). Stafford Northcote recorded that D had gout, 'a good omen for a future premier.' Northcote I 209. On the 4th Wellington would invite the DS to dinner on a day and time of their choosing, an invitation that pleased MA 'amazingly, as the Duke had for many years resented the non-appreciation of his great father by Disraeli'. H B/XXI/W/159; Charlotte de Rothschild to Leopold de Rothschild, 6 February 1864, MS ROTH.

1 See **3817**&n5. In the conflict over the duchies of Schleswig, Holstein and Augustenberg, in 1863 King Frederick VII of Denmark had issued a proclamation and then a constitution defying the 1852 London Protocol of Succession by negating Germany's claims on Schleswig. He had died on 15 November, but it had been signed on the 18th by the new King Christian IX, causing much anger in Germany and risking war with Austria and Prussia, signators of the 1852 protocol. On 24 December, Saxon and Hanoverian troops had invaded Schleswig, and the German Confederation had subsequently appointed Duke Frederick VIII as its head, evoking strong protests from Britain and Russia. The Queen, with close family ties to both sides, was in an awkward position and evidently concerned about parliament's reaction on its Thursday 4 February opening. Lady Ely, a lady of the bedchamber, had written on 'Sunday' (docketed in another hand, 'Feby/64') to acknowledge a gift from MA (possibly that for 'the man at the H of Co[mmo]ns' MA recorded on 2 February). Lady Ely continued: 'I find The Queen looking well, but very low at times ... I think the German & Danish affairs worry her, surrounded as she is, by so many conflicting interests ... she was so anxious for war, & now the sad reality has come & her poor heart is aching she says ... I told her I had had the pleasure of meeting you & Mrs: Disraeli & she asked after you both, with so much interest, fondly.' H acc, B/XIX/D/148. On 4 February the commissioners' speech (in lieu of the speech from the throne) would assert the validity of the 1852 protocol, which (ironically enough) gave King Christian the right 'to all the Dominions then united under the Sceptre of His Majesty the King of *Denmark*'; it also expressed the Queen's desire 'to bring about a Peaceful Settlement of the Differences

I know the question thoroughly. It was the subject of one of the last, long, conversations, that I held with our dear, departed Master;[2] In his little room at Windsor, he had returned from shooting, & sent for me. He went into the whole matter with his sound depth and precision, & encouraged discussion, as he always did, for he was a real lover of truth, so as lawyers say, we could pinch the case.

He threw away all reserve, as he did with me on such occasions. I see him now: his eyes flashing, and his pen-line brow mantling with emotion. I nearly got into a scrape, that day, for tho' little Princesses continually tapped at the door, he would not cease. When he dismissed me at 8 o'clock, I saw him fairly run down the corridor at full speed, to his dressing-room. But where was I?. In a pretty [*blank space*], for if it be a violation of good breeding to be too late for dinners in private life, in the palace of the Sovereign, I should think by common law, it was at least petty treason.

3896 TO: LORD STANHOPE — Grosvenor Gate [Friday] 12 February 1864

ORIGINAL: KCR Stanhope MSS 690(6)1
EDITORIAL COMMENT: Black-edged paper.

The | Earl Stanhope — Grosvenor Gate | Feb. 12. 1864

My dear Lord –

You have much gratified me by your kindness in sending me a copy of the letters of Prince Metternich to yourself, wh: are most / interesting.[1]

Events have given them a fresh relish, but his letters are too full of thought ever to become obsolete.

What a different man he really was to what those fancied him, who formed their judgment / in the glitter of Vienna!

A profound head & an affectionate heart! Had he not been a Prince & a Prime Minister, he would have been a great Professor.

He said to me, once, "Jétais né penseur."

Ever, my dear Lord, | Yours sincerely | & obliged | *B. Disraeli*

which on this Matter have arisen between *Germany* and *Denmark*, and to ward off the Dangers which might follow from a Beginning of Warfare in the North of *Europe*'. In the Lords, the Address would be moved by Lord Sligo, seconded by Lord Abercromby; in the Commons, Lord Richard Grosvenor would move the Address, seconded by G.J. Goshen. Derby and Disraeli in their respective Houses would lead the opposition response, severely criticizing the government's foreign policy while hoping that it would not result in war with Germany on behalf of Denmark. *The Times* next day would comment: 'The conduct of the House of Commons last night was well worthy of its reputation as the first deliberative Assembly in the world. On an occasion peculiarly calculated to stir its feelings and excite its passions, it preserved the most judicial calmness and tranquillity.' *Hansard* CLXXIII cols 3-72, 73-159 (D 86-101).

2 Likely the visit recorded in **3551**&n7, the last time D stayed at Windsor before Albert's death. On that occasion, D told Stanley, he and Albert had also discussed European affairs. *Disraeli, Derby* 165.

---

1 No information on the copy Stanhope sent has been found. Since only the originals are in the Stanhope papers at KCR, perhaps it was a manuscript copy. Information kindly suplied by Michael Carter, KCR.

TO: CHARLES CLUBBE London [Monday] 15 February 1864 3896A

ORIGINAL: RIC [024]

COVER: [1] The | Revd. C.W. Clubbe, | A.M. | Hughenden Vicarage | High Wycomb. | D.; [2] The | Revd. C.W. Clubbe | A.M | Vicarage. | *B. Disraeli*

POSTMARKS: [on cover #1] in circle: LONDON – W | 5 | FE 15 | 64; *on verso,* in circle: HIGH WYCOMBE | FE 15 | 64; the stamp has been removed

EDITORIAL COMMENT: Black-edged envelope (#2) and paper; cover #2 also has a stylized cross on its flap. *Sic:* Wycomb (cover).

The | Rev. C.W. Clubbe | A.M. Grosvenor Gate | Feb. 15. 1864

My dear Mr Clubbe

I send you, on the other side, a cheque for the balance of yr Harvest Home[1] acct. for I am sure, if I do not, it will fall on yr shoulders, which have already, in my opinion, borne too much in this matter.

I don't exactly see / why Mr Hussey was so long about his accts.[2]

I trust the farmers will support you better next autumn, tho' I am sure you will not be able to perform yr own duties more successfully.

With kind remembrances to Mrs Clubbe,

Yrs sincerely, D.

TO: MONTAGU SCOTT Grosvenor Gate [Wednesday] 17 February 1864 3897

ORIGINAL: ILLU XB B365B1 Cards 1,2

PUBLICATION HISTORY: Meynell II 451, a facsimile

EDITORIAL COMMENT: Black-edged paper.

Montagu Scott Esqr[1] Grosvenor Gate | Feb 17. 1864

Dear Sir –

I thank you for your telegram, & I congratulate you on your triumph.[2]

Yours very faithfully,| *B. Disraeli*

TO: LORD STANLEY Grosvenor Gate [Wednesday] 24 February 1864 3898

ORIGINAL: DBP Box 47/2

EDITORIAL COMMENT: Black-edged paper. Endorsed by Stanley on the fourth page: 'Disraeli. Feb. 64.'

Grosvenor Gate | Feb: 24. 1864

Rt Honble | Lord Stanley | M. P.

Dear Comrade –

Should I have the good fortune to find you disengaged, you will please, & oblige,

1 See **3851**&nn3&4.

2 Nothing has been found regarding the role in the Harvest Home of D's tenant George Hussey (for whom *cf* VII **2884**n2 and, in this volume, **3506**n2).

1 Montagu David Scott (1818-1900), of Hove, Sussex (in the parliamentary borough of Brighton), second son of Sir David Scott, 2nd Bt, a barrister (Middle Temple 1840), JP and DL for Sussex, Middlesex and Westminster, would be MP (C) for E Sussex 1874-85.

2 The telegram (not found) presumably told of the 16 February Conservative victory in a hotly contested by-election at Brighton, where Henry Moor had defeated the fractured Liberals with their three candidates.

me very much, if you will dine here on / Saturday next, 27th. Inst., at ½ past 7. o'ck: House of Comm: dinner.[1]

Yours ever, | D.

3899 TO: BARONESS LIONEL DE ROTHSCHILD Grosvenor Gate [Friday] 18 March 1864

ORIGINAL: ROTH RFAM C/2/57
EDITORIAL COMMENT: Black-edged paper.

Grosvenor Gate | Mar: 18. 1864

Dearest Baroness,

Mary-Anne cannot be your guest tomorrow. She was seized, two or three days ago, with bleeding of the nose. I sent for Fergusson. It recurred – & last night, / or rather three o'ck in the morning, when I came from the House of Commons, I found her in an almost alarming state (with a physician Dr Webber[1] &c) the hemorrhage not having ceased for three / hours – & yielding at last ↑only↓ to the most violent remedies.

She begs me to request you not to mention this to anyone, except Lionel, of course. You know, how she dislikes being enquired after. /

I am afraid this is sadly unintelligible, but I ↑& all↓ have been up all night. So excuse me.

She anxiously wishes, that I shd. be your guest today, so I presume to come, tho' very disquieted, & now obliged to go to Ld. Derby's[.]

Adieu dear friend | D.

She must not stir; nor lie down.

3900 TO: BARONESS LIONEL DE ROTHSCHILD Grosvenor Gate [Sunday] 20 March 1864

ORIGINAL: ROTH RFAM C/2/58
EDITORIAL COMMENT: Black-edged paper.

Grosvenor Gate | Mar: 20 1864

Dearest Baroness,

Mary Anne has had a tolerable night, & no recurrence of the attack. There has been no recurrence, since / Friday evening, & that was slight: so it looks well.

No Doctor has been here yet.

She sends her love to you, & begs me to say, that she is, of / course, very weak, but getting on very well.

1 Stanley would reply on 'Thursday' from St James's Square: 'I wish I could accept! It would be a great pleasure – but I have been engaged elsewhere (more than a week) for the 27th, and I fear it won't do to throw over my friend.' H B/XX/S/715. For the guests at D's parliamentary dinner on the 27th see Appendix II.

1 Charles Samuel Webber, of 20 Connaught Square, London W, was Lic. Soc. Apoth. Lond., 1831, MRCS 1836, registered 1859, FRCS 1864. *Medical Register* (1879). Dr Fergusson had been called on the 11th for MA's throat, and both Fergusson and 'Weber' on the 15th for her nosebleed, the latter charging double (*ie,* £2) for a night call. On the 30th she recorded with some asperity that two more surgeons, Mr Shey [Shea?] and Mr Savory, had looked down her throat with an instrument, diagnosed debility and prescribed 'a *tonic,* which I have not taken.' H acc.

I wish your messenger had brought me news, that your own pain was soothed.
Your affectionate | D.

TO: BARONESS LIONEL DE ROTHSCHILD [London] Sunday [20 March 1864] 3901

ORIGINAL: ROTH RFAM C/2/59
EDITORIAL COMMENT: Black-edged paper. *Dating: cf* **3899** and **3900**.

Sunday.

Mary Anne begs me to say, that she is "all gratitude".

She is very much interested by my account of your brilliant party of / yesterday.

What you have so kindly sent her is most acceptable to her, particularly as it is not sweet.

I was very much amused by the extreme tone / of Lord Grey's politics.[1] I have now a more accurate, & precise, conception of what "reactionary" means.

We want to know, when we meet, what / you think of Lady Dufferin.[2]

I must again express my hope, that your suffering has ceased.

Yrs ever | D.

TO: WILLIAM CARLISLE Grosvenor Gate [Tuesday] 22 March 1864 3902

ORIGINAL: MOPSIK [42]
EDITORIAL COMMENT: Paper imprinted 'Grosvenor Gate'. Endorsed in another hand on the first page: '*22nd March 1864 Rt. Hon B Disraeli*'; and in yet another hand: 'Lady Jersey Ceylon Es[ta]te.'

Private Mar: 22 1864

W. Carlisle Esq

My dear Sir –

Lady Jersey asked me yesterday, whether I had heard further from Mr Magenis, & whether he had effected some means to / assist her in her Ceylon troubles, as he kindly said, he wd. try to do.[1]

1 Grey in 1864 published a second edition of his 1858 *Parliamentary Government considered with reference to reform* which included treatments of the reform bills of 1859 and 1861 and suggestions to offset what he saw as the dangers of democracy.

2 This is presumably a reference to the 1863 publication by D's friend Lady Dufferin (see I **234**n14) of *Lispings from Low Latitudes, or, Extracts from the Journal of the Hon. Impulsia Gushington,* a parody of travel writing based on her journey up the Nile.

---

1 See **3800**&n1 for the most recent mention of the Ceylon estates. Lady Jersey's latest letter (15 March), insofar as it can be deciphered, makes no mention of them. In a note (dated '? April 1864' by 'AES') she would write: 'I hear Magennis is *dead* & has left much to a Lady – will she be entitled.' Frederick Villiers would confirm on 6 May that 'MacGennis' had died, leaving most of his money to his 'Lady', a Mrs Carew. He believed the rest, including the Ceylon mortgage, had gone to his natural daughter by Mrs Carew, a Mrs J. Baillie, whose husband had indicated he would act fairly and as the Jerseys wished. On 14 June Villiers would transmit Burley & Carlisle's opinion that the Ceylon property would pass to the legal heir, Villiers's nephew. Since he was a minor, the Chancery Court would be asked to appoint an agent to settle the estate. He added: 'It is therefore all important to ascertain Padwick's real position, as a creditor – and also what power does he take under the deed of gift?' H A/IV/J/253-4, 257, 260. *Contra* VI **2817**n1 and VII **2942**n1, the Frederick William Magenis clearly identified by Burley & Carlisle in 1856 would live until 1866; this must therefore be his half-brother, Richard William Magenis (1789-1863), of Harold Hall, Beds, who had died in December 1863; major 7th Fusiliers, JP and DL, High Sheriff 1830.

Can you tell me?[2]
Yours faithfully, | *B. Disraeli*

3903 TO: PHILIP ROSE Grosvenor Gate [Wednesday] 23 March 1864
ORIGINAL: INU English Literature MSS Lilly Library [2]
EDITORIAL COMMENT: Paper imprinted 'Grosvenor Gate'.

Private & C. Mar 23 1864
Philip Rose Esq
My dear Rose,
I enclose several papers: the amount, rather more than £700, (I think,) place to my acct., as I do not want it.[1]

If Routledge were to publish a shilling edit: of "the Revolutionary Epick",[2] I / believe he would sell 50,000 copies – & it wd go on selling: a shilling book of 200 pages: the profit wd be nearly 2000£.

The offer ought to come from him, & I shd. make difficulties. I would not do it, unless I received a good round sum: at least £500. I have a copy / revised some years ago at Hughenden. If you throw the fly to him, he shd. be impressed with the difficulty of the affair, & that in all probab[ilit]y, I shd not consent.[3]

Yrs ever, | D.

3904 TO: ALEXANDER BAILLIE-COCHRANE Grosvenor Gate [Thursday] 24 March 1864
ORIGINAL: HAS [2]
EDITORIAL COMMENT: Paper imprinted 'Grosvenor Gate'. Endorsed in another hand on the first page: '*Disraeli*'.

Mar: 24 1864
A.B. Cochrane | Esqr. M. P.
Dear Cochrane,
I am glad to hear of your return, and shall be happy to see you today, at three o'ck:[1]
Yrs sincerely, | D.

2 No reply has been found.

---

1 See **3552**&n1 for this money's possible source. Alternatively, it may be an instalment of repayment (£750) of an Italian Domain loan from which D would receive a similar sum through Rose at this time in 1865. H B/XX/R/25. For Baxter, Rose & Norton's involvement in amortization of loans to foreign governments and return of investment capital, see *Norton Rose* 95.

2 On this day, 23 March 1864, Moxon & Co wrote to D from 44 Dover Street: 'We have gone through our stock book in the hope of discovering a copy of your "Revolutionary Epoch" [*sic*] published for you by the late Mr. Edward Moxon. We find that there are no copies in our warehouse, & no trace remains to show what was done with the copies on hand. We have instituted a search for a secondhand copy, & should we succeed in finding one, will let you have it immediately.' H E/VII/E/11. For the cause of renewed interest in *The Revolutionary Epick,* see **3905**&n2.

3 Rose would reply on the 27th: 'I have received your letter and will attend to it.' H B/XX/R/20. See **3905**&n3.

---

1 On 'Wednesday' Cochrane, just returned from the continent (probably Italy), had asked to see D with important documents to do with J. Stansfeld, a lord of the admiralty. The current Paris trial of the conspirators to assassinate the Emperor (see **3741**&n3) had revealed that Mazzini had used Stansfeld's Lon-

TO: PHILIP ROSE Hughenden [Sunday] 3 April 1864 **3905**

ORIGINAL: INU English Literature MSS Lilly Library

EDITORIAL COMMENT: Paper imprinted 'Hughenden Manor'.

Private April 3 1864

P. Rose Esq

My dear Rose

I think, upon reflection, it will not do to publish the R.E. at once in the shilling form.[1] It is quite unknown, only *50* copies having been printed of the original edit:, / wh: appeared thirty years ago. For society, it is, in fact, the same as a *MS* – &, if for no other reason, it shd. be *published,* or it will always be misrepresented, especially from its title, & be thrown in my face, when / it suits[.][2]

When it is read, all that will vanish.

The alterations &c. in the only copy I have here are so considerable, that it is a new work – i.e. in a literary point of view – in no other.

Longman, or some other swell, would bring / out the book, wh:, at this moment, wd. have, in an expensive form, a considerable sale – but I always look to popular editions, & this makes one hesitate about leaving Routledge, if he wishes to do the thing.[3]

Yours ever, | D.

don address to send money to the revolutionaries in London. On 29 February in the House Stansfeld had indignantly denied any involvement with the revolutionaries but had paid warm tribute to Mazzini's character. The matter had come up again on 14 March, when D demanded Stansfeld explain himself, and on the 17th, when D denounced the government for defending a colleague with arrogant dismissals of the French evidence instead of communicating confidentially with the French government to clarify such a serious matter. On the 18th Lord Elcho had inquired whether Stansfeld had offered his resignation. Cochrane told D that his documents, which included some from Mazzini, proved Stansfeld's complicity in Tibaldi's plot in 1857, Orsini's in 1858 and Greco's (in 1862): 'if none of this transpires before the house meets [after Easter] I think that we must on the evidence I possess carry a resolution condemnatory of the government.' When the House reconvened on 4 April, Stansfeld would announce his resignation. See further **3905**&n2. H B/XXI/L/25, D/III/C/417-18; *Hansard* CLXXIII cols 1255-60, 1931-39 (D 1937-39), CLXXIV 189-73 (D 189-90, 270-73), 324-43, 396-401.

1 See **3903**&nn2&3.

2 In the Stansfeld debate on 17 March (see **3904**n1), Bright had tried to counter D: 'I think I have read that the right hon. Gentleman who just sat down, in one of his early writings, expressed opinions – it may be merely to excite a sensation amongst his readers – but still opinions very much like [Mazzini's] to which the hon. Baronet [Stracey] has alluded to-night.' At this D had interrupted: 'There is not the slightest foundation for that statement. I give it the most unequivocal contradiction.' *Hansard* CLXXIV cols 270-86 (D 270-3, 275). On 19 March, *MP* had published a letter dated 18 March from 'OPINION' about D's assertion: 'Mr. Disraeli's "Revolutionary Epick," published with his name in 1834 (when he was not far from 30), is all composed very much in the Mazzini vein, and proposes summary modes of getting rid of kings and priests.' It then quoted passages from Part II of the work, concluding with '"Pharaoh's doom | Shall cool those chariot wheels now hot with blood. | And Blessed be the hand that dares to wave | The Regicidal Steel that shall redeem | A Nation's sorrow with a Tyrant's blood."' On 22 March *MP* had published another letter from 'OPINION', responding to one in D's defence signed '"A Peer"' that had appeared in an unnamed 'morning contemporary'. With more quotations it contended that D's work 'is in every sense of the term a revolutionary epick. It advocates the destruction of monarchy, aristocracy, and priestcraft, and the establishment of universal equality upon their wrecks.'

3 An extensively revised edition of *The Revolutionary Epick,* price 5 shillings, with a preface dedicated to Stanley, would be published in 1864 by Longman, Green & Co. See further **3906**&n3. The preface states: 'The *Revolutionary Epick* is printed from the only copy in my possession, and which, with slight exceptions,

3906 TO: PHILIP ROSE Hughenden [Wednesday] 6 April 1864

ORIGINAL: H R/I/A/170

COVER: Philip Rose Esqr | 6 Victoria Street | Westminster Abbey | *B. Disraeli*

POSTMARK: [*recto*] (1) In a circle: HIGH WYCOMBE | B | AP 6 | 64; (2) In a circle: [*illegible*]; (3) In a double circle: 364; (4) a cancelled one-penny stamp; (5) a large number 2; (6) [*verso*] In a circle: LONDON | AP 7 | 64

EDITORIAL COMMENT: Paper imprinted 'Hughenden Manor'.

P. Rose Esqr April 6 1864

My dear Rose,

I enclose the paper signed, wh:, perhaps, you will witness for me. I am sorry we are not in luck – but it might have been worse – & I am much obliged to you for yr indefatigable friendship / in this, & in all things.[1]

I shall of course be in town tomorrow. As I was obliged to stay for Q. S.,[2] I thought I might as well take another day – & have enjoyed myself much.

I don't think I can let / the matter hang with Routledge. The thing ought to be advertised at once. I cannot postpone my interview with Longman beyond Monday, & shd. prefer seeing him on Saturday, if Routledge is quite at sea.

With / L. I shd. of course make no terms beyond his bearing all costs – & divided profits. I shd insist upon ample advertisemts; tho' his own interest wd. secure that.[3]

Yrs ever, | D.

was corrected in 1837, when, after three years' reflection, I had resolved not only to correct but to complete the work. The corrections are purely literary. The somewhat sudden accession of her Most Gracious Majesty occasioned in that year a dissolution of Parliament, and being then returned to the House of Commons, in which I have since sat without an interval, these dreams for ever vanished.' Stewart *Writings* 54 (item 148); M&B I 241-2, IV 404&n2.

---

1 See **3855**&n1. This letter is connected with the General Credit & Finance Company, chairman Samuel Laing, set up at 7 Lothbury by Baxter, Rose & Norton in 1863 to 'negotiate Loans and ... Foreign, Indian and Colonial Bonds' and offering 125,000 shares. *Norton Rose* 87. On 4 April 1864 the company had advertised a first-issue subscription of £2,500,000, of which £500,000 was paid up, and a 6% Venezuelan loan of £1,500,000 at '60 pm'. On 7 April the company had advertised a first-issue subscription to the British Columbia and Vancouver Island Investment Company of £250,000 in 10,000 shares of £25 each, deposit on application £1, plus £2 on allotment. *The Times* (4-7 Apr 1864). Rose would reply from Victoria Street on 8 April: 'It was our blunder[.] Please sign and return the enclosed at once or what would be better send it on to me at 7 Lothbury... We had *40000* shares paid upon before 2 oClock yesterday. We are steady at £3 pm. & shall be higher. I think by my paying in 500£ for you I may have a chance of getting you *one* hundred or 150. & I shall sell for you as soon as possible'. See **3907**. Also on 8 April Rose would write again from Victoria Street: 'I have paid £500 & hope to get you 100 shares. We are besieged & have had 92000£ paid in already for £35000 and we shall have more tomorrow. I find there was an error in Mackenzies amount & have obtained £2.12.6 more from him today which I have paid to your credit with the London & Westmr. Bank'. H R/I/B/95-96. For Mackenzie, see **3954**&n2.

2 D had attended the Bucks Easter Quarter Sessions at Aylesbury on Monday 4 April; he is not recorded as having contributed to any of the discussions. *BH* (9 Apr 1864).

3 See **3903**&nn2&3 and **3905**&n3. Evidently matters proceeded quickly, as on 11 April Longman would write to D that the printer was sending two proofs, to arrive next day. On 10 May he would write: 'I shall be able to send you the eight copies of your "Epick" tomorrow morning. The presentation copies for the press, of which I enclose a list will be sent out at the same time ... P.S. I understand that we take the cost & risk and divide any profit with you. We print *1000*.' He would advertise on 25 and 29 April that the work would appear 'In a few days, in 1 vol, fcp. 8vo.', on 11 and 12 May that it would 'be published on Friday next, price 5s.', and on 17 May that it was 'Now ready'. On 13 February 1866 he would report that 556 copies were left, and on 20 February gratefully decline D's offer to indemnify him. H E/VII/A/2-5; *The Times* (25, 29 April, 11, 12, 17 May, 1864).

TO: PHILIP ROSE Grosvenor Gate, Friday [8 April 1864] 3907

ORIGINAL: H R/I/A/171

EDITORIAL COMMENT: Paper imprinted 'Grosvenor Gate'. Docketed in another hand: 'April 8 1864'.

P. Rose Esr Friday

My dr R.

You did not *enclose* anything to sign.[1]

I conclude what I enclose will explain what you wanted.

I shall be at home until *three o'ck* in case you send up.

Yrs ever | D.

TO: PHILIP ROSE Grosvenor Gate [Sunday] 10 April 1864 3908

ORIGINAL: H R/I/A/172

EDITORIAL COMMENT: Paper imprinted 'Grosvenor Gate'.

Private April 10 1864

Phil: Rose Esq

My dear Rose,

I saw him.[1] He seemed, generally speaking, against all loans. He said the world was mad, & preferred a bubble share to a good investment. Didn't see, why it shd. be more successful, than the / Danish, wh:, with a cause so popular in the country, was a failure; & so on.[2]

I could observe, that he was disgusted with the interference of the new Companies with the regular financial routine;[3] & all he said must be taken / with this recollection.

Small loans, however, have been successful, even of late, as for example the Egyptian,[4] & to a certain degree, the Portuguese.[5] I am inclined to think myself, that the

1 See **3906**&n1; see further **3908**.

1 Presumably Rothschild, although the Rothschild house was by this time involved in loans to foreign governments. Clapham II 346.

2 For some of Rose's foreign loan dealings, see **3906**n1. *The Times* 'Money-Market' column had announced on 27 February: 'A Danish loan of 500,000£, (being the first portion of a loan of 2,000,000£, authorized for railway purposes) has been announced to-day ... The rate of interest will be 4 per cent ... and the subscription price is 91'.

3 The new companies had proliferated after the Companies' Act of 1862 limited a shareholder's liability to the value of the shares he or she held. See n2 above, and for D's and Rose's investment in the new Land Mortgage Bank of India, see **3855**&n1 and **3924**&n1.

4 *The Times* of 5 April 1862 had reported that 'Proposals for the Egyptian Government Loan have been issued ... for 1,811,040£. sterling, to be represented by 7 per cent. bonds for 2,195,200£., at the price of 82½'. The loan was over-subscribed four times at this price and prompted a second issue. British promoters of a loan through the Anglo-Egyptian Bank in 1864 included Samuel Laing and the General Credit Company. The increasing debt would eventually lead to Egyptian insolvency and D's audacious purchase of the Suez Canal in 1875. L.H. Jenks *The Migration of British Capital to 1875* (1938) 312 ff, 408n42.

5 *The Times* of 19 October 1863 had reported: 'The annexed proposals for a Three per Cent. Portuguese Loan at the price of 48 have been issued ... The nominal amount is 2,500,000£., but 1,000,000£. has been privately subscribed, and 250,000£. is reserved for Portugal, leaving only 1,250,000£. for allotment in London.' The reporter commented that Portuguese credit had now become much more stable. On 6 April 1864, *The Times* had reported that the Portuguese government had repaid its subvention on time and signed a contract for a new railway line.

Swedish[6] would float well, tho' I / shd. recommend my friends not to *remain* in that, or indeed anything else.

I think the prospect is not only of Conference, but even of suspension of arms.[7]

Yours ever, | D.

3909 TO: SAMUEL WILBERFORCE Grosvenor Gate [Monday] 11 April 1864

ORIGINAL: BODL MS Wilberforce c14 ff115-16

EDITORIAL COMMENT: Paper imprinted 'Grosvenor Gate'. *Sic:* embarassed; embarassment.

April 11 1864

The | Lord Bishop of Oxford

My dear Lord,

I was, until this morning, under Royal command to be at Buckingham Palace on Wednesday morning:, wh: greatly embarassed me, as at the same time is / fixed 2nd. Reading of Locke Kings County Franchise Bill: a full house, important debate, & perhaps close division.[1] That embarassment is now removed by H. M. having postponed our reception until Saturday,[2] but / you will see at once, that I cannot be at Oxford, & I sincerely regret it.[3]

Yours ever faithfully | *B. Disraeli*

6 *The Times* the previous day (9 April 1864) had reported: 'It is understood that the new Swedish Four-and-a-half per Cent. Loan for 2,223,000£. will be introduced on Monday ... at the price of 92½'. *The Times* would confirm the report on the 11th. The annual report and general meeting (presumably of a previous issue) of the Swedish Railway Company in London would report disappointing passenger traffic, although partly compensated by freight receipts. *The Times* (28 Apr, 4 May 1864).

7 The conference proposed by England to resolve the Schleswig-Holstein conflict was currently expected to begin as early as Tuesday 12 April, but in the event would open in London on 25 April, only to break up without conclusion on 25 June; see **3933**&n1. *The Times* (8 Apr 1864). The eventual peace treaty would be signed in Vienna on 30 October, after further fighting forced Denmark to relinquish all claims to the disputed duchies.

---

1 The Wednesday 13 April sitting would begin at noon, when the first substantial piece of business would be second reading of Locke King's County Franchise Bill (to extend the county franchise to £10 occupiers). It would pass in a division of 254-227 against the government, D voting with the majority but not speaking in the debate. *Hansard* CLXXIV cols 916-54; *The Times* (15 Apr 1864).

2 The royal invitation had originally been to a court at Buckingham Palace 'on Wednesday the 13th: of April 1864 at ¼ to 3 oClock. Full Dress – Mourning[;] Ladies without Trains[;] Gentlemen – Crape on the left arm'. On 10 April it had been postponed to Saturday the 16th and on the 15th would again be postponed 'in consequence of the Queen's indisposition' with no new date given; MA has docketed the note: 'The Queen suffering from Neuralgia'. On 3 May there would be another invitation, for Wednesday 11 May; see **3921**&n3. H D/V/A/66-67c.

3 On 21 March, at the direction of the Bishop of Oxford, D had been invited 'if possible' to assist at 'the Public Meeting of the 3 Diocesan Societies ... at the Town-Hall, Oxford on April 13th. at 1 o'Clock.' Bishop Wilberforce himself had written on 8 April from Brussels to ask if D could speak at the 1 *pm* Wednesday meeting, pointing out that he could be back at the House within hours: 'I could promise you a great opportunity of moving the young mind of England & a great ovation.' H B/XXI/W/364-5.

TO: [FREDERICK LYGON] Grosvenor Gate, Saturday [16 April 1864] 3910

ORIGINAL: BCP [18]

EDITORIAL COMMENT: Paper imprinted 'Grosvenor Gate'. *Dating:* by context; see n1 and **3911**, which also confirm the recipient. A copy dated '[?19 April 1864]' is in BL (Add MS 61892). *Sic:* aid-de-camp.

Saturday

I am glad to hear from my most brilliant aid-de-camp; I thought you were away – but you are never wanting.

Tomorrow at ½ past one.[1]

Ever Yrs | D.

TO: FREDERICK LYGON Grosvenor Gate, Sunday [17 April 1864] 3911

ORIGINAL: BCP [19]

EDITORIAL COMMENT: Paper imprinted 'Grosvenor Gate'. A copy dated '[?20 April 1864]' is in BL (Add MS 61892). *Dating: cf* **3910**n1.

Sunday

Hon: | F. Lygon

My dear Lygon

It has just occurred to me, that ½ past one may be too late for you, in case you / go down to Ealing, as, I think, may be desirable.[1]

I shall, therefore, be ready for you, as soon as you like.

There is one screw a / little loose in the case – but perhaps you can explain it.[2]

Yrs, | D.

TO: FREDERICK LYGON Grosvenor Gate [Sunday] 17 April 1864 3912

ORIGINAL: BCP [14]

EDITORIAL COMMENT: Paper imprinted 'Grosvenor Gate'. A copy is in BL (Add MS 61892).

April 17 1864

Hon. F.L.

Mon Cher,

Send me, if you can witht. inconvenience, by the bearer, the date of the act, wh: created the V. Prest. Ed: Board.[1]

Yrs | D.

1 Lygon had written from Grosvenor Place on 16 April 1864: 'I have just come from Sir Hugh Cairns. I will try to see R. Cecil tomorrow. If you wish it I will go down to Ealing to "cram" Walpole, in which case I should like to see you & wd call in Grosvenor Gate soon after 1. Please send me a line early tomorrow morning.' H B/XX/LN/23. Walpole's suburban home was The Green, Ealing. *LPOD* (1860). See further **3911**&n1 and **3915**&n1.

1 See **3910**n1. One of Lygon's two letters of 17 April to D was evidently written after returning from Ealing, as he reports: 'I saw Mr Walpole.' H B/XX/LN/25. For Walpole's key support of D's 'Privilege – Under Secretaries of State' speech, see **3915**&n1.

2 The loose screw is possibly clarified by Lygon in another letter of 17 April: 'I take the enclosed from Dodd ... The Third Secretary of State in 1794 appears to have been created by prerogative, & not by Act of Parliament ... The fourth Secretary of State (War) was also created by prerogative.' H B/XX/LN/24.

1 The office of vice-president of the committee of council on education was established in 1856 as that of a minister responsible to parliament. *EB* XI. Robert Lowe had held the office since June 1859. After a reso-

3913 TO: FREDERICK LYGON [London] Sunday [17 April 1864]

ORIGINAL: BCP [1]

EDITORIAL COMMENT: Black-edged paper. *Dating:* by Lowe's resignation; see n2.

Private Sunday 7 o'ck

Hon: Fred: Lygon

Mon Cher –

I am sorry to have missed you[1] – but in my visit I heard some authentic news.

Lowe has resigned, & will make a statement tomorrow. His condition of remaining was, that Palmerston shd. have the vote rescinded.[2] Chichester Fortescue has resigned – and, I believe, Ld. Hartington. If Fortescue is looking / to Lowe's place, it is of the last importance, that we shd. fix the date & ceremony of his appointment.[3]

Look well to Bruce's appointment & also Baring: the latter shifted & changed a good deal. It occurs to me, that he might have been placed in his present post after Hartington accepted U.S.[4]

Also, Bruce: there was great delay / after Clive's illness in filling up U.S. Home.[5]

Yours ever, | D.

lution highly critical of the committee's handling of school inspectors' reports was passed on 12 April, he would resign on the 18th, D attesting to his honour but not his political principles. *Hansard* CLXXIV cols 897-914, 1203-18 (D 1215-16). Lygon's two letters on 17 April deal only with D's upcoming privilege speech; see **3911**nn1&2. H B/XX/LN/24-5. See further **3915**&n1 and **3916**&n1. On this day D visited the Rothschilds 'in wonderful spirits' and chuckling over his 'bit of intended mischief.' Charlotte de Rothschild to Leopold de Rothschild, 17 April 1864, MS ROTH.

---

1 See **3911**.

2 For Lowe's resignation on 18 April 1864, see **3912**n1.

3 D's information about these two men is incorrect. Chichester Samuel Fortescue (1823-1898), MP (L) for Louth 1847-74, was a lord of the treasury 1854-5, under-secretary for the colonies June 1857-8, June 1859-November 1865, PC 7 April 1864; he would be chief secretary for Ireland 1865-6, 1868-70, president of the board of trade 1871-4, created Baron Carlingford 1874, privy seal 1881-5, president of council 1883-5. Hartington (see VII **3360**n2) was under-secretary for war April 1863 to February 1866. The dates of under-secretaries' official appointments were relevant to D's motion on 18 April: '"That the provisions of the Act 21 & 22 *Vict.* c. 106, s. 4, have been violated, and that the Seat of the fifth Under Secretary of State has been and is thereby vacated."' *Hansard* CLXXIV col 1231. That is, it was crucial to determine which under-secretary had been the last appointed. See further **3915**&n1 and **3916**&n1.

4 Henry Austin Bruce (1815-1895), of Duffryn, co Glamorgan, a barrister (Lincoln's Inn 1837), MP (L) for Merthyr Tydvil 1852-68, for Renfrewshire 1869-73, home under-secretary since November 1862, would be appointed Lowe's successor as vice-president of the education board on 26 April 1864 (to 1866) and be made PC the same day; he would be second church estates commissioner 1865-6, home secretary 1868-73, lord president of council 1873-4, created Baron Aberdare 1873, DCL Oxford 1880. Thomas George Baring (1826-1904), eldest son of Sir Francis Thornhill Baring (created Baron Northbrook 1866), MP (L) for Penryn and Falmouth 1857-66, when he would succeed his father as 2nd Baron Northbrook, a lord of the admiralty 1857-8, under-secretary for India June 1859-January 1861, August 1861-April 1864, under-secretary for war January-July 1861, 1868-72, would succeed Bruce as home under-secretary 1864-6; he would be first secretary of the admiralty 1866, viceroy of India 1872-6, GCSI 1872, created Earl of Northbrook 1876, DCL (1876), FRS (1880), first lord of the admiralty 1880-5, head of special mission to Egypt 1884-5, LLD (1892).

5 George Clive (1806-1880), a barrister (Lincoln's Inn 1830), MP (L) for Hereford 1857-69, 1874-80, had been under-secretary for the home department June 1859 to November 1862, when he was succeeded by Bruce (n4).

TO: PHILIP ROSE House of Commons, Monday [18 April 1864] 3914

ORIGINAL: H R/I/A/173a

COVER: *Private* | Philip Rose Esq | Westminster | *B. Disraeli*

EDITORIAL COMMENT: House of Commons paper. Docketed on the first page: '19 April 1864'. *Dating:* the docketed date applies to **3918**, treated in H as the second part of this item. In 1864, 19 April was a Tuesday; 'Monday' fits 18 April: see n1.

Monday

My dear Rose,

I have been trying to get to you every day, for some little time – but this question of ~~Prive~~ Privilege has prevented me / calling: my presence being required at four o'ck:.

I will, however call tomorrow at *four*.[1]

Yours ever | D.

TO: MARY ANNE DISRAELI [House of Commons, Monday 18] April 1864 3915

ORIGINAL: H A/I/A/315

EDITORIAL COMMENT: Docketed by MA on the fourth page: '1864 April'. *Dating:* the context (n1) confirms the docketed date.

My dearest

I thought the affair wd. have lasted all night, but when the Government found that Walpole supported me, they gave / up almost everything.

Walpole did well. I to my satisfaction.[1]

I shall be home tolerably early.[2]

Adieu! | D.

TO: JOHN EVELYN DENISON Grosvenor Gate [Tuesday] 19 April 1864 3916

ORIGINAL: NOT OSC 864

PUBLICATION HISTORY: John Evelyn Denison *Notes from My Journal When Speaker* (1900) 156, dated [2] April 1864, paraphrase

EDITORIAL COMMENT: Paper imprinted 'Grosvenor Gate'. Endorsed in another hand on the first page: 'Mr Disraeli abt. Mr Bruces Writ.'

April 19 1864

Rt Honble | The Speaker

1 See **3915**&n1 for D's privilege speech shortly after the House began at 4 *pm*. See further **3916**&n1 and **3918**.

---

1 On 18 April 1864, D had drawn the House's attention to the unconstitutionality of five under-secretaries of state with seats in the Commons, the law explicitly allowing only four. In the ensuing debate, Walpole strongly supported D's resolution that the last-appointed under-secretary be unseated, and it was passed without division after an amendment that a select committee examine the matter. *Hansard* CLXXIV cols 1218-50(D 1218-31, 1248-9). Frederick Lygon had written on 17 April (**3911**n1): 'Mr Walpole will call upon you tomorrow morning at a quarter before eleven. In the meantime he sends for your consideration the resolution wh: I enclose'; Lygon also detailed the discussion that had determined the wording. H B/XX/LN/25. The solution, announced in the *Express* and reprinted in *The Times* on 22 April, was that in future one under-secretary would be a peer.

2 The House would adjourn just after 1 *am*. *Hansard* CLXXIV col 1274.

Dear Mr Speaker,
It seems to me we have made a mistake about the Merthyr writ, &, if so, the matter is urgent. I tried, but in vain, to prevent the precipitate conduct of the / Govt.

Look at the Statute that appointed the V. Prest of Education – Sess. 1856 – I think c. 116.

There is no analogy betn. the cases of Secy of State, & others, & this office. They may be Secretaries of State & Crs. of Exr. without being Privy-Councillors.

This / is a case of a Statutory P.C. & it seems to me, that the Merthyr seat is not vacant, inasmuch as Mr Bruce could not have accepted the office under the words of the Statute.

I purpose to bring this point before the House / as a matter of Privilege today, & have therefore taken the liberty of troubling you with these lines.[1]

Yours, | dear Mr Speaker, | Ever most sincerely, | *B. Disraeli*

3917 TO: LORD STANHOPE — Grosvenor Gate [Tuesday] 19 April 1864

ORIGINAL: LIV [4]
EDITORIAL COMMENT: Paper imprinted 'Grosvenor Gate'.

The | Earl Stanhope — April 19 1864
My dear Lord,
I am very sorry indeed, that I cannot be present to day at the settlement of our Report, / but I have to bring forward, at four o'ck to day in the House, a question of Privilege of a very grave character.[1] /

Ever, my dr Lord, | Sincerely Yours, | *B. Disraeli*

3918 TO: PHILIP ROSE — 6 Victoria Street [Tuesday] 19 April 1864

ORIGINAL: H R/I/A/173b
EDITORIAL COMMENT: Paper imprinted '6, Victoria Street, Westminster Abbey, S.W. _____*186_*.' The date has been completed to read '19 Apl *1864*'.

---

1 See **3913**n4. After Bruce had been selected to replace Lowe as vice-president of the education board, a new writ for his seat of Merthyr Tydvil had been moved on 18 April, but not passed until after D's speech on privilege that day; see **3915**&n1. On 19 April it would be Col French who would raise D's point succinctly: 'By the 19 & 20 *Vict.* c. 116, the choice of Her Majesty in appointing a Vice-President of the Board of Education was limited to members of the Privy Council; and the hon. Gentleman whose seat was declared to be vacant last night was not a member of the Privy Council. Under these circumstances he could not have accepted an office under the Crown, the House had no power to declare the seat vacant, and the course taken last night was therefore, he believed, totally irregular.' Roundell Palmer, the attorney-general, answered by distinguishing between acceptance of office and completion of the appointment. *Hansard* CLXXIV cols 1194-8 (D 1196-7), 1287-9; *The Times* (19 Apr 1864). The Speaker (see ph) recorded telling D on his arrival at the House that, because of advice he had received since D's letter, this was also his view, to which D had replied: '"Oh, if you think so, I won't make the motion".'

---

1 See **3916**&n1 for the privilege speech D planned for this day. The report was presumably that of the National Portrait Gallery, of which Stanhope was the chairman and D a trustee. On 3 May *The Times* would record the gallery's seventh annual report, listing five donations (including a bust of Thomas Arnold) and seven purchases, among them a portrait of Archbishop Laud attributed to Van Dyck. The gallery reported many working men in the 2,861 visitors on Easter Monday and Tuesday, and it affirmed that under inadequate conditions 'the trustees do their best.' After another meeting on 16 July, D would agree to talk with the secretary, George Scharf, on the 19th. H B/XIV/A/140b.

My dr R.

I was obliged to call, early, as I think there is another case of privilege at 4 o'ck.[1]

Yrs ever | D.

TO: LADY DOROTHY NEVILL Grosvenor Gate [Wednesday 27?] April 1864 **3919**

ORIGINAL: EJM [23]

PUBLICATION HISTORY: Ralph Nevill, ed *The Reminiscences of Lady Dorothy Nevill* (1906) 209

EDITORIAL COMMENT: Paper imprinted 'Grosvenor Gate'. *Dating:* the context (see nn1-3) makes the clearly inscribed date impossible. *Sic:* April 21.

April 21. 1864

Dear Dorothy,

You have made me not only the most graceful, but the most magnificent, of presents.[1] I have never feasted on my favorite fruit so entirely / before: they were not only too plenteous, but really without precedent – superb. Two nights after the house of Commons, &, to day, after a long Council at the Brit: Museum,[2] your / delicious strawberries, as charming as yourself, have refreshed, & renovated, me.

When are you ~~going~~ coming to town? And how do your conifers, & all their graceful companions, flourish? I envy you in your exotic / groves.[3]

What do you think of the P. of Wales & Garibaldi? For a quasi-crowned head to call on a subject is strange – & that subject a rebel![4]

Mary Anne sends you 1000 kind messages, & I am always

Your affectionate | D.

TO: JOHN EVELYN DENISON Grosvenor Gate [Friday] 29 April 1864 **3920**

ORIGINAL: NOT OSC 865

EDITORIAL COMMENT: Paper imprinted 'Grosvenor Gate'.

Rt Honorable | The Speaker April 29 1864

1 See **3914** and **3916**&n1.

---

1 Lady Dorothy had written to MA (the letter docketed 'March 27th/64' by MA): 'It is only today that I heard you were unwell[.] I do hope you will let me know something about yourself pray do as I am so anxious to know how you are [*See* **3899**&n1.] I have not forgotten Mr Disraeli but as yet we have not had a dish of strawberries but you may depend on the 1st being dedicated to him'. H D/III/C/1523. On 26 April MA had recorded paying 'Car[riage] of Strawbs from Lady Dorothy Nevil /9d.' H acc.

2 No mention of this meeting has been found. *The Times* on 11 May would report that "The annual accounts of the British Museum have been laid before Parliament." On Wednesday 27 April, D seems not to have attended the short Commons sitting (until 5:50 *pm*), as he is not listed in a recorded division. *Hansard* CLXXIV cols 1700-55.

3 D's phrase 'exotic groves' became the title of a modern biography of Lady Dorothy, by Guy Nevill (Salisbury 1984).

4 Garibaldi, in England ostensibly to consult about his health, was being lionized by all social classes. D's cynical view was that he was collecting money; see *Disraeli, Derby* 213, and **3923**&n4. The Prince's visit had occurred on 22 April. *The Times* next day reported that Garibaldi had visited Stafford House to give the Prince an opportunity to meet him privately; the Prince walked from Buckingham Palace without attracting attention and stayed at Stafford House for over an hour: 'It is needless to say with what sincere satisfaction the announcement of this visit by his Royal Highness to the General will be received throughout the country.' For the Queen's outrage at the visit, see Weintraub *Edward* 134 (dated erroneously 12 April).

Dear Mr Speaker,
The bottle, wh: is not in a straw cradle, is the wine, wh: I once mentioned to you, & wh: you were so kind as / to say you would taste. I believe it has been in bottle fifty years; but I can only prove by a cellar book, that it was, as bottled, in my father's cellar in 1822: a / great crust & requires care in decanting: color very fine.

The other bottle, in straw cradle, perhaps as old, but then the color has gone. It is said, however, still to / have a remarkable flavor.[1]

Believe me, | dear Mr Speaker, | very sincerely yours | *B. Disraeli*

3921 TO: LORD AUGUSTUS LOFTUS — Grosvenor Gate [Monday] 9 May 1864

ORIGINAL: LUC [1]
COVER: The | Lord Augustus Loftus | K.C.B. | St James' Hotel | *B.Disraeli*
EDITORIAL COMMENT: Paper imprinted 'Grosvenor Gate'. *Sic:* St James' [*cover*].

May 9 1864

Rt Honble | Lord Augustus Loftus | K.C.B[1]
Dear Lord Augustus
There is a meeting of members of the Ho: of Commons, here tomorrow, called somewhat unexpectedly.[2] This will prevent my / having the honor, & pleasure, of receiving you, as you proposed.

On Wednesday, Mrs Disraeli & myself are commanded, in the morning, to the / Palace.[3]

On Thursday or Friday, at three o'ck: I could be at your service.[4]

Yours faithfully | *B. Disraeli*

1 Denison would thank D next day (30th) from Palace Yard: 'The subject shall be treated throughout in a becoming manner. The occasion shall be, when, after due notice, a motion is made, that supply be granted to exhausted nature. There shall be no hurry, a calm state of nerves, and a proper humour. When such a moment will arrive, I know not, perhaps in the Whitsun Holidays. I must add my thanks to Mrs Disraeli for the convoy granted.' H B/XXI/D/162.

---

1 Lord Augustus William Frederick Spencer Loftus (1817-1904), fourth son of 2nd Marquess of Ely, career diplomat (Stuttgart, Baden-Baden, Vienna, Berlin, currently at Munich 1863-6), KCB 1862, GCB 1866, PC 1868, would be ambassador at Berlin 1866-71 (accredited to the North German Confederation 1868), at St Petersburg 1871-9, governor of New South Wales and Norfolk Island 1879-85. For some of D's disparaging references to him in 1876 see M&B VI 23, 89, 111.

2 The meeting was likely to co-ordinate party strategy for second reading of the Borough Franchise Bill (to extend the vote from £10 to £6 occupiers) which, on 11 May after lengthy debate, would be defeated 216-272, D and his colleagues voting with the majority. *Hansard* CLXXV cols 285-351. See further **3923**&n4.

3 See **3909**&n2. The DS are listed among those who attended the Queen's court at Buckingham Palace on 11 May at 3 *pm. MP* (12 May 1864).

4 Loftus's business may have concerned his lobbying the government about this time on behalf of Baron Justus von Liebig's commercial processes for meat extracts. Loftus obtained a naval contract for the product, but Admiralty specifications proved too stringent for fulfilment. *Diplomatic Reminiscences of Lord Augustus Loftus,* 2nd series (1894), vol. 1, 30-5.

TO: DUKE OF WELLINGTON Grosvenor Gate [Wednesday] 11 May 1864 3922

ORIGINAL: HUNT HM 52656

EDITORIAL COMMENT: Paper imprinted 'Grosvenor Gate'. In another hand after 'book': '["Lord George Bentinck"]'.

May 11 1864

His Grace | The Duke of Wellington | K. G.

My dear Duke,

Here's the book. You need not read it, but must accept it as a mark of real regard.

Had / I proceeded with this youthful project, your illustrious father, & his deathless deeds, would have occupied a great portion of it, & I possess a letter from him / *anent;* written thirty years ago![1]

Yours ever, | D.

TO: LORD DERBY Grosvenor Gate [Friday] 13 May 1864 3923

ORIGINAL: DBP Box 146/1 [87]

PUBLICATION HISTORY: M&B IV 344-5, dated at Grosvenor Gate, 13 May 1864, up to 'what I said.' (paragraph 7); 404, the last paragraph

EDITORIAL COMMENT: Paper imprinted 'Grosvenor Gate'. To begin the second sheet, D has repeated 'thing to decide is,' a departure from his usual practice of a single catch word at page breaks. Docketed by Derby on the last page: 'Disraeli B'.

Confidential May 13 1864

Rt Honble | The Earl of Derby | K. G.

My dear Lord,

Conversations with Bernstorff are, in general, so insignificant, that I have difficulty in reproducing to myself the one to wh: you refer, tho' it was so recent.[1]

1 Despite the annotation (see EC), 'the book' is clearly a copy of the new edition of D's *Revolutionary Epick.* Longman sent 8 pre-publication copies on this day; see **3906**n3. For D's failed attempt to dedicate the poem to the Iron Duke, see I **312**&n1. Stanley on this day would record also receiving a copy: 'Disraeli has published a new edition of his almost forgotten poem, which he has dedicated to me. He sent me the volume, but I knew nothing of his intentions, and stumbled on the dedication by mere accident.' *Disraeli, Derby* 215.

1 Derby had written on 12 May 1864 from St James's Square, to thank D for a copy of *The Revolutionary Epick;* he continued: 'I am afraid you will think I am making an ungracious return for your kindness, if I frankly express to you some apprehension, founded on a conversation I had last night with Bernstorff, that in your communications with him you have been rather less guarded than is your wont. For, unless I greatly misunderstood him, he wished to convey to me the impression that you had informed him of your willingness to support, on the Danish question, a project precisely similar to that which Buest had suggested to you. He added, that "considering my position," he was very desirous of knowing my opinion. I answered that "considering my position," I held it to be my duty to keep myself entirely unpledged; and I declined to enter upon any discussion of that, or any other proposal, which might come before the Conference. It is quite on the cards that, if we were in Office, we might find ourselves compelled to admit some such basis; but while we are out of Office, I cannot see the advantage, but quite the contrary, of showing our hands; nor do I think it quite fair to our own Plenipotentiaries in the Conference to give their Opponents any such select encouragement as may lead them to be more unyielding than they might otherwise prove.' H B/XX/S/322. For D's earlier view of the Schleswig-Holstein situation, see **3892**&n2.

On Tuesday / night, at Apponyi's,[2] just as I was going away, he seized me, himself in much excitement, tho' more stupid than usual, if that be possible.

I can only recall the following remarks on my part, wh: formed any exception to the platitudes I usually bestow on him.

He was evidently in a great / fright about war. I said "Why, an armistice is the first step to peace"[.] He reminding me, that it was only for a month, I went on to this effect – "Depend upon it, if you have a long armistice, & nothing settled at the end of it, you *will* be in danger of war: you ought not to lose a moment in solving the real difficulty: / what does the Conference understand by the words "integrity of Denmark": England is not very disposed to go to war with Germany about German territory; Denmark no longer hopes she will, perhaps does not wish her to do so.

Therefore, the future of Holstein ought to be considered by the Conference as a secondary point: the first thing to decide is / "what is Denmark." If you can agree upon that, & if you can, you ought to do it quickly, all the rest will, somehow or other, find its level, & settle itself."

Of course, all this was not said continuously, or so crudely, but this, so far as I can recollect, & I really have racked my brain this morning about it, is the cream / of what I said. I have no recollection of Buest's name ever having been mentioned. I have a very strong impression, that it was not. I assume, always, that Bernstorff & Buest have different objects, & I looked upon Buest's scheme of settlement as Anti-prussian.[3]

Tho' Gladstone's move was matured, & indeed for / a considerable time contemplated, I have no doubt the visit, & reception, of Garibaldi have acted on his impressionable nature & have betrayed him into a far more extreme position, than was at first intended.[4] The consequences must be grave; / tho' I dare say the Cavendishes,

2 There had been a 'numerously attended' assembly at the Austrian embassy on Tuesday 10 May. *MP* (11 May 1864).

3 The London conference convened by the British government, with representatives from Austria, Denmark, France, the Germanic Confederation, Prussia, Russia, Sweden and Norway, had begun meetings on 25 April. Its first achievement, proposed by Russell on the first day, agreed on 9 May and announced in parliament that evening, had been a truce, which the Danish government limited to a month beginning on 12 May. *Hansard* CLXXV cols 176-7, 192, 197-8 (D 197-8). Also on the first day, the representatives had begun to announce their positions; Bernstorff (for Austria) said he would propose annexing the Duchies to Germany under conditions that excluded the Augustenburgs, maintained Denmark's integrity, and made Prussian influence paramount. Count Friedrich Ferdinand von Beust (1809-86), Austrian statesman, imperial chancellor 1867-71, ambassador at London 1871-8, at Paris 1878-82, represented the German diet. On 29 April the British press had published the points announced in Frankfurt that would be Beust's conference proposals – essentially that Holstein and Schleswig be allowed to determine their own futures, disregarding the 1852 protocol or the succession rights claimed by the King of Denmark. *AR* 1864 (Chronicle) 281ff; *MP* (28, 29 Apr 1864).

4 Gladstone, in addition to meetings with Garibaldi, had given a 'great entertainment' for him on 20 April attended by 'Before the door, at night, say a thousand people, all in the best humour'. *Gladstone Diaries* VI 270; *MP* (21 Apr 1864). See **3921**n2 for the 11 May debate in which Gladstone had supported extending the franchise to £6 occupiers, and had polarized his hearers with a ringing call for universal male suffrage. His name, however, does not appear in the division list. Derby (n1) had written: 'What a marvellous exhibition was Gladstone's last night! It was one which cannot but have serious consequences, and, I think must be very embarrassing to his Colleagues, and damaging to the Government. I saw several of their supporters last night who are open-mouthed against him – but I see all the Government supported the motion. Can it be by accident that his own name does not appear as having voted on either side!' Gladstone himself felt that the sensation his speech caused 'was due less to me than to the change in the

Russells, &c, will, in due time, swallow his programme. The smaller Whigs, Beaumonts, Ramsdens, & perhaps Lansdownes & Fitzwilliams, may detach themselves.

Yours sincerely, | D.

TO: PHILIP ROSE Grosvenor Gate [Saturday] 14 May 1864 3924

ORIGINAL: H R/I/A/174

EDITORIAL COMMENT: Paper imprinted 'Grosvenor Gate'.

Philip Rose Esq May 14 1864

My dear Rose,

Will you forward the accompanying to our mysterious ally.

I assume the enclosed requires no attention from me, & must refer to an old transaction.[1]

I mention it, / not to be importunate, but merely apropos, & to prevent possible mistakes – but I have never heard further of the International shares.[2]

Yours ever, | D.

TO: LORD SHREWSBURY & TALBOT Carlton Club [Friday] 20 May 1864 3925

ORIGINAL: H H/LIFE

EDITORIAL COMMENT: Taken from an apparently incomplete MS copy headed: '*To Lord Shrewsbury & Talbot*'. H B/II/66 is a draft in D's hand (see n2).

Copy

Confidential. Carlton Club | May 20 1864.

My dear Lord,

Lord Derby sent for me yesterday afternoon to confer with me on a subject which has frequently, and of late, seriously engaged his anxious attention: vizt, the effect on the prospects, and influence, of the Conservative party, of the Registration Society, of which your Lordship is President.[1]

It is the opinion of Lord Derby, and I entirely concur with him, that the action

hearers & in the public mind from the professions at least if not the principles of 1859.' *Gladstone Diaries* VI 275. See further Morley *Gladstone* II 125-31.

---

1 Adjacent to this letter and presumably the 'enclosed' is a notice of transfer dated at London 11 May 1864, from the Land Mortgage Bank of India, of 140 shares from D to Heyman B. Goldschmidt; near the top is inscribed '1839'. The document states that lack of a response will be taken as confirmation of its correctness. H R/I/A/174a. See **3855**&n1, where Rose's shares are syndicated and locked up for 3-6 months, and **3856**, where D is annoyed that his are also syndicated; he says for 3 months, but if it was in fact for 6 months, that would fit with the date of this letter. For the possible identity of the 'mysterious ally' see **3954**&n2.

2 Perhaps the enigmatic references in **3906**&n1 are relevant here. In *The Times* of this day, 'Inter. Finan. Society' is listed as closing at '6 - 6¼ pm'. The International Financial Society had been established in 1863 as an investment trust specializing in foreign governments and railroads; the second syndicate in the Society's shares had wound up on 7 April 1864. Also in 1863 it had bought the Hudson's Bay Company and refloated its stock. It would make substantial profits underwriting the bonds of the Canadian Pacific Railway in London and, through the HBC, be a major developer of the Canadian west. P.L. Cottrell *Investment Banking in England, 1856-82: A Case Study of the International Financial Society* (1985), chapter 4 *passim*.

---

1 In 1863 Lord Shrewsbury and his son Lord Ingestre, without involving either Jolliffe or Rose, had formed the National Conservative Registration Society, with Henry Smith, the Bucks Conservative agent, as its

of that Society, which has established a double management of the Party in the Country, is highly injurious to us. It was originally formed by a few individuals, some restless, some designing, who unfortunately took advantage of your Lordship's high name and station, and of Lord Ingestre's just popularity, to further their own views and caprices. They have disturbed, perplexed, and tend to break up that concentrated organisation, which it has taken many years to establish by the natural machinery of the party, and are perpetually sowing misconception and dissension enfeebling and distracting our efforts and influence.

There can be no question, that it would be to the advantage of the Conservative party that the Society should cease to exist, but Lord Derby and myself are both alive to the difficulties and perhaps dangers that might attend at this moment such a course. The only mode in our opinion by which the injurious effects may be mitigated and perhaps neutralised is by defining the duties of the Society of which you are President and by strictly confining its operation to the fulfilment of those duties. Its name indicates the remedy. It is a "Registration" Society. Let it confine itself to *Registration* and entirely avoid *Electioneering*. It is its adventures in this province which are doing so much mischief.

As a distinguished member of the Party, as his friend, and as President of the Society Lord Derby looks to you to effect this object; but it must be done thoroughly and completely, and you must not be silenced by any unscrupulous statements to the contrary which are made by underlings. We have in our possession evidence of their unjustifiable and injurious conduct.[2]

The [*end of copy*]

3926 TO: HENRY GEORGE WARREN [London, before 21 May 1864]

ORIGINAL: PS 1471

PUBLICATION HISTORY: *Observer* (22 May 1864); *BH* (28 May 1864)

EDITORIAL COMMENT: The following is the *BH* extract. *Dating:* by context; see n1.

glad to hear that the fund is at length apparently placed on a sound and practical basis.[1]

secretary. On this day, 20 May 1864, Rose complained to Derby that the society was doing more harm than good, and was interfering with Col Taylor's authority. The society would play no part in the 1865 elections, and be replaced by an official party registration association in 1866. Stewart *Conservative Party* 337&n57.

2 The draft (see ec) continues at this point (crossed out): 'I came from the H. to the Carlton in order to take the chance of seeing you on this matter'.

1 The Newspaper Press Fund (for members and families of deceased members) had been founded by parliamentary reporters in 1858, but had not prospered. Its 'inaugural' dinner, with Lord Houghton as president and Henry George Warren as honorary secretary, was held on Saturday 21 May 1864. Warren announced donations amounting to nearly £1,500, and quoted D's letter accompanying his donation of £10. Henry George Warren (b 1809), freemason and publisher, Grand Stewards Lodge 1855, Master 1860, Prestonian Lecturer 1861, published the *Masonic Mirror* 1855-6 and the *Freemasons Magazine and Masonic Mirror* 1856-71 from his office at 2 Red Lion Court, Fleet Street. *BH* (28 May 1864); *MP* (23 May 1864); *The Times* (18 May 1864); *Dickens Letters* IX 350&nn2&3, 361; Colin F.W. Dyer *The Grand Stewards and Their Lodge* (1985). Information kindly supplied by Andrew Prescott, Sheffield University.

TO: PHILIP ROSE 6 Victoria Street [Friday] 27 May 1864 3927

ORIGINAL: H R/I/A/175

EDITORIAL COMMENT: Paper imprinted '6, Victoria Street, Westminster Abbey, S.W. ____*186_*'. D has completed the date to read 'May 27 *1864*'.

Private May 27 1864

P. Rose Esq

My dear Rose,

It is probable, that some important letters may arrive at your house from Copenhagen. As my name would not do for the post I have instructed my friend that they shd be addressed to you; he putting / the initial letter D. in the corner of the direction. Forward them to me at once. If you open them by chance in the hurry of business, wh: is likely eno', dont be annoyed – ↑as it will not in the slightest degree signify.↓[1]

Yours ever, | D.

TO: MARY ANNE DISRAELI [House of Commons? Friday 27?] May 1864 3928

ORIGINAL: H A/I/A/316

EDITORIAL COMMENT: Endorsed by MA on the last page: '1864 May Dear Dizzy'. *Dating:* by context; see n1.

My dearest Love,

Will you send me a great coat. It is very cold: a North-East wind.[1]

Yours | D.

TO: LORD DERBY Grosvenor Gate [Sunday] 29 May 1864 3929

ORIGINAL: DBP Box 146/1

EDITORIAL COMMENT: Paper imprinted 'Grosvenor Gate'. Endorsed by Derby on the last page: 'Disraeli B. *And*'. *Sic:* or is not.

Private May 29 1864

Rt Honble | The Earl of Derby | K. G.

1 D was currently preparing his 6 June speech on Denmark (see **3929**&n3), in which he would chide ministers' secrecy about the on-going conference negotiations in contrast to the other participants' openness with their respective countries: 'I do not want to penetrate the secrets of the Conference, but it has been well said by the Gentlemen who have addressed us, that there is not that reserve in other countries which is observed in England. I myself read in a German paper the other day an absolute account of what took place on a most critical day in the Conference, and that not by way of rumour or *on dit,* but with all the forms of diplomatic accuracy, and I have reason to believe from subsequent inquiry that it was an authentic document.' *Hansard* CLXXV col 1280, whole speech 1279-86. The letters expected from Copenhagen may have been part of D's 'inquiry'. In an undated note (docketed 'June 22d/64' by MA, but written earlier, from a reference to Ascot (9 June) as a future event) Earle would report a letter from Copenhagen, pressing Britain to attack, but non-specific about Danish involvement. If Denmark withdrew, he thought they should publish their reasons for Parliament's edification. There had been a private conference 'yesterday.' On 'Wednesday', he would report another letter from Copenhagen, predicting the dispersal of the conference. H B/XX/E/329, 336. There are two documents in H on Schleswig-Holstein signed only 'IAG'. One suggests 'Possible Solutions of Holstein Schleswig question,' the other (docketed '?July 1864') a response to A.W. Kinglake in the upcoming July debate on D's resolution censuring the government; see **3933**n1.

1 The week of 14 to 20 May 1864 was very hot, but on 27 May there was a heavy frost and gale-force winds. *AR* 1864 (Chronicle) 316.

My dear Lord,

I regret I have not been able to call on you today.

It is highly desirable, that there shd. be "interpellations", in both houses tomorrow, as to the state of the Conference. /

When a government is negotiating, parliamentary reserve usual & right: but then that reserve is conditional: that Parliamt. shd. be acquainted with, & generally approve, the policy pursued by the ministry in their negotiations.

The / policy announced by the Government in the present instance, & sanctioned by Parliament, was founded on treaty of 1852; its object integrity & independence of Denmark; wh: they assured us Austria & Prussia equally desired.[1]

Is it, / or is not, true, as announced in a foreign (– but authentic) – quarter – that the Government, since they entered the Conference, have entirely changed their policy; have given up the treaty of 1852; & instead of supporting integ: & indep: of D. / are actually themselves proposing a programme of dismemberment?[2]

If so, this shd. be declared to Parliament.

I write this, because, if I remember right, ~~you can't~~ ↑it is not usual to↓ ask questions in your house without giving ↑private↓ notice the day before. / I ~~shall~~ ↑propose to↓ give my notice tomorrow morning to Ld. Palmn.

But what is desirable is to have answers in both houses at the same time, as they often vary &c.

I will call to talk over the matter tomorrow / – but from what I hear, it is most important it shd. be done at once & simultaneously.[3]

Yours sincerely, | D.

1 At a London conference in 1852, the five great powers plus Norway and Sweden had declared Denmark indivisible, the separate position of Schleswig and Holstein within the kingdom to be maintained, the Augustenberg line to be excluded from succession to the duchies and the German Confederation's rights in Holstein and Lauenburg to be unaffected. On 19 April 1864 Bernal Osborne had moved that the protocol terms dealing with the order of succession in Schleswig and Holstein not be insisted on in settling the Dano-German dispute. D, by moving the previous question, had successfully opposed the motion as an inappropriate intervention in the conference negotiations about to begin. *Hansard* CLXXIV cols 1292-1376 (D 1360-68, 1376).

2 See **3927**&n1 for some of D's sources of information, not all of them 'foreign' (see his postscript to this letter). On 28 May *The Times* had commented: 'It is asserted in the Continental newspapers that a solution has been found ... and that at last the great Powers of Europe are in accord ... The basis of the arrangement will be the union of Holstein and of the six southern *communes* of Schleswig to Germany, and the incorporation of the rest of [it] ... with the Danish kingdom.'

3 Derby would reply the same day from St James's Square: 'I shall be glad to see you tomorrow, at any hour at which it may suit you to call. I doubt the expediency of asking any questions as to the course of the Conference. My impression is that it will fail: that no agreement will be come to, or, if any, one that will be entirely discreditable to us. I should not look in that light on the proposal which is said to have been before the Conference of the cession (*to whom* is a question) of Holstein & S. Schleswig, which, under certain circumstances, would be no real loss to Denmark. But it is clear that such an arrangement would be a "dismemberment" of Denmark, the sole condition on which Russell declared that France & England were agreed to interfere by force of arms. In my opinion *no* move ought to be made at present, the Government ought to be allowed "rope enough"; and we ought not to move, or to interfere (by which we should take on ourselves the responsibility of an impossible position) but to leave on the Government the undivided charge of untying, or of cutting the Gordian knot which they have been mainly instrumental in framing.' H B/XX/S/323. D would nevertheless make his interpellation on 6 June, first carefully pointing out that it was not the opposition's intention to interfere in the negotiations: 'But when we hear, as we do hear, that the course which the Government is pursuing is one exactly contrary to that which was announced in this House, it is impossible to expect ... that we upon these Benches should

There is no doubt about the fact: I put it for convenience, as announced in a foreign quarter.

TO: FREDERICK LYGON Grosvenor Gate [Sunday] 5 June 1864 3930

ORIGINAL: BCP [15]

EDITORIAL COMMENT: Paper imprinted 'Grosvenor Gate'.

Hon: Fred: Lygon | M. P. June 5 1864

My dearest Lygon

I am grieved, that you shd have had the trouble of writing to me at such a moment.[1] I only called, / that you shd. know my heart was with you, & that, if I could be of any use, I was ready & at hand.

I will say no more / now, but that I am, as ever, | Yours, | D.

TO: LORD BEAUCHAMP Grosvenor Gate [Thursday] 9 June 1864 3931

ORIGINAL: BCP [25]

EDITORIAL COMMENT: Paper imprinted 'Grosvenor Gate'.

Dearest Elmley,[1] June 9 1864

Earle gave me a very cheery account of you. Don't be frightened by Doctors: they are, generally, wrong.

If / ever you feel inclined to see me, I will come. My visit brought you good luck in your first illness, for you / improved ever after.

Ever | your attached, | D.

TO: LORD DERBY Grosvenor Gate [Saturday] 18 June 1864 3932

ORIGINAL: DBP Box 146/1

EDITORIAL COMMENT: Paper imprinted 'Grosvenor Gate'. Endorsed by Derby on the fourth page: 'Disraeli B'.

Confidential June 18 1864

The Conference *most* stormy.

hold ourselves in dignified reserve, and should not expect from the Ministers ... some communication to guide and enlighten public opinion.' He would conclude: 'if it be the fact that Her Majesty's Government in this interval have entirely changed their policy, if they themselves are participating in the partition of Denmark, which only five months ago they were stirring up an European war to prevent, then I say it is a mockery of the House of Commons if, under such circumstances, the noble Lord remains silent.' Derby on 17 June would take the opposite view: 'I conceive the true principle to be, that while matters are in progress – while the Government are engaged in negotiation – it is not the duty of Parliament, with imperfect information, to interfere by advice or by vote.' *Hansard* CLXXV col 1281, 1286, 1924. See further **3932**&n1, **3933**&n1 and **3934**&n2.

1 Lygon had written from 19 Grosvenor Place on 4 June: 'I was very sorry to be unable to see you when you were so kind as to call, but I was in the act of dismissing a visitor in expectation of the Doctor who immediately arrived. I am grieved to say that all I can report is that my brother is free from pain. There are no hopes of a permanent improvement.' H B/XX/LN/27. Lygon's only surviving brother, the current (5th) Earl Beauchamp, would live until 4 March 1866.

1 The former Lord Elmley had succeeded his father as 5th Earl Beauchamp on 8 September 1863. For his brother's recent report on the doctors' pessimism about his health, see **3930**n1.

The Danes have refused arbitration unless accompanied with some pledge of English Govt, that the decision shd. be observed: ↑but this not obtained.↓

They have positively declined to / continue suspension of arms.

Germans, especially Prussians, more arrogant than ever.

At John Russell's earnest request, Conference adjourned to Wednesday; but / that to be final.[1]

Yrs, | D.

3933 TO: [LORD MALMESBURY] Grosvenor Gate, Sunday [3 July 1864]

ORIGINAL: HCC 9M73/460/33

EDITORIAL COMMENT: Paper imprinted 'Grosvenor Gate'. Docketed in another hand: 'July [*written over* 'June'] 3/64.' *Dating:* see n1.

Sunday

In all probability we shall divide on Friday. *We* can keep up the debate; but the question is, whether the Govt. can. I can't answer for ~~them.~~ Friday.[1]

Yours | D.

3934 TO: [CHARLES ROSS] Carlton Club [Tuesday] 5 July 1864

ORIGINAL: HUNT HM 52651

EDITORIAL COMMENT: Carlton Club paper. *Sic:* maint-ain.

Private July 5. 1864

Dear Sir,[1]

I never intrude to correct reports – being quite satisfied with the general ↑result,↓

1 In an undated note (before 17 June) Earle mentions some sources: 'I have just seen my friend. He saw Ld Clarendon yesterday, who told him that the Conference wd. certainly break up, probably tomorrow, – "the sooner the better". Cabinet will not go to war, – they are firm upon this. He had also seen Krieger, who says that Danes must resist, altho' he does not himself believe that we shall do much more for them than Pam.' Another undated note, probably of this day (18 June), states: 'Conference stormy – adjourned till Wednesday – no settlement probable.' H B/XX/E/331, 337. In the Lords on 17 June, Russell had stated his opinion 'that in a very few days either arrangements will have been made for preliminaries of peace, or the negotiations will have been totally broken off, and the war will then of course be resumed.' *Hansard* CLXXV col 1928. At the next, and final, meeting of the conference on 22 June, the Danes would reject outright the British proposal of arbitration by a neutral power. *AR* 1864 (Chronicle) 281-90.

---

1 The London conference had ended in failure on 25 June and hostilities resumed. On the 27th Russell and Palmerston in their respective Houses had announced the government's decision not to get involved in the war. A Conservative meeting on 3 July decided that, since Derby was too ill, Malmesbury would introduce in the Lords on Friday 8 July the same motion of censure that D would introduce in the Commons on Monday 4 July, both using dates scheduled for their motions for papers. Malmesbury recorded: 'I went yesterday [Sunday] to Disraeli to settle about this, he merely pointing to a chair. I did not sit down, but gave him the message Lord Derby had sent, and went away.' Evidently D later sent him this note. The debate would go as planned, the Commons debate lasting until Friday 8 July, when D's motion would be defeated 313-295, and Malmesbury also on the 8th introducing the motion in the Lords, where it would pass 177-168. *Hansard* CLXXVI cols 302-32, 337-55 (D 351-5), 709-817 (D 709-51, 752, 772), 826-930, 952-1073 (D 975, 988, 1003, 1073), 1076-1193, 1198-1305 (D 1287-99); Malmesbury II 326-8. For a detailed discussion of the censure debates, see Keith A.P. Sandiford *Great Britain and the Schleswig-Holstein Question* (Toronto 1975) 131-41.

---

1 Charles Ross (see VII **3162**n1) was chief of *The Times*'s parliamentary staff.

– but in yr report of what I said last night, there is a passage, wh:, I think, ought to be corrected.

Towards the end of the last full column, you make me say "*stained by a policy & expectation wh: I maint-ain ought never to / have been held out to a weak ~~&cn~~ & incapable nation*[.]"

I suppose this means Denmark: I should be sorry to be supposed to have used such words in reference to that unfortunate country. What I did say was this, as I find it in the "Morning Post"[:] "*stained by pledges wh: ought not to have been given, & expectations wh: / ought never to have been held out by ~~a~~ wise & competent statesmen*"[.]

If this can be corrected, I shall, for the reason alleged, feel obliged.[2]

Yrs flly | *B Disraeli*

TO: THOMAS KEBBEL — Grosvenor Gate [Monday] 11 July 1864 3935

ORIGINAL: H H/LIFE

PUBLICATION HISTORY: *Standard* (14 Aug 1906); T.E. Kebbel *Lord Beaconsfield and Other Tory Memories* (1907) 61

EDITORIAL COMMENT: The clipping of the *Standard* article in H H/LIFE is the source of the following. In the *Standard* version Kebbel adds: 'He signed his name with a monogram which I am unable to imitate.'

My dear sir, – Grosvenor-gate, July 11, 1864.

I have just written to Lord Beauchamp, who is an invalid and wanted an agreeable companion in his travels to Brighton and about, to take with him your "Essays."[1] I am delighted with them, and I think they will establish your reputation as a sound critic and a graceful writer.

Very truly yours, | B. DISRAELI

TO: ELIZA FOX BRIDELL — [London late-July 1864] 3936

ORIGINAL: H B/II/123a

EDITORIAL COMMENT: A very rough draft in D's hand on the back of a letter from Eliza Fox Bridell dated 'July 25/64'. Endorsed by D on the bottom of the first page: 'July'.

&c to ackn: ret of yr letter requesting me to unite with others in signing a mem. to

---

2 The passage occurs near the end of *The Times*'s nine-column report of D's 4 July speech moving censure of the government; see **3933**n1. *The Times* next day would publish a correction: 'The sense of the following passage in Mr. Disraeli's speech on Monday night was materially changed by an unfortunate error in the report:– "I find Europe impotent to vindicate public law because all the great alliances are broken down, and I find a proud and generous nation like England shrinking with the reserve of magnanimity from the responsibility of commencing a war, and sensitively smarting under the impression that her honour is stained – and stained by a policy and expectations which I maintain ought never to have been held out to a weak and incapable nation." The latter portion should read thus:– "Stained by pledges which ought not to have been given, and expectations which ought never to have been held out, by wise and competent statesmen."' The corrected version appears in *Hansard* CLXXVI col 748.

1 D's most recent extant letter to Beauchamp is **3931**&n1; the letter mentioned here has not been found. Kebbel's 1864 *Essays upon History and Politics* included a previously published essay on D (326-62); see **3467**&n1. On 12 April 1864 he had written from 6 South Square, Gray's Inn, to ask if D had any objection to the essay being reprinted. On 28 June, he had sent D a copy of the *Essays*, 'in the composition of which Mr Disraeli's kind advice has frequently been of such great service.' On 6 October he would accept D's invitation to Hughenden; see Appendix VII. H B/XXI/K/17-23; Stewart *Writings* 101, 128, 175.

Ld P. "to grant a pension under ↑cert[ain] cir[cumstanc]es↓ from the fund at his disposal."[1]

This is clearly irregular & improper. All pensions ~~esplly from the fund in question~~ are in the gift of ~~H.M.~~ ↑the C[rown]↓ & indeed it is known that with respect to the ↑parti[cula]r↓ fund referred to H.M. ~~exercises~~ ↑in a considerable degree↓ personally controls its distrib[uti]on. The Mem:, shd you ↑on reflecn↓ decide upon one, ~~must~~ ↑shd ther[efor]e↓ be addressed to H.M.

If ~~I may be~~ it ~~is~~ ↑be↓ not presump. / in [my offering *changed to*] me to offer advice, I wd. suggest as a preferable course, that some of the gent: you ment[ion] Mi[lne]r G[ibson?][2] & others who ~~had~~ ↑have↓ a personal relations[hip] with Ld. P. shd. ~~place~~ ↑bring↓ the matter bef[or]e the Min[iste]r so that he may advise H.M. in the ~~course~~ ↑dir[ecti]on↓ you wish

---

3937 TO: MR HARVEY Grosvenor Gate [Wednesday] 27 July 1864

ORIGINAL: MOPSIK [13]

EDITORIAL COMMENT: Paper imprinted 'Grosvenor Gate'.

Mr Harvey July 27 1864

Dear Sir –

In your accts., I observe prem: on Insurance, in Royal Exchange, on house at Bath ↑for £1000↓: but in my banking book at / Drummonds, there is regularly every year prem: on insurance at Sun Fire Office for the same house, Brock St. Bath; £1,500.

Will you look a / little into this?

Yours flly | *B. Disraeli*

3938 TO: GEORGE BUCKLEY MATHEW Grosvenor Gate [Saturday] 30 July 1864

ORIGINAL: PS 1446

PUBLICATION HISTORY: Maggs Bros catalogue 1257 (1998) item 49: 'Autograph Letter Signed ("B. Disraeli") to the diplomat George Buckley Matthew [*sic*], 4 pages 8vo, Grosvenor Gate, 30 July 1864.'

... I hope you are not going to return to your post at present, & that we may be

1 Eliza Fox Bridell had written from 8 Victoria Road, Kensington, on 25 July to ask for D's signature on an enclosed memorial of her deceased father, William Johnson Fox, Unitarian minister and radical reform MP for Oldham 1847-62, in support of an application for a government pension for her mother: 'I am advised ... to have the application based exclusively upon Literary, and in no wise, upon political grounds.' She also enclosed a list of eminent men whose signatures she would ask, and concluded: 'I trust that you will excuse the extreme liberty I take in thus addressing you. My Father's great admiration for your high and brilliant talents is I am aware no claim upon you and I simply appeal to your feelings of kindness towards the memory of an upright and talented man, who is now no more.' H B/II/123a. Eliza Florance Fox Bridell (1823/4-1903), painter and feminist, second of the Foxes' three children, had lived with her father after he and his wife, Eliza Florance, separated in 1834. In 1859 she had married another artist, Frederick Lee Bridell, who had died in 1863. In 1871 she would marry her cousin George Edward Fox, an artist and architect, and thereafter paint and exhibit under the name Eliza Bridell-Fox.

2 The scrawled name in the draft can, with imagination, be rendered thus; Gibson's name is on the enclosed list and he was currently a member of Palmerston's government.

---

1 For a previous mention of the insurance on the house at Bath, see IV **1264**&n17. The recipient is possibly the Harvey listed as Wm Henry Harvey & Co, land and estate agents, 3 Tavistock Square, in *LPOD* (1864); no other reference to him in H has been found.

fortunate enough to induce you to pay us a visit at Hughenden, where we shall be settled in September. Some radiant birds, a little while ago, perched at Grosvenor Gate, & I think, tho' they looked unwearied, they must have flown from Guatemala. Pray accept my thanks for them, & for your kind recollection in sending me a most interesting volume about Mexico.[1]

TO: PHILIP ROSE Carlton Club, Tuesday [2 August 1864?] **3939**

ORIGINAL: H R/I/A/176

EDITORIAL COMMENT: Carlton Club paper. Endorsed in another hand on the first page: 'About Aug 1 1864'.

P. Rose Esq Tuesday

My dear Rose,

I hear at V. S.[1] that you are at the Jun: Carl: Comm[itt]ee.[2] I wish you could make it convenient to come on here for a / few minutes when your business is up, as I want to consult you on a domestic matter, about some horses, wh: requires att[enti]on.[3]

Yrs ever | D.

TO: EMILY CLUBBE Grosvenor Gate [Wednesday] 3 August 1864 **3939A**

ORIGINAL: RIC [025]

EDITORIAL COMMENT: Paper imprinted 'Grosvenor Gate'.

Dear Mrs. Clubbe, Aug. 3 1864

Business, I grieve to say, keeps me in London, tho' I have, every day, been in hopes, I might reach / Hughenden.

Pray permit the enclosed order to swell the amount received at your stall tomorrow.[1]

Sincerely yours, | *B. Disraeli*

1 G.B. Mathew had written from San José, Costa Rica, on 25 January 1864, and sent 'a pair of the celebrated "Quezals" whose plumage was reserved in the olden time of Mexico & these regions, for the wear of the Aztec Emperors'. On 7 August he would write from 9 Augusta Terrace, Ramsgate, to accept D's invitation, with thanks for his 'kindly wish that I may not return to that most odious "apanage" of the Jesuit fathers.' On 25 November he would write from Fryston to suggest a visit before the DS returned to town. H B/XXI/M/236-8. No indication of a visit at this time has been found. After Mexico, Mathew had been minister to the Central American Republics 1861-3, and would next be posted to Colombia 1865-6. D, after asking Charlotte de Rothschild where he should put the birds, at length offered them to her, 'so I suppose we will have the green wonders.' Charlotte de Rothschild to Leopold de Rothschild, 6 August 1864, MS ROTH.

---

1 Victoria Street, the address of Rose's office.

2 For the establishment of the Junior Carlton Club, see **3841**&n3, **3844**&nn1-2 and **3882**&nn1&3.

3 Rose's extant correspondence at this time (30 July and 3 August) makes no mention of horses, but see **3977**&nn1&2,4&5, D to Lovell concerning D's lease of stables. H B/XX/R/22-3, A/V/G/202.

---

1 MA lists 1*s* 6*d* paid to Mrs Clubbe on 2 August 'for Bazaar'. H acc.

3940 TO: SIR EDWARD BULWER LYTTON Grosvenor Gate [Thursday] 4 August 1864

ORIGINAL: HCR D/EK C5 [22]

EDITORIAL COMMENT: Paper imprinted 'Grosvenor Gate'.

The Rt Honble | Sir Ed: Lytton Augt 4 1864

My dear Bulwer,

This is to remind you of your promise to pay us a visit this autumn. I hope, we shall escape from this / early next week[1] – & any time after the close of this month, we shall be most happy to receive you ~~here~~ at Hughenden. It will be our head quarters the whole year.[2] /

The Exeter election seems thriving. At one o'ck Court[ena]y maintained a good majority[.][3]

Yours ever, | D.

3941 TO: SIR HENRY JAMES Hughenden [Monday 15?] August 1864

ORIGINAL: PS 799

PUBLICATION HISTORY: Francis Edwards catalogue 971 (Jan 1973) item 126: 'Two Autograph Letters signed, 5 *pages*, 8vo, *Hughenden Manor* [*Buckinghamshire*] and *Downing Street*, 5 *August* 1864, 22 *January* 1865, to Sir Henry James, Director General of the Ordnance Survey' [*continued below*]

EDITORIAL COMMENT: *Dating:* the extant correspondence (see n1) suggests that the text confusingly described and quoted is from one letter, not two, dated on or about 15 August 1864; D was not at Downing Street on either of the catalogue dates.

[thanking him for information, referring to the Domesday Book facsimiles with which James is concerned adding] I shd very much like to possess Bucks[, thanking him warmly for sending it and inviting him] to one of the Domesday Manors and that is where resides your very obliged and faithful B. Disraeli[, 7 *words added in another hand at the foot of one letter*].[1]

1 The DS would leave Grosvenor Gate for Hughenden on 8 August, taking with them on the train '25 pacages, not counting the Dispatches boxes & little black portmantu & umberellas' which cost them 16*s* in extra luggage charges. H acc.

2 Lytton would respond after a further prompt by D; see **3952**&n1. In July he had sent his regrets for not being able to speak because of his health, instead sending suggestions for D to use in debate. H B/XX/LY/49.

3 At a by-election at Exeter on 4 August after the sudden death of the long-time Liberal incumbent Edward Divett, Lord Courtenay (C) defeated J.D. Coleridge (L) 1096-1070. Edward Baldwin Courtenay (1836-1892), captain 1st Royal Devon yeomanry cavalry, DL for Devon, MP (C) for Devon 1864-8, for E Devon 1868-70, would succeed his father in 1888 as 12th Earl of Devon.

---

1 Sir Henry James had written from the Ordnance Survey Office, Southampton (Topographical Department of the War Office), on 12 August 1864, possibly in response to an unfound letter from D, that in their Cadastral survey they had finished Middlesex on the 25-inch scale and were working on Surrey, Kent and Hampshire. The old one-inch map would be converted, but place names could be corrected now. 'I have therefore had the name "Hitchendon" altered to "Hughenden", and the name of your residence altered from "House" to "Hughenden Manor" and I send with this an impression with these alterations on it. But the Manor of Hughenden is called "Huchedene" in Domesday Book – it is thus referred to.' He quoted at length the Domesday Book information on '"Hatchedene"', lamented the lack of sales in Bucks relative to those of the Domesday Book facsimiles in other counties, and mentioned that they were now printing facsimiles 'of some of our most interesting M.S. Records.' He continued: 'I have had a few copies of [the first part] printed separately on vellum and take the liberty of sending one of them

TO: LADY DE ROTHSCHILD Hughenden **3942**

[Wednesday] 24 August 1864

ORIGINAL: QUA [411]

EDITORIAL COMMENT: Paper imprinted 'Hughenden Manor'. Two corrections in the text may not have been made by D: 'Johnston' has been corrected to 'Johnson', and, in the last line, the word order 'you are' has been corrected to 'are you'. *Sic:* Carlisle.

Augt 24 1864

Dear Lady de Rothschild,[1]

I brought down Mr Arnold with me, but never read him till last night.[2] I feel such a dissipation of mind, when I return to the country after a long absence, / that I am incapable of anything except sauntering on terraces.

I read the paper, however, last night, with great satisfaction, & entire sympathy. There is no doubt, that the characteristic of our literary / age in England is a want of taste. Taste was never, at any time, our forte; but tho' we had not the advantage of a great classical Academy, still the cultivation of belles lettres (we have no English term) by such men as the Wartons, Gray, & Dr / Johnson, did much to sustain the right tone.[3] For years, belles lettres have been extinct. Perhaps Mr Arnold is destined to revive them. I hope so, for he is perfectly equal to the task. The difficulty will be great, & the triumph equal, in a country wh: acknowledges Mr Carlisle a classical historian![4]

Ever yrs, | D.

When are you coming to see us?[5]

for your acceptance.' On 18 August he would thank D for his invitation to Hughenden and tell him that a copy of the Bucks Domesday Book had been sent to him on the 17th. H B/XXI/J/5-6 (the only two letters from James in H). Sir Henry James (1803-1877), superintendent of the ordnance survey since 1854, director of the topographical and statistical department of the war office and colonel in the army since 1857, had been knighted in 1860.

1 There is no extant correspondence in H this year from Louisa, Lady de Rothschild, although the Ds had visited Aston Clinton 27-9 January. H acc.

2 From what follows, D had evidently read 'The Literary Influence of Academies' by Matthew Arnold (1822-1888), the poet, critic and school inspector, published in the August issue of *Cornhill Magazine* (X 154-72). Arnold traces the elevating effect of the French Academy on French literature from before the eighteenth century while he sees literature in academy-less England as having declined from Elizabethan glories to the 'provincial and second-rate literature of the eighteenth century' and, especially with respect to prose, of the current time. The essay would be reprinted in *Essays in Criticism* in 1865. Arnold had visited Aston Clinton in October 1863, commenting to his mother: 'What women these Jewesses are! with a *force* which seems to triple that of the women of our Western & Northern races.' *Letters of Matthew Arnold,* ed. Cecil Y. Lang, vol. 2 (1996), 238.

3 The essay does not deal with the Wartons – Thomas Sr (*c*1688-1745), Joseph (1722-1800) and Thomas Jr (1728-1790) – with Thomas Gray (1716-1771) or Samuel Johnson (1709-84).

4 The reputation of Thomas Carlyle (1795-1881), the essayist and historian, had flourished since his *Collected Works* (1857-8) and the earliest of his six-volume *Frederick the Great* (1858-65), leading one reviewer of the latter, Herman Merivale, to allow that he 'had become, while yet alive and at work among us, something of a classic'. (*Quarterly Review* Vol 118 (July 1865) 225-54, as quoted in *ODNB*). Carlyle, who reciprocated D's view of him despite the deep similarities of their social visions, in 1866 would defeat D to become rector of Edinburgh University and in 1874 reject the GCB and pension that the Queen at D's recommendation offered him.

5 MA made no record of a visit beyond an enigmatic entry on 7 November: 'Lady de Rothschild, Aston Clinton, Tring.' H acc.

3943 TO: LORD CLANWILLIAM Hughenden [Wednesday] 31 August 1864

ORIGINAL: PS 801

PUBLICATION HISTORY: Sotheby's catalogue (13 May 1974) item 236: 'A.L.s., 3 pp., *8vo, Hughenden Manor, 31 August* 1864, to the Earl of Clanwilliam'

[inviting him – since] you said you shd. certainly be hanging about town or the South, for some little time [– to come and stay at Hughenden in September] & taste the air of the Chiltern Hills[1]

3944 TO: LORD JOHN MANNERS Hughenden [Wednesday] 31 August 1864

ORIGINAL: BEA [88]

EDITORIAL COMMENT: Paper imprinted 'Hughenden Manor'.

Right Honorable. | Lord John Manners Augt 31 1864

My dear J. M.

How are you getting on, & where are you?

Not far, I apprehend, from home. How is Lady John, & how is the baby?[1]

My wife wants you all to come to us next month. Pray, let / her wishes, & mine, be gratified!

On the 26th. Sep: (Monday) Lord & Lady Salisbury come, & some other agreeable people, & they will stay with us for some days.[2] Pray join our party. Scotland, we think, must be too far for Lady John, & / especially the baby, who ought not to travel. You will see our new terraces &c., & a nursery, wh: we have made for yours, not for you.

Our kindest regards to Lady John.[3]

Yrs ever, | D.

1 Richard Charles Francis Meade (1795-1879), 3rd Earl of Clanwilliam, under-secretary for foreign affairs 1822-3, ambassador to Berlin 1823-8, GCH 1826, had been created Baron Clanwilliam 1828. He would reply from Edinburgh on 2 September: 'Your letter is an agreeable disappointment. I am much flattered that you shd. have thought of inviting me, and I am vexed that I shall, at the time you name, be in the far North; in fact in Sutherland. Ps. tell Mrs. D.I., w. my best regards, that if I cd. get into that Balloon, (I hope I am right in my 2 *l*'s) & secure a fair wind, I shd. certainly have lit in Hughn. Manor, 29*th*.' H B/XXI/C/235. On 29 August Henry Coxwell, a well-known balloonist, had ascended to 14,000 feet from the Crystal Palace. *Times* (24 Aug, 2 Sept 1864).

1 Edward William John Manners (1864-1903), first child of Manners's second marriage, to Janetta Hughan, had been born on 5 August.

2 See **3946** for D's explanation of the DS' autumn social schedule beginning on 26 September. The party on the 26th would consist of the Salisburys, Lord and Lady Lovaine, Beauchamp, comte Alexander Apponyi and Arthur Russell. Thomas Baring was prevented by the death of his business partner, Joshua Bates. On the 28th Lords Loughborough and Henry Lennox arrived, with Colonel and Mrs Fane joining them for dinner. On the 29th, the Clubbes, Mr Hewett and Algernon Russell came for dinner. The Salisburys, Lovaines and Russell left on the 30th, Beauchamp and Lennox on 1 October. H acc.

3 Manners would reply from St Marys Tower, Birnam, Dunkeld, on 5 September: 'Your letter found us safely established in our Highland home, where we have been reposing for the last ten days! Lady John's recovery was so rapid and unchecked ... [that we undertook] the journey at the end of three weeks, and we came straight through, bag, baggage, baby, servants and all in 13½ hours! She is now quite well and strong again, and the baby (christened yesterday) thrives in this delicious air. You will have already anticipated the answer to your most kind invitation ... [that] being where we are we can only visit Hughenden mentally, and admire the new terraces with the eye of faith ... Here we are very slowly obtaining possession of my Gothic towers, which I please myself with hoping some day to show you.' H B/XX/M/130.

TO: LADY EMILY PEEL Hughenden [Sunday] 4 September 1864 3945

ORIGINAL: NYM [12]

EDITORIAL COMMENT: Paper imprinted 'Hughenden Manor'. Endorsed in another hand on the first page: 'Mr. Disraeli Sepr. 4/64'.

Dear Lady Emily,[1] Septr 4 1864

My wife makes me her secretary, & if the duty were always so agreeable, I should never grumble at its performance.

Could we induce you, & Sir Robert, to breathe / the air of the Chiltern hills? We are only 1½ hours from town; our station High Wycombe, a short two miles from our gates.

Lord & Lady Salisbury, & some other agreeable friends, are coming to us on Monday, 26th Inst:. Will / you join the circle, & then it will be complete.[2]

With our united kind remembrances to Sir Robert, believe me, dear Lady Emily, faithfully yours, | *B. Disraeli*

TO: LORD STANLEY Hughenden [Sunday] 4 September 1864 3946

ORIGINAL: DBP Box 42/7

EDITORIAL COMMENT: Paper imprinted 'Hughenden Manor'. Endorsed by Stanley on the fourth page: 'Disraeli. *Sept. 64* ANSD.'

Sept 4 1864

Right Honorable | The Lord Stanley

My dear Stanley,

When are you coming to the South? When you do, I hope you will remember us.

Our plans are these. We shall receive our friends towards the end / of the month, & so on, till the end of October or November.

Lord & Lady Salisbury are coming here on the 26th. Inst: They will be our first guests.

Suit your convenience, but give me some notice of your intended arrival, / if you can; that you may not, unnecessarily, meet bores.[1]

Yours ever, | D.

I can't receive anyone until towards the end of the month, in consequence of these confounded agricl: / meetings, wh: I must attend this year.[2]

1 Sir Robert Peel, 3rd Bt, in 1856 had married Lady Emily Hay (1836-1924), youngest child of 8th Marquess of Tweeddale.

2 Lady Emily Peel would reply from Drayton Manor on 6 September declining the invitation because of other commitments, hers at the seaside for her health: 'Let us hope fr. better fortune on some future occasion'. H B/XXI/P/181. For the other guests, see **3944**n2.

1 Stanley would reply from Knowsley on 7 September: 'I fear it will not be possible for me to meet the Hatfield party at Hughenden, though I should greatly have enjoyed it. The far west – of Ireland – is my present destination, and I don't expect to be in the south of England till Oct. I shall hope to look in upon you some time in that month, and will take care to give notice.' H B/XX/S/717. See further **3967**&n1.

2 D would speak on agricultural matters at the Royal and Central Bucks United Agricultural Association meeting at Aylesbury on 21 September. To the North-West Bucks Agricultural Association meeting, also on the 21st, he sent a letter and a prize of £5 for the best-kept cottage. At the Royal South Bucks Agricultural Association meeting at Salthill on 5 October, he was accused of ignorance for suggesting on 21 September that sheep farmers cross Southdowns with Cotswolds. D answered the charge gracefully, and a subsequent correspondence supported both sides of the question. On 17 October, he attended Quarter Sessions at Aylesbury. *BH* (24 Sept, 1, 8, 22 Oct 1864).

3947 TO: OCTAVIAN BLEWITT Hughenden [Friday] 9 September 1864

ORIGINAL: RLF M/1077/46 File 1258 Letter 28

EDITORIAL COMMENT: Paper imprinted 'Hughenden Manor'.

O. Blewitt Esq Sept 9 1864

Sir,

Can anything be done for Mrs. Loraine, a poetess, of South Lambeth?[1] Her position seems very grievous. Several years / ago, she received some relief from the Fund, I am told.

She has published some volumes.

Yours faithfully, | *B. Disraeli*

R.S.V.P.[2]

3948 TO: LADY LOVAINE Hughenden [Monday] 12 September 1864

ORIGINAL: NOR G/14/2

EDITORIAL COMMENT: Paper imprinted 'Hughenden Manor'.

Dear Lady Lovaine, Septr 12 1864

Have you forgotten that agreeable promise wh: we have always remembered – to pay us, some day, a visit at Hughenden? I hope not, & if you have, that Lord Lovaine will remind you / of it, as well as myself.

Could we induce you both to taste the air of the Chiltern Hills towards the end of the month? Lord & Lady Salisbury, & a few other agreeable friends, come to us on Monday the 26th Inst., / &, I hope, will remain the week. If you & Lord Lovaine will join the circle, it will be complete.[1]

My wife joins me in kind regards, & remembrances, to Lord Lovaine & yourself, & entreating you / to grant my request, believe me, dear Lady Lovaine,

Ever sincerely yours, | *B. Disraeli*

1 Describing herself as 'a lady of birth and lineage', A.M. Loraine had written to D on 9 August 1864 from 4 Catherina Terrace, Lansdowne Road, South Lambeth, for help in getting financial assistance, her well-reviewed but unsuccessful publications having left her in dire straits. She enclosed some of her poems but did not mention the Literary Fund. Evidently D handed the matter to a secretary, as on 31 August Mrs Loraine had acknowledged to 'Sir' his 'note of the 27th, & Mr Disraeli's very kind offer to write in my favor to the committee of literary fund.' She asked that D be told that this would be useless, as, although she had received a £35 grant twelve years before for her first work, she had been refused for another work seven years later. On 8 September she had written again to ask 'Sir' if D had decided to write to the Literary Fund and, if not, whether he could introduce her to a magazine editor. Amelia Mary Loraine in 1847 had published *Lays of Israel: or, Tales of the temple and the cross,* and in 1858 *Steps on the mountains: a tale.*

2 Blewitt had last written on 14 April 1864 about a duty that D as a vice-president of the Fund had neglected; on 12 September he would reply: 'The case of Mrs. Loraine, and that of her brother Miles Barber, have been known to the Committee for the last 14 years. She received relief on two occasions to an amount which the Committee considered to be fully equal to her literary claim.' She was, however, eligible to apply again. On 25 September she would write to ask D, since her previous letter had not been answered, what was happening. On 26 December Blewitt would report to D that the General Committee had decided to refuse her. H A/IV/M/82-8.

1 Lady Lovaine would write on 17 September, having returned from Northumberland the previous evening: 'We had not forgotten the pleasure you proposed to us, & shall be delighted to pay you and Mrs. Disraeli a visit at Hughenden Manor on Monday the 26th. to remain till Thursday.' H B/XXI/L/348. For her subsequent correspondence, see **3962**&n1; for the other guests, see **3944**n2.

TO: CHARLES ADDERLEY Hughenden [Tuesday] 13 September 1864 3949

ORIGINAL: H H/LIFE

EDITORIAL COMMENT: Taken from a typescript copy.

Copy. HUGHENDEN MANOR | Sept. 13. 1864.

Right Honble C. Adderley, M.P.

Dear Adderley,

I agree with you very much in your general views respecting our colonies, but I can't conceal from myself, that the country is not yet ripe for them.[1] It has been so long accustomed to the idea of what they call Colonial Empire, and the power and profit which they erroneously associate with their obsolete conceptions, that it is, in the highest degree, painful and perplexing for them to contemplate the altered relations, which now subsist between the Metropolis and its settlements.

I think we could count on no united party support in favor of any resolution which, on such matters asserted a principle, but a Committee of Inquiry, as you contemplate, is another affair, and, in my opinion, it would be a feasible move.[2]

I am, therefore, in favor of bringing forward the subject.

Pray present my Compliments to Mrs Adderley, who, I hope, is quite well.

Yours sincerely, | (Signed) D.

TO: SIR WILLIAM JOLLIFFE Hughenden [Thursday] 15 September 1864 3950

ORIGINAL: SCR DD/HY C/2165 [70]

EDITORIAL COMMENT: Paper imprinted 'Hughenden Manor'.

Septr 15 1864

Right Honorable | Sir Wm. Jolliffe Bart: | M. P.

My dear Jolliffe,

We are making up a Hughenden party for Thursday, the 6th. Octr., & we shd. be more than pleased, if we could find you, & your daughters, disengaged on that day, & that you will stay with / us, at least, till the following Monday. The length of the invitation may appear rather absurd, but what with agricl. associations, all of wh: I must attend this year, & other local circumstances, it requires some little management on my part to find myself / at home, when my friends honor Hughenden with their presence.

1 Adderley had written from Hams Hall, near Birmingham, on 3 September to ask if D saw any objections to his proposed motion for a committee of inquiry into British West African settlements. From serving on Joseph Hume's committee in 1859, he felt that British efforts in Africa were both wasteful and harmful, for which one solution might be to amalgamate the Gold Coast with Liberia. Although Palmerston would oppose an inquiry, House feeling in the last session had been in favour: 'Unless you see objection to the committee being moved by me, I think I could now lay foundation of evidence which would lead to a better system with a saving of half a million a year. If you approve, I shall be greatly obliged for any suggestions as to mode of proceeding or whose cooperation to seek.' H B/XXI/A/84.

2 *Cf* **3655**&n1 for Adderley's position on colonial affairs. On 21 February 1865, he would successfully move for a select committee to inquire into the British establishments on the west coast of Africa. He would argue that disease in the four settlements made them unfit for Anglo-Saxon occupation, and that the primary objects of maintaining them – to suppress the slave trade, promote legitimate commerce and civilize the natives – were not being achieved. He favoured consolidation of the four under a single jurisdiction with more British support in order to stabilize and extend its influence into the interior. *MP* (22 Feb 1865).

I hope your daughters are well. My wife joins with me in kindest regards to them, & to yourself.[1]

Yours ever, | D.

3951 TO: [LORD HENRY LENNOX] Hughenden [Friday] 16 September 1864

ORIGINAL: PS 802

PUBLICATION HISTORY: Maggs Bros catalogue 299 (Nov 1912) item 3744: 'A.L.S. "*D.*" 2pp., 8vo. Hughenden Manor, Sept. 16th, 1864.'

EDITORIAL COMMENT: Lennox is almost the only friend to whom D would write in this familiar tone and who received an invitation at this time; see n1.

How are you? Where are you? What are you doing? I hope your engagements will admit of your paying us a visit.[1]

3952 TO: SIR EDWARD BULWER LYTTON Hughenden [Monday] 19 September 1864

ORIGINAL: HCR D/EK C5 [23]

EDITORIAL COMMENT: Paper imprinted 'Hughenden Manor'. *Sic:* to to.

The Right Honorable | Sir Edward Lytton Sept 19 1864

My dear Bulwer,

You were so kind, to to promise to pay us a visit, on the pleasure of wh: we much count.

Should we be so / fortunate as to find you disengaged the 6th. of October, Thursday, & would you stay with us, then, until Monday, at the least?

The absolute necessity, this year, of attending the agricultural meetings renders / it rather difficult for me to arrange the reception of my friends at Hughenden, so, that I should be quite sure of being at home, when they favor me with their presence.

My / wife sends you her very kindest regards.[1]

Yours ever, | D.

1 Jolliffe would reply from Merstham on 17 September that his daughter Mary was obliged to remain at home, but that he and his daughter Cecil would arrive at Hughenden on 7 October and stay until Monday the 10th. Their fellow guests would be Lady Brownlow, General, Lady Mary and Miss Hood, Lord Courtenay, Lord Beauchamp, Bulwer Lytton and Lygon. H B/XX/J/94, acc. See further **3955**&n1.

1 Lennox had written from London on 12 September about the death of the Duke of Cleveland ('The Political results are most disastrous') and other social and political news, ending: 'Tomorrow I return to the solitude of Highcliffe near Christchurch ... I thought you might like to hear of my being in existence'. He had written again, from the seaside resort of Highcliffe, on 16 September, with further news. On 17 September, still at Highcliffe, he would write: 'Many thanks for your letter, which, I received on my return from a day on the ocean. I shall be delighted to pay my respects to you & Mrs Disraeli on Wed Septr 28th.' He would stay until Saturday 1 October. H B/XX/LX/199-201, acc.

1 Lytton at Breadalbane Heall, Perthshire, would reply with thanks on 21 September that he had not forgotten and would be glad to accept about the time D suggested, since it would be after his son's marriage in the first week of October (actually on 4 October). 'I think I can venture to accept your hospitality, therefore, for Friday the 7th & stay till the following Monday.' On 28 September he would write from Brighton to postpone his arrival at Hughenden by a day. On 7 October he would write from Park Lane to confirm his time of arrival early the following evening. H B/XX/LY/149-51.

TO: [EDWARD] GRIFFIN [Hughenden, Saturday] 24 September 1864 **3953**

ORIGINAL: PS 1521
PUBLICATION HISTORY: *MP* (8 October 1864)

– September 24, 1864.

Mr. Disraeli presents his compliments to Mr. Griffin, and regrets that he cannot have the honour of dining at the Princes Risborough Society's meeting on the 5th October; but he has been engaged to dine at the South Bucks Agricultural Society on that day.[1]

TO: PHILIP ROSE Hughenden [Monday] 26 September 1864 **3954**

ORIGINAL: H R/I/A/177
COVER: [*recto:*] Philip Rose Esq | 6 Victoria Street, Westminster | *B. Disraeli* [*verso:*] imprinted: 'Hughenden Manor'
POSTMARK: [*recto:*] (1) in a circle: HIGH WYCOMBE | C | SP 26 | 64 (2) a cancelled one-penny stamp [*verso:*] (1) in a circle: LONDON SW | R | SP 27 | 64
EDITORIAL COMMENT: Paper imprinted 'Hughenden Manor'. *Sic:* checque; meetings ... obliges.

Private Sept 26 1864

Philip Rose Esqr

My dear Rose,

I was delighted to hear of, & from, you; & that your affairs proceeded so agreeably, &, as I trust it will prove, so successfully.[1]

It always gives me pleasure to be of the slightest assistance to you, & to co-operate in advancing your / views, for you have proved, in every way, for a series of years, that you have deserved my confidence, & the interest I always take in your career.

I heard from Mackenzie! very recently & after I had quite given up the thought of the affair: a checque for 120 for 40 shares at 3.[2] /

We shall be here for the next two months certainly, & are beginning, to day, to

1 Edward Griffin (d 1879), of Towersey Manor, Bucks, a JP and county alderman, would chair the meeting of the Princes Risborough Local Agricultural Association on 5 October 1864, when this letter would be read out. *BH* (8 Oct 1864), which wrongly gives his name as 'Griffith.' For the conflict in dates, see **3957**n1.

---

1 Rose had written from Victoria Street on 22 September: 'I have had a most successful and enjoyable visit to Russia and feel the greatest benefit from the change.' He had 'had an interesting audience of Prince Gortschakoff, and made the acquaintance of many of the leading men in Russia besides the Ministers ... [and had] so often felt grateful for your letter to Lord Napier, which ... proved of infinite service to me.' He continued: 'If your anticipations as to the present pressure in the Money Market should be realized I believe my journey will result in a profit upon the transaction arranged of at least half a million Sterling.' H R/I/B/98. Rose's request for a letter of introduction is dated 3 August 1864. H B/XX/R/23.

2 Rose (n1) had written: 'I can find no one in London to tell me about your Anglo Egyptian shares. – Have you received any communication from Mackenzie during my absence?' He hoped to see D soon on various matters, 'and will take an early opportunity of driving over from Rayners in the hope of finding you at home.' See **3906**n1. There is a note by Rose dated in another hand 'July 7 or 27 1864': 'I have been thinking it would be as well for you to write a line to J.T. Mackenzie Esqr 41 Threadneedle St tomorrow morning, stating that I had reported to you his obliging offer respecting the Anglo Egyptian & thanking him. This would *ensure* the allotment for you or at all events Mackenzie would make it up even if he did it out of his own shares. Perhaps you will do this.' H R/I/B/97. Sir James Thompson Mackenzie (1818-1890), 1st Bt, DL for counties Ross and Middlesex, had made a fortune in India before returning in 1850; he was Samuel Laing's business partner and co-founder of the Foreign and Colonial Trust.

receive our friends. If it were not for the agricultural associ[ati]ons, wh:, this year, I must attend, we shd. do so continuously; but these meetings break the reception into parties, & obliges me sometimes to give / absurdly long invitations for the country.

Mrs Disraeli hopes, that you & Mrs Rose will keep yourselves disengaged for Saturday the 8th. Octr.[3] I trust we shall meet, & perhaps often, in the interval. I am,

Ever sincerely yours | D.

3955 TO: SIR WILLIAM JOLLIFFE Hughenden [Saturday] 1 October 1864

ORIGINAL: SCR DD/HY C/2165 [71]

EDITORIAL COMMENT: Paper imprinted 'Hughenden Manor'.

Rt Honorable | Sir W.H. Jolliffe Oct 1 1864

My dear Jolliffe,

We shall be delighted to receive you & Cecil on the 7th. Inst. as you propose, but count on your staying with us now until Tuesday morning.[1]

Yours ever | D.

3956 TO: SAMUEL WILBERFORCE Hughenden [Monday] 3 October 1864

ORIGINAL: BRN [33]

EDITORIAL COMMENT: Paper imprinted 'MAD Hughenden Manor'. Endorsed in another hand on the first page: 'Dizy'.

The | Lord Bp: of Oxford Octr. 3 1864

My dear Lord,

Pardon me for not sooner replying to your letter,[1] but the matter required great deliberation. I shrink from the effort: nevertheless, I / am unwilling to withdraw my hand from the plough; especially at this moment. Therefore, we will, with your permission, have the pleasure of being your guests about the / time you mention. Mrs. Disraeli, however, says, that she shall exact a return from you, or rather, in all probability, an anticipatory visit, for if she receives some agreeable friends, who meditate paying / us a visit, she shall very earnestly request, that you will do us the favor of meeting them.[2]

Believe me, | my dear Lord, | Sincerely yours, | *B. Disraeli*

3 The Roses would dine at Hughenden on 8 October. For their fellow guests, see **3950**n1.

---

1 See **3050**&n1. Jolliffe would reply on 3 October from Heath House, Petersfield, that prior engagements required them to be home on Monday. H B/XX/J/95.

---

1 Wilberforce had written on 23 September: 'Would you come to me with Mrs Disraeli about November 24 & make us a Great Speech at Oxford for our Society for endowing small livings'. He promised a good audience of both university and county people. On 22 October he would write that he had been given the Sheldonian Theatre for Friday 25 November, and hoped the DS could be with him from the 24th to the 26th. H B/XXI/W/366-7. See further **3970**&n1.

2 On 24 October Wilberforce would write that, because of other commitments, he was 'exceedingly sorry not to come to you on the 2nd according to your kind proposal [*not found*].' H B/XXI/W/368.

TO: PHILIP ROSE [Hughenden] Wednesday [5 October 1864] 3957

ORIGINAL: H R/I/A/178

COVER: *Immediate* | Philip Rose Esqre | Rayners | Penn | *B. Disraeli* | ½ pt. 12 o'k | Wednesday

EDITORIAL COMMENT: *Dating:* by context; see n1.

My dear Rose,

I didn't observe in yr letter that Talbot was staying with you, until I had replied, being in a great hurry, on the point of departure to Salt Hill.

I enclose a lre for Tal[bo]t hoping he will come with you on Saty.[1]

Yrs | D.

TO: PHILIP ROSE Hughenden [Friday] 14 October 1864 3958

ORIGINAL: H R/I/A/179

COVER: [*recto:*] Philip Rose Esqr | 6 Victoria Street | Westminster Abbey | *B. Disraeli* [*verso:*] imprinted: Hughenden Manor

POSTMARK: [*recto:*] (1) in a circle: HIGH WYCOMBE | B | OC 14 | 64 (2) a cancelled one-penny stamp [*verso:*] in a circle: LONDON SW | R 7 | OC 15 | 64

EDITORIAL COMMENT: Paper imprinted 'MAD Hughenden Manor'.

Phil: Rose Esq Octr 14 1864

My dear Rose,

I was quite mindful of the affair. I shall be in town at the beginning of the week; immediately after Q.S.; & will do the needful in both respects.[1]

Ever yrs | D.

TO: LORD DERBY Hughenden [Tuesday] 18 October 1864 3959

ORIGINAL: DBP Box 146/1

EDITORIAL COMMENT: Paper imprinted 'MAD Hughenden Manor'. Endorsed by Derby on the last page: 'Disraeli B'.

Right Honble | The Earl of Derby | K. G. Octr. 18 1864

1 Rose had mentioned Talbot in a postscript to his 22 September letter (see **3954**&nn1&2), but nothing has been found to indicate Talbot was staying with him. Presumably Rose had written to inquire what time he and Mrs Rose were to dine with the Hughenden house party on Saturday the 8th (see **3954**&n3), and D had replied to confirm the arrangement; these letters and D's letter to Talbot have not been found. In 1864 D was at Salt Hill on Wednesday 5 October addressing the Royal South Bucks Agricultural Association meeting (see **3946**&n2). *BH* (8 Oct 1864). The above letter was presumably written on his return late that day, perhaps with another note from Rose awaiting him.

---

1 See **3876**&n1. On 30 July Rose had written from Victoria Street about unsatisfactory decorating by Roberts at Hughenden. Lamb had told Rose the 50 guineas allotted for the job should be deducted, but Roberts claimed Lamb had said there should be no reduction. When Roberts offered to re-colour or to deduct £30, Rose advised D to accept the £30, leaving a balance owing of £343.5.7. On 13 October he had written on a torn half-sheet: 'I paid Roberts £343.5.7 and took his receipt in full of all demands 1279.11..7'. H B/XX/R/22, 24. D would attend the Bucks Michaelmas Quarter Sessions at Aylesbury on Monday 17 October (see **3959**). *BH* (22 Oct 1864).

My dear Lord,

Yours[1] reached me yesterday morning, as I was going to Q. Sess: at Aylesbury.[2]

After dinner, the Ld. Lieutenant, very mysterious & disturbed, sought confidential conversation, / & he then told me all that your letter had announced. He said it was so much against his convictions, that, had he not received the intelligence from a quarter, wh: he could only look upon as a notice of preparation for battle, / he wd. not have credited it. ["]Four & twenty, or rather 8 & 40, hours before" he said "nothing would have induced him to treat it as serious; but he did now.["]

He imputed the affair to Gladstone & John Russell, & seemed to think it might have been occasioned by observing / some bad symptom about Palmerston.

Ld. C[arrington] thought it unwise, no solution of difficulties, & leading to another dissolution: nevertheless from the great affection of his speech & manner, & the sort of anguish, with wh: he pressed my hand when we separated, I suspect the Govt. have at last yielded his terms, & that his son will start for the County.[3]

Yours sincerely, | D. /

a hurried letter: just returned: to save post.[4]

3960 TO: PHILIP ROSE — Hughenden [Tuesday] 18 October 1864

ORIGINAL: H R/I/A/180

COVER: Philip Rose Esqr. | 6 Victoria Street | Westminster | *B. Disraeli*

POSTMARK: (1) In a circle: HIGH WYCOMBE | C | OC 18 | 64 (2) a cancelled one-penny stamp

EDITORIAL COMMENT: Paper imprinted 'MAD Hughenden Manor'. *Sic:* checque; Carington.

P. Rose Esqr — Octr. 18 1864

My dear Rose,

The government contemplate dissolving Parlt. next month. My opinion is, they have settled it. I had the news from the highest quarter.[1]

1 Derby had written from Knowsley on 15 October: 'Lord Stanhope, who has been staying here for a few days, told me that he had met the Speaker in Scotland, and ascertained that he thought it probable there would be a dissolution in November'; a letter from Stanhope that morning had repeated the rumour authoritatively from another source. Derby continued: 'I am rather inclined to believe the report. At Palmerston's time of life his colleagues will naturally be desirous of making sure of having the Election under the prestige of his name; and Gladstone's recent "progress" through Lancashire, (not to mention Palmerston's own repeated exhibitions in public) look very much like bidding for immediate popularity. At all events it is right that you should know what I have heard, and on what authority. You may be able to find out whether there is any foundation for it.' He thought Taylor should be alerted so he could find and place candidates; 'He [Taylor] writes me that generally speaking he is satisfied with the registration'. Derby concluded: 'I need say nothing to *you* of the vital importance of the next Election. It will decide the fate of parties, at all events for *my* time.' H B/XX/S/325.

2 See **3958**&n1.

3 See **3873**&n2.

4 Derby would reply on 26 October that he had heard from Stanhope that Palmerston had twice '"stated in the most direct and decisive terms that there was not the slightest intention"' of an imminent dissolution, the rumour was '"unfounded"', and '"it would be an error of policy in the Government to dissolve at present."' Derby continued: 'Stanhope's own theory is that some of the Ministers reckoned on a large gain in the Registration, and thought in that case an immediate appeal to the new Constituency would be desirable; but that they are much disappointed by the result, and have therefore altered their views.' H B/XX/S/326. In the event, parliament would be dissolved on 6 July 1865. For the Bucks registration, see **3960**&n5.

---

1 See **3959**.

I meant to have been in town today, but am / a little indisposed, & must be quiet. If I cannot reach you tomorrow or next day, I shall send my representative in the form of a checque for £1240.[2]

Will you have the kindness to communicate the news to Spofforth, & / Col: Taylor – *our candidates should be all ready.*

Charles Carington, I think, will start for the County.[3] If we can compromise Aylesbury one & one, we shall be fortunate. I have got the thing in hand, but am not very sanguine. It wd. suit the / Rothschilds, & Ld. C. but if the Govt. put on a very strong pressure, I don't much like it.[4]

Of course, they will.

Nobody has written to me a single line about the Registration. Judging from the papers, I fear it has not gone very well.[5]

Yrs ever | D.

TO: C.H. HAWKINS Hughenden [Saturday] 22 October 1864 **3961**

ORIGINAL: RUL Mss Coll Blundell Cat 3, item 37

EDITORIAL COMMENT: Paper imprinted 'MAD Hughenden Manor'.

C.H. Hawkins | Esqre.[1] Octr 22 1864

Sir,

I am honored by the wish of the Colchester Cons: Club, that I should attend their dinner on the 26th. Inst:, but I regret, that it will not be in my power.

For / reasons, with wh: it might be wearisome to trouble ↑you↓, I feel obliged to decline attending any public meetings, wh: are not held in my own County, or Diocese.

I earnestly hope, that / the efforts of the Essex, & Colchester, Conservatives may be crowned with success.[2]

Believe me, Sir, | faithfully yours, | *B. Disraeli*

2 See **3958**&n1.

3 See **3873**&n2.

4 On 21 July 1865, one Conservative (S.G. Smith, an incumbent) and one Liberal (N.M. de Rothschild) would be returned for Aylesbury uncontested.

5 The registration lists drawn up in 1864 would come into effect on 30 November and be the basis for the general election of 1865, for which there would be almost 80,000 more electors than in 1859. F.W.S. Craig *British Parliamentary Election Results 1832-1885* (1977) xiv, 623. D had not yet had reports from local agents, who would tally the party affiliations of those registered in their constituencies, nor from the central agents such as Taylor. On 15 October *BH* had run a long article on registration of voters. Robert Milnes Newton, a barrister appointed to revise the voting lists, had held a court on the 13th at County Hall, Aylesbury, at which Messrs Parrott, Wood and Fell had represented the Conservative interest.

---

1 Probably Charles Henry Hawkins, 3rd son of William Hawkins of Colchester and brother of William Warwick Hawkins, MP (C) for Colchester 1852-7. C.H. Hawkins would be mayor of Colchester 1865-6, 1870-2. http://www.colchester.gov.uk/Info. No correspondence from him has been found.

2 At the anniversary meeting of the Colchester True Blue, or Conservative, Association held on Wednesday 26 October at Colchester, the main speaker would be Charles Du Cane, MP (C) for Essex N, with C.H. Hawkins in the chair. *MP* (29 Oct 1864). The Liberals had a good registration in 1864, and in the 1865 general election would win several seats in Essex from the Conservatives, including one at Colchester.

3962 TO: LADY LOVAINE Hughenden [Monday] 24 October 1864

ORIGINAL: NOR G/14/76

EDITORIAL COMMENT: Paper imprinted 'MAD Hughenden Manor'. *Sic:* been ... been.

Dear Ambassadress, Octr 24 1864

You deserve to be decorée for such skilful diplomacy,[1] & if there were anything better, than a Coventry ribbon[2] in my neighbouring town, I wd. really presume / to send you one.

1000 thanks! All is for the best, for the Duke & Duchess of Welln. proposed, for their arrival here, the very day we were to have been, either at Battle, or at Albury;[3] & tho' their visit has been, from an / accident, been postponed for a few days, we cd., scarcely, have returned in time conveniently to have received them.

I look forward with interest to making the acquaintance of Lord Beverley, but I / fear we are entirely engaged for next month, going to Cuddesdon on the 24th. preliminary to a great ecclesiastical function at the Univy:[4]

The authoritative rumor is, that Parlt. is to be dissolved on the 28th.?[5]

My wife particularly desires me to send her kindest remembrances, & regards, to yourself & Ld. Lovaine. I need not say I join in them, & heartily[.]

D.

3963 TO: MARY ANNE DISRAELI [London, Monday] 24 October 1864

ORIGINAL: H A/I/A/317

EDITORIAL COMMENT: Docketed by MA on the fourth page: '1864 Oct 24th. Dizzy'. *Sic:* Winchelsea.

1 Lady Lovaine had written on 22 October: 'My diplomacy has not succeeded, but you are in no way compromised. My letter suggesting that of course we were no longer expected at [the Duke and Duchess of Cleveland's] Battle Abbey on the 25th. received the answer that we were "depended upon." I then wrote that having been lately staying at Hughenden, I found that you had refused the invitation to Battle thinking it was for the 25th: of Sept when you were engaged, but that on looking back at the letter you found it was for the 25th of October, – & that *I* merely let her know this mistake of yours in case she should not have filled up her numbers. Yesterday evening I got the answer "Alas! I fear we are quite full – if no one throws us over – it is most kind of you to write, & I am much vexed, for I wished particularly to have the Disraelis." Lord Beverley [*Lovaine's father*] has not yet left Leamington, but if we can get him here, I will immediately let you know that you may choose the days most agreeable to you to come to us, for I dare say he will stay a month.' H B/XXI/L/349.

2 Inexpensive woven silk ribbon items including heraldic designs had been widely marketed since 1862 in an attempt to offset the effects of the collapse of the silk industry in Coventry in 1860. Alice Lynes "Thomas Stevens and His Silk Ribbon Pictures" *Coventry City Libraries Local History Pamphlet No 2*.

3 Wellington on 10 and 13 October (his letters evidently crossing ones from D [not found]) had suggested they visit the DS on 2 November. He and the Duchess would be guests at Hughenden 2-5 November, with Lord and Lady Raglan, the Earl of Orford, [Lord] Courtenay and Lady Malmesbury, who arrived on the 3rd. H B/XXI/165-6; H acc. No correspondence has been found on the DS' projected visits to the Clevelands at Battle Abbey or to the Lovaines at Albury Park, nor did they visit either place in the autumn of 1864.

4 The DS would be at Cuddesdon 24-6 November. H acc. See **3956**&n1 and **3970**&n1.

5 See **3959**&nn1&4; *BH* on 29 October would carry several items predicting an imminent dissolution, though without any specific date. See further **3964**.

My dearest Love, Octr 24 1864

Lady Churchill has got a son & heir![1]

Julian Fane is in England & in Yorkshire, at Temple Newsam. I have written to him.[2] /

I have seen Ld. Winchelsea, but he is engaged at Lord Crewe's for races; at Chester.[3]

The luncheon was very good.

I went up with Charles / Carrington, who was going to Newmarket![4]

Your own, | D.

TO: FREDERICK LYGON Hughenden [Wednesday] 26 October 1864 3964

ORIGINAL: BCP [16]

EDITORIAL COMMENT: Paper imprinted 'MAD Hughenden Manor'.

Hon: F. Lygon M. P. Octr 26 1864

My dear Lygon,

The "report" is quite authentic, & there is ~~lit~~ no doubt, that, less than ten days ago, Parliamt. was to have been dissolved on the 28th. Novr: a / coup d'etat – but whether, the cat having got out of the bag, they will venture it, is another question.

The news came to me express from Knowsley, & obtained from a ~~great~~ ↑high↓ quarter.[1] /

It means, I suppose, they have no programme, & they wish to secure dissolution in Palme's lifetime.[2]

Thanks for the Spec: I take it in, fancying of late, that it might perhaps be turned to acct. / Abuse of us is so general, that it must pay eventually to take the other side.

The silence of the Govt journals about Registration is suspicious, & I begin to believe in Spofforth, who tells me the Tories never had so great a one since 1840.

Always yrs | D.

1 *MP* on this day, 24 October, reported: 'Lady Churchill gave birth to a son and heir yesterday at the St. George's Hotel. Her ladyship and infant are progressing favourably.' Victor Albert Francis Charles Spencer (1864-1934), the Churchills' only child, would succeed his father as 3rd Baron Churchill in 1886 and be created Viscount Churchill in 1902. On 27 October Lord Churchill would thank MA for her congratulations. H B/XXI/C/217.

2 Julian Fane (see VI **2352**&n1) was currently first secretary of the embassy at Vienna. D's letter to him has not been found. H.C. Meynell Ingram, owner of Temple Newsam, near Leeds in Yorkshire, used it mainly for house parties during the shooting season.

3 The next race meeting at Chester would be in May 1865. Hungerford Crewe (1812-1894), 3rd Baron Crewe, DL of Wiltshire, FRS (1841), was lord of Crewe Hall, Cheshire, about 23 miles from Chester.

4 The Newmarket Houghton race meeting opened on this day, and would last until Saturday 29 October. *MP* (24-31 Oct 1864).

---

1 See **3959**&nn1&4.

2 Palmerston on 20 October had celebrated his 80th birthday inspecting south-coast fortifications on horseback without apparent ill effects; he would live almost another year, until 18 October 1865. Ridley *Palmerston* 577.

3965 TO: JAMES SHEAHAN Hughenden [Sunday] 30 October 1864

ORIGINAL: UCLA [18]

EDITORIAL COMMENT: Paper imprinted 'MAD Hughenden Manor'. The MS is severely stained.

Private Octr 30 1864

J. Sheahan Esq[1]

Dear Sir,

There is no pension fund set apart for men of letters. It is a vulgar error. Out of a very limited amount, annually placed at the disposition of Her Majesty, £1200 pr annm, the custom has grown up of allotting some portion to the claims of literature, science, / & art: but the Crown has no other fund from wh: it can recognise & reward miscellaneous public services, or even those of the dependents on the Throne. It is, therefore, obviously very difficult to obtain such an arrangement as you intimate, & even that limited patronage depends not only on the advice, / but the personal influence of the Prime Minister.

I need not remind you, that I am not in a position to make an appeal to such an exalted personage either with decorum or effect.

It strikes me that some immediate, & I hope not inconsiderable, relief, might be very properly obtained in your case from the Lity. Fund. Yours is an instance to / [*illegible*] wh: the [*illegible*] was particularly formed & in wh: the aid might be accepted by you with honor & perfect repute. You are a man of letters, of great perseverance in pursuits of public interest & advantage & deserve support.

If I can be of any use in this way, let me know.[2]

I trust I have conveyed to you my general view, but I write to you at a moment of pressure.

Yours faithfully | *B. Disraeli*

3966 TO: RALPH EARLE Hughenden [Wednesday] 2 November 1864

ORIGINAL: H H/LIFE

PUBLICATION HISTORY: M&B IV 370, dated 2 November, first sentence of the third paragraph

EDITORIAL COMMENT: From a typescript headed: 'D. to Mr. R.A. Earle, Hughenden, Nov. 2. '64.' The signature line is in manuscript.

My dear Earle,

It makes me happy to hear, that you have returned home, and I hope you will never

1 For D's prior dealings with Sheahan, see **3619**&n1. Correspondence in August and September 1864 concerned D's subscribed copy of Sheahan's book on Hull (D's other responses not found); on 5 September Sheahan wrote that, after twenty years compiling county history, 'I am in the end so poor that I must now endeavour to procure for myself [a] Secretaryship or Corresponding Clerkship in some Merchants establishment, and in this I fear I shall experience some difficulty.' He gently reminded D that he had not paid the 10*s* 6*d* owing on the book, the receipt for which he sent on 12 September. H B/XXI/S/165-7.

2 Sheahan's letter has not been found, as D forwarded it to Octavian Blewitt of the Literary Fund while Sheahan was considering whether to apply; see **3968**&n1. On 2 November he would thank D for his letter, saying that he had known about the fund and the impropriety of applying to D, but had been persuaded by E.F. Collins, Editor of the *Hull Advertiser*. He would seek Collins's further advice before deciding whether to apply to the Fund. On 7 November he would send Collins's letter endorsing D's advice, and on 24 November (after D had made application for him) write that he would be applying. On 16 December he would report receiving £40 from the Fund, and extend D his profuse thanks. H B/XXI/S/168-71.

have another illness.[1] There is a certain quantity of indisposition, which must be got through in life, and yours has been executed, I hope, in youth.

I have a great lady of the Court here at present; no less a personage, than the Mistress of the Robes.[2]

I am meditating a great ecclesiastical function at Oxford this month,[3] which would have been apropos for the dissolution, had it come off. After that, I hope we shall meet. In the meantime, let me know how you get on, and whether your company is alive, or has vanished in the financial Typhoon.[4]

Yours ever

TO: LORD STANLEY — Grosvenor Gate [Tuesday] 15 November 1864 — **3967**

ORIGINAL: DBP Box 47/2

EDITORIAL COMMENT: Paper imprinted 'Grosvenor Gate'.

Rt Honble | The Lord Stanley — Nov 15. 1864

Dear Stanley,

I thank you for your letter, wh: was kind & considerate.[1]

We must hope, & we may expect, the best.

We have passed three / pleasant months at Hughenden, & ↑are↓ now reconnoitering the old scene.[2]

On the 24th:, we go to Cuddesdon, & then to Strathfieldsaye. I don't, at the moment, see / further, &, when we meet, I hope we may both be as well as I am now.[3]

Yours ever, | D.

1 On 31 October 1864 Earle had reported from 116 Park Street his return on the 29th. On 22 September Rose had written that Earle had 'been at the point of death of miliary fever' but was recovering. H R/I/B/98. On 26 September Earle in Kreuznach had replied to D's of the 22nd (not found) with a dictated letter: 'on the eve of leaving this place I was attacked by a fever, which soon reduced me, & for several days kept me on the verge of life, & death'. Though he was told that afterwards he would be better than he had been for years, he predicted he would not be able to leave for England for three weeks. H B/XX/E/340-41.

2 See **3962**&n3; the Duchess of Wellington was mistress of the robes to the Queen.

3 See **3956**&n1 and **3970**&n1. Earle in his next letter, of 3 December, addressed to D at Beckett House (see **3967**&n3), would write: 'I have not yet told you how much I like & how successful I consider the Oxford Manifesto.'

4 1864 saw great financial fluctuations and joint-stock speculation, with the most critical period in September and October, when many firms collapsed. This caused extraordinarily low prices that attracted buyers, and the crisis gradually subsided by the end of the year. *AR* (1864) 168-71. In his dictated letter of 26 September (n1) Earle had written: 'My company suspended operations until the end of next month, & I seized the opportunity of coming to Germany to be set up.' His company may have been the Ottoman Finance Association, which had issued its prospectus in February, with a capital of £1m in shares of £50. *The Times* (11 Feb 1864). In a letter dated only 'Saturday' Earle wrote from 116 Park Street to ask D to lend him £150 to make up his share of £2,200 'in the syndicate of the Ottoman loan'; he would explain when they next met why he could not get the advance from the Stock Exchange. H B/XX/E/205.

---

1 On 18 and 23 October Stanley had regretfully declined from Hatfield two successive D invitations (not found); on 13 November he had written from Knowsley about his father's health: 'as it is very likely that exaggerated accounts may get abroad, I write to say that there is no cause for anxiety. Last night we were in some alarm ... [but] this morning things are better, and our minds are set at rest. It will be a long affair; he is ordered absolute quiet – rest of body and mind.' H B/XX/S/718-20.

2 The Ds had left Hughenden on 10 November and would return there on the 21st. H acc.

3 See **3970**&n1 for D's Oxford speech on 25 November; the Ds would be guests of the Duke and Duchess of Wellington at Strathfieldsaye 29 November to 2 December, and of Lord and Lady Barrington at Beckett House, Shrivenham, Berkshire, 2-5 December. H acc.

3968 TO: OCTAVIAN BLEWITT Grosvenor Gate [Saturday] 19 November 1864

ORIGINAL: RLF M/1077/64 File 1661 Letter 1

EDITORIAL COMMENT: *Sic:* pennyless.

O. Blewitt Esqr Grosvenor Gate | Nov. 19. 1864

Dear Sir,

The enclosed is a genuine letter, written with no view of appealing to the Lit: Fund, but to another course, over wh: I have, of course, as little control as yourself.[1] /

I have made some enquiries as to this case: & from the labors of the individual; his moral character; & his almost pennyless condition; it appears to me to be one well worthy of the / interposition of our society.

Will you have the kindness to let me know what you think; to Hughenden Manor if you please, as I am only for a day in London.[2]

Yours flly. | *B. Disraeli*

3969 TO: LORD NEVILL Grosvenor Gate [Sunday] 20 November 1864

ORIGINAL: H H/LIFE

EDITORIAL COMMENT: From a manuscript copy.

The Viscount Nevill[1] Grosvenor Gate | Nov. 20. 1864.

My dear Lord,

If this troubles you, you must blame only yourself for having revealed my incognito to Mr. Johnstone of the Standard. He will not let me rest until I write to assure you that belonging to a City Company is not *infra dig* even for a Nevill.

This certainly it is not: any further opinion on the matter I refrain from giving as it wd. be impertinent.

I return to Hughenden tomorrow and on Friday I shall be at Oxford: a great Ch: meeting in the Sheldonian.[2]

Yours ever sincerely, | D.

3970 TO: SAMUEL WILBERFORCE Hughenden [Tuesday] 29 November 1864

ORIGINAL: BRN [35]

EDITORIAL COMMENT: Paper imprinted 'Hughenden Manor'.

The | Lord Bishop | of | Oxford Nov 29 1864

My dear Lord,

I am deeply honored, & gratified, by the request of the Dioc: Board, that what I

1 See **3965**&nn1&2 for the case of James Sheahan, whose letter (not found) D encloses.

2 Blewitt would report on 26 December that Sheahan had been granted £40. H A/IV/M/88. The Ds were at Grosvenor Gate 10-21 November. H acc.

1 William Nevill (1826-1915), Viscount Nevill, eldest surviving son of 4th Earl of Abergavenny, whom he would succeed as 5th Earl in 1868, created Marquess of Abergavenny 1876, KG 1886, was currently chairman of the Junior Carlton Club committee. H A/IV/M/41-2.

2 See **3970**&n1.

said, on Friday last,[1] should be placed in a more permanent form, than it has yet appeared, &, especially, as / that request is headed by yourself.[2] I only wish my words were worthier of the great distinction, but, as I doubt not you perceived, I spoke with doubt how far I might proceed, feeling my way at every sentence; & so omitted several things wh: / might have been expressed with advantage.

We are now first going to Strathfieldsaye, where we shall stay till the end of the week, & then to Beckett,[3] & you, probably, when you receive this, may be hundreds

1 See **3956**&n1. On Friday 25 November at the Sheldonian Theatre in Oxford, at the annual meeting of the Society for the Increasing the Endowment of Small Livings in the Diocese of Oxford, D had made his famous 'apes and angels' speech. His biographer J.A. Froude later described how he 'lounged into the assembly in a black velvet shooting-coat and a wide-awake hat, as if he had been accidentally passing through the town,' a casual appearance that his speech soon belied. Arguing first of all that, in the past four decades since the declaration of the constitutional principle of religious freedom, the established Church had withstood all external attempts to bring it down, he saw the major threat now from within the Church itself, from those clerics who embraced the perspective of the new criticism and philosophical scepticism yet remained within the Church: 'If it were true, as I am often told, that the age of faith has passed, the position of having a hierarchy, vast, opulent, supported by men of high cultivation, brilliant talents and eloquence, and, perhaps, some ambition, with no distinctive opinions, might be a very harmless ... state of affairs. (A laugh.) But when, instead of believing that the age of faith has passed, I observe what is taking place, not only in this country, but on the Continent and in other hemispheres, I hold that the characteristic of the present age is craving credulity. (Cheers.) Why, my Lord, man is a being born to believe (cheers), and if you do not come forward – if no Church comes forward, with all its title deeds of truth sustained by the tradition of sacred ages and the convictions of countless generations to guide him, he will find altars and idols in his own heart and his own imagination. (Loud cheers.)' He predicted that this party within the Church would ultimately fail: 'I find this common characteristic of all their writings, that their learning is always second-hand. (Cheers.) Now, my lord, I do not say that because learning is second-hand, it may not be sound, or that knowledge because it is second-hand may not be true; but this I do say, ... that there is something in original research so invigorating to the intellect, which so braces and disciplines the human mind that those who have undergone that process arrive at their conclusions with great caution and with great circumspection, but that when a man of brilliant imagination has to deal with a vast quantity of facts that have been furnished by the labours of others, he is tempted to generalize with a fatal facility, and often arrives at conclusions which, in time he not only repudiates but often has to refute.' He dismissed recent German biblical scholarship as all anticipated 'by the great Hebrew scholars who flourished in the 18th and at the end of the 17th century', and suggested that the French Revolution had in part been brought about by their ideas: 'I cannot, therefore, believe the views of the new school will succeed. (Cheers.)' In conclusion he addressed the perceived conflict between science and the Church; allowing that science had contributed greatly 'to the convenience of life and the comfort of man', he continued: 'But it is of great importance when science is mentioned that we should annex to it precise ideas. I hold that the highest function of science is the interpretation of nature, and the interpretation of the highest nature is the highest science ... Man is the highest nature, and when I compare the interpretation of that highest nature by the most advanced, the most fashionable, and modest school of modern science with some later teaching with which we are all familiar, I am not prepared to say that the latter is the more scientific. What is the question? It is now placed before society with, I might say, a glib assurance which to me is astonishing – the question is, is man an ape or an angel? (A laugh.) Now, I am on the side of the angels. (Cheers.) I repudiate with indignation and abhorrence these new-fangled theories. (Cheers.) I believe they are an outrage to the conscience of humanity ... On the other hand, what does the Church teach us? What is her interpretation of the highest nature? That man is made in the image of his Creator (cheers) – a source of inspiration – a source from which alone can flow not only every right principle of morals, but every Divine truth.' J.A. Froude *Disraeli* (1905) 173; *The Times* (26 Nov 1864). See Introduction pp xiii-xiv and illustration p lxii. For a full treatment see M&B IV 371-6.

2 Wilberforce had written on 28 November from the County Hall, Oxford: 'A strong wish was expressed to me today at the meeting of our Diocesan Board that you would give us your Grand Speech in a more enduring form. I desired those who asked this to put their wish into writing: this they have done & I have had great pleasure in heading the signatures.' The sheet enclosed with the request has 33 signatures in addition to the bishop's. H B/XXI/W/369, 369a.

3 See **3967**n3.

of miles from Cuddesdon. How shall we act, not to lose / time, wh:, I suppose, is an object?

I will send the report, of wh: I most approve, to the Arch[deaco]n,[4] that it may be set up in type, & then, when I receive the slips from him, I can correct them before they go to press. He will, probably, have them back by return of post, as I will keep him alive to my movements.[5]

Yrs, my dear Lord, | sincerely, | D.

3971 TO: SIR JOHN PAKINGTON Strathfieldsaye [Thursday] 1 December 1864

ORIGINAL: WRC 705:349 BA 3835/7(ii)19

EDITORIAL COMMENT: Endorsed in another hand on the fourth page: '1864 Disraeli'.

Strathfieldsaye | Dec. 1. 1864

Right Honorable | Sir Jno Pakington | G.C.B.

My dear Pakington,

The same post, that brought me your letter & book, brought also a volume & letter from Roebuck.[1] I have only been able to reply to him today for various / reasons, & I let you know at once the purport of my answer: wh: was, that I shd. be prepared to support a motion of enquiry, if brought forward by him, reserving to myself the right, in case / the Government mentioned the subject in the Queen's speech, or gave notice of any course the first night, of taking such a line, as I might then deem expedient.[2]

It wd. be tedious to enter now into the reasons, / wh: prompted this reserve, but, with yr parly. experience, they will, in some degree, be obvious to you.

4 Archdeacon Bickersteth was one of the signatories of the petition (n2).

5 On 1 December the bishop would respond in a note marked '*Secret*': 'There is but one thing in the speech through which I would ask you to strike your pen – the reference to eternal punishment'. H B/XXI/W/370. In his list of practitioners of the new school of criticism D had included 'nebulous professors (a laugh), who appear in their style to have revived chaos (much laughter), and who if they could only succeed in obtaining a perpetual study of their writings would go far to realize that eternity of punishment which they object to (continued laughter)'. The speech, with the objectionable phrase removed, would be published as *Church policy; a speech delivered by the Right Hon. B. Disraeli, M.P., at a meeting of the Oxford Diocesan Society for the Augmentation of Small Livings in the Sheldonian Theatre, Oxford, Nov. 25, 1864* (London: Rivingtons 1864). See further **3973**.

1 Pakington's letter and book have not been found. J.A. Roebuck had written from 19 Ashley Place SW on 1 November for D's opinion of William Galt's *Railway Reform* (1864), 'a proposal to alter our whole railway system & to enable government to take into its own hands the whole railway property of the country'. He asked D to support his motion for a select committee on the matter: 'the motion will be à propos as in 1865 will expire the 20 years, which were given by an act of 1844 for government to ponder upon the scheme then advocated by Mr Gladstone for buying the whole railway property of the country & making railways like the post office, a grand government undertaking. Mr Gladstone wishes I believe to have this matter wholly in his own hands, & to make it strictly a government scheme & proposal. This I desire to prevent & to that end I purpose moving for a select Committee to inquire into the whole subject ... I do not mean ... that your support should go any further than, that you deem inquiry important & even necessary.' H B/XXI/R/103. Pakington's letter may have been about his intention to move for a select committee on the committee of council on education, which he would do on 28 February 1865. *MP* (1 Mar 1865).

2 D's letter to Roebuck has not been found. There would be no mention of the railway issue in the Queen's Speech on 7 February 1865. *MP* (8 Feb 1865). The railways in Britain would not be nationalized until after WWII.

I hope you are well & Lady Pakington, to whom offer my kind Compts[.]
Yours sincerely, | D.

TO: EDWARD KENEALY Strathfieldsaye [Thursday] 1 December 1864 3972

ORIGINAL: QUA [430]
EDITORIAL COMMENT: Paper imprinted 'Strathfield Saye' with a picture.

E.V. Kenealy Esqr Dec 1 1864
My dear Sir,
I am truly sorry, that I cannot have the honor of being yr guest in Janry. next, as / I expect to be, on the 10th: of that month, some hundred miles from home.[1]
Yrs very faithfully, | *B Disraeli*

TO: FREDERICK LYGON Hughenden [Friday] 9 December 1864 3973

ORIGINAL: BCP [17]
PUBLICATION HISTORY: M&B IV 353n1, undated extract from the third paragraph
EDITORIAL COMMENT: Paper imprinted (first sheet) 'Hughenden Manor', (second sheet) 'MAD Hughenden Manor'.

Hon: Fred. Lygon | M. P. Decr 9 1864
Mon Cher!
We arrived here from a run of visits; last from Beckett; the day, or so, before yesterday.[1] I found yr letter[2] – & agree with all it suggests. But the thing is not exactly in my hands, but / in those of the Arch[deaco]n of Buckingham. The B[isho]p had forwarded me a requisition; to print the speech; from the Diocesan Council, & Bickersteth undertook the management after my revision, wh: I sent instantly.[3] His people work slowly, but, perhaps, it is as well, that there shd. / be an interval betn the delivery & the publication.

The publishers are Rivingtons, who have establishments at London, Oxford, & Cambridge: so thats well; & the publication will bear a general, & significant, title; "CHURCH POLICY" being a speech &c.; & thats better; so, on the whole, I think, we shall do pretty well. /

I like, however, your plan, but it wd. lead now to too great delay. Could not we execute it before the dissolution? I have no copy at hand of the *first* Diocesan speech. There was one also previous to that, at a rural decanal meeting, wh: I think might be worth looking at, & wh: wo[ul]d show continuity & consistency of effort. The speech in the H of Comm: on subscription, I think two years ago, would / complete the picture.[4] No one but you could be the Editor, as you know my inmost mind, &

1 Kenealy's invitation has not been found. The DS would go to Gunnersbury (approximately a 25-mile distance) on 7 January but would be back at Hughenden from the 9th to the 20th. H acc.

---

1 See **3967**&n3.
2 On 1 November Lygon had written to D from All Souls College, Oxford, with suggestions for his Oxford speech, and on 4 December had congratulated him, suggesting that Rivingtons publish it and 'that your two former speeches should be reproduced in the same pamphlet.' H B/XX/LN/29-30.
3 See **3970**&nn1&2,4&5.
4 For D's speech to a decanal meeting on 4 December 1860, see **3523**&n2; for his diocesan speech of 14 November 1861, see **3628**&n1; for that of 30 October 1862, see **3734**&n1.

there is entire sympathy between us. The Editor must be a politician & a man of the world.[5]

I read the art: in C & S. with / much satisfaction. I had forgotten it. It was only at the end, that I began to ask myself, whether I were Christopher Sly or not? for the article was written by one in whose career I naturally take an interest, / & by a friend of yours, whom, I think, you love.[6]

Yours sincerely, | D.

3974 TO: LORD DERBY Hughenden [Sunday] 11 December 1864

ORIGINAL: DBP Box 146/1

EDITORIAL COMMENT: Paper imprinted 'Hughenden Manor'. Endorsed by Derby on the fourth page: 'Disraeli B'.

Rt Honorable | The Earl of Derby | K. G. Decr. 11 1864

My dear Lord,

I only received the Homer last night, & lose not a post to assure you, how honored, & gratified, I feel in being the possessor of a presentation copy of / so interesting a production.[1]

Stanley was so kind & considerate, as to give me some bulletins of yr progress.[2] I hear from Lord Stanhope, that he is now at Chevening,[3] but I have learnt from others, / with great satisfaction, that you advance surely, if more slowly than yr friends can desire, & are in good heart.

I will not retard yr convalescence with political cares, & am, ever, sincerely yours, & obliged, | D.

5 Lygon (n1) had also suggested 'a preface somewhat in the sense of an old but very excellent article from the Ch: & State Review wh: I enclose would help in putting before the church party the real method of bringing political aspirations to positive results.' He asked for it to be returned. In a postscript he added: 'perhaps the preface might be the vehicle of more direct statement if written by an Editor.' The result would be *"Church and Queen": five speeches delivered by the Rt. Hon. B. Disraeli, M.P. 1860-1864,* 'Edited, with a preface, by a member of the University of Oxford.' (London: G.J. Palmer 1865) pp xv+79. The contents are: 'Preface – Appendix to preface – On Church rates, Dec. 4, 1860 – On present position of the Church, Nov. 14, 1861 – On future position of the Church, 1862 – On Act of Uniformity, June 9, 1863 – On Church policy, Nov., 1864. For the 1863 speech, see **3821**&n2. For the gist of Lygon's preface, see M&B IV 353.

6 The *Church and State Review* was a monthly periodical 1862-5 edited by the Speaker's brother, the Rev George Anthony Denison, a high-churchman strongly opposed to state intervention in the parochial school system and to all the liberal and latitudinal causes of the time. D's reference is to an unsigned laudatory review in the 1 October 1864 issue of T.E. Kebbel's *Essays Upon History and Politics* (1864). The reviewer especially liked the section on Disraeli, quoting from it at length; for example: '"We have no hesitation in saying, then, that the services of Mr. Disraeli to the Conservative Party have been such as hardly any other living statesman could have performed."' For the time in 1860 that D first saw the essay on him by Kebbel (the man in whose career he took an interest), see **3467**&n1. Christopher Sly is the character in *Taming of the Shrew* who is duped into believing he is a lord. (The information on the *Church and State Review* was kindly provided by Dr Belinda Beaton.)

---

1 Derby published in 1864 (privately printed in 1862) *The Iliad of Homer Rendered into English Blank Verse* (2 volumes).

2 For the most recent report, see **3967**n1.

3 Chevening Place, near Sevenoaks in Kent, was Stanhope's seat.

TO: LORD DERBY Hughenden [Monday] 12 December 1864 **3975**

ORIGINAL: DBP Box 146/1

PUBLICATION HISTORY: M&B IV 405, dated at Hughenden, 12 December 1864, the third and fourth paragraphs

EDITORIAL COMMENT: Paper imprinted 'Hughenden Manor'. Endorsed by Derby at the top of the first page: 'Disraeli B'.

Rt Honble | The Earl of Derby | K. G. Dec. 12 1864

My dear Lord,

I received yr letter this morning, having written to you yesterday.[1] Yr handwriting alone is an excellent bulletin, & yr friends, & the country must find some consolation / for your sufferings in the more than hope, that you will, probably, be free from attack during the period of public business, &, I trust, for a much longer time.

I regret, that our engagements will prevent us / having the honor of availing ourselves of yr obliging invitation to Knowsley in January, but that regret is, in some degree, diminished by the consciousness, that my presence could not be very serviceable or suggestive; for I have nothing to say. Events / must make themselves, & all the energies of the party must be concentrated on the dissolution.

There is only one point wh: I wish to submit to you. To consider, whether it is necessary, that the leaders of opposition in the two houses↑, on the first night,↓ should make those / elaborate & comprehensive surveys of the public situation, wh:, of late years, it has become their habit of doing.

The principle, now conveniently assumed by our opponents, that the Opposition is a body prepared to take office, &, therefore, bound to give its quasi-official opinion on the conduct of every department, seems / to me to have no sound foundation, & is very injurious to us. It forces us to show our cards the first night of the Sess: & the Government profits accordingly. They see where the breakers are ahead, & what perils they have escaped.

Of late years, for example, they / were in great doubt as to the consequences of their American policy, & also particularly of their refusal to join in a Congress: but our declarations, the first night, relieved them on both heads, tho' either, in the course of the Sess:; if we had not become pledged, wd. have proved perhaps a fatal question for the Administration.

So / long as we moved, or move, amendments to the Address, these reviews, on our part, are necessary, but that is a course not adopted by us of late, & wh: will not

1 Derby had written from Knowsley on 10 December: 'For nearly five weeks I have been a prisoner to my room, from which I have not yet emerged; and for a considerable portion of that time I have been confined to my bed: I hope however that I am now shaking off the remains of my renewed attack, and that in a few days I may get out of the house.' He thought that 'we must begin to look forward to the coming Session; in which, though I imagine as of old, our strength will be to sit still, it is well that we should consider our course', and for that purpose invited the DS to Knowsley for a few days from 9 January. He continued: 'The supporters of the Government seem to me to be very nervous about the General Election, and almost to have made up their minds to be beaten whenever it comes.' H B/XX/S/327.

be resumed, probably, next Sess. I wish, therefore, you wo[ul]d consider, whether we may not avoid these displays at present, & assume a politic reserve.[2]

Ever, my dear Lord,

Yours sincerely, | *B. Disraeli*

3976 TO: LORD HENRY LENNOX Hughenden [Wednesday] 14 December 1864

ORIGINAL: QUA [69]

EDITORIAL COMMENT: Paper imprinted 'Hughenden Manor'.

The | Lord H.G. Lennox | M.P. Dec. 14 1864

My dear Henry,

I was very much obliged to you for your letters,[1] wh: are always most acceptable to me. Perhaps I don't deserve them, but my correspondence is very heavy, & in letter / writing, I continue a protectionist, & am more interested in the imports, than the exports.

I saw Elmley as I passed thro' town the other day; I thought looking very well. I have always been sanguine about his case. God grant I may be right, for I can't afford to lose / any more friends.[2]

Let me know how you are getting on.

I hope poor dear Bective is not stranded by this death. He was infamously treated by the old Alderman, but things were righting themselves, I fancy. Will the death derange this?[3]

You will be glad, to / hear that our chivalrous chief has recovered & left his room. We are invited there for Jany. 9th; but cannot go.

As for public affairs, Heaven is above all.[4]

Yrs ever, | D.

2 Derby would speak briefly on 7 February 1865 on the Address to the Speech, simply because not to do so would be discourteous to both Queen and Lords. He did, however, allow himself to observe that the Speech had said virtually nothing, especially on foreign relations and the American civil war's effect on Canada. D would not speak at all until 13 March, in debate on Canada's defences. *Hansard* CLXXVII cols 21-30, 1570-8.

---

1 Lennox had written on 11 November from Pulpit Rock, Bonchurch: 'I am here with Elmley. He is pleased with the House; and the place, has made rather a favourable impression upon him; – but the weather is so cold, that he has, wisely, decided to keep the House, till a change occurs.' On 27 November he had written again, from Bretby Park (Lord Chesterfield), Burton on Trent, to congratulate D on his Oxford speech, and with some political news. H B/XX/LX/202-3.

2 Elmley (actually 5th Earl Beauchamp since 1863), about whose health his brother and heir Frederick Lygon had been giving D discouraging reports, would live only until March 1866. In his reply from Pulpit Rock on 19 December, Lennox would write: 'Elmley is tolerably well. He would be much better, if he would not *worry* himself, about his affairs. He begs his very kindest regards to you & desires I will tell you *how delighted,* he should be, to receive you here.' H B/XX/LX/204.

3 Thomas Taylour (1822-1894), Earl of Bective, eldest son of 2nd Marquess of Headfort, MP (C) for Westmorland 1854-70, when he would succeed his father as 3rd Marquess, in 1842 had married Amelia Thompson (*d* 1864), only child of the very wealthy William Thompson (*d* 1854; see V **2036**n2), alderman of London. After Lady Bective's death on 4 December 1864, the bulk of the vast Thompson estates were inherited by the Bectives' only son, Lord Kenlis, Earl of Bective after his father's succession as Marquess in 1870. *MP* (5 Dec 1864).

4 In his reply (n2) Lennox would include for D's approval a letter about the state of the fleet: 'Earle left us this morning. He thought, that I had better not send my letter to the "Times", without your seeing

TO: WILLIAM LOVELL   Hughenden [Sunday] 18 December [1864]   3977

ORIGINAL: BL ADD MS 37502 f134

EDITORIAL COMMENT: *Dating:* by context; see n5. A pencilled endorsement indicates an 1863 watermark. *Sic:* Dally.

W. Lovell Esqr   Hughenden Dec 18.

My Dear Sir,

Having taken larger stables this season, I let those, wh: I previously rented from Mr. Wrightson M.P. of Brook St., as enclosed.[1]

Donovan was to pay his rent monthly, & in advance, to Mr. Grogan, but I have not required it from that agent.[2]

The term is up on the / 25th. – My butler[3] served a printed notice to terminate the annual tenure on Mr Wrightson's agent, *Mr Dally, Grosvenor Mews, Davies St.*, who has, for many years, received the rent from me.[4]

Will you have the goodness, to take steps that all / is right, as we shall be at Hatfield this Xmas. Receive from Grogan Donovan's rent, & take care, that the stables are given up to Mr. Wrightsons agent, Dallyn, or I shall be burthened with two sets of stables.[5]

Yrs ffly | D.

We / leave this on Tuesday for G.G. & shall go to Hatfield on Thursday.[6]

TO: JOHN MOWBRAY   Hatfield [Monday] 26 December 1864   3978

ORIGINAL: PS 1467

PUBLICATION HISTORY: *MP* (26 Jan 1865); *BH* (28 Jan 1865); *The Times* (25 Jan 1865).

The Right Hon. J.R. Mowbray, M.P.   Hatfield,[1] Dec. 26, 1864.

it.' The letter was presumably that headed 'The Mediterranean Fleet' from 'A Naval Officer' published in *The Times* of 29 December and giving extracts from a correspondent in Malta about the satisfactory condition of ships there.

---

1 See D's earlier letter to Rose, **3939**&n3. The enclosure has not been found. William Battie Wrightson (1789-1879), of Cusworth Hall, near Doncaster, MP (L) for Retford E 1826-7, for Hull 1830, 1831, for Northallerton 1835-65, had a town residence at 22 Upper Brook Street. *LPOD* (1865).

2 Possibly, because both of their addresses are close to Grosvenor Gate, William Frederick Donovan, job master, 5 Shepherd Court, Upper Brook Street W, and William Grogan, estate and house agent, 66 Park Street, Grosvenor Square W. *LPOD* (1860, 1864, 1865).

3 The DS' butler at this time was a Mr Evans. H acc.

4 Richard Dallyn had written to MA from 8 Mount Row (which intersects with Davies Street), Berkeley Square, on 24 June 1859: 'Mr Wrightson has authorized me to receive the rent of Woods Mews'. H D/III/D/913. MA recorded on 4 December 1863: 'Dallyn repairs at stable - £1', on 31 December 1863: 'Stables due Xmas day a check Dis £17/10', and on 30 December 1864: 'Stables ½ year to Oct.' £42.10. H acc.

5 On 24 December 1864, Lovell would write that possession of the stables had been 'delivered up', but that Wrightson's agent had yet to inspect for damage, for which D would be liable. He concluded his note: 'Grogan has received only about £17 but Donovan promises to pay the residue of the rent today, & Grogan is then to pay it to me.' MA had already paid Dallyn 17*s* 6*d* on 2 August 'for repairing hard [?new?] stables'. H A/V/G/203, acc.

6 The DS would leave Hughenden for Grosvenor Gate on Tuesday 20 December, and go to Hatfield on Thursday the 22nd. H acc.

---

1 The DS had arrived at Hatfield (Salisbury) on the 22nd; they would return to Grosvenor Gate on the 27th, and to Hughenden on the 30th. H acc.

Dear Mr. Mowbray, –
I feel truly honoured by the wish of my friend Mr. Benyon, and of Colonel Loyd Lindsay, that I should be present at the dinner which is to be given to them on the 24th of January. But for many reasons, with which I will not now weary you, but which are entirely of a public nature, I have long been obliged to decline attending public dinners except in my own county.

I sincerely hope your gathering will be very successful.

Faithfully yours, | B. DISRAELI.[2]

2 This letter would be read out by Mowbray at the highly successful 'Conservative Demonstration' dinner for Benyon at Reading on 24 January 1865, when 'Colonel Loyd Lindsay' would be also fêted as Benyon's proposed colleague for Berkshire in the next election. Robert James Loyd-Lindsay (1832-1901), Lieut-Col of the Royal Berkshire Regiment of Volunteers, a highly decorated Crimean veteran, equerry to the Prince of Wales 1858-9, would be MP (C) for Berkshire 1865-85, financial secretary for war 1877-80, KCB 1881, and be created Baron Wantage 1885.

APPENDIX I

PRE-1860 LETTERS NEWLY FOUND

These are letters that properly belong in the previously published volumes, but which came to light or were correctly dated too late for inclusion there.

The 'X' following a letter number indicates a new letter to be inserted into the sequence following the letter identified by the number only. The 'R' following a letter number indicates a letter that now replaces the letter with that number which was previously published in part for reasons stated in the headnote for that letter. The letter thus superseded may, however, still contain extracts from other letters not yet found. The 'A' or 'B' following a letter number indicates an additional new letter to be inserted into the existing sequence.

NO	DATE	TO	PLACE OF ORIGIN	LOCATION OF ORIGINAL
47X	[1825?]	MR BRAGG	[LONDON]	JWA
272X	[21 MAY '33]	LADY STEPNEY	[LONDON]	JWA
665R	9 OCT '37	[ROBERT HUME]	BRADENHAM	MOPSIK
690X	[18 DEC '37]	[SARAH DISRAELI]	[LONDON]	GRI
986X	21 AUG '39	E.W. LAKE	BRADENHAM	QUA
1037RR	[27 JAN '40]	SARAH DISRAELI	GROSVENOR GATE	HEY
1542X	18 MAR '47	BARON L. DE ROTHSCHILD	GROSVENOR GATE	ROTH
1562X	[8 JUN '47?]	[HENRY SMITH?]	BRADENHAM	ULR
1617X	26 DEC '47	BARON L. DE ROTHSCHILD	BRADENHAM	ROTH
1619X	3 JAN '48	BARON L. DE ROTHSCHILD	BRADENHAM	ROTH
1619XA	7 [JAN '48]	BARON L. DE ROTHSCHILD	BRADENHAM	ROTH
1619XB	[9 JAN '48]	BARON L. DE ROTHSCHILD	BRADENHAM	ROTH
1669X	22 JUL '48	B. WHEELER	GROSVENOR GATE	HEY
1775R	22 [JAN] '49	SIR ROBERT INGLIS	GROSVENOR GATE	URI
1841X	14 JUN '49	SIR W. MOLESWORTH	GROSVENOR GATE	PS
2132X	11 MAY '51	BENJAMIN LUMLEY	SYON HOUSE	MOPSIK
2156X	25 JUN '51	CHARLES CLUBBE	CARLTON CLUB	RIC
2213X	25 DEC '51	CHARLES CLUBBE	HUGHENDEN	RIC
2224X	[13 JAN'52?]	[WILLIAM COOKESLEY?]	[HUGHENDEN]	H H/LIFE
2365X	16 AUG '52	CHARLES CLUBBE	HUGHENDEN	RIC
2428X	18 OCT '52	[CONSERVATIVE MPS]	DOWNING STREET	JWA
2507X	13 MAR '53	SIR E. BULWER LYTTON	GROSVENOR GATE	NRO
2519X	[MAR '53?]	A.H. LAYARD	[LONDON?]	H
2613X	[5 JAN '54]	SAMUEL LUCAS	[LONDON]	HEY
2637X	27 FEB '54	I.A. BAMPS	LONDON	JAH
2732X	14 FEB '55	CHARLES CLUBBE	GROSVENOR GATE	RIC

NO	DATE	TO	PLACE OF ORIGIN	LOCATION OF ORIGINAL
2837X	[5 APR '56?]	SIR W. JOLLIFFE	GROSVENOR GATE	SCR
2892X	[12 JAN '57]	BARON L. DE ROTHSCHILD	PARIS	ROTH
2949X	5 AUG '57	BARON L. DE ROTHSCHILD	GROSVENOR GATE	ROTH
3111X	7 MAY ['58]	ROBERT HUME	CARLTON CLUB	BRI
3122X	[17? MAY '58]	LORD H. LENNOX	[LONDON]	PS
3181X	15 AUG '58	EDWARD KENEALY	HUGHENDEN	HEY
3300X	[28 FEB '59?]	[PHILIP ROSE]	H OF COMMONS	H
3331X	[7 APR '59]	[T.E. KEBBEL]	LONDON	H H/LIFE
3343X	4 MAY '59	SIR C. EASTLAKE	GROSVENOR GATE	UO
3377X	19 JUN ['59?]	STAFFORD NORTHCOTE	GROSVENOR GATE	HAV
3416X	7 NOV '59	WILLIAM LOWNDES	GROSVENOR GATE	JWA

TO: MR BRAGG [London, 1825?] 47X

ORIGINAL: JWA [4]

EDITORIAL COMMENT: *Dating:* that D's and Evans's account possibly had a favourable balance suggests an early stage in their affair with Messer; see I **21**&nn1&2 and V **1802**&n1.

Mr. Bragg[1]

Dear Sir,

I am so engaged, that I fear I shall not be able to reach you. My friend, Mr. Messer, has kindly undertaken to arrange my business with you at present.

You will be pleased to pay yourself the balance of the old account, but send me a memorandum of / the same, for the satisfaction of Mr Evans, ~~to whom~~ ↑as↓ I some time ago informed him, that the balance was in our favor.

You will be kind enough to deliver the amount remaining due to me, & your account of my separate transactions to Mr. Messer.

I am, dear Sir, | Yours truly, | *B. Disraeli*

TO: LADY STEPNEY [London, Tuesday 21 May 1833] 272X

ORIGINAL: JWA [5]

EDITORIAL COMMENT: The 'X' in the first line may be a crossed-out 'C'. *Dating:* see I **273**.

½ past one

Dear Lady Stepney,

X circumstances have procrastinated my departure to fulfil my inextricable engagement at Hampton / Court this morning to such a degree, that however willing to close my eyes to so very disagreeable a consequence, I cannot / but be conscious that it will be very difficult for me to evince that punctuality at dinner for which I / am distinguished, & which at your house is not only a duty, but a pleasure. Pray therefore do not wait the shadow of a second for

Your faithful Servt | *Disraeli*

TO: [ROBERT HUME] Bradenham [Monday] 9 October [1837] 665R

ORIGINAL: MOPSIK [240]

EDITORIAL COMMENT: Docketed in another hand on the first page: '95 / Aug. *1837 Oct: 10th*'. *Dating:* the year is evident from internal evidence ('new Crown'); see n3.

Dear Sir,[1] Bradenham Oct 9.

I learn this morning by a note from Mr White,[2] that he has received notice of your bill. I write this merely to explain why I cannot be in town, & attend to it. Independent of / several public engagements in the shape of Conservative dinners this week,

1 Possibly the John Bragg listed in *LPOD* of 1832 as a stockbroker at 6 Throgmorton Street.

1 See II **665**ec&n1. See, however, in this appendix **3111x**&n1 to Robert Hume in 1858; the Robert Hume identified in **665** had died in 1853. From the address to which D writes in 1858, 65 Berners Street, he is in fact Robert Hume, carver, gilder & cabinetmaker. *LPOD* (1832, 1860).

2 Archibald White, conveyancer in High Street, High Wycombe, had been D's election agent in 1832 (see I **217**n1).

I must attend the Q. Sessions on the 17th:[3] as I have not yet taken the oaths to the new Crown, & in case of neglect, shall incur a severe penalty.

On the 18th. I shall / be in town, & will see you; I trust this letter will satisfy you I am not neglecting the business, & will prevent any unnecessary steps on your part.

Your obedt sert | *B. Disraeli*

690x TO: [SARAH DISRAELI] [London] Monday [18 December 1837]

ORIGINAL: GRI 6058

EDITORIAL COMMENT: Endorsed in another hand at the top of the first page: 'Disraeli'. *Dating:* the New Year reference implies December; 1837 is the only relevant year the House sat in December; in the special fall sitting (15 November to 23 December) the 18th is the only Monday not ruled out by other evidence. See nn1&3.

Monday

My dearest –

I sent the letter ~~parcel~~ to B.E.L. as I think, as far as I cd. judge, it wo[ul]d be better to defer the visit to the New Year.[1] I dined at Grosvenor Gate yesterday; / only two or three men, Cecil Forester, Holmes & the Horace Twisses & Miss H.T. an ugly likeness of her father & Parnther.[2]

The dinner at Peels on Saturday was / very select; only eight at a round table; an exquisite dinner, our host agreeable & his guests; Chandos[,] Canterbury, Lowther[,] Sir W Follett, Cresswell & Yorke[.][3]

I think we / shall have some fun in the house tonight.[4]

Love | D

986x TO: EDWARD WILLIAM LAKE Bradenham [Wednesday] 21 August 1839

ORIGINAL: QUA [434]

COVER: 1839 | Wycombe ↑1839↓ Augt twenty one | E.W. Lake Esq | Bury Street | St. James' | London | *B. Disraeli*

POSTMARKS: (1) in circular form: HIGH WYCOMBE; (2) in a circle: D | 22 AU 22 | 1839; (3) in rectangle: No. 1; (4) To Pay only; (5) H WYCOMBE | [*illegible*]

EDITORIAL COMMENT: *Sic:* (cover) St. James'.

Bradenham Manor | H. Wycombe

Sir,[1]

Your letter has been forwarded to me here; I expect to be in town for a few

3 See II **665**n2. D attended Conservative dinners on 2 October at Aylesbury, on the 13th at Newport Pagnell, and on the 16th at Great Marlow; at the Bucks Michaelmas session at Aylesbury, he is listed among the magistrates taking the oaths of allegiance on 17 October, and again on the 19th. *BH* (7, 14, 21 Oct 1837).

1 See II **683**&n10 for D similarly posting a letter to his cousin B.E. Lindo; and see **691**, where he similarly suggests to Sarah Disraeli that a visit to Bradenham be postponed until the New Year.

2 Horace Twiss's only child by his first marriage was Fanny Horatia Serle Twiss (1818-1874). She would marry Francis Bacon (*d* 1840) and secondly, in 1842, John Thadeus Delane. From 1853 until her death she would be confined for mental illness. For Robert Parnther see II **646**n22.

3 For Peel's 'first party,' see II **688**.

4 On Monday 18 December 1837 the House would be occupied for five hours with three election petitions. An item on the order paper about a civil list committee caused some disturbance. *MP* (19 Dec 1837).

1 Edward William Lake (see cover) was a solicitor at 30 Bury Street, St James's. *Law List* (1838); *Robson's Commercial Directory* (1840).

days at the / end of the week, when I shall have the hon[o]r to call on you.

Your obedt St | *B Disraeli*

TO: SARAH DISRAELI Grosvenor Gate, Monday [27 January 1840] **1037RR**

ORIGINAL: HEY [1]

PUBLICATION HISTORY: M&B II 91, undated extract from the second paragraph

EDITORIAL COMMENT: *Dating:* the date conjectured in VI **1037**REC is now confirmed; see nn4&5. *Sic:* Earle; Harding; townsmen. In the text, 'Monday' has been written over 'Sunday'.

Gr. Gate | Monday

My dearest –

I write you this in the morng. & therefore it contains no Monday news. The elections seem certainly very bad; but in truth we never had a right to count on any one but Newark, & of that, knowing more of Wilde than the rest of my party, I was never very sanguine. The Whigs are in high spirits, because they can keep what they had – the Tories have kept their only seat that was vacant, & no one notices that triumph.[1] /

I am in great favor with Peel, notwithstanding my speech;[2] perhaps in some degree in consequence of it – but he had taken me to his councils the very morning ↑of the day↓ I ~~had~~ spoke~~n~~.; at least had asked me to consult with his select friends at Whitehall; but this is a secret. I never spoke better. The M. Herald says the speech was "excellently delivd." Sir Rt. Inglis shook hands with me in the middle of the house. Gaskell who dined with me yesterday had just come up from old Ld. Sidmouth at Richmond. / The fine old gentleman now 85 takes the most lively interest in the question, & strange for an old Speaker is on the side of law. He was in raptures with my speech & told Gaskell that "Disraeli bowled Earle out."[3] Harding, Sugden, Pemberton &c. &c., indeed half the house of Commons, congratulated me with genuine warmth. I cannot tell you a tithe of the sayings & doings which wo[ul]d gratify you.

What will happen I can't say, for Sir Roberts blood is up & he will fight on every point. To night he goes down to ~~cut~~ attack the 50000£ a yr.[4] I gave two / parliamentary dinners on Saturday & yesterday – very brilliant indeed.[5]

1 Sir Thomas Wilde (1782-1855), barrister (Inner Temple 1817), serjeant-at-law 1824, king's serjeant 1827, solicitor-general 1839, Kt 1840, attorney-general 1841, 1846, chief justice of common pleas 1846-50, PC 1846, lord chancellor 1850-2, created Baron Truro 1850, was Whig MP for Newark 1831-2, 1835-41; at the 25 January by-election caused by his appointment as solicitor-general, he had defeated Frederic Thesiger QC 541-532. By his second marriage he was son-in-law of the Duke of Sussex. At Beverley on 24 January, the Tory Sackville Lane Fox had held by 556-410 the seat resigned by his elder brother, George Lane Fox.

2 See III **1036**n1.

3 See III **1037**&nn1-3. In the debate on 21 January 1840, after William Erle had defended Commons' rights based on judges' actions at the time of Charles I, D had pointed out that the same precedent could be used to defend the judges by noting the Commons' behaviour at that time. *MP* (22 Jan 1840). William Erle (1793-1880), barrister (1819), KC 1834, was Whig MP for Oxford City 1837-41, judge of common pleas 1844, Kt 1845, judge of queen's bench 1846, DCL (Oxford) 1857, chief justice of common pleas 1859-66, FRS 1860.

4 The House this night would consider in committee the motion to set Prince Albert's allowance at £50,000 a year; see III **1031**&n6. Peel would speak for the successful amendment that reduced the amount to £30,000.

5 For the guests at these dinners, see III **1045**&n5.

Our man bolted from Falmouth in the most unprincipled manner, when he had the winning cards. The Tories put up a townsmen, who ~~registered~~ polled all the votes which require no jigging.[6]

Ld Eliot was warm in the lobby. He sd. he never had heard a speech so spirited.

I have, I make no doubt, much to tell, but am very pressed. I hope you are all well & my father improvd.

Much love | D

1542X TO: BARON LIONEL DE ROTHSCHILD Grosvenor Gate [Thursday] 18 March 1847

ORIGINAL: ROTH RAL 000/848 [68].

Grosvenor Gate | Mar 18 /47

My dear Lionel,

As you blamed me for not mentioning Hampden to you some time back,[1] I tell you now, that Fawley Court, one of the finest estates in Bucks, is, I am privately informed, for / purchase. 'Tis on the border, near Henley, & of course near the river: I shd. think an estate of five or six thousand a year, a splendid park & capital mansion, I believe / in excellent repair. It belongs to a young squire, Freeman, who is constantly resident on his property; & I should think, from his character & habits, that / the farms & buildings were all in excellent order.[2]

Probably you may not be in the humor, at this moment, to buy land, but I thought it best to send you this.

Ever Yours | D.

1562X TO: [HENRY SMITH?] Bradenham [Tuesday 8 June 1847?]

ORIGINAL: ULR [1]

EDITORIAL COMMENT: *Dating:* conjectural; see n1.

Bradenham

My dear Sir –

I regret very much, that it will be quite impracticable for me to reach you on Thursday, but I will not / fail to be with you in good time on Friday, & I shall be very much gratified by accepting your kind hospitality on that night. /

I hope we shall muster strong.[1]

Pray believe me, | my dear Sir, | Your faithful Sert | *B Disraeli*

6 At Penryn and Falmouth on 23 January, E.J. Hutchins (Whig) had defeated William Carne (Tory) 246-238 for the seat previously held by a Whig.

---

1 See V **1880**&n1.

2 Fawley Court, a mile from Henley-on-Thames with the Bucks-Oxfordshire border running through its lawn, had been in the Freeman family since 1684, when it was built to a Wren design in a 250-acre park; it would be sold by auction in 1853 by the current owner, William Peere Williams Freeman (1811-1873), to Edward Mackenzie. Freeman, subsequently of Pylewell Park, Hants, was DL for Oxfordshire, high sheriff 1838, JP for Bucks, Hants and Oxfordshire. Sheahan.

1 This letter is most likely from the 1847 Bucks election, when D altered his plans for Thursday 10 June to give more time in the Newport area before going to Buckingham, where he stayed with his agent Henry

TO: BARON LIONEL DE ROTHSCHILD Bradenham **1617X**

[Sunday] 26 December 1847

ORIGINAL: ROTH 000/848 [61]

EDITORIAL COMMENT: Black-edged paper. *Sic:* Wycomb; 1833.

PRIVATE Bradenham | High Wycomb. | Dec. 26. 1847

My dear Lionel –

I hope by tomorrows post to have a line, giving me the result of your Sunday visit. If it prove of interest & importance, I would, were I you, call upon my friend, who, from a letter of this morning, I apprehend will still be in town, & convey it to / him, as it will animate him to fresh exertions.[1]

I find that *18* men, now Peers, voted against the Jews in the Commons 1833, & only *11* in their favor! I agree with you, therefore, that we must be cautious in publishing the lists of the divisions, & / rather give a précis of them, calling attention only to what is in your favor.[2]

Writing to Ld. John Manners today, I particularly mentioned the anxiety of the Court that the bill shd. pass,[3] as this will be conveyed to the Duke of Rutland, who is a great Courtier.

My friend thinks that a good petition from / King's Lynn would nail Jocelyn's vote for the second reading.[4] Attend to this at once.[5]

Ever yours faithfully | D.

Smith prior to an important meeting on Saturday the 12th; see IV **1563**&nn4&5, **1564**, **1565**&nn1&2 and **1566**. If this date is correct, D must have changed his plans before receiving the Farrer invitation (**1563**&n4) at Chicheley.

---

1 For Rothschild's election as a Liberal for London and the subsequent frustrated attempts to allow him to take his Commons seat by legislation other than the oath on his 'true faith as a Christian', see IV **1607**&nn3&5 and **1617**n2. See also Weintraub, *Charlotte and Lionel,* 103-4, 111-12. Both Lord George Bentinck, who had resigned as protectionist leader on 23 December because of party hostility to his support of Russell's Jewish Disabilities Bill, and D (see the next three letters) were now actively helping Rothschild outside the House as well as preparing speeches for the second reading of Russell's bill. The primary focus at this point was D's collaboration with Rothschild on an anonymous 16-page pamphlet, *Progress of Jewish Emancipation Since 1829,* detailing the argument for removing Jewish disabilities in the Commons; see further **1619X**, **1619XA** and **1619XB**.

2 Researching for the pamphlet, Bentinck had written from Harcourt House on 25 December to correct what he had sent the day before: 'Upon looking again I see I made a blunder about the Duke of Bucks[;] he *did vote* on the 2D. READING *against* the Jews in 1830, but neither voted [n]or paired on the introduction of the Bill. EIGHTEEN MEN NOW PEERS voted AGAINST the Jews & only ELEVEN in their favour!!! In publishing the list of the division therefore they should mind what they are about or they will damage more than they will profit the cause in the Lords.' H B/XX/BE/45-6. The printed pamphlet gives only the totals of favourable divisions and the names of some current peers who voted for a similar bill in 1830. See Appendix VI.

3 See IV **1617**&n5.

4 Bentinck had given this advice on 24 December (n2); Jocelyn, his Peelite colleague for Lynn Regis, is not recorded in the 11 February 1848 division which passed second reading of the Jewish Disabilities Bill 277-204. No petition from Lynn is listed for the days leading up to second reading.

5 Evidently D was acting virtually as Rothschild's campaign manager in this matter. See Introduction pp ix-x.

1619X TO: BARON LIONEL DE ROTHSCHILD Bradenham
[Monday] 3 January 1848

ORIGINAL: ROTH 000/573/6 [59]
EDITORIAL COMMENT: Black-edged paper.

Bradenham | Jan 3. 1848

My dear Lionel –

I have sent you, in two packets, by this post, a sketch of the sort of thing you require.[1]

Altho' it affects to be a dry synopsis, the facts are so disposed, that their impression, / I apprehend, will be highly favorable to your cause among those doubtful, but not very prejudiced. There is not a name introduced without a special reason.

Make what additions & alterations you like before you send / it to the Printer, & let me have a proof before it goes finally to press.[2] Let copies be sent to every member of either house.

I have not had time to revise it, as I cd. only attend to it this morning, & tomorrow our Quarter Sessions commence, / wh: take up three days.[3] Had I delayed it until they were over, too much time co[ul]d have been lost.

Ever yrs | D.

1619XA TO: BARON LIONEL DE ROTHSCHILD Bradenham
[Friday] 7 [January 1848]

ORIGINAL: ROTH 000/573/6 [58]
EDITORIAL COMMENT: *Dating:* the date on the letter is not possible (*cf* IV Chronology); the context (see nn1&2) suggests that D had forgotten the change in month and year. *Sic:* Dec 7. 1847.

Bradm. | Dec 7. 1847

My dear Lionel –

Your packet reached me this morning on my return from Aylesbury.[1]

I have a little enriched the account of the effect of the two statutes.[2] But you sent me the "General abolition of oaths Bill," by / mistake, instead of the "Sheriffs De[c]

1 See **1617X**&nn1-4. From this and the next letter (**1619XA**) it is evident that D was doing more than merely helping Rothschild.

2 For the proof see **1619XA**&nn2&3. The pamphlet, dated 15 January 1848, would be printed by Effingham Wilson.

3 D would attend the Bucks Epiphany Sessions at Aylesbury from Tuesday to Thursday, 4-6 January 1848. *BH* (8 Jan 1848).

---

1 For D's Aylesbury business of 4-6 January 1848, see **1619X**&n3.

2 See **1619X**&n2 for D's request for a proof; it is now in the Rothschild Archive, London, extensively revised and corrected mostly in D's hand and some in another's, presumably Rothschild's; see illustration p lxiii. The following has been added in D's hand at the end of the passage describing the 'Bill for the Relief of Persons of the Jewish Religion elected to Municipal Office' of 1841 and the similar bill of 1845: 'All municipal offices ↑of every description↓, including that of Recorder, were opened to ~~the her Majesty's subjects~~ Englishmen professing the Jewish Religion by this statute. [*caret indicating that* (1 and 2) *are to be inserted*]'. ROTH 000/573/6 [26]. *Progress of Jewish Emancipation Since 1829* 10-11 (see App VI p 421). For the additional insertions, see **1619XB**&n1.

lar[ati]on Bill," & therefore you must ~~see~~ ↑take care↓ that I have properly described its object.[3]

It does not appear, by this statement, when, & how, the Jews became Magistrates. I assume they were disqualified.[4] This should / be looked to.

I think the statement will startle & do good. Circulate it in every possible way, & send your first copy, yourself, to Ld. George.

Yours sincerely | D. T.O /

confidential

From a letter received this morning, I find that the statement about the Château has already had its effect in a certain quarter: i.e. a *certain* effect – of hesitation, & very modified opinion.[5] All depends upon how it is followed up.

TO: BARON LIONEL DE ROTHSCHILD Bradenham 1619XB

Sunday [9 January 1848]

ORIGINAL: ROTH 000/573/6 [60]
EDITORIAL COMMENT: Black-edged paper. *Dating:* by Isaac's illness and D's attendance at Quarter Sessions; see V **1620**n2 and, in this appendix, **1619XA**.

Bradm. | Sunday

My dear Lionel,

Insert the inclosed *after* the paragraph, in wh: it is mentioned, that an English Jew may now be Recorder.[1] I think there can be no mistake, but if you have any doubt, you must / send me another proof.

3 In the draft, after the history of the unsuccessful 1830 bill to repeal Jewish civil disabilities, D has added the following sentence: 'Notwithstanding however this temporary check, the progress of Jewish emancipation ~~ra~~ experienced in the course of the ensuing year a great & unprecedented advance.' The printed draft resumes: 'Towards the end of the Session of 1835, the Attorney-General, Sir John Campbell, introduced the "Sheriffs' Declaration Bill," into the House of Commons. This Bill passed both Houses without opposition, and, receiving the royal assent, on the 21st of August, 1835, became a Law, by which a person professing the Jewish religion might fill ~~the office of Sheriff in county or town.~~' D has replaced the deleted section with the following: 'the high constitutional office of ~~a~~ Sheriff of a County; the little prejudice that lingers on this subject in the community is shown by the fact, that English gentlemen of the Jewish ↑faith↓ ~~religion~~ have since filled the office of Sheriff in the Counties of Middlesex, Kent & Buckingham, & in a manner wh: has given universal satisfaction to their ~~inhabitants~~ fellow subjects.' See *Progress of Jewish Emancipation Since 1829* 7 (see App VI pp 420-1).

4 See **1619XB**&n1.

5 See IV **1617**&n5 and **1617X**&nn3&4. D may be alluding to Manners's letter of 5 January 1848, in which Manners had written: 'I think you will be pleased to hear that Granby quite agrees with us in his estimate of these untoward dissensions [resulting in Bentinck's resignation as party leader]. He has to-day written a capital letter to Stanley ... in which he disavows any knowledge of a wish being entertained by any influential section of the Party for G.B's retirement, and hopes Stanley will consider whether some decided step should not be taken on the part of Members of the H. of Commons to induce G.B. to resume the Leadership ... [T]he flower of the bucolic flock are quite right in their sentiments, and although they claim the right of voting on religious questions as they please, they are not so unreasonable as to demand that their leader shall follow them.' H B/XX/M/19. The 'statement about the Château' would be D's mention to Manners of the court's position on Russell's bill.

---

1 See **1619XA**&n2. In the extant proof D's insertion ends with a caret indicating that '1 and 2' (apparently in Rothschild's hand) are to be inserted at that point, but the text D is here sending to be inserted there is not with the proof. In the printed version (final period changed to a comma) the passage continues: 'which thus placed at the disposal of their fellow-citizens in towns, the services which had been rendered for several years in the capacity of county magistrates, [*footnote inserted here*] For Kent – Mr. David

I returned the first, with some additions, by Friday's post to Piccadilly.

My father, whom I left in perfect health, when I went to Quarter Sess:, was seized, on Friday / night, with Influenza in its aggravated form, & is now lying in imminent danger. 83, with a pulse at 100, seems hopeless! Everything combines to make his loss to me a great blow.[2]

Ever yr | D.

1669x TO: ROBERT WHEELER — Grosvenor Gate [Saturday] 22 July 1848

ORIGINAL: HEY [3]

EDITORIAL COMMENT: Black-edged paper.

R. Wheeler | Esq — Grosr Gate | July 22 1848

Dear Sir,

I am flattered, & honored, by the wish of my neighbours, that I should take the chair, on the 2nd. August, at the school / meeting.[1] The prospect, however, of my finding myself in the County by that time, becomes, every day, fainter – and I am / obliged, therefore, on the present occasion, to decline a proposition, wh: wo[ul]d, otherwise, have been agreeable to me.

Yours truly | *B Disraeli*

1775R TO: SIR ROBERT INGLIS — Grosvenor Gate, Monday 22 [January] 1849

ORIGINAL: URI [1]

EDITORIAL COMMENT: Black-edged paper.

Sir Robt Inglis | Bt. M.P. — Grosvenor Gate | Monday 22. 1849

My dear Sir Robert,

I have arrived; & shall be very happy to see you, tomorrow, betn. 1 & 2, p.m. as you mention: but I am / quite ashamed that you should have the trouble of calling on me.

Believe me, | Very faithfully yours | *B Disraeli*[1]

1841x TO: SIR WILLIAM MOLESWORTH — Grosvenor Gate [Thursday] 14 June 1849

ORIGINAL: PS 1523

PUBLICATION HISTORY: Freeman's Auction House, Philadelphia, as offered on eBay, item 1485: 'Autograph Letter Signed. Disraeli, B(enjamin), ... Grosvenor Gate, June 14, 1849. 3 pp.,' paraphrase and photo of two pages of the MS as given below

EDITORIAL COMMENT: *Sic:* [*the irregular punctuation in the paraphrase*].

Grosvenor Gate | June 14, 1849

Salomons, and Sir Moses Montefiore, Bart.; for Sussex – Mr. Joseph Montefiore; for Surrey – Mr. Benjamin Cohen; for Devonshire – Mr. Emanuel Lousada; for Buckinghamshire – Baron Meyer Rothschild; and for Middlesex – Sir Isaac Lyon Goldsmid, Bart. [*end of footnote*] recommended for that honourable trust by the respective Lords Lieutenant.' *Progress of Jewish Emancipation Since 1829* 9-11. For the complete text, see Appendix VI.

2 Isaac D'Israeli would live only until 19 January 1848; see v **1620**n2.

1 The annual meeting and examination of the British School in High Wycombe would be held on Wednesday 2 August, with Robert Wheeler (IV app I **201**xn1) in the chair. *BH* (12 Aug 1848). His invitation has not been found.

1 See v **1775**&n1.

[*Cataloguer's paraphrase:*] To Sir William Molesworth, thanking him for his ["] contribution, to my library, of the classical edition of The Philosophy of Malmesbury..."[1]

[*The text of the photographed pages:*] me last night. It greatly enriches my shelves; but I value it not only for its intrinsic excellence, but as a memorial of the kind feelings of / its accomplished Editor.

Believe me, | with sincere regard, | Yours, | *B Disraeli*

TO: BENJAMIN LUMLEY Syon House [Sunday] 11 May 1851 **2132X**

ORIGINAL: MOPSIK [241]

B. Lumley Esq Syon – May 11. 51.

My dear Sir,

I am very much pressed with affairs, unfortunately, at this moment, but if I can find a free hour on this day week, I hope / to have the pleasure of availing myself of your gratifying invitation, & paying my respects to your distinguished guest.[1]

Believe me, | Yours very faithfully, | *B. Disraeli*

TO: CHARLES CLUBBE Carlton Club [Tuesday] 24 June 1851 **2156X**

ORIGINAL: RIC [004]

COVER: The | Revd. C.W. Clubbe A.M. | Vicarage. | D.

EDITORIAL COMMENT: cover flap embossed with Carlton Club crest.

The | Rev. C.W. Clubbe | A.M. Carlton Club | June 24. 1851

My dear Sir,

I write you a line, tho' much pressed with affairs, to beg that you will give me notice of your / visit to Hughenden, in order that we may make your temporary stay as comfortable as possible. I hope, also, to see you, as you pass thro' town.

I signed your Institution on Friday last, of wh:, I doubt not, Mr Rose has duly apprised you.[1]

Yours very ffly

B Disraeli

We met your friends the Kerrisons, yesterday.

TO: CHARLES CLUBBE Hughenden [Thursday] 25 December 1851 **2213X**

ORIGINAL: RIC [035]

COVER: The | Revd. C.W. Clubbe. | A.M. | The Vicarage | *B Disraeli*

EDITORIAL COMMENT: Hughenden paper. *Dating:* the year in the text could be read as either 1851 or 1857, but the DS were not at Hughenden on Christmas Day 1857.

Rev. C.W | Clubbe. | A M. Xmas 1851

1 See V **1871**&n6 ('Molesworth ha[s] presented me with a copy of his Hobbes – 18 vols'). Molesworth had edited *The English Works of Thomas Hobbes of Malmesbury* (11 volumes) and *Thomae Hobbes Malmesburiensis Opera Philosophica quae Latine Scripsit Omnia* (5 volumes). Perhaps he included two more volumes of his publications – or D miscounted.

1 See V **2137**&n5 for Lumley's dinner of 18 May 1851 at which D would meet Jules Janin, critic and novelist.

1 See V **2149**&n1 and **2150**.

My dear Sir,

Permit me to enclose you £5: as a contribution to your clothing Club.

With every kind wish to Mrs. Clubbe & yourself, believe me,

Yrs sincerely, | *B. Disraeli*

2224X TO: [WILLIAM COOKESLEY?] [Hughenden, Tuesday 13 January 1852?]

ORIGINAL: H H/LIFE

PUBLICATION HISTORY: M&B IV 350, undated (in chapter dealing with 1860-65) and recipient identified only as 'a clergyman'

EDITORIAL COMMENT: Taken from a manuscript copy. For possible recipient and date, see n1.

... I entirely participated at the time in the feelings that influenced you in the Oxford Movement, which, I believe, had it been directed with a discretion equal to its energy and talents, would have conquered the heart of the nation and placed the strong religious feeling of the country on a basis of unassailable authority.

But on the desolating secession of Newman and his followers, to me so unexpected and still to me so unaccountable, I withdrew from the disheartening struggle, and only resumed my weapons, much against the feeling of my political friends, though accused of party motives, when the enemy seemed desecrating the hearth.

I have a certain reverence for the Church of Rome, as I have for all churches which recognise the divine mission of the House of Israel; but I confess I was astounded that a man of the calibre of Newman should have fallen into the pitfalls of the 17th century, and in his search for a foundation have stopt short at Rome instead of advancing to Jerusalem.

For myself, I look upon the Church as the only Jewish institution that remains, and, irrespective of its being the depository of divine truth, must ever cling to it as the visible means which embalms the memory of my race, their deeds and thoughts, and connects their blood with the origin of things.

There are few great things left, and the Church is one. No doubt its position at this moment is critical, and, indeed, the whole religious sentiment of the country is in a convulsive state; but I believe the state of affairs is only one of the periodical revolts of the Northern races against Semitic truth, influenced mainly by mortified vanity in never having been the medium of direct communication with the Almighty; and that it will end as in previous instances, after much sorrow and suffering, in their utter discomfiture.[1]

1 Of plausible recipients of this letter (*eg*, Henry Drummond, Joseph Wolff, Bishop Wilberforce, T.E. Kebbel), the most likely, from an 1852 correspondence, may be W.G. Cookesley. On 6 January 1852 he had written at length from Eton about *LGB*, feeling that the chapter on the Jews was inappropriate, and fearful that many of D's expressions might 'be interpreted in an ironical, rather Gibbonian sense ... the great glory of the Jewish people at this moment is that they are the most *visible* & unmistakeable subjects of divine prophecy; they are mysteriously, & in their own despite, working out God's will.' D should stand well with the Church – not the extreme High Church, but 'the common majority of the clergy' – and be more definitely opposed to 'papal insolence' in taking the lead of the Church of England party. On 16 January Cookesley would thank D for his reply, 'really a *relief* to my mind ... I am persuaded that all things are tending to the restoration of religious principle, as the great distinguishing political element of Europe.' H E/VI/R/15-16.

to: CHARLES CLUBBE Hughenden [Monday] 16 August 1852 2365x

original: ric [008]

cover: *Private* | The | Rev: C.W. Clubbe. A.M. | Vicarage | with the Chr. of Exchequer's | regards

editorial comment: Black-edged envelope and paper.

The | Rev. C.W. Clubbe | A.M Hughenden | Aug. 16. 1852.

My dear Sir,

It is as well, that you shd. read the enclosed, wh: I ought to have sent you before, & wh: will put you *au fait* to some circumstances with wh: you ought to be acquainted.[1]

Yours very truly | D.

to: [CONSERVATIVE MPS] Downing Street [Monday] 18 October 1852 2428x

original: jwa [2]

editorial comment: A facsimile letter; *cf* vii **3349**ec on mechanically reproduced letters.

Downing Street | October 18 1852

Sir,

The meeting of Parliament has been fixed for Thursday the 4th. Novr, when the House of Commons will immediately proceed to the choice of a Speaker, & to the consideration of business of the highest importance.[1] I take the liberty / of earnestly requesting your presence on that day, & I trust you will also excuse my expressing a wish, that you would let me know, whether it will be consistent with yr. convenience to attend at the opening of the Session.

I have the honor to be | Sir | Your faithful & obedt Servt. | *B. Disraeli*

to: SIR EDWARD BULWER LYTTON Grosvenor Gate Sunday 13 March 1853 2507x

original: nro [1]

editorial comment: For the recipient see nn1&2.

Private Grosvenor Gate | Mar. 13. 53. Sunday

My dear Bulwer,[1]

I shd. like to have some conversation with you today. Wd. 5 o'ck suit you at yr. house? I have engagements here from after Church to that hour nearly.[2]

Ever yrs | D.

1 The enclosure has not been found; for its possible nature see vi **2519**&n1.

1 See vi **2435**&n1.

1 This is d's habitual form of address for his friend and colleague Sir Edward Bulwer Lytton regardless of the latter's name changes.

2 For d's probable business with Sir Edward (getting his support for the *Press*), *cf* vi **2506**, **2507** and **2521**.

2519X TO: AUSTEN HENRY LAYARD [London, late March 1853?]

ORIGINAL: H B/II/73
PUBLICATION HISTORY: Gordon Waterfield *Layard of Nineveh* (1963) 234, the second sentence in different form; see n3
EDITORIAL COMMENT: A draft in D's hand. There is apparent discontinuity between *recto* and *verso*. *Recipient:* see n1.

My dr Sir,
I have just concluded ~~your important & inter[estin]g volume. Never were discoveries of such magnitude narrated in~~ reading the vol. wh: you honored[.][1]

Since Bruce,[2] never were discoveries of such ~~magnitude vast~~ vast interest & importance related in so captivating a style.[3] ~~It will~~ This work will alike confirm your well earned fame & advance yr. future career, wh: I sincerely hope may be prosperous & brilliant. / office wh: I am truly flattered by yr wishing me to assume.[4]

~~I am~~ Believe me, | Sir, | ~~Yours~~ Yr fl Srt | D

2613X TO: SAMUEL LUCAS [London] Thursday [5 January 1854]

ORIGINAL: HEY [2]
COVER: (integral:) S. Lucas Esq
EDITORIAL COMMENT: *Dating:* see VI **2613**&n1.

Thursday | ½ pt 6 o'ck

My dear Sir,
It is of the greatest possible importance that the art: shd. be inserted this week. I have copied it myself & somewhat altered & curtailed it.

Yrs | D.

2637X TO: I.A. BAMPS London [Friday] 27 February 1854

ORIGINAL: JAH [1]
COVER: á Monsr | Le Docteur I.A. Bamps | Attaché au Minre. de la Justice | Rue des Minimes 50 | à *Bruxelles*
POSTMARKS: [*recto:*] in a circle: 1854 | 27FE27 | U ; [*verso:*] in circular form: [*illegible*] Par [*illegible*] Ouest 1854 (enclosing:) 28 FEV.; in circular form: Bruxelles (enclosing) 29
EDITORIAL COMMENT: *Sic:* á [cover].

London. Feb. 27. 54

Mr Disraeli has no cousins:
There is no such person as John Disraeli:
Therefore, the individual mentioned / is an Impostor.

D.

1 A.H. Layard (I **49**n1) in March 1853 had published his *Discoveries in the Ruins of Nineveh and Babylon*, a copy of which is in the Hughenden library.

2 James Bruce (1730-1794) in 1790 had published *Travels to Discover the Sources of the Nile.*

3 Waterfield (ph) quotes only the second sentence of D's letter, as follows: 'Never have such important discoveries been narrated in so animated and picturesque a style since the days of Bruce.'

4 No correspondence has been found to indicate what office this was.

TO: CHARLES CLUBBE Grosvenor Gate [Monday] 14 February 1855 2732X

ORIGINAL: RIC [011]
COVER: The | Rev C.W. Clubbe | A.M. | Hughenden | High Wycomb | *B Disraeli*
POSTMARKS: a cancelled one-penny stamp; on verso, in circular form: HIGH WYCOMBE | FE 15 | 1855 | A
EDITORIAL COMMENT: Grosvenor Gate paper. *Sic:* Wycomb.

Rev. C.W. Clubbe Feb. 14: 1855

My dear Sir,

I wish you would have the kindness to distribute for me £5 in coals. I think that the preferable course. Somehow or other, / they generally contrive to get wood – by fair means or foul.

I like to know the names of the persons who are recipients under these, or similar, circumstances.

I / trust that Mrs. Clubbe is quite well.

Yours very truly | *B. Disraeli*

TO: SIR WILLIAM JOLLIFFE Grosvenor Gate Saturday [5 April 1856?] 2837X

ORIGINAL: SCR DD/HY C/2165 [84]
EDITORIAL COMMENT: *Dating:* conjectural; see nn1-4. The letter has proved extraordinarily resistant to being placed chronologically, and the editors have had eventually to assign a date that most nearly fits all the evidence: a Saturday soon after the DS' return to town (n1); a significant event concerning Julia Jolliffe (n2); parliament in session, with the Conservatives in opposition but planning to attack the government in the next week, if not defeat it (n3); G.A. Hamilton unavailable to assist D (n4, and see VI **2838**, where D escalates to 'despair' about his absence). The two most obvious possibilities, Hamilton's leaving the Commons in 1859 (VII **3277–8**) and Julia Jolliffe's death in 1862, are ruled out, the former because D in this letter is not in power, and the latter because his letter of condolence exists (**3775** in this volume).

Sir W.H. Jolliffe Bart: | M.P. G Gate | Saturday –

My dear Jolliffe,

We are arrived, & I hope to see you tomorrow.[1]

Ours is a war, & we must treat danger as becomes warriors. /

But I am very sorry indeed for Julia, my charming friend, who gave me so many cups of tea![2]

If our fellows are *steady,* for the next week, we may perhaps, / lead them, if not to glory, at least to honor. We cannot undertake to destroy a governmt; but if they will stand to their guns, we may have a chance of obtaining for them / the applause & approbation of the nation.[3]

1 The DS had returned to London from Hughenden after the Easter break on Monday 31 March. D may have delayed getting in touch with Jolliffe until he heard from Derby about renewing attack on the government's handling of the fortress of Kars and from Malmesbury about the date of Clarendon's return. See VI **2838**n1.

2 The Jolliffes' fourth daughter, Julia Agnes (1834-1862), would marry Colonel Richard Howard Vyse on 22 July.

3 For the perception that Kars had fallen because the government had failed to support the British garrison, and a Conservative meeting on the matter planned for 10 April, see VI **2838**n1.

Eheu! Georgio Hamilton![4] Our best man – except yourself.
Ever yrs, | D.

2892X TO: BARON LIONEL DE ROTHSCHILD Paris, Monday [12 January 1857]
ORIGINAL: ROTH RAL 000/848 [76]
EDITORIAL COMMENT: *Dating:* by the ball and the return to London; see VII **2883**n5 and **2893**n1. *Sic:* Thuill:.

Paris Monday.

My dear L.
Since I wrote yesterday, my wife has rebelled, & will go to a ball at the Thuill: on Thursday.

This / will delay us a couple of days.
Ever, | D.

2949X TO: BARON LIONEL DE ROTHSCHILD Grosvenor Gate [Wednesday] 5 August 1857
ORIGINAL: ROTH RAL 000/848 [72]
EDITORIAL COMMENT: Black-edged paper.

Confidential Grosvenor Gate | Aug. 5. 1857
Baron Rothschild | M.P.
My dear Lionel,
The enclosed is not the quarter recently in negotiation, but the result wo[ul]d be equally bad. Joined, they would have a circulation of nearly / 6,000, & would be a very powerful organ of the most rabid description.

The circulation of the P. is 3,000, with a small weekly profit. Its market price, wh: can always be commanded, £3000. The newspaper speculators offered for it £3,500, wh: was refused / by Mr Rose about a fortnight ago, but I am not sure he wd. not accept it, as the season is drawing to a close, & he is anxious to reduce his duties, wh: are very onerous.

These are the rough statistics. I place them before you for yr consideration. If / you like to try the effect for a year, I would attend to yr interests, & at the close of the term, you cd. always get yr money back. I mention the matter again to you, because the opportunity, if lost, can never be renewed, as it has cost nearly £10,000 to establish this Liberal Tory journal.[1]

Yrs ever, | D.

4 For D's reliance on G.A. Hamilton for his current paper on administrative reform, see VI **2838**&n3. Despite Hamilton's vote in the Commons on 7 April, he was apparently ill, and on 10 April D would declare: 'this question, properly worked, may be the turning point: but I am in despair about G. Hamilton'.

---

1 For D's efforts at this time to prevent the sale of the *Press* and for Rose's idea of augmenting its political impact with the addition of a cheap daily, see VII **2937**n1, **2951**&n1, **2955**&nn2-4 (Rothschild was probably the source of one of the loan offers mentioned, if not indeed of D's offer itself), **2957**&n1, **2973**&n1, **2974**&n1, **2975**&n6 and **3060**n1.

TO: ROBERT HUME Carlton Club [Friday] 7 May [1858] **3111X**

ORIGINAL: BRI [1]

EDITORIAL COMMENT: Carlton Club paper. Docketed in another hand on the first page: '~~85~~ 1858'. *Sic:* [*a horizontal line between the second and third paragraphs*].

Confidential May 7.

Mr Hume[1]

Dear Sir –

I mentioned yr name, & it is probable, that you may receive some communication; but the affair is so / *doubtful,* that I am not surprised, that no application has been made.

I recommend you to refuse, & discourage, all offers, & arrangements, of the / kind you mention. They cannot answer.

As for yr other point, *I must not be pressed upon it at this moment*[.][2]

You / must wait till you see me for the reason.

Yrs truly | D.

TO: LORD HENRY LENNOX [London, Monday 17? May 1858?] **3122X**

ORIGINAL: PS 737

PUBLICATION HISTORY: Reginald Atkinson catalogue 22 (1916) item 1305: '[written] on Treasury Bench & handed to Lord H. Lennox who was "under-whip" 1859'

EDITORIAL COMMENT: *Dating:* by Whiteside's speech (n1).

It requests that messengers be sent to certain MP's. Whiteside is impudently dining out[1] ... with a Mr. Butt, not an M.P.[2] He should receive the message about soup time.

TO: EDWARD KENEALY Hughenden [Wednesday] 18 August 1858 **3181X**

ORIGINAL: HEY [4]

EDITORIAL COMMENT: Paper imprinted 'Hughenden Manor'.

E. Kenealy Esq Aug 18 1858

1 In the same collection as this letter is BRI [2], a Carlton Club envelope in D's hand, postmarked London, 26 June 1858, to 'Robert Hume Esqre. | 65 Berners St. | Oxford St | *B Disraeli*', Hume's address in *LPOD* (1860). See in this appendix **665R**n1. On 13 September 1852 at Downing Street, 'R Hume' had asked D for a brief interview. H B/XXI/H/751. He is possibly the Hume cited as a Villiers creditor in VII **3380**n1.

2 See VII **3151**&n2 for a possible connection; the 26 June 1858 envelope (n1) is endorsed in another hand: '*1858 R. Spreye*[?]' In any case, the too-clever identification of Hume in **3151**n1 is negated by the evidence of an on-going correspondence between D and Robert Hume.

---

1 For Whiteside's speech late in the evening of 17 May 1858 against Cardwell's motion of censure on the Derby government, see VII **3122**&n1. Possibly Lennox's post as a junior lord of the treasury 1858-9 included some whip duties; see PH.

2 Probably George Medd Butt (d. 1860), barrister (Inner Temple) 1830, QC 1845, MP (C) for Weymouth 1852-7. On 3 February 1859 he would write from 17 Eaton Square to ask D to consider him for a post as divorce court judge. H B/XXI/M/1415.

Dear Sir,

I received yr second letter yesterday, but I had already sent your first to London. The moment I hear anything, I will communicate to you.[1]

Yours truly | *B. Disraeli*

3300X TO: [PHILIP ROSE] House of Commons [Monday 28 February 1859?]

ORIGINAL: H R/I/A/195

EDITORIAL COMMENT: House of Commons paper. There is no salutation. *Dating:* docketed by archivist: '1866/67?' but see n1 and *cf* VII **3300**&n1.

I must have another copy of the Bill to present.[1]

D.

3331X TO: [T.E. KEBBEL] [London, Thursday 7 April 1859]

ORIGINAL: H B/II/67

EDITORIAL COMMENT: A draft in D's hand. A manuscript copy in another hand in H H/LIFE, headed 'Draft in B. Papers 1864 To anonymous correspondent', changes the draft's 'thought' (paragraph 1) to 'insight', and expands the abbreviations. For the recipient and dating see n1. There is no salutation.

I thank you for yr article wh: I received this morning.[1] I read yr criticisms always with interest bec: they are discriminative & are founded on knowledge & thought.

These qualities are rarer in the present day than the world imagines. Every body writes in a hurry, & the past seems quite obliterated from public memory.

I need not remind you that ~~the~~ Parli[amentar]y Reform was a burning question with the Tories after the Rev of 1688: ↑notably↓ Sir W. W & his friends were in favor

1 Kenealy had written from Gray's Inn Square on 13 August about a position, naming the vacant Woodstock recordership, although he would not oppose another candidate, J.A. Huddleston. On the 16th he had thanked D for his note received that morning (not found; see VII Chronological List lx): 'Now that you have written for me I will not yield to Huddleston or any living man unless indeed Mr Walpole is already committed. If he is not, I have no doubt of the vacant office.' He enclosed a copy of the lengthy note of the 16th that he had left for Walpole at the home office. Later that day he had written that Huddleston's rumoured application was a joke, the position being honorary and paying four guineas a year; however, 'If it were only a penny a year as you have mentioned me to Walpole I will have it if I can.' H B/XXI/K/80-2. On the 28th he would write about another position; see VII **3188**n2.

---

1 The Bill is possibly D's 1859 Reform Bill. The Rose papers in H include two versions of the bill in Rose's hand, dated 21 and 22 February 1859, and a letter of 26 February 1859 from Rose to Earle enclosing 'the Chancellor's final print of the Bill.' H R/I/B/74, 75, 73a.

---

1 On 6 April T.E. Kebbel from 6 South Square, Grays Inn, had sent D his article 'Whigs & Tories' from the second number of the short-lived *Universal Review* (April 1859, 177-200), with another of his from the *Chester Courant*, a 'rather influential Conservative Paper'. H B/XXI/K/17. Ostensibly a review of Russell's *Life of C.J. Fox* and the Duke of Buckingham's *Memoirs of the Court of George IV*, 'Whigs and Tories' traces the history of the two parties since the seventeenth century to establish the true difference between them, contending that on major issues such as peace and war, parliamentary reform, Catholic and Protestant, and trade and finance they have often reversed their positions. Its account of recent Tory history comments: 'The reorganization of this party after the Reform Bill was entirely the work of one mind; and when Peel fell, they fell; and subsequently to that period it is difficult to conjecture what would have been their fate, but for the individual energy of Mr. Disraeli.' It concludes that 'the Whigs are an incorrigible oligarchy ... [and that] this antique theory of Whiggism is what at the present day principally impedes the formation of a durable Government ... What is required is a change in Parliament itself; the Whigs must be dissolved, and their material made use of for the erection of a fresh edifice.'

of annl. Pts. & univl. suff[rage], but Sir J. H. C. advocated the ballot.[2] These were desperate measures agst Whig supremacy. It appeared to me in 1832 that the Ref: ~~Bill~~ ↑Act↓ was ano[the]r ~~186~~ –88 – & that influenced my conduct when I entered publ life. I ↑dont↓ say this ~~not~~ to vindicate my course but to explain it.

So I looked then, as I look now, to a reconciliation betn. the Tory party & the R. C. subjects of the Queen. This led ~~in 1834~~ 30 yrs ↑ago↓ to the O'Cll scandal,[3] but I have never ~~gi~~ relinquished my purpose & have now ↑I hope↓ accomplished it.

If the Tory party is not a national party, it is nothing.

Pardon this egotism wh: I trust is not my wont.[4]

TO: SIR CHARLES EASTLAKE Grosvenor Gate [Wednesday] 4 May 1859 **3343X**

ORIGINAL: UO

EDITORIAL COMMENT: Paper imprinted 'Grosvenor Gate'.

May 4. 1859

Sir Chas Eastlake | &c &c

Dear Sir Charles,

It was, with great regret, that I found myself unable to have the honor of dining with you, & the / Royal Academy, on Saturday last, but I was obliged to leave town, unexpectedly, for my Election.[1]

My dear Sir Charles, | Yours sincerely, | *B. Disraeli*

TO: SIR STAFFORD NORTHCOTE Grosvenor Gate, Sunday 19 June [1859?] **3377X**

ORIGINAL: HAV [1]

EDITORIAL COMMENT: Endorsed in another hand on the second page: 'Benjamin Disraeli 15'. *Dating:* see n1.

Grosvenor Gate | Sunday June 19.

Sir Stafford Northcote | Bart: M.P

My dear Northcote,

Could you call on me tomorrow morning? Eleven o'ck would suit me, if convenient to you – but I shall be / at home until two o'ck, tho' with some short interviews in the interval.[1]

Yrs sincerely, | D.

2 Sir William Wyndham (1687-1740), 3rd Bt, Tory MP for Somerset 1710-40, secretary at war 1712, chancellor of the exchequer 1713-14, and Sir John Hynde Cotton (*c*1686-1752), 3rd Bt, Tory MP for Cambridge borough 1708-22, 1727-41, for Cambridgeshire 1722-27, for Marlborough 1741-52, were luminaries in what Blake (195) calls 'Disraeli's Tory apostolic succession'.

3 See II **396**&nn2-4, **398**, **400**&n1, and **406**&ec&n11.

4 See further, in this volume, **3467**&n1.

---

1 Sir Charles was president of the Royal Academy, which had held its annual dinner on Saturday, 30 April; earlier that day D had had an audience with the Queen. *MP* (2 May 1859). The general election of 1859 had begun on 29 April; for D's unopposed re-election, on Monday, 2 May, see VII **3342**n1, where it will be noticed that D was out of London on 1 and 2 May.

---

1 During the period that D and Northcote interacted, 19 June fell on a Sunday in 1859, 1864 and 1870. In 1859, after the Derby government officially resigned on 18 June, D, in the process of leaving office, would

3416x TO: WILLIAM LOWNDES Grosvenor Gate [Monday] 7 November 1859

ORIGINAL: JWA [3]

EDITORIAL COMMENT: Paper imprinted 'Grosvenor Gate'.

W. Lowndes Esqr November 7 1859

My dear Lowndes,

Your letter[1] reached me as I arrived in town, from Lancashire, en route for Devon.[2]

I wrote to Lord Stanley the day after our meeting at Q. Sess:[3] In his answer, Oct. 25, he says "If I had still on my hands / an unappropriated cadetship, I cd. fill it up any time within three years from the date of its being assigned to me: but none such remain; I gave all away." "It is fair to add" he continues, "that a cavalry cadetship is worth two in the Infantry: but I would gladly have obliged your friend, had the means been in my power."[4]

Thinking, that Lord Stanley might not be precisely aware of the circumstances, & that, probably, in / a little time, he might become aware of vacancies from unsuccessful examinations, I thought it best to delay communicating to Mr Drake, until I had been to Knowsley: Lord Stanley, however, has received no intimation of the kind we anticipated, & assures me, that there is no cadetship in his gift unappropriated.

You can send this letter to Mr Drake, as I am only passing thro' / town, & have been, & continue, greatly hurried with business.

Yours sincerely,

D.

have had several 'short interviews' on Monday the 20th. In 1864, House business was pending about the Canadian Red River Settlement and the Hudson's Bay Company (of which Northcote would become governor in 1869 and in which D had just indirectly bought shares; see in this volume **3924**n2). Northcote seconded a motion for papers on 1 July 1864, something that D as House leader of the party would presumably have asked him to do. In 1870, Northcote had returned in May from a tour of Canada and the U.S., possibly leading to a request by D for an interview. Only the first two conjectures have plausibility, but the case of 1859 is the stronger.

1 In 1857 and 1858 William Lowndes, of Chesham, Bucks, a staunch Conservative, had asked D for a cadetship for his third son. H B/XXI/L/354-7. The letter D mentions has not been found.

2 The DS had returned to Grosvenor Gate from Knowsley in Lancashire on 5 November, and would leave on 9 November for their annual visit to SBW in Torquay. See VII **3410**n8, **3415**&n1 and **3416**&nn1&4.

3 D had attended the Quarter Sessions at Aylesbury on 17 October 1859; see VII **3409**&n2.

4 See VII **3413**&n2 for D's 24 October letter to Stanley about T.T. Drake's request to change his son's infantry cadetship to a cavalry one, and for Stanley's 25 October reply as quoted here.

APPENDIX II

The following are the guest lists as recorded in MA*'s account book (*H *acc, except 4 March, from* MP *of 5 March) for* D*'s political dinners from 4 February 1863 to 12 March 1864 to members of the House of Lords and the House of Commons. For the dinners beginning 11 February see* **3783**&n2 *for* D*'s wish to bring together members from both Houses.*
(denotes House of Lords)*

4 FEBRUARY (FOR THRONE SPEECH)

Lord John Manners
Lord Galway
Lord Stanley
Lord Lovaine
Lord Robert Cecil
Henry Wyndham
General J. Peel
Spencer Walpole
Col T.E. Taylor
Sir John Pakington
Sir John Trollope
Sir Stafford Northcote
Sir Matthew White Ridley
Sir Lawrence Palk
Sir William Codrington
Henry Cecil Lowther
William Ormsby Gore

11 FEBRUARY

*Duke of Buckingham and Chandos
*Lord Normanby
*Lord Shrewsbury
Wilbraham Egerton
Sir Charles Mordaunt
Sir Thomas Hesketh
Sir Massey Lopes
Sir Henry Stracey
Sir George Forster
Charles Turner
William Morritt
Col W.B. Barttelot
William Cubitt
Joseph Somes
Henry Butler Johnstone
John Hardy
William Hornby

14 FEBRUARY

*Lord Salisbury
*Lord Devon
*Lord Coventry
Lord William Graham
Lord Mayor [W.A. Rose]
Col J.S. North
William Legh
Seymour Fitzgerald
A. Baillie Cochrane
Philip Papillon
John Rogers
Thomas Collins
J.W. Malcolm
Henry Whitmore
John Hopwood
Col F.P. Dunne
Major W. Parker

18 FEBRUARY

Lord Edward Thynne
Lord Claud Hamilton
Col R.T. Rowley
John Drax

Maj-Gen George Upton
Sir James Elphinstone
Sir Fitzroy Kelly
Sir Hugh Cairns
Henry Ker Seymer
G. Sclater Booth
G.A.F. Cavendish Bentinck
Fitzwilliam Hume
Robert Peel Dawson
William Ferrand
*Duke of Marlborough
*Lord Carnarvon
*Lord Exmouth

28 FEBRUARY

*Lord Cardigan
*Lord Lonsdale
*Lord Wynford
Lord Bective
Lord Pevensey
Charles Packe
Tyringham Bernard
Richard Hodgson
W.H.P. Gore-Langton
James King King
J.J. Hope Johnstone [Sr]
John Rolt
John Pope Hennessy
Nicholas Kendall
Captain White Jervis
John Chapman

4 MARCH (FROM *MP* OF 6 MARCH 1863)

Lord Stanley
Lord Curzon
Lord Holmesdale
E. Douglas Pennant
Charles Trefusis
Ernest Duncombe
Godfrey Morgan
Sir William Heathcote
Sir John Dalrymple Hay
Sir John Walsh
Thomas Baring
Robert Holford
Col Powlett Somerset
George Beecroft
John Laird
George Cubitt
*Lord Mount Edgcumbe
*Lord Derby 'prevented by indisposition'

18 APRIL

Lord George Gordon-Lennox
Lord Henry Thynne
William Addington
Charles Lennox Cumming Bruce
Charles Jasper Selwyn
Gathorne Hardy
Maj Henry Edwards
John Gellibrand Hubbard
William Ormsby Gore
Samuel Kekewich
John Perry Watlington
William Townley Mitford
Col William T. R. Powell
*Lord Colville
*Lord Tankerville
*Lord Stanhope
*Lord Hardwicke
*Lord Verulam 'prevented ... by a domestic affliction'

9 MAY

Lord Robert Montague
John Edward Redmond
Capt Roger W. Palmer
Arthur Edwin Way
Michael Sullivan
*Lord Belmore
*Lord Ravensworth
*Lord Westmorland
*Lord Sandwich
Hedworth Hylton Jolliffe
Eliot Yorke
Stuart Knox
Sir Edward Lytton
James Whiteside
Sir Henry Hervey Bruce
Sir Edward Grogan
Lionel S.W. Dawson-Damer
Charles Watkin Williams-Wynn

3 FEBRUARY 1864

Lord Burghley
Lord John Manners
Lord Galway
Spencer Walpole
Sir John Trollope
Gen Jonathan Peel

Lord Stanley
Lord Lovaine
Lord Curzon
Lord Robert Cecil
Sir John Pakington
Sir Edward Bulwer Lytton
Sir William Jolliffe
Sir Stafford Northcote
Sir Lawrence Palk
Col T.E. Taylor

13 FEBRUARY

*Lord Salisbury
*Lord Winchilsea
Lord Naas
Charles Adderley
Col Howard Vyse
John George
Edward O'Neill
Robert Bateson Harvey
Samuel Waterhouse
*Lord Waterford
Lord Ingestre
*Lord Inchiquin
Sir William Fraser
C. Du Cane
H. Butler Johnstone
Ion Trant Hamilton
Taverner John Miller

27 FEBRUARY

*Lord Lucan
Lord Hamilton
*Lord Colville
Percy Wyndham
Sir John Walsh
Sir William Miles
Thomas Baring
Capt M.E. Archdall
Col R.P. Dawson
*Lord Verulam
Lord Bective
Frederick Lygon
Sir Brook Bridges
Sir Henry Stracey
[J.R.?] Ormsby Gore
William Stirling
Seymour Fitzgerald

12 MARCH

*Duke of Buckingham & Chandos
*Lord Warwick
Adm Arthur Duncombe
Sir Hugh Cairns
Caledon George Du Pré
Edward Bourchier Hartopp
William Murray
John Reginald Yorke
Henry Moor
*Duke of Cleveland
*Lord Longford
Sir James Fergusson
Col R.T. Gilpin
George Ward Hunt
Stephen Cave
Sir William Verner
Thomas Willis Fleming

APPENDIX III

The following is D*'s account of the royal wedding in 1863 and his subsequent interview with the Queen, taken from his memoirs.* H A/X/A/51. *For the complete text, see* DR 76-84.

~~Th~~ In March the Royal Wedding took place. The Prince of Wales was married to the Princess of Denmark at Windsor. This alliance made a great sensation & excitement in the Country. The long-pent up feeling of affectionate devotion to the Queen & of sympathy with her sorrows, came out with that deep & fervid enthusiasm, for wh: the people of England are, I think, [*illegible deletion*] remarkable. But the excitement of the nation with their public receptions, & addresses, & processions, & splendid gifts, & the long vista of universal festivity, wh: was planned, & wh: lasted the whole season, was quite equalled among the Aristocracy, as to who shd., or rather wd., be invited to the Royal Wedding. /

As the beautiful Chapel of St George was very limited, & as there were a considerable number of Royal guests, & as the principal persons of the Household, the Ambassadors, the Knights of the Garter, & the Cabinet Ministers – were as a matter of course to be invited, it became an interesting question where the line was to be drawn. ~~&~~ At last it was whispered about, that the limit was to be Duchesses. But as time drew on, nobody ~~was~~ ↑seemed to be↓ asked, & some great persons received suspicious invitations to a breakfast at Windsor Castle *after* the ceremony. At the same time, tickets began to circulate in influential quarters, permitting the bearers to places in the Cathedral nave, witht. the chapel, in order to see the procession pass.

At last, however, about a fortnight before the ceremony or less, it was announced, that / as there were only ____ seats in the Chapel, & as ~~Princes~~ Sovereigns & Royal Princes, Knights of the Garter & their wives, ↑Cabinet↓ Ministers & ambassadors ↑& gt. Officers of the Household↓ & their wives would nearly fill it, there were necessarily few seats for H.M's private friends.

The disappointment & excitement [*illegible deletion*] equally increased. I have heard that when the list was finally submitted to her Majesty, there were only four places not, as it were, officially appropriated. Her Majesty named Lord & Lady De la Warr her earliest friends, & myself & my wife.

There is no language, wh: can describe the rage, envy, & indignation of the great world. The Duchess of Marlboro' [*illegible deletion*] went into hysterics of mortification at the sight of my wife, who was on terms of considerable intimacy with her, & said it / was really shameful after the reception wh: the Duke had given the Prince of Wales at Blenheim, & as for the Duchess of Manchester, who had ↑been↓ Mistress of the ~~Wardrobe~~ ↑Robes↓ in Lord Derby's Administration, she positively passed me for the season witht. recognition.

However we went, & nothing cd. be more brilliant, & effective, than the whole affair was. It is the only pageant wh: never disappointed me. ~~The various pro~~ The beautiful chapel, the glittering dresses, the various processions, 1st the Knights of the Garter, of the ~~Princes~~ Royal personages, of the Bridegroom, ~~&~~ ↑of↓ the Bride – the heralds, the announcing trumpets, the suspense before ~~they~~ ↑the procession↓ appeared, the magnificent music, the Queen in widowed [*illegible deletion*] garments in her Gothic cabinet – all / deeply interesting or effective.

I had never seen the Queen since the catastrophe, & ventured, being nearsighted to ~~vie~~ use my glass. I saw H.M. well & unfortunately caught her glance – perhaps she was looking to see whether we were there, & triumphing a little in the decided manner in wh: she had testified "her gratitude". I did not venture to use my glass again.

The Prince of Wales who was habited as a Knight of the Garter deported himself with great dignity,

& conducted himself at the Altar where he was left an unusual time alone, from some accident that occurred in the Procession of the Bride~~groom~~, with grace & tact – all eyes being upon him.

The way in wh: the Royal personages ~~bowed to~~ looked / up & bowed to the Royal Cabinet was singularly graceful & imposing ~~–~~ & in this respect the Princess Mary of Cambridge exceeded them all. Her demeanour was most dignified.

After the ceremony, the festival was very joyous; a great number of guests who had been invited to the breakfast ↑at the Castle↓ then appearing – I should say 5 or 600 persons. The Royal personages breakfasted apart – but the mistake was made of not inviting the Ambassadors & their wives to this exclusive repast, who took rank above ~~most of~~ ↑all↓ the Royal guests ~~who were not~~ who were inferior to their Sovereigns whom they personally represented.

Cte. Appony[i] was wroth on this head, & certainly the Hungarian dress of Made. Appony[i] wh: had only arrived the night before justified any / distinction. It was the most gorgeous & graceful costume ever worn – ~~f light~~ ↑bright↓ blue velvet, richly embroidered in gold, & astounding sables, but the fancy of the dress exceeded its costly materials.

They had lodgings at Windsor, & the ambassadress changed her costume before she left Windsor. This was fortunate, for the arrangements for departures were bad; the ladies were mobbed ↑at the station↓, & as many of them had tiaras of diamonds, they were in danger of being plundered. Me. Appony[i] was separated from the Ambassador, I rescued her, & got her into a railway carriage with my wife & some others – ↑grand dames, who had lost their husbands.↓ I think I had to sit on my wife's lap. When we got to Paddington in the rain, there was no Ambassadorial carr[iag]e – but ours was there & so we took home safe this brilliant & delightful person. /

A great lady of the Court, who was my secret friend, & proved herself on many occasions a real one, told me at the breakfast, that the Queen meant to see me. She repeated, that the Queen said she was determined to see me. From wh: ↑& other things,↓ I inferred that there had been difficulties ~~in~~ put in the way.

Lord Derby had had an audience of H.M. before the wedding, on the ↑alleged↓ ground of conferring about the Memorial – but understood ~~that is was~~ ↑as↓ a token of H.Ms return to public life, & that ~~shd~~ she wd. commence to see her Ministers socially, & exalted persons who had been near her person. Ld. Derby never mentioned any of the details of this audience to me, but his son did. The Queen received him in her closet sitting; the audience was by no means brief, & Ld. Derby stood the whole time, altho' recovering from a severe / fit of the gout. The Queen even alluded to this, & said she feared he would suffer by standing, but offered no seat. So severe was the etiquette.

Notwithstanding my private intimation, time rolled on, & I never heard anything of my audience. Weeks, even months, passed. The Queen had received all her principal Ministers, Lord Clarendon & Lord Derby, & there it stopped. I saw my friend occasionally in society, & once she asked me, whether I had heard anything, & when I replied in the negative, she said, ~~You~~ "Be sure, you will, for H.M. said only the other day, she was determined to see Mr D."

On [*blank in MS; the date was 22 April 1863*] I received an invitation to Windsor Castle for [*blank in MS*] & to stay till the next day. /

When I arrived at the Castle, I received a note from Biddulph telling me that the Queen wd. receive me before dinner, at a ¼ past seven o'ck. He gave me the hint, that I might make my toilette early, & so ~~leave~~ be able to leave the presence chamber for the banquet, wh: was about an hour after. After I was dressed, there came another note to say that Lord John Russell had arrived from town with important despatches, & that the Queen wd. be engaged & would postpone my audience till the morrow after breakfast.

It was the beginning of the Polish Insurrection, & the Ministry were much perplexed. The despatches were about Poland.

I was struck at dinner by the contrast with the somewhat subdued tone that prevailed in former days at ↑the↓ royal dinners.

The / Prince & Princess of Wales were our host & hostess. The party ~~very~~ large tho' consisting only of courtiers (~~they w~~ there were ↑more than↓ two households blended) the only [*illegible deletion*] guests being Earl Russell & myself. The Prince of Wales gave me the idea of a young man who had just come into a large estate & was delighted at entertaining his friends. He took out his sister, the Princess Helena, & sate opposite the Princess of Wales, who was taken out by Prince Alfred. On the other side of Prince Alfred, was the Css of Desart (in waiting) & I sate ~~next to~~ ↑between↓ her ~~& on n~~ & Lady Augusta Bruce↑, sister of Ld. Elgin↓, whom I had met before at Windsor, when she was in attendance on the Dss of Kent. I was glad to renew my acquaintance with her, for, like all her family, she is clever, & told me in the course of the dinner a great deal. /

When the ladies had retired, I ~~sate next to~~ ↑was next to↓ Prince Alfred, who invited me to take Lady Desart's vacated seat. I had not seen him since he was a very young & very little midshipman. Tho' still in his ~~tees~~ teens, he ~~no~~ was much altered, had grown a great deal, a bronzed or manly countenance, with a thoughtful brow; ↑altogether↓ like his father. His brother, the Prince of Wales was a Guelph, not a Coburg. The Queen said he was exactly like a portrait wh: they had there of Frederick, Prince of Wales. I thought him very like a portrait also of Windsor of his [*great-*]grandfather, George the third, ~~when young~~ shortly after his accession. Ld. Malmesbury said, that his general resemblance to his [*great-*]grandfather was so great, that he already was always asking questions & talking loud.

Prince Alfred had just ~~co~~ recovered from a severe, & dangerous fever, wh: had prevented [his] being / at the wedding. He was detained by it at Malta, & the telegrams wh: were constant were so alarming, that one day they feared the wedding cd. not take place. Alluding to his illness & Malta, we naturally talked of his travels – he had seen a great deal, having been at (the ↑Africa↓ Cape) &c. – on all of wh: he spoke with simplicity & sense. He was glad to be home again. I remember he said "What a fine Castle this is. I never saw anyone in any country to be compared with it. I love this Castle; I was born ~~here~~ ↑in it↓."

When we returned to the Saloon, the circle was formed as if the Queen were present, but the Prince & Princess did not make the round. She kept apart, & then the Prince came & addressed Lord Russell in the circle, & then led him to the Princess with whom he conversed for about ten / minutes. Then, after a very short space the Prince came to me, & conversed a little. He asked me, whether I thought the Bill for abolishing the City Police would pass? I replied, that I had not given any personal attention to the subject, but my impression was not favorable to its success. He said he had heard the same, but it ought to pass; there ought to be only one police for the Capital. I perceived from this what I afterwards had proof of, that the ~~capital~~ passing of the Bill was a capital point with the Court. The opposition to the Bill ~~was to~~ turned out to be so general throughout the country, that it was eventually withdrawn by the Ministry witht. a division; not before however several courtiers, who had seats in the House of Commons, making speeches against / it, wh: made the discomfiture more flagrant, as well as the particular animus more obvious.

After this, the Prince proposed that he shd present me to H.R.H. & I went up accordingly. ~~She~~ I had, therefore, ↑at last,↓ a good opportunity of forming an opinion of her appearance; wh: was highly favorable. Her face was delicate & refined; ↑her features regular;↓ her brow well-moulded; her mouth ~~exceedingly~~ beautiful; ~~&~~ ↑her hair good &↓ her ears small. She was very thin. She had the accomplishment of being gracious without smiling. She had repose. She spoke English, but not with the fluency I had expected, & I don't think she always comprehended what was said. The Prince hovered about her, & after a few minutes joined the conversation.

I remember nothing very particular about it except that it fell upon nightingales, & I asked / H.R.H. whether she knew what nightingales fed upon. ~~While she~~ While she was confessing her ignorance & her curiosity the Prince came & she addressed the question to him, wh: he cd. not answer. I told them – upon glowworms; exactly the food wh: nightingales shd. require. The Prince was interested by this & ~~said~~ ↑exclaimed↓ "Is that a fact, or is it a myth?" "Quite a fact, Sir; for my woodman is my authority, for we have a great many nightingales at Hughenden, & ~~yet~~ a great many glowworms.["] "We have got one nightingale at Sandringham" sd the Prince smiling[.] I remember now, that the conversation got to nightingales in this manner. The Princess told me they were delighted with their London residence, they awoke in the morning, & looked into a garden, & heard the birds sing. I said then "I fear not nightingales, Madam"[.]

~~In~~ After this, there was the private band, ~~as~~ just the same as if H.M. were present, & at 11 o'ck ~~we~~ the Prince & Pss & attendants retired. /

On the morrow I breakfasted with the Lady in waiting & the maids of Honor – & Lord John Russell. We had a merry breakfast, for the ladies wished to make Ld. John & myself talk – & I, who was really somewhat nervous from my approaching interview, ~~took~~ ↑was glad to take↓ refuge in raillery. Lord John was genial, wh:, on the whole, he generally has been with me. For notwithstanding our ↑fierce↓ public struggles for long years, & the crusade I have always preached against High Whiggism, of wh: he was the Incarnate creation, there were really some elements of sympathy betn. us, being with all his hauteur & frigid manner, really a man of sentiment, & imagination, & culture.

When breakfast was over, we were left together, & I asked him seriously what was the real state of affairs in Poland. He spoke with great frankness on the matter, & among other things, that the Cabinet had sent a secret / agent to Poland in order to obtain some accurate inform[ati]on (I think, Oliphant) ["]but I can't say" he added "we are much the wiser. The best opinions seem to hold, that it will be put down in the summer – but" & he shrugged his shoulders "it may not be – & then – "[.]

He went to town – & I was left alone with the newspapers. In about a quarter of an hour I was summoned. The attendant ~~had~~ led me down ~~a familiar~~ part of the great Gallery, & then turned off into a familiar corridor, & then thro' an antichamber. I was ushered into Prince Albert's special room: a small Cabinet, decorated with all the objects of art he loved, & in wh: I had frequently ~~listened at great len~~ had the privilege of conferring, & listening at length to his views on public life & politics; when throwing off his reserve & shyness, he warmed into eloquence, not ~~um~~ unmixed with sarcastic humor, but on all subjects on wh: he spoke, distinguished by / his perfect knowledge & his thought. The room was quite unchanged. It was in every respect as if he had resided in it yesterday – the writing materials, the books, all the indications of habitual occupation. Only one change I observed: a plate on ~~th~~ his accustomed chair – ~~"This~~ with ~~an~~ an inscription "This was the Prince Consort's chair from 18– to 1861"[.]

In ~~about th~~ less than five minutes from my entry, ~~the~~ an opposite door opened, & the Queen appeared.

She was still in Widow's mourning, & seemed stouter than when I last saw her, but this was perhaps only from her dress. I bowed deeply when she entered, & raised my head with unusual slowness, that I might have a moment for recovery. Her countenance was grave, but serene & kind – & she said, in a most musical voice, "It is some time since we met"[.] /

Then to some murmuring words of mine ~~she sa~~ H.M. said "You have not had a very busy session this year?" ~~I replied~~ In assenting to this, I expressed my wish, that politics were in general as serene as ~~Parliament~~ the Ho: of Comm: Upon this H.M. entered into the state of public affairs with frankness & some animation, wh: entirely removed the first embarrassment of the audience. It was then like an audience betn. ~~a~~ Sovereign & a Minister.

H.M. expressed her conviction, that whatr. happened, the Amer: Union cd. not be restored. She spoke fully about Poland, nor was it difficult to recognise that the insurrection alarmed her from its possible consequences, on the state of Germany. H.M., however, it was quite clear, was sanguine that the Russians wd. suppress it by the Summer.

She asked me, ↑frankly,↓ whether I thought the present Ministry wd. get thro' the Session. I said they were weak, but there was no desire to displace them / unless a stronger one cd. be established. She said she hoped no crisis wd. be brought about wantonly, for in her forlorn condition, she ~~trembled~~ hardly knew what she cd. do. I said H.M's comfort was an element in all our considerations, & that no action wd. be taken, I felt sure, unless from commanding necessity.

She said "Lord Palmerston was grown very old"[.]

I replied "But his voice in debate, Madam, is as loud as ever"[.]

"Yes!" she exclaimed with ~~his~~ animation "and his handwriting! – Did you ever see such a handwriting! So very clear & strong! Nevertheless, I see in him a great change, a very great change. ↑His ~~fa~~ countenance is so changed"↓[.]

Then H.M. turning from public affairs, deigned to say, that it had given her great pleasure to observe, that I had been chosen trustee of the Brit: Museum in the place of the late Lord Lansdowne – & she spoke for some time on kindred subjects, alluding to what the Prince ~~had~~ ↑had done↓ rather than ~~mention~~ directly referring to him herself. /

At last she asked after my wife & hoped she was well, & then with a graceful bow, vanished.

APPENDIX IV

The following is D*'s memorandum on the death of Lord Lyndhurst in 1863.* H A/X/A/60. See also *DR* 118-19.

Octr 13: 1863. – 1863.

Lord Lyndhurst died this morning. He had a mind equally distinguished for its vigor & flexibility. He ~~ne~~ rarely originated, but his apprehension was very quick & he mastered the suggestions of others & made them clearer & more strong. He had a great grasp ↑thoroughly mastered a subject; deep & acute; & sometimes when you thought him slow, was only exhaustive↓. In ↑his statements↓ ~~He was~~ accurate, complete, & singularly lucid: the clearest mind on affairs with equal power of conceiving & communicating his perspicuous views.

His soul wanted ardor for he was deficient in imagination, tho' by no means void of sensibility. He adapted himself to circ[umstan]ces in a moment tho' he could not create, or even considerably control them. His ambition active, not soaring. Its natural height to hold the great seal *thrice:* but when the / King in 1836 had it conveyed to him that he might be called upon to take the first place, & cd he be ready, he exclaimed "why I am a lawyer not a statesman" & seemed disconcerted – but when he had talked over the matter with a friend ↑[*written in another hand:* (i.e. D. 1873)]↓ he not only arrived at the result that he was a statesman, but let his M[ajest]y be assured that he was prepared to do his bidding, tho' it was one unusually difficult & perilous.

His cultiv[ati]on was considerable: far more than he was given credit for. His reading had been various & extensive, tho' he never sought to display it, & his scientific acquirements notable. He retained & digested everything; supported by a powerful & well ordered memory.

A pleader rather than an orator, & never a debater. Unsuccessful in the H. of Comm:, he rose at once in the Ho: of Lords to a pos[iti]on of unapproached supremacy; the times were favorable to him there. His stately & luminous expositions, in a voice of thrilling music, were adapted / to a senate ↑of wh: he caught the tone with facility↓. His taste almost amounted to austerity, yet he did not appreciate Demosthenes, & was a strong Ciceronian.

He had a sweet disposition, with a temper that nothing could ruffle; ↑indulgent,↓ placable, free from prejudice & utterly devoid of vanity. His feelings perhaps were not very strong, but they were always kind. XX

[*The following paragraph has a line drawn around it, perhaps to be omitted or moved.*] His mind was playful, but not witty, & he had little humor tho' he cd. sympathise with it. His knowledge of mankind was great, but not consummate, for in their management, ↑there was this error↓ he was willing to give them credit for being ↑influenced by↓ amiable, but not ~~for being influenced by~~ elevated ~~thoughts~~ feelings.

XX

He was wonderfully fond of the society of women & this not ↑merely↓ from his susceptibility to the sex, wh: was notorious, but because he was fond of them in every relation of life. He loved to be surrounded by his family who were all females: a mother of 90, a sister nearly his own age, & who survived him in the possession of all her faculties, ↑indulged & devoted↓ daughters. He was happy in two marriages, tho' his wives in every respect were very different. / His person was highly prepossessing. Far above the middle height, his figure was symmetrical & distinguished, & tho' powerfully formed, he never became stout. His countenance was that of a high-bred falcon. Indeed nothing cd. be finer than the upper part of his countenance. His deepset eye gleamed with penetrating fire & his brow was majestic. Nothing could be ~~finer~~ ↑more beautiful↓. It was that of the Olympian Jove. The lower part of his countenance betrayed the deficiencies of his character; a want of high purpose, & some sensual attributes.

[*The following rough notes are added in pencil:*]

How he shrank and shrivelled the last years like Metth. Ld. Melbourne his great adm opponent & greatest admirer always adduced him in affection as the true aristocrat.

Manners – gleams of want of refinement from early associ[ati]ons – wh: the female[s] were not ladies – & having entered polished soc[iet]y late – nearer 50 than 40.

APPENDIX V

The following is D*'s memorandum on the 1864 session of Parliament.* H A/X/A/66, 67. *See also* DR 124-25.

1864.

The Session a very curious one; I was [*illegible deletion*] watching for five months for the proper moment for battle. It was very difficult to restrain our friends. The Govt. every day more ~~p~~ unpopular, & yet it was clear to me that the House wd. not directly censure them. The tactic was to postpone to / the last moment a direct attack, but to defeat them in the interval on some indirect vote, taking advantage of the discontent of the House. Thus on the Ashantee war we ran them to 6 or 7 & on Stansfeld's affair to 10: on either question they wd. have resigned. On the direct vote ↑[*in another hand:* (Their Danish policy. 1873)]↓ their majority was 18, of wh: they affected to be proud, tho' in old days, it wd. have been considered a defeat. Sir Robt Peel on his vote of want of confidence in 1840 ~~was~~ moved by Sir John ~~Buller~~ ↑[*in another hand:*] Buller↓ was beaten by 22 – but was Minister next year 1841.

–

Ld. P. after the division scrambled up a wearying staircase to the ladies' gallery. My informant, who was behind him, had the good taste & tact to linger. He saw the ladies' gallery open & Lady Palmerston advance & they embraced! An interesting scene & what pluck – to mount those dreadful stairs ↑at three o'ck in the morning & 80 years of age!↓ My informant wd. not disturb them. It was a great moment! But silly Lady De Grey who / ↑with other Whig ladies↓ was in the gallery with Lady Palm: would come forward with "O! dear Lord Palmerston! How nice!'" &c. &c, wh: spoilt all.

APPENDIX VI

The following is the text of D*'s and Rothschild's pamphlet (with its appendix) on* The Progress of Jewish Emancipation Since 1829.

So much misconception exists as to the nature of the measures which have hitherto been introduced into Parliament for the removal of the civil disabilities of Englishmen professing the Jewish religion – and as to the manner in which they have at intervals been received, not only by the two branches of the legislature, but, by the most distinguished of our public men, representing very different shades of opinion both in the political and the religious world – that it has been deemed expedient to offer to the public a short summary of what has occurred, in this respect, since the first great parliamentary step to advance Jewish Emancipation was taken in 1830 by Mr. Huskisson, then leader of the friends of Mr. Canning.

On the presentation of some petitions, and especially of the Liverpool Petition in that year, that eminent and lamented statesman made the following declaration: "I wish," he said, "to take this opportunity to express the opinion which I have always held of the impolicy and injustice of imposing civil disabilities on account of religious / opinions. I support the prayer of this petition with all my heart, and express my entire and cordial concurrence in the principle of the Bill about to be brought in by the honourable member for Inverness (Mr. Robert Grant), on this subject. Individuals of the persuasion of the Petitioners have hitherto been considered as cosmopolites, rather than as belonging to any particular country. I trust that they will henceforth find a welcome home in Great Britain." And subsequently he said: "In the petition from the bankers, merchants, and inhabitants of Liverpool, in favour of the emancipation of the Jews, they state, that the exclusion from civil offices, on account of religious opinions, and the other civil disabilities under which the Jews labour, are at once repugnant to the genuine and tolerant spirit of Christianity, and most injurious to the best interests of the state. They therefore pray, that the bill now before the House for the emancipation of the Jews may pass into a law. I may mention to the House, that the petition is signed by upwards of 2,000 persons, comprising not only the mayor of Liverpool and many members of the corporation, but also every banker, and, indeed, every merchant of weight and influence in that great and enlightened town. I am sure that my honourable and gallant colleague [*footnote:* General Gascoyne; who, following Mr. Huskisson in opposition, stated, that he "had not known, for many years, any petition presented from Liverpool more numerously or respectably signed."] will acknowledge / that he has never known any petition presented from that town, which has been more numerously and respectably signed. It has attached to it the signatures of several respectable clergymen of the Church of England – men of all parties have subscribed it. There may be some exceptions; but I believe that, generally speaking, there is but one unanimous feeling in the town of Liverpool, even among those most attached to the established religion and church of this country, in favour of Jewish Emancipation. I trust that, under such circumstances, this petition will have due weight with the House."

Early in the Session, on the ensuing 5th April, 1830, the Duke of Wellington then being Prime Minister, Mr. Robert Grant accordingly moved for leave to bring in a Bill to repeal the civil disabilities affecting British-born subjects professing the Jewish Religion. Sir Robert Inglis took the lead in opposition to this motion; but it was carried, on a division, by a majority of 115 to 97. In the majority will be found the names of the present Duke of Marlborough, the present Duke of Manchester, and the present Duke of Grafton; of Mr. Huskisson, Sir Stratford Canning, Mr. Wodehouse, Mr. Wynn, Sir W. Wynn; of Sir Thomas Baring, Mr. Baring, Mr. Alderman Thompson; of the present Earl of Harrowby, and of the present Lord Stanley.

Previously to the motion for the second reading on the 17th May, 1830, Mr. Alexander Baring (the / present Lord Ashburton) presented a petition in favour of it, signed by 14,000 merchants, bankers, and traders of the city of London. The second reading was lost by a majority of 228 to 165; but in the minority, in addition to the names we have already quoted, will be found those of the present Duke of Norfolk, of the present Earl of Derby, and of Lord George Bentinck, then, as now, member for King's Lynn.

Notwithstanding the defeat of Mr. Grant's Bill in the Commons, the comparatively small majority, the recollection of the distinguished names that were enrolled among its supporters – the flower of the Whig party, the followers of Mr. Canning, and the whole of that influential confederacy known as "the Grenvillites," – emboldened Lord Bexley, who on a religious principle was extremely interested in the success of the measure, to present on the 14th Dec. 1830, a petition to the House of Lords in favour of the removal of these disabilities, to express his cordial support of its prayer, and to signify his intention, on a fitting occasion, of introducing the subject to their Lordships' consideration.

But the exertions of Mr. Robert Grant and of Lord Bexley were interrupted by the fall of the Duke of Wellington's Government, and the introduction of the Reform Bill. It was not, therefore, until the 17th April, 1833, that Mr. Grant moved a resolution, in Committee of the whole House, "That it is expedient to remove all civil disabilities at present existing, affecting her Majesty's subjects of the Jewish religion, with the like exceptions as / are provided with reference to her Majesty's subjects professing the Roman Catholic religion."

This motion, after a murmur from Sir R. Inglis, was agreed to without a division. On the 22nd of May the second reading was moved. It was principally opposed by Sir R. Inglis and Mr. Plumptre, but was carried by a majority of 159 to 52. The Bill proceeded through its various stages, sustained by majorities of equal strength, until the third reading, on the 22nd of July, when it was carried by a majority of 189 to 52.

Three days after, the Bill was read a first time in the House of Lords, on the motion of Lord Bexley. On the 1st of August following, previously to the second reading, a number of petitions were presented in its favor, including one signed by 7,000 inhabitants of Westminster, presented by His Royal Highness the Duke of Sussex. [*footnote:* Not one petition was presented against the Bill.] That illustrious Prince likewise supported Lord Bexley in the debate, as also did Lord Melbourne, the Lord Chancellor, the Archbishop of Dublin, the Bishop of Chichester, and the Marquess of Westminster. On a division, there appeared

	Contents.	Non-contents.
Present . .	29	44
Proxy . . .	25	60
	54	104

Majority against the Bill, 50.

The Duke of Portland and Lord Willoughby d'Eresby voted for the Bill. /

Notwithstanding the result of this division in the Lords, five days afterwards, viz: – on the 6th August, the Marquess of Westminster gave notice of his intention to renew the motion in the ensuing Session.

Early in that Session Mr. Grant, in the House of Commons, again introduced a measure of emancipation similar to the one carried in the preceding year. This measure received a very feeble opposition, chiefly from Mr. Hardy and Mr. Hughes Hughes, and was carried through all its stages by large majorities.

During its progress through the House of Commons, Lord Durham had presented to the Lords a petition in its favour, signed by 23,398 merchants, bankers, and traders of London. His Lordship called attention, on that occasion, to the signatures of Messrs. Robarts, Barnet, Mills, Prescott, Baring, Loyd, Smith, Lubbock, Barclay, Grote, Loch, Tooke, and Jones, and warmly supported the prayer. The Lord Chancellor also presented a petition in its favour from Edinburgh, signed by 6,200 persons. The time, however, was not a fortunate one for the passing of the measure. An unconstitutional agitation against the independence of the House of Lords had been encouraged for some time by an extreme section of the Liberal party, and at this moment particularly prevailed. The Lords were not unwilling to seize an early opportunity of asserting the free exercise of their legislative privileges; and the Bill for the relief of Her Majesty's subjects professing the Jewish Religion appeared / to offer an expedient occasion for this purpose. Notwithstanding the fidelity of Lord Bexley, and the earnestness of the Marquess of Westminster, many Peers voted against the measure, who at a subsequent period evinced a very contrary feeling; among these was the Marquess of Bute, destined to become the first successful champion of the British Jews in the House of Lords. Thus the Bill was lost by a majority of 92.

Notwithstanding, however, this temporary check, the progress of Jewish Emancipation experienced in the course of the ensuing year a great and unprecedented advance. Towards the end of the Session of 1835, the Attorney-General, Sir John Campbell, introduced the "Sheriffs'-Declaration Bill," into the House of Commons. This Bill passed both Houses without opposition, and, receiving the royal assent on the 21st of August, 1835, became a Law, by which a person professing the Jewish religion might fill the high constitutional office of Sheriff of a county. The little prejudice that lingers on this subject in the community is shown by the fact, that English gentlemen of the Jewish faith have since filled the office of Sheriff in the counties of Middlesex, Kent, and Buckinghamshire, and in a manner which has given universal satisfaction to their fellow subjects.

Encouraged by this success, Mr. Spring Rice, in 1836, introduced a Bill, similar to that of Mr. Grant, for the general removal of Jewish Civil Disabilities. It was read a first time on the 13th of June, and, on the 10th of July, Mr. Alderman / Thompson, who from the first had been an influential and consistent supporter of the measure, made use of the following expressions: –

"I have the honor to present the petition of burgesses and inhabitants of Sunderland (signed by 2000 persons), praying that the Jewish Disabilities Bill may pass into a law. I beg to say, that I shall most cordially support the Bill of the Right Honourable Gentleman, the Chancellor of the Exchequer. I have already, on several occasions, supported the same measure, and shall continue to do so."

The bill was carried by decisive majorities in all its stages: indeed, the noes on the second reading were only 22; and the principal speakers against the measure were Sir Robert Inglis, Colonel Sibthorp, Mr. Hardy, Mr. Plumptre, and Mr. Peter Borthwick.

The Bill was introduced into the Lords on the 19th of August, and read a first time; but, on account of the lateness of the session, the Marquess of Westminster postponed its further progress.

At the beginning of the Session of 1841, after the presentation of a petition from Mr. David Salomons – who, in the interval, had been elected an Alderman of the City of London, but had been unable to take his seat in consequence of the declaration contained in the words, "On the true faith of a Christian" – a "Bill for the Relief of Persons of the Jewish Religion elected to Municipal Offices," was introduced into the House of Commons by Mr. Divett, and carried by a majority of 113. This Bill was introduced into the Lords / by the Marquess of Bute, and, although opposed by the Archbishop of Canterbury, was carried on its second reading.

Contents	48
Non-Contents	47
Majority	1

Notwithstanding this Bill was lost in a later stage, opinion had become so favourably disposed towards the emancipation of the British Jews in 1845, that a similar Bill was originated in the House of Lords itself and carried without a division. Lord Lyndhurst, then Lord Chancellor, introduced it, and he was warmly supported by His Royal Highness the Duke of Cambridge.

Sir Robert Peel moved the first reading of the Bill in the House of Commons, supported by Lord John Russell. It was opposed by Sir R. Inglis and Mr. Plumptre, who were assisted on the third reading by Colonel Sibthorp. The Bill went through all its stages by very decisive majorities, and received the royal assent July 31st, 1845. Municipal offices of every description, including that of Recorder, were opened to Englishmen professing the Jewish religion by this statute, which thus placed at the disposal of their fellow-citizens in towns, the services which had been rendered for several years in the capacity of county magistrates, [*footnote:* For Kent – Mr. David Salomons, and Sir Moses Montefiore, Bart.; for Sussex – Mr. Joseph Montefiore; for Surrey – Mr. Benjamin Cohen; for Devonshire – Mr. Emanuel Lousada; for / Buckinghamshire – Baron Meyer Rothschild; and for Middlesex – Sir Isaac Lyon Goldsmid, Bart.] / recommended for that honourable trust by the respective Lords Lieutenant.

Within the two years which have elapsed since the passing of this act, several of the most important corporations of the kingdom, those for instance of London, Birmingham, Bristol, Portsmouth, Southampton and other towns, have received into their bodies members of the Jewish faith, elected by the free voice of their fellow-townsmen, among whom they live, and who are the best judges of their fitness for the trust which is reposed in them; while the Citizens of London, in confirmation of their votes at the late Election, and in testimony of their respect for his character and public conduct, conferred the first Aldermanic gown that fell vacant on Mr. David Salomons, who had already filled the office of Sheriff of London, as well as that of High Sheriff of the County of Kent.

After such testimonies of national respect and confidence as have been exhibited in the foregoing statutes, it is not surprising, that, when the Lord Chancellor introduced his "Religious Opinions Relief Bill," at the commencement of the year 1846, and reviewed, preparatory to their repeal, the obsolete laws inflicting penalties on account of religious belief, which still encumbered our Statute Book, he should have proposed to their Lordships to erase from their pages the Ordinance / of King Henry III., which prohibits persons of the Jewish religion from holding land in this country, and to abolish the famous *Statutum de Judaismo* of his son, which was designedly intended to degrade the Jews, and which required that they should wear a prescribed badge. But the measure of 1846 did more than this. Repealing portions of more than thirty penal statutes, chiefly pressing on English subjects of the Roman communion, it concluded with two special enactments; 1st, "that her Majesty's subjects professing the Jewish religion, in respect to their schools, places for religious worship, education, and charitable purposes, and the property held therewith, should be subject to the same laws as her Majesty's Protestant subjects dissenting from the Church of England," and 2ndly, that there should be extended to them the protection of "the laws against the wilful, malicious, and contemptuous disturbance of religious assemblies and teachers."

This measure, proposed by the Lord Chancellor, passed the House of Lords without a division. In the House of Commons, even Sir Robert Inglis left it to be resisted by Colonel Sibthorp and Mr. Spooner. Ten gentlemen, however, were induced to record their votes in the minority, and the "Religious Opinions Relief Bill" received the royal assent on the 18th of August in the same year.

Thus, in seventeen years, after repeated discussions and divisions in both Houses of Parliament; the controversy never having degenerated into a party question; the claims of the British Jews having / during that period been supported by Lord Melbourne and Lord Lyndhurst; by Lord John Russell and Sir Robert Peel; by Lord Bexley, Sir Thomas Baring and the Duke of Manchester, as well as by Mr. Gladstone and Lord Sandon; by Lord Stanley and by Lord George Bentinck – all the civil disabilities disapproved of by Mr. Huskisson, and attempted to be remedied by Mr. Grant, have been removed, except the exclusion from seats in the Houses of Parliament. The citizens of London, who, under the guidance of Lord Ashburton in 1830, petitioned Parliament to grant to the English Jews this franchise, have recently elected an English Jew for their representative; and the Prime Minister, in accordance with the feeling of the leading members of all political sections, deeming this a fair occasion to complete the settlement of Jewish emancipation, introduced, on the 16th of December, 1847, a Bill for the Relief of Her Majesty's subjects professing the Jewish Religion, which stands for a second reading on the 7th of February next.

15th January, 1848. /

APPENDIX

Extracts from the Debate in the House of Lords,
1st August 1833.

THE ARCHBISHOP OF CANTERBURY. – ... "I do not feel harshly towards the Jewish nation. I look on the Jews as the most remarkable people on earth. Having been separated in the beginning from the nations, they shone forth, in ancient times, like a light in the firmament, proclaiming the attributes of the Creator, and the hope of a Redeemer to a benighted world. Even in their present state of depression they retain their original character as vouchers of Divine truth; they bear a testimony – irrefutable, because it is involuntary – to the faith of the Gospel; attesting the truth of the prophecies which relate to the mission of Christ, by their own misfortunes. In this light I cannot but view them with feelings of admiration and pity – admiration for the constancy with which, through all times, under every vicissitude, they have adhered to their faith; and pity for their errors and their sufferings. I trust, however, that the time will arrive when the veil will drop from their eyes – when they will see the delusion which has led them astray – and will fly into the arms of the Saviour, whom they have despised and rejected, but which are ever open to receive them. I regard them as brothers estranged for a while from the family, but eventually to be restored to the household of faith; under the protection of one common father ...... In fact, my lords, the moral and social code of the Jews I apprehend to be the same as the moral and social code of the Christians. The Jews differ from the Christians in point of religious belief; but I apprehend that every sound believing Jew, – every Jew who is a member of his own communion, – adheres to the same moral and social code as the Christians do."

THE ARCHBISHOP OF DUBLIN.– .... ["]It is urged, that persons who not only do not acknowledge, but who renounce and deny – and some say vilify – the great Author of the Christian religion, ought not to have any voice in the legislature of a Christian country. On this point arises a question, which I own I find it very difficult to answer. The Legislature of this country, – I mean the two Houses of Parliament, – is not confined to what may be called the Civil Government, – the imposing of burdens / which all must bear, and the enacting of laws which all must obey, – but it extends to the government of the Established Church also, even in matters purely ecclesiastical. It is, in fact, at present the only ecclesiastical government – since convocation has long been in a dormant state in England; and in Ireland does not even exist in that state. Whoever, therefore, is admitted to a seat in the Legislature, is admitted to a share in the government, not only of the State, but also of the Church; and that, not only in respect of its temporalities, but also of purely ecclesiastical affairs. If, therefore, the question be asked, "What right can a Jew have, under any circumstances, to legislate for a Christian Church?" I know of no answer that can be given to that question, except by asking another: What right has a Roman Catholic to legislate for a Protestant Church; or a Presbyterian for an Episcopal Church? What right, in short, has any man to legislate in ecclesiastical matters, for any Church of which he is not a member? This anomaly appears to me to exist in all these cases alike. The Jews, it is true, are much farther removed from us than any sect of Christians; but it does not follow that they are more likely to make innovations in our religious institutions. They never attempt to make proselytes, nor to introduce into Christianity any admixture of Judaism; nor is it likely they would attempt, in any way, to interfere with the doctrines or institutions of any description of Christians. Christians, on the contrary, of different persuasions, have often interfered in the most violent manner with each other's faith and worship. The Presbyterians did, we know, at one time, when they gained the ascendancy in this country, eject from every parish in England the Episcopalian clergy, and were, in turn, ejected by them; and I need not remind your Lordships of the many and violent struggles between Roman Catholics and Protestants in this, and in many other countries. In fact, the nearer approach to each other in point of faith between different denominations of Christians than between Christians and Jews, instead of diminishing, increases the risk of their endeavouring to alter or to overthrow each other's religion. Although, therefore, I cannot, in the abstract, approve of Jews being admitted to legislate for a Christian Church, or of the ecclesiastical concerns of any Church being, in any degree, under the control of such as are not members of it, I cannot on that ground consent to withhold / civil rights from the Jews, when Roman Catholics and Dissenters have been admitted into Parliament; since, in the case of the Jews, the anomaly is not greater, and the danger is even less. The nearer any class of men approach to ourselves in their faith, the more likely they are to interfere with ours. If, indeed, an erroneous faith be regarded in the light of a sin against God, and if we were authorised to visit this sin with civil disabilities, we might then look to the greater difference in faith of the Jews, than of any Christians. I trust I may dismiss, without argument, the notion of our having a right to punish men on account of their religious opinions, either with a view of forcing them to renounce those opinions, or of inflicting retribution on them for erroneous belief. Often as that principle – which is, in fact, that of persecution – has by many been implied in their practice – no one, I imagine, will be found, in the present day, to defend it in the abstract. If, indeed, we were to admit the principle of punishing religious error, then, as I have said, the greater error of the Jews might be consistently assigned as a reason for harsher and less indulgent treatment of them than of any sect of Christians; but the only ground which any one will distinctly avow as authorising penalties and restrictions imposed on any class of religionists, is that of self-protection – to guard ourselves either against religious corruption, or against some alarming civil danger. And in this point of view – looking to self-protection, and not to punishment, – it is plain, that the nearer any persons approach to us in religion, the greater the danger, when there is any to be apprehended, of admitting them to an equality of rights with ourselves. We know that the Roman Catholics have persecuted the Protestants, and the Protestants, in their turn, the Roman Catholics; – in short, we know that the various sects of Christians have done more, in molesting each other's faith and worship, than any Jews or Pagans have done against Christianity. When, therefore, it is said, that although not an exclusively Protestant, we have still an exclusively Christian, Legislature, I cannot but confess that a Christian Legislature, as such – simply as Christian – does not necessarily afford religious, or even personal security to a Christian. The most merciless persecutions, we know, have been (it is with shame and sorrow I speak it, but it is notorious) those inflicted by Christians on each other. From the mere circumstance, / therefore, of being under a Legislature exclusively Christian, I can derive no security; and, what is more, I am certain that your Lordships think with me in this: for, there is no one of us, professing Protestantism, who would not prefer living in Turkey or Persia, where he would be allowed, on paying a small tribute, the free exercise of his religion, to living under an exclusively Christian government in Spain or Portugal, or any country in which the Inquisition was established. The mere circumstance, therefore, of our having a Christian Legislature is not of itself any ground of security. But, on the other hand, there is not necessarily any danger, or any incongruity, in persons of any religious persuasions, different from that of the Church of England, legislating upon matters distinct from religion.....

"If any Jews are returned to Parliament, it must be by the choice of a great majority of Christian constituents. I own it does, therefore, appear to me to be a scandal, rather, on our own faith, to consider it so frail and brittle as not to bear touching – to proclaim that Christianity is in danger unless the hands of Christians are tied to preclude them from the election of Jews. I am not discussing the question whether Jews are the fittest persons to be returned to Parliament; but whether Christians should be left free as to that question, or should be prevented from electing them if they think fit. This Bill, it should be remembered, differs materially, in this respect, from that by which the disabilities of the Roman Catholics were removed; because, by the latter, many persons, being already Peers, were by that Bill at once admitted to Parliament. That will not be the case in this instance; because no Jew can set foot in Parliament until he has been freely elected by a Christian constituency.["]

THE BISHOP OF LONDON. – ... "As to the personal character of the Jews themselves, so far as I have had an opportunity of forming an opinion, the results of my observations are highly favourable. I once had the care of a large parish in which a number of that people resided; and I found them amongst the most liberal, loyal, and quiet of the inhabitants."

Effingham Wilson, Printer, 11, Royal Exchange.

APPENDIX VII

Chapter III of T.E. Kebbel Lord Beaconsfield and Other Tory Memories (*1907*) *30–7*.

It was early in October, 1864, that I first received an invitation to Hughenden. Mr. Disraeli had very kindly asked me to come when he had some people staying in the house whom he thought I might like to meet; among them, I remember, was the Duchess of Somerset, the Queen of Love and Beauty at the Eglinton Tournament; but, unfortunately, I could not go on the day fixed, and thus just missed meeting her Grace, who had left the day before I got there.

I remember the journey well – I started from Oxford, and drove in a dogcart to Thame, where I caught a train to High Wycombe. Here I got a fly to take me up to Hughenden. The driver was drunk, and several times nearly upset me. But it was a pitch dark night, and he may not have been so drunk as he looked. Mr. Disraeli, when he heard the story, congratulated me on having had an adventure. I was too late for dinner, but that did not signify, as I had practically dined at Oxford; and after I had dressed I was shown into the drawing-room, where I found Mrs. Disraeli by herself, whom I now saw for the first time. We were soon joined by her husband – and you do not see such a couple as they made every day in the week. The contrast was striking. It is enough to say that I liked Mrs. Disraeli very much. She was very good-natured; had nothing of the fine lady about her; and I dare say frequently astonished those who had much of it. Later on I was regaled with sandwiches and sherry, Mr. Disraeli assuring me that Hughenden was famous for its sandwiches. I do not know how they were made, but I remember I thought they were particularly good – as good, that is, as it is in the nature of a sandwich to be. The only two guests remaining in the house when I got there were Mr. Lygon, afterwards Lord Beauchamp, and a Buckinghamshire country gentleman, whose name I have forgotten, but who, like Dandie Dinmont, as described by Dominie Sampson, was learned "in that which appertaineth unto flocks and herds," and was possessed of a fine herd of Alderneys, which occupied a large share of our attention before we went to bed. No smoking-room was mentioned, and we retired early.

When I looked out of my window the next morning I saw Mr. Disraeli walking up and down between his two friends on the terrace which ran along the front of the house, and afforded a pretty view of the little valley of the Wye, from which Wycombe takes its name, and the woods and hills which encircle it. The other side of the house looked out upon the lawn. Mr. Disraeli's costume was a black velvet shooting coat – the very same, perhaps, which he wore when he made his famous speech at the Oxford Diocesan Conference, as described by Mr. Froude; a tall, sugar-loafed hat, with, if I remember right, some kind of feather attached to it; and a dark green tie, a colour to which he was always partial. I joined them on the terrace as soon as I could, and then Mr. Disraeli told me a great deal about the house and the estate, and the Norris family who had formerly possessed it, and was interested in hearing that many years ago an uncle of my own had once had thoughts of buying it. He forgot to add that the Manor of Hughenden belonged to the Priory of Kenilworth, and that he himself was one of those "gentle proprietors of abbey lands" whom he denounced in "Sybil."

Of course, he knew the whole neighbourhood thoroughly, and seemed to take pleasure in talking about it. He was fond of Buckinghamshire, its woods and waters, for a great love of trees was one of his marked characteristics; and here, perhaps, a highly imaginative person fond of far-fetched resemblances might be reminded of the political differences between Mr. Disraeli and Mr. Gladstone, the one a great conservator of trees, the other a great destroyer. Mr. Disraeli was proud, too, of the place which Buckinghamshire filled in history, and of the continuity of its character down to the present time. When asked once where were the four thousand Buckinghamshire freeholders who followed John Hampden, "Why, where you would expect to find them," was the answer, "in Buckinghamshire, to be sure." After breakfast, he took me into his library, and it was a pleasure to see him among his books. He pointed out several scarce volumes, touching each of them as he spoke with a slender forefinger, indicative both of race and of character. He was a scholar, his favourite classics being Sophocles and Horace. But he made little parade of either his scholarship or his literature; and his conversation did not often turn on books, either ancient or modern.

On quitting the library, he retired to his own den – a small room upstairs, which I was shown on a subsequent visit to Hughenden after Mr. Disraeli's death – and I was left in charge of Mrs. Disraeli, with whom I walked round the garden, and was introduced to the peacocks, the cedar brought direct from Lebanon, and some other plants or trees which came from the Far East. Then we set out for a ramble through the woods, my hostess being attired in a short skirt, with stout gaiters – a costume which has since become comparatively common among ladies, but was new to me at the time. In the month of October the woods are apt to be wet, and, as it was a damp morning, I rather envied her. But her conversation would have made amends had I got twice as wet as I did. "*Namque canebat uti.*" For she told of her first acquaintance with "Dizzy," as she always called him; of the sums she had spent on electioneering down to that date – I think she said a hundred thousand pounds – and that she was well rewarded by the devotion of so brilliant a husband. She spoke of his position as a country gentleman and his popularity with the farmers and peasantry. He was no sportsman, she said, and kept neither hunters nor pointers – I believe a pair of carriage horses were the whole of his stud. The tenants supplied him with game as he required it, and that much-maligned character, the gamekeeper, was never seen on the estate. Then she showed me the walks which had been cut through the woods, to each of which some fanciful name was given. One was Italy; another, I think – but of this I am not sure – was named after some Spanish province. Then there was "The Lovers' Walk," and all, as I understood, were planned by Mrs. Disraeli herself, with the approval and sympathy of the statesman. She spoke of his favourite flowers and favourite trees, his love of birds, and of the garden songsters in particular – the thrush, the black-cap, the goldfinch, and the whole tribe of warblers. She showed me, in fact, a side of his character but little understood by the world in general at that time, though since then it has been better appreciated, and, coming fresh from the lips of so clever a woman as his wife, it is easy to understand the deep impression which it made on me. She gave me also anecdotes and illustrations of his great good nature, his kindness to unfriended talent, his fidelity to his friends and magnanimous contempt for his enemies.

My hostess brought me back to luncheon about the usual hour, and after that meal the carriage came round to the door, and Mr. Disraeli took his two other guests and myself for a drive round the neighbourhood. It is full of historic memories, and it is needless to say that our host was steeped in them. It was good to be with the great satirist of the "Venetians" on this, to him, classic ground. It was the home of his childhood, and here he imbibed ideas which never afterwards deserted him. His father, Isaac Disraeli, was living at Bradenham, only a few miles distant, when he was writing his life of Charles I., and ransacked the whole district for facts or traditions relating to the Rebellion and the families concerned in it. But all family papers belonging to that period, said our host, were destroyed at the Restoration. "The conspiracy was hatched in these hills," he said, ["]and whatever evidence of it still existed in the bosom of the Chilterns was carefully removed when the Stuarts reappeared upon the scene." Our drive took us through a beautiful country, through the lovely beech woods from which Buckinghamshire derives its name, till at last we came to a spot where the hills slope down into a little valley, called Velvet Lawns, the slope being covered with natural boxwood, said to be indigenous to only one other county in England besides Buckinghamshire. Velvet Lawns, he said, at one time was a favourite place for picnics, and even parties came down from London to hold their revels on its turf. But they behaved so badly that leave had to be withdrawn. I remember staring at Mr. Disraeli, and trying to imagine him at a picnic.

Mr. Disraeli talked a good deal about the Civil War, and had evidently persuaded himself that the Chiltern Hills were the cradle of an aristocratic conspiracy, intended by the authors to regain for their own order the power which they had wielded under the Plantagenets. Charles I.'s mistakes gave them the opportunity they wanted. They were the excuse for the Rebellion, but not the cause of it. This already existed. Such was the general tenour of his conversation on this particular subject, to which he had given deep and serious attention independently of the information for which he was indebted to his father. It was impossible to doubt, as you listened to his voice and marked the play of his features, that he was perfectly sincere in this belief. We may take different views of the policy of the Parliamentary party, and of the results of its ultimate victory in 1688, without doubting that Mr. Disraeli's theory of its origin came very near the truth. This was a memorable afternoon, and I remember what struck me at the time was that Mr. Disraeli, in his sugar-loaf hat and black cloak which he wore in the carriage, resembled anything but a Cavalier.

If I remember rightly, we assembled before dinner in the library, and when dinner was announced Mr.

Disraeli led out his wife and left the three of us to follow. The dinner, I recollect, was very good. But Mr. Disraeli talked very little, leaving the lady of the house to lead the conversation. I remember mention being made of Harper Twelvetrees, and Mr. Disraeli seemed really to take a lively interest in counting up the number of names which had been formed from trees. I had the honour of making a remark which attracted his attention on the subject of portrait galleries. I asked him if he had ever noticed, in looking at collections of family portraits, how the general type changed as you passed from the seventeenth century into the eighteenth, the long or oval face predominating in the former becoming the rounder and fatter one most common in the latter. He said he never had, and turned to Mrs. Disraeli to tell her what I had said. The change, I thought, was coincident with the change from claret and sack to port and punch, together with the deeper potations which the Germans made fashionable in England. He seemed to think it might be so; but he pointed out that claret and Burgundy continued to be the drink of the higher classes nearly all through the century, and in support of the assertion he quoted his two favourite heroes, Bolingbroke and Carteret, who both drank Burgundy in large quantities. Yet George I. and Walpole drank punch together till the small hours, and we have all heard of Savage "roaring for hot punch at five o'clock in the morning." Mr. Disraeli said that men in those days had less fear of mixing their liquors, and that this might be one cause at least of the greater amount of drunkennness.

We did not sit long after dinner. Nor did Mrs. Disraeli remain long with us after we returned to the drawing-room. When she was gone, Mr. Disraeli sat and chatted with us for an hour very pleasantly: told some good stories and said some good things – a joke upon an inn called the King's Arms (at Berkhampstead, I think) is the only one that I remember. Mr. Disraeli said he did not remember the inn, upon which the owner of the Alderneys assured him that he must be mistaken. "You must remember the house, sir: there was a very handsome barmaid there – monstrous fine gal – you must have been in the King's Arms, sir." "Perhaps," said Dizzy, "if I had been in *her* arms I might have remembered it." Mr. Lygon looked grave. But Mrs. Grundy has now retired from the stage, and I think I may repeat the above without giving offence.

APPENDIX VIII

The Hughenden renovations 1862-4 by architect E.B. Lamb involved reconstructing the exterior in Victorian Gothic style, retaining a pergola along the south front, adding a 'Jacobean' parapet with pinnacles, repositioning windows and installing red brick facing. The interior was given vaulted and ribbed ceilings. Lamb also replanned the garden, with personal supervision from Mary Anne Disraeli. (Hughenden Manor guidebook.)

The following extracts from Mary Anne Disraeli's accounts and Disraeli's letters itemize the expenses of renovation, furnishing and decorating. Cash amounts have been standardized (£1.1s.1d.); spelling and punctuation have been corrected or supplied only when necessary. Where possible, London shops and dealers have been identified in square brackets.

1862	
18 Feb	Signor Fentanove – for statue – a check Dis £26.5s.
4 Mar	Burton Ironmonger [39 Oxford St] a cabinet plate warmer £6 bag of fuel 5s. 6d.
27 May	Vokins [carvers & gilders] 14 Gt Portland St 2 frames, with true lovers knot The Queen & the late Prince Consort Given by her Majesty to Dizy [*for which see* **3667**&*n2*]
3 Jun	E.B. *Lamb Esqr* for the Monument – a check self £200 £300 – total the Monument £500
4 Aug	Signor Fentanove Sculptor 67 Berners St. Oxford St. for 2d. statue £2.2s.
7 Aug	Drew from Drummonds by Dizy £350 £250 for Hughenden &c part of the 350 drawn for Lady Jersey's statu by [*blank in text*]
8 Aug	Check Mr Lamb £300
	[Thomas] Scowen[,] Allen Road, Stoke Newington An expanding Canopy blue & red for the garden £5.10s.
13 Aug	Pictures, 2, from G Gate (large) 6s.1d.
20 Aug	Two Sygnets arrived a present from Mr. Hussey, taken to the Island
26 Aug	About 18 yards left of the striped red & w[h]it[e]
4 Sept	Turner for Magnolias 2 &c on May last £2.6s.3d.
	[Thomas] Raftery [105 Upper St Islington] Green Desert Service £3.5s. 2 doz best cut wine glasses 24/10 £1[.] 6 best cut tumblers 12s. One doz moulded 14s. cream jug 1s. Toy [?] tumblers 3s.3d. 12 plates, 4 Dishes, & compo[te] Green [*total*] £5.2s.2d.
	A carpet stool
21 Sept	15 yds & ½ & 3½ Chintz – in White room pink & green like my bedroom
15 Sept	Carpet from London from Waterloo House 1s.2d.
	Bill at [Robert] Powlesland [tailor, 8 Great Vine St, Regent St] Mason[?] for toilets 11s.2d. 19½ yds. 18 8½ thread & needles £1.0s.7½
	Ann Dobson for damask at Waterloo House & pink callico, & binding[,] a post Office order £2.10s.
22 Sept	Carpet from London 1s.7d.
29 Sept	Carpet from London 1s.8d.
	2 bushells of grass seed 12s. on the Ru^{t} [?]
7 Oct	Raftery, pr of decanters £1 pan for water brown, 4s.3d.
14 Oct	Making 3 table & mending £1.5s.
	Mrs. Lovegrove 4 days making carpet for blue room 18s.
	Ward china & glass pitcher for water

	Fontana. Magic lantern 18s.6d. & slides
	repairing tea pot & toast rack 1s.6d.
21 Oct	Thos Husseys bill repairing chairs in Housekeepers room 9s.
Nov	At International Exhibition D buys statue of 'Hero expecting Leander' by Ignazio Villa. (**3709**n3)
4 Nov	2 Telagrams from & to Mr Lamb London 2s.
	Johnson – Timepiece upstairs 5s.6d.
	Mrs Aldhous black binding for Hall curtains 4s.
8 Nov	[George] Diack upholsterer 213 Oxf[ord] St Curtains for Hall at Hugh[enden] £12.5s. packing picture £1.11s.
	George Pratt upholsterer 12 Denmark St Soho Sq black Pedestal for Statue, Hero, £4.10s.
11 Nov	Halling & Pearce & Stone [linen drapers, 1-4 Cockspur St] Waterloo House Brussels carpet 4s.3d. 23 & 21 – pd. sent to Hugh[ende]n in Septr £9.6s.9d.
12 Nov	Lapworth [22 Old Bond St], Kidderminster carpet pink & white 3s.9d. same as before £2.7s.
18 Nov	Mr Lamb commenced height[en]ing the rooms with Mr Roberts today
	Hussey for repairing
4&15 Dec	Four dozen fine Scotch firs planted in the Ladys walk at 1s.6d., each
5 Dec	'Hughenden is now a chaos, for Mary Anne is making a new garden. She never loved her old one: &, now, she has more than twenty *navvies* at work, levelling & making terraces. We have as many workmen inside of the House, for altho' I always thought that, both from form, & situation, I was safe from architects, it turns out that I was wrong, & Hughenden House will soon assume a new form & character' (**3747**)
9 Dec	24 Scotch firs from Slough 1s.2d.
12 Dec	S Lessard[?] for new locks & keys £1.11s.2d.
	Mr Simmonds, a check Dis £38.4s. all paid for except the little wardrobe to be painted white & red. Mr Simmonds has a drawer for pattern
	Mr Lamb 300
1863	
Jan?	Robert Roberts, builder, paid £500. (**3876**n1)
17 Jan	Mr Roberts builder on account a check Dis £200
21 Jan	'I could not well go to Hughenden [for quiet], as it is full of workmen.' (**3777**)
18 Feb	Roberts paid £200. (**3876**n1)
14 Mar	Mr Lamb for Roberts a check Dis 200
28 Mar	Settled to give Diack for the 2 chairs to be *made* & guilded, for my work, by the Marchioness of Ely – £9
1 Apr	Hughenden is now 'a very noisy place, for we are restoring the house inside & out.' (**3777**n2)
15 Apr	'My strict injunctions not to destroy small birds, at Hughenden, have been successfully carried out.' (**3805**)
27 Apr	[Henry & John] Gardner [oil refiners] 453 Strand Lamp for Hero £4.4s. Pillar lamp £2.15s. Ormolu & ruby pillar Candlelabra £5
7 May	Mr Lamb, a check Dis £200 for Hughenden
5 Jun	Lewis & Allenby [silk merchants, 193–7 Regent St] quilting 24 yds. 4s.6d.
24 Jun	a check Dizy to Mr Lamb £200
21 Jul	plants to Hug[hende]n from K[ew?] gardens 2s.4d.
25 Jul	Diack £10.2s.6d.
1 Aug	Hindley & Sons late Miles, 1340 Ox[ford St] for a Persian carpet (small) £2.15s.
3 Aug	Andrews Oxf[ord] Bazaar 2 Swiss stools 9s. little armed chair 10s.
7 Aug	'Here, we are living in two rooms; Hughenden House being still full of architects, builders &c &c. We have made an Italian Terrace, which would delight you, & which, in time, is entirely to be dressed up with statues & vases, like Isola Bella.' (**3838**)
11 Aug	Van with lug[gage] to Hug[hende]n 4s.6d. ca[rriag]e of bronze statue piping Fa[un] 4s.6d. pa[rce]l of carpets 6d. Cr. of stove from London 3s.6d.
13 Aug	Roberts paid £300. (**3876**n1)
21 Aug	'We have passed two or three weeks here most happily: my wife in an infinity of creation, & I seeing only books & trees, but both good of their kind' (**3843**)
25 Aug	Ca[rriage] of fender 2s. Ca[rriage] of 2 marble chimney pieaces for bedrooms 8s.2d. Marble chimney piece Mowsney Mashl [Mowlem, Freeman & Burt, stone & granite merchants] 7s.9d. Mrs Lovegrove work woman altering curtains (10s. 5days)

3 Sept	The terrace walk 125 feet by 12, 20 feet with the grass from one side to the other
7 Sept	Mr Hussey mending 2 chairs 1s.6d.
8 Sept	Black cord for Library 1s.6d.
15 Sep	Ca[rriage] of Mows [Mowlem] B[urt] 6s.8d.
	Bill at Powlesland, flan[ne]l for Library curtains, at 9s.2d., 60 yds £2.7s.11d.
	Mr Gibb[o]ns gardner from Easter May 22d, &c £1.11s.
22 Sep	seeds grass 1s.
28 Sep	'When we left Hughenden last year we sent in an architect & suite, & tho' ten months have elapsed, some workmen still linger about. We have realised a romance we had been many years meditating: we have restored the House to what it was before the civil wars, & we have made a garden of terraces, in wh: cavaliers might roam, & saunter with their ladye-loves! ... In making the alterations here, a great number of owls have been disturbed among the yew trees, but they have been religiously cared for' (**3853**).
	'The house internally is still much in the hands of artisans, but [the] library ... is enriched & improved' (**3854**).
8 Oct	'I see, now, no chance of getting the workmen out of Hughenden this year. I have got rid of them externally, but I have only one bedroom finished, & I see a prospect of increased internal paint, wh: will soon drive me into Devonshire' (**3857**).
13 Oct	C[ar]r[iage] of carpet for dining room 3s.9d.
17 Oct	The ash tree cut down today 74 feet long & 10 feet round[.] The back north front near the Icehouse, all the part by the root decayed [...] cut down with all its branches, most of them dying
21 Oct	'Mary Anne has been very busy the whole year, & still remains so. She has nearly finished some rooms, wh: are named after [Baroness de Rothschild]' (**3861**).
24 Oct	Grass seed sowed in North front
24 Oct	Turner – Ordered by Mr. Gib[b]on gardner flowers &c £4.8s. 10s.6d. baskets deducted
	Grass Lawn grass 12 lb best 19s.
27 Oct	Brackets clock 5s.6d. little timepiece 2s.
1 Nov	Tins 1 bowl collander 1 slice mending[?] 2 cans [£8.5s.]
5 Nov	'I can't tear myself away from this place. This is my great planting time; and I have got a new batch of workmen in the dining room putting down a new floor. I feel, if I leave any workmen here, they never will go out' (**3870**).
8 Nov	'Mrs Disraeli['s] drawings of what we were doing, or proposing to do, here. The workmen have been here now, more than a year, & they have not yet entirely disappeared. She has been very much amused, wh: is something for your money' (**3875**).
9 Nov	Biggs & Palmer [upholsterers, 267 Holloway Rd] for sheeting Table cloth brown holland for a bag for cloths dusters
	Honey [ironmonger, 261 Regent St] for Door Mat 18s.6d. too much
11 Nov	Roberts paid £400 (**3876**n1).
30 Nov	Waterloo House Haley & Co [upholsterer, 37 George St Portman Sq] for an Axminster carpet a check Dis £33.12s.
	W Burton ironmonger 4 stoves £11.8s.
Dec	Mapel [Maple, 145-7 Tottenham Court Rd] upholsterer for Hughenden a check Dis £132.10s.8d.
4 Dec	Mansell, Tagya [*sic*], Hughenden, in Au[gus]t last, £10
	Burke & Company Warwick House [142-4] Reg[ent] St Marble chimney pieces 4, a Tagya [*sic*], a bas[k?]et candlestick &c A check Dis £27
19 Dec	Walter & Barry one pr. of candlestick with Lead on enameled china & 2 glass for tops for dear Dizzy on his birthday the 21st
1864	
26 Jan	booking 32 pces of [glass?] to H Manor 2s.
2 Feb	Burtons bill for Chim[ney] pces 5s.6d. *Four dining room glaces* 2s.
	Smiths bill for bedroom curtains white muslin
	Fishers for glass & plates &c £1.0s.6d.
10 Feb	Simmonds upholsterer a check Dis £62
	W. Broughton stone mason Dis £8.18s.9d.
12 Feb	Mason Ironmonger High Wycombe for stove in dining room, the *brass* work £15 workmens time taking down & putting up again £9.17s.4d. oil, repairing fenders &c a check Dis £21.0s.11d.

April Big[g]s & Palmer, 1 Damas[k] cloth 2/2 long 2/2 wide £1.8s.6d.
D[itt]o 2 yds/2 wide 3 yds long £2.15s.
Two D[itt]o. 3 yds wide 4 long, both the same pattern £12.12s
Eighteen napkins to match £4.19s.
Big[g]s & Palmer 2 yds Winery[?] 18d/12, 20 yds £1.10s.10d.

18 Apr [Frederick] Arthur 3 Sakvill St for the brown room at G Gate, & 3 bedrooms & a dressing room at Hughenden £21.13s.6d.
See bill Augt 1st. and 5 pieces more of the same paper & note in July, for the same rooms total pieces 37

25 Apr Arrowsmith & Co. Upholsterers &c Marquet floor at Hughenden for dining room, a check Dis £62.13s.10d. 80 New Bond Street

4 May [Thomas] Woodgate [antiques, 94-6 High Holborn], for, 4 biscuit[?] white china figures, the Seasons, for the garden at Hughenden, a check Dis £60

19 Jul [Henry] Nurse [carver & gilder] black enameld whatnot guilded 19 Old Cavendish Street £4

20 Jul Leach plum[ber] to this day a check Dis £41.4s.4d.

28 Jul Ramas[?] 148 Strand – 2 pr. of Berlin Corbeilles [flower baskets] – for dinner table at Hughenden, boys & foliage £10.10s.

30 Jul Houbigant [perfumers & glovers, 216 Regent St] a Cache – for flower pot 2s.6d.
Roberts's decorating at Hughenden unsatisfactory; £30 deducted. (**3958**n1)

1 Aug Arthur for 5 more pieces of paper (total 37) sent to Hugh[end]en for the 3 bedroom and a small dressing d[itt]o £1.2s.6d. NB all the railings and rooms £7.4s., total £8.6s.7d.
[Charles] Hancock [silversmith, 152 New Bond St] a silver Lily, or Lotos, in *pot* (*guilded*) silver & fronded leaves for centre ornament a check Dis £82.5s. with a case – after allowing £16.15s. for an oblong magazine
Walter & Barry making a mosaics gold rims, my own mosaic service gold – £5 24 more sett in gold by Mr Barry £4.4s. a check by Dis £8.15s. NB 49s for the marking, 5gns sett in gold – 6 Mosaics
Settled with Arthur to clean the Blue paper in dining room & cealing

4 Aug Carpet with blue velvet & mosaic left with London & Rider [jewellers, 17 New Bond St] to have more gold on it – received the above Augt.28th.

5 Aug A china tray tea pot cream & sugar bason £1.5s. roses & blue border, 1 plate to match 2s.
Houbigant 6 cases for flower pots 15s.
Diack upholsterer – a check Dis £17.9s.

8 Aug Wilson & Cy. 18 Wigmore St Estimate workmen 5 to 6s pr. day Carpets beating 2s.6d. to 3s. each stair carpet 6s., Making wardrobe with a looking glass, small size from 10 to 12 pounds
Mr Benjamin [curiosity dealer] 32 Glasshouse Street *Golden Sqr. Regent Street*

10 Aug Benjamin a check Dis £93 for marble Statue Dancing F[aun] & an inlade table of pearl & tortoishell

11 Aug Furniture from London July 19th. 7s.1d. C[ar]r[iage] of carpet 4s.3d.

23 Aug Shepard, bill handels two rooms for locks &c Decr. 27th. 1863 to April 6th 1864 £5.11s.6d.
2 cases by rail for the hall £16.4s.

30 Aug Broughton for Portland stone pedestal for Bronze figure & fixing Dancing marble Faun & the 4 china figures &c – with Cement 6s &c £5.14s.11.
Powlesland 5/2 callico 10/12 4/10 for lining curtains rib[bon] 2d. 5s.

7 Sep Cr for cases of furniture 17s.10d. from London G Gate

20 Sep Cr of carpet Lapworth 2s.6d.

28 Sep Cr of carpet 1s.3d goods from London 7s.4d.
Mr Gibbons Gardener expences & flowers Sepbr. 20th. 1864 £1.1s.6d.

4 Oct Carriage of chairs from 3s. from Diack 4s.9d. Cr. of large brass fender from Jackson for Dining room 2s.4d.

12 Oct parcel from Mapel 1s.8d. Hobigant for flower pots 1s.4d.
Biggs & Palmer 1 marcella quilt 19s.6d. 1 D[itt]o £1.5s.

13 Oct Roberts paid £343.5s.7d., gives final receipt for £1,279.11s.7d. (**3958**n1)

18 Oct Mrs Bignell, for making 12 pillow cases large ones 6s.
Powlesland, for Blankets & Counter[panes?] pillowcases &c £27.18.11.

22 Oct Westfield furniture for new bed rooms &c. £2 Hancock for painted glass in garden door &c our own painted glass

1 Nov Angelo Sedley & Co. [cabinet makers, 38 Conduit St] for blackboy £10.10s. Tapestry &c a check Dis £33

14 Nov	Maple upholsterer, bed furniture sent to Hughenden, a check Dis £99.12s.3d.
	Fertham[?], Iron Monger, for [b]rass fenders, & guilded gate for D[itt]o. a check Dis £260 (after deducting £23.12s.6d.)
	Kettle holder 8d.
	[William & George] Phillips [earthenware manufacturers 155 New] bond St Tiles for Hug[hende]n £2.17s.
	Noyell [?], for 2 looking glass[es], for the Brides room Hughenden
	Diack for chairs sent to Hughenden &c £10.18s. after deducting a charge for the cases
	Houbigant for 9 Corbells, sent Sepr 1st to Hu[ghende]n 7s.6d. each for flower pots £3.6s.
15 Nov	Nurse for mounting 2 china Dishes one at Hugh[enden] the other at G.Gate over charge £11.10s.
12 Dec	Simmonds a check Dis £117
30 Dec	Eleven yards of red & white carpet Like the stair carpet Birds nest & White room
31 Dec	London & Rider, gold for casket, repaired card case 14s. a check Dis £16.14s.

1865

14 Jan	Ward, China &c Chests of drawers cloth for table &c a check Dis £26.5s.6d.

RECIPIENTS, VOLUME EIGHT

INDEX TO VOLUME EIGHT

The references in this index are to letter numbers; bolded numbers denote main notes for persons; numbers ending in 'X' 'XA', or 'R' refer to letters in appendix I unless preceded by a roman numeral denoting a previous volume.